THE PAPERS OF WILL ROGERS

From the Broadway Stage to the National Stage

Volume Four

September 1915–July 1928

Will Rogers, ca. 1925. Photograph taken at the White Studio, New York, and used on the cover of Rogers's lecture tour program. *(OkClaW)*

The Papers of Will Rogers

From the Broadway Stage to the National Stage

Volume Four

September 1915–July 1928

EDITED BY

Steven K. Gragert

AND

M. Jane Johansson

UNIVERSITY OF OKLAHOMA PRESS : NORMAN

Library of Congress Cataloguing-in-Publication Data

Rogers, Will, 1879–1935.
　　The papers of Will Rogers / edited by Steven K. Gragert and M. Jane Johansson.
　　　p.　　cm.
　　Contents: v. 4. From the Broadway Stage to the National Stage, September
1915–July 1928.
　　ISBN 0-8061-3704-5
　　1. Rogers, Will, 1879–1935—Archives.　2. Rogers, Will, 1879–1935—Correspondence.　3. Performing arts—United States—History—20th century—Sources.
I. Steven K. Gragert.　II. M. Jane Johansson.　III. Title.
PN2287.R74A25　1995, vol. 4
792.7'028'092—dc20
　　　　　　　　　　　　　　　　　　　　　　　　　　　　　　94-24165
　　　　　　　　　　　　　　　　　　　　　　　　　　　　　　CIP

Book and series design by Bill Cason.

The paper in this book meets the guidelines for permanence and durability of the
Committee on Production Guidelines for Book Longevity of the Council on Library
Resources, Inc. ∞

1　2　3　4　5　6　7　8　9　10

THE WILL ROGERS PAPERS PROJECT IS A DOCUMENTARY HISTORY PROJECT OF
THE WILL ROGERS MEMORIAL COMMISSION, CLAREMORE, OKLAHOMA. MICHELLE
LEFEBVRE-CARTER IS PROJECT DIRECTOR AND DIRECTOR OF THE MEMORIAL.
FUNDING FOR THE PROJECT HAS COME FROM THE SARKEYS FOUNDATION, THE
WILL ROGERS HERITAGE, INC., AND THE STATE OF OKLAHOMA.

THIS BOOK IS ALSO PUBLISHED WITH THE GENEROUS ASSISTANCE OF THE WILL
ROGERS MOTION PICTURE PIONEERS FOUNDATION, TOLUCA LAKE, CALIFORNIA,
AND THE EXECUTIVE DIRECTOR OF THE FOUNDATION, TODD VRADENBURG.

Contents

Documents

1. BROADWAY STARDOM

2. FROM BROADWAY TO HOLLYWOOD

3. BACK TO BROADWAY

4. RETURN TO HOLLYWOOD

5. ON TO EUROPE

6. ON TO POLITICS—WITH A SMILE

Illustrations

Acknowledgments

THE WILL ROGERS PAPERS PROJECT IS ESPECIALLY INDEBTED TO TWO PRIVATE entities for crucial underwriting of the volumes. The Sarkeys Foundation, Norman, Oklahoma, provided a grant in the early years that met much of the start-up costs of the project and helped significantly to fund the research and publication of the first three books in the series. More recently, the Will Rogers Motion Picture Pioneers Foundation, Toluca Lake, California, and its executive director, Todd Vradenburg, stepped forward to provide substantial funding for the publication of volumes four and five. We greatly appreciate the commitment of both groups to the preservation and dissemination of the legacy of Will Rogers.

We also extend our gratitude to Governor Brad Henry of Oklahoma for his endorsement and advancement of the project. State Senator Stratton Taylor and Representative Tad Jones, with the backing of Representatives Curt Roggow and Randall Erwin, Senators Jeff Rabon and Rick Littlefield, and other members of their committees and of the entire Legislature of Oklahoma, helped provide the public means to augment private funds. We are exceedingly grateful to the citizens of Oklahoma for their support of this multivolume tribute to their native son.

Rogers State University, Claremore, Oklahoma, played a key role, with the Will Rogers Memorial, in sponsoring the final volumes of the Will Rogers Papers. We owe a tremendous debt of gratitude to Dr. Joe A. Wiley, president of the university, and to Drs. Richard Boyd, Ray Brown, Frank W. Elwell, Abe Marrero, Larry Minks, and Carolyn Taylor for their affirming support, advice, and guidance.

The Will Rogers Papers project would never have been possible without the endorsement and leadership of several other key individuals. We are especially thankful for the encouragement in the early years of the project of the late sons of Will Rogers: Will Rogers, Jr., and Jim Rogers. Rogers's grandchildren, Kem, Chuck, and Bette, all of whom have strongly believed in the mission of the project, have given it their abiding interest and continuing support. We thank them.

We are also very grateful to the members of the Will Rogers Memorial Commission for their affirmation of the project and attention to its work. Commissioners Pat Crume, Jim Hartz, Paul Johnson, Stephen R. Pazzo, Jr.,

Kem Rogers, Bob Schulz, and Steve Turnbo have taken a keen interest in the project's progress and completion.

We greatly appreciate the generous time and invaluable effort the staff at the Will Rogers Memorial has invested in the *Papers*. Joseph H. Carter, executive director of the Memorial for ten years, conceived the project, gave it vision, and guided it for many years. His successor at the Memorial, Michelle Lefebvre-Carter, has enabled seamless continuity through her affirming leadership and support. Patricia Lowe, Memorial librarian and archivist extraordinaire, has contributed an enormous amount of time and energy over the years to various facets of the project. Her knowledge of the vast Will Rogers Memorial collection of correspondence and other papers has proved incomparable and indispensable. Greg Malak, curator of the Memorial, graphics designer Rick Mobley, and past staff member Tammy Humburg also made significant contributions.

The Interlibrary Loan Office of the Stratton Taylor Library, Rogers State University, responded promptly and professionally to our many requests for documents, books, and other reference sources for the project. The ILL staff at RSU, headed capably by Janice Ferris, kept us well supplied with critical materials and often went to extra lengths to meet our research needs. We are indebted to Jan and assistants Sharon Bean, Jennifer Clark, and Shangri-La Holdren for their diligence and patience.

We also received significant research aid from librarians, archivists, and other staff members at the libraries of the University of Oklahoma, Norman, and Oklahoma State University, Stillwater. Especially helpful at the former institution was Kay Womack, head of the Reference Department, Bizzell Library. The following individuals provided key assistance at Edmon Low Library at OSU: Sheila G. Johnson, professor and dean of the libraries; Jennifer Paustenbaugh, professor and head, Kay Bost, assistant professor and assistant head, and David C. Peters, coordinator, Special Collections and University Archives; John B. Phillips, professor and head, Documents Department; Richard T. Paustenbaugh, associate professor and head, Steve Locy, associate professor and assistant head, and David Oberhelman, associate professor and librarian, Humanities and Social Sciences Division; Carolyn Warmann, head, Access Services; and Barbara Muret, senior library technical assistant.

We are also indebted to the following librarians and archivists who assisted with our on-site and remote document collection and annotation research at libraries and other research institutions throughout the country: Lori Curtis, head, and Lisa Inman, librarian assistant, Special Collections, McFarlin Library, University of Tulsa, Oklahoma; Barbara DeWolfe, curator, and Janet Bloom, William L. Clements Library, University of Michigan, Ann Arbor;

Mike Shadix, librarian, Archives, Roosevelt Warm Springs Institute for Rehabilitation, Warm Springs, Georgia; William S. Bryans, professor and head, and Michael M. Smith, professor, Department of History, Robert Ward, assistant professor, Department of Music, and Emilia Brunner, staff member, Department of Theatre, Oklahoma State University, Stillwater; Timothy Walch, curator, and Lynn Smith, archivist, Herbert Hoover Presidential Library, West Branch, Iowa; Rodger Rainwater, director, Special Collections, Mary Couts Burnett Library, Texas Christian University, Fort Worth; Janet Moulding, assistant director, Forbes Library, Northampton, Massachusetts; Kerry McLaughlin, Historical Society of Pennsylvania, Philadelphia; Leslie A. Morris, curator of manuscripts, and Jennie Rathburn, archivist, Houghton Library, Harvard University, Cambridge, Massachusetts; Fred Bauman, manuscript reference specialist, Manuscript Division, Library of Congress, Washington, D.C.; Susan Conley, registrar, Taylor Museum for Southwestern Studies, Colorado Springs Fine Arts Center, Colorado; Jim Orr, image services coordinator, Benson Ford Research Center, Henry Ford Museum, Dearborn, Michigan; Cyndy Bittinger, executive director, Calvin Coolidge Memorial Foundation, Inc., Plymouth Notch, Vermont; Heather M. Crocetto, research librarian, Eric Friedheim Library, National Press Club, Washington, D.C.; Jean Ashton, director, Rare Book and Manuscript Library, Columbia University, New York; Alan Loehr, director of Alumni Relations, Debrah Fox, Alumni/Development, and Robert B. D. Hartman, historian and archivist, Culver Academies, Culver, Indiana; Lora Korbut, Archives, New York Times Company, New York; Sherry Phillips, reference librarian, University of Missouri–Kansas City; Susan Weiss, reference librarian, Freeport Memorial Library, Freeport, New York; Fanny Witherspoon, archivist, *Kansas City Star*, Kansas City, Missouri; and Mildred Murphy DeRiggi, historian, Nassau County Division of Museum Services and Long Island Studies Institute, Hofstra University, Hempstead, New York.

We are grateful to the following individuals who also provided key help in obtaining and researching documents: Todd Vradenburg, executive director, Will Rogers Institute, Toluca Lake, California; Mary Rulinski, *Farm Journal* magazine, Philadelphia; Rochelle N. Booth, curator, Will Rogers State Historic Park, Pacific Palisades, California; John Bolig, Dover, Delaware; Ann Baker Horsey, curator, Johnson Victrola Museum, Dover, Delaware; Bert Atkinson, producer, *Charles F. Lummis: The Lion of the Southwest*, Los Angeles; Steve Barse, program analyst and public affairs liaison, Oklahoma City Area Indian Health Service; Lisa Proctor, Indian Health Service, Claremore, Oklahoma; Jocille Hoffman, CPA, Stillwater, Oklahoma; Bob Boze Bell, executive editor, and Carole Compton Glenn, general manager, *True West* magazine,

Cave Creek, Arizona; Beth Wright, tour director, News/Talk 750 WSB radio, Atlanta; and Jason McGarvey, editor, *Outdoor America* magazine, Izaak Walton League of America, Gaithersburg, Maryland.

Several retired employees of the Western Union Telegraph Company supplied key information about institutional operations and history, and shared anecdotes of Will Rogers's unique relationship with the company. We extend our thanks to Robert McCluskie, Allendale, New Jersey, secretary of the Retired Western Union Employees Association; John J. Durkin, Franklin Lakes, New Jersey, editor of the group's newsletter; and fellow association members William H. Rank, Grandy, North Carolina, and Edward J. Gander, Kansas City, Missouri.

Librarians, archivists, or curators at the following additional institutions provided important help in the documentation and production of this volume: Special Collections, Princeton University Library, Princeton, New Jersey; Museum of Modern Art Film Center, New York; Western History Collections, University of Oklahoma, Norman; Western Historical Manuscript Collection, University of Missouri, Columbia; Amon G. Carter Museum, Fort Worth; Will Rogers Public Library, Claremore, Oklahoma; Kansas City Public Library, Kansas City, Missouri; Charles Lummis Collection, Southwest Museum, Pasadena, California; Tulsa City-County Public Library; Oklahoma Historical Society library and archives, Oklahoma City; Sophia Smith Collection, Smith College, Northampton, Massachusetts; Margaret Herrick Library, Academy of Motion Picture Arts and Sciences, Beverly Hills, California; Chelsea Public Library, Chelsea, Oklahoma; and Tutt Library, Colorado College, Colorado Springs.

We are extremely grateful to Gordon Kuntz, who provided several outstanding items from his private collection of Will Rogers film memorabilia to help illustrate this volume. Gordon has been a generous and invaluable supporter of the mission of the Will Rogers Memorial Museums through the years.

A special salute goes to Helen Koons Gragert and David Hjalmar Johansson for their constant support and encouragement, and to our predecessors, Arthur Frank Wertheim and Barbara Bair, for the exacting standard they set as documentary editors of the first three volumes. Personal recognition is also due Robert Kreitmeier, J. B. Roberts, Peter C. Rollins, Bryan B. and Frances N. Sterling, and Joseph A. Stout, Jr., for their interest and kindness in the production of the present volume.

We extend warm thanks to our associates at the University of Oklahoma Press. We are especially grateful for the continuing support and advice of John Drayton, director, and Charles Rankin, editor-in-chief. Alice Stanton, managing editor, has provided her usual careful and expert guidance of the manuscript through the editorial process, and as with the previous three books in the series, Lys Ann Shore Weiss of Post Hoc Academic Publishing Services, Friday Harbor, Washington, has skillfully copyedited the work and prepared it for publication. We appreciate her professionalism and the quality contributions of all of our colleagues at the University of Oklahoma Press.

THE PAPERS OF WILL ROGERS

From the Broadway Stage to the National Stage

Volume Four

September 1915–July 1928

Introduction

BY THE SUMMER OF 1915, A FEW MONTHS SHY OF AGE THIRTY-SIX, WILL ROGERS had already proven to be remarkably adaptable. He had managed to turn an ill-planned adventure to become an expatriate gaucho in Argentina into a budding career as a cowboy entertainer in South Africa. He had allowed his eventual stage act to evolve from a roping and riding routine with occasional funny asides into a stand-up monologue of topical humor with occasional rope spinning. He had maneuvered a careful course through the politics and struggles rampant among rival organizations of vaudeville managers and artists, and his career had survived and prospered. He had moved from a Wild West persona, complete with trick roping and women bronc riders, showcased in vaudeville houses coast to coast, to stage performances in London and a successful run in a Broadway musical comedy.

Even on the personal side, he had shown the ability to change and adapt. He had seen his relationship with his father mature from contention to reconciliation, from misunderstanding to respect. He had buried the romantic relationships from the vaudeville circuit to marry a sweetheart from his past and to establish a growing family. He had traded a life of hotel rooms for a roomy house in a Long Island suburb of New York City with enough acreage to teach his children to ride and rope. He had left behind the vastness and openness of Indian Territory prairie for the ever-increasing density and closeness of urban America.

Readers of the first three volumes in this series have witnessed the adaptability of Will Rogers. Through the pages of *The Papers of Will Rogers*, they have had the privilege of a front-row seat, an intimate look at the transformations in his life and at many of the factors that shaped who he was and what he became. Through him they have caught a reflected image of American society of the times. His writings and sayings have given them a mirror through which to view selected trends and changes in the cultural life of the United States: in forms and choices of popular expression, in style and content of mass entertainment, in the venues of artistic performance.

The first three volumes of *The Papers of Will Rogers*, expertly edited by Arthur Frank Wertheim and Barbara Bair, provide a documentary account of much of Rogers's life and career, from his birth in November 1879 to the moment of his breakthrough on Broadway in September 1915. Volume one covers most of the first twenty-five years of his life. It relates his heritage and birth in Indian Territory, his primary years and family history, his challenges and successes in school, his earliest experiences as a performer, his adventures as a young man on an unplanned journey around the world. Volume two takes the reader through four years, 1904 to 1908, that saw Rogers transformed from a still uncertain performer in Wild West productions to a well-accepted entertainer on the professional vaudeville stage. It follows the subtle evolution of his public persona and shows him capitalizing on the prevailing fascination with the American West. Through the correspondence of Will Rogers and Betty Blake, volume two also gives us a close look at an on-again, off-again relationship that ran the gamut of emotions and expressions. Embracing the years 1908 to 1915, volume three opens with Rogers not yet fully committed to a career on stage but then making a complete commitment in his personal life with marriage to Betty Blake. The wedding virtually coincided with his move from flirting with a life in vaudeville to total immersion in the art form. As his career evolved and expanded, so did his family life. Although Will Rogers lost his father in 1911, he and Betty welcomed their first child shortly before Clem Rogers's death. Two other children were born to the couple over the next four years, and for their sake Rogers worked to solidify his career, his finances, and his future. A successful life on the vaudeville circuit was complemented by opportunities on the New York musical stage and even performances abroad.

Over the thirteen-year time span of volume four, as he moved into the most productive years of an increasingly diverse career, Rogers continued to experience transforming moments in his professional and personal life. A significant development came in August 1915 with his debut appearance in New York in the *Midnight Frolic*, commencing a long and mutually successful association with famed theatrical impresario Florenz Ziegfeld, Jr. The *Frolic* led the next year to Rogers's big break on Broadway amid the dazzle and glamour of the *Ziegfeld Follies* and its trademark chorus line of beauties. In intentionally obvious contrast to his surroundings, Rogers played off the perceived down-to-earthness and innocence of his humor, while continuing to evolve more fully into a monologist of topicality. His work on stage with the Ziegfeld organization spanned much of the period from 1915 to 1928 and brought him into prominence on Broadway and along the route of the touring road shows. It provided him with valuable contacts in the entertainment world and, perhaps more important in the long term, in social, political, and business circles. It also opened opportunities for him in other media, such as writing and film.

When confronted with an opportunity to take up a different medium, Rogers seemed rarely to hesitate to make the move, to try a new avenue to express himself, to reach an additional audience or expand a present one. He had experienced one such moment earlier in his professional life when he wrote a short piece on roping for a rodeo program. His career as a writer began to bud and blossom in 1916, when he started producing articles for newspapers, first in New York, and then within months for newspapers in other major cities. Within three years he had authored his first two books. Although his early literary efforts ranged in style and substance, as often as not they were simply his stage act set in type, one gag feeding or following another. His writing matured over time, and new opportunities arose, some originating from his own initiatives, others resulting from someone seeking him out. Rogers reached a milestone in his literary career in December 1922 with the syndication and first publication of what became popularly known as the "Weekly Article," a column that he would continue to produce until his death. Other syndicated writings followed over the next two years, the most noteworthy being the debut in the fall of 1926 of what would become his signature piece, the so-called "Daily Telegram." Along with his regular newspaper columns, Rogers also managed to write four more books, scores of newspaper articles covering the national political conventions during this time period, a few hundred pieces of advertising copy, and several articles, single and serialized, for national mass-circulation magazines.

During those same years, 1915–28, Rogers tested his talents in two other media, both relatively new and still evolving: film and radio. Each presented different as well as similar challenges; each offered him a chance to reach new, broader audiences. His work in motion pictures, especially, proved transforming in terms of his career, as well as in his personal and family life. His film debut in *Laughing Bill Hyde* in 1918 resulted from mutual relationships and his presence on Broadway; it led to a multipicture deal with Goldwyn Pictures that took him and his family from their long-time residence on the East Coast to the new capital of filmdom in southern California. Rogers's foray into film acting produced mixed results. He received generally good reviews from critics, but his movies failed to gain overwhelming favor at the box office. He tried his own hand at film production in 1919 after financial difficulties developed at Goldwyn, but the pictures he produced lacked a ready distribution network. He chalked it up as a lesson not to be repeated. Rogers would appear several more times on film during the silent era, and his gags often reached theater audiences through the on-screen subtitles he supplied for his own movies and for other ventures. His real success in motion pictures, however, would have to wait for a further change in film technology—the advent of sound.

Rogers spoke his first words on radio in 1922, when the medium was still very much in its infancy. He would make a few other on-air appearances over the next six years, including a disconcertingly controversial one in 1926 when he imitated the voice of President Calvin Coolidge during a national broadcast. In 1923 he also took his humor to another medium of sound, phonograph records, but the recordings he made on discs consisted mostly of replays of speeches and little original material. His work in the relatively early years of sound media, both disc and radio, was not a fully satisfactory experience for him, because he lacked the chance to play his humor off a live audience. He would enjoy greater success as his broadcast career and the technology of radio progressed in the 1930s.

At the same time he was dabbling in radio broadcasting, Rogers was also scoring success in the live arena of the lecture circuit. For two and one-half years, from the fall of 1925 through the spring of 1928, he took his humor, his chewing gum, and his rope to concert hall stages in cities both small and large throughout the country. He adapted his after-dinner speaking, his Ziegfeld monologues, and his newspaper commentary to the lecture venue, bringing to new audiences in new ports of call the same topical, homespun humor that had won him favor through other media. At each stop, he would add a local twist, following the pattern he had long before established in Ziegfeld road productions.

Throughout the years 1915–28 Rogers willingly sought and tried new ways to convey his humor. He adapted when necessary. He broadened his career with ventures into silent films, radio broadcasts, sound recordings, syndicated writings, magazine articles, and lecture tours. Not all proved successful, but each added a new dimension to his professional life and enabled him to reach an ever-widening public. His national appeal and stature grew with each new stage in his performing career, and even his prominence abroad would be enhanced during those years by such experiences as his five-month stay in Europe in 1926. This period in Rogers's life of increasing exposure, of widening diversity in his professional life, of a maturing of his humor and philosophy brought him the national recognition that would evolve into universal endearment.

Chronology, 1915–1928

1915

23 August 1915–
ca. 16 January 1916 — Rogers appears in "Just Girls," a revue in *Midnight Frolic* on roof of New Amsterdam Theatre, New York City.

23 September–
17 November — Performs in *Town Topics*, Century Theatre, New York City.

5 December — Participates in benefit for *New York American* Christmas Fund, New York City.

19 December — Benefit show for *New York American* Christmas Fund.

1916

24 January–ca. 9 April — Rogers entertains in new edition of *Midnight Frolic*, New Amsterdam Theatre, New York City.

20 February — Seventy-first Regiment Gala, Liberty Theatre, New York City.

27 February — Benefit for Hebrew Infant Asylum, New York City.

28–29 February — B. F. Keith's Palace Theatre, New York City.

5 March — Benefit for Battleship Fund.

19 March — Benefit for Actors' Fund, Century Theatre, New York City.

17–22 April — Benefit for Flower and Sydenham Hospitals, Century Theatre.

19 April — Matinee benefit for Bronx County Society for the Prevention of Cruelty to Children, Bronx, N.Y.

23 April — Two Easter benefit performances for Permanent Blind Relief War Fund and Allied Charities, Hippodrome, New York City.

5–ca. 6 May — Lassoes at least two deer during roundup by game rangers at Shelter Island, Long Island, N.Y.

7 May	Presides at benefit for New York newsboys, Hippodrome.
28 May	Performs in *Friars' Frolic*, New Amsterdam Theatre.
29 May	Begins tour in *Friars' Frolic*, New Nixon Theatre, Atlantic City, N.J.; Forrest Theatre, Philadelphia.
30 May	*Friars' Frolic*, New Academy of Music, Baltimore. President Wilson and entourage are in audience.
31 May	*Friars' Frolic*, Nixon Theatre, Pittsburgh.
1 June	*Friars' Frolic*, Keith's Hippodrome, Cleveland.
2 June	*Friars' Frolic*, Emery Auditorium, Cincinnati.
3 June	*Friars' Frolic*, Olympic Theatre, St. Louis.
4 June	*Friars' Frolic*, Auditorium, Chicago.
5 June	*Friars' Frolic*, Detroit Opera House.
6 June	*Friars' Frolic*, Majestic Theatre, Buffalo; Lyceum Theatre, Rochester, N.Y.
7 June	*Friars' Frolic*, Hollis Street Theatre, Boston.
8 June	*Friars' Frolic*, Opera House, Providence, R.I.
12 June–9 September	Appears in summer edition of *Midnight Frolic*, New Amsterdam Theatre.
16 July	Thespian Society entertainment, Astor Theatre, New York City.
ca. 23 July–16 September	Joins cast of *Ziegfeld Follies*, New Amsterdam Theatre.
5 August	Attends Stampede rodeo competition, Sheepshead Bay, Brooklyn, N.Y.
6 August	Article by Rogers about Stampede appears in *New York American*, marking his newspaper writing debut.
8 August	*New York American* publishes second article about the Stampede.
5 September	Several of Rogers's stage gags are published in newspaper article copyrighted in Great Britain.
ca. 16 September 1916– ca. 31 March 1917	*Ziegfeld Follies*, with Rogers apparently in cast, makes annual road tour, including stops in Boston, Philadelphia, Chicago, and Baltimore.
26 November	Rogers helps roast Enrico Caruso at banquet, Friars Club, New York City.

1917

11–20 January	Rogers performs in cabaret at Allied Bazaar, Chicago.
2 April	Injures leg in automobile accident involving W. C. Fields as driver.
2–ca. 24 April	Appears in new edition of *Midnight Frolic*, New Amsterdam Theatre, New York City.
19 April	Participates in *Wake Up, America!* Carnegie Hall, New York City.
6 May	Appears in benefit for theatrical group, Hudson Theatre, New York City.
10 May	Guest contribution for newspaper column "Ye Towne Gossip" is published.
5–ca. 9 June	Performs in tryout run of *Ziegfeld Follies of 1917*, Atlantic City.
12 June	Appears as auctioneer at Lambs Club charity auction, Hudson Theatre.
12 June–15 September	Performs in *Ziegfeld Follies of 1917*, New Amsterdam Theatre.
22 July	Benefit for *New York Sun* Tobacco Fund, Winter Garden Theatre, New York City.
5 August	Benefit for LIGHTS, Astor Theatre, New York City.
2 September	Benefit for emergency fund of Twelfth Infantry, Manhattan Opera House, New York City.
16 September	Benefit for Army Athletic Fund, Hippodrome, New York City.
ca. 17 September 1917– 20 April 1918	Performs in road tour of *Ziegfeld Follies of 1917*. Stops include Boston, Philadelphia, Washington, Pittsburgh, Chicago, St. Louis, and Montreal.
23 September	Benefit for Seventy-first Regiment, Hippodrome.
ca. 29 October– 10 November	*Ziegfeld Follies*, Forrest Theatre, Philadelphia.
ca. 19–23 November	*Ziegfeld Follies*, Washington.
ca. 26 November– 1 December	*Ziegfeld Follies*, Nixon Theatre, Pittsburgh.
15 December	Article by Rogers published in *Detroit Journal*.

ca. 22 December	Second article by Rogers appears in *Detroit Journal*.
23 December 1917–	
2 March 1918	*Ziegfeld Follies*, Illinois Theatre, Chicago.

1918

17 February	Article by Rogers appears in *Chicago Sunday Tribune*.
21 February	Article by Rogers, *Chicago Examiner*.
ca. 3 March	Article by Rogers, *Chicago Examiner*.
24 April–ca. 25 May	Rogers performs in new edition of *Midnight Frolic*, New Amsterdam Theatre, New York City.
10 May	Appears as auctioneer in benefit for American Red Cross, Liberty Theatre, New York City.
20–26 May	Benefit show for American Red Cross, various theaters, New York City.
21 May	Pledges $100 a week to wartime fund of American Red Cross.
10–15 June	Appears in tryout run of new *Ziegfeld Follies*, Apollo Theatre, Atlantic City.
18 June–14 September	Performs in *Ziegfeld Follies of 1918*, New Amsterdam Theatre.
15 July	Fred Stone Rogers is born in Amityville, N.Y.
Summer	Rogers begins work on his first motion picture, *Laughing Bill Hyde*.
12 September	Registers for draft, Elmhurst, N.Y.
22 September	*Laughing Bill Hyde* opens at Rivoli Theatre, New York City.
ca. 24 September 1918–	
April 1919	Performs on road in *Ziegfeld Follies of 1918*, but flu outbreak in Boston forces troupe to replay Broadway during part of tour schedule. Other road stops include Philadelphia, Washington, Cleveland, Detroit, Chicago, and Montreal.
30 September	*Laughing Bill Hyde* is given general release.
2–3 October	Rogers uses flu-induced temporary closing of *Follies* to visit family and friends in Claremore, Okla.
7–26 October	*Ziegfeld Follies*, Globe Theatre, New York City.
13 October	Attends Lambs Club Gambol, Collie Theatre, New York City.

14–26 October	Appears in *Midnight Frolic*, New Amsterdam Theatre.
17 November	Participates in *Friars Frolic* in benefit for United War Work Campaign Fund, Metropolitan Opera House, New York City.
30 November	Signs film contract with Sam Goldfish of Goldwyn Pictures Corporation at $2,250 weekly.
ca. 14 December	Article by Rogers is published in Detroit newspaper.
ca. 16–21 December	*Ziegfeld Follies*, New Detroit Opera House.
ca. 22 December	Article by Rogers in Detroit newspaper.
22 December 1918–ca. 8 March 1919	*Ziegfeld Follies*, Colonial Theatre, Chicago.
24 December	Receives "Certificate of Honor" from President Wilson for volunteer service to promote war effort.

1919

16 February	Rogers serves as master of ceremonies at benefit, Colonial Theatre, Chicago.
25 February	Speaks at luncheon of Traffic Club of Chicago, Hotel La Salle.
ca. February	Prepares screen subtitles for use in motion picture theaters.
24 April	Benefit at Knights of Columbus hall, New York City.
12–31 May	Performs on alternate nights in *Revue* at nine o'clock and in *Midnight Frolic*, New Amsterdam Theatre, New York City.
25 May	Appears in benefit for Salvation Army, Hippodrome, New York City; speaks at Friars dinner for Stage Women's War Relief, Hotel Astor, New York City.
2 June	Makes unexpected final appearance in *Midnight Frolic*.
ca. 4 June	Leaves New York City for West Coast to start film work.
5 June	Appears at opening of new motion picture theater, Kansas City, Mo.
6 June	Arrives in Los Angeles.

16 June	Begins work at Goldwyn Studios, Culver City, Calif.
ca. 29 June	Harper & Brothers releases *Rogersisms: The Cowboy Philosopher on the Peace Conference*, Rogers's first book.
ca. September	Buys space in *Wid's Year Book* to announce and explain his venture into motion pictures.
12 October	*Almost a Husband*, starring Rogers, opens at Strand Theatre, New York City.
ca. 19 October	Rogers's second book, *Rogersisms: The Cowboy Philosopher on Prohibition*, is published.
7 December	*Jubilo*, Rogers's third movie, premieres at Strand Theatre, New York City.
20 December	Benefit for *Los Angeles Examiner* Christmas Fund, Clune's Auditorium, Los Angeles.

1920

2 January	Rogers and wife, Betty Blake Rogers, visit Charles Lummis at his home in Santa Barbara, Calif.
8 February	*Water, Water Everywhere*, with Rogers in lead, is given general release.
11 February	Rogers receives California driver's license.
ca. 12 February	Shoots scenes for *Jes' Call Me Jim* on location in Santa Cruz, Calif.
20 February	Contract with Marion H. Kohn to produce *The Illiterate Digest* series of motion picture screen subtitles at $750 weekly.
21 February	Entertains visitors, including John Burroughs, at home of Charles F. Lummis, Santa Barbara.
12 March	Appears on cover of *Variety*.
May	*The Strange Boarder*, his fifth motion picture, is released.
30 May	*Jes' Call Me Jim*, Rogers's sixth film, opens at Strand Theatre, New York City.
ca. 6–12 June	From California, covers Republican national convention, Chicago; provides copy to syndicate for distribution to newspapers.

17 June	Fred Stone Rogers dies of diphtheria. After hearing of illness, Rogers rushes from location shooting near San Francisco but arrives too late.
ca. June–December	Article by Rogers is published in unidentified newspaper.
28 June–3 July	Reports on Democratic national convention, San Francisco, but is not present; remains in Los Angeles following death of son.
25 July	*Cupid, the Cowpuncher* premieres at Capitol Theatre, New York City.
7 September	Debates Dr. James Whitcomb Brougher at luncheon at Advertising Club, Los Angeles.
19 September	*Honest Hutch*, Rogers's eighth movie, is released.
Fall	Rogers writes article for anthology. His contribution is reprinted in a newspaper.
26 December	*Guile of Women*, starring Rogers, opens at California Theatre, Los Angeles.

1921

2–8 January	Rogers visits New York City.
21 January	Visits New Orleans with his wife.
28 January	Appears at Old Mill Theater, Dallas; makes appearances in Fort Worth, Tex.
27 February	*Boys Will Be Boys*, Rogers's ninth film, premieres at California Theatre, Los Angeles.
1–3 March	Will and Betty Blake Rogers visit family and attend events in Claremore and Chelsea, Okla.
May	Contract with Goldwyn Pictures is not renewed.
8 May	*An Unwilling Hero*, Rogers's tenth picture, opens in Los Angeles.
29 May–4 June	Visits New York City.
11 August	Purchases motion picture rights to *Rip Van Winkle, Jr.*
ca. 20–21 October	Makes personal appearances at first two screenings of *Doubling for Romeo*, Miller's Theater, Los Angeles.
27 October	Returns to New York City to perform in vaudeville.

29 October	*The Ropin' Fool*, a Will Rogers Productions film, opens at Roxy Theatre, New York City.
ca. 1–6 November	Covers preliminary meetings of Conference on Limitation of Arms, Washington, D.C., for Universal Service; writes newspaper article about his observations.
2 November	Visits U.S. Senate.
7–19 November	Appears at Shubert's Winter Garden Theatre, New York City, at salary of $5,000.
17 November 1921– 7 January 1922	Performs in *Midnight Frolic*, New Amsterdam Theatre, New York City, at $1,000 weekly.
20 November	Guest of honor at Friars Club dinner; speaks at banquet of Author's League Fellowship, Hotel Astor, New York City.
29 November	Entertains inmates at state prison, Ossining, N.Y.
ca. 30 November	Newspaper article by Rogers is published through Universal Service news bureau, Washington, D.C.
December	*A Poor Relation*, Rogers's thirteenth and final Goldwyn production, is released.
1 December	*Fruits of Faith*, a Will Rogers Productions film, premieres at Rialto Theatre, New York City.
12–17 December	Performs four times nightly at various Loew's theaters, New York City, for salary of $1,500.
18 December	Benefit for *New York American* Christmas Fund, Hippodrome, New York City.
19 December	Benefit for Big Sisters charity, Sherry's restaurant, New York City.

1922

8 January	Rogers arrives in Philadelphia with his wife.
9–28 January	Performs in road edition of *Ziegfeld Frolic*, Garrick Theatre, Philadelphia.
20 January	Benefit for Actors' Fund, Century Theatre, New York City.
29 January	*One Glorious Day*, a Famous Players–Lasky production starring Rogers, opens at Rivoli Theatre, New York City. Rogers arrives with his wife in Pittsburgh.

30 January–4 February	*Ziegfeld Frolic*, Pittsburgh. Rogers makes his first radio broadcast over KDKA, Pittsburgh.
5 February	Arrives in Washington, D.C.
6–11 February	Rogers meets President Harding at White House. Performs in *Ziegfeld Frolic*, National Theatre, Washington.
10 February	Watches from U.S. Senate gallery as President Harding presents disarmament treaties negotiated at Washington Naval Conference.
ca. 11 February	Writes newspaper article about his visit to Senate.
13–18 February	*Ziegfeld Frolic*, Baltimore.
20–ca. 26 February	*Ziegfeld Frolic*, Lyceum Theatre, Rochester, N.Y.
24 February	Appears at Lion's Club luncheon, Powers Hotel, Rochester.
27 February–5 March	*Ziegfeld Frolic*, Cleveland.
ca. 6–11 March	*Ziegfeld Frolic*, Toronto.
13–18 March	*Ziegfeld Frolic*, Detroit.
ca. 19 March	Article by Rogers is published in *Detroit Sunday News*.
19 March–3 June	*Ziegfeld Frolic*, Colonial Theatre, Chicago.
24 March	Benefit for Actors' Fund of America, Auditorium Theatre, Chicago.
26 March	Article by Rogers is published in *Chicago Herald and Examiner*.
5 June 1922– 31 May 1923	*Ziegfeld Follies of 1922*, New Amsterdam Theatre, New York City.
11 June	Speaks at benefit for Lambs Club, Knickerbocker Hotel, New York City.
19 June	Signs his last will and testament.
10–16 July	Stays at Hotel Astor, New York City.
July–August	In production on *The Headless Horseman*, including on location near Tarrytown, N.Y., and Hackensack, N.J.
7–12 August	Stays at Hotel Astor.
13 August	Presides as toastmaster at dinner for Fred Stone at LIGHTS Club, Freeport, N.Y.
13–28 August	Stays at Nassau Hotel, Long Beach, Long Island, N.Y.

20 August	Appears in LIGHTS vaudeville show, Columbia Theatre, Far Rockaway, N.Y.
29 August– ca. 3 September	Stays at Hotel Astor.
10 September	Serves as toastmaster at dinner for National Vaudeville Artists, Forty-sixth Street Clubhouse, New York City.
24 September	Attends testimonial dinner for Eddie Cantor, Friars Club, New York City.
8 October	Benefit for Saranac Day Nursery, Lexington Theatre, New York City.
13 October	Speaks at luncheon for Associated Motion Picture Advertisers, New York City.
26 October	Speaks at campaign event for congressional candidate Ogden Mills, Town Hall, New York City.
ca. 28 October	"Will Rogers' Sayings This Week" is published in *Evening World*, New York City.
November–December	Produces gags for regular publication in *Life* magazine.
4 November	"Will Rogers' Sayings This Week" appears in *Evening World*, New York City.
5 November	*The Headless Horseman* opens at Capitol Theatre, New York City.
6 November– 2 December	Stays at Hotel Astor.
7 November	Brief article by Rogers is published in *New York American*.
10 November	Submits manuscript of screen subtitles to *Selznick Newsreel*.
17 November	Speaks at luncheon for Merchants' Association, Hotel Astor.
3 December	Speaks at dinner for Pleiades Club, Hotel Brevoort, New York City.
7 December	Speaks at luncheon for Advertising Club, New York City.
16 December	Delivers speech at event for American Bond & Mortgage Company, Hotel Astor. Appeal by Rogers is published in *New York Times* for contributions to newspaper's Hundred Neediest Cases fund.

17 December   Speaks at rally sponsored by Molly Pitcher Club for Association against the Prohibition Amendment, 39th Street Theatre, New York City.

24 December   Rogers's first article in *New York Times* is published.

30 December   Receives gold trophy from Ziegfeld organization following performance of *Follies*.

31 December   Rogers's first syndicated "Weekly Article" appears in *New York Times* and other newspapers.

1923

3 January   Rogers speaks at Sherry's Restaurant, New York City, on occasion of *Life* magazine's fortieth anniversary.

7 January 1923–
15 September 1935   Rogers's "Weekly Article" continues to run in national syndication; a total of 666 are eventually published.

7 January   Speaks at frolic for Authors' League, Hotel Astor, New York City.

9 January   Delivers speech to Dutch Treat Club, New York City. Speaks at dinner for National Automobile Chamber of Commerce, Commodore Hotel, New York City.

10 January   Addresses manufacturers of automobile accessories at dinner in New York City.

11 January   Speaks at dinner for paint manufacturers, Biltmore Hotel, New York City.

13 January   Addresses Ohio Society dinner, Hotel Astor.

14 January   Attends Progress Club dinner, Newark, N.J.

16 January   Delivers after-dinner speech to Board of Aldermen, New York City.

19 January   Benefit for Actors' Fund of America, Century Theatre, New York City.

20 January   Speaks to 24 Karat Club, Waldorf-Astoria Hotel, New York City.

21 January   Entertains cadets at U.S. Military Academy, West Point, N.Y.

25 January   Speaks at dinner for Electric Railway, Commodore Hotel, New York City, and at banquet for Furriers Trade, McAlphine Hotel, New York City.

26 January	Signs contract with Hal Roach Studios to appear in two-reel comedies at $2,000 weekly with deal to commence on closing of current *Follies*.
28 January	Benefit for Actors' Fund, Hippodrome, New York City.
6 February	Victor Records releases Rogers's first phonograph recording.
13 February	Speaks at event for bicycles trade group, Hotel Astor.
18 February	Benefit at Earl Carroll Theatre, New York City.
19 February	Addresses Retail Milliners, Hotel Astor.
20 February	Speaks at Corset Manufacturers Association banquet, Waldorf-Astoria Hotel, and then at Allied Shoe and Leather Industries event, Commodore Hotel.
23 February	Speaks at banquet at Delmonico's Restaurant, New York City.
25 February	Appears at Salvation Army event, Selwyn Theatre, New York City.
28 February	Testifies in New York Supreme Court in injunction suit brought by Shuberts against Gallagher & Shean.
11 March	Speaks at Salvation Army dinner, Pennsylvania Hotel, New York City.
13 March	Addresses Sphinx Club dinner, Waldorf-Astoria Hotel.
16 March	Appears at luncheon for Child Adoption League, New York City.
17 March	Speaks to American Committee for Devastated France, Madison Square Garden, New York City.
18 March	Gives speech at Newspaper Women's banquet, Ritz-Carlton Hotel, New York City.
21 March	Speaks at National Association of Waste Material event, Hotel Astor.
31 March	Speaks during benefit minstrel show for New York Building Superintendent's Association, Carnegie Hall.
4 April	Addresses representatives of Carpet and Rug Manufacturers, Commodore Hotel.

5 April	Speaks at Hosiery and Underwear Manufacturers event, Philadelphia.
8 April	Benefit for former chorus girl hospitalized with tuberculosis, Casino Theatre, New York City.
10 April	Speaks at National Council of Importers and Traders event, Hotel Astor.
11 April	Addresses paper manufacturers, Waldorf-Astoria Hotel.
14 April	Speaks at dinner for New York City detective force.
26 April	Addresses Newspaper Publishers' Association banquet, Waldorf-Astoria Hotel. Event is broadcast by WJZ.
29 April	Benefit for Treasurers' Club of America, Hudson Theatre, New York City.
3 May	Addresses international conference of law enforcement chiefs, Commodore Hotel.
5 May	Speaks at dinner for American Society of Newspaper Editors, Waldorf-Astoria Hotel.
9 May	Appears in theatrical event for U.S. Chamber of Commerce, Hippodrome.
13 May	Performs at Metropolitan, Hippodrome, and Manhattan Theatres, New York City, for Sick and Benefit Fund of National Vaudeville Artists.
15 May	Speaks at luncheon for National Association of Manufacturers, Waldorf-Astoria Hotel.
31 May	Victor Records releases second Rogers sound disc.
ca. 1 June	Rogers takes out $250,000 life insurance policy.
2 June	Victor Records issues Rogers's third sound recording.
ca. 3 June	Rogers leaves New York City for Los Angeles to begin work for Hal Roach Studios.
11–23 June	Works on production of *Jus' Passin' Through*, Roach Studios, Culver City, Calif.
25–30 June	Filming of *Hustling Hank*.
2–7 July	Filming of *Jus' Passin' Through*.
13–17 July	Filming of *Hustling Hank*.
18 July	Retakes of *Jus' Passin' Through*

19 July–11 August	Filming of *Hustling Hank*.
15 August–4 September	Filming of *Uncensored Movies*.
19 August	*Hollywood*, a Famous Players–Lasky film with Rogers in cameo appearance, is released.
5–19 September	Filming of *Gee Whiz, Genevieve*.
20 September	Filming of *Uncensored Movies*.
21 September– 4 October	Filming of *Two Wagons, Both Covered*.
23 September	Rogers and crew travel to Elsinore, Calif., to shoot on location.
5–6 October	Shoots retakes of *Hustling Hank*, Roach Studios, Culver City.
8–9 October	Filming of *Two Wagons, Both Covered*.
10 October	Filming of *Hustling Hank*.
11 October	Filming of *Two Wagons, Both Covered*.
12–13 October	Filming of *Uncensored Movies*.
14 October	*Jus' Passin' Through* is released.
15–16 October	Filming of *Gee Whiz, Genevieve*.
18–29 October	Filming of *The Cowboy Sheik*.
30 October– 5 November	Filming of *The Cake Eater*.
6–16 November	Filming of a movie bearing studio designation of R-8.
11 November	*Hustling Hank* is released.
17 November– 8 December	Filming of *Big Moments from Little Pictures*.
9 December	Retakes on *The Cake Eater*. *Uncensored Movies* is released.
10–11 December	Filming of *Big Moments from Little Pictures*.
12 December	Filming of *High Brow Stuff*.
13 December	Retakes on *The Cake Eater*.
14–26 December	Filming of *Highbrow Stuff*.
27 December 1923– 1 January 1924	No production work is scheduled.

1924

2–3 January	Filming of *Highbrow Stuff*.
4 January	*Life* magazine publishes column of gags by Rogers.
6 January	*Two Wagons, Both Covered* is released.

19–30 January	Filming of *Going to Congress.*
26 January	*The Cake Eater* is released.
29 January	Rogers signs contract with Alphonzo E. Bell Corporation, Los Angeles, to purchase 159.721 acres of land in Santa Monica Mountains for $319,442.
3 February	*The Cowboy Sheik* is released.
4–6 February	Filming of *Gee Whiz, Genevieve.*
18–20 February	Filming of *Highbrow Stuff.*
21 February–12 March	Filming of *Don't Park There.*
14 March	Last day passes for Hal Roach Studios to assume option on Rogers's contract.
17–29 March	Filming of *Our Congressman.*
30 March	*Big Moments from Little Pictures* is released.
2 April	Filming of *Don't Park There.*
11–29 April	Filming of *A Truthful Liar.*
24 April	Rogers speaks at dedication of new Metro-Goldwyn-Mayer studios, Culver City, Calif.
27 April	*High Brow Stuff* is released.
5 May	Retakes of *Our Congressman.*
12 May	Rogers's production unit at Hal Roach Studios is terminated.
16–18 May	Rogers and his wife visit family and friends in Chelsea and Claremore, Okla.
16 May	Rogers speaks at Chelsea Chamber of Commerce meeting.
ca. 20 May	Arrives in New York City.
25 May	*Going to Congress* is released.
26 May	Meets with film executives in New York City and submits proposal for "Will Rogers Weekly" newsreel.
28 May	Visits gallery of U.S. House of Representatives, Washington.
8 June	Leaves for Cleveland.
9–12 June	Covers Republican national convention in Cleveland as syndicated writer.
18–21 June	Performs in "tryout" run in Atlantic City of new *Ziegfeld Follies.*
24 June–9 July	Reports on Democratic national convention, Madison Square Garden, New York City.
24 June–ca. 29 October	Headlines *Ziegfeld Follies of 1924,* New Amsterdam Theatre, New York City.

22 June	*Don't Park There* is released.
29 June	*Jubilo, Jr.* is released.
4 July	Rogers receives two half-votes for Democratic nomination for president.
6 July	Speaks at campaign rally for presidential candidate William G. McAdoo.
20 July	*Our Congressman* is released.
28 July	Addresses convention of Royal Order of Moose, Carnegie Hall, New York City.
17 August	*A Truthful Liar* is released.
31 August	Stars in polo match at Westchester Biltmore Field, Rye, N.Y.
3 September	Entertains at dinner for Prince of Wales, Piping Rock Country Club, Long Island, N.Y.
4 September	Dines with Prince of Wales at luncheon, Long Island.
6 September	Attends dinner at Piping Rock Country Club at invitation of the prince.
16 September	Watches International Polo Tournament match at Meadow Brook Club, Westbury, Long Island.
28 September	*Gee Whiz, Genevieve* is released.
29 September	American Tobacco Company offers Rogers twenty-six-week contract to write advertising copy for its Bull Durham tobacco at $500 weekly.
12 October	Speaks at testimonial dinner for Eddie Cantor hosted by Solax Club, Pennsylvania Hotel, New York City.
27 October	Addresses luncheon of Catholic Actors Guild, Hotel Astor, New York City.
30 October 1924– 7 March 1925	Stars in fall edition of *Ziegfeld Follies of 1924*, New Amsterdam Theatre.
4 November	Appears on election night radio broadcast from Waldorf-Astoria Hotel, New York City. Rogers's forty-fifth birthday.
20 November	Leases house and acreage in East Williston, Long Island, for one year at $7,000.
23 November	Benefit for *New York American* Christmas and Relief Fund, Earl Carroll Theater.

26 November	Speaks at luncheon at YWCA, New York City.
4 December	Delivers remarks at Alexander Hamilton Dinner of the Alumni of Columbia College, New York City.
14 December	*New York Times* reviews Rogers's third book, *The Illiterate Digest.*
ca. 18–24 December	Rogers and son Jimmy visit Chelsea, Okla., to be with Rogers's sister, Maud, who is seriously ill.
25 December	Returns to stage of *Ziegfeld Follies*, New York City.

1925

ca. 1 January	Rogers begins to provide advertising copy for Bull Durham tobacco.
4 January	Entertains at banquet at Hotel Astor, New York City.
7 January	Appears at luncheon for automobile dealers, Commodore Hotel, New York City.
8 January	Performs in *Red Pepper Revue*, a tribute to the Columbia Burlesque Circuit, Columbia Theatre, New York City.
13 January	Appears at luncheon for Big Brother and Big Sister Federation, Hotel Roosevelt, New York City.
19 January	Speaks at dedication held in Manhattan of new E. F. Albee Theatre, Brooklyn, N.Y.
20 January	Shares podium with Carl Sandburg at annual luncheon of National Association of Book Publishers, Yale Club, New York City. Later, speaks at U.S. Polo Association event, Biltmore Hotel, New York City.
23 January	Addresses Pennsylvania League of Women Voters, Philadelphia.
24 January	Participates in morning benefit at Manhattan Opera House. Son Bill Rogers and nephew Bruce Quisenberry leave New York City for extended tour of Europe.
31 January	Rogers and his wife dine in New York City with actor William S. Hart and artist Charles Russell and wife Nancy.
1 February	Speaks at banquet for Jewish Theatrical Guild of America, Commodore Hotel.

6 February	Entertains executives of Standard Oil Company of New Jersey at dinner at Biltmore Hotel.
12 February	Benefit for children's clinic in New York City.
18 February	Performs at World Court Ball, Plaza Hotel, New York City, sponsored by League of Nations Non-Partisan Association.
22 February	Provides entertainment at Lighthouse for the Blind, New York City.
27 February	Speaks at Genesee Society Dinner, Commodore Hotel. Radio station WJY broadcasts the event.
28 February	Benefits for Cathedral of St. John the Divine, Palace and Hippodrome Theatres, New York City.
6 March	Presides as master of ceremonies at supper-dance for Newspaper Women's Club, Ritz-Carlton Hotel, New York City.
10 March–4 July	Performs in spring edition of *Ziegfeld Follies of 1925*, New Amsterdam Theatre, New York City.
22 March	Roasts Gov. Al Smith at Friars Club dinner, Hotel Astor. Event is broadcast on radio.
29 March	Performs in annual *Friars' Frolic*, Manhattan Opera House, New York City.
14 April	Participates in cabaret to benefit a children's clinic in New York City.
15 April	Meets Bill, Jr., on his return from Europe.
19 April	Appears at dinner for American Woman's Association, Plaza Hotel.
21 April	Speaks at Pennsylvania Society luncheon, Waldorf-Astoria Hotel, New York City.
23 April	Visits with President Coolidge at his office in Washington. Speaks at Gridiron Club dinner, New Willard Hotel, Washington.
24 April	Takes airplane ride with Brig. Gen. William (Billy) Mitchell, Bolling Field, Washington.
26 April	Appears at Lambs Club Spring Gambol, Metropolitan Opera House, New York City.
28 April	Spends several hours with residents of Salvation Army Industrial Home, New York City.
3 May	Appears at five theaters in New York City in benefit for National Vaudeville Artist Fund.

25 May	Rogers's first edition of new syndicated piece, "The Worst Story I Have Heard Today," is published in *Tulsa Daily World*. He receives $300 weekly for the column.
ca. 1 June 1925–15 January 1927	"Worst Story I Have Heard Today" appears almost weekly in *Tulsa Daily World* and other newspapers.
4 June	Agrees to start national lecture tour under management of Charles L. Wagner on 1 October for total fee of $82,500.
15 June	Sister Maud Rogers Lane dies in Chelsea, Okla.
15–ca. 18 June	Rogers is away from New York City to attend his sister's funeral.
6 July–19 September	Stars in summer run of *Ziegfeld Follies*, New Amsterdam Theatre.
13 July	Wires newspaper editor in Bartlesville, Okla., to squelch boom for governor of Oklahoma.
16 September	Speaks at radio industries dinner, Commodore Hotel. Twelve radio stations broadcast the event.
1 October	Begins lecture tour with The de Reszke Singers, Park Church, Elmira, N.Y. Article by Rogers appears in tour program.
2 October	Lecture tour, Kalurah Temple, Binghamton, N.Y.
3 October	Auditorium, Canton, Ohio.
4 October	First Christian Church, Canton; Masonic Hall, Cleveland.
5 October	Memorial Hall, Columbus, Ohio.
6 October	Carnegie Music Hall, Pitttsburgh.
7 October	Memorial Hall, Springfield, Ohio.
8 October	Woodland Auditorium, Lexington, Ky.
9 October	Odeon Theatre, St. Louis.
10 October	Ivanhoe Temple, Kansas City, Mo.
11 October	Auditorium, St. Joseph, Mo.
12 October	Civic Center Auditorium, Bartlesville, Okla.
13 October	Convention Hall, Tulsa.
14 October	Visits family and friends in Claremore and Chelsea, Okla., where he stays overnight at sister's home.
15 October	City Auditorium, Ponca City, Okla.
17 October	Shrine Auditorium, Oklahoma City.

18 October	Joplin Theater, Joplin, Mo.
20 October	Auditorium, Denver. Rogers speaks in afternoon at YMCA dinner.
21 October	Municipal Auditorium, Omaha, Nebr.
22 October	Central High School Auditorium, Madison, Wis.
23 October	Coliseum, Toledo, Ohio.
24 October	Orchestra Hall, Detroit.
25 October	Murat Theatre, Indianapolis.
26 October	Park Theatre, Youngstown, Ohio.
27 October	Des Moines, Iowa.
28 October	Auditorium, St. Paul, Minn.
29 October	Auditorium, Saginaw, Mich.
30 October	Pabst Theatre, Milwaukee.
31 October	Memorial Hall, Dayton, Ohio.
1 November	Auditorium, Chicago.
2 November	Shrine Mosque Auditorium, Springfield, Mo.
3 November	Municipal Auditorium, Birmingham, Ala.
4 November	Ryman Auditorium, Nashville, Tenn. Rogers visits with governor at state executive's mansion.
5 November	Auditorium, Memphis.
6 November	Municipal Auditorium, Jackson, Miss.
7 November	Montgomery, Ala.
8 November	Attends dinner in his honor at Antoine's Restaurant, New Orleans. Lengthy remarks by Rogers are published in *Times-Picayune*.
9 November	Jerusalem Temple, New Orleans.
10 November	City Auditorium, Houston.
11 November	Auditorium, Waco, Tex. Betty Rogers is in audience.
12 November	Central High School Auditorium, Fort Worth.
13 November	City Auditorium, Houston; Fair Park Auditorium, Dallas.
15 November	Spends "free" day in Wichita Falls, Tex.
16 November	Junior College Auditorium, Wichita Falls.
17 November	Wichita, Kans. Charters special train to reach Wichita in time for concert.
18 November	City Auditorium, Lincoln, Nebr.
19 November	Central High School Auditorium, Sioux City, Iowa.
20 November	New Armory, Duluth, Minn.

21 November	High school auditorium, Hibbing, Minn. Betty Blake Rogers accompanies her husband on tour.
25 November	Hill Auditorium, Ann Arbor, Mich.
26 November	Elmwood Music Hall, Buffalo, N.Y.
27 November	Convention Hall, Rochester, N.Y.
28 November	Auditorium, Washington. Rogers visits at White House with President Coolidge.
29 November	Palace Theatre, Waterbury, Conn.
30 November	City Auditorium, Richmond, Va.
1 December	Charlotte, N.C.
2 December	Auditorium, Asheville, N.C.
3 December	Reynolds Memorial Auditorium, Winston-Salem, N.C.
4 December	Atlanta.
5 December	Bijou, Chattanooga, Tenn.
7 December	Palais Royale, South Bend, Ind.
8 December	Emery Auditorium, Cincinnati.
9 December	Market Auditorium, Wheeling, W.Va.
10 December	Carmichael Auditorium, Clarksburg, W.Va.
11 December	Lyric Theatre, Baltimore. Rogers attends the court-martial trial of Billy Mitchell in Washington, D.C.
13 December	Broad Street Theatre, Newark, N.J.
15 December	Symphony Hall, Boston.
17 December	Appears with The de Reszke Singers in "Artistic Mornings," Plaza Hotel, New York City.
26 December	Hosts benefit horse show at his home for Beverly Hills Woman's Club.

1926

20 January	Rogers arrives in Miami Beach, Fla., accompanied by his wife.
21 January	Plays polo at Nautilus Polo Fields, Miami Beach.
27 January	Auditorium, Daytona Beach, Fla., with The de Reszke Singers.
29 January	Betty Rogers purchases 84.373 acres in Santa Monica Mountains for $120,231.52.
30–31 January	Davis Island Coliseum, Tampa, Fla.
1 February	Coliseum, St. Petersburg, Fla.
5 February	City Auditorium, Raleigh, N.C.

6 February	Rogers visits Bull Durham factory, Durham, N.C., and then travels to nearby Chapel Hill.
7 February	Arrives in Greenville, S.C.
8 February	Fine Arts Auditorium, Greenville.
9 February	New Princess Theater, Columbia, S.C.
10 February	High school auditorium, Little Rock, Ark.
16 February	Rogers is guest of governor of Texas at luncheon in Austin.
18 February	High school auditorium, Breckenridge, Tex.
19 February	Auditorium, Amarillo, Tex. Rogers visits ranches in area.
20 February	Liberty Hall, El Paso.
24 February	American Legion War Memorial Building, San Diego.
1 March	Rogers visits Salt Lake City.
3 March	City Auditorium, Pueblo, Colo.
4 March	Albert Taylor Hall, Emporia, Kans.
6 March	Armory, Akron, Ohio, for twenty-fifth anniversary banquet of Davey Tree Specialists.
15 March	Stops in Chelsea, Okla., for visit.
16 March	Hippodrome Theatre, Okmulgee, Okla.; Orpheum, Muskogee, Okla.
18 March	Memorial Auditorium, Coffeyville, Kans.
19 March	City Auditorium, Newton, Kans.
1 April	National Theater, Greensboro, N.C.
3 April	Mason Theatre, Goldsboro, N.C.
5 April	Eastern Carolina Exposition, Greenville, S.C.
ca. 8 April	Stops in Dayton, Ohio, to visit Annie Oakley and Frank Butler.
9 April	City Auditorium, Huntington, W.Va.
10 April	Maryland Theater, Cumberland, Md.
11 April	Carnegie Hall, New York City.
12 April	Visits with *New York Times* publisher Adolph S. Ochs, New York City.
15 April	Stops in Philadelphia to confer with *Saturday Evening Post* editor George H. Lorimer.
19 April	Massey Hall, Toronto.
20 April	Closes lecture tour with performance in Philadelphia.

26 April	Receives passport.
1–7 May	Rogers and son Bill sail to Europe aboard the S.S. *Leviathan*.
7 May	Arrives in Southampton, England.
9 May	Gives interviews in London.
11 May	Visits Parliament and meets Lady Nancy Astor and other members.
12 May	Speaks at American Club, London, as guest of honor.
13 May	Dines with U.S. ambassador and others at Lady Astor's residence.
14 May	Visits with Prince of Wales at St. James Palace and applies for visa to visit Russia.
15 May	Flies with his son from London to Paris.
17 May	Leaves Paris for Geneva.
18 May	Attends session of League of Nations Preparatory Commission for the Disarmament Conference, Geneva.
20 May	Leaves Geneva by train for Rome by way of Milan.
21 May	Arrives in Rome and spends day writing.
22 May	Writes while son Bill tours Rome.
23 May	Tours Rome with his son.
24 May	Hosts group for dinner in Rome while Bill goes to movies.
25 May	Visits Italian cavalry school in Rome and speaks at banquet, American College.
26 May	Visits Vatican with his son and is accorded papal audience.
27 May	Speaks at banquet and ball for Alliance Internationale de l'Hotellerie, Excelsior Hotel, Rome.
28 May	Meets Premier Benito Mussolini in private session.
ca. 8–22 June	In Spain with son Bill.
12 June	Interviews Spanish dictator Miguel Primo de Rivera, Madrid.
ca. 23 June	Returns to London.
ca. 3 July	Attends event at American Club in Paris.
ca. 4–6 July	Visits Moscow.
ca. 7 July	Arrives in Warsaw.

10 July	Addresses American Club, Hotel Adlon, Berlin.
12 July	Returns to England.
ca. 13 July–	
ca. 7 September	London.
14 July	Signs contract to appear in British film *Tip Toes*.
19 July–ca. 14 August	Performs in *Cochran's 1926 Revue*, London Pavilion, Piccadilly.
25 July	Visits with Lord Thomas R. Dewar.
29 July	Sends brief cable to *New York Times* about Lady Astor sailing for United States.
30 July	*New York Times* publishes Rogers's cable, first of what will become known as "Daily Telegrams."
31 July–27 September	Rogers continues to provide *New York Times* with almost daily cables, forty-six in all.
7 August	Betty Blake Rogers and children Mary and Jimmy arrive in England to join Rogers and elder son, Bill.
14 August	Rogers works on filming of *Tip Toes*.
ca. 17 August–	
ca. 4 September	Performs at supper club in London.
17 August	Appears on radio broadcast in London and then donates his fee to local hospital charity.
8 September	Stages benefit at La Scala Theatre, Dublin, for victims of a fire.
ca. 8–ca. 20 September	Visits several sites in Europe to film scenes for series of travelogues.
11 September	Berlin.
16 September	Germany.
17–20 September	Paris.
21 September	Leaves England by ship for United States.
24–26 September	Stages three-night benefit aboard S.S. *Leviathan* for victims of Florida hurricane.
27 September	Arrives in New York City.
29 September	Receives telegram to visit overnight at White House. Lunches in Philadelphia with *Saturday Evening Post* editor Lorimer.
30 September	Dines at White House with President and Mrs. Coolidge and stays overnight.

1 October	Arrives in New York City by plane via Philadelphia.
4 October	Opens his second year on lecture circuit with The de Reszke Singers, Bronxville Theatre, Bronxville, N.Y.
5 October	High school auditorium, Passaic, N.J.
6 October	High school auditorium, Binghamton, N.Y.
7 October	Massey Hall, Toronto.
8 October	Auditorium, Ottawa.
10 October	Montreal.
11 October	Buffalo, N.Y.
11 October 1926– 16 August 1935	Rogers's "Daily Telegrams" run in national syndication; total of 2,771 are syndicated.
12 October	Market Auditorium, Wheeling, W.Va.
13 October	Emery Auditorium, Cincinnati.
14 October	Ryman Auditorium, Nashville, Tenn.
15 October	Municipal Auditorium, Birmingham, Ala.
16 October	New City Auditorium, Macon, Ga.
17 October	Spartanburg, S.C.
18 October	Montgomery Theater, Spartanburg.
19 October	Wesley Memorial, Atlanta.
20 October	High school auditorium, Gulfport, Miss.
21 October	Auditorium, Memphis.
22 October	Ada, Okla.
23 October	Muskogee, Okla.
24 October	Joplin Theatre, Joplin, Mo.
25 October	Visits the 101 Ranch in Ponca City, Okla.
26 October	Okmulgee, Okla.
27 October	Convention Hall, Tulsa. Rogers visits his boyhood ranch at nearby Oologah.
28 October	University Auditorium, Norman, Okla.; Shrine Auditorium, Oklahoma City.
29 October	First Baptist Church Auditorium, Fort Worth.
30 October	San Antonio.
31 October	San Antonio. *New York Times* publishes review of Rogers's newest book, *Letters of a Self-Made Diplomat to His President.*
1 November	City Auditorium, Houston.

2 November	University Men's Gymnasium, Austin. Rogers dines with Gov. Dan Moody.
3 November	Fair Park Auditorium, Dallas.
4 November	Lubbock, Tex.
5 November	Lyric Theatre, San Angelo, Tex.
6 November	Auditorium, Waco, Tex.
7 November	Fort Worth.
8 November	Municipal Auditorium, Amarillo, Tex.
9 November	Junior college auditorium, Wichita Falls, Tex.
10 November	First Baptist Church, Abilene, Tex.
11 November	Texarkana, Tex.
12 November	High school auditorium, Corsicana, Tex.
13 November	High school auditorium, Little Rock, Ark.
14 November	Visits in Chelsea, Okla., en route to Kansas.
15 November	Theater, Independence, Kans. Rogers participates in national broadcast to inaugurate NBC radio network.
16 November	Ivanhoe Temple, Kansas City, Mo. Rogers also speaks at national 4-H banquet.
17 November	Topeka, Kans.
18 November	Wichita, Kans.
19 November	Denver.
20 November	Macky Auditorium, Boulder, Colo.
21 November	St. Joseph, Mo.
22 November	Auditorium, St. Joseph.
23 November	Orchestra Hall, Chicago.
24 November	Memorial Hall, Lima, Ohio.
25 November	Carnegie Hall, Pittsburgh.
26 November	State Arsenal, Springfield, Ill.
27 November	National Guard Armory, Indianapolis.
28 November	Louisville, Ky.
29 November	Rogers gives impromptu performance at son Bill's school, Culver Military Academy, Culver, Ind.
30 November	Kalamazoo, Mich.
1 December	Coliseum, Toledo, Ohio.
2 December	Akron, Ohio.
3 December	Shrine Auditorium, Fort Wayne, Ind.
4 December	Grand Rapids, Mich. Rogers receives telegram from Douglas Fairbanks informing him that he has been "elected" mayor of Beverly Hills, Calif.

5 December	Chicago.
6 December	Henry H. Stambaugh Auditorium, Youngstown, Ohio.
7 December	Utica, N.Y.
8 December	Carnegie Hall, New York City.
9 December	Elizabeth, N.J. Rogers presides as master of ceremonies at dedication of new Ziegfeld Theatre, New York City.
10 December	Lyric Theater, Baltimore.
11 December	Auditorium, Washington. Rogers also visits U.S. Senate and speaks at National Press Club.
12 December	Washington.
13 December	Scranton, Pa.
14 December	Jamestown, N.Y.
15 December	Syria Mosque, Pittsburgh.
16 December	Irving Theatre, Wilkes-Barre, Pa.
17–18 December	Chicago.
19–20 December	Travels home by train.
21 December	Arrives in Los Angeles. Rogers and family members are escorted to Beverly Hills Hotel, where he is inaugurated as mayor of Beverly Hills.
22 December 1926–2 January 1927	Spends time with his family at Santa Monica ranch.
31 December	Purchases 418.69 feet of beach-front property in Santa Monica for $357,000.

1927

3–5 January	Rogers travels east by train to resume lecture tour.
6 January	Masonic Temple Auditorium, Detroit.
7 January	Hill Auditorium, Ann Arbor, Mich.
9 January	Coliseum, Richmond, Ind.
10 January	Washington University Fieldhouse, St. Louis.
11 January	Chicago.
12 January	Armory, Grand Rapids, Mich.
13 January	Masonic Temple, Detroit. Rogers visits with Henry Ford at his home.
14 January	Memorial Hall, Columbus, Ohio.
15–ca. 17 January	Lexington, Ky.
18 January	Knoxville, Tenn.

19 January	Spartanburg, S.C.
20 January	Armory Auditorium, Norfolk, Va.
21 January	Charleston, W. Va.
22 January	Lynchburg, Va.
23–26 January	Travels in state of New York, making stops in New York City, Syracuse, and Utica.
27 January	Garden Theatre, Atlantic City. Rogers signs his last will and testament in New York City.
28 January	Town Hall, New York City, and Music Hall, Troy, N.Y.
29 January	Convention Hall, Camden, N.J.
30 January	New York City.
31 January	Roanoke, Va.
1 February	City Auditorium, Raleigh, N.C.
2 February	Daytona Beach, Fla.
3 February	Visits with John D. Rockefeller, Sr., at his winter home at Ormond Beach, Fla.
4 February	Biscayne Fronton, Miami.
5–6 February	Miami.
7 February	St. Petersburg, Fla.
8 February	Pensacola, Fla.
9 February	Sarasota, Fla.
10 February	Palm Beach, Fla.
11 February	Municipal Auditorium, Tampa, Fla.
12 February	Colonial Theater, Athens, Ga.
13 February	Aiken Theater, Aiken, S.C.
14 February	Columbia Theatre, Columbia, S.C.
15 February	Asheville, N.C.
16 February	Pinehurst, N.C.
17 February	High school auditorium, Florence, S.C. Rogers purchases six lots in California Riviera section, Los Angeles County, for $75,000.
18 February	Municipal Auditorium, Montgomery, Ala. Afterward, Rogers addresses Alabama legislature.
19 February	Jackson, Miss.
20 February	Hot Springs, Ark.
21 February	Auditorium, Hot Springs.
22 February	University of Arkansas Gymnasium, Fayetteville, Ark.

23 February	Fort Smith, Ark.
24 February	High school auditorium, Breckenridge, Tex.
25 February	Brownwood, Tex.
27 February	Amarillo, Tex.
28 February	Armory, Albuquerque.
1 March	Liberty Hall, El Paso.
2–3 March	Tucson.
4 March	Santa Barbara, Calif.
5 March	In ad in *Exhibitor's Herald*, Rogers "warns" theater owners about release of his travelogue series, *Strolling Through Europe with Will Rogers*.
7 March	Riverside, Calif.
8 March	Pomona, Calif.
9 March	Philharmonic Auditorium, Los Angeles.
10 March	Fresno, Calif.
11 March	Scottish Rite Auditorium, San Francisco.
12 March	Orpheum, Oakland, Calif.
14 March	San Jose State Teachers College, Calif.
15 March	Addresses the California state assembly in Sacramento.
16 March	Speaks to members of Nevada legislature, Carson City.
17 March	Flies to Salt Lake City.
18 March	Frazier Hall, Pocatello, Ida.
19 March	Pinney Theatre, Boise, Ida.
20 March	Portland, Ore.
21 March	First Baptist Church, Tacoma, Wash.
22 March	Civic Auditorium, Portland, Ore.
23 March	Aberdeen, Wash.
24 March	Eagles' Auditorium, Seattle.
25 March	Armory, Yakima, Wash.
26 March	American Theater, Spokane.
27 March	Spokane.
28 March	Missoula, Mont.
29 March	Broadway Theater, Butte, Mont.
30 March	Marlow Theater, Helena, Mont.
31 March	Grand Theater, Great Falls, Mont.
1 April	Babcock Theatre, Billings, Mont.
2 April	Lotus Theatre, Sheridan, Wyo.

4 April	Purchases 1,420.51 feet of beach property adjacent to Santa Monica ranch for $307,500.
5 April	Manhattan, Kans.
6 April	Shrine Temple Auditorium, Des Moines, Iowa.
7 April	Milwaukee.
9 April	Lyceum Theater, Minneapolis. Addresses Minnesota house of representatives in St. Paul.
10 April	Chicago.
11 April	Danville, Ill.
12 April	Vincennes, Ind.
13 April	Bedford, Ind.
14 April	Armory, Lafayette, Ind.
15 April	Masonic Hall, Cleveland.
ca. 16–ca. 18 April	Cleveland.
19 April	Warren, Ohio.
20 April	Pittsburgh.
21 April	Morgantown, W.Va.
22 April	Majestic Theater, Harrisburg, Pa.
23 April	Williamsport, Pa.
24 April	Appears at Lambs Club Gambol, Metropolitan Opera House, New York City.
25 April	Philadelphia.
26 April	High Point, N.C.
27 April	Winston-Salem, N.C.
28 April	City Auditorium, Richmond, Va.
29 April	Staunton, Va.
1 May	Performs at Ziegfeld Theatre, New York City, to benefit Red Cross relief fund for Mississippi River flood victims.
3 May	Albany, N.Y.
4–5 May	New Haven, Conn.
6 May	Leroy Theatre, Pawtucket, R.I.
7 May	Montpelier, Vt.
8 May	Appears at four different theaters in New York City in benefit for Vaudeville Artists Benefit Fund.
9 May	Springfield, Mass.
10 May	Northampton, Mass.
11 May	State Armory, Bennington, Vt.

12 May	Opera House, Boston.
13 May	Playhouse Theatre, Rutland, Vt.
14 May	University of Vermont Gymnasium, Burlington, Vt.
15 May	Modern Theatre, Providence, R.I.
16 May	Oneonta Theatre, Oneonta, N.Y.
17 May	Auditorium, Brattleboro, Vt.
18 May	Pittsfield, Mass.
19 May	Parson's Theatre, Hartford, Conn.
20 May	Concord, N.H.
22 May	New York City.
23 May	City Hall Auditorium, Portland, Me.
24 May	Auditorium, Springfield, Mass.
25 May	Glens Falls, N.Y.
26 May	Charlottesville, Va.
27 May	Bluefield, W.Va.
29 May	New York City.
30 May	Hershey, Pa.
31 May	Atlanta.
1 June	Performs at Saenger Theatre, New Orleans, to benefit Red Cross flood relief fund.
2 June	Takes air tour of flood damage along lower Mississippi River.
3 June	Springfield, Mo.
4–5 June	Visits family in Chelsea and Claremore, Okla., and stays overnight at family ranch, Oologah.
6–7 June	Travels by train to West Coast.
ca. 8 June	Returns to Beverly Hills but suffers from stomach ache.
14 June	Continues to feel pain from what is diagnosed as nervous indigestion.
16 June	Rogers enters hospital in Los Angeles as his condition worsens.
17 June	Undergoes troublesome but successful operation to remove gallstones.
18 June–ca. 1 July	Remains at California Lutheran Hospital to recover from surgery.
19 June	*Tip Toes*, a British National Pictures production starring Rogers, is released in United States.

26 June	Rogers's newest book, *There's Not a Bathing Suit in Russia & Other Bare Facts*, is reviewed in *New York Times*.
27 June	Receives notice that American Red Cross has elected him life member.
2 July	Leaves hospital and returns to Beverly Hills home to continue to recuperate.
3 July–20 August	Remains in southern California, either at Beverly Hills home or at Santa Monica ranch.
29 July	Receives word that new state law will eliminate his position as mayor of Beverly Hills.
ca. 1 August	Rogers begins work on new film, *A Texas Steer*.
12 August	Attends Old Spanish Days Fiesta, Santa Barbara, Calif.
13 August	Speaks at luncheon, Santa Barbara.
20–24 August	Travels by train from Los Angeles to Washington, D.C., for on-location filming of *A Texas Steer*.
25–31 August	Works on location in Washington in film role of newly elected congressman.
27 August	Receives title, "Congressman at Large for the United States," from National Press Club, Washington Auditorium.
1–4 September	Travels back to West Coast.
5 September–4 November	Remains mostly in southern California, where he continues work on *A Texas Steer*.
21 September	Speaks in San Diego at reception honoring Charles Lindbergh.
22 September	Flies with his wife from San Diego to Los Angeles in plane piloted by Lindbergh.
18–21 October	Flies on airmail planes from Los Angeles to New York City and back as postage-paid passenger.
6–9 November	Takes vacation tour of Southwest by train with his wife.
11–17 November	Travels as far east as Detroit and makes stops in Chicago, Culver, Ind., and South Bend, Ind., before returning to California.
18–27 November	Beverly Hills.
25 November	Obtains certificate to travel to Mexico.

28 November	Departs for Mexico.
30 November– 19 December	Visits Mexico as invited guest of U.S. Ambassador Dwight Morrow.
1–7 December	Tours parts of Mexico with President Plutarco Calles and Ambassador Morrow aboard presidential train.
4 December	Rogers's newest film, *A Texas Steer*, opens at Strand Theatre, New York City.
14 December	Greets Charles Lindbergh when aviator arrives in Mexico City for goodwill visit.
ca. 22 December 1927– 6 January 1928	Rogers spends several days at home in Beverly Hills.

1928

4 January	Rogers impersonates President Coolidge during broadcast from his home as part of nationwide radio hook-up.
6–ca. 10 January	Travels to Washington, D.C.
ca. 10 January	Sends letter of apology to President and Mrs. Coolidge for his on-air imitation of president.
11 January	Receives note from President Coolidge dismissing matter of impersonation.
12 January	Appears before House Flood Control Committee and speaks at Democratic party's Jackson Day banquet.
15–19 January	Travels with his wife to attend Sixth Pan American Conference, Havana, Cuba, as unofficial "Representative at Large."
20–ca. 25 January	Travels home to California.
26 January– ca. 17 February	Spends three weeks in southern California before returning to lecture circuit.
20 February	Resumes lecture tour with solo appearance at Tech High, Omaha, Nebr. The de Reszke Singers are no longer part of program.
21 February	Coliseum, Sioux Falls, S.D.
22 February	Shrine Auditorium, Des Moines, Iowa.

23 February	Odeon, St. Louis, Mo. *Life* magazine launches campaign for Rogers as Anti-Bunk party candidate for president.
24 February	Waterloo, Iowa.
26 February	Omaha.
27 February	Shrine Mosque, Pine Bluff, Ark.
28 February	Camden, Ark.
29 February	Auditorium, Memphis.
1 March	Florence, Ala.
2 March	Municipal Auditorium, Birmingham, Ala.
4 March	Visits Tuskegee Institute, Tuskegee, Ala.
5 March	Albany Theatre, Albany, Ga.
6 March	Charlotte, N.C.
7 March	Asheville, N.C.
8 March	Greensboro, N.C.
9 March	Municipal Auditorium, Savannah, Ga.
11 March	Miami Beach, Fla.
12 March	Orlando, Fla.
13 March	St. Petersburg, Fla.
14 March	Armory, Jacksonville, Fla.
15 March	Daytona Beach, Fla.
16 March	Municipal Auditorium, Tampa, Fla.
18 March	Benefit performance for Salvation Army, West Palm Beach, Fla.
19 March	Ocala, Fla.
20 March	Rose Theatre, Thomasville, Ga.
21 March	Raleigh, N.C.
22 March	Atlanta.
23 March	Pinehurst, N.C.
25 March	Ormond Beach, Fla.
26 March	Ohio Theater, Mansfield, Ohio.
27 March	Carnegie Music Hall, Pittsburgh.
28 March	Masonic Hall, Cleveland.
29 March	Armory, Akron, Ohio. Rogers flies in blimp for first time.
30 March	Cincinnati.
31 March–1 April	Lexington, Ky.
2 April	Hill Auditorium, Ann Arbor, Mich.
3 April	Battle Creek, Mich.

4 April	Purdue University, Lafayette, Ind. Rogers acquires lighthouse and 306.94 feet of beach property near Santa Monica ranch for $214,872.
5 April	Anderson, Ind.
6 April	Indianapolis.
8 April	Columbia Auditorium, Louisville, Ky.
9 April	Columbus, Ohio.
10 April	Emery Auditorium, Cincinnati.
11 April	Finney Chapel, Oberlin, Ohio.
12 April	Rochester, N.Y.
13 April	Philadelphia.
15 April	Performs at Gallo Theatre, New York City, with proceeds donated to charity.
16 April	High school, Montclair, N.J.
17 April	Visits New York City.
18 April	Hagerstown, Md.
19 April	High school auditorium, Parkersburg, W.Va.
20 April	Armory, Fairmount, W.Va.
21 April	High school auditorium, Charleston, W.Va.
22 April	Armory, Indianapolis.
23–24 April	Chicago.
25 April	Speaks at banquet, Merchantile Exchange, Chicago.
26 April	St. Paul, Minn.
27 April	Cedar Rapids, Iowa.
28 April	Kansas City, Mo.
30 April	Salina, Kans.
1–2 May	Visits family and friends in Chelsea, Okla.
2–3 May	Flies home to Beverly Hills.
4 May–5 June	Remains in southern California.
6–7 June	Flies to Chicago.
8 June	High school auditorium, Jackson, Mich. Rogers purchases 100 additional feet of beach property at Santa Monica for $80,000.
10–17 June	Covers Republican national convention, Kansas City, Mo.
11 June	Benefit performance at Shubert Theater, Kansas City, for Salvation Army children's programs.
17 June	Stages benefit show at Ivanhoe Auditorium, Kansas City, for family of local police officer killed while on duty.

18 June	Visits Gordon (Pawnee Bill) Lillie at his ranch, Pawnee, Okla.
19–20 June	Spends two days visiting family and friends in Chelsea and Claremore, Okla. Meets Andy Payne, from nearby Foyil, winner of recent transcontinental footrace.
22–ca. 29 June	Reports on Democratic national convention, Houston.
ca. 30 June–1 July	Visits King Ranch near Kingsville, Tex.
1–3 July	Returns by train and plane to California.
4–17 July	Remains in southern California.
18–20 July	Travels eastward to make some personal appearances.
21 July	Auditorium, Ocean Grove, N.J.
23 July	Casino Theatre, Newport, R.I.
24 July	Symphony Hall, Boston.
25 July	New York City.
26 July	Winona Lake, Ind.
27 July	Chicago.
28–29 July	Returns to California by air.
30 July	Arrives home in Beverly Hills.

Editorial Principles and Practices

DOCUMENT SELECTION FOR VOLUME FOUR

VOLUME FOUR OF *The Papers of Will Rogers* PRESENTS THE READER WITH PRINTED transcriptions of several kinds of documents. These include handwritten and typewritten, personal and business correspondence; telegrams of both a personal and business nature; correspondence printed in a newspaper; published newspaper articles, advertisements, and columns by and about Will Rogers; his notes for speeches and performances, and newspaper records of such events; manuscripts intended for publication; a typescript of a lecture tour performance; personal records, including a payroll statement and income tax documents; insurance inspector's reports; business records, including contracts; transcripts of sound recordings by Rogers; and notes and a transcript for motion picture subtitles. This collection includes a sampling of all documents collected by the Will Rogers Papers project for the time frame of 1915–28, a period during which Rogers and his family had begun to accumulate and retain a greater volume of materials than in previous years. None of the documents contained in this volume have been previously published in comprehensive form in a scholarly work.

The selection of documents for volume four emphasizes the growing diversity of Rogers's professional life, which took him from success on Broadway to his first immersion in filmmaking in Hollywood, and from a return to stardom in New York to a prosperous run on the national lecture circuit. It also covers the development of his career as a writer; his initial work in sound media; and passages in his personal life, as he and wife, Betty Blake Rogers, gained and lost a son, a favorite sister of Rogers died, and the family made a permanent transition from New York to California. Correspondence selected for this volume records and explains Rogers's personal life and relationships involving his family, friends, and work. Letters and telegrams written by, to, and about Rogers help delineate his connections with members of his immediate and extended family, and record and describe the nature and evolution of his professional life. They provide the reader with an understanding of his feelings about his work, his travels, and the people with whom he interacted. Business and personal records follow the progression of his career; document, often in intimate financial detail, the successes and challenges in his work; and provide a view of the changing fortunes and situations in his private life. The notes he prepared for stage monologues, theatrical skits, speeches, lecture appearances, and film subtitles help document the topicality, thrust, and maturation of Rogers's humor during this period. Along with his published material in the volume, these unpublished items also hold a mirror to the times, capturing for the reader a unique perspective of the events, people, views, and cultural themes of both critical and incidental interest to American society at all levels. The published articles by Rogers included in this book help complete a documentary record of his miscellaneous work in print. The several manuscripts of other writings meant for publication provide a sampling of his syndicated columns and of his efforts at writing advertising copy, complementing previous scholarly editions of such material. Published articles by and about Rogers help the reader follow the schedule of his public appearances, sample reactions to his performances and to his person, and sense his rise to national prominence. The transcripts of his sound recordings provide a readily accessible record of a little-known medium for his humor. Records of his lecture appearances, from a published account of his first performance on the circuit to a virtually verbatim transcript of one of his final lecture appearances, document ways he modified his lecture monologue over time. To maximize space for original documents, annotations concerning the people, events, places, and concepts mentioned in the materials have been kept brief. They generally give concise background information and explain the immediate context, although longer explanations are given as required.

PLACEMENT OF DOCUMENTS

Documents are presented in chronological sequence, determined by date of authorship, performance, or publication. In cases where the date of the author's creation is not known and a document appeared in published form, the date of publication is used to determine placement. Incompletely dated documents are placed at the end of a given time frame (e.g., a document dated February 1919, with no specific day given, would appear following all other documents for February 1919); similarly, a document dated with only a year or season (e.g., 1919 or fall 1920) is placed at the end of that year or in context within the seasonal period of time. Dates construed by editors are indicated in document headings as "circa" (ca.) a given date, usually with some explanation of the choice of date given in the notes. Questionable dates or errors in dating in place and date lines are noted or corrected within square brackets. Dates have been construed either from the content of the document (e.g., mention within the document of a particular event or date or allusion to a stage in Rogers's chronology) or from other material (e.g., a hotel letterhead that indicates context with other similar letters or a postmark on an envelope in which an original, undated letter was received). The date designation of documents created on more than one day (e.g., a letter written over a course of several days or a composite document containing a series of reviews from a particular time period) indicates a time span (e.g., November–December 1922), and the document is placed according to the first date in that span. Two or more documents of the same date are arranged according to historical sequence or in the best contextual relationship to documents that directly precede or follow.

Volume four consists of six thematic sections, each with its own introduction. Section divisions reflect discrete stages in Rogers's personal life or career. Part one, "Broadway Stardom," focuses on his breakthrough on the Broadway stage and the beginning of his long, successful association with the Ziegfeld organization. It documents his initial appearance before a sitting U.S. president and covers the early stages of his writings for newspapers. Part two, "From Broadway to Hollywood," opens with Rogers's initiation into the world of motion pictures and then takes the reader through the transitional period preceding his shift from the theatrical stage to the movie set. It continues to document his published writings and introduces his new opportunity for expression in producing intertitles for motion pictures. Part three, "Back to Broadway," starts with the permanent relocation of the growing Rogers family to the glamorous new film capital of Hollywood. It covers the immersion of Rogers in the motion picture industry, first as an actor and occasional scenarist for a major film production company and then as a struggling producer and performer within his own motion picture operation. It then follows Rogers back to New York and Broadway, where he returns to the Ziegfeld stage, makes scores of appearances as a banquet speaker, and churns out more writings for publication and the screen, all in a successful effort to recover the financial position lost by his foray into film production. Part four, "Return to Hollywood," eventually finds Rogers back in California and once more making pictures, this time for someone else. Along the way, he begins a national syndicated weekly newspaper column, tries his voice at sound recordings, and writes his third book. Part five, "On to Europe," opens with his reportorial experience at the interminable Democratic national convention of 1924 and his final run in the *Ziegfeld Follies*. It also documents the grief felt in the extended Rogers family over the fatal illness of a favorite sister. It records the growing reach and significance of Rogers's syndicated writings, chronicles his early seasons on the national lecture circuit, and culminates with accounts of his five-month-long, career-enhancing experience in Europe. Finally, part six,

"On to Politics—With a Smile," brings Rogers back to the United States and the lecture circuit and documents his growing prominence in national political circles, concluding with Rogers on the brink of his satiric "run" for the presidency in 1928.

In each section of the volume, introductions set the context and identify some of the major themes that appear in the documents that follow. Headnotes introduce particular documents, further establishing their context and supplying brief, pertinent information.

PRESENTATION OF DOCUMENTS AND EDITORIAL ELEMENTS

All documents are presented with a caption or document heading, a date and place line, a descriptive source note, and, wherever appropriate, annotations.

Captions of correspondence assume that Will Rogers is either the author or the recipient of the letter and indicate only the other party in the correspondence (e.g., "To Will Rogers, Jr." or "From Florenz Ziegfeld, Jr."). While correspondence by letter is implied in the caption, telegraphic correspondence is noted in the document heading by the use of the word *telegram*. Primary documents other than correspondence, and published third-party documents, are given descriptive titles (e.g., "Notes for Appearance at Friars Club" or "Article in *Elmira Advertiser*"). Document headings also include the date of the document and the place where it originated. The day-month-year dating style is used in the captions, and the abbreviation *ca.* (for *circa*) is used with editorially construed dates.

Place and date lines are printed flush right at the beginning of the documentary text, regardless of where this information may have been presented in the original document. Line breaks of the place and date information are structured in accordance with the original, unless they are of such length as to demand alteration. When no place or date appears on the original document, the place and date line is left blank.

For letters where a recipient's address is given on the original document, the address is set flush left above the salutation, regardless of where the information may have been given in the original. Salutations are similarly set flush left, no matter how they appear in original correspondence. Headlines of printed documents taken from newspapers are centered and, if abridged, are so described in the source note.

During the years embraced in the present volume, Rogers moved steadily from producing documents by hand to typing them on a typewriter. By the mid-1920s he had almost completely turned to his trusty Corona, sometimes a Royal, and had forsaken pen and pencil, except for editing. Using mostly a two-finger style at a pace that seems to have gradually increased, he managed to produce an impressive volume of work. Carefulness on the keys, however, was never a Rogers trademark. His typewritten documents in volume four reflect his relative lack of expertise at the keyboard, his indifference to typing perfection, his rush, his style. Mistyped letters, extra spacing between words and even between letters within words, omission of apostrophes, improper lower- and uppercasing, all the idiosyncrasies of a Rogers typewritten document have been left intact.

All documents, not just those produced by Rogers, are presented with as little editorial intervention as possible. Texts are reproduced as written, with irregularities in grammar, punctuation, and spelling left intact. Paragraphs are indented. Rogers often wrote without punctuation and with irregular use of capitalization. In transcriptions of most documents written or typed by him, extra spacing has been added at the end of a sentence or phrase break where no period or other punctuation was supplied in the original, in order to make the text easier to read. Italics are used to render single-underlined words in autograph texts and italicized text in printed documents. Double-underlined words in autograph texts are rendered in italics with underline. For ease of reading and sake of space, the editors chose to use small capital letters in instances of words given in all capitals. This substitution of small for large capitals applies to all documents, whether printed, typewritten, or handwritten and whether from Rogers or another source. Documents such as letterheads with printed place and date lines or application forms that include blanks filled out by hand are presented with the filled-in words in roman type and the blanks indicated by underlining. Minor typographical errors in published documents have been silently corrected. Misspellings or abbreviations that occur in original documents are clarified if necessary in notes or with the use of square brackets. Illegible words or missing or mutilated text are indicated by an editorial message in italics and square brackets (e.g., [*word illegible*] or [*page torn*]). Interpolations are indicated by the use of the appropriate symbol, ▲, ▶, ▼, or ◀, at the beginning and end of the inserted text. Unless noted in a bracketed editorial message or in the descriptive source note, all interpolations in autograph text are handwritten and all interpolations in typewritten text are type-inserted. Marginal notes are inserted as interpolations at the point of the intended insertion or are quoted in annotations. Some documents that were not written by Rogers have been abridged. Abridgments are indicated by unbracketed ellipses. The source of an ellipsis is indicated either in the descriptive source note or by an annotation.

Closings of letters are set flush right or are run into the last paragraph of the letter, as they are in the original document. Signatures are set flush right, no matter how they were rendered in the original. Postscripts follow signatures, and mailing addresses, endorsements, or docketing are set flush left above the source note.

Descriptive source notes contain the following information: the type of document, given in abbreviated form (e.g., ALS for "autograph letter signed"); a brief indication of the nature of the document (e.g., rc for "recipient's copy"); the source of the document (repository, manuscript collection, or printed source); and any further information pertaining to the physical nature of the document or its content and presentation, including letterhead data. Facts printed, metered, stamped, or written on an envelope or telegram are given if pertinent. All abbreviations used in the source notes are explained in the list of symbols and abbreviations that follows this section.

Annotations are used to clarify the text, to provide cross-references, or to identify people, places, events, and terms. Cross-references to other documents in the volume are given by description and date of the document, with a designation of whether the document is printed "above" or "below" (preceding or following) the cross-reference. Places, events, organizations, and institutions are identified when they are significant to Rogers's life and career or are not widely known. Annotations fully identify individuals who are referred to in the text by initials only or by first or last names (unless an individual appears frequently). Biographical annotations of individuals are presented at first appearance and additional contextual information is given, if appropriate, on subsequent appearances. In some cases, biographical searches either revealed no data or were limited by the obscurity of the individual and lack of public information. Cross-references to biographical annotations in previous volumes are presented at the first mention in the current volume. Bibliographic source citations in the annotations are given in either abbreviated or short-title form. Complete listings of all sources appear either in the list of symbols and abbreviations or in the bibliography.

Symbols and Abbreviations

TEXTUAL DEVICES

[roman]	Editorial clarification or addition to text.
[roman?]	Conjectural reading for missing, mutilated, or illegible text.
[*italic*]	Editorial message regarding the nature of the original text (e.g., [*line missing*], [*page mutilated*], or [*word illegible*]).
. . .	Text editorially abridged.
~~canceled~~	Word deleted in original.
▲ ▲	Text that appears between markers is inserted above the line in the original document.
▼ ▼	Text that appears between markers is inserted below the line in the original document.
◄ ◄	Text that appears between markers is inserted in the immediate left margin in the original document.
► ►	Text that appears between markers is inserted in the immediate right margin in the original document.
► ◄	Text that appears between markers is inserted on the line of copy in the original document.

DESCRIPTIVE ABBREVIATIONS

AD	Autograph document
ALS	Autograph letter signed
AM	Autograph manuscript
AMS	Autograph manuscript signed
ANS	Autograph note signed
CG	Cablegram
PD	Printed document
PDS	Printed document signed
SRT	Sound recording, transcript
TD	Typed document
TDS	Typed document signed
TG	Telegram

TL	Typed letter
TLS	Typed letter signed
TM	Typed manuscript

cc	Carbon copy
cy	Copy other than carbon (correspondence)
dc	Draft copy (of printed article or correspondence)
sc	Sender's copy (correspondence)
rc	Recipient's copy (correspondence)

MANUSCRIPT COLLECTION AND REPOSITORY ABBREVIATIONS

AGC-TCU	Amon Carter Collection, Special Collections, Mary Couts Burnett Library, Texas Christian University, Fort Worth.
BFRC-HFM	Benson Ford Research Center, Henry Ford Museum & Greenfield Village, Dearborn, Mich.
CLSU	University of Southern California, Los Angeles.
CMA	Culver Military Academy, Culver, Ind.
CPpR	Will Rogers State Historic Park, Pacific Palisades, Calif.
CSC-GKC	C. S. Clancy Papers, Gordon Kuntz Private Collection, Woodbury, Minn.
FL-CCPLM	Forbes Library, Calvin Coolidge Presidential Library and Museum, Northampton, Mass.
HHPL	Herbert Hoover Presidential Library, West Branch, Iowa.
HL-HU	The Houghton Library, Harvard University, Cambridge, Mass.
LC-UT	Robert W. Love and Paula McSpadden Love Collection, Department of Special Collections, McFarlin Library, University of Tulsa, Tulsa, Okla.
MD-LC	Manuscript Division, Library of Congress, Washington, D.C.
MoU-WHMC	Western Historical Manuscript Collection, University of Missouri, Columbia.
NNC	Columbia University, Butler Library, New York, N.Y.
NYT-A	Archives, The New York Times Company, New York, N.Y.
OkClaW	Will Rogers Memorial, Claremore, Okla.
OSU	Special Collections, Oklahoma State University, Stillwater.
RFP-DLM	Rogers Family Papers, Doris L. Meyer, Bartlesville, Okla.
URL-CLU	Department of Special Collections, University Research Library, University of California, Los Angeles.

ABBREVIATED CITATIONS FOR PUBLISHED SOURCES

CH	*Chicago Herald,* Chicago
CP	*Claremore Progress,* Claremore, Okla.
CR	*Chelsea Reporter,* Chelsea, Okla.
EA	*Elmira Advertiser,* Elmira, N.Y.
HA	*Huntington Advertiser,* Huntington, W.Va.
HC	*Houston Chronicle,* Houston
KCS	*Kansas City Star,* Kansas City, Mo.
LAE	*Los Angeles Examiner,* Los Angeles
LAEH	*Los Angeles Evening Herald,* Los Angeles
LAT	*Los Angeles Times,* Los Angeles
MPN	*Motion Picture News*
NYMT	*New York Morning Telegraph,* New York, N.Y.
NYT	*New York Times,* New York, N.Y.
ON	*Oklahoma News,* Oklahoma City
PGT	*Pittsburgh Gazette Times,* Pittsburgh
SEP	*Saturday Evening Post*
TDW	*Tulsa Daily World,* Tulsa, Okla.
WD	*Wid's Daily*
WDT	*Wichita Daily Times,* Wichita Falls, Tex.
WES	*Washington Evening Star,* Washington, D.C.
WST	*Wyoming State Tribune,* Cheyenne
WYB	*Wid's Year Book*

REFERENCE WORKS AND FREQUENTLY CITED SOURCES

AFIC F1CS *The American Film Institute Catalog of Motion Pictures Produced in the United States. Feature Films, 1911–1920: Credit & Subject Indexes.* Edited by Patricia King Hanson and Alan Gevinson. Berkeley: University of California Press, 1988.

AFIC F1FE *The American Film Institute Catalog of Motion Pictures Produced in the United States. Feature Films, 1911–1920: Film Entries.* Edited by Patricia King Hanson and Alan Gevinson. Berkeley: University of California Press, 1988.

AFIC F2CS *The American Film Institute Catalog of Motion Pictures Produced in the United States. Feature Films, 1921–1930: Credit & Subject Indexes.* Edited by Kenneth W. Munden. New York: R. R. Bowker, 1971.

AFIC F2FE	*The American Film Institute Catalog of Motion Pictures Produced in the United States. Feature Films, 1921–1930: Film Entries.* Edited by Kenneth W. Munden. New York: R. R. Bowker, 1971.
AFIC F3CS	*The American Film Institute Catalog of Motion Pictures Produced in the United States. Feature Films, 1931–1940: Credit & Subject Indexes.* Edited by Patricia King Hanson and Alan Gevinson. Berkeley: University of California Press, 1991.
AFS	*American Film Studios: An Historical Encyclopedia.* Gene Fernett. Jefferson, N.C.: McFarland, 1988.
AmCar	*The American Car since 1775: The Most Complete Survey of the American Automobile Ever Published.* Editors of *Automobile Quarterly.* 2d ed. New York: L. Scott Bailey, 1971.
ANB	*American National Biography.* Edited by John A. Garraty and Mark C. Carnes. 24 vols. New York: Oxford University Press, 1999.
AVWWI	*American Voices of World War I: Primary Source Documents, 1917–1920.* Edited by Martin Marix Evans. London: Fitzroy Dearborn, 2001.
BBDM	*Baker's Biographical Dictionary of Musicians.* Edited by Nicolas Slonimsky. 8th ed., rev. New York: Schirmer Books, 1992.
BDAC	*Biographical Directory of the American Congress, 1774–1996.* Alexandria, Va.: CQ Staff Directories, 1997.
BDAJ	*Biographical Dictionary of American Journalism.* Edited by Joseph P. McKerns. New York: Greenwood Press, 1989.
BDASBase	*Biographical Dictionary of American Sports: Baseball.* Edited by David L. Porter. New York: Greenwood Press, 1987.
BDASBask	*Biographical Dictionary of American Sports: Basketball and Other Indoor Sports.* Edited by David L. Porter. New York: Greenwood Press, 1989.
BDASFoot	*Biographical Dictionary of American Sports: Football.* Edited by David L. Porter. New York: Greenwood Press, 1987.
BDASOut	*Biographical Dictionary of American Sports: Outdoor Sports.* Edited by David L. Porter. New York: Greenwood Press, 1988.
BDSU	*A Biographical Dictionary of the Soviet Union, 1917–1988.* Jeanne Vronskaya with Vladimir Chuguev. London: K. G. Saur, 1989.

BDUSCong	*Biographical Directory of the United States Congress, 1774–1989, Bicentennial Edition.* Senate Doc. No. 100–34. Washington, D.C.: Government Printing Office, 1989.
BDWWI	*Biographical Dictionary of World War I.* Holger H. Herwig and Neil M. Heyman. Westport, Conn.: Greenwood Press, 1982.
BE	*The Baseball Encyclopedia: The Complete and Definitive Record of Major League Baseball.* Edited by Jeanine Buck et al. 10th ed., rev. New York: Macmillan, 1996.
CA	*Convention Articles of Will Rogers.* Edited by Joseph A. Stout, Jr., and Peter C. Rollins. Stillwater: Oklahoma State University Press, 1976.
CAMT	*A Chronology of American Musical Theater.* Vol. 2, *1912–1951.* Edited by Richard C. Norton. Oxford: Oxford University Press, 2002.
CB	*Current Biography: Who's News and Why, 1947.* Edited by Anna Rothe. New York: H. W. Wilson Co., 1948.
CCBH	*The Columbia Companion to British History.* Edited by Juliet Gardiner and Neil Wenborn. 1995. Reprint. New York: Columbia University Press, 1997.
CEPMJ	*The Complete Encyclopedia of Popular Music and Jazz, 1900–1950.* Vol. 1, *Music Year by Year, 1900–1950.* Roger D. Kinkle. New Rochelle, N.Y.: Arlington House, 1974.
CHE	*The Cambridge Historical Encyclopedia of Great Britain and Ireland.* Edited by Christopher Haigh. Cambridge, U.K.: Cambridge University Press, 1985.
DAB	*Dictionary of American Biography.* Edited by Allen Johnson et al. 20 vols., 10 supps. New York: Charles Scribner's Sons, 1928–95.
DATH	*Documents of American Theater History.* Vol. 2, *Famous American Playhouses, 1900–1971.* William C. Young. Chicago: American Library Association, 1973.
DBD	*The Dickson Baseball Dictionary.* Paul Dickson. New York: Facts on File, 1989.
DE	*The Dance Encyclopedia.* Compiled and edited by Anatole Chujoy and P. W. Manchester. Rev. ed. New York: Simon & Schuster, 1967.
DIH	*A Dictionary of Irish History since 1800.* D. J. Hickey and J. E. Doherty. Totowa, N.J.: Gill & Macmillan, 1980.

DNB	*The Dictionary of National Biography, 1922–1990.* 22 vols., 11 supps. Edited by J. R. H. Weaver et al. Reprint. London: Oxford University Press, 1953–96.
DSUE	*A Dictionary of Slang and Unconventional English: Colloquialisms and Catch-phrases, Solecisms and Catachreses, Nicknames and Vulgarisms.* Eric Partridge; edited by Paul Beale. 8th ed. NewYork: Macmillan, 1984.
DT 1	*Will Rogers' Daily Telegrams.* Vol. 1, *The Coolidge Years, 1926–1929.* Edited by James M. Smallwood and Steven K. Gragert. Stillwater: Oklahoma State University Press, 1978.
EABAuto	*Encyclopedia of American Business History and Biography:The Automobile Industry, 1920–1980.* Edited by George S. May. NewYork: Facts on File, 1989.
EAH	*Encyclopedia of American History.* Edited by Richard B. Morris. NewYork: Harper & Brothers, 1953.
EAR	*Encyclopedia of American Radio, 1920–1960.* Luther F. Sies. Jefferson, N.C.: McFarland & Co., 2000.
EBP	*The Encyclopedia of the British Press, 1422–1992.* Edited by Dennis Griffiths. NewYork: St. Martin's Press, 1992.
ECB	*Encyclopedia of Consumer Brands.* Vol. 1, *Consumable Products.* Edited by Janice Jorgensen. Detroit: St. James Press, 1994.
EG	*Encyclopaedia of Golf.* Compiled by Webster Evans. New York: St. Martin's Press, 1971.
EM	*Encyclopedia of Mexico: History, Society, and Culture.* Edited by Michael S. Werner. 2 vols. Chicago: Fitzroy Dearborn, 1997.
EMF	*Esquire's Encyclopedia of 20th Century Men's Fashions.* O. E. Schoeffler and William Gale. New York: McGraw-Hill, 1973.
EMJR	*Ether and Me or "Just Relax."* Will Rogers. 1929. Rev. ed. Edited by Joseph A. Stout, Jr. Stillwater: Oklahoma State University Press, 1973.
EMT	*The Encyclopedia of the Musical Theatre.* Kurt Gänzl. 2 vols. NewYork: Schirmer Books, 1994.
ENYC	*The Encyclopedia of New York City.* Edited by Kenneth T. Jackson. New Haven, Conn.:Yale University Press, 1995.
ENYS	*The Encyclopedia of the New York Stage, 1920–1930.* Edited by Samuel L. Leiter and Holly Hill. 2 vols.Westport, Conn.: Greenwood Press, 1985.

EPM   *The Encyclopedia of Popular Music.* Compiled and edited by Colin Larkin. 1992. 3d ed. 8 vols. New York: Muze UK, 1998.

EV   *The Encyclopedia of Vaudeville.* Anthony Slide. Westport, Conn.: Greenwood Press, 1994.

EWMeth   *The Encyclopedia of World Methodism: Sponsored by the World Methodist Council and the Commission on Archives and History of the United Methodist Church.* 2 vols. Edited by Nolan B. Harmon et al. Nashville, Tenn.: United Methodist Publishing House, 1974.

FE   *The Film Encyclopedia.* Ephraim Katz. 2d ed. New York: HarperPerennial, 1994.

Film   *Filmarama.* Vol. 1, *The Formidable Years, 1893–1919.* Compiled by John Stewart. Metuchen, N.J.: Scarecrow Press, 1975.

FWR   *The Films of Will Rogers.* Compiled by Anthony Slide. Beverly Hills, Calif.: Academy of Motion Picture Arts and Sciences, 1998.

GLA   *Greek and Latin Authors, 800 B.C.–A.D. 1000.* Michael Grant. New York: H. W. Wilson, 1980.

HBPUS 3   *A History of Book Publishing in the United States.* Vol. 3, *The Golden Age between the Two Wars, 1920–1940.* John Tebbel. New York: R. R. Bowker, 1978.

HCTR   *"He Chews to Run": Will Rogers' Life Magazine Articles, 1928.* Edited by Steven K. Gragert. Stillwater: Oklahoma State University Press, 1982.

HDFI   *Historical Dictionary of Fascist Italy.* Edited by Philip V. Cannistraro. Westport, Conn.: Greenwood Press, 1982.

HDGWR   *A Historical Dictionary of Germany's Weimar Republic, 1918–1933.* C. Paul Vincent. Westport, Conn.: Greenwood Press, 1997.

HDM   *Historical Dictionary of Morocco.* Thomas K. Park. New ed. African Historical Dictionaries, No. 71. Lanham, Md.: Scarecrow Press, 1996.

HD1920s   *Historical Dictionary of the 1920s: From World War I to the New Deal, 1919–1933.* James S. Olson. New York: Greenwood Press, 1988.

HDPE   *Historical Dictionary of the Progressive Era, 1890–1920.* Edited by John D. Bruenker and Edward R. Kantowicz. New York: Greenwood Press, 1988.

HEBM	*The Heritage Encyclopedia of Band Music: Composers and Their Music.* William H. Rehrig; edited by Paul E. Bierley. 2 vols. Westerville, Ohio: Integrity Press, 1991.
HFVVC	*Halliwell's Filmgoer's and Video Viewer's Companion.* Leslie Halliwell. 9th ed. New York: Perennial Library, 1990.
HTBF	*"How to Be Funny" & Other Writings of Will Rogers.* Edited by Steven K. Gragert. Stillwater: Oklahoma State University Press, 1983.
IBP:E	*International Book Publishing: An Encyclopedia.* Edited by Philip G. Altbach and Edith S. Hoshino. New York: Garland Publishing, 1995.
ID	*Illiterate Digest.* Will Rogers. 1924. Reprint. Edited by Joseph A. Stout, Jr. Stillwater: Oklahoma State University, 1974.
IDFF 1	*The International Dictionary of Films and Filmmakers.* Vol. 1, *Films.* Edited by Nicholas Thomas and James Vinson. 2d ed. Chicago: St. James Press, 1990.
IDFF 2	*The International Dictionary of Films and Filmmakers.* Vol. 2, *Directors/Filmmakers.* Edited by Christopher Lyon and Susan Doll. Chicago: St. James Press, 1984.
IDFF 3	*The International Dictionary of Films and Filmmakers.* Vol. 3, *Actors and Actresses.* Edited by James Vinson et al. Chicago: St. James Press, 1986.
IDTL	*An International Dictionary of Theatre Language.* Edited by Joel Trapido et al. Westport, Conn.: Greenwood Press, 1985.
IFI:HD	*The International Film Industry: A History Dictionary.* Anthony Slide. New York: Greenwood Press, 1989.
IGEA	*The International Geographic Encyclopedia and Atlas.* Boston: Houghton Mifflin, 1979.
LSMD	*Letters of a Self-Made Diplomat to His President.* Will Rogers. 1926. Reprint. Edited by Joseph A. Stout, Jr., et al. Stillwater: Oklahoma State University Press, 1977.
ML	*More Letters of a Self-Made Diplomat.* Will Rogers. Edited by Steven K. Gragert. Stillwater: Oklahoma State University Press, 1982.
MT	*Mark Twain, A to Z: The Essential Reference to His Life and Writings.* R. Kent Rasmussen. New York: Facts on File, 1995.
NatCAB	*The National Cyclopaedia of American Biography.* 63 vols. New York: James T. White, 1898–1984.

NAW	*Notable American Women, 1607–1950: A Biographical Dictionary.* Edited by Edward T. James et al. 4 vols. Cambridge, Mass.: Belknap Press of Harvard University Press, 1971–80.
NEAW	*The New Encyclopedia of the American West.* Edited by Howard R. Lamar. New Haven, Conn.: Yale University Press, 1998.
NGDMI	*The New Grove Dictionary of Musical Instruments.* Edited by Stanley Sadie. 3 vols. London: Macmillan, 1984.
NGDO	*The New Grove Dictionary of Opera.* Edited by Stanley Sadie. 4 vols. London: Macmillan, 1992.
NHD	*The New Historical Dictionary of the American Film Industry.* Anthony Slide. Lanham, Md.: Scarecrow Press, 1998.
NOCM	*The New Oxford Companion to Music.* Vol. 2, *K–Z.* Edited by Denis Arnold. Oxford: Oxford University Press, 1983.
NWAT	*Notable Women in the American Theatre.* Edited by Alice M. Robinson et al. New York: Greenwood Press, 1989.
NYTFR	*The New York Times Film Reviews, 1913–1968.* Vol. 6, *Appendix, Index.* New York: New York Times & Arno Press, 1970.
OCAH	*The Oxford Companion to American History.* Thomas H. Johnson. New York: Oxford University Press, 1966.
OCAL	*The Oxford Companion to American Literature.* Gerald Bordman. New York: Oxford University Press, 1984.
OCAT	*The Oxford Companion to American Theatre.* Gerald Bordman. New York: Oxford University Press, 1992.
OCEL	*The Oxford Companion to English Literature.* 1932. 5th ed., revised. Edited by Margaret Drabble. Oxford: Oxford University Press, 1995.
OCMT	*The Oxford Companion to Mark Twain.* Edited by Gregg Camfield. Oxford: Oxford University Press, 2003.
OCSS	*The Oxford Companion to Ships and the Sea.* Edited by Peter Kemp. London: Oxford University Press, 1976.
OCT	*The Oxford Companion to the Theatre.* Edited by Phyllis Hartnoll. 4th ed. Oxford: Oxford University Press, 1983.
OCWSG	*The Oxford Companion to World Sports and Games.* Edited by John Arlott. London: Oxford University Press, 1973.
ODM	*The Oxford Dictionary of Music.* Edited by Michael Kennedy and Joyce Bourne. 2d ed. Oxford: Oxford University Press, 1994.
Papacy	*The Papacy: An Encyclopedia.* 3 vols. Edited by Philippe Levillain et al. New York: Routledge, 2002.

PrivCU	*Private Colleges and Universities.* John F. Ohles and Shirley M. Ohles. 2 vols. Westport, Conn.: Greenwood Press, 1982.
PSI	*Popular Song Index.* Patricia Pate Havlice. Metuchen, N.J.: Scarecrow Press, 1975.
PubCU	*Public Colleges and Universities.* John F. Ohles and Shirley M. Ohles. Westport, Conn.: Greenwood Press, 1986.
PWR 1	*The Papers of Will Rogers.* Vol. 1, *The Early Years, November 1879–April 1904.* Edited by Arthur Frank Wertheim and Barbara Bair. Norman: University of Oklahoma Press, 1996.
PWR 2	*The Papers of Will Rogers.* Vol. 2, *Wild West to Vaudeville, April 1904–September 1908.* Edited by Arthur Frank Wertheim and Barbara Bair. Norman: University of Oklahoma Press, 2000.
PWR 3	*The Papers of Will Rogers.* Vol. 3, *From Vaudeville to Broadway, September 1908 – August 1915.* Edited by Arthur Frank Wertheim and Barbara Bair. Norman: University of Oklahoma Press, 2001.
RHHDAS	*Random House Historical Dictionary of American Slang.* Edited by J. E. Lighter. 2 vols. New York: Random House, 1994.
SWBD	*Southern Writers: A Biographical Dictionary.* Edited by Robert Bain et al. Baton Rouge: Louisiana State University Press, 1979.
TB	*Total Baseball.* Edited by John Thorn et al. 7th ed. Kingston, N.Y.: Total Sports Publishing, 2001.
TCA	*Twentieth Century Authors: A Biographical Dictionary of Modern Literature.* Edited by Stanley J. Kunitz and Howard Haycraft. New York: H. W. Wilson, 1942.
TNBSR	*There's Not a Bathing Suit in Russia & Other Bare Facts.* Will Rogers. 1927. Reprint. Edited by Joseph A. Stout, Jr. Stillwater: Oklahoma State University Press, 1973.
TYS	*Twenty Years of Silents, 1908–1928.* Compiled by John T. Weaver. Metuchen, N.J.: Scarecrow Press, 1971.
UDFT	*The Ultimate Directory of Film Technicians: A Necrology of Dates and Places of Births and Deaths of More than 9,000 Producers, Screenwriters, Composers, Cinematographers, Art Directors, Costume Designers, Choreographers, Executives, and Publicists.* Billy H. Doyle. Lanham, Md.: Scarecrow Press, 1999.
UDSSEP	*The Ultimate Directory of Silent and Sound Era Performers: A Necrology of Actors and Actresses.* Billy H. Doyle. Lanham, Md.: Scarecrow Press, 1999.

USFWW	*The United States in the First World War: An Encyclopedia.* Edited by Anne Cipriano Venzon. New York: Garland Publishing, 1995.
VO	*Variety: Obituaries.* 14 vols. New York: Garland Publishing, 1988.
WA 1	*Will Rogers' Weekly Articles.* Vol. 1, *The Harding/Coolidge Years, 1922–1925.* Edited by James M. Smallwood and Steven K. Gragert. Stillwater: Oklahoma State University Press, 1980.
WA 2	*Will Rogers' Weekly Articles.* Vol. 2, *The Coolidge Years, 1925–1927.* Edited by James M. Smallwood and Steven K. Gragert. Stillwater: Oklahoma State University Press, 1980.
WA 3	*Will Rogers' Weekly Articles.* Vol. 3, *The Coolidge Years, 1927–1929.* Edited by James M. Smallwood and Steven K. Gragert. Stillwater: Oklahoma State University Press, 1981.
WA 4	*Will Rogers' Weekly Articles.* Vol. 4, *The Hoover Years, 1931–1933.* Edited by Steven K. Gragert. Stillwater: Oklahoma State University Press, 1981.
WA 6	*Will Rogers' Weekly Articles.* Vol. 6, *The Roosevelt Years, 1933–1935.* Edited by Steven K. Gragert. Stillwater: Oklahoma State University Press, 1982.
WhAmer	*Who Was Who in America.* 11 vols. Chicago: A. N. Marquis, 1960–96.
WhJour	*Who Was Who in Journalism: 1925–1928.* Gale Composite Biographical Directory Series, No. 4. Detroit: Gale Research, 1978.
WhScreen	*Who Was Who on Screen.* Evalyn Mack Truitt. 1974. 3d ed. New York: R. R. Bowker, 1983.
WRHolly	*Will Rogers in Hollywood.* Bryan B. Sterling and Frances N. Sterling. New York: Crown Publishers, 1984.
WWBoxing	*Who's Who in Boxing.* Bob Burrill. New Rochelle, N.Y.: Arlington House, 1974.
WWHolly	*Who's Who in Hollywood: The Largest Cast of International Film Personalities Ever Assembled.* David Ragan. 2 vols. New York: Facts on File, 1992.
WWOkla	*Who Is Who in Oklahoma.* Lyle H. Boren and Dale Boren. Guthrie, Okla.: Co-Operative Publishing Co., 1935.
WWRodeo	*Who's Who in Rodeo.* Willard H. Porter. Oklahoma City, Okla.: Powder River Book Co., 1982.

1. BROADWAY STARDOM
September 1915–August 1918

Will Rogers dressed for the stage of the *Ziegfeld Follies*. (*C. White Studio photo, OkClaW*)

BY AUGUST 1915 WILL ROGERS HAD PAID HIS PROVERBIAL SHOW BUSINESS DUES. For slightly more than a decade he had made the circuit of the United States, spinning his rope, lassoing horses and humans, giving impressions of other performers, riding a unicycle. He had trouped the Orpheum Circuit and the Keith Circuit and had performed in independent theaters from Davenport to Butte, San Francisco to Boston. He had worked Wild West exhibitions, horse shows, vaudeville houses, and variety theaters in scores of cities around the country. He had played some of the least-known venues, as well as those ranked among the most famous, including Hammerstein's and the Palace[1] in New York City. He had even taken his act to Berlin and London, the latter twice. He had appeared on bills with dog acts and freak acts, song-and-dance duos and solo comedians, impressionists and contortionists, female impersonators and blackface singers.

During the same time, Rogers had managed to marry and start a family. On 25 July 1915 he and his wife of almost seven years, Betty Blake Rogers, celebrated the birth of their second son, James Blake (Jim or Jimmy) Rogers.[2] Along with their other two children, three-year-old William Vann (Will, Jr., or Bill) Rogers, and Mary Amelia Rogers, age two, they lived comfortably in a rented house in Amityville, N.Y.[3] There on Long Island they found sufficient space to rear their expanding family, to keep a stable of horses, and to ride and rope.

In the midst of such relative ease, Rogers nevertheless faced the inevitable pressure of how to provide for his growing brood. At the same time, he probably also sensed that his vaudeville career had neared its peak. After ten years of traveling hard the theatrical road—and along the way, building and earning a well-deserved reputation as a solid, popular performer—Will Rogers had arrived in the late summer of 1915 at a transforming moment in his professional life.

The momentous break came that August. Gene Buck, the assistant to famed Broadway impresario Florenz Ziegfeld, Jr., and a chief writer for Ziegfeld's Broadway production, the *Follies*, signed Rogers for the *Midnight Frolic*, a late-night cabaret atop the New Amsterdam Theatre, home also of the *Follies*.[4] On 23 August 1915 Rogers made his debut at the *Midnight Frolic*, performing his rope tricks and dropping his humorous asides amid the splendor and dazzle of a typical Ziegfeld production. The Oklahoman proved immediately popular. Significantly for his career, his success that fall in the *Midnight Frolic*, as well as in the Broadway revue *Town Topics*, led to his engagement the next July in the *Ziegfeld Follies of 1916* and the launch of a long and prosperous association—financially and professionally—with the Ziegfeld organization.[5]

During these early years with the *Midnight Frolic* and the *Follies*, Rogers honed and fine-tuned his stage routine, working hard to craft and time his gags for best effect. He expanded and refined his use of topical humor, something he had first tried in his vaudeville routines. He more frequently joked about politics and politicians, and played off people in the audience and his fellow performers. Gradually his characteristic rope and chewing gum became mere diversions on stage, handy props to finger while letting a gag take hold or during a transition of thought.

His jokes never spoke malice, yet they could be daring. The *Follies* and *Midnight Frolic* drew some of the most prominent people in New York City. Rogers rarely missed introducing them during a performance and then poking gentle fun at some recognizable foible. Their mention in the morning's headlines would almost guarantee a joke that night. No one, no matter how well known, no matter how powerful, could hope to escape Rogers's wit. Rarely did they want to.

Along with his successful work in the *Midnight Frolic* and the *Follies*, Rogers began at this time to move professionally in new directions. This began in August 1916, when the *New York American* published his first two newspaper articles, both of which concerned a huge rodeo competition being staged in suburban New York City by some of Rogers's old pals from out West.[6] By April 1918 seven more articles had appeared, at least four of which were published in Chicago and Detroit during road tour stops of the *Follies*, and one as a guest contribution to a syndicated column of topical poetry.[7] These early writings were the foretaste of much to come.

Like his humor on stage during these years, Rogers's topics in print mirrored life as he read it in the newspapers and heard it on the streets. His subject matter varied from baseball in Philadelphia to transit strikes in Detroit to crime in Chicago to upheaval in Russia. Increasingly at this time, it also concerned war. This pivotal period in Rogers's life, September 1915 to August 1918, fell squarely within World War I, from the anxious time leading to U.S. entry into the conflict through most of the trying months of American involvement. Reflecting its impact on American society, the war in Europe became a primary focus of Rogers's commentary, spoken and published.

Despite the pain of war, Rogers felt comfortable enough to make the conflict a thrust of his humor. At the same time, he confidently took comedic aim at the president of the United States.[8] One evening in May 1916, about a year before the United States entered the war, President Woodrow Wilson and his entourage descended on a theater in Baltimore to attend the *Frolic*, a touring variety show that featured Rogers and other members of a club of entertainers. Apparently aware in advance that the president would be in the audience, Rogers, in his usual bashful, self-deprecating style, cracked gag after gag about the Wilson administration and its handling of foreign affairs. Much to Rogers's relief and delight—and that of his fellow performers—Wilson laughed loudly and often. On another occasion, less than a month before Congress voted to declare war, Wilson attended a *Follies* performance where Rogers again targeted the administration, the shape of the war, and the national debate over American involvement.

Rogers's professional life took another dramatic new course in the late summer of 1918. That July he and Betty had welcomed into the family their fourth child, Fred Stone Rogers.[9] Shortly thereafter, Rogers began making his first motion picture. His entry into movies soon spelled the end of his career with the Ziegfeld organization, at least for a few years, and a change in geography for the Rogers family. Within a year Will and Betty Rogers, their four children, and their horses had moved to southern California in the heart of the burgeoning new film industry.

For Rogers, the thirty-six months from September 1915 to August 1918 witnessed dramatic, successful turns in his professional life, occurring in the midst of turbulent times in the political, economic, and social life of the United States and the international community. Throughout this period, Rogers continued to communicate in humorous tones to his public the issues, flaws, perfections, and values prevailing in the country. Although he had paid his dues in show business, he continued to find many and new ways of expression.

1. For Oscar Hammerstein and Hammerstein's Theatre, see *PWR*, 2:156–57n.1; for the Palace Theatre, New York City, see *PWR*, 3:322–23n.1.
2. For Betty Blake Rogers see *PWR*, 1:531–33; for James Blake Rogers see *PWR*, 3:431–38.
3. For William Vann Rogers see *PWR*, 3:438–47; for Mary Amelia Rogers see *PWR*, 3:406–11.
4. For Gene Buck see *PWR*, 3:396n.1; for Florenz Ziegfeld, Jr., and his *Midnight Frolic* and *Follies*, see *PWR*, 3:396–98n.1.
5. The revue *Town Topics* opened on 23 September 1915 at the Century Theatre on Central Park West. The extravagant musical production received lukewarm reviews

overall, although the *New York Times* singled out Rogers as "best" of a large cast of entertainers, "so genuinely amusing and likable." The show closed after only sixty-eight performances, but Rogers had already left after being asked to take a 50 percent reduction in salary (*NYT*, 19, 24 September 1915; *EMT*, 2:1532–33; Yagoda, *Will Rogers*, 132–33; undated clipping, *NYMT*, CPpR files, OkClaW).

6. See Newspaper Article by Will Rogers, 6 August 1916 and 8 August 1916, below.

7. See Newspaper Article by Will Rogers, ca. 5 September 1916; Guest Newspaper Column by Will Rogers, 10 May 1917; and Newspaper Article by Will Rogers, 15 December 1917, ca. 22 December 1917, ca. 17 February 1918, 21 February 1918, and ca. 3 March 1918, below.

8. See Notes for Appearance in *Friars' Frolic*, 30 May 1916, below.

9. Fred Stone Rogers, the fourth child of Will and Betty Blake Rogers, was born in Amityville, Long Island, N.Y., on 15 July 1918. Named for the family's close friend, entertainer Fred Stone, the infant died in Los Angeles of diphtheria on 17 June 1920 (Yagoda, *Will Rogers*, 162; certificate of death, Fred Stone Rogers file, OkClaW).

Telegram from Gene Buck
23 September 1915
New York, N.Y.

Rogers received several telegrams from well-wishers before the opening of the revue Town Topics. *Perhaps none signified better this pivotal time in Rogers's theatrical life than the one below. The message itself was typically brief for such first-night greetings; more significant was the sender. Only a month earlier, Gene Buck had given Rogers a break on Broadway that would eventually transform his career.* [1]

66 NY FE 9PM 11

SI NEWYORK CITY NY SEPT 23,1915

WILL ROGERS.

CENTRURY THATRE [*sic*] NEWYORK

HERES HOPING THE OKLAHOMA STRING AND GAB TOSSER IS A HIT.

GENE BUCK

TG, rc. OkClaW, 1975.31.0328. On Postal Telegram–Commercial Cable letterhead.

1. Although brief, Buck's telegram conveyed a crucial element of what attracted Buck to Rogers: his western contrast to the usual Broadway act. Buck had signed Rogers in August 1915 to appear in Florenz Ziegfeld's late-night cabaret *Midnight Frolic*. Rogers made his debut in the *Frolic* on 23 August, dressed as a cowboy, spinning a rope, and delivering a monologue of gags and topical commentary. His appearance in the show would lead within a year to a regular spot in the *Ziegfeld Follies* and mark his transition from a traveling performer on the vaudeville circuit to a featured entertainer on Broadway. Credit for this career change would go in part to Buck and

his faith in the Oklahoman's appeal to the New York theater-going public (Wertheim, ed., *Will Rogers*, 6, 9–10; Yagoda, *Will Rogers*, 132–33, 139–40, 146–48).

From Solomon Wolerstein and Marcus L. Chasins
7 March 1916
New York, N.Y.

Throughout his career—on his own initiative or by invitation—Rogers participated in scores of events to benefit charitable institutions and causes, usually without remuneration. The following letter is the earliest known note of appreciation to Rogers for his services at a benefit performance.

New York, <u>March 7, 1916.</u> 191

Mr. William Rogers,
% New Amsterdam Roof,
New York City.
Dear Mr. Rogers,

In behalf of the Young Folks League of the Hebrew Infant Asylum[1] we desire to sincerely thank you for your kind assistance at our recent Benefit Performance at the Hippodrome, Sunday Evening, February 27th, 1916.[2]

We deeply appreciate your very material aid and beg to assure you that your help was in the interest of a cause than which there is none worthier or more deserving.

Please accept our warmest gratitude in which all our "Little Babies" join us, and wishing you every success, we remain

Sincerely yours,
Sol Wolerstein[3]
President
Marcus L. Chasins[4]
Chairman-Ent. Committee

TLS, rc. OkClaW, 1975.22.0002. On letterhead of Young Folks League of the Hebrew Infant Asylum, 71 West 88th Street, New York. Printed above letterhead: "'All for the Babies'".

1. The Hebrew Infant Asylum was founded in Bronx, N.Y., in 1895. Renamed the Hebrew Home for Infants in March 1916, it provided care for as many as four hundred chronically ill, abandoned, and orphaned Jewish children up to the age of five. The facility closed in 1943. The Young Folks League, an association of young working people, provided philanthropic and social service support for the orphanage (Bernard, *Children*, 107–16; *NYT*, 18 January 1915, 12 March 1916, 10 May 1920, 18 July 1921).

2. The benefit raised "several thousand dollars," according to a brief mention in the *New York Times* the next morning. The show featured selections from the Hippodrome's regularly scheduled program, as well as from other entertainers, including Rogers, who at the time was headlining as "The Oklahoma Cowboy" at the Palace and appearing at the New Amsterdam in the *Midnight Frolic* (*NYT*, 27–28 February 1916; Chronology, 1914–16, OkClaW).

3. Solomon (Sol) Wolerstein, a composer of march music for bands, served as president of the Young Folks League from at least 1916 to 1920 (*NYT*, 10 May 1920; *HEBM*, 2:830).

4. Marcus L. Chasins (ca. 1884–1931) was an attorney in New York City and a former schoolteacher (*NYT*, 31 December 1931).

From Arthur F. Simonson
14 April 1916
Stapleton, N.Y.

The following letter is the earliest surviving example of the enormous quantity of correspondence and special requests Rogers received from fans during his lengthy performing, writing, and broadcasting career.

STAPLETON, N. Y. CITY April 14, 1916.

My dear Mr. Rogers:-

Ordinarily, busy people have little time to devote to common place matters, and were this of that character I would surely follow the rule and avoid wasting your time and mine–Here is an exception and I must of necessity take longer to cover the point.

We were considerably disappointed upon your failure to answer my letter and I got more jawing over it than I really deserved–yet, subsequent events more than recompensed me. The arrival of your very kind and thoughtful package containing the wonderful rope and letter and the more wonderful autographed photo set my household into a pandemonium of "Wild West" shrieks.

When I went home for my luncheon Charlie met me at the door and immediately began quizzing me concerning the package-I refused to tell him anything other than that the box had been sent to him by a friend–He lost no time in ripping off the cord and if you could have seen the expression on his face as he beheld your photo it would no doubt have pleased you beyond measure–The boy was absolutely speechless for at least a minute and then broke out with a big roar, Oh! Mother! see what Will Rogers has sent me!–Bounded out to the nearest neighbors and proceeded to tell everyone of his great prize.

The articles in question fill a much needed requirement in the boys' division of my household and incidently I might mention the fact that the rope has been used continuously since it arrived and the photo occupies the most conspicuous spot of Charlie's dresser where it awaits framing–(order having been given.)

Those of us who are blessed with young Americans are in a position to appreciate what a real boy wants, and I desire to take this opportunity of expressing my thanks for your generosity, and if ever I can be of service to you or yours, comman▶d◀ me.

Again thanking you and with best wishes from my gang to yours, I am,

Sincerely yours,

Arthur Simonson.[1]

TLS, rc. OkClaW, Correspondence, Fan Letters, Box 6. On letterhead of Arthur F. Simonson, Attorney and Counselor-at-Law, Savings Bank Building, Stapleton, N.Y. Sans serif type in place/date-line indicates preprinted text. The interpolation was hand-inserted.

1. A Charles A. Simonson, a member of the class of 1931 at Dartmouth College, married Celia Merriam Howard in Plainfield, N.J., on 31 August 1935. The announcement in the *New York Times* the next day mentioned his parents as Mr. and Mrs. Arthur Simonson of St. George, Staten Island. The wedding took place not many days after Rogers's death (*NYT*, 24 July, 1 September 1935).

Notes for Appearance at Friars Club
ca. 28 May 1916
New York, N.Y.

Despite a world war, commemorations took place throughout Europe and the United States in the spring of 1916 to mark the tercentenary of the death of English poet and dramatist William Shakespeare. The Friars Club[1] noted the occasion during its yearly entertainment event, the Frolic,[2] at the New Amsterdam Theatre in New York on 28 May 1916. A member of the Friars, Rogers may have delivered the following remarks during his scheduled appearance.[3]

FRIAR ABBOTT, MR. SHAKESPEARE, BROTHER FRIARS:

In assigning me the   task tonight   of introducing William Shakespeare, you have handed me a dead one. His death occurred three hundred years ago, and now everybody is celebrating it. The whole   world is so happy over his death that for the past month   it has been holding a Tercentenary Celebration, giving parades, pageants and dinners. Three years ago occurred the 350th anniversary of Shakespeare's birth and nobody   paid any attention to it.[4] William Shakespeare had to die to make a hit.

The first recorded mention in history of any Shakespeare   was that of one of his ancestors, who in the year 1248   was convicted of robbery and hanged.[5] Our guest   was born in 1564 in Stratford -o on- the- Avon   and on the bum. His name Shakespeare in its derivation means "carrying a spear", and right away his father ►f◄eared his baby son would grow up to be a Winter Garden chorus man.[6] Young Shakespeare became a butcher, working in the *bacon*   department. He always dealt a great deal in *bacon*. In November, 1582, he took out a license to marry Anne Whateley. On the appointed day of the wedding, however, he did not marry her, but married instead Anne Hathaway   - by request.[7] Anne Hathaway owned a cottage in Stratford, and Shakespeare moved right in and lived there. That   was the origin of the Only Their Husbands Club. Subsequently he became very prolific, producing thirty-seven plays and a pair of twins.[8]

The night the twins were born   William told Anne that he was going down town   and have a couple of flagons of ale with some of the boys. He said he would be back early. He ▲stayed out later than he expected, for he▲ was gone from home eleven years. During that entire time he forgot to telephone Anne. When next heard from he was in London. He had walked the whole distance. That long walk gave him the idea of becoming an actor . In those days English actors were called vagabonds. Today they are called Lambs.[9] It is   said that he left Stratford because he was accused of poaching. Young William   already had been convicted   of stealing deer, of stealing pheasants, of stealing a coat of arms, and of stealing quail. Now, ~~how did where~~ ▲how▲ did he get his plays?

In London he obtained a job holding horses in front of the Globe Theatre. That was before Dillingham owned it.[10] After he had held horses for a few nights Shakespeare opened a livery stable. If Dillingham had been at the Globe then, it would have been *his* livery stable. Finally Shakespeare obtained control of a theatre. He wrote his own ~~play~~ plays, produced them and acted in them. He was the George Cohan of his time.[11] In casting plays he always gave himself parts like the First Grave Digger in "Hamlet", and Friar Laurence in "Romeo and Juliet" – characters that came on late ~~thus   sg~~ ▲so▲ that he would have a chance to count the house before makingn   up. One day he met "Diamond Jim" Brady.[12] That gave him the idea for the character of Romeo. The role of Benedick was suggested by De Wolf Hopper.[13] Then he met ▲William Jennings Bryan[14]▲ ~~Eugene Kelso allen~~, and wrote "Much Ado About   Nothing." In the course of his theatrical career he became involved in many lawsuits. He was always being sued . His lawyer was William Klein.[15] Klein finally protected him by transforming him into a dozen corporations.

He became William and Lee Shakespeare, Incorporated; William and Jake Shakespeare, Incorporated; and Lee and J. J. Shakespeare, Incorporated.[16] He was ffequently sued for plagiarism, but he always brought home the *bacon*.

The Friars are honored to have Mr. Shakespeare in our midst   tonight. We like him in spite of his whiskers. It makes us~~n~~ proud to welcome the dramatist who has ruined more th▲e▲atrical managers than all the other playwrights combined, and who cost the Founders of the New Theatre a half-million dollars. He has heard that several of his plays were being revived, and he has come over from England to try to collect a few back royalties. Also he is trying to dispose of the moving picture rights. Since he is an English citizen and is now in New york, there is one question the Friars would like to ask of you, William:"Why are you not at the front?"

TD. OkClaW, Will Rogers, Jr., Collection, Original Notations, Folder 15. All interpolations were handwritten but not in Rogers's hand. Double strike-throughs indicate hand-deleted text; single strike-throughs indicate type-deleted copy.

1. Organized in New York City in 1904 by theatrical press agents, the Friars Club expanded and diversified its male-only membership within a few years to include many of the leading figures from vaudeville and musical theater (*EV*, 197–98).

2. The Friars produced their first *Frolic* in 1907. The variety show became an almost annual event that helped sustain the organization and showcase members' talents. The group staged the *Frolic* of 1916 just six days after opening a new clubhouse and as celebrations continued worldwide to mark the three hundredth anniversary of the death of Shakespeare. Billed as the Friars's biggest production to date, the new *Frolic* featured an all-star ensemble (*EV*, 197–98; Dougherty, *New York Friars*, 15–30; *NYT*, 29 May 1916).

3. The evening's printed program listed the final routine as "A Travesty on the Now Famous Friars Dinners," an apparent take-off on the club's annual banquets at which the Friars traditionally honored in a lighthearted manner a prominent individual, usually an entertainer, oftentimes a member. In this instance, the surprise "guest" was William Shakespeare, in the person of Friar Louis Mann. Given the notes he prepared for that evening, Rogers apparently was assigned the role of introducing the guest of honor (*EV*, 197–98; "The Friars Souvenir Book for the Sixth Annual Frolic," OkClaW; *NYT*, 29 May 1916).

In the files at the Will Rogers Memorial is a typewritten document (OkClaW, 1975.14.0215) that contains content similar to the above notes. In it, however, Rogers addresses his remarks to "Mr. Toastmaster, Ladies and Lights" and then opens with several references to the LIGHTS, an acronym for Long Island Good Hearted Thespians Society, an organization of New York theatrical performers who lived and sometimes also worked on Long Island. Like the Friars, the LIGHTS also opened a new clubhouse in 1916. The group staged its annual entertainment extravaganza in New York City on 16 July 1916. Rogers was listed on the bill with scores of other performers and may have delivered his Shakespeare remarks on that occasion (Smith, "Actors' Colony," 183; Metz, *Freeport*, 32; *NYT*, 16 July 1916).

4. Parish records in Stratford, England, show that Shakespeare was christened on 26 April 1564; most scholars give his birth as three days prior. The commemoration of the three hundred fiftieth anniversary of the event occurred in 1914, although celebratory activities that year were far fewer than what took place two years later on the occasion of the tercentenary of Shakespeare's death, 23 April 1616 (Schoenbaum, *William Shakespeare*, 24–26; Habicht, "Shakespeare Celebrations," 450–55).

5. The name Shakespeare, and its many variations in spelling, appears frequently in historical records in the region surrounding Stratford. The earliest mention is that of a William Sakspere of Clopton, Gloucestershire, who was executed by hanging in 1248 for the crime of robbery (Schoenbaum, *William Shakespeare*, 13).

6. The Winter Garden opened on 20 March 1911 and became one of the most popular theaters in New York City, known widely for its presentations of musical comedies and revues (*DATH*, 23; *OCT*, 898).

7. Recent biographers of Shakespeare hold that Anne Hathaway and Anne Whateley were the same person but that the latter name was erroneously entered into the official record of the marriage. A court clerk in Worcester, who is known to have made other careless entries in the legal register, recorded the marriage license on 27 November 1582 (Schoenbaum, *William Shakespeare*, 83–86; Wells, "William Shakespeare," 296).

8. William and Anne Shakespeare had three children: Susanna, christened on 26 May 1583, and twins Hamnet and Judith, christened on 2 February 1585. Hamnet, the only son, died young; the girls lived well into adulthood. For several years after the birth of the twins the documentary record of Shakespeare's life remains blank, although legends abound. It is not known exactly when Shakespeare left his family to travel to London, but a pamphlet published in 1592 shows him already well engaged as a dramatist and actor in the capital (Schoenbaum, *William Shakespeare*, 3, 93–94, 95, 149–51, 318).

9. Harry Montague and other actors in London founded The Lambs in the 1860s as a dinner club, but the group disbanded three decades later. In the meantime, Montague, an American, had returned to New York City, where he started a similar club in 1875, also called The Lambs. When the London club dissolved, the accoutrements of its Shepherd, or chairman, passed to the American body, which became one of the most prominent theatrical organizations in the country (Laurie, *Vaudeville*, 304–10; *OCT*, 471, 557–58).

10. Charles Bancroft Dillingham (1868–1934), theater manager and Broadway producer, opened the Globe Theatre—named after the London playhouse most popularly associated with Shakespeare—in New York City on 10 January 1910 (*EMT*, 359–60; *NYT*, 31 August 1934; *DATH*, 21–22).

11. George Michael Cohan (1878–1942), celebrated American composer, producer, and performer, starred in several musical productions on Broadway in the early 1900s, eventually adding the responsibilities of producer and playwright. He also operated and managed theaters in New York. By 1916 he had become one of the busiest and most popular figures in the entertainment industry (*EMT*, 292–93; Morehouse, *George M. Cohan*, 125).

12. James Buchanan (Diamond Jim) Brady (1856–1917), colorful American financier and philanthropist, was well known for his vast collection of jewelry and gems, his elaborate gifts of jewels to favorite women, and his immense size, daily fed by a robust appreciation for hearty food. He sat in the front row at the *Frolic* the night of the Shakespeare event (Morell, *Diamond Jim*, 4, 5–7, 221, 240, 249–51, 257–61, 270; unidentified clipping, CPpR files, OkClaW).

13. De Wolf Hopper (William d'Wolf Hopper, 1858–1935), a popular comedy star of the American musical stage, appeared in a series of Gilbert and Sullivan productions in New York in the 1910s. He attempted a move to motion pictures in 1915 but quickly returned to musical theater (*NYT*, 24 September 1935; *EMT*, 676; McNamara, *Shuberts*, 96).

14. For William Jennings Bryan see *PWR*, 3:59–60n.3.

15. William Klein (ca. 1875–1966), a New York attorney, served as counsel and public spokesman for the Shubert brothers and their theatrical management company. He played a major role in helping the Shuberts build their vast empire of theaters and real estate properties (*NYT*, 18 January 1966).

16. For brothers Lee (Levi), Samuel, and Jacob J. Shubert see *PWR*, 3:384–85n.3.

Notes for Appearance in *Friars' Frolic* 30 May 1916 Baltimore, Md.

To celebrate the club's new clubhouse and to raise funds to help pay for it, the Friars took their annual Frolic on tour for the first time. In a two-week period, they played several cities in the United States as far west as St. Louis and generated more than one hundred thousand dollars for the building fund. Among the troupe's first stops—and perhaps its most memorable—was Baltimore, where an enthusiastic audience included President Woodrow Wilson[1] and an official party that had motored from Washington, D.C., for the performance.[2] As was his usual custom, Rogers prepared notes for that evening's routine. The lead gag shows that Wilson's appearance that night did not come as a surprise to Rogers. As he explained several years later, he would always give extra effort in preparing to perform before a president.[3]

1 This is really my second Presidential appearance   Bryan spoke in our town and I was to follow him and rope   it was so dark when he got through they couldent see the Rope. ▲What ever become of him.▲

2. Peace White flag. Vernon Castle[4] and Portugals entrance[5] Will about decide it. Portugal. I[t]aly.[6] christian science.[7]

3. Preparedness   Okla Senators send home more Garden Seed[8]   300 thousand Fords[,] Man to every car.[9] Russian Ballet[10]

4. Not facing a crisis. Lusitania.[11] Illegal. Gargoyle

5 Notes Behing [behind?].[12] Some Note Paper.

VILLA[13]   Atlantic Pacific. Man on Guard. Red Tape   Machine Gun Plattsburg[14]   another Gun.

American in Morning Journal[15]   let him go in eve[ning].

Escapes Net and Fleas. We will never get him.

Self destroying Submarine. Aeroplane.

~~Let your Ka Jasbo~~. ▼(Used in other Book)▼ Panama Canal. RR. coming
▲this Way▲

New Y[ork] New H[aven] and H[artford].

Girls out of Trenches by Xmas.

Belgian Night.

Littlest country but with most friend[s] of any country in World   only

King[16] Wont be looking for a job after War is over.

May a Mitchell[17] dancing Mayor. told of other bows [?].

AD. OkClaW, 1975.14.0156. Handwritten, in Rogers's hand, top margin: "Act Did before President
Wilson in Baltimore With Friars".

1. Woodrow Wilson (Thomas Woodrow Wilson, 1856–1924), a former president
of Princeton University and governor of New Jersey, served as president of the United
States from 1913 to 1921 (*DAB*, 19:352–68).
2. The presidential party in Baltimore included Woodrow Wilson's wife, daughter,
and members of the administration and the diplomatic corps. During an intermission
the president went backstage where he shook hands with Rogers and other members
of the Friars troupe. According to an account the next day in the *New York Times*,
Wilson told them, "Gentlemen, you have complimented me by helping me put aside
my cares." George M. Cohan, the presiding Abbot of the Friars, thanked him for
making the trip from the capital, to which Wilson reportedly responded, "I'd travel ten
times that distance to listen to a man as wise as Will Rogers" (*NYT*, 31 May 1916;
Dougherty, *New York Friars*, 28–30; *WA*, 1:193–96; Rogers, *Will Rogers*, 163–65;
Yagoda, *Will Rogers*, 144–46; Betty Blake Rogers to Wesley W. Stout, 1 July 1940,
OkClaW; Tape T7–023–T7–074, OkClaW).
3. For Rogers's account of the evening in Baltimore see *WA*, 1:193–96. In the
piece, which he wrote as a tribute to President Wilson two weeks after his death,
Rogers explained the circumstances of his first performance before the president and
recounted his monologue. He had saved the notes reproduced here and used them in
the retelling of the events of that night. The article illustrates how Rogers often structured his act, used his prepared notes as primer, and conveyed the intention of his
humor.
4. Entertainer Vernon Castle (see *PWR*, 3:419–23) left New York in February
1916 to join the Royal Flying Corps in his native England. He flew several missions
over France and engaged in more than one skirmish with German aircraft (*NYT*, 18
February 1916; Castle, "My Memories," *Everybody's*, January 1919, 42, February
1919, 50, 52–53).
5. Portugal abrogated its treaties with Germany in April 1916 out of concern that
its colonies would become bargaining chips among the warring nations and in
response to the German seizure of Portuguese-claimed territory in east Africa. The
first troops from Portugal, however, did not arrive in France until February 1917 and
did not see action until mid-June (Gallagher, *Portugal*, 25; *NYT*, 23 April 1916;
Gilbert, *First World War*, 308, 341).
6. Initially a neutral in the war, Italy joined the Allies on 20 May 1915 after being
promised substantial territorial gains. In March 1916 the Italian army lost considerable ground to Austrian troops and in the process failed to bring relief to the French
at Verdun (Di Scala, *Italy*, 201; Gilbert, *First World War*, 165–66, 235).

7. After the war began, the *Christian Science Monitor*, a daily newspaper in Boston that was part of the Christian Science Church, took a decidedly pro-Allied position and editorialized for U.S. intervention, a stance that seemed to conflict with church principles (Mott, *American Journalism*, 559–60).

8. Oklahoma was represented in the U.S. Senate by two Democrats, Thomas Pryor Gore (1870–1949) and Robert Latham Owen (1856–1947). While Owen distinguished himself in the Senate in matters of banking, monetary, and economic reform, Gore focused largely on agricultural issues. As chairman of the Senate Agriculture Committee, he played a significant role in the passage of legislation in May 1916 to establish federal farm loan banks. Rogers may have been referring to an issue related to the bill (*BDUSCong*, 1078, 1601; Keso, *Senatorial Career*, 5; Billington, *Thomas P. Gore*, 3, 64).

9. Henry Ford (1863–1947), pioneer automobile manufacturer and champion of mass production, had built Ford Motor Company by 1915 into an industrial giant responsible for 35 percent of all automobiles (308,000) manufactured annually worldwide. Ford, thoroughly antiwar, spent millions of dollars to oppose preparedness in the United States (*DAB*, Supp. 4:291–304; Nevins and Hill, *Ford*, 2:9, 28–49; Harries and Harries, *Last Days*, 54–55).

10. The Ballets Russes, or Russian Ballet, arrived in the spring of 1916 for its second tour of the United States. Although the troupe featured famed Russian dancer and choreographer Vaslav Nijinsky in his American debut, the tour suffered from financial and artistic handicaps (Krasovskaya, *Nijinsky*, 299–307; Garafola, *Diaghilev's*, 204–6).

11. For the wartime sinking of the British liner *Lusitania* see *PWR*, 3:379n.1.

12. Until the United States entered the war, its relations with the conflicting powers involved several exchanges of diplomatic notes, sometimes in furious succession (Zieger, *America's Great War*, 43; Blum, *Woodrow Wilson*, 102–6).

13. Francisco (Pancho) Villa (ca. 1878–1923) was a rebel leader in northern Mexico in the revolution of 1910–11 and the turbulent years thereafter. Angered by President Woodrow Wilson's recognition of a government led by a rival revolutionary, Villa led a raid on the border town of Columbus, N.M., on 9 March 1916 that resulted in seventeen deaths. In response, Wilson ordered the U.S. army to pursue the raiders into Mexico, a futile chase that received wide and excited attention in newspapers. The day before the *Frolic* opened in Baltimore, American soldiers uncovered the first cache of arms attributed to Villa since the troops had crossed the border (Blum, *Woodrow Wilson*, 87–94; Stout, *Border Conflict*, 1, 4–21, 33–37, 43–46, 59, 62, 83, 142; *NYT*, 30 May 1916).

14. The so-called Plattsburg movement originated in the summer of 1915 among young New York businessmen and professionals who sought to promote military training as a form of patriotism and in opposition to the Wilson administration's neutral stance. The group arranged for the use of a training facility at Plattsburg, in upstate New York, and in August 1915 sent the first batch of trainees to the camp. Similar installations soon opened elsewhere (Zieger, *America's Great War*, 35–36; *NYT*, 6 August 1916).

15. Virtually companion newspapers, the *New York American*, which published in the morning, and the *New York Journal*, an afternoon daily, had earned reputations for reckless, sensational journalism. Both opposed U.S. entry into the war, especially on the side of the Allies; nevertheless, they supported and cheered armed intervention in Mexico (Mott, *American Journalism*, 520–44, 615–17; Nasaw, *Chief*, 248–49).

16. Albert I (1875–1934) ascended to the throne of Belgium in 1909. Popular as a monarch in his homeland, he gained international acclaim for his leadership in resistance

to the German invasion and occupation of his country (*BDWWI*, 64–65; Cammaerts, *Albert*, 59–72, 143–274, 442–49).

17. John Purroy Mitchel (1879–1918) served as mayor of New York from 1913 to 1917. Although Mitchel's administration earned some praise for municipal reform, it became increasingly unpopular, especially among wage-earners in the city who saw the young mayor as tied to wealthy society (*DAB*, 13:37–38).

Newspaper Article by Will Rogers
6 August 1916
New York, N.Y.

The following was Rogers's first contribution to a regularly distributed publication. Three years earlier, an article of his had appeared in the printed program for the Winnipeg Stampede,[1] but this is the first known instance of his writings being published in a newspaper or magazine. Within about eighteen months, he would see publication of eight articles of varying style in at least four different newspapers.[2] Likely, it was no coincidence that Rogers's first three published pieces—the one in 1913, this one, and the one immediately following it—concerned rodeo productions by the same man, Guy Weadick, an accomplished promoter.[3] Eventually, Rogers would produce about a million words in print, published in books, magazines, and newspapers.

STAMPEDE[4] BIG
EVENT, SAYS
WILL ROGERS

———

ROPE-THROWING CHAMPION WRITES
OF COWBOY WORLD'S SERIES AT
SHEEPSHEAD BAY FOR AMERICAN

———

THRILLING SPORTS SEEN BY 25,000[5]
AS RIVALS OF THE PLAINS
MEET IN CONTESTS FOR PRIZES

———

The twenty-five thousands persons were thrilled with hair-raising feats at the opening of the "Stampede," the great Western Cowboy and Cowgirl contest at the Sheepshead Bay Speedway yesterday.

It was the first time such a show has been given in this city and one of the most remarkable ever presented here. Wild horse races; wild buffalo races; bulldogging steers and other dangerous sports brought the huge crowd to its feet in breathless excitement every moment of the afternoon. The show lasted until seven o'clock in the evening. It will be continued every day next week.

Will Rogers, the champion cowboy of the Ziegfeld Follies, is describing the Stampede for the American. This is his story:

By Will Rogers.

Well, here goes. I thought about everything had happened to me since I gave up trying to rope steers and came back to New York. I worked in a Ziegfeld show, danced with a girl, sang a song—once. Even wore a dress suit in one show.[6] But the worst is yet to come.

I was asked to write for a paper—like those great authors and writers, Christy Mathewson[7] and Ty Cobb.[8]

I am going to lay my chips a little different from what they say those birds do. I am not only going to sign my name, but I am going to take a shot at the whole works myself, and I want it to go as she lays, even if the guy that has to set up the type has to get drunk to do it.

OVERLOOKING BEST BET.

I want to tell you about the bit Stampede down at Sheepshead Bay. If you haven't been down to take gapeins at it, you're overlooking the best bet that ever hit this old village.

I know a lot of you all will say, well, Will, why aren't you out there showing us some[t]hing?[9] Say, I don't see any of you fellows fighting Willard.[10] My "rep" as a rope tangler was mostly east of the Hudson River and it started vanishing to-day.

Besides acting a fool in one show and trying to keep New Yorkers awake the rest of the night in another one,[11] and day herding three young Rogerses in a yard to keep 'em from catching this disease—I can't even spell it[12]—a man don't get a whole lot of time to practise.

PAID THEIR OWN FARE.

I'll bet it took as much as a couple of days for these boys to learn some of the stunts that they're pulling. I want to tell you what makes it so great. It's not a show. Do you know that every one of these boys and girls paid their own fare here for themselves and horses from all over the United States and Canada, and they don't get a cent, even paying their own expenses while here. You've got to win it to get it. And you'll win it fair, you'll bet your case card on that.

They have three judges in each event, the most competent men with whom neither money, influence nor friendship would cut any ice. There are as high as fifty entries in some events. Only about four of these get any money.

Now you're not going to see much laying down, are you? A man has got to know he's a pretty fair hand to enter a thing like that. Now, I know more than two-thirds of these boys personally and have met all of 'em. Several of 'em are right from my home, and I know that every one of them has won prizes in various contests all over the West. But never has there been as many good ones in one contest.

RIVALS TO MEET HERE.

Boys will meet here who have dreaded each other for years. I got a pretty good line on it and I couldn't tell you of a man that's anyways sure of winning any event. The money is worth going for and, believe me, they're going for it.

These people who put it on have got the limit and no expense. And Guy Weadick—"guy" in name only—who manages the whole thing and produces it, has had a lot of experience in this line and has made this one the biggest ever held and the biggest prizes ever offered.

By the way, it was our friend, Fred Stone who originally conceived the idea of having it here.[13] As he didn't have the time to devote to it, he sent for Weadick, and Guy put it over.

Now, if you all want to see something plumb good and on the level by the world's greatest horsemen, look it over. This is the World's Series of Cowboy Sports.

HAD THEM STANDING UP.

Now when a bunch of New York people stick to see a show that lasts till after seven o'clock it's good, and, say, these old Western boys sure had 'em standing up and yelling like drunken Injuns.

There was quite a mess of excitement in the ladies' relay race, when one of the Irwin girls—that's Charley Irwin's daughter, the man who produces "Frontier Days at Cheyenne," who's brought his whole family here[14] (he is to the Wild West game what Eddie Foy is to the stage[15])—and another lady rider both tried to run their horses over the same spot at the same time. All went down, but not for the count. They came up grinning and went right after 'em.

One old bucking pony turned a complete somersault with a girl. If he keeps that up every day somebody's liable to get hurt.

NEW THRILL FOR NEW YORK.

How the crowd did eat up the bulldogging. That's something plumb new for New York. Imagine a big old longhorn breezing down across space going about two-nothing, and a man on a fast horse, jumping from the horse to the brute's head and twisting his neck and throwing him and holding him with only his hands.

Say, if the Humans want to look into anything they ought to X-ray these boys after this is over. But any of you boys who might have lost an arm or a hand in one of our recent Mexican wars, why, don't feel downhearted, for John Spain,[16] who only has one hand, his other being off at the wrist, goes in for this little parlor game. John would be considerable boy if he had his other hand.

Ed Lindsey[17] laid one on his flat side in forty-one seconds, quicker than a chorus girl can order a drink. Art Accord,[18] the movie boy, upset one quick, but was fined thirty seconds for starting too quick. Some movie fan hollered "Action" at Art too quick. I am leaving it up to Fred Stone[19] to uphold the "rep" of the stage. He sure is doing it. He did some fine roping, and, believe me, there's boys in there that eat rope.

PD. Printed in *New York American*, 6 August 1916. A clipping of the article in Scrapbook 15, OkClaW, bears an identification of the *New York Times*, but references in the text of the article and further research substantiated that the piece was published in the *New York American* (see advertisement, *NYT*, 8 August 1916).

1. See Article by Will Rogers from *The Stampede*, 9–16 August 1913, *PWR*, 1:307–13.
2. See articles below in *New York American*, 8 August 1916; unidentified publication, ca. 5 September 1916; *Detroit Journal*, 15 December 1917; *Detroit Journal*, ca. 22 December 1917; unidentified publication, ca. 17 February 1918; *Chicago Examiner*, 21 February 1918; and *Chicago Examiner*, ca. 3 March 1918.
3. For Guy Weadick see *PWR*, 3:457–59.
4. The Stampede was promoted as the first large-scale rodeo in New York. Produced by Guy Weadick and staged at a year-old automobile racetrack at Sheepshead Bay in Brooklyn, N.Y., the Stampede drew many of the best rodeo competitors in the country. They were attracted by the rare opportunity to show easterners the sport and to win a share of $500,000 in advertised prize money, the largest purse to date. The Stampede ended as a financial failure, with $17,500 still owed to winners and scores of contestants left stranded from lack of funds (*NYT*, 6, 17 August 1916; *ENYC*, 1065; King, *Rodeo Trails*, 178–79; Hanes, *Bill Pickett*, 141; Woerner, *Belly Full*, 16).
5. The *New York Times* reported that only 15,000 people attended the Stampede on 5 August, the first day of the event. The crowd had grown to full capacity of 25,000 by the end of the week (*NYT*, 6, 12 August 1916).
6. Never comfortable in top hat and tuxedo, or "dress suit," Rogers shunned dress even on occasions that specifically called for such special wear. One notable exception was in *Town Topics*, the short-lived musical of a year earlier. The *New York Times* reviewer noted on opening night that Rogers "sheepishly astounds in evening clothes (he stows the rope under the hat)" (*NYT*, 24 September 1915).
7. Christopher (Christy) Mathewson (1880–1925) set several season and World Series records as pitcher for the New York Giants from 1900 to 1916. His gentlemanly and scholarly qualities made the college-educated Mathewson a model for juveniles. A series of youth-oriented books were ghostwritten under his name (*DAB*, 12:407–8; *BDASBase*, 391).
8. Tyrus Raymond (Ty) Cobb (1886–1961), one of the greatest all-around players in the history of baseball, starred in the field, at the plate, and on the base paths for the

Detroit Tigers from 1905 to 1926. By 1916 he had ghostwritten a book and several syndicated newspaper articles (*DAB*, Supp. 7:127–29; *BDASBase*, 98–100; Stump, *Cobb*, 231, 244).

9. Rogers probably attended the Stampede every day and participated in some events. In addition, several of the Stampeders saw him perform at the *Midnight Frolic* that Tuesday, 8 August, and as advertised, Guy Weadick and others joined him on stage to entertain the crowd with lariat and whip tricks (*NYT*, 6, 8, 9 August 1916; Hanes, *Bill Pickett*, 142–43).

10. Jess Willard (1881–1968) won the world heavyweight boxing title by knocking out the much older champion, Jack Johnson, on 15 April 1915 in a classic but controversial bout in Havana, Cuba. Willard defended the world title only once between the battle with Johnson and an unsuccessful defense against Jack Dempsey in July 1919 (*BDASBask*, 476–77; Roberts, *Papa Jack*, 197).

11. At the time Rogers was appearing in both the matinee and evening performances of the *Ziegfeld Follies* at the New Amsterdam Theatre, as well as late at night in the *Midnight Frolic* on the theater's roof.

12. The most serious epidemic to date of poliomyelitis, or infantile paralysis, swept the United States between June and October 1916. The crippling, death-dealing disease struck hardest in New York, with a larger proportion of cases reported on Long Island, where the Rogers family lived, than in Manhattan. The cause of the disease being unknown, parents reacted with self-quarantine: locking their children indoors, regardless of summer heat, as a defense against infected children and unclean air (*NYT*, 6 August 1916; Rogers, *Dirt and Disease*, 2, 6, 10–14).

13. For Fred Stone see *PWR*, 3:451–57.

14. Charles Burton Irwin (1875–1931), a Wyoming rancher and showman, was the arena director and provided the stock for the Cheyenne Frontier Days, one of the premier rodeo contests in the country. All of Irwin's children—son Floyd Leslie Irwin, adopted son Roy Kivett, and his daughters, variously named in sources as Pauline, Joella, Frances (or Francis), and Edith—competed in rodeo events (*WWRodeo*, 64–65; *WST*, 23 March 1931; LeCompte, *Cowgirls*, 60; Stansbury, *Lucille Mulhall*, 99; *NYT*, 6 August 1916; Hanes, *Bill Pickett*, 141, 147; Riske, *Cheyenne*, 30–32; Clancy, *My Fifty Years*, 62).

15. For Eddie Foy and the Seven Little Foys, see *PWR*, 3:357n.3.

16. Johnathan E. Lee (John) Spain (b. ca. 1893) was a saddle bronc rider from Tennessee, who with his brother Fred was involved in the early years of the Pendleton, Ore., Roundup as promoters and stock providers (Allen, *Rodeo Cowboys*, 163; Hanes, *Bill Pickett*, 12).

17. Ed Lindsey, a leading competitor from New Mexico in both bronc riding and bulldogging, won $4,700 at the Stampede in New York. He gave part of it to friends who failed to receive their prize winnings or found themselves otherwise strapped for money to get home (*NYT*, 6, 14 August 1916; Hanesworth, *Daddy*, 163; King, *Rodeo Trails*, 28, 29).

18. Art Acord (1890–1931) was a working cowboy from Oklahoma who performed in rodeos and, beginning in 1909, as a stuntman in motion pictures. After a brief stint in a Wild West show, he returned to movies, where he had risen to star status by 1916 through several two-reel westerns (Corneau, *Hall of Fame*, 53–55).

19. Fred Stone participated in a fancy roping contest on opening day of the Stampede, demonstrating his skills by roping six horses with riders at one time (*NYT*, 6 August 1916).

Newspaper Article by Will Rogers
8 August 1916
New York, N.Y.

TOSSING THE
HE-OXEN WITH
WILL ROGERS

CHAMPION COWBOY ENTERTAINS
MARY PICKFORD[1] AS HE WATCHES
THRILLING FEATS AT STAMPEDE

"BULLDOGGING" CARRIES THE CROWD
BY STORM- I. B. DAM AND ANT-
EATER, BUCKING HORSES, AT WORST

By Will Rogers.
Champion Cowboy of Ziegfeld Follies.

Well, I sho' never did think I would last this long. That mess of junk I had in Sunday's paper got by, 'cause I reckon the censor was out getting a drink when it slipped by, and they let her ride just as she lay. I think they figure them about like the Cherry Sisters[2]– so bad, they're funny.

Well, yesterday was the first day I got to take a peek at the whole show at the Stampede. Saturday I was away for about an hour and a half at matinee: but I sho' did get moon-eyed yesterday trying to see everything and talk to all my old friends at once.

She sho' was a fast moving and clever moving performance. Don't ever think you see the same thing at one of these any two days. A whole bunch of different riders were up today to try to qualify for the big final.

I finally left the arena and went around up in the grand stand, and there's where I step on a mule's shoe and have me some luck. I am invitationed to join Miss Mary Pickford and Mr. Douglas Fairbanks[3] and a lot of other poor, struggling moving picture actors.

BULLDOGGING FEATS.

Say, I lost quite a bit of interest in that show, as much as I love it. How Ziegfeld ever overlooked that Pickford party, I don't know.

Well, the big feature of the day, the one that the crowd seemed to enjoy most, was the bulldogging. That's where they jump from the back of a running horse onto the head of a wild bovine and gently lay him down with hands only.

You know, tossing the old he-oxen has long been the favorite pastime of New York, but here was a brand new way to do it. Those boys sure did do some fine work throwing them old steers, but I think Fairbanks and I held our own doing the same thing right there in the box.[4]

I didn't know how easy it was to improve on another man's work until I sat and watched it. Why, we rode buckin' horses and roped steers all over the box for Miss Pickford's benefit. I have to say it, but I believe she enjoyed the work in the arena as much as she did ours.

Then we had a drink, which Mr. Fairbanks paid for. Say, he's a great fellow. I always did like him. (I wonder if he'll be there to-day.)

OLD "BILL" PICKETT.

It did me good to see old negro "Bill" Pickett, whom I first knew at a contest in St. Louis in 1899.[5] (No, I didn't win anything there either.) Him, up here, after all these years, showin' these young men how to do it.

You know, I believe in giving some credit for originality and if ever a man originated anything, he originated this game. There's not a bone in his body that ain't bent up some way. The Lord knows how old he is. And say, he's not a Jack Johnson, he's a credit to his race.[6] He laid one down in twenty-six seconds, the fastest up to that time. Then came Jess Stahl, another Polangus (a black boy), also in twenty-six seconds.[7]

In numbering the men, Stahl said to Mr. Weadlick [Weadick], "Give me number forty-foh and I know I won't have to walk back to California."

But, hurrah! The white race to the front, as usual, when "Jim["] Massey popped one against the ground in 22½ seconds.[8] That's quicker than a woman can change her mind. They made wonderful time, according to the new rules they have to work by back here, on account of the humane society.[9]

"HOOLIHANNING" BARRED.

They are not allowed to bust 'em or Hoolihan 'em (that's where they jump from the horse to the head and throw him somersault all at, one move).[10] According to the new rules, you have to stop 'em and then throw 'em.

Say, they turned loose some buckin' horses there. You know the horses out West have a bigger "rep" than the men, and they get all the bad ones.

I. B. Dam is one that gets his man every time out. I asked Henry Grammer, an old friend of mine from Kaw, Okla., who used to be a great rider down home,[11] what he would take to set on this I. B. Dam bird. Henry says, "I would want just ten cents less than I'd die for."

Anteater was out yesterday. "Johnny" Mullins[12] says he just bucks and looks back at you and winks and says, "I've carried you 'bout long enough. So long!" But a good old cowpuncher, "Charlie" Aldrich, stayed with him yesterday.[13]

"Tex" McCloud broke his record.[14] The picture taking guys get some wonderful pictures of "Tex" parting company with his bronco, and they were all set yesterday; but "Tex" fooled 'em and stayed on. It was a big disappointment to everybody but "Tex".

I want to tell you a little later on about all the fancy ropers. Naturally that's a line I'm sort of interested in.

PD. Printed in *New York American*, 8 August 1916. CPpR files, OkClaW.

1. Mary Pickford (Gladys Louise Smith, 1892–1979), known through her film work as "America's Sweetheart," had become by 1916 the best loved and most recognizable star in motion pictures (*DAB*, Supp. 10:634–36; *IDFF*, 3:500–501).

2. For the Cherry Sisters see *PWR*, 3:301n.2.

3. Douglas Fairbanks (Douglas Elton Ulman, 1883–1939), stage and motion picture actor, had established himself by 1916 as a leading star in silent films. Pickford and Fairbanks, the undisputed king and queen of Hollywood, were married in 1920, after both had divorced their respective spouses within the year (*DAB*, Supp. 2:172–73; Slide, *Silent Players*, 311).

4. Douglas Fairbanks and several other film stars were scheduled to test their rodeo skills two days later on Movie Actors' Day at the Stampede (*NYT*, 10 August 1916).

5. Willie M. (Bill) Pickett (ca. 1871–1932), an African American, demonstrated his unique bulldogging skills in Wild West exhibitions and as a competitor in rodeos. He originated the unique, so-called bite-'em-down style of bulldogging, by which a person downs a steer by biting its upper lip (*WWRodeo*, 96–97; Hanes, *Bill Pickett*, 3, 20, 26–27). For Pickett and Rogers in St. Louis in 1899 see *PWR*, 1:181–84.

6. John Arthur (Jack) Johnson (1878–1946), an African American boxer, held the undisputed world heavyweight title from 1910 to 1915. A classic fighter who was considered one of the best of all time, Johnson aroused much hostility among many whites and even some blacks because of his arrogance, flamboyance, and success. He fled abroad in 1913 after being convicted, in a controversial decision, of violating a federal law prohibiting the interstate transportation of women for prostitution (*DAB*, Supp. 4:432–34; *BDASBask*, 408–11).

7. Jesse Stahl (1883–1938), a native of Tennessee who settled in California, began riding bucking horses in 1913 and thereafter competed in rodeos throughout the country, earning a reputation as the best bronc rider never to win a championship. His failure to garner a title was widely attributed to his being an African American in a sport dominated by white competitors and judges (*WWRodeo*, 124–25; Hanes, *Bill Pickett*, 141).

8. Jim Massey, an expert practitioner of the bite-'em style of bulldogging, was acknowledged as one of the best early-day competitors in the event. His time of twenty-two and a half seconds in the bulldogging contest on 7 August did not turn out to be the fastest posted at the Stampede. A then world's record of twelve seconds was set four days later (Hanes, *Bill Pickett*, 10; King, *Rodeo Trails*, 29; *NYT*, 12 August 1916).

9. A representative of the American Society for the Prevention of Cruelty to Animals attended the Stampede and censored at least one event (*NYT*, 6 August 1916).

10. An accusation of hoolihanning led to a confrontation between Charles Irwin and Ed Lindsey during competition at the Stampede on Monday, 7 August. Fueled also by a rivalry between the northern and southern factions, the argument devolved into fisticuffs in front of the crowd of several thousand. During his visit the next day, former president Theodore Roosevelt used his mediation skills to get the two men to shake hands and end their hostility (Hanes, *Bill Pickett*, 142; *NYT*, 8, 9 August 1916).

11. Henry Grammer was considered one of the outstanding steer ropers of all time, as well as a strong competitor in saddle bronc riding. He captured the overall steer roping title at the Stampede (Hanes, *Bill Pickett*, 58, 144).

12. Johnnie Mullens (John or Johnny, 1884–1978) earned a reputation as one of the best saddle bronc riders in the country, an expert on "outlaw" horses, and a top manager of such prime bucking stock (*WWRodeo*, 92–93; Woerner, *Belly Full*, 19–20).

13. Charlie (or Charley) Aldridge (1875–1951), a native of Colorado, was a veteran performer in Wild West shows and rodeo competitions. A Rogers favorite, Aldridge competed in relay racing at the Stampede. He later became caretaker of Rogers's horses during the road tours of the *Follies* (Woerner, *Belly Full*, 11, 22; Hanes, *Bill Pickett*, 141; Clancy, *My Fifty Years*, 65; Rogers, *Will Rogers*, 139).

14. A. D. (Tex) McLeod (1889–1973) was a champion rodeo competitor, Wild West show performer, and vaudevillian, whose stage act included a monologue and rope spinning in the style of Rogers. He competed in saddle bronc riding and cowboy trick and fancy roping at the Stampede (*WWRodeo*, 201; Hanes, *Bill Pickett*, 141; *NYT*, 14 February 1973).

Newspaper Article by Will Rogers
ca. 5 September 1916
[New York, N.Y.?]

Ziegfeld has a way of dressing a chorus girl so that you don't know whether she has or whether she hasn't; and you go away and wonder about it two or three days, and then you come back to have another look.

They say that a shark won't bite at a leg that has a stocking on it.[1] These theatre goers must think they're sharks, the way they strain their eyes to determine whether they're being worn or not.

The ladies say that getting a job with a Ziegfeld show is largely a matter of form. Then how did William Rock's crooked shanks get into the Follies?[2] He has the lumpiest knees I ever saw; I wouldn't be the first to knock 'em, but they knock each other.

And Rock's partner, Miss White,[3] is a peach. If I could work with her, I'd be willing to look like Rock.

The girls of the Frolic wear a little less each year. I only ask that my life be spared until I see three more Frolics.

Every time I see one of these shows I go out and put a dollar and a tear of sympathy in a blind man's cup.

Well, the Summer is about over, and what will these butterflies do then? Some of these girls don't know where their next limousine is coming from.

People think I can't be a real cowboy, or I wouldn't work in a show where there's nothing but calves.

One fellow in the audience said he could do things with a rope that I couldn't do. I confessed that he was right when I saw him lighting a Pittsburgh stogie.[4] He could smoke a rope, and I can't.

So many exciting things have happened this Summer that people haven't had time to laugh at the Palm Beach suits.[5] When a fellow puts across something funny, he ought to get a laugh; and those little half-hearted belts and ruffles are as good as anything Charlie Chaplin ever pulled.[6] Wouldn't those suits be just as cool if they fit?

Well, Germany got her submarine back,[7] Shackleton got his Polar party back,[8] and if the Giants get back without losing their uniforms we'll all be happy.[9]

It begins to look like Brooklyn.[10] Colonel Ebbets[11] may have to make another speech. Once at a banquet he said: "Baseball has grown and grown until now it is in its infancy!"

Roosevelt[12] said: "I'm out of politics. I'll be found in the Hughes camp."[13]

Hughes said: "I'm for America first."[14] After the way America has kept him in office all his life, we didn't expect he'd come out for Venezuela!

Bryan said: "Every day the war is nearer its close."[15] And yet he wonders why he never could be elected President.

The Erie Railroad claims it can't run trains on the eight-hour-day plan.[16] They say that if they mustn't run a train more than eight hours at a shift they'll have to put the stations closer together all along their line.

The boys that are back from the Mexican border say the reports were wrong that said it was 115 in the shade down there. They say that's a lie. There *wasn't any shade there.*

They say the Mexican soldiers fight without making any trenches. That's right. Unless the Mexicans have a changed a lot since I knew them, they'd rather be shot than go to work and dig a trench.

The Mexican soldiers get 10 cents a day for serving in the army. And the only day they earn it is the day they try to collect it.

The Mexicans eat so much chili pepper that when they're killed the coyotes can't eat their bodies. But if Uncle Sam ever has to pepper them with his machine guns there won't be a big enough piece left to burn a buzzard's mouth.

PD. Unidentified clipping, ca. 5 September 1916.[17] CPpR files, OkClaW. The clipping carries the heading "The Inimitable Will Rogers The Laugh Maker at the 'Follies'". Printed in the bottom margin, right of center: "Copyright, 1916, by the Star Company. Great Britain Rights Reserved."

1. Sightings of sharks and human encounters with them were reported along the East Coast in greater than usual numbers between July and late August 1916. Shark attacks claimed the lives of several bathers and swimmers, and received excited coverage in the press and even attention from President Wilson (*NYT*, 3, 7, 13–15 July, 6, 8, 21, 25 August 1916).

2. For William Rock see *PWR*, 3:236n.13.

3. Frances White (1898–1969), a chorus girl, and William Rock, a veteran vaudevillian, debuted as a song-and-dance team in New York in May 1916. They went on to perform in that year's production of the *Ziegfeld Follies*, with White becoming the star of the duo (*EV*, 424–26; Ziegfeld and Ziegfeld, *Ziegfeld Touch*, 316).

4. By 1915 the city of Pittsburgh had become the leading producer of stogies, manufacturing more than 400 million of the cigars noted for being made from the long leaves of tobacco (*PGT*, 12 July 1915).

5. Introduced in the 1910s and refined in the next decade, the so-called Palm Beach suit became the first successful all-white, lightweight suit for men (*EMF*, 12).

6. Charles Spencer (Charlie) Chaplin (1889–1977), English-born actor, made his motion picture debut in 1914. In his trademark costume of baggy pants, floppy shoes, and tightly buttoned coat, and in his comedic portrayals of the "Tramp," he soon became the most popular star in American films and one of the most financially successful (*DAB*, Supp. 10:114–18).

7. To break the Allied blockade on its ports, Germany built and launched large, cargo-carrying submarines. Although the fate of one, the *Bremen*, was uncertain by late August, the *Deutschland* arrived in Germany to much fanfare on 23 August with a cargo of dyestuffs from the United States. Nearly a year passed before the Germans confirmed that the *Bremen* had been lost at sea (Crane, *Submarine*, 146–47; *NYT*, 9, 12, 24–25 August 1916, 16 June 1917).

8. Ernest Henry Shackleton (1874–1922), an English explorer who led an expedition that reached the South Magnetic Pole in 1909, attempted a major trans-Antarctic journey in August 1914. One of his two groups of men, however, became stranded on a remote island in the polar region. Shackleton and others were not able to rescue them until 30 August 1916. Word of the rescue did not reach the public until 5 September (*DNB*, Supp. 4:758–60; Landis, *Antarctica*, 242–43).

9. The New York Giants saw the composition of the team shaken up considerably during the last half of the major league baseball season in 1916. Team management traded and sold nine players in the summer of 1916 in an attempt to recover from a rare last-place finish the previous season and a lackluster start in 1916 (McGraw, *Real McGraw*, 256–57; *NYT*, 21, 30 July, 3, 26, 29 August 1916).

10. The Brooklyn Dodgers won the National League pennant in 1916, the team's first since 1900 (*BE*, 295; *NYT*, 19 April 1925).

11. Charles Hercules (Charlie) Ebbets (ca. 1858–1925) was president and owner of the Brooklyn Dodgers (*BDASBase*, 165–66; *NYT*, 19 April 1925).

12. Former president Theodore Roosevelt ran unsuccessfully as a third-party presidential candidate in 1912 and was promoted as the nominee of both the Republican and Progressive Parties in 1916 (*DAB*, 16:135–44).

13. For Charles Evans Hughes see *PWR*, 2:323n.1. Although his relations with Roosevelt had cooled over the years, Hughes nevertheless received the former presi-

dent's endorsement in 1916 after Hughes won the Republican presidential nomination and stated his support of preparedness (Miller, *Theodore Roosevelt*, 551).

14. In his acceptance of the presidential nomination and in campaign speeches, Charles Evans Hughes spoke often of "America first," a phrase used at the time generally to indicate disapproval of Americans whose loyalties appeared to be divided between U.S. interests and those of their ancestral countries (Pusey, *Charles Evans Hughes*, 1:338).

15. William Jennings Bryan, an ardent pacifist who supported Wilson in part because he believed the president would keep the United States out of the war, campaigned not only against intervention but also in opposition to preparedness (Coletta, *William Jennings Bryan*, 3:38–39).

16. Railroad workers threatened to strike on 4 September 1916 unless accorded an eight-hour day without a reduction in pay. With the public encouragement of President Wilson and in the face of aggressive opposition by railroad operators, Congress averted a walk-out with passage of the Adamson Eight-Hour Act on 3 September (Canfield, *Presidency*, 76–77).

17. Dating of the document was determined from references to historical incidents and to Rogers's chronology (see Chronology, 1914–16, OkClaW).

Statement of Salary from Ziegfeld Follies, Inc.
16 September 1916
New York, N.Y.

New York.

Sept. 16ᵗʰ, 1916.[1]

Mr. Will Rogers

ᵃ/c U. S. Income Tax[2]

For Salary Paid By Ziegfeld Follies, Inc.

> *Danse de Follies*

3	Weeks	ending	Jan'y 22/16	@	$275.	825
15	"	"	May 6"	"	300.	4500
<u>17</u>	"	"	Sept 16	"	350	<u>5950</u>
35	"		Total			11275[3]
			Credit Exemption			<u>4000</u>
						7275

	To Tax 1%	72[.]75
July 3	By Cash	<u>34[.]25</u>
	Bal. due	38[.]50

AD. OkClaW, 1975.24.0231.

1. The *Follies of 1916* ended a lengthy run at the New Amsterdam Theatre on the same day, 16 September. The show then embarked on a road tour of several weeks

that included engagements in Boston and Philadelphia. Rogers remained in New York (Chronology, 1914–16, OkClaW).

2. The federal government began collecting corporate and individual income taxes in 1913, but compliance in the early years was minimal. Initial tax legislation allowed exemptions of $3,000 for an individual and $4,000 for a married couple, and provided for some deductions. Congress enacted a new tax measure on 8 September 1916 that doubled individual rates and brought other changes (Carson, *Golden Egg*, 81–83, 86–87, 100–103; Myers, *Financial History*, 267).

3. Rogers's federal income tax return for 1916 is unavailable. As a gauge of his salary in 1916, the estimated per-capita annual income in the United States was $332 in 1910, the year of the most recent census. The average household income at the time, when more than 61 percent of the population lived on farms or in communities of less than 8,000 population, was $1,494 (King, *Wealth*, 16, 129, 224).

Published Remarks from Friars Club Banquet
ca. 26 November 1916
New York, N.Y.

Will Rogers—I want to speak a few words to Mister Caruso[1] in his own language. It is a language that everybody here will understand. I am not much of a poet, but I will give you a little jingle. I have some silver dollars here that I will rattle.

I never went to hear Caruso but twice. The first time, I went with my wife as a wedding present. The second time I went on a bet. When my wife came here with me she said there were two things in New York that she had always wanted to see. They were Caruso and Grant's Tomb.

I got some opera tickets from a speculator and my wife made me dress up in my wedding clothes for the event. So my whole evening was spoiled before I ever got to hear Caruso. My wife had heard that the only proper way to go to the opera was in a cab. Well, we were living just across the street from the Metropolitan,[2] but I went and hired a cab, as my wife insisted on. And so we rode across the street in our cab and got out and showed our tickets. Then we began climbing stairways as high as the Rocky Mountains.

Before we reached the seats our checks called for I realized that we had turned loose of that darn cab just when the main part of our trip was beginning. From the place we were located we could just see the drummer in the orchestra and about six inches of the stage. We figured that if Caruso exited on the left side we would get a shot at him. Well we stuck until the first intermission, and then we went up to Hammerstein's and saw some regular acts.

We stayed up until the morning papers came out and then we eagerly read what had happened at the opera. We found that Caruso had played the part of some sort of a clown.[3] That was the first we knew which one was Caruso.

But I guess the show wasn't any good. For I went past there the next day, and I saw that they had taken it off and put on another show.

PD. Unidentified clipping, ca. 26 November 1916. CPpR files, OkClaW.

1. Enrico Caruso (1873–1921) was considered one of the greatest singers in the history of opera. The beauty, range, and power of his voice brought him wide acclaim and immense success. The Italian tenor was the guest of honor on 26 November 1916 at the annual dinner of the Friars Club in New York, where Rogers was among others who paid him tribute (*NGDO*, 4:746; Rogers, *Will Rogers*, 105; Jackson, *Caruso*, 233; Caruso and Goddard, *Wings*, 108; *NYT*, 27 November 1916).
2. Will and Betty Blake Rogers's first known residence in New York was at the Albany Hotel at Broadway and 41st Street. The opulent Metropolitan Opera House was nearby at Broadway and 39th (*PWR*, 3:132n.1; Burrows and Wallace, *Gotham*, 1074).
3. Based on Rogers's description of the opera they attended, the couple probably heard Enrico Caruso sing the role of the clown, Canio, in *Pagliacci*. Caruso appeared in the two-act opera at the Metropolitan in New York every autumn-winter season from 1903 to 1920. According to Rogers's known chronology, the most likely date of the performance he and Betty attended was on Saturday, 26 December 1908, a month and a day after their marriage (Caruso and Farkas, *Enrico Caruso*, 675; Chronology, 1908–09, OkClaW).

Notes for *Ziegfeld Follies* Performance
21 March 1917
Washington, D.C.

In the same week that he issued a call for a special session of Congress to consider a declaration of war, President Wilson attended a road-tour performance of the Ziegfeld Follies *in Washington.[1] It was Rogers's second opportunity to entertain the president.[2] The notes that Rogers prepared for the second performance—typically in much abbreviated form—do not reveal that he knew that Wilson would be in the audience.*

Have to do something while Girls change

Agravating Clothes   only want to live three more ▲years▲

Only one dont own Car. Limouzine.

Street car Strike[3] – Brought car back.

Move Inauguration. Rep[ublicans] want to Move Election ▲after Thanksgiving.▲

Weather too Uncertain. Dont see how could be more ▲certain   Storms every time▲

Ask Man about Inau'g [Inaugural] Parade. hadent got sand out of ▲eyes.▲

Memorial Bridge to Arlington in Spring – late Spring.

Arlington Hotel – three Men and boy.

White House Pickets.[4] What were they suffering ▲for.▲

Jeanette R– [Rankin][5] likes Chaplin. She will like Cong[ress? *part of document torn and missing*]

Back yard Garden– Plow the town up.

B.O. R.R. Strike[6]– dident get word to Man in t[time? *part of document torn and missing*]

Base Ball Team Win drill Prize. Girls in Alley

Congress vote on Prohib[ition].[7] Just feel like voting

Drug Store.–Wear Badges. 14 Miles of Bryan Speech

Bryan speeches in Jail. Czar Escapes Net and Fleas[8]

China best Jap army in World.[9]

Pres called Congress.–give another chance. La Follette[10] ▲speech in System▲

New Rule[:] Senator could talk all day ▲WOULD NOT HAD TO CALL CONGRESS▲ Now when talk all ▲know must sit down▲

Root[11]–H[ughes?]–Roosevelt – declared War last Night[12]– Hughes told what would ▲*of*▲ our 8 hours▲

Root longer than Bryans   Bryan got by election– Root—Mesopotamia[13]

Missed three years good War might of been in–   Split Egg.

Mrs Astor Child.[14] German-Belgian Brother in law   *Ford Trench*

AD.[15] OkClaW, Will Rogers, Jr., Collection, Notes and Other Writings, Folder 4. Hand-written, top margin, center: "Act did for President Wilson at Washington." Approximately one inch of document, midway along right margin, was torn and missing.

1. On Wednesday, 21 March 1917, President Wilson issued a call for a special session of Congress to meet on Monday, 2 April. On that day Wilson addressed the full Congress and asked for a declaration of war. The Senate approved the war resolution two days later, and the House of Representatives concurred on 6 April (*EAH*, 308–9; *NYT*, 8 April 1917).

2. See Notes for Appearance in *Friars' Frolic*, 30 May 1916, above.

3. A strike by streetcar and railway workers chiefly over wage issues paralyzed the transit system in New York City and its suburbs in the summer and fall of 1916. Although no long-term gains came from it, effects of the strike and criticism of its leaders continued to be reported in the local press in March 1917 (*NYT*, 23, 28, 31 July, 22 August, 22 September, 30 November 1916, 13 March 1917).

4. Members of the National Woman's Party, a group formed in 1916 to advocate for the equality of women throughout the world, began to picket the White House on 10 January 1917. Supporters, usually carrying banners and signs urging the vote for women, continued to picket silently at the presidential mansion and at other political sites in Washington, D.C., for the next three years. The picketing eventually resulted in violent confrontations and generated criticism from other suffragists, who considered it disrespectful, undignified, and damaging to the cause (Barber, *Marching*, 72–73; *HD1920s*, 247).

5. Jeannette Pickering Rankin (1880–1973), a suffragist and social worker in her native Montana, won election to the U.S. House of Representatives in 1916. She took her seat on 2 April 1917, becoming the first woman to serve in Congress (*DAB*, Supp. 9:640–41).

6. The Baltimore & Ohio, along with most other railroad companies in the country, began to prepare in early 1917 for a nationwide strike. With the prospect of war, however, President Wilson declared on 18 March that a strike would not be allowed. A government commission stepped in and negotiated a settlement the next day (*NYT*, 17, 19, 20 March 1917).

7. On 4 March 1917 Congress passed and President Wilson signed one of the first major pieces of federal legislation affecting the prohibition of liquor. The new law forbade the transportation of alcoholic beverages into any state—about one-half of all states at the time—that prohibited their manufacture or sale (Colvin, *Prohibition*, 441; *NYT*, 5 March 1917).

8. Nicholas II (Nicholas Romanov, 1868–1918) reigned as tsar of Russia from 1894 until his abdication in March 1917, marking the end of the monarchy in Russia and the ascendency of a provisional government. After Nicholas's abdication his whereabouts were not immediately known to the public. Soon, however, he and his family were arrested and taken to the palace of Tsarskoye Selo near St. Petersburg (*BDWWI*, 260–63; Perry and Pleshakov, *Flight*, 12, 153, 168; *NYT*, 23 March 1917).

9. China, a virtual protectorate of Japan, severed diplomatic relations with Germany on 14 March 1917 and entered the war with the financial backing of the Japanese government and in support of Japan's claim to certain German possessions in the Pacific region (Kawamura, *Turbulence*, 71–72; *USFWW*, 601). Rogers's use of such ethnic and national pejoratives as "Jap" or instances of his singling out of ethnic or immigrant groups can be found scattered among his papers, especially his unpublished materials (for example, see "Jewish audiences" in Letter to Florenz Ziegfeld, Jr., 13 February 1918; "Polok" in Notes for Lecture Tour Appearance at Carnegie Hall, 11 April 1926; and "Wop" in Notes for Remarks at Mayoral Inauguration, ca. 21 December 1926, below). Reflective of sentiments commonly felt in U.S. society at the time, such stereotypical language, some of it new to the vernacular since 1900, was very much a part of the culture of vaudeville comedy (*DSUE*, 904, 1351; *PWR*, 3:214, 357–58n.6).

10. Robert Marion La Follette (1855–1925), former governor of Wisconsin, served as U.S. senator from 1906 until his death. Progressive and anti-British, he openly opposed U.S. entry into the war and led a filibuster in the Senate in early March 1917 that effectively blocked legislation providing for the arming of merchant vessels (*DAB*, 10:541–46; Cashman, *America*, 481–82).

11. Elihu Root (1845–1937) was a former U.S. secretary of war, secretary of state, and senator from New York (*DAB*, Supp. 2:577–82).

12. Elihu Root and fellow Republicans and interventionists Charles Evans Hughes and Theodore Roosevelt addressed the Union League Club in New York on 20 March 1917. Not much unlike the bellicose remarks of Hughes and Roosevelt that night, Root's speech asserted that Germany was already making war against the United States and that Americans should stand with the Allies (Leopold, *Elihu Root*, 115; *NYT*, 21 March 1917).

13. Mesopotamia, an ancient region in southwestern Asia traditionally defined as the land between the Tigris and Euphrates Rivers and in modern-day terms as Iraq, was the scene of fierce combat during the war. A major assault by British forces beginning in

February 1917 resulted in a major victory over Turkish troops with the capture of Baghdad on 11 March (Falls, "Turkish Campaigns," 208–9; *IGEA*, 473).

14. Madeleine Talmadge Force Astor Dick (ca. 1893–1940) had become the second wife of John Jacob Astor IV only a few months before the sinking of the *Titanic*, the luxury liner on which they were returning to the United States from their honeymoon trip abroad. One of the wealthiest men in the world at the time, Astor went down with the ship after having put his pregnant wife aboard a lifeboat. By 1917 his widow had remarried and relinquished rights to her share of the estate. Nevertheless, she sought, and was awarded, an increased daily allowance for the support of her son, John Jacob Astor VI (1912–92), on 16 March 1917 (*NYT*, 17 March 1917, 28 March 1940, 27 June 1992).

15. Dating of the document was determined by historical references in the text.

Guest Newspaper Column by Will Rogers
10 May 1917
New York, N.Y.

Rogers occasionally wrote song lyrics for use in skits or other performances, but the following is the only known published poem to be credited to him.

YE TOWNE GOSSIP
BY K.C.B.[1]

By Bill Rogers.

DEAR FRIEND K.C.B.[2]

ALL I know is what I see in the papers.[3]

AND IN other cities.

THEY CHARGE two cents for their papers.

AND IN New York.

THEY ONLY charge one cent.

BUT I guess they know here.

ABOUT WHAT their papers are worth.

AND MARSHAL Joffre.[4]

(I CAN spell it but I can't pronounce it.)

IS IN New York today.[5]

AND HE'S going to be remembered.

ABOVE EVERYTHING else.

FOR BEING the general.

THAT TOOK the red pants.

OFF THE French soldiers.

AND MADE them look.
LIKE THE real fighting men.
THEY'VE SHOWN themselves to be.
IF WE can produce.
JUST ONE general.
WHO WILL undertake.
TO REMOVE.
THOSE PALM beach suits.[6]
OUR WAR.
WILL NOT have been in vain.
AND HE can start in.
RIGHT NOW.
BY LOWERING the belts.
ON THOSE comedy overcoats.
THE MEN wear
AND DON'T you remember.
THAT THE custom used to be.
TO GIVE notables.
WHO VISITED our country.
A FEW jewels.
OR OTHER junk like that.
BUT NOW.
SINCE WE'VE grown so wealthy.
I SEE.
THAT MRS. Woodrow Wilson.[7]
HAS SENT Madam Joffre.
A WHOLE Virginia ham.[8]
AND K.C.B.
I CAN tell by your articles.
THAT YOU like kids.
AND I thought maybe.
THAT YOU wouldn't mind.
IF I mentioned mine here.
THEY NEVER get their names in the papers.
THERE'S THREE of them.
BILL IS six.
AND MARY is a four-year-old.
AND JIM is a yearling.
AND IT will please their mamma.

TO SEE their names here.
AND HER name is Betty.
AND LIKE you.
AND LIKE me.
SHE BELONGS out there.
IN THE big West.
IF I'D mention the names.
OF FRANCES White.
AND ED. Martindel.[9]
AND I have.
AND IF you cut anything out of this.
DON'T CUT out the stuff.
ABOUT THE children.
OR MAMMA.
AND IF there's room.
YOU CAN mention Bill Rock.
HE ASKED me to put his name in.
MUCH OBLIGED to you.

PD. Printed in *New York American*, May 1917. Scrapbook 8, Part 1, OkClaW. Imprinted below the column heading in small type: "(Reg. U.S. Pat. Off.)". To the left of the column heading is an illustration of a man dressed in colonial attire reading the *New York American* and holding in his right hand a rod-like instrument that is pointed at the heading. Handwritten, though not in Rogers's hand, diagonally across the body of the poem: "This is a corker." A line drawing of a Rogers-like figure, dressed in chaps and other western attire and spinning a rope above his head, appears between the last two lines of the poem. For literary effect the editors chose to retain the use of capitals in this printed document.

1. The identity of K.C.B. is unclear. The column, "Ye Towne Gossip," probably was syndicated in some fashion. Almost concurrent with the publication of this item in the *New York American*, work by a writer using the same initials and an identical informal style of poetry appeared in the *Seattle Times* (Jackson, "Politics of Gender," 4).

2. K.C.B. used his column the previous week to publicly challenge Rogers to be a guest contributor to "Ye Towne Gossip." In his unique style the poet columnist wrote of having recently attended the *Midnight Frolic* with a friend. The two were so taken with Rogers's cleverness that the friend dared K.C.B. to give Rogers a chance to write a guest column (transcript in Early Articles, 1916–22, OkClaW).

3. The poem's initial line closely approximated a saying that became a Rogers trademark: "All I know is what I read in the papers." Its appearance here marks Rogers's first known published use of the line.

4. Joseph Jacques Césaire Joffre (1852–1931) was the chief of staff of the French army at the outbreak of the war. Although he scored some early success in the war, major losses and minor results led to his removal from command in December 1916.

With the largely ceremonial title of marshal of France, he was one of several Allied leaders to visit the United States in the spring of 1917 to greet their new partner in the war. Joffre arrived on 24 April and encountered large, enthusiastic crowds throughout his tour (*BDWWI*, 198–99; [Joffre], *Personal Memoirs*, 2:575–77).

5. Marshal Joffre arrived in New York on 9 May for a three-day stay. An estimated one million people—"a human sea," Joffre recalled—thronged the streets to greet his arrival. Rogers was in New York at the time performing in the *Follies* ([Joffre], *Personal Memoirs*, 576–77; Chronology, 1917–19, OkClaW).

6. In the urgent chaos of the first weeks after U.S. entry into the war, officer candidates and enlistees often arrived at the newly erected military camps dressed in their best clothes. Once there many had to undertake basic training while clad in civilian wear because the supply of uniforms and boots ran well behind the demand (Zieger, *America's Great War*, 87, 88).

7. Edith Bolling Galt Wilson (1872–1961), the wife of Woodrow Wilson and one of his most trusted advisors, had married the president in December 1915, about sixteen months after the death of his first wife (*DAB*, Supp. 7:795–96).

8. When the Wilsons presented Marshal Joffre with the gift of a Virginia ham, he expressed his regrets that his wife was not present to enjoy it; whereupon the Wilsons gave him another to take home (Wilson, *My Memoir*, 137).

9. In his challenge to Rogers, K.C.B. had asked him to mention in his guest column the names of Frances White, whom K.C.B. claimed to have known in California, and Ed Martindel, who was with K.C.B. and his friend at Rogers's performance in the *Midnight Frolic*.

From J. Thomas McSpadden
7 July 1917
Chelsea, Okla.

In addition to owning or leasing several hundred acres of ranch land at his birthplace near Oologah, Okla., by the summer of 1917 Rogers had accumulated various real estate holdings in Claremore, the seat of Rogers County. Much of the latter property, some of it rental houses, came from the estate of his father, Clement Vann Rogers, who had died in October 1911.[1] Will Rogers had either acquired it as part of his one-quarter interest in his father's estate or had purchased it over time from the other heirs: his sisters, Sallie and Maud, and the children of his late sister, May.[2] Sallie's husband, J. Thomas McSpadden, helped manage the property for Rogers for several years.[3]

July 7 – 1917

Dear Willie & Bettie

I have about finsohed [finished] up at claremore & will Send you a kind of a statement that will give you some Idea of my expenditure of your money. I am surprised at the cost, but I have done my best. you have sent me $3650^{00} I have collected in rents about $900^{00} I have spent all of this money & $600^{00} of my own. So if conveint [convenient] send me the $600^{00} if not I can take it out of the rents as they come in   The rents will amt to 194^{00} from now on. all the rents are collected except on[e] fellow– he is about 15^{00} behind—

I have collected $97.^{50}$ on the garrarge which pays it up to the 1ˢᵗ of ~~agu~~ ▲aug▲. It sure looks good   I counted 27 cars in it the other morning & that about filled it.[4] The renter said he could use twice the floor space. I had the south entrance to the garrarge fixed & the curbing put in & The workmen are finsohing [finishing] the side walk in front of the little new dwling [dwelling] & the Hutchens house to day. The Theater was to open to night   Brophy[5] was to Phone me if he opens to night   It looks good & I am told it is up to "now"   The front with its discorations sure looks good to me

all very well   With love

J T McS–

[*separate page:*]

on this sheet I will give you a few items to give you some idea how I spent some of the money   about $800 was spent on the little dwelling

Taxes & back Taxes	770	– on house & claremore —
Cabin " "	75	
Out on loan	96	includ[es] some on Cabin Creek & ▼garrarge▼
Lumber bill	1200	cement sand roofing
Electric wiring	125	wire put in pipes garrarge
gas Plumbing	150.	Including closet "
gasoline Tank	150	& fixtures
Pd for cement floor	280	in Theater
White washing	100	garrarge
Pd out for Labor	1050.	I have the items for you when you ▼come home▼

ALS, rc. OkClaW, 1975.24.0329. On Maplewood, Chelsea, Oklahoma, letterhead. J. T. McSpadden, Owner.

1. For Clement Vann (Clem) Rogers see *PWR*, 1:536–43, 3:259n.1.

2. For Sallie Clementine Rogers McSpadden see *PWR*, 1:511–15; for Maud Ethel Rogers Lane see *PWR*, 1:499–501; for May Rogers Yocum Stine see *PWR*, 1:554–58. For the disposition of the estate of Clement Vann Rogers see *PWR*, 3:259n.2.

3. For John Thomas (Tom) McSpadden see *PWR*, 1:510–11.

4. The Sequoyah Garage occupied one-half of a stone building owned by Rogers that had once been a livery stable. The operator rented space in the garage to people wanting to store their automobiles during the winter months (*CP*, 1 November 1917, OkClaW).

5. L. W. Brophy founded the Yale Theatre Company in Muskogee, Okla., in 1908. By early 1917 he had opened movie houses in four eastern Oklahoma communities. His company, which McSpadden assured Rogers was "strong" (autograph note on

Lease Contract, 9 January 1917, OkClaW), paid fifty dollars a month to Rogers to rent one-half of a former stone barn in downtown Claremore. Brophy spent several months remodeling it for use as a movie theater, part of the cost of which was covered by Rogers (L. W. Brophy to J. T. McSpadden, 24 February 1922, OkClaW; Collings, *Old Home Ranch*, 63).

Manuscript for Magazine Article
ca. 3 November 1917
[Philadelphia, Pa.]

To Charles P. Shoffner[1]—

Now the Editor has asked me to write and tell you boys how to make and throw a rope or lasso. Say thats harder than learning to do it, trying to tell about it. I wish I could see you all and show you what little I know of it   that would be easier all around.

Now in the first place it is a whole lot easier than you think so dont let it get its bluff in on you.

Now a lot of you may think you have to have a certain kind of rope   thats all wrong   any kind will do   its all in what you practice with and what you get used too

of course for fancy Roping and spinning of the rope the best kind is an ordinary Cotton Rope that you can buy at any hardware store   its just like Wi[n]dow sash cord only bigger and for a small boy that is all right as it is light   I use a No. 10. Sampson *Spot cord*   it has a colored stran[d] running through it but any kind will do

then get in the same place a spool of this copper wire and use it to make your ~~toop~~ eyelet or Hondo as we call it. just double the end of your rope back three or four inches and wrap this copper wire around it tight   dont tie any knots in the rope to make this eyelet   this wire will give it weight[,] not much   you dont want it heavy at the loop for most things. use this wire to wrap this back just as you would tie it with a string   wrap it around say about 10 or 15 times   then cut your rope off say from 15 feet depending on the size of the boy   make a short rope at first as it will get all tangled up on you and the shorter it is the easier it will be for you to handle it

you dont need one of those Brass Hondos, or heavy ones[,] till you get so you want a Rope that you want to jump through from side to side   thats the only kind of trick [for which] you [would] want a heavily weighted rope   we use a different rope for that, thats something when I learned we did not know and we tried to do everything with a heavy rope and we were working about twice as hard and as fast as nessary. and lots of tricks are impractible with a hevily weighted rope

this piece of rope and the wire and all wont cost you over 25 or 30 cents and you are ready to go to fighting it or if you cant afford that get any old piece of discarded rope you might find and if you havent got the wire wrap enough string around there where you fasten the loop and you can learn just as much as the other boy   its not in the rope   its in keeping after it and dont think your rope is not fixed right. its all right   its you thats wrong   for the plain tricks of just spinning it around and jumping in and out and those things I can take a cable wire[,] a rope as big around as your arm[,] ~~and~~ or a garden hose or anything of that kind and tie a temarary loop in it and spin it and so can you if you can spin any rope at all. So you cant go wrong   just keep after it. It would be about impossible to fix a rope so you could not spin it. Every boy can learn in a Week or so to keep the loop going.

After you fix your loop or Eyelet in it then you are ready to start in   run the other end through this one you have made and make a loop[,] say using about three or four feet of your rope   you Want to spin a small loop[,] not too small, till you get so you can keep it going good   then you increase the size of it by letting it slide through your hand and increase your speed at the same time.

Now the one thing to remember[:] *always let the rope turn in your hand*   dont hold it tight   hold it and let it turn so the kinks can twist out of the other end. thats the whole secret of the thing   it will at first get all tangled up an[y]way   so when you take the twists out of it take them all out ~~so they~~ by letting your whole rope down to no loop at all and then make it over again and each time spin the rope the opposite way. that is if you tried to keep it going with your hand turning forward   the next time turn it backwards as that helps keep it from getting so twisted and you have to learn both ways anyway

Now you try this and later on I will try and tell you more about how to do the different tricks. Any of you write me to the show or to the Editor and I will try and help you any way I can.

Dont get discueraged and just stay with it and any of you can get it

yours,

Will Rogers.

AMS. OkClaW, Will Rogers, Jr., Collection, "How to Throw a Lasso" Original Manuscript.[2] The salutation is not in Rogers's hand.

Will, Jimmy, Mary, Bill, and Betty Blake Rogers on Long Island, N.Y., during Rogers's early years with the *Follies*, ca. 1916–17. (*OkClaW*)

1. Charles Pennypacker Shoffner (ca. 1873–1946) was associate editor of *Farm Journal* from 1913 to 1924. The magazine, known for its practical information for farmers and their families, had been published in Philadelphia since 1877 (*NYT*, 6 May 1946; *WhJour*, 353; Wood, *Magazines*, 173–77).

2. Rogers's manuscript was acquired by the Will Rogers Memorial several years after Charles Shoffner's death. With the papers was the following note from Shoffner describing his visit with Rogers at the *Follies* and the circumstances that led to the article:

> At the time Will was with the "Follies", I was editing a Young Folks Department for "The Farm Journal.["]
>
> I wrote to Will in New York and he wrote "meet me in Philadelphia". I met him and suggested he write an article on "How to Throw a Lasso" for the boys. He was enthused over the subject and after several meetings with him the enclosed article was handed me by Will one Saturday matinee during the "Follies" run in Philadelphia. He also gave me five (5) photographs, with appropriate inscriptions. These photographs are very unusual and show Will with his three children, then Bill, 6; Mary, 4; and Jim, 2.
>
> At the "Follies" he introduced me to Bert Williams, the comedian, saying "Shoffner, shake hands with the whitest man God ever made." Bert's reply was "Aw—Bill".
>
> The Fairbanks twins came rushing in and Will caught one in each arm saying, "Here's the friskiest ponies we have." (OkClaW, Will Rogers, Jr., Collection, "How to Throw a Lasso" Original Manuscript)

The dating of the manuscript was determined by Shoffner's references to the ages of Rogers's children and to the schedule of *Follies* performances in Philadelphia. There is no evidence that the manuscript was published (Chronology, 1917–19, OkClaW; Mary Rulinski to editors, September–October 2002).

From Oscar A. Price
12 November 1917
Washington, D.C.

Rogers and other theatrical personalities in New York were among groups of prominent individuals who were specially targeted in the Liberty Loan drives that swept the country following U.S. entry into the war in April 1917. While the campaigns sought to raise much needed government revenue, they also became a testing ground for demonstrating a person's patriotism.[1]

November 12, 1917.

Mr. Will Rogers,
Lambs Club,[2]
130 W. 44th St.,
New York City.
My dear Mr. Rogers:

Permit me in behalf of Secretary McAdoo[3] to express to you the very sincere appreciation of the Treasury Department for the valuable assistance you rendered in the Second Liberty Loan campaign.[4]

The participation in it by thousands and thousands of patriotic Americans was what made it the great success it was. The splendid result in New York City and District is something that must be particularly pleasing to the citizens of the city and district, more especially those who aided in bringing about that result.

Very sincerely yours,
Oscar A Price[5]
Director of Publicity.

HM P[6]

TLS, rc. OkClaW, 1975.21.0043. On letterhead of Treasury Department, Liberty Loan of 1917, Office of Director of Publicity, Washington. In the first paragraph "Secretary McAdoo" has been underscored by hand.

1. To finance the war effort, the Wilson administration decided that borrowing would prove more immediate and less politically sensitive than increased taxation. Beginning in the spring of 1917, the government used a succession of highly publicized and emotionally charged Liberty Loan drives to promote and sell war bonds to the public. The campaigns produced an oversubscription of $20 billion and helped to mobilize the American people (Zieger, *America's Great War*, 75–76; Canfield, *Presidency*, 108–9).

2. At the time of this correspondence, Rogers was on the road, touring with the *Ziegfeld Follies*. He was a member of the Lambs, so it would not have been unusual for him to receive mail in care of the theatrical group's clubhouse (Chronology, 1917–19, OkClaW; Laurie, *Vaudeville*, 306).

3. William Gibbs McAdoo (1863–1941), attorney and former railroad executive, became U.S. secretary of the treasury in 1913. As secretary, he initiated and led the Liberty Loan campaigns, which included using entertainers and patriotic speakers as volunteers to address mass rallies throughout the country (*DAB*, Supp. 3:479–82; Zieger, *America's Great War*, 75–76).

4. The second Liberty Loan drive was launched on 1 October 1917 with great fanfare and ceremony throughout the country and a nationwide goal of $3 billion in government bonds. By the end of the campaign in November, New York sources had purchased 41 percent of the total accepted allotment of bonds (*NYT*, 2 October, 9, 11 November 1917).

5. Oscar A. Price, an auditor in the U.S. Interior Department, was appointed publicity director of the second Liberty Loan campaign on 1 August 1917 (*NYT*, 2 August 1917).

6. "HM P" was probably a clerical notation.

Newspaper Article by Will Rogers
15 December 1917
Detroit, Mich.

EXTRA! STREET RAILWAY

PROBLEM IS SOLVED

WILL ROGERS, FAMOUS COMEDIAN WITH ZIEGFELD FOL-LIES, MAKES EXHAUSTIVE INVESTIGATION AND SUB-MITS HIS REPORT TO THE JOURNAL

By Will Rogers.

I have been asked to tell about Detroit and its street car troubles.[1] They are both linked together just like Mexico and the revolutions.

Now, I have investigated the whole thing and even gone so far as to ride on some of their cars.

Now, in my article, I am going to give all sides to this mess an equal show because they are all so bad I can't pick out the worst.

We'll start in with the street car line first. Now in the f[i]rst place, they could be arrested for treason in these war times. Treason means anything that causes trouble or annoys our people, thereby giving aid or comfort to the enemy. Why, the Kaiser[2] would almost pull a human grin if he knew what was happening in Detroit.

The D. U. R. were the originators of camouflage, by running tractors and calling them street cars.

And those stoves they have in the cars—the motorman puts his bottle of beer in there to keep it cool till he gets to the end of the line. Last Monday two women had their feet frostbitten by putting them too close to the stove.

Then they have a Carnegie library[3] in their cars, consisting of a pamphlet telling all (not quite all) about the company. It's bad enough to have to ride in the cars—much less have to read about them. These pamphlets told everything but that the fare was to be increased.

Now, on the other hand, the system is trying to do better.

They are putting another car on the Harper line just like the one they have now.

Now there are features on this D. U. R.—DO U RIGHT—that no system in the world has.

Take the Fourteenth street line, for instance. It will take you any place in Michigan, if you stay on long enough. I asked a conductor on that line if he went to Trenton. He says, "No, we haven't been out there for the last few days, but we can go out that way today if you want to." You see the company issues the conductor an automobile Blue Book so they'll know how to get back. That line don't need a library—it should have a sleeping car trailer.

The fare on most lines is three or five cents, but on this line it's twenty-five cents a day and fifteen cents extra if you want to stay on at night. It crosses Grand River so many times that you are really over water more than you are over land. Instead of giving transfers, they issue life-preservers.

Now, this sk[*obliterated*]op that you hear so much about—[*obliterated*]if you live near a corner—the car skips your corner.

Now, there's one thing that the company did that [I] claim was legitimate—It is operating on a day-to-day agreement. Well, the day they raised the fares, they got up early that morning and raised the fares before the council had made the daily agreement with them—Give 'em credit—also a nickel if you want a ride.[4]

Now, we will take up the COMMON Council.[5] Whoever named it knew something. Now, they're a good bunch of boys—all love one another—no dissension—except perhaps most of them would like to poison each other—and do they love their Mayor[6]— Why sure they do. They get along just like Villa and Carranza.[7]

The Common Council appropriated $35,000 to have the street car lines investigated—and the Committee turned in a report—"We find the car system in pretty bad shape and recommend additional appropriations to carry on the investigation."

Any man with a nickel could have found that out.

The Common Council say they will make the company take their cars off the street.

The people waiting on the street these cold nights to get home claim the company has already taken their cars off. The Common Council don't like anybody—not even their Couzens—especially Jim.[8] Yes, they have severed diplomatic relations. Each claims the other has committed the overt act. I would tell you what they call each other, but this is not asbestos paper.

They used to charge three bucks to get your car out of pound, but so many people didn't call for their cars, they had to reduce it to a dollar so they'd come and get 'em.

The Mayor don't like the idea of this Common Council of 42—count 'em. He wants the short ballot consisting of 9 men.

An old fellow down home in Oklahoma wanted a bill passed to reduce a jury from twelve to six men; asked why he said: "Well, the fewer men, the more chance an innocent man has got going free." I guess that's the way the Mayor figures these birds. Then the Council would not be so common with 9 men.

Most controversies have only two sides, but this mess here—talk about Russia and all her factions;[9] it's a garden of Eden stacked up side of this. But, one thing I am glad to say—that during it all there is absolutely NO POLITICS.

Everybody is acting for the good of Detroit. AMEN.

Now, I don't believe anyone should criticize anything unless they have a better suggestion to offer. Well, I have and here is the solution to the whole problem.

1—Take all the street cars, rails and equipment—melt 'em all up in old junk, sell it, take the money and buy smokes for the solders.

2—Take everybody's automobile away from them, send all the cars to France—when a soldier comes back from the front line trenches, give each one an automobile and tell him to go to Paris and put on a show till they need him again.

3—The Ford and Dodge cars send to the poor Belgian children to play with for Christmas.

4—Take this cop up in that watchful waiting tower on the Campus—He should make a good aviator by now.

This is the ONLY way you will ever make the streets of Detroit FREE FOR DEMOCRACY.[10]

PD. Printed in *Detroit Journal*, 15 December 1917. Scrapbook 20, OkClaW.

1. The Detroit United Railway, known popularly as the D.U.R., operated an interurban network that connected most of the major municipalities in the southeastern part of Michigan, allowing people to commute several miles to work each day. A major point of agitation, however, concerned ownership and operation of the rail lines. Constant pressure was applied throughout the 1910s toward municipal ownership, but the city of Detroit did not acquire possession until 1922 (O'Geran, *History*, 241–308; Dunbar, *Michigan*, 565–66).

2. For KaiserWilhelm II see *PWR*, 2:287–88n.4.

3. Andrew Carnegie (1835–1919) amassed a large fortune from several enterprises, especially steel. He distributed his wealth to many causes, including public libraries. By 1918 Carnegie had given almost $40 million for library buildings in 1,405 communities in the United States (*DAB*, 3:499–505; Bobinski, *Carnegie Libraries*, 13–14).

4. In the fall of 1917 the operator of the streetcars, Detroit United Railway, raised fares from three cents to five (Beasley and Stark, *Made in Detroit*, 255).

5. When describing the common council, or city commission, a local writer noted at the time, "We still employ forty-two aldermen to do the work of half a dozen" (Nimmo, "Detroit," 36).

6. Oscar Bruno Marx (1866–1923) served as mayor of Detroit from 1913 to 1919 (Marquis, ed., *Book of Detroiters*, 339; *NYT*, 24 November 1923).

7. Venustiano Carranza (1859–1920), leader of the Constitutionalist forces in the Mexican Revolution in the 1910s, seized control of Mexico City in August 1915. Despite having once agreed to serve under Carranza's leadership, Pancho Villa grew to hate and distrust him. The feeling was mutual: Carranza announced in early 1916 that his rival must be eliminated (*Diccionario Porrua*, 290–91; Stout, *Border Conflict*, 9–11, 21, 48).

8. James Joseph (Jim) Couzens, Jr. (1872–1936), was a partner in Ford Motor Company and its former business manager. As chairman of the Detroit Street Railway Commission from 1913 to 1915, he failed to win municipal ownership of the streetcar system. In 1915 he became police commissioner (*DAB*, Supp. 2:125–27).

9. Within a period of about nine months, from March to November 1917, Russia underwent dramatic, turbulent shifts in government: from the monarchial rule of the tsar to parallel provisional and soviet governments to the culmination of the revolution with the coming to power of the Bolsheviks on 8 November (Gilbert, *First World War*, 314–15, 326, 374).

10. In his message to Congress on 2 April 1917 asking for a declaration of war, President Wilson drew the loudest roar of approval with the words, "to make the world safe for democracy." That phrase, or variations thereof, became the prevailing justification for U.S. participation in the war and the message conveyed in the psychological mobilization of the American people (Harries and Harries, *Last Days*, 71–72; Zieger, *America's Great War*, 83–84).

Newspaper Article by Will Rogers
ca. 22 December 1917
Detroit, Mich.

STUFFY M'INNIS[1] IS MARTYR
TO BASEBALL PROFESSION
DECLARES WILL ROGERS.

By Will Rogers.
(Star of the Ziegfeld Follies.)

This guy Beasley,[2] who signs a pay check from the paper just to follow Ty Cobb around and tell how many bats he carries up to the plate—

Well, he was out last night and in no shape to tell you anything today. So he asked me to pinch hit for him, and, like all of them, I suppose I will take my three healthies and sit down.

Of course, you all know about both Philadelphia leagues selling their teams.[3] Well, today, I want to bat out a few lines about Cornelius McGillicuddy,[4] Bush,[5] Schang[6] and Strunk.[7] Now I don't think it will be taken so hard in Phi, as very few people there ever saw them play.

———

One thing is a cinch: They can't lose any more games than they did; of course, now they can lose by more runs.[8]

An opposing player used to have just four chances of being put out when Bush, Schang and Strunk were playing; now he has only one. If he hits out of reach of McInnis he can bat a thousand.

Of course, the sympathy of all of us goes out to poor McInnis. I don't know what terrible things Connie must have it in for him for, to make him stay all the time.[9]

Poor Stuffy is a martyr to the baseball profession.

―――――

Now personally, I think Connie made a good deal, as his park is located in a good part of Phi and I don't think he will have any trouble cutting it up in lots and selling it.[10]

Or, he can plow it up and plant it in something. That's a good scheme. When a town is no good plow it up and sow it in something.

The beauty about Mack farming is that he could still sit on the bench with his program and give his gardeners signals when and what to plant.[11] Suppose he wags his program for a double plant; the gardener, right away, plants a few rows of succotash. Suppose he wants to pull off a delayed plant; the coacher drops his hoe. That tips the field gardener and he sows winter wheat.

When Mack crosses his legs and writes on his program, that's the pick and run sign. It means that a patch of beans are ripe and the short gardener is to pick 'em and run to market with them, not spilling one as Connie himself did the winter after playing the Braves.[12]

―――――

You see, he could pick up young inexperienced college boys who had never worked in a big city garden before and develop them into big league trucksters.[13]

You see, it is a lot different gardening in a big league city. A weed may be growing right towards you and then take a crooked growth and you fail ►to cut it◄, or a man might fumble a radish right in the heart of the season.

On days when he wanted to sow wild oats he could use his left-handers.

Can you imagine what a large garlic field Bodie[14] could cover and what a treat it would be for Hughey Jennings[15] to play on a field like that instead of picking the grass and eating it? Think what he would do to the turnip tops and young onions. Hughey would eat up the profits.

This scheme would have the endorsement of Emperor Ban Johnson[16] of the league cause when he asked for exemption for his gardeners, Hoover would see to it that it was granted.[17]

―――――

They would have the same crowd out to see 'em garden as to play ball, as those fellows go out there to knit every day, anyway—both of them.

And my only and last request is that I hope they won't draft any of the Athletics, as we want to win this war.

PD. Printed in *Detroit Journal*, ca. 22 December 1917.[18] Scrapbook 20, OkClaW. The interpolation was handwritten and inserted in lieu of a torn and missing portion of the clipping.

1. John Phalen (Stuffy) McInnis (1890–1960) began his major-league baseball career in 1909 with the Philadelphia Athletics. Playing mostly at first base, McInnis became one of the team's best performers, both at the plate and in the field (*BE*, 1343; *BDASBase*, 357–58).

2. Norman B. Beasley (ca. 1877–1963) was a reporter and sports editor for the *Detroit Journal* from 1907 to 1919 (*NYT*, 4 July 1963; Marquis, ed., *Book of Detroiters*, 43).

3. In mid-December 1917, at the winter meetings of the major league baseball teams, owners of both of the Philadelphia squads, the Athletics of the American League and the Phillies of the National, made deals that sent star players to rival teams (Lieb and Baumgartner, *Philadelphia Phillies*, 141; Lieb, *Connie Mack*, 190–91).

4. Connie Mack (Cornelius Alexander McGillicuddy, 1862–1956), manager and part-owner of the Philadelphia Athletics, was one of the pioneers in baseball's American League when it began operations in 1901 (*DAB*, Supp. 6:414–16; *BDASBase*, 358–59).

5. Leslie Ambrose (Joe) Bush (1892–1974) was rated the strongest pitcher in the Philadelphia Athletics organization. Bullet Joe won eleven games and lost seventeen, and recorded an earned run average of 2.47 in 1917. He was traded to the Boston Red Sox in the off-season (*BE*, 1867; Lieb, *Connie Mack*, 191).

6. Walter Henry (Wally) Schang (1889–1965) played mostly catcher for the Philadelphia Athletics for five seasons, beginning in 1913. After hitting .285 in 1917 and having one of his best years as a fielder, he was traded to the Boston Red Sox (*BE*, 1560).

7. Amos Aaron Strunk (1889–1979), a native of Philadelphia, starred in center field for the Athletics from 1908 to 1917. Fleet of foot and reliable with the glove, Strunk was among the team's top players sent to the Boston Red Sox on 14 December 1917 (*BE*, 1639; *CH*, 15 December 1917; Lieb, *Connie Mack*, 190).

8. Although they finished last in the American League in 1917 for the third consecutive year, the Athletics actually lost fewer games than in the previous season: 98 vs. 117 (Jordan, *Athletics*, 76–78).

9. Connie Mack traded McInnis to the Boston Red Sox in January 1918 (*BDASBase*, 357).

10. The Athletics opened Shibe Park in 1909. Located in a working-class neighborhood and near two areas of Philadelphia known locally as Swampoodle and Goosetown, it was considered a show place among major-league baseball stadiums at the time (Lieb, *Connie Mack*, 122; Jordan, *Athletics*, 43).

11. Known as "The Tall Tactician," Connie Mack proved keenly adept at managing his players during games, often waving his ever-present scorecard as he moved his players defensively or signaled them in hitting and running situations (*DAB*, Supp. 6:415; *BDASBase*, 359).

12. The Athletics won their second consecutive American League pennant in 1914, but the Boston Braves swept the World's Series in four games. In December of that year Connie Mack began selling and releasing key players. The Athletics finished the next season in last place (Lieb, *Connie Mack*, 165, 175, 179, 181).

13. A superb judge of talent, Connie Mack was well known for signing collegians who became some of his team's finest players (*BDASBase*, 359; Lieb, *Connie Mack*, 84, 105).

14. Ping Bodie (Francesco Stephano Pezzolo, 1887–1961) played only one season, 1917, with the Philadelphia Athletics. Although a favorite of the fans and a reasonably good hitter, the outfielder struggled to stay in the major leagues because of his weak fielding (*BE*, 800; Jordan, *Athletics*, 77).

15. Hugh Ambrose (Hughie) Jennings (1869–1928) managed the Detroit Tigers from 1906 to 1920. One of the sport's most colorful personalities, Jennings was known for stomping his feet, grabbing clumps of grass, and yelling a piercing "Ee-yah!" during critical moments in a game (*BDASBase*, 281–82; Lieb, *Detroit Tigers*, 86).

16. Byron Bancroft (Ban) Johnson (1864–1931), attorney, sportswriter, and baseball executive, served as president of the American League from 1900 to 1927. He established the upstart American League as a legitimate rival of the National League and became a dominant figure in the sport (*BDASBase*, 285–86).

17. Herbert Clark Hoover (1874–1964), who would become the thirty-first president of the United States, headed the Commission for Relief in Belgium during the early years of the war. His success in that position led to his appointment by President Wilson in April 1917 to head the wartime Food Administration. As food administrator, Hoover promoted heavily in the fall of 1917 the voluntary conservation of food through "meatless" days, "wheatless" days, and even the "gospel of the clean plate" (*DAB*, Supp. 7:357–59; Nash, *Life*, 229).

18. The dating of the document was determined from historical references and from the fact that Rogers's previous article in the *Detroit Journal* had been published on a Saturday.

To Florenz Ziegfeld, Jr.
13 February 1918
Chicago, Ill.

The Follies of 1917 *closed in New York on 15 September and embarked on a forty-eight-week tour. The road show opened in Chicago on 23 December and staged its final performance at the Illinois Theatre there on 2 March 1918. Apparently at some point during the road tour, Rogers became aware that* Follies *producer Flo Ziegfeld would give him his own show. Excitedly, Rogers sat down and produced the following outline of ideas for the production, which he titled "A Mess of Junk."* [1]

Chicago, February 13, 1918.[2]

Mr. Ziegfeld,

Dear Boss:

As I didn't get to see you, I thought it might do no harm to write you out as well as I can a few ideas of a show.

Now, in the first place, I have an idea of a title that I know is unique and different and, especially, if it is a piece with no connected story: it is "A Mess of Junk". Now, you think that over and see if you don't think its good.

The scene where we use horses , I think should be early and be my first appearance on the stage as it will be a surprise as they do not know that I have kept up on that kind of work and, if it makes a good impression, it will help me in what I do later. Its a big, full stage set of Western scenery and a moving picture company are at work. They set up the camera, a big, loud talking director (we could use Wayburn);[3] now, he explains "I have found a guy to do these stunts, but I don't think he's any good; he looks like a 'nut' to me and I don't think he can throw a rope in the creek, but we will have to try him. All right, come on out here ; I will think of the tricks and you do them. He names some trick that he wants done and all I say is "Well, I don't know but I'll take a crack at it". He criticises the costume, says 'You don't look like a moving picture cowboy" and everything with him is all wrong; even when you do a trick right, its wrong to him . Then he'll announce another trick and I say 'I'll take a crack at it'. He says– 'You wont do, you don't look at the camera and smile like Fairbanks', and you don't look mean enough for W.S.Hart".[4] Now, its my idea that he can have all the talk with the other people standing on the stage, but I never say a word; just do as he says and he keeps bawling me out, telling me how bad I am.

Now,during this scene,I have a lot of good tricks on horses that have never been done before;you see by him asking me that announces the trick and lets the audience understand what I am going to do, but other people on the stage have all the talk and comedy; all I do is the work. Now, here are a few of the tricks ,- I can rope all the horses in one throw that you can get on the stage; I think about five , maybe six .

I do part of the catches while I am sitting on one horse and catch the other horse as he goes by. Now, here are a few of the original tricks that I have been practicing on all this time. I rope a horse by the neck, the rope crossing in a perfect figure 8 on his chest and catching his front feet; I rope a horse by the neck, the rope crossing in a figure 8 and catching the rider with the upper part of the loop; throwing two ropes at once, catching the horse by the head and tail; throwing three ropes at once and catching the horse by the feet and by the neck and the rider .

Here is one no one has ever tried; throwing four ropes at once, the fourth with my foot;all catching different places. Standing down over the footlights on a horse with a rope about 90 feet long, spinning it clear out over the audience.

Now,for a comedy finish, he keeps hollering at me what to do;he gets over by the camera and operator; I am on my horse. I throw a big loop over him,camera, operator and all; I have it tied to my saddle and drag him off the stage.

Now, I have an idea of a sensational, dangerous looking stunt; just as the curtain comes down on this full stage scene, run around into one, and have a horse standing there ready;this horse dashes across the stage in one right over the footlights at a dead run with me hanging down on his side by one leg and one leg over the saddle horn; and pick up a handkerchief backwards and out at the small entrance in one on the other side. It looks like he is going to scrape me off as he goes out; you see its so quick, I think it would be a good stunt and it would be easy.

Now, I have an idea of a way to do a lot of my newspaper stuff. Its a country Post Office; got an old stove and three or four fellows around talking; I am the old Rube that reads all the papers and knows about everything they ask me and all the time I am moving around and doing something; for instance, they say "I see by the papers that so-and-so, has happened"; all I do is "Yes, so-and so-etc" You see,they are doing the straight for me and it will make a gag go better than if I had to repeat it all myself. Not one of these musical comedy Rubes ,but a legitimate character like you really see. I will have all the gags necessary for it.

Now, I am practicing on a new dance   to do with a girl in a rope;a fast Texas-Tommy,where we do all those fast spins ;that would go good in a show, following some other dances.

Now,the blackface idea: I am made ~~of~~ up as Bert Williams[5] , the colored chauffeur; come on to a scene where it is one of those gasoline filling stations and I come on ;this mule of mine,- its not a donkey, its a big mule and its white and black and blue and every color;the funniest looking thing you ever saw; looks like Urban had painted it.[6] Now,he is made up like an automobile. I steer him with a wheel; the saddle is all made up like the seat of a car, different brakes, and levers, mud guards and a bumper. Now,some other comedian is running this filling station. We take the hose and put them into the mule's mouth and he starts pumping. Could get a lot of comedy out of "How much does the tank hold" and talk about the car. The end of this hose is sweetened and the mule chews on it. I unscrew a cap from the top of the mule's head,like the radiator cap on a car,and have smoke in there that comes out as if it was a hot radiator;then pour in water. Now, he backs and turns just like a car; as I am on him and leaving, I arrange an explosion or shot on the opposite side of the mule from the audience and it is supposed to be a blowout and I have no extra tubes. I and the other fellow are down looking at the mule's front foot;I tie a handkerchief around his leg in such a way that,when I get back on him and start off, he limps off on three legs; also showing as he exits a red tail light and a license tag fastened on his tail . Now, I come right back on and,regardless of that roof thing, I can sing a Bert Williams song; I kid about it and the leader says "Why don't you sing a song?" I say "I'll take a crack at it" and make that a ~~e to~~ catch line that runs through the show.

Now,I have the song all ready; a black faced comedian used it in vaude-ville and it is sure fire for he has a lot of good extra choruses; I would use a lot of local topics in each chorus and do his dance at the finish; I know I can do this as out home at the minstrel shows we used to sing coon songs. Put a sure fire gag in each chorus and it is sure to go.

Now,for my specialty in one, most of the talk would be on the show, kidding myself, but doing a lot of new tricks with the rope all the time. I have an idea of a dressing room scene on the stage where a lot of the male principals and I dress and we could talk on the show and how it was going and name people who really were out front and what really had happened that night,with all the acts kidding me about being the star and wouldn't I like to be back with The Follies and see an audience? Each act tells how good they have gone;there is a wonderful scope to a scene like this. It would be my idea to have it closing the show, instead of closing the show with a number. I come off just ahead of it from my specialty in one and right into the dressing room with all of them asking me how I did and we talk and discuss things and gags and how they have gone that night and who we saw out front. You see, you cover the Hitchcock idea only in a different way .[7]

Now,the people, one by one, dress and leave saying "good-night". Some are to meet the girls ; some say they are going out to hit you for more money; well I am the last one and I am not satisfied with the way I have done and feel disappointed. Someone impersonating you comes in and says- "Oh, cheer up, you didn't do so bad", or something to that effect. You go out and I am alone; watchman comes in and says "all out" and I leave with either some little pathetic touch,- "Well I guess that act was right; this thing is too fast for me; back to The Follies and just be one of the mob, or some comedy line after this little pathetic scene as I went out and the curtain comes down.

Now,what do you think of that for a novelty ending to a musical show? You see,they have never had a men's dressing room with performers talking about what really happened. There is your intimacy without getting fresh with the audience and they are being let in on something.

Now,get some novelty opening to the show with the stage hands making the set in full view of the audience,which would be a novel opening and same a scene and number. Now, there is any amount of comedy to be gotten out of this dressing room as all your principals are there and,besides, the pathetic touch,there would be any amount of things to discuss and get laughs.

All of these things I have explained mean a third of your show;you don't need a story;the other third is taken up with numbers and the other third with sure-fire vaudeville specialties. What I think would be one of the best acts in the world for a show would be the Avon Comedy Four;[8]they are the surest fire act in the show business;the best singing Quartette; can do a full stage scene; all lead numbers and you would get all the Jewish audiences in America to come see them as they are big favorites.

Now, I wont tell you what I want for all this as I want your wife to take the body back to New York alive; Iwant some real money next year, but if some man gives me the chance I will work my head off to show him I am worth it. I wouldn't do any one of these things next year unless it was in my own show and do them all at once. I figure it would be the surprise of doing them all that would help me.

Now,just to kind of sum up;the horse thing with good roping I know will go and develop into a good comedy number. The Rube,with sure ,up-to-date sure fire laughs should go; the mule idea I think is funny and,with the big Jew of the Avon Comedy Four[9] to do it with me,it would be good. The Bert Williams song I simply talk off;I have the dialect and,if the song is good and good extra choruses on up-to-date topics, it should go. A dance with a girl is sure, especially as we have never done it before theatre audiences, and this new one is faster and better than the old one. My specialty in one I have enough new rope tricks for it;besides up to then you have not done any talking in my own character, so you see this is the first time they really see you as you are. I don't think you want a great big show; get good people and we might put it over. Now,you don't have to have a story with this;that title covers it all,- "A MEss of Junk".

I may be all wrong on this, but I think a show framed up this way would be the easiest to get together and the cheapest; I can put on everything I explained to you here with four weeks' work; if you would let me leave this show about three weeks before it closed and send on an act in one from the Roof, like Savoy and Brennan,[10] of [or] Van & Skenk,[11] we could put it on out of town in at least six weeks and would not interfere with rehearsals of The Follies; then,if it was no good , take whatever scenes in it that did go and put them in the follies. Lets try it and get it off our chest. There is sure to be something in the show to be fit to go in The Follies.

If I left the show about four or five weeks before it closed, then we would have plenty of time to see what we had before The Follies rehearse. I would want to play the Roof while rehearsing as I have to work to keep myself up to date.

Now,you and Mr.Erlanger put this on and don't spend a lot of money on it and maybe you can make some money out of it.[12]

How about coming to Chicago for a Summer run if it proved any good ?Wire me on receipt of this what you think of it all.

Well,after writing these few lines, I'll stop. Tell Mrs.Ziegfeld I have two sure-fire gags about her for the new show.[13]

Regards to both,   Yours truly,

                                                                        [Will Rogers]

TL, rc. OkClaW, 1975.21.0208.

1. When it closed, the *Follies of 1917* ended its most profitable season to date. The revue then started its annual circuit, performing in Boston, Washington, D.C., Baltimore, Philadelphia, and Pittsburgh, before stopping in Chicago (*NYT*, 20 August, 10 September, 4 November, 2 December 1917; *CH*, 23 December 1917).

2. Although this document bears the date of 13 February 1918, Rogers may have first typed the outline in January, when news of a Ziegfeld-produced show for Rogers became public. Although the show apparently never moved beyond the concept stage, some of Rogers's ideas were not wasted. The setting in a rural post office compares closely to "The Country Store," a scene in the *Follies of 1925* that featured Rogers as a philosophizing Vermonter. Another element, the lariat tricks, found their way into *The Ropin' Fool*, one of Rogers's own silent film productions (Yagoda, *Will Rogers*, 155, 365; *NYT*, 20 January 1918; Ziegfeld and Ziegfeld, *Ziegfeld Touch*, 258; Wertheim, ed., *Will Rogers*, 153).

3. Edward Claudius (Ned) Wayburn (1874–1942), choreographer and stage director, helped mount several *Follies* productions and produced his own revue, *Town Topics*, in 1915, featuring Rogers (*EMT*, 1532–33).

4. William Surrey Hart (ca. 1862–1946) moved from a successful career on the stage to become one of the most widely recognized performers in early Western silent films, known for his commanding presence on the screen (*DAB*, Supp. 4:362–63).

5. For Bert Williams see *PWR*, 2:526–32.

6. Joseph Urban (Josef Karl Maria Georg Urban, 1872–1933), an Austrian-born architect and theatrical designer, achieved great fame for his spectacular, brilliantly colorful sets for the *Ziegfeld Follies*, beginning in 1915, and for operatic, straight theater, and musical productions (*DAB*, 19:132–33; Carter and Cole, *Joseph Urban*, 12, 45).

7. Raymond Hitchcock (ca. 1865–1929), popular comedian and actor, produced an annual revue, *Hitchy-Koo*, beginning in 1917, which among other entertainment elements featured a disjointed collection of his far-ranging monologues, rapid-fire singing, and physical antics (*DAB*, 9:78–79; *EMT*, 660).

8. The Avon Comedy Four was a vaudeville act, a comedy and singing quartet, that formed about 1900 with Joe Smith and Charlie Dale as its mainstays. Rogers had occasionally appeared on the same bill with them during his vaudeville career (Laurie, *Vaudeville*, 75–76; *PWR*, 3:225n.1, 3:383n.2).

9. In the Avon quartet's act, Joe Smith played the part of a Jew, or more commonly "Hebe," a role often found in vaudeville comedy routines at the time (Laurie, *Vaudeville*, 75).

10. Bert Savoy (Everett McKinzie, ca. 1888–1923), an outrageously flashy female impersonator, teamed with Jay Brennan (ca. 1883–1961), portraying a debonair straight man, in a vaudeville comedy act that first scored success at the Palace Theatre in New York in 1916. They made their *Follies* debut in the same year and subsequently appeared in the *Follies* in 1918 and in several editions of the *Midnight Frolic* (*EV*, 455–58; Ziegfeld and Ziegfeld, *Ziegfeld Touch*, 311).

11. For Van and Schenck see *PWR*, 3:335n.7.

12. For Abraham L. Erlanger see *PWR*, 2:367–68n.1.

13. Billie Burke (Mary William Ethelbert Appleton, 1885–1970), a star of musical comedies and revues, married Florenz Ziegfeld, Jr., in 1914. Thereafter, she appeared mostly in straight theater and motion pictures. She never performed in the *Follies*, but she did appear in other productions by her husband (*EMT*, 192; Ziegfeld and Ziegfeld, *Ziegfeld Touch*, 54–58, 90, 101, 104–5).

Newspaper Article by Will Rogers
ca. 17 February 1918
[Chicago, Ill.?]

CASTLE "A REGULAR GUY"

WILL ROGERS, OKLAHOMA COWBOY,
PAYS TRIBUTE TO DEAD AVIATOR.[1]

"HE WAS DOING HIS BIT JUST AS MUCH
AS IF HE HAD BEEN TRYING TO
DROP A BOMB ON THE
KAISER'S BEAN."

Will Rogers, Oklahoma cowboy comedian, whose rope throwing act and monologue is a never failing source of joy to vaudeville audiences in the East and West alike, was one of Vernon Castle's warm friends. He pays this tribute to the dead aviator in the Chicago Tribune:[2]

On the opening night of a new show at Ziegfeld's Midnight Frolic in New York I came out to do my little act, and at a front table sat Vernon Castle and his wife.[3] He had only returned from France that day.[4] I walked over and shook hands with him and told the audience:

"Here is one tango bird that made good."

They gave him an ovation.

I told them that I took a pride in Vernon, as Fred Stone and I had got him on a bucking horse down at Fred's place, and that was where he got his idea of aviating from. I says:

"Vernon, you have not been through anything in the war compared to what your wife has here in moving pictures."

And every time he was in the audience we had a good time kidding.

"HE WAS GAME."

Now I will tell you I knew he was game before he enlisted. He and Fred Stone had a polo team, and had been playing quite a while—at least, they knew the rules. Well, the first day I played I didn't know a polo ball from Bolo Pasha.[5] I could ride, but I couldn't hit the ball with a rake. I was in everybody's way, missing the ball farther each lick.

Finally I came a-tearing across at right angles at Castle, thinking I would scare this dancer off the ball. It was a foul, as I was crossing him. But say, that

Englishman didn't scare worth a darn, he kept a-coming at me, too. Well, we hit, and there were dancers, horses and rope throwers scattered all over Long Island. What did he say when he got up?

"That's all right. I did that, too, when I was learning."

We all had many a tilt with him and he never flinched.

That bucking horse—he knew he couldn't ride him, but he got on.

"A REGULAR GUY."

At a big benefit one night on the Manhattan Opera House stage Castle, Sloane, Tinney,[6] Carillo[7] and I put on a Wild West act called "The Horse Thief." Castle was the only one game enough to volunteer to play the thief. In the act, as he was running away on the horse, I was to rope him from another horse, have the rope tied to my saddle, drag him off at a dead run, and then drag him around the stage.

Well, I put it on real and he went through with it, and I'll tell the world he was game.

He was the most skillful and fearless driver of a motor car I ever saw.

Now I just want to say to you people who didn't know him, he was a regular guy, and I was mighty hurt to hear of his death, because he was doing his bit just as much as if he had been killed trying to drop a bomb on that kaiser's bean.

Few men gave up more to enlist and it should teach us all a lesson that no matter how frail or small or physically unfit, and no matter what kind of work he has been doing, if the old heart is in the right place he is there.

PD. Unidentified clipping, ca. 17 February 1918. Scrapbook 20, OkClaW.

1. Vernon Castle died in a flight training exercise at a military airfield near Fort Worth, Tex., on 15 February 1918 (*EV*, 90).

2. Rogers eulogized Vernon Castle in an article that appeared in the *Chicago Sunday Tribune* two days after Castle's death (see *PWR*, 3:423).

3. For Irene Castle see *PWR*, 3:419–23.

4. Vernon Castle arrived in Canada on Monday, 23 April 1917, after ten months of service on the British front in France, and journeyed the next day to New York. That night, he and his wife and dance partner, Irene, attended a performance of *The Century Girl* and then the season opening of the *Midnight Frolic*. The returned air hero received special recognition during both shows (*NYT*, 25 April 1917).

5. Paul Marie Bolo was convicted of treason on 14 February 1918 in his native France for obtaining funds from Germany that he had used to generate "defeatist" propaganda. He had acquired the title of "pasha" (or "pacha" in France) from the then ruler of Egypt, who allegedly had abetted his scheme. Bolo was executed on 17 April 1918 (*NYT*, 17 April 1918; "Who's Who: Paul Bolo").

6. Frank Tinney (1878–1940), a veteran blackface performer in Ziegfeld productions, was appearing in *The Century Girl* on the night of 24 April 1917 when he spotted the Castles in the audience and requested the orchestra to honor Vernon's return from

the war with a special tune (*EV*, 503–4; Ziegfeld and Ziegfeld, *Ziegfeld Touch*, 114; *NYT*, 25 April 1917).

7. Leo Carrillo (1880–1961), member of one of California's founding families, left the newspaper profession to enter show business as a dialect comedian in vaudeville in 1896. He started working in legitimate theater in 1915 (*EV*, 87–88; *UDSSEP*, 93).

Newspaper Article by Will Rogers
21 February 1918
Chicago, Ill.

SAYS WILL ROGERS

I HATE TO WRITE ABOUT
CROOKS FOR FEAR I LOSE
SOME FRIENDS. THERE'S
THIS ABOUT CHICAGO'S
CROOKS: THEY KILL WITH-
OUT FAVORITISM.

By Will Rogers
Cowboy comedian with "The Follies," who is writing some pieces for the Examiner.

Some guy up in the Press Club asked me to write and tell about the crooks. I don't know why he picked on me; I don't know much about crooks; I've only been in Chicago six weeks and I don't know all of them yet.

But I tell you, if they keep on arresting them at the rate the papers say they do it is time to call a halt, as it will interfere with the attendance at the theaters. They are good spenders—come easy, go easy.

Now, it's kind of hard to write about crooks, as you don't know whose toes you are stepping on, and I may lose a lot of good friends.

They call this "a crime wave,"[1] but it's not a wave, for a wave hits the shore sometime.

Of course, you will hear some fellow say "there are no more killings here than any other place." It's all right for him to say that, but he is probably one of the few men that have not been murdered.

FEWER VICTIMS NEXT YEAR.

Now, Mayor Thompson[2] says there were fewer murders here last year than the year before; why, sure there were, and there will be fewer next year than this, and keep on getting fewer each year until the last two men fight a duel.

One thing I must say for the crooks here—they have no favorites in whom they kill, policeman or civilian. Most crooks have to have something against you to kill you; not these.

If these fellows have a notch on their guns to account for each one, like the old-time westerners did, they would have to use Winchesters to have room to put them on.

The policemen are all right, but for the risk they run they don't pay them enough money.[3] The city tells them, "Why, we pay you a living wage," but the cops say, "Yes, but few of us live to collect it."

I haven't seen any of the robberies here, but if I have time before I leave I want to go out and see some.

A fellow invited me to see a murder next Tuesday. I told him I couldn't get away, I was so busy. So he said, "Well, let me know when you have some time off."

And automobile robbers—there are so many of them! I wanted to buy a car, but I am afraid to do it, as I know everybody will wonder where I got it.

Of course, they have this cleanup here every year and make them all get out; sometimes they make them stay away a week or ten days.

You see, what has made it bad here this Winter, there have been a lot of scab crooks here from other places that have robbed and killed for less than the scale. No doubt about it, they have cheapened the trade.

QUARREL OVER AMMUNITION.

There was little argument this Winter over "How much will you charge me to 'croak' so-and-so?" but several good murders have fallen through because the party who wanted a guy killed and the fellow who was to do the killing could not agree on who was to furnish the ammunition.

If it keeps on like this, by next Winter you will have to conscript people to get them to come here. If some playwright were to write a play of Chicago life and stage it real and as it is, all the actors would be dead at the end of the show and the audience would have to let down the curtain.

Still, advertising is a wonderful thing, and it's better for people to knock a town than it is to never hear it mentioned at all, as a lot of them are.

I understand how the crooks got in bad here this time: They robbed some aldermen. I always thought they had a kind of secret understanding that they never bothered each other.

But now, all kidding aside, I want to say that everything will be all right soon, as they are going to be more stern with the crooks; from now on, when they do anything, they are going to publish their names.

PD. Printed in *Chicago Examiner*, 21 February 1918.[4] Photocopy of clipping, Notebook 3, OkClaW.

1. An increase in murders, payroll robberies, and holdups prompted Chicago police to begin arming themselves with rifles in early February 1918 and to take other measures to counter an apparent wave of crime. Concerned business and political leaders in the city met with the governor of Illinois on 18 February to seek his assistance in addressing the problem. A chief concern was a large number of parolees, many from outside Chicago, who had been recently arrested for various crimes, ranging from murder to vagrancy (*NYT*, 11 February 1918; *CH*, 16, 19 February 1918).
2. William Hale Thompson (1867–1944) was mayor of Chicago from 1915 to 1923 and again from 1927 to 1931. Although he had campaigned in 1915 as a reform candidate, Thompson, popularly known as "Big Bill," declared after taking office that Chicago would be an open city for gambling. His encouragement of gamblers contributed to an increase in criminal activity, despite the efforts of the police who staged several raids on gaming establishments in 1917 and 1918 (*DAB*, Supp. 3:771–73; Browning and Gerassi, *American Way*, 322–23).
3. Two days earlier, Chicago aldermen had defeated a proposal for a 10 percent salary hike for desk and patrol sergeants. The police had asked for a 15 percent boost for the entire department (*CH*, 10, 20 February 1918).
4. This article was published in the *Chicago Tribune* on the same day, 21 February 1918. It appeared there under Rogers's byline but with the heading, "Will Rogers Pities Crooks" (see clipping, Scrapbook 20, OkClaW).

Notes for Performance or Publication
ca. 2 March 1918
[Chicago, Ill.]

Kaiser has [told?] the duke[1] that it is better ~~to be~~ ▲Have German[y]▲ surrounded by a lot of little countries than ~~all~~ ▲bou[n]ded by▲ Rep[ublican] ones   they are more handy to go through.[2]

Thats why Pres Wilson wants to carry the war on into extra innings to protect these bush League Nations.

We are Pinch Hitting for Russia[3] now and as soon as the Kaiser gets it through his square head that the Lord is umpiring instead of him why the Game will be over.

Russia team work in the early part of the Game was not bad

————

Russia had more men signed up than any other team in the L[eague].[4]

————

Haig ~~made~~ ▲hit▲ a ~~wonderful~~ ▲hard▲ wallop that looked like a ▲sure score▲ ~~home run~~[5]   tried to stretch it into a home Run instead of playing it safe and the whole play went for N. [naught?]

Italy our outfielder either played sensationally or Muffed em   there was no between.[6]

Roumania a raw recruit should never have even been permitted in in the Game as they went out on three strikes at a ~~time~~ ▲critical▲ part of the Game (or let em get a Run that they never should of had[)][7]

The crown Prince ▲had the NERVE, time after time,▲ tried to steal Second on France catching but was thrown out further each time[8]

Canada furnished a short stop but he ▲was▲ ~~early~~ spiked in the Game, but they came back with another one.[9]

A Guy named Turkey was [*illegible*] when the Game started to be the dirtiest player in Baseball But the other players on the Central Team had tricks that made [*sentence ends*]

A ▲Player named▲ Germany ~~Base~~ ran clear off off the field and slugged a fellow named Belgium who wasent even playing in the Game.

America originally had the Ticket Speculating Priv[ilege].

Japan was under contract to the Allies (But wants a share of the Profits) But wont play as he says he can do better by having the Peanut and Sandwich priv[ilege] at the Game.[10]

There was a dirty little Runt in the Game named Submarine. Who under the rules should never be[en] allowed in a Big League Game. He starts an a[r]gument with a Guy named America who is sitting with his ~~family~~ ▲wife and C.– [children]▲ in a box. He throws a bat ~~into~~ ▲at▲ this [box] not caring who he hit and ducked back in the Game.

Now the only way this A. [America] could get at him was get in the Game himself. Since then they are curing this [*illegible*] Sub bird as every time he comes up to bat some Allied Pitcher Beans him[11]

AM.[12] OkClaW, Will Rogers, Jr., Collection, Folder 2. On letterhead of Hotel Sherman, Randolph Street at Clark, Chicago, Ill. A preprinted dateline appears below the letterhead, with the following printed in the position of the year: "191__". The pagination of the text begins with "4" and continues sequentially through "8." The handwritten heading "Base Ball" appears on the letterhead of each page, except the second. A large, hand-inserted "X" overwrites the first paragraph, possibly indicating the deletion of the paragraph. The short horizontal lines that appear between some paragraphs replicate similar hand-inserted marks that appear in the original document, likely indicating breaks between gags.

1. Rogers may have referred to Albrecht (1865–1939), the duke of Württemberg and at one time the heir apparent to Kaiser Wilhelm II. The duke successfully commanded German forces in Luxembourg and Belgium and was the first officer in the war to employ poison gas. In February 1917 he was transferred to a command in southern Europe and thereafter saw little action (*BDWWI*, 65–66).

2. After war had been declared, Germany attacked France by routing German forces through the small, neighboring countries of Belgium and Luxembourg (Gilbert, *First World War*, 165–66, 282–83).

3. In December 1917, soon after the overthrow of the provisional government, the new Bolshevik government in Russia signed an armistice with Germany, effectively breaking the Russian alliance with the Allies (Gilbert, *First World War*, 374, 386).

4. Over the course of the war, Russia mobilized about 12 million men, of whom 1.7 million died, the largest loss of lives among the Allied nations (Gilbert, *First World War*, 37, 541).

5. Douglas Haig (1861–1928) became commander in chief of British troops in Europe in December 1915. Under his command, a combined British and French force launched a major assault in July 1916 to break through German lines. The Battle of the Somme resulted in heavy losses and little gain in territory; however, it did relieve pressure on French forces at Verdun, allowing them to recover most of the ground they had lost there (*DNB*, Supp. 4:373–80; Gilbert, *First World War*, 258, 299).

6. On the heavily contested Italian front, Austrian troops launched an offensive on 23 December 1917 with the goal of reaching Venice by Christmas. Despite an initial loss of territory and significant casualties, the Italians regrouped and counterattacked, halting the Austrian advance with the aid of the first heavy snow of the season (Gilbert, *First World War*, 390).

7. By February 1918 the German army had overrun Romania, prompting government officials to begin discussing peace terms with the Central Powers (*NYT*, 5 February 1918).

8. Friedrich Wilhelm (Frederick William, 1882–1951), the crown prince of Germany, commanded German forces in several engagements between August 1914 and spring 1918. His Fifth Army assault against the French at Verdun in February 1916 resulted in the loss of 300,000 crack German troops and made Verdun into a symbol of French determination (*BDWWI*, 383–84; Gilbert, *First World War*, 233, 614).

9. Although they scored some success at Vimy Ridge in France in April 1917, Canadian forces lost more than 15,000 troops in a six-day battle. Canadians also played a key role in the final days at Passchendaele in Belgium. The battle there ended on 10 November 1917 with the Canadians gaining the final five hundred yards of a total Allied advance of four and one-half miles (Gilbert, *First World War*, 321–22, 377).

10. Although Japan declared war on Germany in late August 1914, it did not commit troops to the European theater; rather it sought to expand its influence in China and elsewhere in East Asia. Its military forces joined the British and Australians in moving against German possessions in the Far East (Gilbert, *First World War*, 46, 84, 123; *USFWW*, 601).

11. On 26 January 1918 Allied naval forces sank three German submarines, two of them in the English Channel. All told, 180 German submarines were sunk in the war (Gilbert, *First World War*, 41, 396).

12. Dating of the document was determined by historical references in the text and by Rogers's chronology.

Newspaper Article by Will Rogers
ca. 3 March 1918
Chicago, Ill.

Says Will Rogers:

Take Russia: You can always fear the worst about Russia and never be disappointed. They can't fight without a national anthem. Let's send 'em "Poor Butterfly."[1]

By Will Rogers

Now they've asked me to write about Russia. That's fine! There's some sense to that. I can write about Russia for I know that my readers don't know any more about Russia than I do; even as great a man as President Wilson passed up mention of it in his last speech.

There is always this to look forward to with Russia. Pick up the morning paper and look for Russian news and have a fear of reading the worst; you won't be disappointed.

I will give the Russians credit for one thing: They didn't sign a peace with Germany. They said: "What's the use signing something? We just quit."[2]

You see, Germany was willing to treat for peace as long as Russia did all the treating.

Now they have given German freedom to some province called Ukrainia;[3] sounds like ukulele, and I doubt if it will flourish even as long as that short-lived instrument.[4]

The ukulele had this advantage: Not even a trained musician could tell if you were playing on it or just monkeying with it, but the Ukrainian liberty can't fool anybody; those poor independents have "Made in Germany" stamped all over it.

You see, the Kaiser has the dope on it this way: It is better to be surrounded by a lot of small nations than by a couple of regular ones; they come in handier to go through.

Germany wants to make peace with Roumania. She says, "We will take a chunk off you and give it to Bulgaria; as we promised them something. After looking it all over they seem to like your country best. But for what we give Bulgaria of yours, we will take a small hunk out of Russia and you all can have that."[5]

You see, if Russia's land holds out long enough, German[y] should be able to make a very generous peace with her eastern foes. One thing I will say for the Germans they are always perfectly willing to give somebody else's land to somebody else.

Of course, we will admit that they were handicapped by not having a national anthem to fight by; it's hard to fight without a good anthem.

If we had only known it, we could have loaned them "Poor Butterfly," but only on one condition, that is, that they keep it.

I guess that old nut monk over there had about the only right dope on Russia.[6] He could throw sticks in the water and make any of them go out and get them. Some bird over there shot at this guy, Lenine, the other day, and missed him.[7]

If they got any shooting to do, why don't they get some of their American wives to do it. There hasn't been a husba[nd] missed in this country in two [*portion of page missing; handwritten:*] years.

PD.[8] Printed in *Chicago Examiner*, ca. 3 March 1918. Photocopy of clipping in Will Rogers, Jr., Collection, Miscellaneous Original Writings, Folder 8, OkClaW.

1. The hit song "Poor Butterfly" was introduced in *The Big Show*, a revue that opened at the Hippodrome in New York on 31 August 1916 and ran for 425 performances (Bloom, *American Song*, 1:100; *CEPMJ*, 79).

2. The Bolshevik government in Russia signed an armistice with the Central Powers on 15 December 1917, less than a month after the new government had come to power (Gilbert, *First World War*, 386).

3. Independence for the Ukraine came officially on 3 March 1918 with the signing of the Treaty of Brest-Litovsk. By the terms of the agreement with Germany, whose troops at the time were advancing rapidly toward Russia despite an armistice between the two countries, the Bolsheviks surrendered all claims to the Ukraine and other western provinces (Gilbert, *First World War*, 401).

4. The small, guitarlike ukulele was introduced in Hawaii in the late nineteenth century and had begun to gain popularity in the mainland United States by the mid-1910s. By 1916 ukulele music had reportedly reached fad status, particularly on college campuses (*NGDMI*, 3:696–97).

5. Romania started negotiating peace terms with Germany in February that included surrendering a portion of its southeastern territory to neighboring Bulgaria, a member of the Central Powers, in return for Bessarabia, once a part of western Russia. The agreement was signed on 5 March 1918 on the condition that the Romanians convince the Bolsheviks to agree to the deal (*NYT*, 18 February 1918; Gilbert, *First World War*, 402).

6. Although not a cleric, Grigory Efimovich Rasputin (Grigory Novykh, ca. 1863–1916) used mysticism and his seemingly miraculous powers to exert great influence in the family of the tsar and in the government of Russia before and during the early years of the war (*BDWWI*, 293–94; Fuhrmann, *Rasputin*, 3).

7. Vladimir Ilich Lenin (Vladimir Ilich Ulyanov, 1870–1924), founder of Bolshevism, led the revolution in Russia that overthrew the provisional government and established the world's first socialist state in November 1917. More than once a target of assassins, Lenin survived unscathed two separate attempts by gunmen in January 1918 to kill him (*BDWWI*, 222–23; Service, *Lenin*, xvii, 1, 13, 315, 335–36, 478–79; *NYT*, 17 January, 2 February 1918). The name "Lenin," a pseudonym, appeared often in newspapers in the United States at the time as "Lenine" (see, for example, *NYT*, 26 February 1918).

8. The clipping of the article was undated. The dating of the document corresponds to the last day that the *Follies* troupe performed in Chicago.

Published Remarks from *Ziegfeld Follies*
ca. 16 April 1918
[Great Britain?]

SOME OF WILL ROGER'S FUND OF FUN AT THE FOLLIES

The Follies give men an opportunity to come here with their new wives to see what their old wives are doing. If they come early they can see just where their alimony is going to!

Anybody who does anything nowadays writes about it, like my four years here or there. When I round out this season I'm going to write a book on "My Four Years in the Follies and Prominent Men I Have Met at the Stage Door!"

I hear that Charley Chaplin is going to war.[1] Now I can see the Kaiser hit with a custard pie square in the face! There sure is good news from the front nowadays. There's one thing about the Italians. They're either coming or going! There's no standing still with them! Austria and Germany are priding themselves on the many substitutes they have found. But somehow they can't find a substitute for the most important thing, food.[2] It was Austria's war in the first place, but Germany took it away from her. Now let Germany suffer!

I see where Ham Lewis got up in the Senate the other day and made a long speech on Russia.[3] Whenever anybody wants to make an impression in the Senate and wants to make sure that the rest of the members don't know whether he's right or wrong he speaks on Russia!

If the United States had sent Roosevelt to Russia instead of Root,[4] you can bet your bottom dollar the Russians would be fighting somebody now! According to a report somebody shot at Lenine the other day, but missed him. We ought to send over a few American wives. There hasn't been a husband missed in this country in the last three years! But don't be sore at Russia. She'll soon be in the fight. They're rehearsing among themselves now!

England is debating about giving Ireland home rule.[5] Somebody should tip England off to give Ireland home rule, but reserve the moving picture rights! There's one thing about an Irish Parliament. There's never going to be a dull moment there!

A U-boat sunk a Norwegian vessel last week. I guess Norway, Sweden and Denmark intend to remain neutral down to the last ship![6] But you've got to hand it to Uruguay. That country's got the right idea. It declared war on Germany without much fuss.[7] Germany hasn't sunk any of her ships, you bet. But she's building one now!

Our shipping board is going to do some active work now and turn out one ship after the other.[8] Schwab[9] is already wearing his uniform! I see where they appointed Ford to the Shipping Board, too.[10] I hope if he builds any ships that he'll change the front![11] They've got an awful time in Washington over this here prohibition fight. I read that Wilson doesn't want to do away with the two per cent alcoholic drinks.[12] What good is this drink anyway? Who wants to drink fifty bottles to get 100 per cent drunk?

The Republicans are jealous over the way the Democrats are running the war. I bet when peace is declared and the Republicans get in power they'll start another war to show how much better they can run one! Still there's one thing we can say about Wilson; he's not partial in handing out jobs. Just look at all the one dollar a year men.[13] They're all Republicans! Look at Colonel House.[14] Some people fight their way into fame, others walk into fame, but for the first time in history a man has listened his way into fame!

The Government wants 2,000,000 more men, but they're not going to be gotten from the draft. They want more officers! After they're in, they're going to reduce 'em! Down in Washington the other day I met an honest to goodness private! Poor fellow, he saluted so much he was all in!

You can't kick about the women in this war. They're all doing their bit. Some of them can't wait until they get into a crowd to knit! You know, women are wonderful things. To me they're like an elephant. I like to look at 'em, but hate to own one! The girls in this show are patriotic all right. One of the girls came up to me yesterday and said: "Will, I've already sent five sweethearts to France and am still out recruiting!"

PD.[15] Unidentified clipping, ca. 16 April 1918. Scrapbook 20, OkClaW. Printed at the bottom of the article: "Copyright 1918 by the Star Company Great Britain".[16]

1. Charles Chaplin, who allegedly had been refused enlistment in the U.S. army in June 1917 for being underweight, wrote an English reporter in February 1918 that he was ready to serve in his home country's forces if England needed him to fight more than its soldiers needed his humor on screen. Although he never served in either the British or U.S. military, Chaplin helped to counter cries of "slacker" by heavily promoting war bonds in the United States in the spring of 1918 (Maland, *Chaplin*, 36–38, 380).

2. Reduced bread rations and scarcity of other foodstuffs led to reported rioting in Vienna and other parts of the former Austro-Hungarian empire in early 1918. At the same time, similar stories of low food supplies in Germany and disease and death attributed to hunger gained wide circulation in the press (*NYT*, 9, 13, 18, 19, 24, 29 January 1918).

3. James Hamilton Lewis (1863–1939) served as Democratic U.S. senator from Illinois from 1913 to 1919 and from 1931 to his death. Addressing the Senate on 21 February 1918, Lewis, the majority whip, warned against German-provoked threats by Russia to regain Alaska and seize other American territory on the Pacific rim (*DAB*, Supp. 2:381–82; *NYT*, 22 February 1918).

4. Elihu Root led an official U.S. mission to Russia in June 1917 to show American support for the new provisional, post-tsarist government, but the mission received scant attention in Russia and accomplished little. President Wilson, who had appointed Root, gave the commission's subsequent reports minor notice and never again consulted him on Russian affairs (*DAB*, Supp. 2:581; Jessup, *Elihu Root*, 364, 367–68).

5. Opposition by Ulster unionists in Ireland had forced the British government to postpone until after the war implementation of the Home Rule Act of 1914. In the meantime, the nationalist Sinn Fein movement, which had grown so strong that it won a majority of Irish seats in the British Parliament in 1918, demanded an Irish republic independent of the British crown (*CHE*, 307, 308).

6. A Norwegian merchant vessel was sunk by a German U-boat, or submarine, in early March 1918. Norway's significant trade with Great Britain during the war made the ships of the officially neutral Scandinavian country a target of German warfare. As a result, the Norwegians lost more ship tonnage during the war than any other country except Britain (*NYT*, 7 March 1918; Larsen, *History*, 509–10).

7. Uruguay severed relations with Germany in October 1917 and immediately seized several German vessels that had sought refuge in Uruguayan waters early in the war. Uruguay leased the ships to the United States in the spring of 1918 (Fitzgibbon, *Uruguay*, 253).

8. The U.S. Shipping Board was a five-member body created in September 1916 to develop the naval preparedness of the United States. Through its agency, the Emergency Fleet Corporation, the board worked to enlarge both the naval and commercial fleets of the United States (*EAH*, 276).

9. Charles Michael Schwab (1862–1939), American industrialist whose Bethlehem Steel Company had been a major arsenal for the Allied powers before U.S. entry into the war, was appointed director general of the Emergency Fleet Corporation on 16 April 1918. Schwab focused on motivating greater production and left day-to-day administration in the hands of a general manager (*DAB*, Supp. 2:601–3; Smith and Betters, *United States*, 23; *USFWW*, 521).

10. Henry Ford joined the U.S. Shipping Board on 7 November 1917 (Nevins and Hill, *Ford*, 2:69).

11. Although the Ford Motor Company developed small escort vessels and began producing them in Michigan in the spring of 1918, only two of the so-called Eagle

Boats arrived on the East Coast before the end of the war (Nevins and Hill, *Ford*, 2:72–74; *USFWW*, 209).

12. In August 1917 Congress effectively shut down the distilling industry in the United States by forbidding during the course of the war the use of foodstuffs in the production of distilled liquor. The new law exempted wine and beer but gave the president the power to reduce their alcoholic content. In December 1917 President Wilson used that opening to lower the alcohol in beer to 2.75 percent (Pegram, *Battling*, 146–47).

13. Dollar-a-year men were individuals from the private sector who provided services to U.S. government agencies during the war. Enlisted to help in the mobilization effort, these businessmen received a full-time compensation of one dollar a year. Despite regulations to the contrary, however, they often earned salaries from other sources (Koistinen, *Mobilizing*, 214–15).

14. Edward Mandell House (1858–1938) served Woodrow Wilson as his chief and most trusted advisor during his presidency. House acquired the honorary title of "Colonel" while active in Democratic politics in his native Texas in the 1890s (*DAB*, Supp. 2:319–21).

15. Dating was determined by historical references within the document.

16. The Star Company may have been related to the *Star*, a prominent evening newspaper in London founded in 1888 (*EBP*, 530).

To William Fox
21 May 1918
[New York, N.Y.]

May 21st, 1918.

Mr. William Fox,[1]
Chairman, Allied Theatrical and Motion Picture Team,
American Red Cross,
1465 Broadway, City.

Dear Mr. Fox:-

I have tried hard during the last week to figure out what I personally consider my duty in the amount that I should contribute to the Red Cross Fund.[2]

While not a wealthy man, I earn a very good salary. I calculate my income for the next year at $52,000. I am pleased and grateful, therefore, for the opportunity to contribute ten (10%) percent. of my next year's income to the Red Cross and put me down on the books for $5,200.

I wish I had greater wealth so that I could give a larger amount.

Very truly yours,

[Will Rogers]

P.S. I pray to God this terrible war will be over in less than a year, but if not I hereby pledge myself to continue my subscription of $100. a week for the duration of the war.

TL, rc. OkClaW, 1975.15.0002. On letterhead of American Red Cross War Fund Committee of New York, William C. Breed, Chairman, Allied Theatrical and Motion Picture Team, William Fox, Captain, Headquarters, 1465 Broadway, Corner 42nd St.

1. William Fox (1879–1952), owner of a large chain of movie theaters, organized the Fox Film Corporation in 1915. His work as chairman of the theatrical division of the American Red Cross campaign during the war generated important publicity for his motion picture enterprises (*DAB*, Supp. 5:229–30).
2. The American Red Cross drive in New York opened on 18 May 1918. The campaign to raise $100 million nationwide, one-fourth in New York, was the organization's second effort, both highly successful, to fund its wartime relief and emergency assistance (*NYT*, 19 May 1918; Dulles, *American Red Cross*, 130).

From Theodore Roosevelt
4 August 1918
Dark Harbor, Me.

Rogers may have met Theodore Roosevelt in July 1900 in Oklahoma City at a reunion of the Rough Riders,[1] the volunteer unit that Roosevelt had organized in the Spanish-American War and that Rogers had attempted to join. Regardless, the former president had an impact on Rogers in his entertainment career: the Oklahoman named his performing horse Teddy and used Roosevelt often as the topic of his political jokes. It is not surprising, therefore, that Rogers preserved this brief message, the first known correspondence he received from a president. Equally noteworthy is that it was written slightly more than two weeks after Roosevelt had received news of the death of his youngest son in the war in France.[2]

Aug 4th 1918

To Will Rogers NY

Dear Mr. Rogers,

My old friend Eddy Riggs[3] has told me of your more than kind and friendly allusion to my boys[4] and incidentally to me. I wish to thank you, very warmly. With all good wishes,

Faithfully yours

Theodore Roosevelt

ANS, rc. OkClaW, 1975.21.0150.[5]

1. For Rogers and Roosevelt in Oklahoma City, see Yagoda, *Will Rogers*, 43.
2. Roosevelt received news on 17 July 1918 that his youngest son, Quentin, a pilot, had been killed in an aerial dual over the Marne battlefield in France (Renehan, *Lion's Pride*, 193–97).

3. Edward Gridley (Eddy) Riggs (1856–1924), a long-time political reporter at the *New York Sun*, retired from the newspaper in 1913 to provide public relations services for the president of a railroad. Through the years, he befriended many political leaders of the day, including Roosevelt (*NYT*, 18 November 1924).

4. Roosevelt and his second wife, Edith Kermit Carow Roosevelt, had five children: Theodore, Jr., Kermit, Archibald Bullock, Ethel Carow, and Quentin. All four sons served in the war, but only Kermit escaped death or injury (Renehan, *Lion's Pride*, 4, 11).

5. Roosevelt's note to Rogers was sent from Dark Harbor, Me., where the Roosevelt family had sought refuge after the death of Quentin (Renehan, *Lion's Pride*, 198). It was enclosed in a letter from Riggs to Rogers, dated 6 August 1918. In the latter, Riggs explained that he had attended a *Follies* performance "a couple of weeks" earlier and had enjoyed Rogers's monologue, especially the references to the former president. "You said, in your whimsical way," Riggs wrote, "people had and would criticize Theodore Roosevelt and then, turning full face to the audience you said with force something like this — BUT NO MAN ALIVE OR DEAD EVER DARED SAY HE WASN'T AN AMERICAN! — and when the audience cheered I was happy." Riggs felt so moved that he wrote Roosevelt, who in turn sent a message for Rogers, which he asked Riggs to forward (Edward G. Riggs to Will Rogers, OkClaW, 1975.21.0146). For Rogers's depth of appreciation for Roosevelt's personal message, see Article in *New York Times*, 27 October 1922, below.

2. FROM BROADWAY TO HOLLYWOOD
September 1918–June 1919

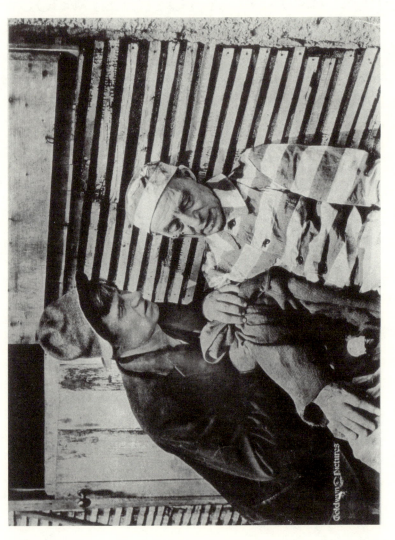

Lobby card for Rogers's first motion picture, *Laughing Bill Hyde.* A Goldwyn Pictures release, the film premiered at the Rivoli Theatre in New York City on 22 September 1918. Rogers and Dan Mason played fellow prisoners in the silent comedy. (*Gordon Kuntz Private Collection*)

WILL ROGERS MADE HIS MOTION PICTURE DEBUT IN LATE SEPTEMBER 1918. AS with his gags, his timing could not have been better. His entry into the relatively new world of filmdom came at a time when the industry was consumed with an eagerness to discover stars, to introduce new personalities. For years the industry had relied on proven veterans from the era of the nickelodeon, but by mid-decade film producers had begun to compete fiercely to sign top talent from the theatrical world and other entertainment sectors. Even many untested performers, backed with aggressive prerelease publicity campaigns, succeeded in breaking through to stardom.[1]

Rogers benefited from this demand for new talent. The producer who recruited him, Samuel Goldfish,[2] not long to the business himself, had sought out Rogers in the summer of 1918 at the suggestion of a mutual acquaintance, Edith Crater Beach, the sister of Allene Crater, who was the wife of Rogers's dear friend, Fred Stone.[3] Goldfish had recently added Edith's husband, author Rex Beach, to his largely female stable of talent at Goldwyn Pictures, a two-year-old partnership of Goldfish and playwright Edgar Selwyn that took its name from an amalgamation of theirs. Edith thought Rogers would fit perfectly the lead character in *Laughing Bill Hyde,* a forthcoming Goldwyn adventure film based on a Rex Beach story.[4] After Goldfish apparently caught Rogers's act at the *Midnight Frolic,* the film producer was convinced that the Oklahoman fit the role of Bill Hyde. In August the Ziegfeld star began his film work at the Goldwyn studios at Fort Lee, New Jersey, and at the same moment added a new line to an ever more diverse résumé.

In the months that followed the film's general release on 30 September 1918, Rogers began to reap the benefits of budding screen stardom. Some of the initial attention came from the press. His performance in *Laughing Bill Hyde* drew favorable comment from several reviewers, and *Variety,* a venerable voice in the entertainment industry, gave space to welcoming the newest talent on film.[5] Box office returns even proved strong enough that Goldfish on 30 November—within days of petitioning to take the name Goldwyn as his own—offered a year's contract to Rogers with an option for renewal.[6]

Although Rogers signed, his decision to put name to paper likely involved some serious thought. Exciting as it might appear, the business of performing in motion pictures brought with it much that was strange, unknown, unattractive to a man who had settled well into the routine of a set schedule of shows, some speaking engagements, and an occasional writing assignment. His life on Broadway left time for what was especially important to him: his family, horses, roping, and friends. His account of his first day on a motion picture set reveals an uncertain fascination, a sure hesitancy. Not surprisingly, he found much that seemed silly and contrived. His view was that of an outsider looking in, the interested but quizzical observer.[7]

Rogers's decision to commit to the life of a film actor, at least for a year, came at a time when he probably realized that he needed a break from Broadway. He had introduced his act in Ziegfeld's *Midnight Frolic* in late summer of 1915 and then had joined the *Follies* the next year. He had spent countless nights on stage at the New Amsterdam Theatre and had toured with the road production. He constantly had to come up with fresh material for his monologues, and each *Follies* season required at least one new skit. What probably had a greater effect on his decision-making, however, was a rising note of criticism. Overspread, suggested one reviewer about his Ziegfeld work; another offered faint praise for Rogers himself and only criticism for the role he played. One of his skits in the new *Follies* season barely survived opening night before being mercifully dropped.[8]

By signing the Goldwyn contract, Rogers made a commitment that transcended work. With the studio already preparing by November to relocate to the West Coast, to the pulsating new scene of motion picture production in Hollywood, Rogers knew that his decision would have a great impact on his family, but he also probably anticipated that relocation to California would prove beneficial and familiar. Southern California certainly was not Oklahoma, but it was less strange and "foreign" than New York and Long Island.

Between the time he first set foot in the Goldwyn studio in the summer of 1918 and the moment he boarded the train for Hollywood the following June, Rogers kept busy. The *Follies* closed at the New Amsterdam on 14 September, but he continued to perform nightly in the *Frolic*. He then joined the *Follies* troupe as it embarked in the fall on its annual road tour. Sunday nights often found him making special appearances at charitable events. The war had finally ended with the armistice on 11 November, but relief drives and soldiers' benefits continued.[9] In addition his budding career in films introduced him to a new opportunity as a writer: he began providing on-screen gags to movie exhibitors and producers. A chance to recycle on film, joke by joke, his stage monologue delivered to him an expanded audience.[10] He used much the same formula to produce during these months his first book, *Rogers-isms: The Cowboy Philosopher on the Peace Conference,* a collection of his gags about the lengthy conference in Paris that followed the armistice.[11] Soon after reaching California, he would produce a second volume, one filled with his humorous comments about Prohibition, which by then had become nationally instituted, not necessarily universally accepted.

The nine months following Rogers's introduction to film "stardom" proved transitional. He used the time to complete his obligations to Broadway and Ziegfeld, and to prepare for the full plunge into the world of Hollywood. Characteristically, he remained busy and involved. Typically, he discovered new outlets for his talents, new means to earn a living. With his departure for California in early June 1919, Will Rogers made an important shift in career focus, one that would add a lasting dimension to his life and that of his family.

1. Koszarski, *Evening's Entertainment*, 259, 261.

2. Samuel Goldfish (Schmuel Gelbfisz, 1879–1974), a former traveling salesman, entered the film business in 1913. He formed Goldwyn Pictures Corporation in November 1916 as a joint venture with other investors, including stage producer and playwright Edgar Selwyn (see *PWR*, 3:272–73n.5) as a principal partner (*DAB*, Supp. 9:322–25; *UDFT*, 240).

3. Edith Greta Crater Beach (d. 1947) was an actress and the wife of Rex Ellingwood Beach (1877–1949), a best-selling writer of adventure stories. As sister of Allene Crater (1876–1957), also a veteran of the stage and the wife of Rogers's closest friend, Edith Beach was well acquainted with Rogers and had seen him perform in the *Follies* (*DAB*, Supp. 4:59–60; *WA*, 6:252–53; Fields, *Fred Stone*, 106, 282).

4. Rex Beach's contract with Goldwyn Pictures gave the studio film rights to his vast and popular treasury of western adventure tales. Among the first adaptations of his work was *Laughing Bill Hyde,* a novel that had been published in 1917 and set mostly in a gold-mining camp in Alaska. With Rogers in the title role, the film was released nationally on 30 September 1918 after less than two months in production. It scored a modest success at the box office (*DAB*, Supp. 4:59–60; *TCA*, 92; *FWR*; Berg, *Goldwyn*, 85).

5. Berg, *Goldwyn*, 84–85.

6. See Contract with Goldwyn Pictures Corporation, 30 November 1918, below.

7. See Unpublished Manuscript by Will Rogers, ca. 30 September 1918, below.

8. Yagoda, *Will Rogers*, 162.

9. Chronology, 1917–19, OkClaW; Ziegfeld and Ziegfeld, *Ziegfeld Touch*, 245. See Notes for Appearance at Benefit Event, 25 May 1919, below.

10. See Letter from Pell Mitchell, 30 December 1918, and Notes for Motion Picture Intertitles, ca. February 1919, below.

11. See Letter from William H. Briggs, 1 May 1919, below.

Unpublished Manuscript by Will Rogers
ca. 30 September 1918
[New York, N.Y.?]

In this unique account of his first day of filming, which may have been used or intended as a studio press release, Rogers provides evidence of the trepidation he felt about the new venture, while positioning himself as the outsider looking in, a trademark of his career in films, both silents and talkies.

I have been asked to tell somet[h]ing of these bucking pictires and ~~TAH~~ as I have been in only one I have naturally like most peoplpe starting in something new been in just long enough to know all about it, But to ~~try and~~ be original I am not going to try to rewrite the business   let them go on making their millions out of [it] ~~and have to give it to the Income Tax man,~~if they want to I wont tell them how to fix it ,

  I horned into this Eldarado a little different from most of them   I had been going along peacefully working for a living on the stage and really felt a little hurt that I hadnever been offered a job in them

  One day Mrs Rex Beach who you ~~really~~ hear very little of but whois really the Ram Rod of the Beach outfit Mrs Beach after a late supper co[n]sisting of a Rarebit had a very bad night and thought of some terrible things, She arose early and commanded ~~to~~ James to Taxi out the favorite Limouzine and give it the gun for where I was bedded down for the mosquieto season on Long Island

  She drifted in on me early one morning ~~about the time I was~~ when I had just started in licking on my third Kid and I was a little vexed at being thrown behind in my daily routine

  Well she climbed out of this royalty on the Spoilers[1] and chirped above the wail of young rope throwers , Will you are going into the Flickering photos (now I live at the same town and its not a coincidence on the island where the Asylum is located so I winked at her chouffer and said you brought this Woman to the wrong house

  Now I tried to tell the Lady that I never bothered anybody and never annoyed over one Audience at a time and that these were war times and a man could be arrested for treason as treason meant any thing that causes pain to our peoplethereby giving aid to the enemy   but she still insisted that the people of Oolagah Okla, and Higgins Texas would grow up in ignorance if I did not enlighten them with my Art on the old muslin , said education for which they could obtain for a jitney and war tax,

I told her that I vouldent [couldn't] afford to earn any more   that I was just on the verge of the Income tax now , all that saved me was that the Gov[ernment] allowed two hundred for each child and my children and my income just come out even and that I would have to speak to my wife ~~before~~ and see if we could afford to increase our income,

I told her that i had heard that some of these movable Actors sometimes appeared personallyat the Theatre where their pictures were showing , she said yes   some of them do but most of them dont or wont, she says you wont have to and i would advise you not tolet them know ever where you live,

Of course she had one corking good argument that Caruso and myself were the last two singers to go in[2] and look what it would mean to Caruso when someone after looking at his picture asked him why he went in he could say well Will went in, us artists have to stick togeather   I showed her that Caruso had used up his only means of publicitygetting married[3] and going into the movies and that the firs t thing you knowche [know he] would be back singing again

I w[a]nted time to think it over but she kept on insisting she know at once asshe said if it got nosed around and Fairbanks and Chaplin and Ha[r]t heard about it they might get to me with a bigger offer to stay out, She told me will its the only business in the world where you can sit out front and applaud yourself so you cant absolutely flop ✗

Its the only way you can play a town and not have to worry about the hotels,

In fact I dont think you realize what a tremendous business it is   it stands fourth   Fords are first[,] Uneeda biscuits[4] are second and Gillettes ▲[*handwritten*:]R. [razor] BLADES▲ are third , she says you are thinking of ~~an~~ essential Industry[5] ▲[*handwritten*:]s.▲ You forget that Kings have appeared on the screen   I told her ify my ~~earl~~LIFelooked asshort as theirs I dont blame them from appearing   Then she put it up to me in such a sympathetic way that I could not refuse   It was the first thing he had written he had had excepted [accepted] and it meant everything for them to get an established legitamate Actor of my sterling worth to go into it and that if I did not it would just about mean the ruin of them and they would have [to] go back down to Greenwich Village and live with all those long haired nut writers,

Well I stayed up all one night so I would be over at Fort Lee N.J. to start in at Eight thirty sure   I arrived at eight and woke up the night watchman , About nine a few extras commenced straggling in, My Director[6] come and said I must make up ,Now I had been on the stage a few years   I had never yet had any of that junk on my face   he said I would photograph black if I dident make up   I asked him to make it a blackface part then I could play it straight,

WEll they had tob [to] put a ttwich on my upper lip to get me to smear paint all over my contour, even that could not disguise this old homely pan of mine , They said the day of the pretty actor is gone   you are so ugly you are a novelty

We then go up into what they call the studio   Its a big glassed in place like those up in Bronx Park where they stable those big South American Palm Trees , It reminded me of Amiralla Texas in the old days with about six heards [herds] waiting to ship ate once

It was a bad day outside and it had hazed all these companies under cover, You couldent move aroundwith out stepping on a five or six thousand dollar a week star, And moving picture cameras were thicker around there than Army commission hunters in Washington,

I got lost from my Director and started to take a near cut across when some guy balled me out   [He] sounded like a Roosevelt speech

I was only between Mabel Norman and three Cameras and them all a cranking on her most particular scene in a picture called a perfect 36[7] , so I had really gone in movies quicker than I had figured on, Imagine me [as a] principal ае in a perfect 36.

When they all got through cussing me afellow said what company are you working for   I told him Goldwin   He said its all Goldwin   I mean who is your Director   Miss Norman was looking at me and I couldent think of that guys name to save my life,

This bird says he must be in Madge Cannedys[8] scene ▲company▲   they are taking a Bowery Lodging House scene, I got pretty sore at that and walked   Now you wouldent think afellow could pull the same bonehead wtwice but leave it to an old country boy to horn in wrong   so I am feeling my way around among more scenery and sets trying to locate my man When a big burly [guy] nabbed me by the coat tail and yanked me back and said You poor boob   I saved your life   thats Miss Geraldine Farrah[9] taking close ups for the hell cat,[10] I had heard what she did to Caruso one time[11] and I thanked him   I watched her a while in hopes she would sing , but I tell you what she did have   she had an orchestra playing approp[r]iate music in all of her scenes , This man said he would show me where i belong   so we passed through an irish farmhouse of Tom Moores[12] , Stopped to see May Marshes[13] Propagander picture choking the Kaiser

We passed through Metropolitan Opera House and Cheyenne Joes saloon on the way to my gang , By the time I got there they thought I had given up the picture and gone back home

It was now ten thirty and I thought I waslate   we took the first scene at exactly three forty five in the afternoon

The Director says now Will we are going to take the scene where your old pal dies   you have broken out of jail and he gets hurt and you are bringing him into the Doctors office at night to get him treated and he dies , Its the dramatic scene of the whole opera , I says but I havent got out of Jail yet , He says no you wont for a couple of weeks yet, besides the jail is not built yet, Thats the first time I learned that they just hop around any old way , WE took a scene [of] the start of afellow and I fighting out doors and alot of rainy weather come and a weeek later he knocked me down in the same fight   I thought we were trying to beat the european war ~~record~~,

He says have you ever had any Camera experience   I said only with a little Brownie No 2 I used to have,[14] He says moving Picture experience , I told him I worked with Miss Norman once but I dident know how it turned out yet,

He saysif you havent I can tell you something   thats more than I can do with a lot of them, He says I am not going to tell you how to act , I said to him why these correspondence schools do   He instructed me as follows[:] now thought photographs   if you are thinking a thing the camera will show it , so I told him I would try and keep my thoughts as clean as possible,

now we will reherse the scene and then take it , now carry your old pal in , Ha [Hey], Wait a minute   you wouldent carry him in that way would you   you will hurt him worse than he is even suposed to be in the ~~picture~~ story, I told him to change the story around and let me be hurt and him do the carrying   that the other fellow was the biggest , but those guys are set in their ways and [w]ont change anything, Then we took it , him a ballehooing at me through a megophone just what to do , he says thats fine very good,then I heard him say to the camera man mark that N.G.[15] The next take I really was getting along fine on it   I was just dramaing allover the placeholding this pal a[nd] pleading with the Doctor to do something for him when my mind was more on my art than on the load I had and I dropped him, Well I want to tell you folks   somebody could of bought my Moving Picture future pretty cheap right then,

He kept impressing on me that my only pal was dying , well he dident have any thing on me   I was almost dying, he looked and he saw I had tears in my eyes and he says thats great   he thought I was crying aboutmy pal and I was crying about going into the darn thing

TM.[16] OkClaW, 1975.28.0003. Handwritten, bottom right corner, page one: "632 Words". Typewritten, top margin, center, pages two and three: "BREAKING IN THE MOVIES." Double strike-through indicates hand-deleted text; single strike-through indicates type-deleted copy. Interpolations were typewritten, unless otherwise noted.

1. Rex Beach's second book and first novel, *The Spoilers*, became a best seller at 700,000 copies. It was first made into a movie in 1914 (*DAB*, Supp. 4:60).

2. Enrico Caruso began work in his first movie, *My Cousin*, in the summer of 1918. Although the opera star disliked the filmmaking experience, the picture opened in New York in late November to favorable reviews (Jackson, *Caruso*, 250; *NYT*, 25 November 1918).

3. Caruso, at the age of forty-five, married Dorothy Benjamin of New York on 20 August 1918. It was his only marriage (*DAB*, 3:549–50).

4. Uneeda biscuits, a cracker produced by the National Biscuit Company, became a best seller in the early 1900s as one of the first consumer food products marketed in sealed inner packaging as a way to combat food contamination and short shelf life (*ECB*, 1:183).

5. The term *essential industry* was commonly used by U.S. government officials during the war for industries such as munitions, minerals, metals, food, and clothing, whose output was critical to wage the war or to meet consumers' basic needs (Cuff, *War Industries*, 88).

6. Hobart Henley (1886–1964) was a motion picture producer and director whose earliest known film, *Courtmartialed*, was released in 1915. Three years later, he directed Rogers in the *Follies* star's first movie (*AFIC*, F1CS:105; *UDFT*, 119; *NYT*, 23 May 1964).

7. Mabel Normand (1892–1930), one of the most popular comediennes of the silent film era, first appeared in movies in 1910 at the age of eighteen as an extra. She began work for Goldwyn in 1918 and made at least nine films for the studio that year, including *A Perfect 36* (*IDFF*, 3:474–75).

8. Madge Kennedy (1892–1987) made her acting debut on Broadway in 1912 and in motion pictures five years later. Rogers may have been referring to the production of *A Perfect Lady*, a light comedy that opened in New York on 1 December 1918 (*FE*, 740; *NYT*, 2 December 1918, 13 June 1987).

9. Geraldine Farrar (1882–1967), world-renowned, American-born opera singer, made her motion picture debut in 1915. Her success in films paved the way for other opera stars, including Caruso, to work in the same medium (*DAB*, Supp. 8:168).

10. Farrar did not enjoy making *The Hell Cat*, a melodrama that was shot at the Goldwyn studio in New Jersey and on location in Wyoming. It was released at the same time as Caruso's *My Cousin* (Farrar, *Such Sweet Compulsion*, 181–82; *NYT*, 25 November 1918).

11. Caruso, a tenor, and Farrar, a soprano, often shared the operatic stage. One of their memorable appearances together occurred on 17 February 1916 during a particularly charged performance of *Carmen* at the Metropolitan Opera in New York. At an intense moment in the final scene, Farrar, singing the title role, marched up to Caruso as Don José and slapped him across the face with her fan in a pronounced, violent manner. He in turn grabbed her and tossed her to the stage, seat first, while continuing to sing. The incident caused an avalanche of attention from the public and press. Despite the brouhaha, which made tickets for *Carmen* almost impossible to purchase, Farrar and Caruso soon resumed their close friendship and mutual admiration (Ybarra, *Caruso*, 241–43; Jackson, *Caruso*, 229–30).

12. Tom Moore (1885–1955) was an Irish-born stage, screen, and vaudeville performer who made his first of many motion pictures in 1912. He played Madge Kennedy's leading man in the feature film *The Kingdom of Youth,* which was released in October 1918 (*WhScreen,* 518; *NYT,* 15 October 1918).

13. Mae Marsh (Mary Warne Marsh, 1895–1968), a leading actress of the silent screen era, began her movie career in 1912 but delivered one of the finest performances in silent films three years later in *The Birth of a Nation.* She became known as the original "Goldwyn Girl" of Goldwyn studios (*IDFF,* 3:409–10; *WhScreen,* 487).

14. The Brownie No. 2 was one in a series of box cameras marketed by the Eastman Kodak Corporation of Rochester, N.Y., and designed to use recently developed daylight-loading roll film. The popular Brownie line, supposedly named for its inventor, Frank A. Brownell (1876–1939), originated in 1900 and continued until 1935 (Auer, *Illustrated History,* 129–30; *NYT,* 4 February 1939).

15. "N.G.," or "no good," was used in filmmaking to signify a bad take that would need to be reshot (*FE,* 1009).

16. Dating of the document was based on the national release date of *Laughing Bill Hyde.*

Insurance Inspector's Report
2 October 1918
New York, N.Y.

BUREAU OF INSPECTION AND REVISION

Inspector's Report on Applicant

Name <u>Will Rogers,</u>   Space Reserved for Home Office
data.

  Address <u>Forest Hills, L. I.</u>   Agency <u>Metropolitan C. H.</u> No. <u>5599</u>

  Date of report <u>October 2nd</u> 1918   Applying for $ <u>40,000</u> In force
$____

  Points covered in report:

1. Age
2. Health, past and present
3. Health of family
4. Habits, past and present
5. Character

6. Domestic environment
7. Sanitary conditions of residence
8. Occupation
9. Finances

This man's age is the same as stated. He is of medium height, good build, has a tanned out of door complexion, and has the appearance of good health and habits.

During the time he has been known to my informants which is from two to ten years he has not had any serious sickness and so far as I could learn he is said to be in good health at the present time.

Very little is known here of his family history.

My informants say that applicant has always been so far as they know a total abstainer from tobacco and alcoholic beverages, and has never been addicted to any injurious vices, and although he is very popular in his profession he has never been a mixer in the sense that he would stay out at night gambling or carousing. He has always led so far as is known a clean and regular life and takes excellent care of his health.

He is of excellent moral character and professional standing.

He is the father of five children,[1] is devoted to his family and is said to reside at the above address with his wife and family in a private residence which he is believed to have purchased recently.[2]

He was for years a cow boy on a ranch in the West; he then joined a circus, where his act consisted of lassooing wild horses and steers and exhibitions with the lariat. About ten years ago he made his first appearance in New York City in vaudeville, in which his act consisted of lariat exhibitions, with the assistance of a horse on the stage. Later the horse in the act was discarded and he gave exhibitions of lariat throwing and added a small monologue, which became very popular. His act was first produced by Frank Jones[3] of the United Booking Office and who booked his act for a short time, and for the past ten years he has been managed by Max Hart,[4] booking agent, Palace Theatre, this city. Applicant became very popular and was in great demand as a head line act and appeared on the best circuits throughout the country. For the past few years he has been under the management of Florenz Ziegfeld, Jr. under a five year contract and has appeared in his annual reviews. At present he is the leading man in Ziegfeld's Midnight Frolics on the roof of the Amsterdam Theatre, this city, doing his specialty with the lariat and his monologue. His act is in no way hazardous, he does no acrobatic work of any kind and his specialty is confined principally to his monologue. He has always had steady employment, has lost very little time in the past few years and is said to be under a contract of $450 a week. He has always been a careful liver, and is said to have saved some money and has ample means to pay for the amount of insurance applied for. In April 1918 he opened an account with the Broadway Branch of the Greenwich Bank, 46th Street and Broadway, on the recommendation of Florenz Ziegfeld and carries a large and satisfactory balance.

Respectfully submitted,

Jos. J. F.[5]

TDS. OkClaW. Sans serif typeface indicates printed matter. Stamped at the top of the first and second pages of the two-page document: "2526950." Time of "1918 OCT 2 PM 2 33" and "COM-MITTEE CASE" are stamped in the form box "Space Reserved for Home Office data" on the first page. The form box "Space Reserved for Home Office data" also includes smaller "Read" and "Checked" boxes. Within the "Checked" box is stamped: "OCT 2 1918". An illegible signature or set of initials also appears in the "Space Reserved for Home Office data" area.

1. Just a few months earlier, on 15 July 1918, Will and Betty Blake Rogers had celebrated the birth of their fourth, not fifth, child, Fred Stone Rogers.
2. The Rogerses were residing at 5 Slocum Crescent, Forest Hills, Queens, N.Y. (see Will Rogers's military registration card, OkClaW, 1975.16.WRM).
3. A Frank Jones was the assistant manager at Hammerstein's vaudeville theater as early as 1911. The Hammerstein family and United Booking Offices, a theatrical agency, were closely associated (Laurie, *Vaudeville*, 394; *NYT*, 11 September 1915).
4. For Max Hart see *PWR*, 3:424–27.
5. See Insurance Inspector's Report, ca. 31 May 1923, below, for a later report by the same agent.

Notes for Stage Appearance or Speech
ca. April 1917–November 1918
[New York, N.Y.?]

. . . Want to speak about the training of these officers in this war of Wash[ington], or how to get a higher Com[mission], In all my gags ilike to take the part of the private against the officers as it is always more popular to uphold the few against the many.

First thing is to come to Was[hington.] Thats the most essential thing   THen try to get a room   thats the hardest thing   No previous experience neessary ▲TO BE AN [O]FFICER▲ unless it is that you are in danger of being drafted as a private by your own board   Then pick out the branch of the service whos office hours are the shortest, Then get your home senators address   Await your turn in line and if you draw only a Capt why dont feel discouraged   you may meet a cabinet officer and be promoted before night.

Next and the most essential thing is your uniform   without it you wouldent want the office   Then decide whether you want to take your savings of years and get an officers equipment or pay aw weeks room rent with it   they both cost the same   Unfortinately our uniforms are mostly alike   When we have had as many wars [as] theeuriopean [the European] countries we can remidy that to the satisfaction of our officers, Your only chance of ranking above your fellow officers is to get a more expensive grade of cloth, Now you wont have time to have this made to order AS Foch[1] is holding up this war now waiting tillyou get in . Besides you have a date at the photographers at

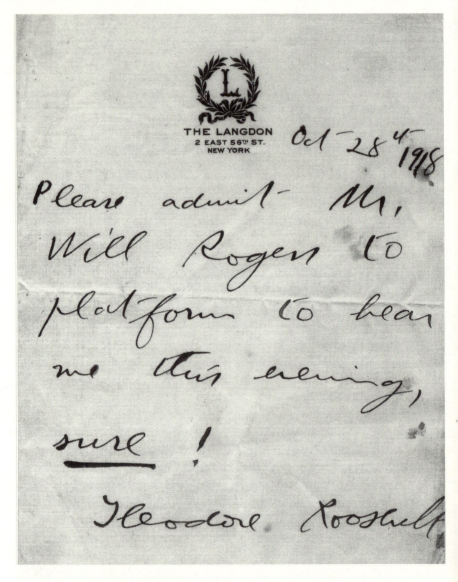

THE LANGDON
2 EAST 56TH ST.
NEW YORK

Oct 28th 1918

Please admit Mr,
Will Rogers to
platform to hear
me this evening,
sure !

Theodore Roosevelt

Theodore Roosevelt provided Rogers with this note as special admission to hear what turned out to be the former president's last major speech of his political career. Speaking to a packed house at Carnegie Hall in New York on 28 October 1918, one day after his sixtieth birthday, the ever-fiery Roosevelt attacked the record of Woodrow Wilson and the president's call for a Democratic Congress to be elected that November. Not long afterward, Roosevelt was admitted to a hospital with inflammatory rheumatism. He never recovered and died at his home on 5 January 1919. (*OkClaW*) four oclock   so go to the best ready made store   He will fit you till you can have a suit made and will show you what insigna to put on your shoulderand which end of your putees[2] go on top,

If you decide as most of them do to get boots and spurs be sure to get spurs without the ~~rowels~~or sharp things in them , as you may cut your boots up with them, besides they are apt to catch in your clutch and youcant shift your gears as well with them,

Now when you have found a coat that is uncomfortably tightand pants with the neesary bigness about the knees the clerk for a small extra fee will show you how to salute as you may in going out meet a cadet who has only been in WEst point three years and you as a superior officer must return his humble salute. Now with the salute learned you are a full fledged American Officer in the Great War of Washigton D C

Now try and think of some humble unpatriotic friend whom you used to know before you entered this awful conflict who is toiling trying to make enough to pay his taxes and meet his payments on his Liberty Bonds and ask him out to dinner with you, and you cant afford to go in any but the best now as you may be humiliated by being next to alot of non com officers

Now be sure and tell your friend confidentially that you got it straight but he must not mention where it come from   that turkey was about through and that the only thing you are sore about is that it may end before you can get across, Now the follies are playing in town so you take your friend   Now its perfectly proper for an army ▲WASH▲ officer to admit ignorance of the war but its gross negligence to admit he is not acquainted with at least five of the girls, When the usher comes back and says there is no answer[,] ball him out before your friend and tell him you bet he gave it to the wrong girl and was he sure he hold her it was capt jasbo

From now on you pan the show   its the worst youve ever seen and yuove seen them all

Now its tomorrow morning and you are to start in as about the deciding ▲FACTOR▲ in this war   when you get to your office building your hardest war work is trying to find a place to park your car,

Now make sure of one thing and that is as to whereyou are to be located   The saddest case that has happened in this war was a fellow dident notice how his appointment read and he found he had been put with a regiment that was to go to the European War   But that was ▲THE▲ only ~~one~~ case,

You spend your first day being introduced to your typewriters   by night you will gegin to realize what a tremendous war this is   Now its time to dress for dinnerso you return ~~home~~ to your rest billets brush your new suitsee that your shoulder tags are on straight and make for a cafe   get a table where you can get a good view of all these new officers who have only been appointed today

Tonight you start in on your millitary training   you atte[n]d a school for twelve leessons to learn how to dance with agirl without catching your spurs in her dress

Carry a french book in your pocket   you know you are not going to use it but it lends a certain amount of atmosphere,

Youve now been in about long enough to commence figureing on a promotion   By this time you should be receiving the paper from home that is one of the most anxio[u]s moments of your entire military career[22][:] wondering how the picture will turn out and if its on the front page

You know one of the most unfortunate cases in this war was a boy after *
sacrificing a good home and all his social standing to enlist as a 2nd, Lieut in this civil conflict returned home on furlough and didedt look well in his uniform   well his people were just ▲SIMPLY▲ killed by it,

Now they dont know whether to try and get him out of the army or get anothr Tailor , You know the ordinary person dont realize the chances these men take when they enlist in this service   why i have seen them pouring out of those goverment buildings after a hard days struggle with three Austrian notes and the ink on their hands up to their wrists,

Why the casualty list in one day out of a miillion and a half officers in Washington was ten wounded getting in and out of Taxicabs, Two choked through their collars being too tight,61 hands hurt through typewriters choking up,

~~50~~500 prostrated when they heard war was over and they would have to go back to work,

It will take two years to muster all of them out of Willard Hotel Lobby,[3] It will take all the Drawing room space on Mcadoos Railroad[4] for years to get them home again,

Then people at home will have to listen for another year why they dident go ▲[*typewritten:*]over,▲ The hardest part of it is trying to look like an officer, and how to act in the presence of some one who has been across,

Also how to properly thank astaff officer for past performances and ask for future ones,

I met one officer here who could tell me what he was doing without explaining   Also trained how to make your uniform look worn somewhere else besides the trouser seat,

They are also allowed to keep their uniforms to show their children and grand children the desk marks on them,

One officer has been recomended for gallantry   he has only missed one show and no dances since the war started,

TD. OkClaW, 1975.14.0135 and 1975.14.0138 (transcribed as one). Typewritten, top margin, page one: "TINNEY AND OFFICERS,[.]" Interlineations were handwritten, unless otherwise noted. Ellipsis inserted by editors.

1. Ferdinand Foch (1851–1929), field marshal of France, was commander in chief of Allied forces from April 1918 through the close of the war (*BDWWI*, 151–54).

2. Puttees, leather or woven wool that was wound around a man's legs up to the knees, were sometimes worn by soldiers. A tubular, plain-knitted variety became popular with civilians during and immediately after the war (Linton, *Modern Textile*, 453).

3. The historic Willard Hotel, with its classical art features, stood at Pennsylvania Avenue and Fourteenth Street in the heart of Washington, D.C. Its lobby had long been a favorite gathering place of the capital's power brokers and prominent visitors (Lewis, *District of Columbia*, 22, 27, 85).

4. Secretary of the Treasury McAdoo's responsibilities in the Wilson administration included serving as director general of the railroads following their seizure by the government in late December 1917. Under McAdoo's direction the U.S. Railroad Administration coordinated and improved rail transportation so effectively that both military and industrial demands on the system were being met by May 1918 (Zieger, *America's Great War*, 71; Bryant, *History*, 239).

Notes for Stage Appearance
11 November 1918
[New York, N.Y.?]

Night Peace Sig ned

Well everybody sobered up ,

Only a rehersal   wait till the real thing,

Best rehersala I ever saw,

I thoug h[t] something was wrong when I heard Hearst got his news from t hem[1]   Good bye Bill   take care of yourself,

Take anot her war to get rid of Crowned heads,

14 days   g ive prize fighter 10 seconds,

If war hadent stopped would of been out of France alot quicker,

History will say Austria ran agood war,

Got Italy all in trying to keep up,

Another   war to make Phila[delphia] Free for the Democrats

Get alot of votes if anybody would ever count them

Roumania found they wwre shooting   real Bulletts,

Germans were playing areturn date across Belgium

U B [U-boat] attacks Doroty Barrett, Knew our gir[l]s were followed by terrible things, Hide U B in Subway and nobody ever see you,

Turks want   Armenian Massacreeing privalege,[2]

If it took as long to muster an Army as did to get Casualty list,[3]

1$ a year men

Fig ht   Bolsheviki with hose,

_ov _ardner[4] in at K C   his Wife[5]   Col House, 'iaduct , Ford Passed t hrough

$peech Bonehead and Highbrow, 5elephones cant get anumber over two lines

Men have to go to Europe to escape these high Prices[6]

Bolsh[eviks] under control   just little weaker than Prohib[ition],

Must be g reat to be little Country and have smart men plan for yo[u][7]   Guess it will be to late to do anything for us,

Must of been terrible in old days to Have men like LIN[coln,] Was[hington, and] Jef[ferson], could ont [only] take care of own country   This seems to have reached clear down to R[oosevelt's] time

Europe wouldent   understand it If we elected Rep[ublicans.] Some parts of A[merica?] dident[8]

Not averse to Rep[ublicans] in war as afig ht er

Guess war soon be o ver   Pres said Pol[itics] adjourned till after war And I see whe r e he has started Pol[itics],[9]

Surrendered in American   started in Journal,

Looks like Foch or Pershing[10] would know it if they had surrendered,

I would hate t o stop all the Bullet ts that were fired from now on,

Base ball in London, Practiceed for weeks to throw out ball   some nut put net up there, Pres Wilson have to learn to pour tea at A Cricket g[ame.]

Amer[icans] stood u p in seventh Inning to stretch and cops tried to make them sit dowm

Shoulder to shoulder nobody can run that fast,

Captured Kimmell   I knew that stuff would get t hem sooner or later,

Women marrying 3[,] 4 soldiers [and] g etting paid for it   Others hace [have] to live a lifetime with one old Kodger and get   nothing   for it,

Women t aking up smoking   cant   hardly wait till get in Cafe t o start

Took shot   at another King   This King [business] is as Hazardous as living in Chi[cago.] there is no closed season on shooting, Those guys over there are such rotten shots, Not aone hurt during the war,

Havent h eard much of King of Port[ugal],[11]   If he starts send Gaby[12]   put him back on ▲bum▲

Ger[many] been in peculiar position since war   nobody to look after but herself,

---

TD. OkClaW, 1975.33.0015. A bracket was hand-inserted in left margin of paragraph 23 ("Must be g reat to be . . .").

1. For William Randolph Hearst see *PWR*, 2:323n.1. After England barred Hearst correspondents in October 1916 because of the newspaper organization's very public pro-German and anti-British bias, Hearst had to rely on reporters and sources in Germany for gathering and transmitting news from Europe (Nasaw, *Chief*, 244–45).

2. Fear of an uprising by the ethnic Armenian population in the Turkish part of the Ottoman empire in April 1915 prompted the Turks to seize and kill more than fifty thousand Armenians and to deport hundreds of thousands of others in death marches to distant regions. News of the atrocities brought an outcry in Europe and the United States, but the killings continued. More than one million Armenians perished at the hands of the Turks between 1915 and 1919 (Gilbert, *First World War*, 142–43, 166–67, 540; U.S. Congress, House, *Hearing*, 4–5).

3. Reasonably reliable records of military casualties showed that the United States during the war suffered 116,708 dead, 204,002 wounded, and 4,480 captured or missing in action, out of a total mobilized force of 4,743,826 (*AVWWI*, 219–20).

4. Frederick Dozier Gardner (1869–1933), a coffin manufacturer, was elected governor of Missouri in 1916 as a Democrat. He served a single, four-year term (*NYT*, 19 December 1933).

5. Jeannette Vosburgh Gardner was the wife of the governor (*NYT*, 19 December 1933).

6. The inflationary policies of the Wilson administration in waging the war contributed to an almost 74 percent increase in the cost of living in the United States between 1917 and 1920 (Harries and Harries, *Last Days*, 285).

7. Presidential advisor Edward House and other representatives of the Allied nations had met in Paris since 29 October 1918 to discuss peace terms, including such issues as territorial gains, self-determination, disarmament, reparations, and the proposal for a postwar league of nations (Harries and Harries, *Last Days*, 411–13).

8. Republicans gained control of both houses of Congress in the general election on 5 November 1918 after a bitter campaign (Zieger, *America's Great War*, 166–67).

9. President Wilson appealed to the public in late October to elect a Democratic Congress to maintain his prestige abroad and to validate his conduct of the war and the peace terms he had proposed. Wilson's plea drew vehement criticism because of his prior call for a wartime moratorium on political partisanship (Knock, *To End All Wars*, 178–79).

10. John Joseph (Black Jack) Pershing (1860–1948), general in the U.S. Army, was commander of the American Expeditionary Force in the war (*DAB*, Supp. 4:653–58).

11. Manuel II (1889–1932) became king of Portugal in 1908 but was dethroned two years later in a revolution that established a republic. He lived in exile in England after his abdication (*NYT*, 3 July 1932).

12. Gaby Deslys (Gabriele Caire, 1881–1920), a dancing and singing star of French music halls, had become an international sensation by 1910 because of the highly publicized infatuation of King Manuel (*EV*, 128; *NYT*, 9 September 1911, 12 February 1920).

Notes for Speech, Performance, or Publication
ca. 21 November 1918
[Washington, D.C.?]

See Mr Ford was defeated for the Senate,[1]   I dont see how he ever figured on being elected when every voter in the state owned one,

Guess he figured the ford owners would vote for him on the theory if he was in Was[hington], he could not make as many cars,Then on the other hand they were just as liable to vote against him[,] keeping him in Detroit so he could make more cars[,] thereby helping them to get even with more peo[ple.] I see in all his statements he says he is a self made man   anyone can ride in one of his cars and tell that,

~~He came in for a great deal of censure cause his~~ ▲Edsel▲ ~~son would not go to war I think he was exempted on account of his first name,~~

~~Ford claimed he was essential to the factory now any one that has ever ridden in one knows nothing is essential to one of those things,~~

I think he would of been a big drawing card in the Senate and you know business has fallen off in that gallery since Proh[ibition], came[2] you know ~~no one can sit and listen to those Senators talk without a certain amount of liquor in him~~ ;

He would of been the only man that ever went to the Senate on   a joke   there are a lot of them in there but they were not elected on one, You know Mark Twain[,][3] George Ade[4] and lots of other men besides Ford have made fortunes out of jokes but still they cant be elected to the biggest one in the U S

It would of been wonderful to see him in there when the Senatepulled one of those long stalls like they do all the time   he would of lifted up the hood to see what was the matter,

His first bit of legislature would of been to make all roads free for Young Hennerys,

He is a wonderful Man and does a lot of g ood besides ediuuatating [educating] people to higher price cars   he pays the best wages to his people[5]

and he dont have to either as he does not manafacture a nessesity   neither would I say that you could callit a luxury, Just comes under the heading of Knick Nacks,

You know he has enough money that he could be appointed Embassadr to some Country but he dont like ocean travel,

He voted years ago and cant remember who he voted for   Ill bet i[t] was for Road Commissioner,

If he had gotten in the Senate those guys are about mean enoughto of nick named him Lizzie,

Mcadoo would been against him as they run opposition transportation systems   (only difference Henrys works),

I dont see why Michigan did not also honor her other great Statesman Mr Kellog[6] , As Fords and Grape Nuts are Michigans principal commodities ~~First two men to take a~~ tin can and a saw log and run it into a fortune, No what really beat him was he said he would not spend a cent, he lost the Politicians vote right there, ~~If you are not going to split with anybody in politics you better not goin you havent got a chance,~~

Mr Ford could of made one speech and been elected, if he had said people if I am elected I will change the front on ~~tem,~~ them,

Personally I dont see why he ~~was not p~~ is not in the~~y~~ Senate asthey are everywhere else,

---

TD.[7] OkClaW, 1975.14.0139. Typewritten, top margin, near center: "FORD." Double strike-through indicates hand-deleted text.

1. Running as a Democrat, Ford lost his bid for the U.S. Senate by less than eight thousand votes in the general election on 5 November (Nevins and Hill, *Ford*, 2:117, 121).

2. On 21 November 1918 Congress passed the Wartime Prohibition Act, which forbade the manufacture and sale of intoxicating beverages in the United States beginning approximately mid-1919 and continuing until the end of demobilization. With the new law, national Prohibition effectively began, even while some states were still debating ratification of the Eighteenth Amendment (Pegram, *Battling*, 147).

3. Mark Twain, the pseudonym of Samuel Langhorne Clemens (1835–1910), was a humorist and novelist, whose standing as one of the premier figures in American literature and observer of political and social life had been well established long before his death (*DAB*, 4:192–98).

4. For George Ade see *PWR*, 3:315n.4.

5. The Ford Motor Company made national headlines in January 1914 when it instituted a daily wage of five dollars for qualified employees, twice what rival firms paid their skilled automobile workers in Detroit at the time (*DAB*, Supp. 4:297).

6. Brothers John Harvey Kellogg (1852–1943) and Willie Keith (Will) Kellogg (1860–1951) originated flaked cereals and other breakfast foods, including Grape

Nuts. Personal differences caused them to split in 1905, with John thereafter concentrating on his work as a surgeon and health promoter and Will focusing on management of the highly successful Battle Creek Toasted Corn Flake Company (*DAB*, Supp. 3:409–11, Supp. 5:378–80).

7. The dating of the document was determined by historical references in the text.

To Maud Rogers Lane
ca. 29 November 1918
Washington, D.C.

Washington.

Dear Maud and folks.[1]

Say here is $2000 for the second payment on those bonds. I think it is due about today.

We played to the President last Night[2]   I will write you all about it in a letter in a day or so. I joked all about the Peace Ship going to Europe[3]   he sure enjoyed it

I had lunch today with Mr and Mrs Nick Longworth[4] at their home   tomorrow at McCleans[5]– you remember the people [with] the hundred Million dollar Baby[6] we used to read about   thats theirs   he is about 9, now   I wouldent give one of *mine* for him.

their home you could put all Rogers County in it   I made a hit with them   they are very fine and friendly.

Will write you all.

Love.
Willie.

folks all well
It looks like my picture thing goes through for Cal. about May.[7]

ALS, rc.[8] LC-UT, IV:B:1.

1. For Maud Ethel Rogers Lane and family, see *PWR*, 1:494, 498–501, 506, 521–22.

2. President Wilson apparently attended a road-show performance of Rogers and the *Follies* in Washington, D.C., in late November 1918. It would have been Rogers's third known appearance before the president.

3. Wilson had announced on 18 November that he would head the U.S. delegation to the peace conference in Paris. Although the American peace party did not embark for Europe aboard the *George Washington* until 4 December, Wilson's proposed trip stirred much controversy, in part because no sitting president had ever traveled outside the country (*NYT*, 18 November 1918; Zieger, *America's Great War*, 167).

4. Nicholas (Nick) Longworth (1869–1931), a wealthy Republican congressman from Ohio, and his wife, Alice Lee Roosevelt Longworth (1884–1980), the outspoken eldest daughter of President Theodore Roosevelt, were leading figures in the social and political life of the nation's capital (*DAB*, 1:394–95, Supp. 10:464–66).

5. Edward Beale (Ned) McLean (1886–1941) and his wife, Evalyn Walsh McLean (ca. 1887–1947), both came from extremely well-to-do families, his in newspaper publishing, including the *Washington Post*, and hers in gold mining. They entertained lavishly at their two residences in Washington, D.C., the McLean family's seventy-five-acre estate and the Walshes' sixty-room mansion (*DAB*, Supp. 3:491–92; *NYT*, 27 April 1947; Roberts, *Washington Post*, 135). See Telegram from Evalyn W. McLean, 28 December 1926, below.

6. When the McLeans' first child, Vinson Walsh McLean, was born in 1909, he became known as the "one hundred million dollar" baby because he was heir to the immense fortunes of the McLean and Walsh families. He was killed in May 1919 at the age of nine when he was struck by an automobile near his parents' estate (*NYT*, 19 May 1919; Roberts, *Washington Post*, 115).

7. Rogers apparently had been in contact with Sam Goldfish about a long-term motion picture contract. The two would soon meet in Cleveland to complete the deal, which would require Rogers's relocation with the Goldwyn studios to southern California (see Contract with Goldwyn Pictures Corporation, 30 November 1918, below).

8. The dating was determined by historical references in the text of the document and by the approximate schedule of *Follies* performances in Washington, D.C.

Contract with Goldwyn Pictures Corporation
30 November 1918
[Cleveland, Ohio]

AGREEMENT made and entered into this 30th day of November, 1918 by and between GOLDWYN PICTURES CORPORATION, a corporation duly organized and existing under and by virtue of the laws of the State of New York, hereinafter called the "Producer", party of the first part, and WILL ROGERS of the City and State of New York, hereinafter called the "Artist", party of the second part,

WITNESSETH:

FOR and in consideration of the sum of one dollar lawful money of the United States by each of the parties to the other in hand paid, at or before the ensealing and delivery of these presents, the receipt whereof is hereby acknowledged, the parties hereto have agreed and do hereby agree as follows:

FIRST:- The Producer shall and hereby does employ the Artist for and during the term hereinafter provided as an actor in and about its business of producing plays and scenes and taking, making and producing motion pictures thereof. The Producer shall pay to the Artist as and for compensation the sum of two thousand two hundred and fifty dollars during each week of the term hereof.

SECOND:- The Artist hereby accepts said employment and agrees that he will throughout the term hereof or throughout any extension thereof as herein provided for act, pose and appear solely and exclusively for and as directed by the Producer in and about the production of plays and scenes and the taking, making and production of motion pictures thereof.

THIRD:- The Artist agrees that he will not during such term or during any extension thereof act, pose and appear in or for any other motion picture production or productions ~~or render any services of any kind or nature in any way connected with dramatic, theatrical or motion picture productions~~, for any other person, firm or corporation; and that he will not ~~contract or~~ permit himself to be advertised, exploited or exhibited in any motion picture or in any one, more or a series of pictures in which he may appear at any time prior to or for twenty four weeks after the expiration of the term herein provided for, or if the term is extended for a like period of time after the expiration of such extended term, ~~without first obtaining the written consent of the Producer, and that he will exact such a covenant for the benefit of the Producer when contracting for his services after the termination of this agreement, Anything herein contained to the contrary notwithstand~~ing, the Artist shall have the right, at his option, to contract for his services for his appearances upon the speaking stage immediately upon the termination of this agreement.

FOURTH:- The Artist hereby expressly authorizes and consents to the photographing by the Producer of all the acts and plays of any kind and all kinds in which the said Artist shall pose, perform, act or appear, taken by the Producer pursuant to the terms hereof, and the production and reproduction thereof, by photographing, printing and all other methods.

FIFTH:- In the event that by reason of the inability or sickness or otherwise, the Artist shall be unable to perform the terms and comply with the covenants and conditions of this agreement on his part to be performed, thereupon the same shall be suspended both as to services and compensation during such sickness or inability of the Artist.

SIXTH:- The Producer agrees to feature the name of the Artist as the star upon all positive prints of those motion pictures in which he shall appear pursuant to the terms hereof and upon all advertising material connected with such motion picture photoplays issued by the Producer, and the Producer further agrees, so far as it is practicable and to the best of its ability, to make known the name of the Artist to the public by publicity and advertising.

SEVENTH:- The term of employment hereunder shall commence on the 16th day of June, 1919 at which time the Artist shall report to the Producer at its studio in Culver City, California, or as otherwise directed by the Producer, and shall continue for a period of one year from and after such date. The Artist hereby grants to the Producer the right, at its option, upon notification in writing to the Artist on or before March 16, 1920, to extend the term of employment of the Artist for an additional period of one year from and after the expiration of said one year period, upon the same terms and conditions herein contained, except that the salary or compensation to be paid to the Artist for the said additional one year period shall be the sum of three thousand dollars per week instead of Twenty two hundred and fifty dollars per week.[1]

EIGHTH:-   The Producer shall furnish to the Artist first class transportation, parlor and sleeping car expenses from New York to California, and to pay the transportation and expenses of the Artist to and from locations or places other than the studio of the Corporation in the event that the Artist shall be called upon to leave the said studio and proceed to such locations or places in connection with rendering his services to the corporation in or about the making of said motion pictures.

IN WITNESS WHEREOF the Corporation has caused these presents to be signed by its officers thereunto duly authorized and its corporate seal to be hereunto affixed, and the Artist has hereunto set his hand and seal, the day and year first above written.

GOLDWYN PICTURES CORPORATION
By <u>Samuel Goldfish</u>[2]
President

Attest:

_____
Secretary

<u>Will Rogers.</u> (LS)

TD, with autograph insertions. OkClaW, Income Tax Return, 1921, Folder 16-B. Centered and stacked (/) on cover page: "AGREEMENT / between / GOLDWYN PICTURES CORPORATION / and / WILL ROGERS". Double strike-through indicates hand-deleted text. Hand-inserted and stacked (/) in the left margin, adjacent to the first section of double strike-through text, are the following sets of initials: "S. G. / W. R."

1. The Goldwyn contract more than doubled the salary Rogers was earning at the time with the Ziegfeld organization (Yagoda, *Will Rogers*, 162).
2. On 2 December 1918, two days after signing the contract with Rogers, Goldfish petitioned a state court in New York to change his name to Goldwyn. The request was granted later that month, allowing the producer to assume legally the name with which he had become so closely identified (Berg, *Goldwyn*, 82–83, 522).

From Thomas A. Johnston
6 December 1918
Boonville, Mo.

December 6, 1918.

William P. Rogers,
New York, N.Y.

Dear Rogers:

My daughter, Mrs. R. J. Foster, of Washington, D. C., wrote me of her meeting you there recently when your company was playing in that city; she gave me a very pleasant impression of you and your art, confirming what I had already learned of you through newspapers. It is a source of great satisfaction to me when any Kemper boys make good and achieve distinction. I very heartily congratulate you.[1]

She informs me that your company is making a tour of the larger cities as far west as Kansas City. Can you not improve the opportunity of being near Kemper to visit us and re-new acquaintance, and entertain our cadets? We would all appreciate it very highly, and consider this an urgent invitation.

I am informed that you are the star in the movie film "Laughing Bill Hyde" by Rex Beach. We have a moving picture machine at the school, and are trying to secure this picture through the regular channels. In case we have any difficulty about it, can you assist us?

I visit Chelsea, Oklahoma, occasionally and met Cap Lane[2] and your sister, Mrs. Lane. They are good friends, whose hospitality and acquaintance I very much enjoy.

Hoping to have a favorable answer to this invitation,[3] I am

Very sincerely,
T A Johnston[4]
Superintendent.

TAJ/ER.

TLS, rc. OkClaW, Miscellaneous Schools, binder. On Kemper Military School, Boonville, Mo., letterhead.

1. For Rogers at Kemper School see *PWR*, 1:131–35, 142–44.
2. Cap Lane (see *PWR*, 1:498), whose wife, Maud Ethel Rogers Lane, was a sister of Rogers, was a graduate of Kemper.
3. No evidence was found that Rogers was able to visit Kemper during the *Follies* road tour in 1918–19 or secure a copy of *Laughing Bill Hyde* for showing at his former school.

4. Thomas Alexander Johnston (1848–1934), a veteran of the Confederate army, had been associated with Kemper Military School since 1872. He served as president and superintendent from 1909 to 1928 and then president until his death (*WhAmer*, 1:644; *PWR*, 1:83n.26).

Newspaper Article by Will Rogers
ca. 14 December 1918
[Detroit, Mich.]

THE NO. 2 PEACE SHIP[1]

AN EDITORIAL ON PRESIDENT WILSON'S JAUNT TO FRANCE.
By Will Rogers, of "The Follies."

Well, I see the No. 2 Peace Ship arrived all O K yesterday.

By sending this Commission over there we are going to get even with them for some of their visits over here.

You know here for awhile we sure was lucky to know what flag to put out each day.

Now this article is not only up to the times, but I figured it should be of special interest to Detroiters as it was in this town that the original Peace Ship idea was conceived.

You know it's the same in anything; the fellow who originates or starts something is generally called a Nut. The next fellow comes along, takes his idea, gets away with it and is a smart man.

Of course this company has the advantage of the first as this one waited till the war was over to go.

I claim that Mr. Ford only made one great mistake and that was there were some people on his boat that should never have had return trip tickets.[2]

Through Holland receiving some of his crowd is where the Kaiser got his idea of going there.[3]

A lot of people think it is a bad omen arriving on Friday 13, but I think it started out alright. I see they arrived at a town called Brest, the only port they could have landed at that we could pronounce.

About everybody that amounts to anything met them at the boat, including a delegation of Ladies' Milliners and Dressmakers.

Col. House was there listening to everything.

A lot of people were not in favor of this trip but I was. I think it gave the people of this country a chance to at least hear who was vice-president.[4]

The paper today does not state anything about landing the Republican they took along.[5] They may of chucked him overboard. They only took him to argue with and when the peace talk starts they won't need him.

I think they were going to let him wait on the peace table.

Paper mentions Admiral Dr. Grayson.[6] Hope he stood his maiden sea voyage well.

They would of taken Sectry Daniels, but he hates the ocean.[7]

Mr. McAdoo would of gone with them but the salary was not big enough.[8] So Mr. Wilson told him to stay at home and try to hustle a job so he could make his wife a living, cause there is nothing worse than having a jobless son-in-law on your hands.[9]

Some wanted Mr. Hughes to go. While the others were signing up he could of been investigating. He would of had his report about ready to turn in the day before the next election.[10]

I wanted to get to go along for Jester. The president will miss his comedy when he gets away from congress. No, I wanted to represent the United Press.[11] I could have them there before they had ever started.

Hope the president gets back before March 1, or these Republicans will want to charge him a tariff to get back in again.

Mr. Creel goes along to suppress any scandal that may crop up.[12] They wanted Mr. Bryan to go but nobody knew where he was.[13]

We have no prime minister like these other nations to send, unless we send Billy Sunday.[14]

If Ireland is represented at the conference I can see France saying take this fight away and bring us back war.

Now they have sent over for the Industrial Board.[15] We may not of had as many men in the war as these other nations but we are going to swamp them at the peace table.

Some day next week if I don't get killed for this I will tell what will happen at the peace table.

PD.[16] Clipping from unidentified newspaper, Detroit, Mich., ca. 14 December 1918. Will Rogers, Jr., Collection, Miscellaneous Items, News and Magazine Articles, Folder O, OkClaW. Hand-inserted cross-marks appear adjacent to each paragraph, right margin or left margin, beginning with paragraph 11 ("Col. House was there ...").

1. The *George Washington*, carrying President Wilson and fellow members of the U.S. delegation to the peace conference in Europe, docked in Brest, France, on 13

December. Three years earlier, the first so-called Peace Ship, *Oskar II*, landed in Norway with Henry Ford and other pacifists aboard who were on a controversial mission to end the war in Europe. Ford, ill and dispirited, quickly returned home. The peace initiative failed overall to achieve its purpose but did dramatize the issue (*NYT*, 14 December 1918; *DAB*, Supp. 4:298; *USFWW*, 233–34).

2. Among the more controversial delegates aboard Ford's Peace Ship in 1915 was Rosika Schwimmer, a writer and lecturer and one of the organizers of the crusade. As a Hungarian, she technically was an enemy alien, a fact widely reported in the press. Generally, however, the group consisted of distinguished and eminent individuals (Nevins and Hill, *Ford*, 2:26, 35–37).

3. Wilhelm II fled into exile in the Netherlands on 11 November after his abdication as kaiser of Germany two days before. He remained in Holland until his death (Cowles, *Kaiser*, 405, 430).

4. Thomas Riley Marshall (1854–1925), former governor of Indiana, served as vice president of the United States from 1913 to 1921. With the first instance of a president absent from the country while in office, the question arose as to who would serve in his stead. Wilson continued to conduct the affairs of office during the time he was away, and Marshall acted as ceremonial head of state (*DAB*, 12:330–31; *NYT*, 20 December 1918).

5. Henry White (1850–1927), a wealthy American career diplomat, was selected by President Wilson as one of the five official U.S. delegates to the peace conference. The only Republican in the group, White nevertheless exerted influence in the negotiations (*DAB*, 20:102–3; Canfield, *Presidency*, 159).

6. Cary Travers Grayson (1878–1938) was a naval physician who served as personal doctor to three U.S. presidents, including Woodrow Wilson; he became a close confidant and friend of Wilson (*NYT*, 15 February 1938).

7. Josephus Daniels (1862–1948), a newspaper editor in North Carolina and a national leader in the progressive wing of the Democratic party, served as secretary of the navy in the Wilson administration despite a lack of naval experience. His record in office, however, proved exemplary (*DAB*, Supp. 4:215–18).

8. William G. McAdoo, citing his health and finances, submitted his resignation on 22 November 1918 as secretary of the treasury and director general of the railroads (*DAB*, Supp. 3:481).

9. McAdoo, whose first wife had died in 1912, had married Eleanor Randolph Wilson (ca. 1889–1967), a daughter of the president, in May 1914 (*DAB*, Supp. 3:480; *NYT*, 7 April 1967).

10. Charles Hughes had conducted a twenty-two-week investigation of alleged scandalous mishandling of the wartime aircraft program. In the report that he delivered on 31 October 1918, just days before the general election, he cited instances of unsatisfactory management and minor violations of the law but no gross negligence or corruption (Pusey, *Charles Evans Hughes*, 1:374–79; Cramer, *Newton D. Baker*, 152).

11. The news service United Press Association, picking up on a rumor behind the front lines in Europe, had cabled in error the signing of the armistice on 7 November, four days before the actual event. The news release caused premature celebrations and excitement worldwide (Gilbert, *First World War*, 494–95; *NYT*, 8 November 1918).

12. George Creel (1876–1953), a muckraking journalist, was chairman of the wartime Committee on Public Information, a federal agency that sought to mobilize public opinion in support of the war. He headed the administration's press office at the peace conference (*DAB*, Supp. 5:141–43; Creel, *Rebel*, 206–7).

13. William Jennings Bryan aggressively sought appointment to the U.S. commission to the peace conference, but President Wilson rejected him, in part because he

thought Bryan might prove too accommodating in the peace negotiations (Coletta, *William Jennings Bryan*, 3:84–85).

14. William Ashley (Billy) Sunday (1862–1935), a popular Christian revivalist, drew crowds of thousands to tent meetings and tabernacles throughout the country during the peak of his evangelistic career in the 1910s (*DAB*, Supp. 1:679).

15. The War Industries Board was created in July 1917 to mobilize American wartime industry. The civilian agency's chair, Bernard M. Baruch, had resigned on 30 November but did not accompany Wilson to the peace conference. By mid-December, however, the president requested that Baruch and an associate join the U.S. delegates in Paris (Cuff, *War Industries*, 1–2, 262, 263; Schwarz, *Speculator*, 109).

16. Dating of the document was determined by historical references in the text.

Newspaper Article by Will Rogers
ca. 22 December 1918
[Detroit, Mich.?]

POOR BILL DIDN'T
PLAY THE REGENT

By Will Rogers.

When we were playing in Cleveland two weeks ago, the old fellow that rattles the bones in the Old Soldier Fiddlers,[1] a vaudeville act at the Regent last week, came back of the stage at the Euclid avenue opera house to see me. We had played together in vaudeville about five years ago and had got to be good friends.

He looked around the big stage where I was practicing with the ropes and said:

"What is this act you're with?"

I told him the Ziegfeld Follies.

"How many people in your act?"

"About 100 to 125," I told him.

He whistled and then said: "Must get 'em pretty cheap."

I told him Ziegfeld paid pretty good salaries.

"Do you carry this scenery or is some of it house stuff?" he asked.

I told him we carried it all.

His comment was: "Don't see how you do it."

Then he asked where I was playing the following week, and when I told him Detroit, he asked what theater. I told him the Detroit opera house.

"Well, you wouldn't be playing where we are," he said with an air of superiority. "We play a new house and a big house, too. It's the Regent, out near Ford's factory."

Then he asked: "What are you getting, Will?"

I told him I was getting a pretty good salary.

"Getting as good as $40?"

I told him I was.

"Well, it's funny," he said, with pity in his voice. "It's funny you had to go with this act. You could get $40 in vaudeville, couldn't you? Why, every time I saw you, you always did all right. ["]

And he went away, sorry because that promising youth, Bill Rogers, had been reduced from a vaudeville act to playing in the Follies.

PD.[2] Unidentified clipping, ca. 22 December 1918. CPpR files, OkClaW. To the right of the article is a dropped-out publicity photograph of Will Rogers, apparently on stage, dressed in western attire and holding a rope. Above the image is the heading "THE ROPE AND ITS TRAINER."

1. For the Old Soldier Fiddlers see *PWR*, 3:247n.2.
2. Dating of the document was determined from Rogers's chronology (see Chronology, 1917–19, OkClaW).

From Pell Mitchell
30 December 1918
Flushing, N.Y.

As the following letter gives evidence, more than one film organization recognized Rogers's potential as a humorous interpreter of current events.

December
Thirtieth
Nineteen Eighteen.

Mr. Will Rogers

C/o The Follies

Chicago, Ill.

My dear Rogers:–

I had a talk with Sam Rothapfel[1] the other evening and he showed me some of your "stuff" on the Peace Conference,[2] which he expects to put on at either the Rialto or Rivoli[3] this week in title form.

Seeing this stuff, brought back to mind the talk we had together on the train, from New York to St. Louis, last October when you were on your way home for a visit.

I don't want to "butt into" any arrangements you have made with Rothapfel, but since we discussed the thing prior to any present plans, I feel that if you are not tied up in any way with other picture people, I can give you an opportunity to get the widest possible publicity for yourself, for very little effort on your part.

I presume you are familiar with the prestige and circulation of our weekly news reels, the Gaumont News and the Gaumont Graphic?[4] We go into all the first class houses in this country, and enjoy the biggest circulation in England, France and South America, - - in fact we have branches in every important capital in the world.

I will feature your sayings and your personality each week, and will make you the best known individual in the world within a short time.

I would like to hear from you as soon as convenient, and if you are in a position to take up this form of publicity on an exchange basis, will be glad to tie up with you.

Kindly let me hear from you as soon as possible, with your advance route, so that I can put a cameraman on your trail.

With kindest regards and best wishes for a happy and prosperous New Year, I am,

> Sincerely yours,
> Pell Mitchell
> Editor
> GAUMONT NEWS & GRAPHIC.

PM/D

[*handwritten:*] I want to start this stuff right away if agreeable to you

TLS, rc. OkClaW, 1975.22.0015. On letterhead of Gaumont Co., Factories, Congress Ave., Flushing, N.Y.

1. Samuel Lionel (Roxy) Rothafel (also Rothapfel, 1881–1936), a successful motion picture theater operator, pioneered the concept of elaborate musical presentations and other unique entertainment to accompany the film feature. Among his most prominent movie venues were the Rialto and Rivoli in New York (*DAB*, Supp. 2:584–85).
2. See Notes for Motion Picture Intertitles, ca. February 1919, below.
3. Rogers's first film, *Laughing Bill Hyde*, opened in New York on 22 September 1918 at the Rivoli, a theater advertised as "The Triumph of the Motion Picture" (*NYT*, 22 September 1918; *EV*, 439).
4. *Gaumont Graphic* was a newsreel produced by one of the oldest film companies in Europe. The U.S. branch of the Gaumont Company announced in May 1919 that Rogers had agreed to provide a monologue feature for its weekly productions (Low, *History*, 286; *IFI:HD*, 176, 177; *Variety*, 23 May 1919). For subtitles that Rogers prepared for Gaumont, see Notes for Motion Picture Intertitles, ca. February 1919, below.

From Harry R. Durant
8 February 1919
New York, N.Y.

The following letter from an associate of film producer Samuel Goldwyn contains the earliest known written proposal to Rogers of a motion picture adaptation starring the Oklahoman.

509 Fifth Ave;
New York City.
February 8, 1919

Mr. Will Rogers,
Ziegfeld Follies,
Colonial Theatre,
Chicago, Ill.

My dear Rogers:

Do you remember Sol Smith Russell?[1] He was a splendid actor and a great favorite all over the United States, which he toured year after year.

One of his best plays was "A POOR RELATION" by E.E. Kidder.[2] We can get this play at a reasonable figure and are inclined to buy it if you like it. I enclose a synopsis. This synopsis does not do the play justice, but I am afraid to send the play itself through the mail as it is the only copy in existence.

Please read this synopsis over and tell me what you think of it. And please bear in mind these very important facts-----that a good love interest will have to be added to "A POOR RELATION"[3] and two or three more dramatic situations built up. This done, I think we would have a splendid vehicle for you and one in which you would make a fine rep.

Please answer as soon as possible, and with all good wishes, I remain

Sincerely yours,
H. R. Durant[4]

HRD/MK

TLS, rc. OkClaW, 1975.22.0016. On letterhead of Goldwyn Pictures Corporation, 16 East 42nd Street, New York. Handwritten note in upper left corner: "Changed my mind about synopsis and am sending the *play* by Ex[press]. Please return by Ex. Durant".

1. Sol Smith Russell (1848–1902) was an American actor and singer who after several years in stock productions began appearing regularly on the New York stage in 1874, mostly in comedies of quaint country life (*DAB*, 16:249).

2. Edward E. Kidder (ca. 1849–1927), American playwright, wrote thirty-one plays, including the successful *A Poor Relation*, a comedy drama and one of several pieces he wrote for actor Sol Smith Russell (*NYT*, 17 November 1927).

3. Bernard McConville adapted *A Poor Relation* for the screen. Goldwyn Pictures Corporation released the five-reel film, with Rogers in the lead role, in December 1921 (*FWR*).

4. Harry R. Durant (ca. 1869–1957) was a freelance writer and newspaper editor, who also wrote more than fifty scripts for motion pictures and worked as an agent for several theatrical and film stars (*NYT*, 23 April 1957).

Notes for Motion Picture Intertitles
ca. February 1919
Chicago, Ill.

A new opportunity for Rogers's humor to reach the public opened for him in early 1919 when he submitted to the Rothafel organization his first set of gags for its motion picture screens.[1] Drawn from his Follies *act, Rogers's brief commentaries on current events probably appeared on screen between film offerings. As the following notes indicate, he supplied Gaumont with at least one batch of intertitles, also known as subtitles, and provided others to an unidentified source in Cleveland, Ohio, and possibly to* Ford Weekly *as well.[2]*

SENT TO DIFFERENT ONES TO BE USED ON THE SCREEN.

I am going to horn into this big anniversary week that this Rothafel Birdis pulling off, Wiyh a few commemts of mine on the No 2 Poace [Peace] ship,[3]

See where they took one Republican along So they would have somebody to argue with on the way over,

They are going to let him wait on the Peace Table,

Wanted Bryan to go along but nobody knew where he was,

Asked Mr Ford to go but he said no[,] One trip cured me,

Mr Garfield is going over[4]   Says he is not going to stay here and freeze another winter

See where Admiral Dr Grayson stood his Maiden Voyage well

You dont hear much news from the Peace Conference, First few weeks they are all complimenting each other, Wait till t hey go to divide up something,

Each Nation is g oing to share in the Peace terms according to what t hey have done in the war   Holland gets the Kaiser, Mexico t he Crown Prince,[5]

I am playing out in Chicago   if you like tis Junk I will send you some more next week   It cant be worse than the Subway, SO LONG.

FOR CLEVELAND ON REEL I HAVE .

Thought   would get chance to find out who was Vice Pres,

Everybody amounted to anything met them   Col House was there in listening capac[ity.]

Havent   heard much   wait till [they] divide up something,

Not as many men in the war but we will swamp them at the Peace Table, Mr Garfield,

Mcadoo salary not big enough,

Took Rep[ublican] t o wait   on the Table,

Senator no dress suit,

If Pres can handle P[eace] C[onference] like Con[gress] we need have no fear of results,

Make Russia shave,

Now if you like these will send you some more   SO LONG.

2 BATCH TO RIVOLI THEATRE.

Heres old Pest again   See you entertained amess of Ships[6]   The war Depart was goint t o send one to the Great Lakes Naval Stat on when war stopped,[7]

Our Pres is playing atour of one night st ands through Italy this week,[8]

He passed t hrough Paris grabbed aclean shirt and lit out for Italy,

When he finished in Italy he asked his asvance man where do we go from here,

Caruso gave him alet ter of int roduct ion so he would meet some of best peole [people.][9]

We were lucky he was our Repres[entative], in Eng land   he is only one could have spoke

Can you imagine how sore these Republican[s] are when [they] read about a Dem sleeping

Czar and Emperor[10] used to kid King Georg e[11]   say he had no authority,

After eating off 15 mil, dollar Gold plates habnobbing with Kings and Dukes

When they g et   through wining him he will have Gout so bad agree t o anything

These Jokes cant be any more behind the times than Roth, he just caught the Flu[12]

3rd Batch to Rivoli Theatre

League getting on pretty good[13]   all but 30 or 40 small nations

Wilson said if dont   do something AmericansDel[egates] will pick up wives and go home

Sent t hem t heir Quest ionnaire,

Handle meeting like Congress,

Disease called t he Gimmees,[14]

Get back before Mar 1st when country goes into hands of Rep[ublicans],

Think He will trade America off for a Couple of Golf Clubs,[15]

England put embargo [in place.][16]   good thing he visited there when he first went   over,

League to prevent   war going fine   Go ahead with big Navy,

SENT GAUMONT.

Good thing   its warm Winter   with Prohib[ition] coming on no place in cellar for coal[17]

There will be husbands t ending Furnaces next winter never knew where [they] were bef[ore.]

People want   Proh, and we owe all our success now to Haig and the Tanks,[18]

Hop on Cigaret t s and Room and Bath next,

We are now in a class with Turkey and Russia

Who wants t o drink 50 bottles to be 100 percent d runk,[19]

SENT FORD FROM KANSAS CITY.

Passed through K C   Mcadoo   FORD   Guess Bryan and I only ones ever stopped, (re Buildi[ng] car to compete with Street cars   wont take much to compete with these he [has.)]

Wilson speech Bone Head[,] High brow get it same way,

Had to come back to explain it to Congress,

Good joke [to] not call them at all,

Women send Del forget this is aPeace Conference,

Germans much chance as Democrat in next Con[gress],

Make Russians shave,

If Pres Frees allother nationsand says nothing about Ireland [*page torn*] etter land assum G[*page torn*] way to solve Prohib 50 50 let Prohib quit drinking [*page torn*]

TM.[20] OkClaW, 1975.28.0020. Typewritten underscoring of variable but short lengths appears between each gag in the third group of subtitles.

1. See Letter from Pell Mitchell, 30 December 1918, above.

2. *Ford Weekly*, also known as *Ford Educational Weekly*, was a regular series of news subtitles produced by Ford Motor Company and distributed by Goldwyn Pictures (Nevins and Hill, *Ford*, 2:115; *WYB, 1919–1920*, 7). The actual on-screen dates of the various series of gag intertitles could not be determined.

3. Sam Rothafel announced on 7 January 1919 that he had resigned as manager of the Rivoli and Rialto Theatres, effective 1 February (*NYT*, 8 January 1919).

4. Harry Augustus Garfield (1863–1942), the son of President James A. Garfield, took leave as president of Williams College to serve as unpaid head of the U.S. Fuel Administration, overseeing a wartime agency that sought to ensure sufficient coal production and stable fuel prices to meet both consumer and military demands. He did not participate in the peace conference (*DAB*, Supp. 3:292–94).

5. Like his father, Crown Prince Wilhelm of Germany fled into exile in Holland after the war (*BDWWI*, 354).

6. Several destroyers and other ships of the U.S. fleet that had served in the Atlantic returned to Boston and Philadelphia in early January and to New York on 12 February 1919 (*NYT*, 4, 9 January, 13 February 1919).

7. The Great Lakes Naval Training Station, located near Chicago and far from the ocean, became the world's largest naval training facility during the course of the war. Although the navy trained tens of thousands of officers and enlisted men at Great Lakes, it did not serve as a naval port (Farwell, *Over There*, 70; Daniels, *Our Navy*, 310).

8. Wilson spent a few days in Italy before the peace conference opened in Paris in mid-January. His Italian tour began on 2 January and included stops in Genoa, Rome, Turin, and Milan before his arrival in Paris five days later. Large, enthusiastic crowds greeted Wilson throughout the trip (*NYT*, 2–8 January 1919).

9. No such letter from Caruso was found in Link et al., eds., *The Papers of Woodrow Wilson*.

10. Francis Joseph I (1830–1916) became ruler of the Hapsburg Empire in 1848 and eventually emperor of the dual monarchy of Austria-Hungary. By the time of his death in 1916 he had surrendered all hope of victory in the war. His great-nephew, Charles I (Charles Francis Joseph, 1887–1922), succeeded him as emperor of Austria (*BDWWI*, 114–15, 155–56).

11. George V (George Frederick Ernest Albert, 1865–1936) succeeded to the throne of the British Empire in May 1910 on the death of his father, Edward VII. President Wilson visited England and met with George V in late December 1918, marking the first meeting of a U.S. head of state and an English monarch (*DNB*, Supp. 5:313–34; *NYT*, 27–31 December 1918, 1 January 1919).

12. Although the identity of Roth is unknown, he apparently was another victim of a pandemic of influenza that swept the world from June 1918 into early 1919. The disease took an estimated 20 million to 30 million military and civilian lives worldwide. More U.S. army troops (62,000) died in the pandemic than were killed in battle during the war (Gilbert, *First World War*, 437, 479, 540; *USFWW*, 573–74).

13. The concept of a league of nations, an international organization to maintain peace in the postwar world, had been formulated and proposed by President Wilson as the final element of his so-called Fourteen Points for lasting peace, which he outlined in a war message to Congress on 8 January 1918. Wilson succeeded in effecting the establishment of the League of Nations through the negotiations at the peace conference in Paris (Walworth, *Wilson*, 1–4, 106–24, 194–97, 378–81).

14. Several countries voiced strong interest in the colonial territories of the defeated Central Power nations. The conquered possessions were placed under Mandates of the League of Nations and then distributed to various countries under the Mandate system (Gilbert, *First World War*, 509).

15. Although not an enthusiastic golfer, Wilson, on the advice of the White House physician, took up the sport during his presidency as a means of exercise (*NYT*, 15 February 1938).

16. Great Britain instituted on 29 January 1919 an embargo on certain imports in an effort to help domestic manufacturers recover from the war. The restrictions, including limits on shoes and other leather goods, prompted demands in the United States for retaliation (*NYT*, 30–31 January, 5 February 1919).

17. Prohibition became part of the U.S. Constitution on 16 January 1919 when Nebraska became the thirty-sixth state to ratify the Eighteenth Amendment (Pegram, *Battling*, 148).

18. General Douglas Haig, the commanding officer of British troops in the war, was the son of a distiller. During the war, the British army developed and introduced a new armored weapon, the tank, which helped overcome the obstacles of trench warfare with caterpillar tractor mobility. The word *tank* was also used at the time in reference to consuming alcoholic beverages, especially beer (*BDWWI*, 177; Gilbert, *First World War*, 229–30, 458; *USFWW*, 590; *DSUE*, 1202).

19. Because the newly ratified Eighteenth Amendment did not define an intoxicating beverage, many beer producers continued to brew the beverage with 2.75 percent alcohol, a level that the administration had allowed during the war (Pegram, *Battling*, 149).

20. The dating of the document was determined from historical references within the text.

To Sallie Rogers McSpadden
ca. 1 March 1919
[Chicago, Ill.?]

Well I received your letter tell[*small portion of page missing*] the matrimonial plans of another Neice,[1] Altho not being ask[*missing text*] give my consent,

The war is over and the Armistace has [*missing text*] signed but if they dont know it down there I cant help it,

Why a man should marry and no draft in sight I dont know, I cant figure it out unless it is one of those old fashioned marriages where they loved each other,

I am so glad that bot h Families agree, Even if it is only for awhile, I am tickled that one of the Girls is marrying an Electrician, There was not a person in our whole family that could change a tire, We can always use him,

Now as to the various other suitors that are soaking up your heat these cool evening s Kindly give preference to one that knows somet hing about Farming As we havent a one of those in our whole Family either   How [Now?] th e Peace Conference means little to Sallie but how t o hem the most Napkins and Pillow Slips in the short est time is her great est problem for the next few years,

Be abou t my luck for Haviland China[2] to be higher aft er t he war

I can cut down on the number of pieces and make up some of it

As people dont have as much to eat as they used to and as for having people to Dine with you that is a lost Art nowadays,

As the prospects seem bright for various forthcoming   marriages in the Family[3] I am just going to leave a standing order with Marshall Fields[4] For several sets of China and a gross of Baby Buggies and you all just wire t hem direct which to send,

Now a few words about the Cupid affairs of my own immediat e Family William (thats the oldest boy)is a bit like your Herbert[5](who seems to like t he Horses and Poetry better than Women)   Well William seems more of a mechanical naturethan affection   he is continually working on some scheme to make a Toy Train run, His task seems hopeless with the opposgsition he encounters from the next nearest of kin,

Now there Mary thats our Female of the specie, Kinder takes after your Helen[6]   She cant seem to keep her mind on any particular fellow any longer than the Candy lasts,

We fear she is a bit frivolous , All of which I lay to breeding on the Arkansaw side, She is very patriotic however and is now keeping   company with a Boy Scout, I havent met the family yet although t hey have lived next door for years, And must be people in moderate circumstancesas   they have ~~not~~ had no new Car this year,

Now James Rogers named rightly after t he James Boys[7] is a regular Loung e Lizard   He is to the Ladies of our town what your Pau[*portion of page missing*] [Pauline?][8] is to the younger Male Set of Rogers Count y, He h as Kicked up more disturbances and circulated more inside Propoganda concerning t he inner workings of people both in and out of his set than Count Von Bernot. And as for family affairs he has the key to the Sceleton Closet, I personally am hoping he dont marry till after he g ets out of Jail,

Now Freddy[9] our youngest he only made his Debutt   into Scoiety last Summer   He is such a ladies man that he never goes out alone and really recieves more attention from the opposite sex than any of the older ones

But my Wife and I feel that they are all young yet and that a Son or a Daught er in law would be rather an incumbrance on us as we are permanent ly fixed for t hem as you all are there,

Well will close by offering our best   wishes to both parties, And cong rat ulate them on th e fact as they both have the worst of th eir first y ears t roubles over, As they have already seen Niagra ~~F~~ Falls, Grants Tomb Statue of Liberty , Bushes Sunken Garden and the Cliff House,

Come RIGHT ON LADIES AND GENTLEMEN   DONT PUSH DONT SHOVE WHO WILL BE NEXT LUCKY PERSON,

Suppose Herb says he will take a Wife if he can g et 10 other men to t ake one

TL, rc.[10] LC-UT, IV:A:1. Typewritten, bottom margin, left side: "(Letter Sister Sallie McSpadden)". Handwritten, bottom margin: "about 1919".

1. The letter from Rogers's sister, Sallie Rogers McSpadden, was not located. Rogers probably was referring to May (Mazie) McSpadden, the second daughter of Sallie and J. Thomas McSpadden. May married Walton Charles Poole in Chelsea, Okla., on 22 May 1919 (see *PWR*, 1:528–29).

2. David Haviland (1814–79), an American, founded what became Haviland & Company, a premier porcelain manufacturer, in Limoges, France, in 1840. Haviland china, available in many price ranges, earned a worldwide reputation for its beauty and quality (*NYT*, 14 December 1879; Cruikshank, "Haviland").

3. At the time Sallie and Tom McSpadden had four other unmarried children.

4. Marshall Field (1834–1906) acquired in 1862 a partnership in a dry goods store in Chicago that eventually became Marshall Field & Company. Under his merchandising management the firm prospered and grew, over time becoming one of the leading and most respected department store operations in the country (*DAB*, 6:366–67).

5. For Herbert Thomas (Herb) McSpadden see *PWR*, 1:509–10.

6. For Helen McSpadden Eaton see *PWR*, 1:488–89.

7. Jesse James (Jesse Woodson James, 1847–82) and his brother Frank James (Alexander Franklin James, 1843–1915) led a gang of bank and train robbers that gained legendary stature in the outlaw history of the American West (*NEAW*, 564–65).

8. For Pauline Elizabeth (Paula) McSpadden Love see *PWR*, 1:505–6.

9. This was one of Rogers's rare references to his youngest child, Fred Stone Rogers, then less than a year old and whose death from diphtheria would occur about fifteen months later.

10. The dating was determined by historical references in the document and an inference to Rogers's presence in Chicago at the time. His final performance in Chicago in early 1919 appears to have been on 1 March (Chronology, 1917–19, OkClaW).

Interview in *Kansas City Star*
11 March 1919
Kansas City, Mo.

Countless interviews with Rogers appeared in newspapers, magazines, and other publications throughout his public life. The following one appeared in a local newspaper the day after the Follies *opened a week-long engagement in Kansas City.[1] Although not extraordinarily probing, it does provide an understanding of Rogers's approach to humor—or the telling of a gag, as he more likely would term it.*

MAKES JOKES AS HE GOES

. . . "No gag is any good that is more than six hours old. . . . That's why I must use impromptu stuff on the stage. A funny story travels so quickly I sometimes find it is old before I get out of the theater. I claim no credit because people laugh at what I say, although I do think I am correct in believing in the success of my method of attack. I have found out two things. One is that the more up-to-date a subject is the more credit you are given for talking on it—even if you really haven't [said] anything very funny. But if the subject is old, your gag must be very funny to get over.

"Audiences like to have you believe they are 'getting' you—that they know just what you are talking about, because they, too, are smart folk and read papers. Therefore, your gag must be founded on facts. You can make it ridiculous by exaggeration, but what the crowd most likes to say is: 'Well, that's just about right, at that.'

"No audience is so quick to 'get' you as the after dinner audience. In Minneapolis one time I was at a dinner where the mayor had just made one of those beautiful speeches, praising the Lord because we all were good Americans, but adding pleasantly—as he believed—that he was glad that 'some good people from the South were with us, too, for the South now is part of the United States, you know.' I live far enough in the South to know how real Southerners felt about that, so when I was called on to speak I said, so the mayor of Minneapolis could hear me:

"'I am glad to get back to Minneapolis again. I haven't played here for five or six years. The last time I was here was the year they started teaching English in the Minneapolis public schools.'

"Of course, that got a yell, because that mayor, in spite of his little dig at sectionalism, was of Swedish descent and spoke with a noticeable accent.

"More recently I talked before the Traffic Club in Chicago. The audience was made up chiefly of railroad officials and shippers—all eager to have the administration turn the roads back to them. The toastmaster introduced me as the young man who made at least a thousand people laugh every day. I said I felt complimented, but that I had nothing on the railroads which were making monkeys out of hundreds of thousands of folk every day.

"In the theater, of course my comment must be more general and that is one reason I get laughs out of national topics. Some public men always are subjects; some an audience won't let you say anything complimentary about."

... "The [newspaper] paragraphers are my best friends, ... but I don't get my gags from their columns. I read the papers for the topics, for the subject matter, just as they must do, but I can't 'lift' their paragraphs. They seldom fit my style. For instance, all the leading paragraphers quarreled some months ago about the gag concerning the man who said he had been drafted, but was asking exemption.

"'Why?' was the answer, 'You look fit to fight, and able to go to war.'

"'Yes,' he said, 'but I'm asking exemption on the grounds of dependency—you know, I have a new car with wire wheels.'

"All the leading paragraphers said they had originated that story, and some inferred that I had 'lifted' it. But the truth is, it came out of a little country paper, and when I told it on the stage I changed it to: 'I must be exempt because I have a Ford. Who'd keep it going while I'm away? It's utterly dependent on me.'"...

PD. Printed in *Kansas City Star*, Kansas City, Mo., 11 March 1919. *Kansas City Star* file, OkClaW. Ellipses inserted by editors.

1. Edward Bernard (Ruby) Garnett (d. 1968), the drama critic and editor of the Sunday edition of the *Kansas City Star*, conducted the interview. A few months later when Rogers stopped in Kansas City on his way to Hollywood, he called Garnett and invited him to the grand opening locally of a new motion picture theater, where Rogers was scheduled to entertain (*KCS*, 7 July 1968). The visit that night led to a letter from Rogers that was published in the *Star* and claimed erroneously by Garnett to be the Oklahoman's first published writing (see Letter to *Kansas City Star*, ca. 5 June 1919, below).

From William H. Briggs
1 May 1919
New York, N.Y.

A proposal for a series of six books of Rogers's sayings offered a new opportunity for him to reach a wider audience. The first effort, Rogers-isms: The Cowboy Philosopher on the Peace Conference, *was published by Harper & Brothers in the fall of 1919 and was soon followed by a second,* Rogers-isms: The Cowboy Philosopher on Prohibition.[1] *Both books contained about two hundred paragraphs, each one essentially a gag from Rogers's* Ziegfeld Follies *routine.*

May 1,1919.

Will Rogers, Esq.,
The Colonial Theatre,
Boston, Massachusetts.
My dear Author:

Enclosed herewith are contracts[2] covering the series of humorous books we talked about this morning. I think you will find them in proper form and, if so, will you kindly sign one and return it to me, keeping the other for your files.

The more I think about it the more tickled I am about undertaking these books. There is going to be real joy in publishing them, and we want to start the first one off with bells. We will begin manufacturing it immediately, and I think we shall be all ready for you to O.K. the proofs when you come back to town on Monday, May 12th.

I certainly want to thank Rex Beach for his happy thought in heading you in this direction.[3] I hope that some time you will have a chance to mill with the Harper crowd.

Meanwhile, all good wishes.

Cordially yours,
William H. Briggs[4]

2 enclosures - contracts
William H. Briggs-KD.

TLS, rc. OkClaW, 1975.26.0065. On letterhead of Harper & Brothers, Publishers, New York and London, Franklin Square, New York.

1. See Stout and Rollins, eds., *Rogers-isms: The Cowboy Philosopher on the Peace Conference;* and Stout and Rollins, eds., *Rogers-isms: The Cowboy Philosopher on Prohibition.*
2. Copies of the contracts were not found with the letter or elsewhere in the archives of the Will Rogers Memorial.
3. Harper & Brothers, the second oldest publishing house in the United States, founded in 1817, published several of Beach's novels, either as first editions or as reissues (*IBP:E*, 148; for example, see Beach, *Spoilers*).
4. William Harlowe Briggs (1876–1952), a former newspaper editor and drama critic, joined the book department at Harper & Brothers in 1908. At Harper he edited the works of Mark Twain, as well as other prominent writers (*NYT*, 1 August 1952; *WhAmer*, 3:104).

Notes for Stage Appearance
ca. 21 May 1919
[New York, N.Y.]

See President W is up to his old tricks   wrote Americans a note,[1]

Lot of people critisize it but I think it is one of the best notes Col H[ouse] ever ▲(wrote▲

He gave Congress their Peace terms and gave them 30 days to sign,

If they dont sign he ~~will invade congress personally,~~ has ordered the George Woodrow Wahington[2] to stand ready and he will invade congress personally

In some quarters the terms laid down to Congress is considered more strict than the ones last fall to the voters,

The Peace terms to Congress consist of 5 points,

1st is Womans Sufferage,Pres says if they are going to insist on going ever-where with their Husbands   why we may as well let em vote,

2 point,Labor the Pres made it very plain on this that he is for labor,But not against Capital, they must get their pay somewhere else,

3 point, Railroads, says give them back to their owners and if they wont take them for the lord sake give them to somebody,

4 point, Telegraph and cables, He says give them back and slip in Burleson[3] as a Bonus,

5 point The freedom of drink,He is for light wines and light beers, evi-dently he has not tasted any of our beers latelyor he would realize that if they were made any lighter you would [have] to be an aviator to drink them

The Peace terms were received by congress with various degrees of emo-tion   Some even going so far as to show their disrespect by replying to it while sitting down,

Senator Randall[4] Prohibitionist of Colorado,replied, prepostrous, that last point shall never pass, the Pres has doubled crossed us, somebody has been sending him news of American sentiment, No I will never agree to sign for such ~~democratic~~ principle as freedom of peoples rights, in the name of that illustrious commoner William Jennings Bryan I again say no,If you call that reason make the most of it,

Senator Penrose[5] Republican, I dident hear the terms (I stopped up my ears) But I will never agree to sign anything written by a Democrat,

Senator Moses[6] Republican (no relation of Gentleman of Bullrushes fame) Cutting the number of points down from 14 to 5 only leaves me 7 less to missunderstand

Senator Poindexter [7] Republican, Why the terms are enslaving   if we sign ~~the~~ them the Rep[ublicans] will be back where they were before the last election,

Representative Mondell[8] Republican Floor walker, We₊ will give his points all careful consideration before voting against them,

Senator Owen Democrat, I am for signing provided they amend it to read that the Senate is higher in authority than the Supreme Court,

~~I will sign~~ Senator Gore Democrat, The terms are very fair but should guarantee my constituents 5 dollar a bushell wheat,

Senator King[9] Democrat, The phrasing of the terms are wonderful   no one but a ~~true~~ democrat could written it,

Senator Lodge[10] republican, The phrasing of the terms is terrible   no one but a democrat could have written it,

Senator Borah[11] Republican, [*text ends*]

TD. OkClaW, 1975.33.0009.

1. Wilson forwarded a message to the U.S. Senate and House on 20 May 1919 at the opening of a special session of the new Sixty-sixth Congress. The first document to be transmitted to Congress from overseas by a U.S. president, Wilson's remarks included several controversial recommendations: improvements in the conditions of workers, the repeal of wartime prohibition, the enactment of women's suffrage, and the return of the railroads to private control (Link et al., eds., *Papers*, 59:289–97; *NYT*, 21 May 1919).

2. Wilson and other members of the U.S. commission to the postwar peace conference traveled to Europe aboard the transport ship *George Washington* (*NYT*, 14 December 1918).

3. Albert Sidney Burleson (1863–1937), a Texan, served as U.S. postmaster general in the Wilson administration. Probably the most unpopular cabinet member of the day, he wielded the power of patronage and used wartime legislation to ban from the mail publications critical of the draft and in support of higher taxes. As head of the telegraph and telephone administration during the war, he clashed with workers over pay and collective bargaining and with business groups that feared nationalization (*DAB*, Supp. 2:74–75).

4. Charles Hiram Randall (1865–1951), a newspaper publisher in California, was first elected to Congress on the Prohibitionist party ticket in 1914. He served from 1915 to 1921 (*BDUSCong*, 1689).

5. Boies Penrose (1860–1921) served in the U.S. Senate from 1897 until his death. A partisan Republican from Pennsylvania, he was known for his scalding comments (*DAB*, 14:448–49).

6. George Higgins Moses (1869–1944) was elected to the U.S. Senate as a Republican from New Hampshire in a special election in 1918. He served until 1933. As a member of the Senate Foreign Relations Committee, Moses played a key role in opposition to Wilson's international agenda, including membership in the League of Nations (*DAB*, Supp. 3:542–44).

7. Miles Poindexter (1868–1946), a progressive Republican from the state of Washington, served as U.S. senator from 1911 to 1923. An opponent of the League of Nations as a threat to American sovereignty, Poindexter was one of the so-called Irreconcilables, senators who opposed the peace treaty and blocked its ratification (*DAB*, Supp. 4:669–70).

8. Franklin Wheeler Mondell (1860–1939), who served in the U.S. House of Representatives from 1895 to 1897 and 1899 to 1923, was the Republican majority leader during his final four years in Congress (*BDUSCong*, 1518).

9. William Henry King (1863–1949), one of the first U.S. representatives from Utah after statehood, was elected as a Democrat to the U.S. Senate in 1916, serving from 1917 to 1941 (*BDUSCong*, 1314).

10. Henry Cabot Lodge (1850–1924), Republican U.S. senator from Massachusetts from 1893 until his death and chair of the Senate Foreign Relations Committee, led opposition in the Senate to ratification of the peace treaty and the covenant creating the League of Nations. Although favorable toward the League, he objected to coupling it with the treaty (*DAB*, 11:346–49).

11. William Edgar Borah (1865–1940) was U.S. senator from Idaho from 1907 until his death. Although considered a progressive Republican, he proved a maverick in the Senate, often opposing Wilson's reform agenda and his own party's congressional leadership. A leader among the Irreconcilables, he opposed all compromises toward the peace treaty (*NYT*, 20 January 1940; *DAB*, Supp. 2:49–53).

Notes for Appearance at Benefit Event
25 May 1919
New York, N.Y.

Rogers participated in several postwar charitable events. He prepared these notes for remarks he delivered at a dinner held by the Friars Club in tribute to the Stage Women's War Relief.[1] More than one hundred women from the organization attended the benefit, which was held at the Friars' clubhouse, a place that had long been reserved for men.

Those rehersals we held in the Club on how to conduct ourselvs in the presen[ce] of ladies ~~wehh~~ was agood Idea,

Glad to see the club get on so well in its maiden effort entertaining Ladies
That boisterious element that generally prevails at other dinners is eliminated tonight, showing you that that therehersals that were held instruc [instructing us ?] at the club last week did a lot of good, and the management showed rare judgement in eliminating Felix adler[2] and tommy Gray,[3]

I represent the Jass of the entertainment,

I am here tonight to do honor to another of our veterans who though not fortunate enough to see oversea[s] service, I refer to that veteran of old gags Capt Frank Tinney,[4]   The first man of business ability enough to take out the controlling interest in a soldier show,

Frank was unfortunate in getting in to the Army so near the finish , Had he been in earlier he would have done better,

Capt Gleason[5] was given Com[mission] to find out how Tinney got in, Now Frank got out and Gleason is still in trying to find out how he got out and how much he ~~Work~~

Women did wonderful Knitting, keep it themselvs, red cross, running elevators   ~~Women to the Peace conference,~~

Mrs Wilsons dresses,[6] Her trip did some good after all,

Womans war relief and salvation army,[7] Dident take a war to make them great   were just as goodbefore the war to the fellow who was broke

were not as fashionable, Thats only trouble I am afraid of if [in] society   If they can just survive this temporary invasion of Society they will be the greatest organization in the world,

Everyone seemed to overlook what to me seems the most remarkable part of these these ladies part in this great work and that was that they did all this and had no uniform,

Most women enlisting in war work would pick out the branch of the service whose uniforms were the prettiest,[8]

Why I know ladies who after they got in and then found that that particular uniform was not suited to their complexion they would have to be transfered till they found a uniform that suited their comp[l]exion,

The ladiy ambulance drivers seemed on account of being the more mannish of any of the costumes to be the most sought of branch of the service,

Their instructions consisted of aperiod of 32 days[,] 2 days to leard [learn] how to drive the car and the other 3p0 [30] to get fitted for their uniform,

War of Wash[ington], Take three years to muster out of lobby,

Casualty list

Croix de Jasbo,

[*handwritten reverse side:*]

Houdini.[9] Ireland

Austria.

Divide up Something

Gimmes. . .

You can [*illegible*].

Tuesdays.

Russia & a Note.

R.R.

Soldiers.

Prohib[ition].

TD. OkClaW, 1975.14.0003. Handwritten, top margin, center right: "women DiNNE[R] ON WAR." Four large, hand-inserted exes appear between the sixth ("Capt Gleason . . .") and seventh paragraphs. Double strike-through indicates hand-deleted text; single strike-through indicates type-deleted copy.

1. During the war, the Stage Women's War Relief in New York operated a home for soldiers. The group planned to continue to use the house as a refuge for disabled men (*NYT*, 26 May 1919).

2. Felix Adler (1884–1963) was a comedy writer, actor, and scenarist (*UDFT*, 2; *VO*, 27 March 1963).

3. Thomas J. (Tommy) Gray (1888–1924) wrote comedy sketches, songs for musicals, and humorous subtitles for silent films (*UDFT*, 105; Laurie, *Vaudeville*, 49; *NYT*, 1 December 1924).

4. Tinney held the rank of captain in the U.S. Army Quartermasters Corps during the war (*NYT*, 29 November 1940).

5. John J. Gleason (ca. 1872–1923) was a stockbroker, prizefight promoter, and a member of the Friars Club. During the war he served as a captain in the intelligence division of the army (*NYT*, 14 March 1923).

6. During the war, Edith Wilson could often be seen in a Red Cross uniform of motherly dress and apron as she doled out cigarettes and gum to soldiers at the train station in Washington, D.C. The wartime attire did not match her usual well-chosen designer wear, which she on several occasions supplemented while in Paris during the peace conference (Hatch, *Edith Bolling Wilson*, 52, 108, 156, 170).

7. A star-studded benefit for the Salvation Army was held at the Hippodrome in New York on 25 May 1919, the same night as the Friars' tribute to the Stage Women's War Relief. Rogers was scheduled to appear at both. In addition to contributing to the women's cause, the audience at the Friars event donated $5,000 to the Salvation Army (*NYT*, 25–26 May 1919).

8. About forty-one thousand women served in the military branches of the United States during the war and approximately sixteen thousand in England and France, mostly in clerical or medical care positions. Although they wore uniforms and were subject to military regulations, some of the women who served with the army in Europe were not aware until after the war that they had not been officially engaged in military service (Zieger, *America's Great War*, 141–43; *USFWW*, 803).

9. For Harry Houdini see *PWR*, 2:486–88.

To *Kansas City Star*
ca. 5 June 1919
[Kansas]

Ruby Garnett, an editor at the Kansas City Star,[1] *considered Rogers "the brightest mind he ever encountered in public life."[2] When Rogers paused in Kansas City en route to Hollywood on the California Limited,[3] Garnett suggested that he should put his humor in print. Rogers denigrated his own ability to write, but he did admit that he had packed a typewriter. The newspaperman encouraged him to put it to use and to send him a letter as he headed west. Garnett promised that the* Star *would print whatever Rogers submitted. Several days later the following letter arrived. Garnett promptly published it on 15 June 1919, giving it special treatment in the letters section of the* Star. *Years later, Garnett would claim—inaccurately—that he had given Rogers his start as a published writer.[4]*

You asked me to drop you a few lines on my way west to Los Angeles, where I hear the call of ART to act a fool for the bucking Pictures, I think they want to use me as the horrible example in some picture, But you can never tell what amovie fan will fall for, Look last night at that mob trying to get into that new Theatre,[5] Waiting for hours as though it was their last chance, They will get achance to see it   if the Grand has stood for a thousand years this one ought to stand a million[6]   Those people last night when they went to bed dident know whether they had been to a fight or a show,

We are making good time crossing Kansas, If it was not for having to stop to unload express packages for the bootleggers we would make it all in one Hop,

I have discovered a way to tell a Bottlegger from a citizen in kansas[:] the bootlegger will be sober,

As I readthe news today I see where Sectry Baker[7] replied to Gov Allen[8] His reply was just as clear as the income tax blanks,

Baker says he is willing to~~m~~ have an investigation but that Gov Allen ca cant expect his investigation to take preference over all the others ahead of it,

If Mr Baker stays in to see all these investigations[9] through he will hold office as long as Unc e Jojo, [Uncle Joe] Cannon[10]

In the words of the M▼o▼vie Director the Gov has called for a retake,

The Gov claims when the 35th went into action the artillery that should have backed them up claimed exemption,

He claims they had plenty of aeroplanes there but they all belonged to the Germans,

He says the only barrage our Dough boys had was laid down by the Krupps[11]

While the boys were fighting the officers in the rear were debating " Resolved that west Point turns out better Shimmie dancers[12] than Plattsburg

The Gov says the whole thing was aframe up   It was aPrairie Division and they made them fight in a Forrest,

He says they made a mistake by removing the National Guard Officers as the men were used to them,[13] That speaks pretty well for them as most officers are hard to get used too,

Gov says he will see this thing through if he has to be elected Gov of Kansas again to do it,

Congressman Anthony[14] of Leavenworth ▲(father of the Susan B Anthony amendment)[15]▲ went to France and looked it all over   His report was, ~~It~~ " I think it was but I wont be sure"   now he says he was missquoted and what he said was" " I feel definite that they were"   I claim if you are going to investigate the 35th not being properly supported in the Argoynne, That you should go further and investigate why the Democrats were not properly supported in November,

Will Rogers.

P S   Wallace Read[16] is on this train   still got on his dress suit,

I fell [feel] more encouraged in my new endeavour as the Porter just told me this was the same train Mary Pickford went out on her first trip, In fact everybody on this train is going to Cal to go in ghe [the] movies   Its the Movie Special, The Porters will tell you they are not black   they are only made up for a part,

The Dining car serves for Breakfast what they call a Close Up, I had a Fade out steak for Dinner, They have a feature Dinner consisting of 5 reels, I

wrote on my chech for bottle of beer , The Dining car conductor who used
to be a director said mark that check N,*G*,

    There is a Carona Typewriter in every birth writing Scenarios,

TLS, rc.[17] Kansas City Star Article, OkClaW. Handwritten, in Rogers's hand, in top margin: "on
Board Cal Limited try▼ing▼ to get out of Kansas". The reverse side bears the carbon image of
the text caused by Rogers's failure to properly insert the carbon sheet. Handwritten on reverse
side, in Rogers's hand, top margin: "could have turned the carbon Paper the other way but—
Never thought of that."

1. See Interview in *Kansas City Star*, 11 March 1919, above.
2. *KCS*, 20 September 1956.
3. Since its inaugural run in 1896, the California Limited had offered three-day
deluxe service from Chicago to Los Angeles. A part of the Santa Fe railroad system, it
became a popular train in the early 1900s for motion picture stars and others bound
for the West Coast (Bryant, *History*, 328).
4. Garnett, "Will Rogers."
5. Rogers was the special guest at the dedication in Kansas City of an elegant,
new cinema theater, the Newman. He entertained the huge crowd with a few minutes
of gags (Garnett, "Will Rogers").
6. The Grand Theatre played host to the *Follies* during its week-long stop in
Kansas City in March 1919 (*KCS*, 10 March 1919).
7. Newton Diehl Baker (1871–1937), a former mayor of Cleveland, Ohio, served
as secretary of war from 1916 to 1921 (*DAB*, Supp. 2:17–19).
8. Henry Justin Allen (1868–1950), a newspaper publisher and Republican,
served as governor of Kansas from 1919 to 1923. Allen wired Baker on 18 May 1919
with charges that mismanagement by regular army officers had led to troops in the
35th Division, a National Guard unit from Missouri and Kansas, receiving the heavi-
est casualties among American forces in the battle in the Argonne forest in September
1918. Baker issued a lengthy reply on 5 June that essentially said an investigation was
pending. An eventual inquiry by the army cited "poor discipline, lack of leadership
and probably poor preparation" (*DAB*, Supp. 4:11–13; *NYT*, 20 May, 6 June 1919;
Farwell, *Over There*, 226–27).
9. During the war, Baker and the War Department faced more than fifty congressional investigations and special inquiries into questions of waste, fraud, incompe-
tence, and profiteering (Cramer, *Newton D. Baker*, 149–53).
10. Joseph Gurney Cannon (1836–1926) served in the U.S. House of Representatives from 1873 to 1891, 1893 to 1913, and 1915 until his retirement in 1923 at the
age of eighty-six. Popularly known as "Uncle Joe" for his folksy, sometimes coarse
manner, Cannon ruled the House as speaker for eight years until his overthrow in 1911
(*DAB*, 3:476–77).
11. The Krupp family's armament factories in Essen, Germany, supplied much of
the firepower for the German military during the war. The family patriarch, Gustav
Krupp von Bohlen und Halbach (1870–1950), was arrested for war crimes and served
time in prison (Batty, *House of Krupp*, 11, 12, 20).
12. The shimmy evolved from African-based dancing that involved much body
movement, often suggestively sexual. Mae West's "Shimmy Schwabble" in the musical
comedy *Sometime*, which opened on Broadway in October 1918, contributed to a
shimmy craze that swept the country at the time (*NOCM*, 2:1680; *EMT*, 2:1345).

13. U.S. Army procedures at the time called for regular army officers to replace their National Guard counterparts, regardless of their comparative level of competence. Poor leadership was blamed in the disaster that befell the 35th Division (Farwell, *Over There*, 227).

14. Daniel Read Anthony, Jr. (1870–1931), a newspaper editor in Leavenworth, Kans., served as a Republican in the U.S. House of Representatives from 1907 to 1929 (*BDUSCong*, 542).

15. The Nineteenth Amendment to the U.S. Constitution, providing the vote for women, was submitted to the states on 5 June 1919 for ratification. The dedication and work of Susan Brownell Anthony (1820–1906), a leading suffragist and women's rights advocate, had helped pave the way for the amendment. Congressman Anthony was a nephew of Susan Anthony (*NAW*, 1:51–57; *NYT*, 6 June 1919, 5 August 1931).

16. Wallace Reid (William Wallace Reid, 1891–1923) made his film debut in 1910 but did not achieve stardom until five years later with the release of *Birth of a Nation*. He thereafter starred in scores of films, becoming the motion picture industry's first matineé idol, often portraying the all-American hero (*IDFF*, 3:529–30; Slide, *Silent Players*, 250).

17. Dating of the item was determined from historical references in the document.

3. BACK TO BROADWAY
July 1919–December 1922

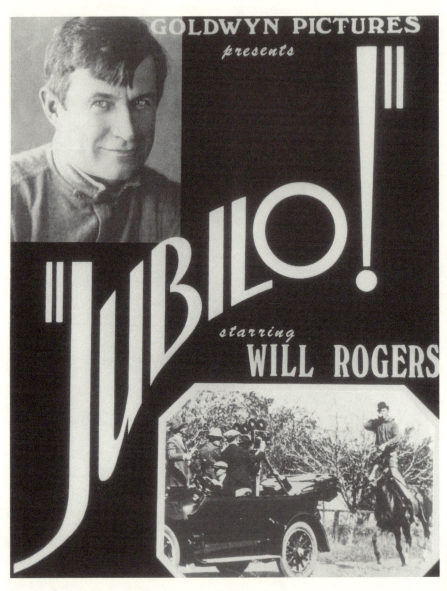

Poster for *Jubilo*. When Goldwyn Pictures thought about changing the title of Rogers's third film, he fired off a telegram of spirited protest. Goldwyn got the message. The movie was released in early December 1919 as *Jubilo*. (*OkClaW*)

HOLLYWOOD BY 1919 HAD BEGUN TO EMERGE AS THE MECCA OF MOVIES. IT already claimed many of the world's most famous motion picture personalities, and every day seemed to bring another trainload of cinema stars and hopefuls from the East. The town and its environs offered the allure of bright sunshine and bountiful flora, a boomtown pulse of a region tripling in population in ten years, an easy optimism of quick wealth. Indeed, when one of the film industry's newest discoveries, Will Rogers, headed west in June 1919 to start a full-time career as an actor in motion pictures, Los Angeles had already begun to live up to the nickname it would soon acquire, "City of Dreams."[1]

Rogers stepped from his first-class rail berth into the frenzy of southern California in early June. While his family spent the summer among Betty Blake Rogers's kin in Arkansas, Rogers immersed himself in work at the freshly opened Goldwyn studios in Culver City, a newly born town within a few miles of Hollywood that had been created expressly to serve the film industry. Beginning with *Almost a Husband,* which reached theaters in October, Rogers would star as the lead character in eleven feature-length motion pictures for the Goldwyn organization over the next two years. Only one, *Doubling for Romeo*—a favorite of Rogers's but not among film exhibitors—was intended as a comedy. Several delivered some humorous moments, but the Goldwyn people saw Rogers, probably rightly so, as best suited to portray the country-rube-turned-hero. Silent film did not allow him to showcase his full comedic talents—in particular, his verbal skills in conveying a gag. His screen presence, however—his characteristically easygoing demeanor, the head bowed in innocent embarrassment, the casual brushing back of his hat in studied interest, the quizzical scratch of the head, the wide-eyed look of earnest amazement—suited well the depiction of a man willing to do good and win the girl before the final fade-out.[2]

The constant pace of filmmaking failed to separate fully Rogers from his typewriter. As he was known to have done much later in his film career, he likely packed his trusty Corona to the set each day and pecked away at the keyboard between camera calls. His output continued to be impressive in its volume, although far from the production level he would reach years later. Apparently, not long after arriving in California, he completed the manuscript for his second book, *Rogers-isms: The Cowboy Philosopher on Prohibition*. Although four other proposed volumes in the same series seem to have quietly faded away, Rogers found on the West Coast other outlets for his writing talents through articles for newspapers and even for a trade publication of the film industry.[3] Understandably, much of his written humor during this period centered on the local scene, happenings on and off the set, the artificiality and reality of this new cinema world of which he was now a part.

He continued to produce film intertitles, often called subtitles, the on-screen text used in silent movies for explanation, transition, and dialogue. In the absence of his spoken humor, his words on the silent screen gave movie audiences their best opportunity to appreciate the full Rogers. Most of the intertitles he worked up on paper, but sometimes they occurred informally, as when a Goldwyn staff member would trail him on the set, jot down his asides and remarks, and then transfer them to film.[4] Evidence of his writing appeared early in his motion picture work, although he failed to receive on-screen credit. His second movie, *Almost a Husband*, featured several gags and one-liners that strongly suggest Rogers as contributor.[5] The studio listed him as title author in only one instance, *Doubling for Romeo*,[6] his twelfth film for Goldwyn.

In addition to his written contributions at Goldwyn, Rogers also began in the fall of 1919 to produce copy for his own series of film subtitles. Adapting much the same topical humor he used on stage, he created *The Illiterate Digest*, a title not by accident akin to *Literary Digest*, a leading magazine of the day.[7] He introduced the on-screen gags, usually just one-liners, at a Los Angeles cinema house in October and eventually succeeded in getting the series into general distribution. His use of the name *Illiterate Digest* prompted a threat of legal action by the attorney for the magazine, but Rogers in characteristic good humor turned it aside.[8] He continued to use the name for his subtitle series and would recycle it in later writings.

His work in films kept him busy, but it also afforded him time for a home life. The family rented a comfortable, roomy house on Van Ness Avenue in Los Angeles. It came complete with a swimming pool, which no doubt caught the attention of at least the three oldest children. Young Bill was approaching eight when the family arrived in California, Mary was six years old, and Jimmy had recently turned four. No space for horses was available at the house, but Goldwyn provided Rogers with a building on the studio lot in Culver City that was converted into a stable. There the kids could ride and Dad could practice his roping. Within a year, the family moved into a new house, their first as owners, in the still developing residential community of Beverly Hills. It, too, featured the ever-present southern California pool, but the lot was large enough to accommodate also a stable and a riding circuit for the horses. The move to Beverly Hills, however, was preceded by a tragedy in the Rogers family: in July 1920 little Freddie Rogers died of diphtheria just shy of his second birthday.[9]

Despite the grievous loss, the family settled comfortably into the lifestyle of southern California. When Goldwyn chose not to renew Rogers's contract in May 1921—due more to precarious studio finances than to the less-than-glowing box office returns of Rogers's films—Will could have returned to New York and the Ziegfeld stage, but he chose to remain. He decided to produce and star in his own films, each just a couple of reels long, known in the trade as "shorts." He gathered his resources, hired a director and small crew, wrote and acquired scripts, and produced his first movie, *The Ropin' Fool.* More a clever demonstration of Rogers's unique skills as a rope-meister than a story on film, the two-reeler made a brief appearance on screen in November 1921 before being shelved for a year until Rogers found a distributor willing to take it national.[10]

Rogers underwrote and produced three films, but the lack of a distributor and the need to recoup his investments forced him to shut down the short-lived Will Rogers Productions and return to New York to replenish his finances. Once there, he seized every opportunity to lasso a dollar. He performed on stage for the Shubert organization, started a long run in Ziegfeld's *Midnight Frolic* on the roof of the New Amsterdam, made personal appearances in movie houses, toured several cities in a road production called the *Ziegfeld Frolic,* delivered after-dinner speeches at almost every turn, became a headliner in the *Follies of 1922,* and even starred in another motion picture, his longest to date and one shot in New York. Somehow, he also found time to crank out material for publication, producing articles for newspapers in cities where the *Frolic* paused during its road tour and supplying gags to a major, nationally distributed humor magazine.[11]

Rogers's initial foray into film during this period was the prelude of far more to come. He had taken another turn in an ever-expanding career, and despite some unfortunate twists along the way, he had found it to his liking. In California he had also discovered a desirable environment for his family and his lifestyle, a place to sink some roots, a chance to build a future. Indeed, Betty and the children had remained behind when he returned to New York. That alone guaranteed that he would be back in California as quickly as circumstances allowed.

1. Starr, *Material Dreams,* 65–70; Berg, *Goldwyn,* 88–90.

2. *FWR*; *WRHolly*, 17–39; Yagoda, *Will Rogers*, 165–66.

3. See Advertisement by Will Rogers, ca. September 1919; Article by Will Rogers, ca. 1919; and Newspaper Article by Will Rogers, ca. Fall 1920, all below.

4. Yagoda, *Will Rogers*, 166.

5. Rogers, *Will Rogers*, 145; *Wid's Daily*, n.d., OkClaW; *NYT*, 13 October 1919. See also Draft of Intertitles for *Almost a Husband*, ca. 12 October 1919, below.

6. *WRHolly*, 37.

7. See Screen Subtitles for *The Illiterate Digest*, ca. 31 March 1920, below.

8. *WYB*, 1919–20, 156. For complete transcriptions of Rogers and Winslow's correspondence, see *ID*, 1–3; see also William Beverly Winslow to Will Rogers, 21 November 1921, OkClaW, 1975.22.0027.

9. Rogers, *Will Rogers*, 144, 147; Yagoda, *Will Rogers*, 171, 176.

10. Rogers, *Will Rogers*, 149–50; Yagoda, *Will Rogers*, 179–80; *WRHolly*, 46–48. See Notes for Premiere of *The Ropin' Fool*, ca. 7 November 1921, below.

11. Yagoda, *Will Rogers*, 187–88, 190–92. For example, see Newspaper Article by Will Rogers, ca. 11 February 1922; Notes for Banquet Speech, 16 December 1922; and Gags for *Life* Magazine, ca. November–December 1922, below.

Advertisement by Will Rogers
ca. September 1919
Hollywood, Calif.

Only a few months in California and with just one released movie to his credit, Rogers apparently decided to announce his presence by placing an advertisement in Wid's Year Book, *a huge source book of the film industry published by Wid Gunning.[1] Composed and presented in a style not unlike his other writings to date, Rogers's "contribution" to* Wid's *contrasted sharply, and perhaps effectively, with the hundreds of slickly produced ads of more obvious self-promotion. It was the first known published advertisement by Rogers.*

I have been asked to contribute (at so much a contrib) to Wid's Year Book. Being new in this business I didn't know who this bird (with that dehorned name) was and as for his Year Book, I didn't know they issued an almanac in the Moving Picture Business. He said in his letter that he was deserving and had done a lot for the business. Now before I jarred myself loose from any coin (as Goldwyn don't pay for this ad) I looked up this guy's references and found that he had done a lot for the business. He had told the truth about it and I found that his publication was as much sought after in the movie industry as the Police Gazette used to be in the Barber Shops.[2] He says his book is rehash of last year's pictures—personally I think the dead should be allowed to remain. President Wilson and I each have fourteen points. He took his to Paris where they not only saw his fourteen but raised him twelve more,[3] I brought my fourteen points to the coast. The first five and the principal of mine are a wife and four children in itself constitutes a novelty in this business, that is provided you still live with them.

Point number six: I heard there was a movement on to revive moving pictures.

Point number seven: Producers decided to make fewer and worse pictures. They may make fewer but they will never make worse.

Point number eight: I hold the distinction of being the ugliest man in pictures.

Point number nine: Caruso and I and Jesse Willard[4] were the last to go in.

Point number ten: Goldwyn figured by getting a good cast and good story, it would about offset the action of the star.

Point number eleven: I can't roll a cigaret with one hand and can't whip but one man at a time (and he must be littler than I am).

Point number twelve: I made a picture last year and some theatres bought it. So they figured if I made another one they could double the sale on this one. Get two to use it.

Point number thirteen: Moving pictures are the only way in the world that you can play a town and not have to worry about the hotels.

Point number fourteen: It's the only business where you can sit out front and applaud yourself.

WILL ROGERS.

P.S. If I don't last in the business till the next Year Book is issued I take this means now of wishing everybody Good Luck as I have certainly met some fine folks out here in the business. I love it and only hope I am able to string along with you even if its in the rear and Oh you know what I like, to forget the climate, isn't it dear? Turkey is the only other prohibition country in the world besides us. If we enjoyed a few of their privileges it wouldn't be so bad.

PD. Printed in *Wid's Year Book, 1919–1920*, ca. September 1919.[5] Photocopy, Wid's Year Book file, OkClaW.

1. F. C. (Wid) Gunning (1886–1963) was a publisher of trade periodicals about the film industry and a motion picture producer. *Wid's Daily* featured current news of the movie business and film reviews, while *Wid's Year Book* carried more than three hundred pages of news highlights in the industry, commentaries from major film figures, various listings of companies involved in motion picture production, and promotional advertising (*UDFT*, 109; *WYB, 1919–1920;AFIC*, F2CS:1431, F3CS:1130).

2. The *National Police Gazette* began publication in 1845 and by the end of the century was the leading magazine of sex, crime, and sports stories, especially prize-fighting. A mainstay in such male-dominated establishments as bars and barbershops, the *Gazette* had seen its circulation decline considerably by 1920 (Mott, *History*, 2:325–37).

3. President Wilson had outlined his Fourteen Points, a foundation for peace, in an address to Congress on 8 January 1918. He had insisted that the fourteenth, an association of nations to ensure the independence and integrity of all countries, be a crucial element of the peace negotiations in Paris. The covenant of the League of Nations was presented at the peace conference on 14 February 1919. It contained twenty-six articles and was incorporated into the Treaty of Versailles in April 1919 as Article I. The U.S. Senate, however, rejected the treaty in March 1920, in part because of opposition by some so-called irreconcilable senators to U.S. participation in the League (*EAH*, 310–11, 316; Walworth, *Wilson*, 120, 563–70; *USFWW*, 333, 336–37).

4. Jess Willard, a tall, powerful boxer from Kansas, gained the world heavyweight title in 1915. He lost it to Jack Dempsey in a bloody bout on 4 July 1919, only a few days after his first, and last, motion picture, *The Challenge of Chance*, had opened in New York (*BDASBask*, 476–77; *AFIC*, F1CS:217, F1FE:131).

5. Versions of the same article appeared in the *New York Times*, 11 January 1920; the *Houston Post*, 15 February 1920; the *Wichita Beacon*, ca. 28 February 1920; and possibly other newspapers (see *NYT*, 11 January 1920; Scrapbook 15, OkClaW; and Will Rogers, Jr., Collection, OkClaW).

Telegram to Samuel Goldwyn
7 October 1919
[Los Angeles, Calif.?]

OCTOBER 7 1919

SAMUEL GOLDWYN

469 FIFTH AVENUE

NEW YORK CITY NY

THOUGHT I WAS SUPPOSED TO BE A COMEDIAN BUT WHEN YOU SUGGEST CHANGING THE TITLE OF JUBILO[1] YOU ARE FUNNIER THAN I EVER WAS. SUPPOSE THE SAME JURY SUGGESTED ARE THE ONES SUGGESTED SELLING OVERLAND RED[2] THE BEST STORY WE HAD. I DONT SEE HOW LORIMER OF THE POST[3] EVER LET IT BE PUBLISHED UNDER THAT TITLE.[4] THAT SONG[5] IS BETTER KNOWN THROUGH THE SOUTH AND BY OLDER PEOPLE THAN GERALDINE FARRAR'S HUSBAND.[6] WE HAVE USED IT ALL THROUGH BUSINESS IN THE PICTURE BUT OF COURSE WE CAN CHANGE THAT TO EVERYBODY SHIMMIE NOW. SUPPOSED IF YOU PRODUCED THE MIRACLE MAN[7] YOU WOULD HAVE CALLED IT A QUEER OLD GUY. BUT IF YOU REALLY WANT A TITLE FOR THIS SECOND PICTURE I WOULD SUGGEST JUBILO. ALSO THE FOLLOWING:

A POOR BUT HONEST TRAMP

HE LIES BUT HE DONT MEAN IT

A FARMERS VIRTIOUS DAUGHTER

THE GREAT TRAIN ROBBERY[8] MYSTERY

A SPOTTED HORSE BUT HE IS ONLY PAINTED

THE HUNGRY TRAMP'S REVENGE

THE VAGABOND WITH A HEART AS BIG AS HIS APPETITE

HE LOSES IN THE FIRST REEL BUT WINS IN THE LAST

THE OLD MAN LEFT BUT THE TRAMP PROTECTED HER

WHAT WOULD YOU HAVE CALLED THE BIRTH OF A NATION[9]

WILL ROGERS

TG, rc. OkClaW, 1975.13.0001. On Western Union Telegram Co. letterhead.

1. Rogers's third motion picture was released by the Goldwyn Pictures Corporation on 7 December 1919. Rogers, cast as Jubilo, a homely tramp, witnesses a train robbery and then ends up at a ranch, where he discovers a plot by the same thieves to frame the ranch owner for the robbery. Jubilo helps thwart the scheme and convict the outlaws. In the end he wins the love of the rancher's daughter. Perhaps because of Rogers's enraged telegram, Goldwyn released the film under its original title, *Jubilo* (*FWR*; *AFIC*, F1FE:478).

2. The novel *Overland Red*, written by Henry Herbert Knibbs and published in 1914, concerned the misadventures of a tramp prospector in the goldfields of California. A motion picture version by Universal Film was released in March 1920 (*AFIC*, F1FE:692).

3. George Horace Lorimer (1867–1937) became editor-in-chief of the *Saturday Evening Post* in 1899. He guided the editorial direction of the popular, general-interest magazine until his retirement in 1936 (*DAB*, Supp. 2:393–94).

4. The film *Jubilo* was based on Ben Ames Williams's story of the same name, which was serialized in three parts in the *Saturday Evening Post* in 1919 (see *SEP*, 28 June, 5, 12 July 1919).

5. Williams's story concerned the adventures of a hobo whose nickname comes from his frequent singing of a southern folk tune of the Civil War era, "Jubilo." The song and the story line became so identified with Rogers that he starred in another adaptation, *Too Busy to Work*, years later, after the introduction of talkies (Arnold, *Folksongs*, 11; *AFIC*, F1FE:478; Yagoda, *Will Rogers*, 167–68).

6. Lou Tellegen (Isidor Van Dameler, 1881–1934), Dutch-born actor considered one of the handsomest stage and screen actors of his day, married Geraldine Farrar, star of opera and of Goldwyn films, in 1916. Tellegen signed a film contract with Goldwyn in May 1919 to co-star with his wife (*FE*, 1337; Berg, *Goldwyn*, 90; Beardsley, *Hollywood's Master*, 61; *WYB, 1919–1920*).

7. *The Miracle Man* was based on a novel and a play of the same title, both dating from 1914. The acclaimed feature-length motion picture premiered in New York on 11 August 1919 (*AFIC*, F1FE:614).

8. *The Great Train Robbery*, released in 1903, was one of the first films to feature a story line, thus ensuring its significance in the history of motion pictures. It attracted a wide following among viewers worldwide (*IDFF*, 1:363–64).

9. *The Birth of a Nation*, directed by film pioneer D. W. Griffith and released in 1915, was the longest, costliest, and most profitable motion picture of its day. An epic about the American Civil War from a southern perspective, it became one of the industry's best known and most controversial films (*DAB*, Supp. 4:350; *IDFF*, 2:231).

Draft of Intertitles for *Almost a Husband*
ca. 12 October 1919
[Culver City, Calif.?]

Almost a Husband *set the tone for the type of motion picture that Goldwyn produced for Rogers: the rube melodrama.*[1] *Although* Almost a Husband *and Rogers's other films at Goldwyn featured some humorously acted scenes, most of the fun came through the intertitles, the on-screen text also known as subtitles. Goldwyn allowed Rogers to write or help create them, but he did not always receive on-screen credit for his work. The following draft for* Almost a Husband *gives evidence of the contributions that Rogers made to the production of intertitles for his movies.*[2]

1. "ALMOST A PICTURE"   cut out from "ALMOST A HUSBAND" (almost a picture)

2. Entire production of this masterpiece under the sole supervision of William Rogers, assisted by Walter Futter.[3]

3. This picture will set moving pictures back five years.

4. Originally(before Goldwyn got ahold of it) it was a very good story by Opie Read.[4]

5. Misdirected by CLARENCE BADGER[5]

6. Spoiled, as usual, in continuity by BOB HILL.[6]

7. Art titles by "BULL" MONTANA[7]

8. Photographed in broken inglish by MARCEL LE PICARD[8] with a Brownie number 2 Camera.

9. Most pictures are passed by the [*obliterated*] Censor Board[9] -- here is the gang of yeggs[10] this picture couldn't get by ---

10. ABRAHAM LEHR:[11] Foreman of the jury:
    "MAKE GOOD PICTURES BUT DON'T USE SO MUCH FILM"

11. J.G. HAWKS:--[12]
    ["]PUT IN THE RUN ON THE BANK-- IT'S ALWAYS BEEN GOOD, SO WHY QUIT USING IT."

12. TOMMY BUCHANAN;-[13]
    Author if [of]   "THE WORLD AND IT'S WOMEN"[14]

13. LOUIS SHERWIN,[15] number four on the jury: --
    (who sees that none of Roger's gags get into the titles)

14. JACK DENNIS;-[16]
    The more you cut out the less you have to fit in.

15. The part of Sam Lyman is taken by that dignified, legitimate actor, WILL ROGERS.

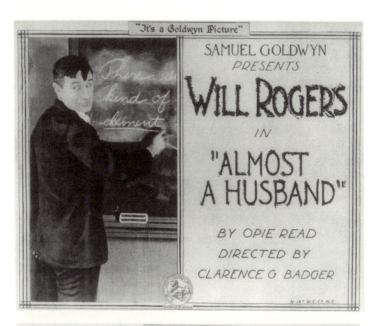

Lobby cards for *Almost a Husband* (1919). In his second film, the first to be produced in California, Rogers played a teacher in a small southern town (*top*). In a scene from the film, Clara Horton watches as Rogers passes a sack to Cullen Landis (*bottom*). (*OkClaW,* top; *Gordon Kuntz Private Collection,* bottom)

16. The star in repose.

17. The landing of the Mississippi River steamboat at Sacramento, Cal.

18. The school trustees of Old Ebenezar have come to welcome the new school teacher from Vermont.

19. "I'M Jasper Staggs.[17] We're here to make you welcome. I got a room fixed up at my house -- three dollars a week."

20. "You didn't have to fix it much for three dollars ."

21. <u>"</u> Most pictures use hundreds of feet of film showing you coming and going. We just show you three.

22. "They must think I'm Jack Dempsey."[18]

23. SCENE MISSING --(a good one)

24. "You're all wrong audience. He only wanted to see his mother."

25. "He hit me."

26. "Sure, if he three [threw] at you, he hit you."

27. "I'm going to let you go -- a man should never strike a woman he's not married to."

28. Shows how quick mail can be delivered when Mr. Burleson has nothing to do with it.

29. NOTE INSERT:

> Goodbye Jane:[19]
> I can't stand to see your love for another. I'm going to kill Sam Lyman with a baseball bat and drown myself,
>
> Jerry,[20]

30. WHo's going to kill you and drown himself."

31. "If he's going to do both, tell him to drown himself first."

32. Grabbing the bat gives me excuse for the baseball game.

33. "How's the score?"

34. "Eighteen to nothing."

35. "Who's favor?"

36. "Theirs."

37. "They're kinda hangin' one on you, ain't they."

38. "No, we haven't been to bat, *yet.*"

39. SCENE MISSING (not so good)

40. Story starts. Enter villians. Two of them. McElwin, the banker,[21] and Zeb Sawyer, the mule trader.[22]

41. Plot of story. Mules wants banker's daughter[23] or he'll draw out his money.

42. We put this in just to show you that we can take pictures moving.

43. Since last reel I have been made a lawyer. You can do it that quick in pictures.

44. I overhear the girl say she don't wish to crave the mule person for a husband.

45. Griffith[24] made his rep. with human touches. Here is the greatest human touch there is.

46. I try to touch the old gur [guy] for 500 berries.

47. "That old ~~gu~~ crab is so stingy he wouldn't perspire in hell."

48. We hold a mock marriage which turns out to be on the level account the minister having just been ordained.

49. "We can be divorced by a petition signed by a notary, or by my staying out of the state for a year."

50. We put this in to add class.

51. To get sympathy from the audience, I give poor child a nickel. It's in every film but never in real life.

52. "Good morning, gentlemen."

53. "You too, papa."

54. "Take your papers. I won't sign for two more reels."

55. "It looks like a Goldwyn stockholder's meeting."

56. Through the banker's influence I am canned as teacher. From now on the children can grow up in ignorance.

57. Wednesday morning.

58. The two villians plotting. Looks bad for the star.

59. Thursday noon.

60. In the original picture here's where I received a check for $10,000 for a story I had written. If I had a story worth $10,000 I would have used it instead of "Almost a Husband".

61. In same mail I also receive these cheerful tidings.

62. INSERT--

~~Y~~OU BETTER GET OUT OF TOWN WITHIN THE NEXT TWENTY-FOUR HOURS OR LOOK OUT.

63. To show you I am not a real movie-hero I couldn't whip all of them.

64. If more stars were horse-whipped, moving pictures would be better--

65. Lets get a gag for the Madge Kennedy stuff in here)

66. I pull a Houdini and get lose~~:~~ [loose] and for the sake of two more reels I'm still in town.

67. "I heard what they did to you last night and to show you I'm a fighting juvenile I'll go and get them."

68. "You've got to force her to make him sign or I'll start a run on your bank."

69. No use introducing the mob. You know them. They're are the same one who appeared in every picture.

70. Gotta give Zeb credit. His run looks like the Goldwyn pay window on Saturday night.

71. Oh, yes. I forgot to tell you I have also been made a printer.

72. I grab a motorboat, go to another town and get my draft cashed.

73. "Sam sent this money - - and I forgot to make-up my neck."

74. "Here's enough money to pay off every extra on the set."

75. They three [threw] him in shallow water and he swam out to deep water so I could rescue him.

76. One hour later I found a high bank to jump off. In the meantime he had dressed and gone home.

77. You can't tell‡ which one is doing the saving.

78. "I'm sorry ,Sam. Forgive me."

79. "Good thing it's summer or I would never have jumped in after you."

80. Give the old villian a hand -- it's the last time you will see him.

81. Different morning -- same week.

82. Director has picked out a pretty spot.-- it must be nearing the end.

83. How did I know the girl was here? Director told me. He KNOWS EVERYTHING.

84. "This is the end of a terrible picture."

85. Ought to have a gag for Tom Moore in kissing   scene.

TD. OkClaW, 1975.28.0019. Typewritten, top margin, center, page one: "TEMPORARY TITLES OF "ALMOST A PICTURE."

1. *Almost a Husband,* Rogers's second picture and the first under his contract with Goldwyn, had its premiere at the Strand Theatre in New York on 12 October 1919. In it, Rogers portrayed a country schoolteacher, Sam Lyman, who marries his secret love as part of a parlor game, then must overcome the dastardly attempts of the evil Zeb and the girl's father, a banker, to drive poor Sam from town. Zeb's misdeeds include an attempted run on the father's bank. In the end Sam prevails, and the almost husband becomes a real husband (*FWR*; *Variety,* 17 October 1919).

2. No one received on-screen credit for the intertitles in *Almost a Husband,* but one reviewer noted, "For once, spectators also enjoy some of the subtitles flashed on the screen, which are surely from Rogers himself" (*WD,* undated, OkClaW; *NYT,* 13 October 1919). See also Notes for Motion Picture Intertitles, ca. February 1919, above.

3. Walter A. Futter (1900–1958) started in motion pictures as an editor. He later wrote and produced films (*NYT,* 5 March 1958; *UDFT,* 93; *NYTFR,* 4285).

4. Opie Percival Read (1852–1939) was a newspaper editor, founder of the humorous weekly *Arkansaw Traveler*, and prolific writer of novels and stories. His fictional work *Old Ebenezer*, published in 1897, formed the basis for *Almost a Husband* and was typical of his tales of life in the southern backwoods (*DAB*, Supp. 2:549–50; *SWBD*, 374; *UDFT*, 218; *TCA*, 1153–54).

5. Clarence Badger (1880–1964) was a veteran film scenarist and director of two-reel comedies. He joined the Goldwyn organization in 1918 as a contract director and eventually was assigned to *Almost a Husband*. Rogers became so enamored with Badger that he insisted on always working with him. Badger directed Rogers in fourteen films (*FE*, 23; *FWR*).

6. Robert F. Hill (1886–1966), a screenwriter and director, was credited with adapting Ben Ames Williams's "Jubilo" for the screen. He also may have contributed to the continuity of *Almost a Husband*, although no such credit appeared on film (*FE*, 626–27; *MPN*, 20 December 1919).

7. Bull Montana (1887–1950), an Italian-born actor and former professional wrestler, appeared in several motion pictures and silent serials between 1919 and 1929. He was not listed in the credits of *Almost a Husband* (*NYTFR*, 4565; *UDSSEP*, 388).

8. Marcel A. Le Picard was a cinematographer from France who had worked in the United States since at least 1913. Le Picard and Norbert F. Brodine were listed variously as cameramen for *Almost a Husband*. Le Picard also contributed photography on all subsequent Rogers films at the Goldwyn studios in California (*UDFT*, 158; *AFS*, 127; *FWR*).

9. The National Board of Censorship of Motion Pictures, a citizens' body, was established in 1909 with the encouragement of motion picture exhibitors interested in avoiding official censorship of the films they screened. The Board of Censorship, which became the National Board of Review of Motion Pictures in 1916, issued a seal of approval, but the development of local censorship bodies lessened the value of the national sanction. Filmmakers paid the agency a fee per reel for each film submitted for approval (*NHD*, 140; Mitchell, "Ties," 1).

10. *Yeggs*, a slang term, generally referred to petty criminals (*DSUE*, 1360).

11. Abe Lehr (Abram or Abraham Lehr, 1880–1952), a pal of Sam Goldwyn since their teenage years, joined his friend's film corporation in 1917 as vice president of studio production. He remained with Goldwyn Pictures Corporation for nineteen years (*UDFT*, 156; Berg, *Goldwyn*, 18, 73, 286; *NYT*, 25 August 1936).

12. John G. (Jack) Hawks (or Hawkes, 1875–1940), head of the writing department at Goldwyn studios, contributed to the scenarios for several films between 1914 and 1929. He did not receive credit for work on *Almost a Husband* (*VO*, 17 April 1940; *UDFT*, 117; *AFIC*, F1CS:103, F1FE:16, F2CS:1145; Easton, *Search*, 53).

13. Thompson Buchanan (1877–1937), a newspaper drama critic in New York, began writing for the stage in the early 1900s and for motion pictures in 1916. He was credited with adaptation work on *Jes' Call Me Jim*, Rogers's sixth film (*OCAT*, 109; *AFIC*, F1CS:43; *FWR*).

14. Buchanan wrote the story for the film *The World and Its Woman*, a Goldwyn feature that starred Geraldine Farrar and Lou Tellegen and opened in Philadelphia on 1 September 1919 (*AFIC*, F1FE:1069).

15. Louis Sherwin began writing film scenarios in 1918 for Select Pictures Corporation and appeared in one movie for the same company. He later worked briefly as a scenarist for Goldwyn (*AFIC*, F1CS:188, F1FE:62, 392).

16. Jack Dennis worked as a motion picture film editor from about 1924 to 1941 (*AFIC*, F2CS:1054, F3CS:196).

17. Gus Saville (1856–1934), a veteran character actor often seen in western films, played the part of Jasper Stagg in *Almost a Husband* (*WWHolly*, 2:1502; *UDSSEP*, 487; *FWR*).

18. Jack Dempsey (William Harrison Dempsey, 1895–1983), a former itinerant boxer from the mining camps of Colorado, gained the coveted world heavyweight title in July 1919 by soundly thrashing the reigning champion, Jess Willard, in three rounds (*BDASBask*, 373–74).

19. Clara Horton (b. 1904), who appeared in the minor role of Jane in *Almost a Husband*, had acted in motion pictures as early as 1914 and was still active in films in 1923 (*FWR*; *TYS*, 177; *Film*, 135).

20. Cullen Landis (1895–1975) started working in pictures in 1917 as a director and starred as a leading man in several silent films before his retirement in 1929. Jerry in *Almost a Husband* was one of his first movie roles (*FE*, 781; *FWR*).

21. Herbert Standing (Herbert Standing, Jr., 1884–1955), English-born actor of stage and screen, played the part of the banker, McElwyn (*WhScreen*, 676; *VO*, 28 September 1955; *FWR*).

22. Ed Brady (Edward J. Brady, 1889–1942), who played the main villain, Zeb Sawyer, in *Almost a Husband*, often appeared as a character actor in western and action pictures during his twenty-five-year film career (*TYS*, 59; *VO*, 8 April 1942; *FWR*).

23. Peggy Wood (Margaret Wood, 1892–1978) started in show business in 1910 as a chorus girl in New York and by 1917 had established herself as a musical comedy star. Her co-starring role as Rogers's romantic interest, Eva, in *Almost a Husband*, marked her first work in films, after which she returned to the stage (*NWAT*, 928–32; *FWR*).

24. David Wark Griffith (1875–1948) made his entry into motion pictures in 1907 as an actor and scenarist. He directed his first film a year later and scored his earliest acclaim with *The Birth of a Nation* in 1915. He became one of the most important and innovative directors in the early years of American movies (*DAB*, Supp. 4:348–51).

Article by Will Rogers
ca. 1919
[New York, N.Y.?]

Rogers's "voice" reached the public in myriad ways. One of the more unusual instances occurred via the pages of a California automobile dealer's in-house publication. The following article, a reprint of Rogers's story of his automotive trials and tribulations, suggests that others found his humor relevant and repeatable regardless of the origin. It also tells us something about his taste in cars.

WILL ROGERS BRINGS FORTH
REASONS HE LIKES CADILLAC

One of the interesting house publications by a motor car firm is the "Don Lee Spirit," published in the interest of Cadillac owners and the Don Lee organization in California. The feature story last issue was an article by Will Rogers, the rope-swinging monologist, who is in California in pictures.

The following is part of Rogers' article:

"When I bought a Cadillac from these birds[1] I thought I was through, but now I find that owning a Cadillac is a serious business. You have to write them articles and have your picture taken, and the deuce knows what else. Guess they want me to tell how I like the car. They are pretty safe there, 'cause I have had it only three days and what else could I say but good? I will be here a year and maybe I will write again, who knows?

"Then they want to know why I bought a Cadillac. Well, if they got to know I will tell them.

"Up to the time I came out here I made my living by telling jokes on the stage, and some of the best jokes I ever told I thought of while riding in a Cadillac. Bet that's an argument no salesman ever thought of before.

"When I got out here I also heard that Miss Geraldine Farrar had bought one and as I sang a song in the 'Follies' last year I thought that us singers kind-a oughter hang together, for what is good enough for Geraldine and Lou is good enough for me.

"I also understand that when you want to soak one, or sell it a Cadillac will bring you more than any other car, and at the price they charge moving picture people for everything out here I may not have it long.

"Now, the reason I got a closed car is because in an open car I had a lot of trouble losing some of my children. I could never seem to arrive with the same number I started out with. With this roof, and doors, with locks I don't have to count the children when they come out.

"I hope that I have better luck with this car than I did with a certain brand of hayburner I had in New York. Just before I was coming away I sold it but had not delivered it. Now it happens that this car was insured for twice as much as I had sold it for and when someone stole it from in front of the theater I figured I was in luck again. I was feeling pretty good over having my car stolen when darn if the police didn't find it. There ought to be a law passed making a man keep what he steals; that is the only way to stop automobile thievery.

"W. C. Fields, the comedy juggler and comedian of the 'Follies' for the four years we were together,[2] made all his jumps from city to city in a Cadillac and always beat our special train to its destination. But I guess after all that isn't much of a boost when you consider how some of the trains have been running.

"You might notify the Chamber of Commerce of Los Angeles that now is the time to take the census.[3] I took Mrs. Rogers, four children and four horses to Southern California."

PD.[4] Unidentified clipping, ca. 1919. Scrapbook 20, OkClaW.

1. An invoice and a credit statement from Don Lee Motor Cars for automobile parts and repair costs were found in the Rogers files at the Will Rogers Memorial. They date from June 1919 and indicate that the company had offices throughout California (statements, Don Lee Cadillac, 17 June and 30 June 1919, Income Tax Returns, Folder 16, OkClaW). Rogers's income tax return for 1919 included a $1,500 deduction for a new $6,000 car, which Rogers had claimed as a business expense "to transport him to and from locations" in his motion picture work. As his personal secretary explained to the Internal Revenue Service during an audit inquiry several years later, "The studios do not furnish him with an aut[o]mobile, but demand that he have one to expedite the travelling" (E. H. Hayden to The Commissioner of Internal Revenue, 3 March 1923, Income Tax Returns, Folder 16, OkClaW).

2. W. C. Fields (William Claude Fields, 1880–1946) began his entertainment career as a juggler, eventually becoming a vaudeville headliner in both the United States and Europe. He made his *Follies* debut in 1915, a year before Rogers, and appeared in the Ziegfeld productions through 1921 (*DAB*, Supp. 4:269–70; *FE*, 450–51).

3. Plans for the national census of 1920 were announced in the fall of 1919. The start date was set for 24 January 1920 (*NYT*, 30 December 1919).

4. The dating of the document was determined by historical references in the text.

Letter of Agreement with Marion H. Kohn
18 February 1920
[San Francisco, Calif.?]

February
Eighteen
Nineteen
Twenty

Mr. Will Rogers,
c/o Goldwyn Studios,
Culver City, California.
Dear Sir:

This is to confirm the agreement I have this day made with you; concerning furnishing by you of original gags for a period of ▶6◀ months, beginning with the first day of March, 1920.

You are to deliver to me at least fifteen original sayings or comments or witticisms, of the same general character as are now being exhibited at the California Theatre in the City of Los Angeles, California,[1] for every week of the term of this agreement, and you also agree to allow me to use at least one hundred feet of moving pictures of yourself in some of your characteristic attitudes, to acompany and illustrate these sayings, it being understood that these rights given to me are to be exclusive, and that I am to have the sole right to sell and exploit these sayings with such characteristics pictures of yourself throughout the world during the period of this contract.

I am to pay you for the above privileges the sum of Seven Hundred Fifty ($750.00) Dollars per week for each set of fifteen original sayings, and I agree to pay you the first six weeks in advance.

Said sayings are to be delivered to me, in care of Consolidated Film Company, 90 Golden Gate Avenue, San Francisco, California,[2] each week under this contract.

Yours very truly,

Marion H. Kohn

I hereby agree to the above arrangement, and to be bound thereby.

Will Rogers

We consent to the making of the above contract.

GOLDWYN PICTURES CORPORATION

by Samuel Goldwyn

Pres.

TLS, rc. OkClaW, 1975.26.0064. The interpolation was handwritten. The signatures of Rogers and Goldwyn were autographed on type-inserted lines.

1. Rogers produced a series of humorous subtitles in late 1919 for the California Theatre, a showcase movie house in Los Angeles that had recently undergone extensive renovations. After its reopening, it became the exclusive venue in the city for Goldwyn films, including *Almost a Husband.* The screen gags that Rogers provided the California followed the topical style of those he had written months earlier for Roxy Rothafel's Rialto and Rivoli Theatres in New York. Rothafel had since relocated to southern California, where he managed the California Theatre (Beardsley, *Hollywood's Master Showman,* 61; see Notes for Motion Picture Intertitles, ca. February 1919, above).

2. Marion H. Kohn apparently headed Marion H. Kohn Productions, Inc. The Consolidated Film Company may have been a subcontractor or another organization with which he was connected. By this agreement with Rogers and Goldwyn, Kohn acquired the rights to produce, market, and distribute a national edition of Rogers's screen gags. Both the local and national series bore the same title, *The Illiterate Digest,* a name borrowed in jest from *Literary Digest,* a popular magazine of the time ("Good Things Come in Small Packages," *Exhibitors Herald,* 24 April 1920, Scrapbook 20, OkClaW). Kohn's actual participation or role in *The Illiterate Digest* project remains unclear. Rogers later claimed that he produced, promoted, and marketed the series of films at a personal cost of several thousands of dollars (Miscellaneous Letters, OkClaW). See also Screen Subtitles for *The Illiterate Digest,* ca. 31 March 1920, below, and deposition by Will Rogers, 5 January 1924, OkClaW.

From Mortimer M. Newfield
4 March 1920
Chicago, Ill.

March 4, 1920.

Mr. Will Rogers,
c/o Goldwyn Studios,
Culver City, Cal.
Dear friend Will:

Enclosed herewith I beg to hand you your Income Tax Return for 1919. I assume that you have received the two telegrams which I sent you.[1] In your letter to me you said that I should let you know what the approximate tax would be and you surmised that it would "knock you loose from your appetite." You will have to fast a long time to save enough to pay the tax.[2]

Regarding the payment of the tax a very important change was made in the law last year. The taxes may be paid in four installments, the first with the return and the others on the 15th day of the third, sixth and ninth month after the time fixed by law for filing the return, which is March 15th. No discount is allowed for payment in advance. You will observe this gives you nine months in which to pay the total tax.

I am returning to you the copy of your schedule for 1918, and by comparing it with that of this year you will readily see how the tax was arrived at.

If I have omitted anything, please wire me and I shall make such corrections as you desire.

I am also enclosing herewith advertisement from a newspaper in a small town in Indiana.[3] It is self-explanatory.

I am incorporating a moving picture company for the purpose of starring Bill Fields in two-reel comedies.[4] We expect to make the first two pictures in New York, and if they get over we shall probably be neighbors of yours this fall. Bill said that you wrote him that when one gets out to Los Angeles, he never wants to go East again.

Your name is prominently billed in front of most of the theatres around 32d and Broadway. In front of one of the theatres you were billed as W. Rogers, - probably because of lack of space.

I hope that you will have continued success, and that I shall get to see you soon.

With kindest regards and best wishes, I am,

Faithfully yours,
Mort[5]

P. S. I am also enclosing two simple forms which you are supposed to fill out and file with your return if you paid any employe[e] of yours over $1,000, during the past year.

M.N.N. [*sic*]

Encls.

TLS, rc. OkClaW, Income Tax Return, 1921, Folder 16-B. On letterhead of Burkhalter and Newfield, Attorneys and Counselors, Edison Building, Chicago.

1. The two telegrams were not found in the collections at the Will Rogers Memorial.
2. According to Rogers's federal income tax return of 1919, he incurred a tax liability of $12,275.04, almost twice the amount for the previous year. Although the wartime tax rate was higher in 1918, Rogers's greater income in 1919—$85,000 combined from the Goldwyn and Ziegfeld organizations, less losses from his rental and agricultural properties—resulted in the larger amount owed. His tax return for 1919 did not escape the scrutiny of the Internal Revenue Service. An audit in 1922 that continued into 1923 questioned much of the $21,758 that Rogers claimed in business-related deductions (Individual Income Tax Return, 1919, OkClaW; Individual Income Tax Return, 1918, OkClaW; W. B. Swafford to Will Rogers, 13 March 1922, OkClaW; W. B. Swafford to Will Rogers, 9 June 1923, OkClaW).
3. The clipping of the advertisement was not filed with the letter.
4. Other than two one-reel films in 1915, the filmography for W. C. Fields begins with *Janice Meredith*, a feature-length movie released by Metro-Goldwyn in 1924. Mortimer M. Newfield and Fields collaborated on at least one comedy routine, "Just before the Battle Mother," a sketch probably written during the war and similar to known *Follies* skits that involved Fields (Gehring, *W. C. Fields*, 209; Louvish, *Man*, 218).
5. Mortimer M. Newfield's legal firm had prepared tax returns for Rogers since at least 1918 (see Burkhalter & Newfield to Will Rogers, 2 March 1918, OkClaW; and Mortimer M. Newfield to Will Rogers, 7 March 1919, OkClaW).

Screen Subtitles for The Illiterate Digest
ca. 31 March 1920
[Culver City, Calif.?]

Rogers wrote a series of gags that appeared on motion picture theater screens as The Illiterate Digest. *Initially produced for use at the California Theatre in Los Angeles as early as October 1919, Rogers's subtitles eventually received national circulation.[1] The following group may have been among the first set of gags that Rogers supplied to Marion H. Kohn Productions for general distribution.[2]*

1. Mr. Hearst got out an injunction to stop the Government from selling our ships.[3] Be a good joke on all these other papers if Hearst turned out to be an American.

2. In California they are making these Ouija Boards[4] of old Ukeleles. The knocking is an improvement over the music you used to get from them.

3. The Ouija has grown till it's the 4th largest industry in the U.S. Presidential Candidates come first, Fords second, Robberies and Murders third and Ouija fourth.

4. I really do believe you can commune with the departed, as I hear some man talked with Bryan the other day.

5. I got some departed friends I want to call up on the Board, but I am afraid to have Ouija tell me where they are.

6. The only thing that could equal the Pickford and Fairbanks marriage[5] would be for Charlie Chaplin to wed Theda Bara.[6]

7. Mary could have gotten her divorce[7] in Los Angeles, but she didn't want to stand in line to wait her turn.

8. Suppose Ben Turpin will be marrying as soon as he can see his way straight to do so.[8]

9. REMEMBER THE 18TH OR PROHIBITION AMENDMENT TO KEEP IT HOLY.[9]

10. Be good joke on Ireland if England said we will give you freedom just like America, including prohibition.

11. If I was England I would give Ireland Home Rule[10] and   reserve the Moving Picture Rights.

12. Guess France and Germany have their peace all signed up, I see where they have gone to fighting again.[11]

13. A Senator in Michigan was convicted for buying his seat in the Senate.[12] The law says you can buy your seat but you must not pay too much for it.

14. Ford could have been elected in the first place if he had only made one speech: "Voters, if I am elected I will change the front on them."

15. Hope the audience has horse-sense like you. They may as well stick it out 'cause they're goin' to get more of the same stuff here next week.

Illiterately yours,
WILL ROGERS.

TD.[13] OkClaW, Will Rogers, Jr., Collection, Illiterate Digest typescripts, Folder 9-M. Typewritten, top margin, center left, stacked (/): "NATIONAL EDITION / WILL ROGERS' # 2". Hand-inserted horizontal lines below numbers 1, 5, 8, 11, and 14 in the list. Hand-inserted "3" to left of numbers 1 through 6.

1. Rogers's choice of title, *The Illiterate Digest*, prompted a letter of complaint in November 1920 from William Beverly Winslow (ca. 1862–1944), an attorney for the *Literary Digest*, a prominent magazine at the time that was producing its own newsreel, *Topics of the Day*. Winslow claimed that "the prestige of 'The Literary Digest' is being lowered by the subject matter of your film as well as by the title of your film because the public naturally confuse the two subjects." He threatened legal action if Rogers failed to cease using the name, *The Illiterate Digest*. Rogers responded that he had quit writing for the screen six months earlier because the producers of the subtitles had

fallen behind in their remittances, in fact he noted, "After a few months of no payments I couldent think of a single joke." With typically deflating humor, Rogers told the lawyer to inform his client that its "most dangerous rival has withdrawn" (for complete transcriptions of Rogers and Winslow's correspondence see *ID*, 1–3; see also William Beverly Winslow to Will Rogers, 21 November 1921, OkClaW; *WYB, 1919–1920*, 156).

2. See Letter of Agreement with Marion H. Kohn, 18 February 1920, above.

3. Hearst, who was considered by some detractors a traitor because of his opposition to U.S. involvement in the war, brought suit on 13 February 1920 to enjoin the U.S. Shipping Board from selling seized German vessels to British interests. By the end of the fiscal year, the board had disposed of all German cargo ships and several passenger vessels (*NYT*, 14 February 1920; Nasaw, *Chief*, 268–71; Smith and Betters, *United States Shipping Board*, 42).

4. The Ouija board, a centuries-old folk device that was used to seek messages from the spirit world, grew in popularity in the United States in the early 1900s through the creative marketing efforts of its primary manufacturer. Sales soared during the war when Americans spent their extra time at home using the boards to communicate with their loved ones serving abroad (Hunt, *Ouija*, 4–5).

5. Pickford and Fairbanks, companions in public since the late 1910s, were married quietly in Los Angeles on 28 March 1920. They did not announce the marriage until three days later (Whitfield, *Pickford*, 199–200; *NYT*, 31 March 1920).

6. Theda Bara (Theodosia Burr Goodman, ca. 1885–1955) emerged from virtual obscurity to capture the public's imagination in 1914 with her title role performance in the film *The Vampire*. Portraying a succession of sultry, sexually assertive women, Bara saw her movie career peak three years later with a highly publicized, near-nude appearance in *Cleopatra*. She attempted a comeback in legitimate theater in March 1920, but rejection by critics and audiences prompted her to retire (*DAB*, Supp. 5:37–38; Genini, *Theda Bara*, 2).

7. Pickford had obtained a quiet, quick divorce in Nevada on 2 March from her first husband, Irish-born motion picture actor Owen Moore (1886–1939). They had starred together several times in the early years of her film career and had wedded secretly in 1911 (Whitfield, *Pickford*, 198; *FE*, 966).

8. Bernard (Ben) Turpin (1869–1940) became permanently cross-eyed early in his vaudeville years from the effect of balancing a playing card on his nose. He parlayed the handicap into a highly successful career as a slapstick comedian on stage and screen (*DAB*, Supp. 2:672; *UDSSEP*, 550; *FE*, 1370).

9. While the Eighteenth Amendment, ratified more than a year earlier, had prohibited the manufacture, sale, and distribution of alcohol, the passage of the Volstead Act on 27 October 1919 provided its enforcement guidelines and procedures. Prohibition brought about a cultural crisis in the United States. Illegal distillers, bootleggers, smugglers, and speakeasies flourished, and many ordinary individuals made creative and crude attempts at home brewing, distilling, and wine production that sometimes led to tragic results (Pegram, *Battling*, 150–52; *HD1920s*, 269–70).

10. A bill to provide home rule for both the substate of Ulster and the rest of Ireland was first read in the British House of Commons in late February 1920. Intended by the ruling cabinet to ensure the safety of a Protestant-dominant Ulster and to appease opinion abroad, the Government of Ireland bill met virulent opposition in Parliament and Ireland; nevertheless, it became law on 23 December 1920 (Curran, *Birth*, 27, 28, 29–30).

11. Prince Joachim of Prussia and several companions assaulted members of a French postwar military mission on 7 March 1920 in Berlin. When reports followed of

similar incidents in other parts of Germany, French army leaders threatened reprisals. German government officials soon moved to quell the disturbances (*NYT*, 8, 11–12, 18, 28 March 1920).

12. Truman Handy Newberry (1864–1945), a wealthy businessman and former U.S. secretary of the navy, defeated Henry Ford in November 1918 in a race for a Senate seat in Michigan. A year later, a federal grand jury indicted Newberry and others for violations involving campaign contributions and expenditures. He and sixteen aides were found guilty on 20 March 1920 (*DAB*, 549–50; *NYT*, 21 March 1920).

13. Dating of the document was determined by historical references in the text.

From Herbert T. McSpadden
18 August 1920
[Chelsea, Okla.?]

Will Rogers's nephew, Herb McSpadden, oversaw his uncle's ranch property and boyhood home near Oologah, Okla. He lived in nearby Chelsea and leased the Oologah farm and house to tenant operators. Several years later, he moved his family to the property and took charge as on-site manager. The following letter offers a picture of conditions at the ranch during the years of tenancy.

Aug 18 1920

Dear Uncle Willie

I guess its about time for me to make a little report and it is a little one this year. It was a little better than a failure though. I dont remember the exact number of bu. [bushels] threshed on your place but it is all over there in the granaries. All next to the river though is in corn and the corn is pretty good for a dry year. Alfalfa is about run out, I am going to have that put in some thing else next year as it doesnt pay what it ought to.

I have got some fellows from Arkansas on the place for next year. My natt is to[o] much of a stock man to make a good renter[1] so I would n't rent him the place again. I can't spend as much time over there as I ought too and just have to get things done the best I can and am not above making mistakes my self but am doing the best I can with it.

I am sending you a note for $1000. I put $84.*61* to your credit in the bank and my $120, com. [commission] makes the $1284.*61*   I should have done this sooner but neg lected it

I dont expect these farms ever will pay ag ain what the[y] have paid during these war prices, but I am holding your grain this year, partly because of the low price now and I could n't have gotten it hauled off   I had wanted it sold   Grain is always higher along in the winter though.

Saw one of yours & Jimmie's pictures[2] in Chelsea the other night. It was the first one I'd seen. It was great

Must close   Best regards to all.

Herb.

ALS, rc. OkClaW, 1975.24.0323.

1. According to Collings, Rogers began to take a keener interest in conditions of the Oologah property in late 1919. One of his first moves was to hire a tenant farmer, Austin Hart, who could capably operate the ranch (Collings, *Old Home Ranch*, 110). This letter, however, suggests that such changes may not have occurred by August 1920.

2. *Jes' Call Me Jim*, Will Rogers's sixth motion picture and the second in succession to include his son Jimmy, who had turned age five by the time of this writing, was released on 5 June 1920. Jimmy made his film debut in *The Strange Boarder*, which had opened a month earlier (*WRHolly*, 24–27).

Notes for a Debate
ca. 7 September 1920
[Los Angeles, Calif.]

Rogers was sometimes challenged to a congenial public debate. He prepared the following notes for what may have been the first such occasion, a good-natured measuring of cowboys and preachers.[1]

I want to apologise for my long shaggy hair and unkept personal appearance but I am right in the middle of a Picture and and am playing the part of a Preacher,[2]

Now I want it understood before we start in that I had nothing to do with this thing   this Preacher Guy (   ) started it, And I am glad to say that I have en enough christian spirit in me to assist the Church in any advertising scheme that I may be called on to assist, and anything that I am able to do or sayh here is entirely for the opposition as my clients the Cowboys have enough advertising wlready , In fact too much,

The Cowboys need no word of praise from me   they are already understood and honored and appreciated by the whole civilized world and this is the only instance in all the record of our great and glorious U S   of America where one   [o]f us has ever been called upon to defend our honored calling against any profession in the world , much less against the Preachers, and what makes it especially degrading and humiliating is that in this first case we are called to defend it against Preachers, Had it been against the Landlord or the

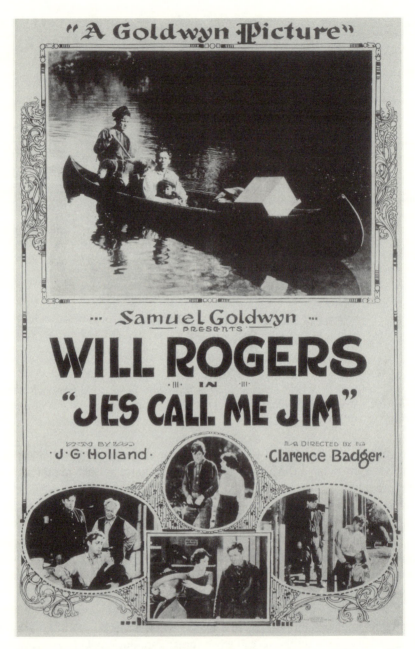

Rotogravure sheet for *Jes' Call Me Jim*. Goldwyn Pictures released the film, Rogers's sixth and the second for his son Jimmy, in late May 1920. Pictured in the canoe with Will and Jimmy Rogers is veteran character actor Raymond Hatton, the on-screen father of Jimmy's character, Harry. (*Gordon Kuntz Private Collection*)

or the groceryman the case might have at least been or the bootlegers fairly egual and then I would have to have had to produce some arguments for our foe would have been worthy of our mettle but as the case is now comparing a preacher to a cowboy is like comparing one of our present Presidential candidates to Roosvelt, William Jennings Bryan of [or?] Lincoln Dakota   But this defending themselvs is the first thing that a preacher has to l learn   Now I claim that any profession that you have to offer an excuse for existence is no profession , Nessity created the Cowboy   he is an essential, In the early days he was nessary to c[a]re for the herds and tend the Ox that people might be fed   in later years he has been called upon to do various things principally to double for the Star when there is an especially rough hill to run down, Where I ask you would your Bar room fights at the end of the each reel be if it wasent for the Cowboys,

I feel in meeting Dr Br[ougher]   that I am not meeting one of the ordinary or repres sentative preachers   I know that I am meeting the smartest man in his line in Americaincluding Beverly hills, He is the only preacher that ever knew enoug to ~~not~~not have a church but to preach in a Moving Picture Theatre,[3] And to show you how Foxy he is He leaves the Billing up there of the Picture that is playing there during the week

Dr, they took that from our Hon profession of Medical Drs of the U S of Ame and Rochester Minn, Was that a hiss I heard when isaid hon Drs   was that a Ki ropractic i heard hiss, The first thing a preacher does is to take advantage of his middle name

Now they are called Sheperds or men who tend their flocks, Now Gentlemen you know the Cowboys contemt for a lowly sheephered   A sheepherder is just two degrees lower than than an uninstructed deligate, to a presidential convention,

Republican party more dessention than ministers,

more preachers in the jails and in the U S senate than there are cowboys,

Statistics show thatere were fewer last year   why were they fewer   because they got to be trustys and then escaped,

two things in common[:] driving the Bulls and Preachers throw it,

Cowboys opened up this great country, what happened then   the Preachers come here from Iowa and closed it,

Bartenders missfortune to have this c[o]nvention come just two weeks after Pro[hibition?]

Churches are wonderful things cause there is where they hold the Sunday scho   The only disatvantage is what yo learn at the Sunday School will be contradi[cted] if you stay for church,

WhenI realized It was before Add men I knew that Any gramatical or his-torica mistakes that I may make would not be recognized by any one butmy opponent,

I doubbt if my side will get a fair showing here as i know that Advertising and preaching have much in common,

and Iwould advise myopponent that on account of the limited knowledge and ~~memory~~hom our listeners to not delve into history farther than the enactment of the 18th amendment

TD.[4] OkClaW, 1975.14.0077. Hand-inserted vertical marks appear in the left margin of several lines of the text.

1. Rogers faced Dr. James Whitcomb Brougher, Sr. (1870–1967), a Northern Baptist minister who served as pastor of Temple Church in Los Angeles from 1910 to 1926, in a lighthearted discussion of the comparative virtues of cowboys and preach-ers. The event was staged at the Advertising Club of Los Angeles on 7 September 1920. Earlier in the year, Brougher had presided at the wedding of Mary Pickford and Douglas Fairbanks (*WhAmer*, 5:89; Thompson, *Indiana Authors*, 48; Whitfield, *Pick-ford*, 199). He and Rogers met in a friendly debate on at least one other occasion (see Newspaper Article, ca. 9 December 1923, below).

2. Rogers may have referred to *Honest Hutch*, his eighth picture, which was released by Goldwyn in late September 1920. Rogers starred in the title role, which was not a minister, but rather a lazy, no-account social outcast who stumbles onto good fortune (*FWR*; *AFIC*, FEF1:419–20).

3. Brougher, of whom Rogers would later remark, "has proven that talking and not preaching is appreciated," held Sunday services at Auditorium Theatre, the largest cinema house in Los Angeles (*WA*, 1:154).

4. The date was determined from a newspaper columnist's contemporary account of the event (see clipping, unidentified newspaper, 8 September 1920, Scrapbook 18, OkClaW).

Newspaper Article by Will Rogers
ca. Fall 1920
[Los Angeles, Calif.?]

WHAT THE ACTOR IS DOING FOR
HUMANITY TOLD BY WILL ROGERS

By Will Rogers

Will Rogers, Goldwyn star, wrote the following articles [*sic*] for The One and Only, the book of original manuscripts by famous authors,[1] which is to be given to the holder of the lucky number at the benefit for the Actors' Fund in the Beverly Hills Speedway[2] today.

Along with all the class and Highbrow Everything must have a Common or jazz touch nowadays. So in this Masterpiece of Fiction I am jazz.

And that's only a start of what the Actor is doing to-day for Humanity.

Having been for years indirectly associated with Actors, I was given the subject, "What the Actor Is Doing for Humanity."

First, it is not generally known that I am an Author. In fact, the discussion finally reached my publishers (Harper & Bros.) and after looking over their sales they decided I was NOT.[3]

That only gives you a kinder rough Idea of what the Actor is doing for Humanity.

But the best Books are only read by their Writers.

There are Authors to-day cutting their mouths with my knives who will be forgotten when Rogers Silverware will be in our best Plated Houses.

That's only an inkling of what Actors are doing in the cause of Humanity. My Principal Contribution to Liter[ar]y Fame was a Novel entitled PROHIBITION. When I penned that Gem of Free Thought I naturally imagined that we were to have Prohibition. But as the Idea seems to have fallen through my VOLUME was a total loss. It was a case of a Man writing 5 years ahead of the Times.

And that's what the Actor has done for Humanity.

Of course if the Democrats are ever unfortunate enough to get in again[4] and decide to enforce Prohibition, Why then I will revive my Book and reap a harvest.

That's one of the things actors are doing to-day to uplift Humanity.

It was during the great Campaign to defeat Prohibition that I became acquainted with so many Eminent Authors.[5] Among the more Zealous workers in the cause were Rupert Hughes,[6] Governor Morris,[7] Mr. Knoblock,[8] LeRoy Scott,[9] Rex Beach,[10] George Ade[11] and Bull Montana. Also Miss Elinor Glynn,[12] who came all the way from England to help defeat the cause and keep true love on the Alcoholic Pedistal, where it had been for LO these many.

That's what Actors are doing for Humanity Daily.

Another Reason I am on good terms with these Garona [Carona?] Hounds is that I have never played in any of their Pictures. I was in one of Rex Beach's. But since then he casts them Himself. I wish I had time and space to tell you half the Actor is doing.

If you can show me any class that has done more for Humanity let's see you do it.

PD.[13] Unidentified clipping, ca. Fall 1920. Scrapbook 20, OkClaW.

1. Evidence of the publication of "The One and Only" could not be found.

2. The Beverly Hills Speedway, a mile-and-a-quarter wood oval near Beverly Drive and Wilshire Boulevard, attracted thousands of spectators in the early 1920s for automobile races that featured some of the most prominent drivers of the day. Increased demand for residential development led to demolition of the racetrack in 1924 (Basten, *Beverly Hills*, 56–61).

3. Rogers's first two books, *Rogersisms—The Cowboy Philosopher on the Peace Conference* and *Rogersisms—The Cowboy Philosopher on Prohibition*, both of which were collections of gags from his stage routines, were considered best sellers at the time. The earliest available sales figures, however, date from 31 December 1922, more than three years after the original publication of the books. The semiannual royalty statement from Harper & Brothers showed sales for the period totaled 490 copies of each title. Rogers netted $19.36 in royalties (*HD1920s*, 288; see Income Tax Returns, 1922 and 1923, OkClaW).

4. In the general election on 2 November 1920, the Democrats lost the presidency in a landslide of popular and electoral votes and the Republicans solidified their hold on Congress, eventually claiming 303 out of 435 seats in the House and 59 of 96 in the Senate (*HD1920s*, 105–6; Murray, *Harding Era*, 66).

5. Sam Goldwyn organized Eminent Authors in 1919 as a division of his film company. Hoping to increase the quality and profitability of his motion pictures, he assembled an impressive stable of popular novelists and short story writers and exploited their talents to produce movie scripts (*DAB*, Supp. 9:323; Easton, *Search*, 50–51).

6. Rupert Hughes (1872–1956), an editor and author, wrote plays, poetry, novels, short stories, and biographies. He turned several of his works of fiction into screenplays. His *The Old Nest* was the only movie script produced by a member of the Eminent Authors that proved successful at the box office (*DAB*, Supp. 6:108–10; Berg, *Goldwyn*, 92).

7. Gouverneur Morris (ca. 1876–1953), the namesake and great-grandson of a noted figure in the Federalist period, began his writing career as a student at Yale. A prolific author of novels and short stories, he was among the original Eminent Authors. One of Goldwyn Pictures' best efforts, *The Penalty*, was based on a story by Morris (*NYT*, 15 August 1953; Easton, *Search*, 50–51; *NHD*, 84).

8. Edward Knoblock (also Knoblauch, 1874–1945) wrote his first play in 1895 and produced at least one new work every year for the next forty years. Although born and educated in the United States, he spent most of his professional life in England and became a British citizen. He wrote his first film scenario in 1921 (*NYT*, 20 July 1945; *OCT*, 461; *AFIC*, F2CS:1195).

9. Leroy Scott (1875–1929) started his writing career in newspapers but also spent time in social work. After he returned to writing full time in 1904, he often focused on social reform as subject matter, producing several novels and short stories in a career that included a brief, undistinguished stint in Hollywood (*DAB*, 16:496–97; Berg, *Goldwyn*, 92).

10. Rex Beach, whose association with Goldwyn Pictures long preceded Eminent Authors, helped to select the writers for the highly publicized venture (Berg, *Goldwyn*, 91; Easton, *Search*, 51).

11. Ade was credited with stories, adaptations, and subtitles for five Famous Players–Lasky films in the 1920s (*AFIC*, F2CS:940).

12. Elinor Sutherland Glyn (1864–1943) published her first novel in 1900 in her native England. Noted for her glamour and good looks, Glyn captured wide attention with her romantically sensational novels and a lifestyle and personality to match. After the creation of Eminent Authors, a Goldwyn rival lured her to Hollywood. She arrived in the fall of 1920 and enjoyed several years as a successful screenwriter (*DNB*, Supp. 6:302-3; Glyn, *Elinor Glyn*, 273, 276).

13. Dating of the document was determined by historical references in the text.

Newspaper Article by Will Rogers
ca. June–December 1920
[New York, N.Y.?]

"Only Person I Saw Hit at the Fight
Was the Referee," Says Will Rogers

By Will Rogers.
American's Famous Humorist and Movie Star.

This scrap with the director of the duet was an unfortunate affair—unfortunate for the fellow who got hit.

Don't hit hard, fellows, or I'll have to tell Dr. Atticus Webb[1] about you.

I'd rather write up a Republican national convention than this fight. Old Boise Penrose at least kept things moving.[2]

Hoped they'd put a kick in the last reel, but instead they shook hands.

Ought to give the decision in this fight to the crowd. They worked harder than anybody else.

I don't see why they want to stop prizefighting in Dallas because it's rough and brutal. Looks like a parlor game to me. Were they playing tag?

To be continued in the next round. Is this a serial or something?

Seeing these ring fighters makes me remember we've got a bunch of fighters in Siberia.[3] We'd send after them, only no one in the War Department knows where the place is.

No wonder the fight went up in smoke.

Lots of fans out there—but they needed fans. I didn't have any.

Only person I saw hit at the fight was the referee.

I'm glad I wasn't the referee. If I'd been hit I'd go home.

These fellers aren't working. Now we have it tough in the movies, sometimes we don't get lunch till 12:15.

I'd rather write politics than fights. Of course, about the only difference is that political fights didn't last 12 rounds and Penrose did make things interesting.

Speaking of thrillers, this fight had nothing on a six-day bicycle race.[4]

Looked like the fight was going to get good when the fans jumped the ropes.

It seemed the four-legged stools were in danger of becoming bipeds.

This is a funny game where you knock a fellow down and pick him up again.

I read somewhere that Bill Brennan[5] does not want his wife to see him fight. I wouldn't either, cause I'd be [*text ends*]

PD.[6] Unidentified clipping,[7] ca. June–December 1920. Scrapbook 20, OkClaW.

1. Atticus Webb (b. ca. 1869), a former college president and an ardent prohibitionist, became head of the Anti-Saloon League in Texas in 1918 and served in that position until at least 1936 (*WhAmer*, 5:763; Barns, *Texas Writers*, 458).

2. Rogers reported on both the Republican and Democratic national conventions in June and July 1920 in a series of articles syndicated to newspapers. His film work and the death on 17 June of his youngest child, Fred Stone Rogers, prevented his presence at either venue. He wrote the articles in California and, in the instance of the Republican gathering in Chicago, pretended to be in Philadelphia picking the brain of Boies Penrose, one of the party's most powerful leaders in the Senate. Although seriously ill at the time, the Pennsylvania political boss kept in contact with the convention by telephone and telegraph wired into his bedroom (*CA*, 5–7). See *CA* for a full record of Rogers's political convention reports.

3. The United States and other Allied nations had dispatched naval and army units to Russia following the revolution in 1917, ostensibly to protect their countries' business interests but more to help Russian anti-Bolshevik forces and to contain Japan. With prospects of the latter having dimmed noticeably and public opinion rising against continued intervention, the United States evacuated its troops in northern Russia in July 1919 and then announced on 9 January 1920 that its military forces in Siberia would be withdrawn. The last American soldier departed Russian soil on 1 April 1920 (White, *Siberian Intervention*, 330, 331, 352, 354, 362; *USFWW*, 512–13).

4. Six-day bicycle races were popular indoor events, especially in New York, during the early decades of the 1900s. The first such two-man-team race at Madison Square Garden occurred in 1900, and a competition at the same venue in December 1920 drew record crowds and gate receipts. A local writer, however, questioned the peculiarity of the sport and of the people who would spend countless hours watching weary cyclists pedal around an oval (Riess, *Sports*, 174–75, 184, 189–90; *NYT*, 13 December 1920).

5. Bill Brennan (William Schenck, 1893–1924) began his professional boxing career in 1914 and had experienced mixed success by the time he challenged world heavyweight titleholder Jack Dempsey on 14 December 1920. The champion knocked out Brennan in the twelfth round in a closely contested fight that one reporter termed "vicious" (*WWBoxing*, 29; *NYT*, 15 December 1920).

6. Dating of the article was determined by historical references in the text.

7. The by-line identification suggests that the source of the clipping was the *New York American*.

From Lan Renny
23 May 1921
Dallas, Tex.

May 1921 found Rogers at one of those career-altering moments that he faced and overcame on several occasions. Financial difficulties at Goldwyn Pictures and in the film industry as a whole left him without a movie contract and without solid prospects of landing another.[1] Although the author of the following letter wished in ignorance that the Goldwyn-Rogers partnership would continue, it is more important

Poster for *The Ropin' Fool*. Self-produced by Rogers, the two-reel silent became a classic of lariat throwing and spinning. He filmed it in 1921, gave it an abbreviated release that November, and then had to wait a year before finding a distributor willing to take it national. (*OkClaW*)

that he expressed the same encouragement that Rogers probably heard from others and from himself: stay in Hollywood and stay in pictures.[2]

May 23, 1921.

Mr. Will Rogers,
Goldwyn Producing Company,
Culver City, Cal.
My dear Will:

I regret very much that my time was so taken up that I could not avail myself of the opportunity and visit with you in your home, as this is one of the pleasures I looked forward to on my trip to California. You know we troopers who have been riding rails for twenty years, a trip to California means nothing, but to meet a real, honest to God he-man like yourself means a lot. Then further, we showmen of the old school are getting few and far between; the last three years the theatre business has been over run with butchers, barbers, Jews and others, who have reaped the harvest of the inflated prosperity through our efforts, but we can all set back and come into our own from now on, as it is not a question now of unlocking the door, it is a question of showmanship to get deposits at the box office.

I do hope that you remain with the organization, as I told you, your pictures are being sought after by the small towns daily; it is only a question of putting you over in the big centers. I really believe that you would map out a tour of the larger towns, appearing in person and giving a few showman stunts, it would put you over to an extent that you would be a permanent fixture in the motion picture industry, for there is only one Will Rogers on the speaking stage and there would be only one Will Rogers on the silent screen. Men of your type and character are not made—they are born; there was only one David Mansfield,[3] there was only one Al Jolson[4] and there is only one Will Rogers.

The screen needs Will Rogers, and anything that I can do to help the screen keep Will Rogers, I will feel that I performed a great task if I could do it. If I can be of any service to you personally, please do not hesitate to ask.

Hoping that you and yours keep well and happy, believe me,

Sincerely your friend,
Lan Renny

TLS, rc. OkClaW, 1975.22.0024. On letterhead of Goldwyn Distributing Corporation, 1922 Main Street, Dallas, Texas.

1. Despite a significant infusion of cash from investors in late 1919, Goldwyn Pictures was in serious financial straits by May 1921. Sam Goldwyn had spent lavishly on

production, sunk considerable capital in questionable acquisitions, and watched major, expensive new films lose at the box office. The climax came when a recession swept the entire motion picture industry in late May and pushed Goldwyn and other film companies to the brink of bankruptcy. The company cut expenditures by 22 percent and either canceled major contracts or refused to renew them. Among the casualties was Rogers (Berg, *Goldwyn*, 94–95, 99, 101, 102–3; Yagoda, *Will Rogers*, 179).

2. Rogers could have returned to Broadway and the *Ziegfeld Follies*, where offers awaited him. Instead, he took the lead of other Hollywood actors, including his Beverly Hills neighbors, Douglas Fairbanks and Mary Pickford, and formed his own motion picture production company. To save costs, he employed only one star, himself, and shot two-reel shorts, rather than the five-reel features common at Goldwyn. He started production on his first small-scale effort, *The Ropin' Fool*, in the summer of 1921 (Yagoda, *Will Rogers*, 179; Rogers, *Will Rogers*, 149; *WRHolly*, 46).

3. The writer possibly referred to David Mansfield, an actor who was credited with only one motion picture role, a minor character in *The Last Chance*, a western melodrama released in 1921 (*AFIC*, F2CS:1245).

4. For Al Jolson see *PWR*, 3:144–45n.5.

From Charles F. Lummis
20 July 1921
Los Angeles, Calif.

California continued to offer opportunities for Will and Betty Blake Rogers to start and broaden friendships with an array of fascinating figures. They developed a warm relationship with Charles F. Lummis,[1] and as this letter reveals, through him they met John Burroughs[2] and other intellectuals, among whom they moved comfortably.

July
20
1921.

Dear Will and Betty:-

The bright idea of framing for you the "Miracle Picture" which I was lucky enough to get of the beloved old philosopher John Burroughs only six days before he died[3]—it occurred to me only after I was talking with you over the wire, and Will so generously consented to bring his Magic Rope down to tickle my four Infants,[4] whom I had together for the first time in fourteen years. I knew that it was his father-heart that made him appreciate how I was feeling at this reunion, and it just occurred to me then and there that perhaps he would like the picture of "Uncle John" who so greatly admired his magic at our "Noise," February 21, 1920,[5] and never tired of talking about it. And as it was a busy day, and my supply of glass was short, and I had a deuce of a time to cut a piece to fit the frame which Quimu gladly framed and burned for me—that I had no chance to finish the backing. It must have strips gummed over the cracks of the backing so the cursed little silver moths won't get in and eat up its face. So I will ask you to do that for its safety, and pardon my shortcoming.

And I send with this a sheet which I should have pasted on the back if I had had time for the finishing—perhaps you will also paste it there.[6]

I cannot tell you how deep in my heart I felt Will's generosity, which fascinated and astounded my four dear children, as well as everyone else present. And I could appreciate thoroughly that he was putting his whole heart into it for friendship—and I am sure he never did it more wonderfully. We shall all remember it always.

Quite aside from that, it was Good Medicine to see the two of you here again—but one of these days when you can find time, I want to hold you down while I deliver the Sermon that is burning in my noddle; and which I think I honestly ought to preach to you. And I am sure you know my friendship well enough to let me be absolutely honest and frank.

God bless you and your dear youngsters and all your interests.

With a great deal of love

Always Your Friend

Chas. F. Lummis–.

CFL:AM

[*handwritten in bottom margin, page two*:]*Also*, I want to make a portrait of Will, some foggy Day. He hasn't the picturesque Whiskers; but I know *exactly* the *crisis* in his face that I want to catch, *if* I can — just as I caught a crisis in J B's face when the Man was Right at Home.

TLS, rc. OkClaW, 1975.22.0025. On letterhead of Charles F. Lummis, 200 East Ave. 43, Los Angeles.

1. Charles Fletcher Lummis (1859–1928), a writer and editor, arrived in 1885 in southern California, where in addition to his literary work, he became a leading scholar and preserver of the history, ethnography, and archaeology of the Southwest (*DAB*, 11:501–2).

2. John Burroughs (1837–1921), internationally respected author and philosopher, published his first book, *Notes on Walt Whitman as Poet and Person*, in 1867. During his lifetime he produced many other well-regarded volumes and essays that spoke to his passion for nature and its preservation (*DAB*, 3:330–34).

3. Lummis took the last known photograph of Burroughs on 23 March 1921, two days before the famous writer, quite ill, left California by train to return to his home in

upstate New York. He died en route. The image, which Lummis titled "Facing the Mystery," shows the full-bearded Burroughs eyeing the camera with a calm, inquisitive gaze (Barrus, *Life*, 415, 463; Fiske and Lummis, *Charles F. Lummis*, 167).

4. Lummis had four children living at the time: Bertha Belle Page (b. 1879), whom her father first met when she had already reached her late teenage years; Turbesé Lummis Fiske (Dorothea Lummis, 1892–1968); Quimu Lummis (Jordan Lummis, b. 1900); and Keith Lummis (b. 1904). His first son, Amado Bandelier Lummis (b. 1894), had died at the age of six (Gordon, *Charles F. Lummis*, 41).

5. Lummis's frequent, famous "noises" were gatherings of friends enjoying food, music, dance, literature, and abundant fellowship. The one held on 21 February 1920 attracted about seventy-five people, including Rogers and Burroughs (Fiske and Lummis, *Charles F. Lummis*, 166). "The thing Mr. Burroughs most enjoyed," according to his biographer, "was the magic rope performance of Mr. Will Rogers. . . . Close to the performer he stood in abject amazement while that gentleman gave his unbelievably clever exhibition of complicated coördination — his side-splitting monologue carried on with unremitting gum-chewing and the bewildering rope-magic" (Barrus, *Life*, 382–83).

6. With the letter Lummis enclosed a typewritten provenance of the photograph and the circumstances of its origin. In the bottom margin he inscribed in pen, "This sepia enlargement I have framed today with These Fists, for Will Rogers — whom I love & admire; & whose wizardry with the Live Rope gave my old friend John Burroughs never-forgotten wonder & delight, that memorable night at my house, Feb 21, 1920. He often spoke to me afterward about the extraordinary mentality as well as physical dexterity of Will Rogers. With Love to Will & Bonny Betty   Charles F. Lummis." The note was dated "July 17, 1921" (see 1975.22.0026, OkClaW).

Uncanceled Check from Will Rogers Productions
16 August 1921
Los Angeles, Calif.

One of the few surviving documents of Will Rogers Productions, Rogers's brief and costly entry into the business end of motion pictures, was the following check made payable to Walter Cain[1] and signed by Rogers. Its uniqueness was enhanced by Cain's full-color illustration and accompanying message.[2]

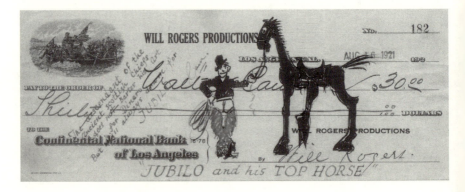

PDS. OkClaW, 1975.17.0087.

1. Walter Cain (1862–1929), a long-time Tennessee journalist, became editor of the *Nashville Banner* in 1921 and worked at the newspaper until the year of his death. His work with Will Rogers Productions was not identified (*WhAmer*, 1:182; *NYT*, 22 May 1929).

2. Cain's hand-printed message reads: "The descendant of the Ancient scottish Chiefs does not Barter his Art for Dinero. But will always draw for JUBILO   *Cain*."

Telegram from Arthur S. Kane Pictures Corporation
23 August 1921
New York, N.Y.

August 23 1921

Mr Will Rogers
Care Hollywood Studios[1]
Hollywood Los Angeles Cal

CAN CLOSE DISTRIBUTION CONTRACT WITH PATHE AS FOLLOWS STOP PATHE TO ADVANCE TWENTY THOUSAND DOLLARS EACH PICTURE PAYABLE TEN THOUSAND DURING PRODUCTION TEN THOUSAND ON DELIVERY OF NEGATIVE STOP IN CASE OF PICTURES ALREADY PHOTOGRAPHED TWENTY THOUSAND DOLLARS EACH ON DELIVERY OF NEGATIVE STOP PATHE ALSO TO ADVANCE COST PRINTS STOP TERMS SIXTY FIVE THIRTY FIVE UNTIL YOUR SIXTY FIVE PERCENT OF GROSS AMOUNTS TO SUM SUFFICIENT TO REIMBURSE PATHE FOR ALL MONIES ADVANCED PLUS REIMBURSING YOU FOR ALL ADDITIONAL CERTIFIED NEGATIVE COST ABOVE THE TWENTY THOUSAND DOLLARS ADVANCED THEN TERMS TO BE FIFTY FIFTY STOP CONSENSUS OPINION ALL CONCERNED EACH RELEASE SHOULD GROSS SEVENTY FIVE TO ONE HUNDRED THOUSAND DOLLARS STOP PATHE ASKS ACCEPTANCE OR REJECTION THIS PROPOSITION BY CLOSE OF BUSINESS AUGUST TWENTY FOURTH ACCOUNT OTHER DEALS PENDING STOP WE THINK PROPOSITION BETTER THAN OBTAINABLE ANY OTHER DISTRIBUTOR AND URGE ACCEPTANCE STOP IF NOT UP TO YOUR EXPECTATIONS WILL ENDEAVOR NEGOTIATE BETTER PROPOSITION ELSEWHERE IF YOU CARE TAKE RISK LOSING OUT WITH PATHE BY NOT ACCEPTING BEFORE CLOSE BUSINESS WEDNESDAY STOP WIRE DECISION EARLIEST POSSIBLE MOMENT STOP REGARDS

Postal Day Letter   ARTHUR S KANE PICTURES CORPORATION[2]
179 Words 1:35 P.M.

Charge: ARTHUR S. KANE PICTURES CORPORATION
          25 West 43d Street, New York City.

JCR:DSD

TG, rc. OkClaW, Income Tax Return, 1921, Folder 16-B. On Postal Telegram – Commercial Cables Telegram letterhead. Typewritten below letterhead, centered: "D A Y L E T T E R". A hand-inserted check mark appears to the immediate right of the preceding. Typewritten to right of first address line: "*Confirmation*". The latter appears to have been inserted with a different machine and probably at a different time.

1. Hollywood Studios, also known as Hollywood General Studios, was built in 1919 and was one of almost fifty motion picture production facilities in southern California. It operated during the silent film era as a rental lot for independent producing outfits. Rogers may have used Hollywood Studios for film work on one or two of his self-produced two-reelers (*NHD*, 93–94; *AFS*, xii, 184, 186).

2. Arthur S. Kane (ca. 1874–1945) worked as a sales manager with several organizations in the movie industry before his retirement in the 1930s. Rogers had wired him on 4 August, apparently asking him to find a distributor for his new line of short films. Kane's reply a few days later cautioned against the likelihood of a favorable arrangement, certainly not a quick one (see Telegram from Arthur S. Kane Pictures Corporation, 9 August 1921, File Folder 16-B, OkClaW). Thanks to Kane's work, Rogers closed a deal sometime in 1921 with Pathé Exchange, the American branch of the French firm Pathé Frères, then the world's largest film production and distribution company. The distribution arrangements took an unexpected turn, however. After Rogers had three of his two-reel pictures ready for release—*The Ropin' Fool*, *Fruits of Faith*, and *One Day in 365*—Pathé abruptly informed him sometime before 21 September 1921 (see F. B. Warren Corporation to Will Rogers, 21 September 1921, OkClaW) that it would need several more finished films before commencing distribution. With thousands of dollars already spent and prospects of quick returns now slim, Will Rogers Productions ceased operations and Rogers moved to remedy his family's threatened financial position (Yagoda, *Will Rogers*, 180–81; *NHD*, 156; *WRHolly*, 46, 47, 49–50; *AFS*, 162).

Telegram from Max Hart
18 October 1921
New York, N.Y.

25GSA 15 1014a

SI New York Oct 18-21

Will Rogers

Famous Players   Lasky Studio[1]
Hollywood Calif.

Okay three weeks three thousand   dollars   exclusive engagement opening winter garden Oct thirty first[2] confirm

Max Hart[3]

TG, rc. OkClaW, 1975.31.0478. On Postal Telegram–Commercial Cable letterhead.

1. Famous Players–Lasky started in the early 1910s as separate film studios of Adolph Zukor and Jesse L. Lasky, a brother-in-law of Sam Goldwyn. The merged firm

was one of the pioneer film production companies in Hollywood. In late October 1921 Rogers was finishing work on *One Glorious Day*, a Famous Players–Lasky picture that opened in New York on 29 January 1922 (*AFS*, 158–59; *WRHolly*, 74).

2. Rogers arrived in New York a few days before the start of his engagement at the Winter Garden. He played only two weeks at the Broadway location, but during the second week he appeared in Brooklyn at another theater in the Shubert chain. His performance fee from the Shuberts totaled $8,600, a vaudeville record, according to the company (Chronology, 1920–22, OkClaW; Yagoda, *Will Rogers*, 187).

3. Hart, a long-time agent in the entertainment industry, netted a commission of $860 from Rogers for arranging the bookings with the Shubert organization (see Statement of Net Income, ca. 15 March 1922, below).

Notes for Premiere of *Doubling for Romeo*
ca. 21 October 1921
Los Angeles, Calif.

Doubling for Romeo, *advertised as "Five Centuries of Laughter in Six Reels of Super Comedy," was one of Rogers's final films to be produced and released by Goldwyn Pictures. He prepared these notes for a personal appearance at the movie's premiere screening in Los Angeles.*[1]

Me appearing with one of my Pictures is like adding insult to injury.

I hope that my first Shakespeareian effort has met with your approval.

In doing Shakespeare you always have one consolation. somebody has done it just as bad as you have.

of course the principal reason the Goldwyn people decided to do it was they dident have to buy the story.

Then they had some tights out there that Geraldine Farrar and Lou Telligan had worn in a Picture so we used them . I am proud to say I wore jerrys [Geraldine's]. There may have been a few baggy spots but by a little padding applied properly why I made quite a showing.

I think we did very well considering no one of us coneected with the company had ever read Romeo and Juliet.

But the detail was perfect for the company sent back to Philadelphia and found a man who had seen the play .

Now in one scene where I think Juliet is dead I really cry. someone asked me if that wasent hard . No it is not   now it used to be but the way the movie business has been for the last few months its no trouble to get an act[or] ~~or or a produ~~ to cry   in fact you cant hardly keep them from it. and a Producer will cry if you look at him.

You see we had to extend ourselvs in this picture for it had been done twice before in the Movies once by Theda Bara[2] and once by Francis X Bushman[3]   In fact thats what gave me courage to do it. . . .

TD.[4] OkClaW, 1975.28.0018. Parts of the document were stained by adhesive tape that had deteriorated. Ellipsis inserted by editors.

1. *Doubling for Romeo*, Rogers's twelfth motion picture, had been in production since at least March 1921. Rogers liked the finished film, which received acclaim from reviewers, especially for Rogers's work. A prerelease viewing by Goldwyn salesmen, however, drew nary a laugh. Their reaction devastated Rogers and nearly led him to abandon film work. It might also have prompted him to make personal appearances at the initial screenings in Los Angeles in October—hence these notes—in hopes of boosting the film. Advertising for the event invited fans to "Come and Hear Bill Tell How It Feels to Play the World's Most Famous Lover" (*WRHolly*, 37–38; *NYT*, 11 August 1929; clipping of advertisement in *LAEH*, ca. 21 October 1921, Scrapbook 20, OkClaW).
2. Bara starred as Juliet in 1916 in a Fox Film version of Shakespeare's classic story of an ill-fated love affair (*AFIC*, F1FE:785).
3. Francis Xavier Bushman (1883–1966), one of the great early-day romantic leads in motion pictures, was rated by legions of female film fans as "the handsomest man in the world." In October 1916 Bushman appeared in a Metro Pictures production of *Romeo and Juliet* that opened only four days before the Fox film with Theda Bara. The release of both movies coincided with the tercentennial anniversary of Shakespeare's death. Bushman's highly successful movie career crashed in 1918 following scandalous revelations about his marital and family life (*DAB*, Supp. 8:65–67; *UDSSEP*, 83; *FE*, 198–99; *IDFF*, 3:113–14; *AFIC*, F1FE:785).
4. Dating of the document was determined by the date of the premiere of the film.

Notes for Speech
ca. 26 October 1921
Los Angeles, Calif.

In case this is not a respectable party I left an assumed name as I came in in case I was called on to testify.

Adam and Eve made the Rib famous   Corbett made the Solar Plexus wtand out[1] but it remained for Roscoe to bring the ▼[*handwritten:*]bladder▼ into a prominence that was never before enjoyed by any other organ.[2]

Now at all the fashionable teas and gatherings ▲sooner or later the c[onversation] drifts to▲ [the bladder.] ~~it is the principal topic~~ it has supplanted the appendix as a conversational [topic.]

There is some talk now in fashionable society about having them retreaded. Every day they take him into a new court and charge him with something[3]

A bunch of Women will say why you havent had him out in our court we want to see him . the judge will say well what will we charge him with. weell the club will hold a meeting and decide just what we will charge him with   oh its just such a nice day for vharging something.

The toughest charge he has now against him is being from Los A.

The Gra[n]d Jury is out now aand sre going to turn in a verdict favoring cremating everbody south of Bakersfield.

The District attorney[4] has been promised if he can hang Arbuckle he will be Mayor And if he can hang ten other Picture people with him he will be made Govenor

There hasent been a dish washed in Frisco since the trials started. all the women are down at the trial.

If A[rbuckle] come clear once a day on every count he would still be in for life[5]

I am working over at Laskys now[6]   it looks like V[alentino?] is going to be rewarded.[7] For a while it looked very discouraging.

I was on the verge of leaving a good wife . not that I wanted too but I was simply in need of notririety. In fact mr Jackson mapped out the campaign[8]

Now as you all know i am not an educated person. I never grazed educationally past the fourth reader.[9] Well now all these Birches and Obenchains and all that mees are college graduates.[10] The Boneheaded way they committed thatis the biggest blow against ~~prohibition~~ learning. so that shos that us ignorant are gradually coming into our own

I have left Goldwyn and am over at   L[asky].[11] Of course everbody says which do you like best. well I think Goldwynns have the prettiest lawns[12] but I think Las[ky] have the best Pictures. you see I was unfortunate in working for G[oldwyn] that I did not get in the Old Nest[13]   consequently the advertising said nothing about me being there . Goldwyn have rather a unique way of advertising . they put adds in that on a certian week three months from now they are going to adver[tise.] well while they are advertising that they are going to advertise why these other firms advertise.

I am playing Lila Lee lover[14] in this one and if I get an O K I am to get a chance in A Demille Love special[15] . There I hope to meet a class of audience that havent been familiar with my work heretofore.

I am going down tonight to see his affairs of Alcahol.

I went to Klunes auditorium[16] to see Foxs version of the Bible.[17] From my readin of the Bible I dont remember any exciting Chariot races but of course he fig[ures] to play to the 90 percent who hadent read the original script. If

Queens dressed like she did they would never have gotten half way through the old Testa[ment.]

Want a press agent not to exploit but to suppress.

Morality clause.

Read Arbuckles confession in next months Examiner. L[os Angeles?] press agents work on a Percentage of what they get about their stars in the Papers   now they are trying to collect on the arbuckle case.

Frisco Whiskey from Los A

TD. OkClaW, 1975.28.0021. Handwritten and underscored, possibly in Rogers's hand, top margin, left side: "Arbuckle". Interlineations were typewritten unless otherwise noted.

1. Jim Corbett (see *PWR*, 2:195n.2) lost the heavyweight boxing title in 1897 when his opponent knocked him out with a blow to the stomach, a devastating punch that made many Americans aware of the solar plexus for the first time (*DAB*, Supp. 1:200–201; *BDASBask*, 368–69).

2. Roscoe Conkling (Fatty) Arbuckle (1887–1933), actor, director, and screenwriter, had become one of the most popular and successful comic performers in motion pictures by 1921. His career was shattered on 10 September of that year when news first broke that he had been charged with capital murder. A young actress had died the day before of a ruptured bladder, after allegedly having been sexually assaulted by the ample-bodied Arbuckle during a drunken spree in the comedian's hotel room in San Francisco (*FE*, 44–45; Oderman, *Roscoe "Fatty" Arbuckle*, 153–56).

3. A grand jury in San Francisco in September failed to indict Roscoe Arbuckle for first-degree murder, and an inquest before a local judge later the same month resulted in a reduced charge of manslaughter. Inconclusive forensic evidence, conflicting testimony, and a lack of credible witnesses hurt the prosecution's case. In early October, in a related development, Arbuckle was arrested by federal agents in Los Angeles for violating the law against the "consumption of intoxicating liquor" (Oderman, *Roscoe "Fatty" Arbuckle*, 165–71, 173).

4. Matthew Brady, district attorney in San Francisco, served as the chief prosecutor in the Arbuckle case (Oderman, *Roscoe "Fatty" Arbuckle*, 162).

5. After Arbuckle's first two trials ended in hung juries, a third concluded on 12 April 1922 with a verdict of acquittal. Although Arbuckle received apparent vindication in court, his career, finances, and persona had suffered irreparable damage. The scandal also led to greater self-censorship in the film industry and reinforced the prevailing opinion of Hollywood as a modern-day Sodom (Oderman, *Roscoe "Fatty" Arbuckle*, 185, 189, 192; *FE*, 44).

6. Jesse Louis Lasky (1880–1958) started his entertainment career as a musician but achieved success as a talent manager and a producer, initially in vaudeville and by 1913 in motion pictures. His Jesse L. Lasky Feature Play Company merged with Famous Players Film Company in mid-1916, and the resulting firm evolved into the production arm of Paramount Pictures (*DAB*, Supp. 6:368–69; *NHD*, 154–55).

7. Rudolph Valentino (Rodolpho Alfonzo Raffaelo Pierre Filibert Guglielmi di Valentina de'Antonguolla, 1895–1926), a native of Italy, spent his first years in American motion pictures in minor character roles. In 1921 he struck stardom, especially among

women filmgoers, as the lead in *The Four Horsemen of the Apocalypse*. As public excitement rose in anticipation of his next picture, *The Sheik*, also a Famous Players–Lasky release, a Los Angeles judge granted Valentino's wife a separation in a highly publicized decision on 25 October (Arnold, *Valentino*, 19; *FE*, 1400–1401; *IDFF*, 3:627–28; Shulman, *Valentino*, 131–32).

8. Joe Jackson (Joseph Jackson, 1894–1932) was a drama editor at the New York *World* who began working in motion pictures as a scenarist in 1918 (*UDFT*, 133; *NYT*, 28 May 1932).

9. For William H. McGuffey and his *Eclectic Readers* see *PWR*, 1:80n.1.

10. Madalynne Obenchain and Arthur Cowbrey Burch, former classmates at Northwestern University in Evanston, Ill., were indicted on 11 August 1921 for the late-night ambush slaying in Beverly Hills, Calif., of John Belton Kennedy, a local insurance broker. Obenchain and Burch allegedly had conspired to murder Kennedy, also a graduate of Northwestern, when the latter had balked at marrying the divorced Obenchain. The sensational nature of the crime and the collegiate backgrounds of the main subjects captured the attention of the press and public. Separate, multiple trials ended in hung juries (*NYT*, 7–8, 12 August, 14 September, 1 December 1921, 17 January, 20 March, 23 May, 1, 10 December 1922).

11. Rogers made two films at the Lasky studios in the early 1920s. The first, *One Glorious Day*, an imaginative picture involving spiritualism, opened on 29 January 1922. Rogers stepped into the lead role when the studio dropped the original star, Roscoe Arbuckle, after news broke of the scandal in San Francisco. In the second, *Hollywood*, Rogers shared cameo appearances with other film celebrities. The picture was released in August 1923 (*WRHolly*, 74–75, 76–77).

12. Sam Goldwyn spent lavishly on his production facilities in Culver City, Calif., and on beautification of its expansive grounds. Income from the box office, however, could not keep pace with the capital outlay at the studios (Berg, *Goldwyn*, 95, 99, 102, 103).

13. *The Old Nest*, a melodrama released in October 1921, realized almost a million dollars for Goldwyn Pictures. One representative of the studio was told not to market the box office hit without "wrapping around the exhibitor's neck" a few of Rogers's films (*AFIC*, F2FE:562; Berg, *Goldwyn*, 92–93).

14. Lila Lee (Augusta Appel, 1901–1973), a vaudeville performer as a child, began making motion pictures at age seventeen. Although she starred as Rogers's love interest in *One Glorious Day*, her appearance opposite Rudolph Valentino in *Blood and Sand* later the same year brought her wider popularity (*FE*, 807; *WRHolly*, 74).

15. Cecil Blount DeMille (1881–1959), a long-time associate of Sam Goldwyn and Jesse Lasky, produced and directed some of the most sensational and spectacular motion pictures in the industry's first fifty years. Several of his most popular, immediate postwar movies took aim at the lives and loves, frailties and foibles of the upper class (*DAB*, Supp. 6:158–60; *FE*, 350–51; *IDFF*, 2:125–26; Hayne, ed., *Autobiography*, 6–7).

16. William H. (Billy) Clune (1862–1927), Los Angeles real estate developer, built motion picture theaters and also produced films to exhibit in his own and other cinema houses. He constructed and operated two of the earliest theaters in Los Angeles: the Cameo (also known as Clune's Broadway) and Clune's Auditorium, called "the big house on Fifth street" (*VO*, 26 October 1927; Berger and Conser, *Last Remaining Seats*, 9–10; *LAT*, 2 December 1919).

17. *The Queen of Sheba*, a motion picture spectacular produced by William Fox, depicted the title character as the lover of Solomon, the king of Israel. Although the

movie had its official premiere in early September 1921 and its general release in December, it had opened several months earlier in New York, where one reviewer likened it to a "gorgeous circus." Like Rogers, the same critic questioned the authenticity of the chariot race, as well as other curiosities in the film (*AFIC*, F2FE:625; *NYT*, 11 April 1921).

Newspaper Article by Will Rogers
3 November 1921
New York, N.Y.

[H]OW WILL [R]OGERS
VIEWS ARM MEET

Will Rogers, cowboy-actor and screen star, reported for duty at the Washington Bureau, Universal Service[1] as a commentator on the Conference on Limitation of Armament.[2] He will be a regular contributor.

BY WILL ROGERS.

WASHINGTON, Nov. 2.—Well, here I am in Washington to write you all about this Number 2 Peace Conference. You see there seemed to have been some jealousy over the last on[e,][3] so they are holding another und[er] another name.

This is really the third attempt a[t] international peace. Ford conducte[d] the first one. The only mistake he made was in bringing his troop back to this country.

I arrived direct with the Japanese delegation. If the conference had been put off two years they wouldn't have to send them from Japan. They could send them from California.[4]

The Japanese delegation came over on battleships.[5]

While waiting around here for this disagreement conference to start I went up to the Senate to-day and I want to tell you they got the best show in town. Jim Reed has got the funniest act he has had in years.[6]

Disarmament can't hurt this country. We were disarmed when we entered the last war and got away with it. Maybe we can do it again.

To-morrow I will have some real news for you. I am to go to the White House and meet Laddie Boy[.][7] Why that pup is better known than the [D]emocratic party. So long.

PD. Printed in *New York American*, 3 November 1921. OkClaW, WRM, Early Articles (1916–22) Folder. Bracketed copy infers text that is missing because of the torn and distorted condition of the clipping on file.

1. Universal Service was a news association that the Hearst organization established in 1917 to serve its own and other morning newspapers. Until its demise in 1937, Universal provided client papers with uniform dispatches, supplementary news, feature columns, and other special services (Mott, *American Journalism*, 711).

2. Amid rising tensions in the Far East and the threat of a naval arms race, President Warren G. Harding invited eight other nations to participate with the United States in a naval disarmament conference in Washington, D.C. Although the Conference on the Limitation of Armaments, often referred to as the Washington Naval Conference, officially convened on 12 November 1921, delegates from the conferring nations, including Japan, had begun arriving as early as 3 November (Murray, *Harding Era*, 140–47; *NYT*, 4 November 1921).

3. That is, the Paris Peace Conference of 1919.

4. In 1920 the Japanese population in California reached 72,000, an increase of 80 percent in ten years. The growth had occurred despite the Alien Land Act of 1913, a state law that forbade ownership of land by aliens ineligible for citizenship, particularly the Japanese. Loopholes in the law had made possible a continuing influx of Japanese immigrants and the leasing and subleasing of farm acreage (Rolle, *California*, 165).

5. At the time Japan had 494,528 tons of battleships and battle cruisers in its arsenal, but the United States had 728,390 tons and Great Britain boasted 1,015,825. Although Japan and the United States each had fifteen capital ships planned or under construction in 1921, while Britain had only four, the American expansion program had slowed and prospects of additional appropriations had dimmed. Japan's position, therefore, appeared the more aggressive (Buckley, *United States*, 23–24).

6. James Alexander Reed (1861–1944), a fiercely independent and famously outspoken Democrat, served as U.S. senator from Missouri from 1911 until his retirement in 1929 (*DAB*, Supp. 3:621–63).

7. Laddie Boy, President Harding's Airedale terrier and constant companion, received much attention in the press and from the public. Harding and his dog often appeared together in publicity photos, and Laddie Boy even accompanied him to cabinet sessions and on his frequent golf outings (Russell, *Shadow*, 444).

Notes for Premiere of *The Ropin' Fool*
ca. 7 November 1921
New York, N.Y.

With his own money at risk, Rogers's first self-produced film, The Ropin' Fool,[1] *opened at the Capitol Theatre in New York the week of 7 November 1921. At the time, Rogers was performing across the street at the Winter Garden and may have arranged the screening to gauge critical and audience reaction and to entice a distributor for his finished films. Another year would pass, however, before general distributor Pathé released* The Ropin' Fool *and another Rogers short subject,* Fruits of Faith, *nationwide.[2] Rogers likely prepared these notes for a personal appearance at the initial showing in New York of* The Ropin' Fool.

I got a little 2 reel Picture here if ~~you folks aint~~   I would like to have you folks stay and look at if you are not in too big a hurry to [get] your todays Prescription filled

I dident think Mr Rothafel would run it in a swell ~~da~~ joint like this bur [but] he said Sure I will run it[3]   I have put over worse Pictures than it in here.

You see I made this Picture myself   its my own Doe in it so you Critics and Bootlegeers treat it kindly.

~~When I was with Goldwyn~~

~~On account of~~ being a Cowboy they always put me in some acting part and ~~The Story~~ 90 percent of the Moving Pictures have no story but this is the o only one ever admitted it.

Theatre owners tell me that its generally about the middle of the third reel when audiences go to sleep . I am going to beat them to it with this short Picture.

I tried to get D W Griffith to direct it but he would be too old by the tome [time] he finishes the 2 Ophans [Orphans].[4]

~~If it~~ flops as it is

Griffith   they say D W Griffith advances Movies 4 years with one of his Picur [Pictures.] Well here s one that will set em right back where they started.

If it ~~dont go~~ flops I will put on a Beard and swear it was made in Germany[5]   then it will be a Riot.

It may bnot be Aartistic but there is

I dont know what you might consider Art . But there is 30 years of hard Practice ~~in thiese little 2 reels~~ in ti

TD, cy. OkClaW, Will Rogers, Jr., Collection, Folder 8. On letterhead of The New Willard, Washington, D.C. Typewritten below letterhead: "2ill 4ogers says [Will Rogers Says]".

1. Directed by Clarence Badger and photographed by Marcel Le Picard, two of Rogers's most reliable associates from Goldwyn days, *The Ropin' Fool* starred Rogers as Ropes Reilly, "The Ropin' Fool." Thin of plot, the film nevertheless served as a cinematic display of Rogers's remarkable roping skills, an opportunity to bring his vaudeville act to the screen (*WRHolly*, 47; *Variety*, 11 November 1921).

2. With Pathé's general release of the movie on 29 October 1922, followed late the same year by that of another Rogers-produced short subject, *Fruits of Faith*, Rogers eventually recovered more than two-thirds of his investment in his production company (*WRHolly*, 47, 49; Yagoda, *Will Rogers*, 179, 191). See also Statement of Moving Picture Receipts, 14 April 1923, below.

3. *The Ropin' Fool* debuted at the Capitol Theatre on an eclectic "Armistice Week" bill that included another comedy short subject, a symphony, a travelogue, and an orchestral tribute to the end of the war. A showcase cinema house at Broadway and Fifty-first Street in New York, the Capitol stood across the street from the Winter Garden Theatre, where Rogers opened the same week for the Shubert organization. Roxy Rothafel, who had transformed and managed other prestige movie theaters in

New York and had introduced Rogers's on-screen gags in New York and Los Angeles, had assumed management of the Capitol in 1920 (*NYT*, 7 November 1921; Chronology, 1920–22, OkClaW; *EV*, 439–40).

4. Griffith started production on *The Two Orphans*, a motion picture spectacle of the French Revolution adapted from a stage classic of the same title, in the spring of 1921. His efforts to complete the fourteen-reel picture became complicated by questions of copyright infringement, competition from similar films under way elsewhere, the immensity of the project, and a scarcity of underwriting. The issue of ownership of rights forced Griffith to release the movie as *Orphans of the Storm*. It premiered in Boston in late December 1921 (Schickel, *D. W. Griffith*, 454–55, 457–58, 459).

5. The war had allowed the film industry in Germany to develop free of foreign influences and to establish significant, independent production facilities. The end of the war marked the advent of a golden decade of German cinema, characterized in part by the rise of expressionism. The dark, foreboding, exaggerated style of expressionistic German film was symbolized by *The Cabinet of Dr. Caligari*, a motion picture considered a masterpiece in Germany but whose showing in New York in April 1921 provoked a near riot of rebuke (*FE*, 519; Berg, *Goldwyn*, 98, 101).

Newspaper Article by Will Rogers
ca. 30 November 1921
[New York, N.Y.?]

WILL ROGERS
HAS OWN WAY
TO END WARS

PROPOSES TO MOVE NATIONS
WHEN THEY WANT
TO FIGHT.

By WILL ROGERS,
Motion Picture and Vaudeville Star.
(Written Expressly for Universal Service.)[1]

WASHINGTON, D. C., NOV. 29.[2]—I got a scheme to really stop wars, not just get together and talk about it.

The guy who laid out the location of all these nations was coo coo.

If I live next door to a man and can't get along without fighting I will move. Now that's my scheme. It wouldn't cost anything but the transportation of changing places.

Now separate France and Germany. France trades places with Japan. Let Japan live by [Germany.] They are both war-like an[d if] they wa[nte]d to fight each ot[her no]body in [the] world would care. [At] present Japan is a great gr[eat] country.

Let England go to Canada or Australia and live off her sons-in-law.

That would also solve the Irish question for Lloyd-George.[3] Put Ulster where England is now. Let Ireland keep all of Ireland till they become tired of it, which would be perhaps six or eight months. That would give us a chance to get rid of Mexico. Trade it for Turkey, harems and all.

Leave Sc[otl]and where they are as they wo[uld] not want to pay railroad fare.

That's th[e] only way in the world they will [eve]r stop war. Every time they [th]reaten to fight move 'em.

Now this is only a rough idea of mine. I haven't gone into it technically. But if Mr. Harding[4] wants to call a conference on it I would be only too glad to co-operate. That's of course in case this present chautauqua don't function.[5]

As a committee of delegates to help me draft this and get it into good enough English so England would understand it, I want Bugs Baer[6] Ring Laudinum[7] and William J. Bryan. I want the last named in case we want to make it longer.

Now, of course, this may never receive any consideration—nothing with any merit ever does.

PD. Unidentified clipping, ca. 30 November 1921. OkClaW, Early Articles, 1916–22. Bracketed copy infers text that is missing because of the torn and distorted condition of the clipping.

1. See also Newspaper Article by Will Rogers, 3 November 1921, above.

2. Rogers entertained at the state prison at Ossining, N.Y., the night of 29 November and probably was not in Washington, D.C., on that day (see Chronology, 1920–22, OkClaW). He could have forwarded the article to the Universal Service office in Washington, and the bureau might have issued it from that city on 29 November.

3. David Lloyd George (1863–1945), leader of the Liberal party, served as prime minister of Great Britain from 1916 until his resignation in October 1922 (*DNB*, Supp. 6:515–29).

4. Warren Gamaliel Harding (1865–1923), former Republican senator from Ohio, was elected president of the United States in a landslide victory in 1920. He served from 1921 until his death in office (*DAB*, 8:252–57).

5. That is, the Conference on Limitation of Armaments.

6. Arthur (Bugs) Baer (1886–1969) started his newspaper career as a sports columnist and artist, whose caricatures of a baseball-shaped insect provided him with a nickname. He eventually turned to writing humor. His long-time column of wit, "One Word Led to Another," in the New York *World* brought him much popularity (*NYT*, 18 May 1969; Meyer, *Pundits*, 436).

7. Ringgold Wilmer (Ring) Lardner (1885–1933), journalist and author, worked for several newspapers in the Midwest, primarily as a sports writer, from 1905 to 1919. He then began writing a syndicated column and producing humorous magazine articles and books. By 1922 he had written at least nine books (*DAB*, Supp. 1:482–83).

Newspaper Article by Will Rogers
ca. 11 February 1922
[Washington, D.C.?]

HARDING GOES SLUMMING IN SENATE,
AS WILL ROGERS SEES IT

Will Rogers sat in a United Press seat in the Senate press gallery when President Harding submitted the armament conference treaties,[1] and reported the historic event as it looked to a cowpuncher.

By Will Rogers

President Harding went slumming and took in the Senate late yesterday.

He carried his bale of treaties along. They were all bundled up in wrapping paper so you couldn't tell whether he was a President or a bootlegger.

La Follette was doing a monologue when the President come in and had to stop.[2] Otherwise the Sunday adjournment was all that would have stopped him.

ONE OF BEST SPEECHES HUGHES EVER WROTE

Harding made quite a speech. In fact, it sounded like one of the best speeches Hughes ever wrote.[3]

He said it was different from the league of nations because the league of nations commences with an L and this was to start with an A.[4]

He said lots of people will ask, well if it ain't binding, why have it? But he said it looked like a good year for treaties, so he thought he would bring up a bunch of them.

OUGHT TO LIKE SOME OF THEM

He said he brought along six or eight of them and the Senators would be pretty hard to please if they didn't like some of them.

One treaty says there is to be no war and another tells how many submarines you can have in case there is a war.

Japan did pretty well. She used to have a treaty that she wouldn't go to war without England. Now she has one she won't go to war without England, America and France.[5]

He said, if you don't sign these treaties I won't bring any more.

SORRY HE COULDN'T GIVE PHILIPPINES AWAY

President Harding apologized for not being able to pan the Philippines off on some nation.[6] But he said they divided China up so nice that even she don't know it.

He intimated that in spite of prohibition it was one of the most successful conferences ever held.

If the Senate reads them all they can't ratify for at least a year.[7]

PD. Unidentified clipping, ca. 11 February 1922. Scrapbook 20, OkClaW.

1. The Washington Naval Conference, which had opened in November 1921, resulted in several agreements that addressed postwar issues of balancing the size of the navies of the major powers, subjecting submarines to the usual international laws of naval warfare, banning the use of gas warfare, restoring to China some Japanese-held territories, and respecting the general territorial and commercial rights of China. On 10 February 1922, only four days after the conference's adjournment, Harding presented the treaties to the Senate for ratification. Rogers, who was performing at the National Theatre in Washington with the road production of *Ziegfeld Frolic*, witnessed the event from the gallery of the Senate (Murray, *Harding Era*, 150–58; Chronology, 1920–22, OkClaW).

2. La Follette, who had lost favor among many Americans during the war for suspected pro-German feelings, spoke in the Senate on 10 February against a bill to reduce the wages of railway workers (*DAB*, 10:545; *NYT*, 11 February 1922).

3. Charles Evans Hughes had returned to private law practice after losing his bid for the presidency in 1916. He became secretary of state in the Harding administration in 1921 and served in the post until 1925. Hughes chaired the Washington Conference and served as the chief U.S. negotiator and spokesman. His dramatic speech on opening day set the tone for the assembly's successful conclusion (*DAB*, Supp. 4:405; Buckley, *United States*, 32, 70–73).

4. None of the several treaties signed at the conference provided for U.S. participation in the League of Nations (*HD1920s*, 338–39).

5. The Four-Power Treaty was the most unexpected of the international pacts signed at the Washington Naval Conference. By its terms Japan, Great Britain, France, and the United States agreed to respect the sovereignty of each other's territories in the Pacific region and to meet and communicate in the event of a related controversy or an outside threat (Murray, *Harding Era*, 154–55).

6. The outcome of the Washington Naval Conference had a significant impact on U.S. strategic development of the Philippines, which the United States had acquired in the Spanish-American War of 1898. The arms limitation treaty precluded a build-up of naval forces in the Pacific sector, but the Four-Power Treaty effectively conceded Japanese dominance in the region. Although the Harding administration in the fall of 1921 had expressed its commitment to the Philippines, the new treaty restricted its ability to fortify the islands, leaving them more vulnerable to attack (Murray, *Harding Era*, 345–46; Brands, *Bound*, 145).

7. The U.S. Senate ratified all of the treaties by 31 March 1922 (Murray, *Harding Era*, 160–61).

To Edward H. Hayden
10 March 1922
Detroit, Mich.

Dear Hayden.[1]

Enclosed find two checks for the Taxes. Now this one reaching New York may be a little late but even if we are fined it wont be much.[2] I only hope this charging off these Pictures go. I have not done anything with them and they are a loss so far.[3]

We open the 19th at the Colonial Theatre in Chicago for a run   think we will be there 6 or 8 weeks.[4] we have a pretty good show

I have a pretty good deal to go to Hal Roach to make 2 reel Comedys.[5] Still.our Show might run into the Summer.

Best to you and Wife.

Yours

Will Rogers.

TL, rc. OkClaW, Income Tax Return, 1921. On letterhead of King Edward Hotel, Toronto, Canada. Filed with the letter is an envelope bearing a Toronto, Canada, postmark, dated 10 March 1922 and rubber-stamped "REGISTERED". The envelope is from the King Edward Hotel, but the name of the hotel has been struck-through by hand. Handwritten, in Rogers's hand, immediately below and stacked (/): "Will Rogers / Detroit Opera House / Detroit, Mich."

1. Edward H. Hayden worked for Will and Betty Blake Rogers as both private secretary and bookkeeper during the early 1920s. He had prepared federal income tax returns for 1921 for both Will and Betty, and a New York state return for Will. He had mailed the documents a month earlier to Washington, D.C., where Rogers was performing at the time. In the fall of 1927 Hayden closed his tax preparation business and began work as a business manager at Fox Studios. Less than two years later, a federal grand jury in Los Angeles indicted him for preparing false tax returns for four prominent motion picture actors and directors. Disposition of the case was not found (Business Records, 1921–25, OkClaW; Edward H. Hayden to Will Rogers, 7 February 1922, OkClaW; Edward H. Hayden to Betty Blake Rogers, 29 September 1927, OkClaW; *NYT*, 16 March 1929).

2. Will Rogers owed a balance of $2,902.46 on his federal return and an unknown amount to the state of New York. He had apparently enclosed those checks for Hayden to forward with the completed returns. The state return likely did not reach New York before the deadline of 15 March (Income Tax Return, 1921, OkClaW).

3. Rogers declared more than $45,000 in deductions on his tax return in 1921 for expenses related to Will Rogers Productions. The three films he produced remained on hold (see Statement of Net Income, ca. 15 March 1922, below).

4. Rogers and the *Ziegfeld Frolic* appeared at the Colonial Theatre in Chicago from 19 March to 4 June 1922, a run of eleven weeks (Chronology, 1920–22, OkClaW).

5. Harold Eugene (Hal) Roach (1892–1992) formed his own motion picture company in 1915 and eventually produced and directed some of the most popular film comedies of the 1920s and 1930s. Roach approached Rogers after a *Midnight Frolic* performance in Chicago in the fall of 1921 with an offer for a starring role in two-reel comedies. The two men, however, did not sign a contract until more than a year later. Rogers's arrangements with the Ziegfeld organization may have prevented an earlier commitment (*FE*, 1156; *NYT*, 3 November 1992; Yagoda, *Will Rogers*, 205; see Letter from Charles H. Roach, 10 March 1924, below).

Statement of Net Income
ca. 15 March 1922
[Los Angeles, Calif.?]

	Will Rogers.	1921
INCOME STATEMENT		
SALARIES:		
Goldwyn Picture Co	24 weeks @ $3000.	$72,000.00
Famous Players-Lasky	one picture	7,583.30
Shuberts Theatres, New York	$3000.-$5000. -$600.00	8,600.00
Zeigfield, New York	7 weeks @ $1000.	7,000.00
Marcus Loew, New York[1]	one week	1,500.00
Capitol Theatre,	personal appearance	500.00
	TOTAL INCOME	97,183.30
DEDUCTIONS:		

Commissions to Max Hart, New York on Shubert Contract.	$ 860.00	
Bill of Hotel Astor	736.96	
Transportation to N.Y. to accept engagements, including drawing room meals etc.		535.56
Salary paid to Betty Rogers	9.600.00	
Taxes on Beverly Hills property	969.80	
Interest on notes Continental Bank	1,207.77	
Interest on notes, Culver City Bank	1,572.68	
Dues paid to professional clubs,	266.00	
Charitable contributions	447.00	
Salary paid to T. Roy Barnes, Famous Players-Lasky, "THE EK"[2]	1,000.00	

Make-up		75.00
Wardrobe		750.00
Laundry		200.00
Advertising (Folders, stamps etc)		700.00
Horses, used in profession) Upkeep and part salary of groom		3,000.00
Automobile, Pierce Arrow, 2/3rds of upkeep.		3,444.07
Attorney, E. B. Edington		200.00
Loss Aero Club, Goldwyn		200.00
Bad debts: W. B. Harkness,	$200.00	
Clyde E. Miller,	126.67	326.67
Will Rogers Productions, as per schedule attached.[3]		45,135.07

Transportation from New York to Washington D. C. and return to Washington D. C. and return to appear at Kieth [*sic*] theatre, total expense covering transportation and weeks stay at New Willard 150.00 71,226.58

Net income 25,956.72

TD.[4] Income Tax Return, 1921, OkClaW. Hand-inserted check marks and dots appear to the immediate right of each of the figures in the full column of deductions. A hand-inserted "x" appears to the immediate left of each of the deduction entries for "Horses" and "Automobile." A handwritten "16" appears to the right of the gross deduction figure for "Bad Debts." A handwritten "37" appears immediately above the gross deduction total of "71,226.58." A handwritten "13" appears to the right of the deduction for "969.80"; a handwritten "12" appears to the right of "1,207.77"; and a handwritten "15" appears to the right of "447.00."

1. Marcus Loew (1870–1927), a pioneer in the film industry, developed and operated one of the largest chains of motion picture theaters in the country. Rogers made four personal appearances a night for seven nights at different Loew theaters in New York during the week of 12 December 1922. Each evening, Rogers also headlined the *Midnight Frolic* on the roof of the New Amsterdam (*DAB*, 12:355–56; *FE*, 837; Chronology, 1920–22, OkClaW).

2. T. Roy Barnes (1880–1937), a comedian, was a veteran performer in vaudeville, musical comedies, and stage revues. He was credited with his first feature film role in 1920 and continued to appear in character parts for many years. Barnes was not listed among the credits of *One Glorious Day*, a Famous Players–Lasky production that had the working title of "Ek," the name of the unborn spirit that temporarily took residence in the body of Rogers's lead character in the film. According to cast credits, John Fox played the part of Ek (*NYT*, 31 March 1937; *UDSSEP*, 33; *AFIC*, F1CS:29, F2CS:962; *WRHolly*, 74).

3. The printed schedule was not found, but a handwritten itemization of costs for Will Rogers Productions listed the following: salaries, $25,660; "Travelling Expense," $3,358.69; railroad fares, $1,621.82; taxes, $1,727.49; interest, $2,792.47; dues,

$266.00; charitable contributions, $300.00; makeup, $349.52; wardrobe, $355.00; ropes, $300.00; laundry, $156.00; automobile, $3,627.08; horses, $928.42; entertainment, $3,600.00; camera, $200.39; and arena, $450.00 (see AD, Income Tax Return, 1921, OkClaW).

4. The document was probably compiled by Hayden while preparing Rogers's income tax return for 1921. The date assigned coincides with the filing deadline.

Newspaper Article by Will Rogers
ca. 19 March 1922
Detroit, Mich.

WILL ROGERS WRITES A DRY STORY
AND WILL FIELDS PICTURES IT

By Will Rogers.

I have been asked to write a little article for The Sunday News, as the solicitors fell down on an ad they had figured on and it left a blank space.

I asked them what they wanted me to astonish the Fordites with, and they said. "Oh, anything. No one will read it much anyway."

Then I happened to think why have I the time to write an article? Because I have no drinking to do. Then why not write an article on why I have no drinking to do? Ah, prohibition!

I could have said prohibition was my object at first without all this introductory stuff, but it took up space and space is what I am trying to cover. I think it is the space that the Eagle Boat ad was to have gone in.

Now, my friend of the Follies, W. C. Fields, the habitual golfer,[1] has helped me on several wet articles and always he has held up his end wonderfully. I hope he can do himself proud on a dry subject like this.

If you read this article and like it, you can say, "Look what prohibition has done! it is directly responsible for this literary masterpiece."

If you don't like it (as you probably won't), you can say, "If this town had stayed wet, we wouldn't have had to read such junk as this."

So I feel that this article will give prohibition a real test.

The first thing is what is a prohibitionist?

A prohibitionist is a man (or perhaps a woman) who is so self-satisfied that he personally presents himself with a medal called the Croix de Perfect He.

He gives himself this medal because he is now going to start to meddle in everybody's business but his own.

Look what prohibition has done to this town! After 8 o'clock in the evening you can see dogs chasing rabbits up and down Woodward avenue.[2]

And if you drop into a cafe after the show at night, they'll wake up the night watchman to cook you something.

Have you ever seen a jolly crowd around a table here? They look as if the war had been just declared back on again.

Your automobile factories are all changing and going to turn out Jamaica ginger and lemon extract.

If a residence gets on fire here now, the firemen don't run to save the people or the valuables: they rush to the basement to save the liquor.

What is life in Detroit without a cellar!

Prohibition has made good cocktail mixers out of a lot of fellows who never amounted to anything before. If you praise the way the host mixes them, you are sure of a return invitation.

And about getting stuff in here, there are people who, if they put half the time on a mechanical invention that they put on studying how to smuggle liquor, would be as great as Edison.[3]

They have brought it in in extra tires, and they have even put it in tires they are riding on. One day a fellow had a couple of blowouts on the trip from Toledo and lost all his profits.

But there is really only one successful way, and that is the most satisfying. You drink it just before you get to the state line. Then you can bring in all you can carry.

I saw a box of Armour's meat[4] drop off an express wagon yesterday and broke every bottle.

You Detroiters have one chance of getting a new bridge built to Bell Isle.[5] That is to vote the island wet.

But, after all, the people of Michigan have the natural ingredients of one of the best jags in the world. Take a bottle of Stroh's mixture and pour it over a bowl of Grape Nuts. Michigan's second national commodity. Eat this hurriedly, then take a five-mile ride over a rough road in a Ford. And you have as good results as any souse would want.

PD. Printed in *Sunday News*, Detroit, ca. 19 March 1922. Scrapbook 15, OkClaW.

1. Fields performed his famous golf routine as early as 1915 and first introduced it in the *Follies* in 1918. A favorite of audiences and of the performer himself, the golf act was one of the first comedic sketches that Fields registered with the copyright office of the Library of Congress (Louvish, *Man*, 204, 205, 206–7, 213).

2. Woodward Avenue, running north and south, had long been one of the two main arteries in Detroit. As late as 1910 the heavily traveled thoroughfare was lined

with towering elms, spacious mansions, and imposing churches (Beasley and Stark, *Made in Detroit*, 20–21).

3. Thomas Alva Edison (1847–1931) began inventing at the age of sixteen and by the turn of the century had developed the phonograph and patented or made improvements in stock tickers, telegraphic devices, and incandescent lamps. Long before 1922, he had been recognized as the country's leading inventor and technical innovator and accorded the name "Wizard" (*DAB*, Supp. 1:277–81).

4. Jonathan Ogden Armour (1863–1927) assumed management of his family's meat-packing company in 1901. Over the next twenty years, the sales of Chicago-based Armour & Company grew 500 percent and its meat products dominated the market. The effects of the war, however, so irreparably damaged Armour's financial position that he was forced to relinquish control of the company in 1923 (*NYT*, 17 August 1927).

5. Belle Isle, long a favorite recreation and rest haven for Detroit residents, lies in the middle of the Detroit River at the entrance to Lake St. Clair. The island's only bridge burned down in 1916 and was not replaced until 1923. In the meantime, Belle Isle continued to be accessible by ferry (Beasley and Stark, *Made in Detroit*, 39; City of Detroit, "Belle Isle Timeline").

From William Randolph Hearst
2 August 1922
New York, N.Y.

August 2nd, 1922

Mr. Will Rogers,

New Amsterdam Theatre,

New York City.

Dear Mr. Rogers:

I hope when you are in the neighborhood of either my Mexico ranch at Chihuahua or my California ranch near San Luis Obispo, you will take occasion to visit them.

If I am on the ranch at the time   I shall be doubly gratified; but if I am not, please use   this letter as an introduction and ask the managers to give you every facility for visiting the property, and every liberty to enjoy yourself thereon.

By so doing they will confer a favor upon

Yours very sincerely,

W R Hearst

[*handwritten:*] The California ranch is at San Simeon about 45 miles north of San Luis Obispo[1]   San Luis is the nearest railroad station.

WRH

TLS, rc. OkClaW. On New York American letterhead.

1. San Simeon, Hearst's ranch on the coast near San Luis Obispo, Calif., embraced 375 square miles and included a magnificent, sprawling estate house. Rogers, who had been acquainted with Hearst as early as the fall of 1915, probably made his first visit to San Simeon in December 1925 or January 1926 (*DAB*, Supp. 5:287; Yagoda, *Will Rogers*, 139).

Article in *New York Times*
27 October 1922
New York, N.Y.

WILL ROGERS MAKES
HIT AS SPELLBINDER

LASHES "SCOUNDRELLY" OPPO-
SITION AND "TOOLS OF INTER-
ESTS" AT TOWN HALL.

COMEDIAN EVOKES LAUGHS

SUPPORTS OGDEN MILLS[1] FOR CONGRESS
AND GIVES HIS OWN VERSION
OF FAMILY HISTORY

Will Rogers, the cowboy comedian, made his first political speech last night when, at the invitation of Kermit Roosevelt,[2] he addressed the Ogden Mills mass meeting in Town Hall. His talk was something new for a political meeting and won a large number of laughs. After being introduced by George W. Wickersham,[3] the comedian spoke as follows:

"I have spoken in all kinds of joints from one of Mrs. Vanderbilt's parties on Fifth Avenue[4] to Sing Sing in Ossining,[5] but this is my first crack at a political speech, and I hope it flops. I don't want to go over and then have to go into politics, because up to now I have always tried to live honest.

"A great many think I was sent here by Mr. Mills's opponent,[6] but this is not the case. I don't know him. But he must be a scoundrel. From what I have read of politics every opponent is. He must also be a tool of the interests. I believe the least you can do is to say that in a political speech.

"Now, as to Mr. Mills, I have read up on his family history. He comes from the old Mills family of New Jersey. There was Eleanor[7] and Ogden. Eleanor, being rather wild, went into the choir, while Ogden, being of a more divine, spiritualistic nature, took to politics.

"Events of the last few weeks have proved that Ogden's judgment was the better of the two. Statistics of the last Congress show that not a Congressman was shot. The country has been wondering why. Probably it is on the old theory, 'He ain't worth the powder and lead.'

"Mr. Mills is quite a novelty. He is one of the few men that didn't go into politics through necessity. He was wealthy when he started. Not as wealthy as he is now, but he had some money, and he went into politics to protect it. He figured, if he stayed out of politics, they would take it away from him and he went in to protect it, for they say there is honor among thieves.

PUTS HIM IN SHADY SIDE.

"Mr. Mills represents Fifth Avenue and Broadway, and in the old saying of the great poetical Commoner, William Jennings Bryan, 'East is West and West is East, and never the twain shall meet'—except at the stage door of a musical show. His dividing line is Park Avenue, so he also represents the shady side of Park Avenue.

"I met Jimmy Walker,[8] Senator from Greenwich Village, and I asked Jimmy about him. Jimmy said Ogden was a good fellow. You know, Jimmy was the fellow who put through the fake boxing bill for Greenwich Village, and it was a wonderful thing for him to get through for his constituents. If a boxing glove was put in Greenwich Village, they would think it was a pillow and sleep on it. Jimmy also put through Sunday baseball, whereby the Giants could play baseball on Sunday and the Yanks could practice.

RECOUNTS CAMPAIGN PLEDGES.

"Here are a few of the things which he has promised to do:

"He represents Broadway and the theatrical district. He has promised to keep all of us actors working.

"He is a hundred per cent. for the ticket speculators.

"He is for every industry in his district.

"He is for a living wage for the bootlegger.

"He is also for the lesser interests of his district. He will go just as far for the two Jewish people that live in his district as he will for the rest of his constituents.

"He is the only Congressman we can send to Congress who can go into a Fifth Avenue home without delivering something.

"He is the only one you can accept a campaign cigar from and feel a perfect safety in smoking it.

"Now I will tell you why I am here. I have no politics. I came here because a Roosevelt asked me to come here. A Roosevelt hint is the same as one of my wife's commands. I have no politics. When Colonel Roosevelt died, as far as I am concerned, the Republican Party was buried right alongside of where the Democrats had been."

Mr. Rogers said that during the war he had said some complimentary things about the Colonel and his family and some friend who heard it wrote to Colonel Roosevelt and repeated it to him.

ROOSEVELT WROTE TO HIM.

"Colonel Roosevelt," he continued, "wrote me a nice letter from a trip he was on in Maine and wrote the letter in longhand in his own hand. He was about the busiest man in the United States at the time.[9]

"I have said, along with my little knocks, nice things about men in public life, but he was the only man who ever took the time to write and thank me for it. He is the only big man who ever did a thing like that, so far as I know.

"Now this gentleman Mills was a friend of his and is a friend of his family. That is all I know about him. That is all I want to know about him. That is all you need to know about him."

In telling how far he would go to do anything asked of him by a Roosevelt, Rogers said:

"I would even make a speech in favor of Harding, if one of them asked me."

The candidate, Ogden L. Mills, sat throughout the speech with a stolid expression of countenance, but seemed pleased toward the end.[10] . . .

PD. Printed in *New York Times*, 27 October 1922. Scrapbook 8, Part 2, OkClaW. Ellipsis inserted by editors.

1. Ogden Livingston Mills (1884–1937), scion of a wealthy and socially prominent family in New York, won election to Congress in 1920 as a reform Republican. He was reelected in 1922 and served until 1927 when he made an unsuccessful run for governor (*DAB*, Supp. 2:459–60).

2. Kermit Roosevelt (1889–1943), the second son of Theodore Roosevelt and Edith Kermit Roosevelt, headed an international shipping company in New York from 1920 to 1931 (*DAB*, Supp. 3:667–68). The original invitation to Rogers to speak had come from A. Perry Osborn (ca. 1883–1951), a prominent New York attorney long active in state and national Republican politics. Osborn then elicited the aid of Roosevelt to land Rogers as headline speaker. In his note to Rogers, Roosevelt asked, almost forgivingly, "I rather suppose you know [Mills] and I certainly do not wish to be put in the position of asking you to speak for any one, any where, but if you are going to do so, there could be no better man to speak for than Ogden Mills, for he has an excellent record and has never been afraid to come out and say what he felt" (Kermit Roosevelt to Will Rogers, 10 October 1922, OkClaW, 1975.21.0001; *NYT*, 8 July 1951).

3. Samuel George Woodward Wickersham (1858–1936), U.S. attorney general in the administration of William Howard Taft, was a partner in an influential New York law firm and a leading advisor to the Republican party (*DAB*, Supp. 2:713–15).

4. Virginia Graham Fair Vanderbilt (d. 1935) was the daughter of a multimillionaire silver miner, and the wife—then separated, later divorced—of an heir to one of the great family fortunes in the United States. Her large, ornate residence long stood as a landmark on fashionable Fifth Avenue in New York. Rogers entertained on 19 December 1921 at "The Big Sisters," a philanthropy of Vanderbilt's that supported several other organizations (*NYT*, 20 December 1921, 8 July 1935; Virginia G. F. Vanderbilt to Will Rogers, 13 December 1921, OkClaW, 1975.21.0051).

5. Rogers made a personal appearance at Sing Sing, the state prison at Ossining, N.Y., in late November 1921 (Chronology, 1920–22, OkClaW).

6. Herman August Metz (1867–1934), a manufacturer of dyes and chemicals, served as U.S. representative from New York from 1913 to 1915. A Democrat, Metz challenged Mills in 1922 in an unsuccessful effort to regain his old seat (*NYT*, 18 May 1934; *BDUSCong*, 1495).

7. Eleanor Reinhardt Mills (b. ca. 1890) and the Rev. Edward Wheeler Hall (b. 1881) died in a lovers' lane near New Brunswick, N.J., on 14 September 1922. The double homicide of the Episcopal cleric and a member of his church choir became one of the most sensationalized and examined stories in the annals of crime in the United States. Several individuals came under suspicion for the murders, but no one was ever convicted. The case remained unsolved (Kunstler, *Hall-Mills*, vii–viii, 9–10, 35, 49, 61, 63, 69, 70–74, 87, 102, 106, 303).

8. James John (Jimmy) Walker (1881–1946), colorful Irish Catholic, Democratic politician, held the Greenwich Village seat in the New York state assembly from 1909 to 1914 and in the state senate from 1914 to 1925. As a state senator Walker helped secure legalized boxing in New York and professional baseball on Sundays (*DAB*, Supp. 4:854–56; *ENYC*, 134, 1233).

9. See Letter from Theodore Roosevelt, 4 August 1918, above.

10. An editorial writer for the *New York Times* pondered Rogers's effectiveness in behalf of Mills's candidacy, while subtly questioning his credentials: "it is impossible to predict in which direction the quips of a humorist will fly. Mr. Rogers was characteristically amusing in his speech in behalf of Mr. Mills, but laughs are not votes, and whether the candidate whom Mr. Rogers was ostensibly supporting gained more by the performance than did his opponent it would be hard to say. Probably the professional engagements of Mr. Rogers will prevent his further entertaining excursions into the political field. Undoubtedly he would prove a great attraction at any political meeting, but that he would attract votes for his man is by no means certain. The only thing certain is that he would make the task of the grave speakers who preceded and followed him so difficult as to be almost impossible" (*NYT*, 28 October 1922).

Remarks by Will Rogers in *Evening World*
ca. 28 October 1922
New York, N.Y.

WILL ROGERS'S SAYINGS THIS WEEK

"Well," said Will Rogers, the cowboy comedian of the Ziegfeld "Follies," to-day, "we've had a right smart smatterin' of notables out in front this week. It's always nice to have famous people in the audience as well as on the stage because it sort o' makes a cordial entente, or cocktail entente, whichever it is, and I like that.

"Now, the other night we had Doug and Mary in a box. I dropped my rope over Doug and hauled him to his feet and then tripped him for a bow. Doug's had a lot of tough luck lately. You know, he made a picture called 'Robert Hood'[1] and they put some archery in it. If I'd 'a' done the film on my salary they'd 'a' called it bow and arrow shootin', but, o' course, Doug is different with that bankroll. You know Doug is stoppin' at the Ritz. Well, one day he crawled out on the roof of the next buildin' to show some newspaper friends how he could archery. He shot at the side of the Ritz, missed it and hit a fat man over on Second Avenue.[2]

"'Now, Doug,' I says to him up at the show stop, 'you've been out in the sticks so long you might not know it, but we've got bigger hotels here than the Ritz. We'll fix it so you can stand on Gimbel's store[3] and see if you can hit the Pennsylvania House.[4] If you miss that you better go back to California, stand on the beach and archery at the Pacific Ocean. You'd be apt to hit that.'"

"John McCormack dropped in durin' the week to get an eyeful an' I introduced him to the customers as the greatest American Ireland ever produced.[5] I tried to get him to spill a little singin', but he smiled me off. Finally we compromised by me singin'.

"John,' I says, 'when you got sick of recent date they started warmin' me up.'

"I sang, an' John had to admit he never could sing like me.

"Tom Lipton[6] did us the honor of lookin' in, too. I told him he was the world's best loser an' he liked that.[7] I got him all het up with praise an' then says: 'Sir Tom, you see what we think of you in this country, but as much as we like you, your tea—well, that's another thing.' I had to jolt him good-natured like. He was gettin' too happy.

"Mary Fairbanks, the time she was there with Doug, stood up too an' took a bow. You know, I'm the Fairbanks's official pointer-out away out yonder in California. I live at the bottom of the hill an' they live at the top. All the tourists come to my place an' ask where Doug an' Mary hang out. Then's when I do my pointin' out.

"Al Smith single-footed in, too, one night.[8] When I see him I dropped the lariat over him and stood him up. Rudolfo Valentino, lookin' right pretty, he was there likewise. I got him up on the stage. You know, he acted the bull wrastler in that film, 'Blood an' Sand.'[9] In it he does some heroic work with the front end of an old steer that everybody who needs a steer uses in films out West. I know that steer well an' I love the gentle old thing like a brother.

"'Well, Rudy,' I says to him, 'what did you tie that old steer's hind legs to when you attacked him?' It got over big with most of the audience, but some of the ladies was mad, they wantin' to believe Rudy was just as heroish as the films showed him to be.

————

"Then Pola Negri[10] come in one night, along with Mr. A. Zukor, her manager.[11] All I done was praise her a heap, but she's not convivial with English an' never got a word I said. Neither did Mr. Zukor.

————

"You know I made a speech for Ogden Mills, don't you? Well, it was in the papers, but they missed one point. I told the crowd about Mr. Mills maintainin' apartments at the hotel that bears his name down on Seventh Avenue.[12] I reckon Ogden will be elected to whatever he's runnin' for. If he ain't, he don't need to blame me, for I certainly shot his opponent full of holes, if he's got one.[13]

————

"Well," concluded Will, "now I got to go over to the New Amsterdam Theatre and help keep Ziggy from starvation. The old boy an' me are good friends, the only difference bein' he's got a lot of money an' I ain't. So long!"

PD.[14] Printed in *Evening World*, New York, ca. 28 October 1922. OkClaW, Early Articles, 1916–22. Handwritten in the left margin: "Eve. World. Sat–".

1. *Robin Hood*, starring Fairbanks in the title role, opened in New York on 30 October. The screen idol's newest film followed the swashbuckling style he had introduced in *The Mark of Zorro* two years earlier and then repeated in *The Three Musketeers* in 1921 (*NYT*, 31 October 1922; *DAB*, Supp. 2:173; Slide, *Silent Players*, 312).

2. Several days before the premiere of *Robin Hood*, Fairbanks was on the roof of his New York hotel, the Ritz-Carlton, showing acquaintances one of the bows from the film. In the course of the demonstration, someone, perhaps Fairbanks, fired an arrow that wounded a furrier in his shop on Fifth Avenue. When Fairbanks discovered what had happened, he visited the gentleman at his home and apologized (*NYT*, 5 October 1922).

3. Gimbel's, a leading department store, began operations in New York in 1909 at a prime location between Thirty-second and Thirty-third Streets in Herald Square. Brothers Jacob Gimbel (1850–1922) and Isaac Gimbel (1856–1931) were the principal organizers and operators of the store, which became famous for its aggressive marketing (*DAB*, Supp. 8:212; *ENYC*, 468; *NYT*, 8 November 1922, 12 November 1931).

4. The twenty-two-story Hotel Pennsylvania opened in 1919 on Seventh Avenue between Thirty-second and Thirty-third Streets. With twenty-two hundred rooms it ranked at the time as the largest hotel in the world (*ENYC*, 985).

5. For John Francis McCormack see *PWR*, 2:55n.23. The Irish-born tenor made his home in New York during the war and became an American citizen in 1919, actions that aroused bitter feelings in the British Commonwealth, despite his overt expressions of

loyalty to Ireland. McCormack had returned to New York on 11 October 1922 after one of his first trips to England since the war (*DAB*, Supp. 3:483–85; *NYT*, 12 October 1922).

6. Thomas Johnstone Lipton (1850–1931) was a multimillionaire Scottish grocer, food processor, and tea plantation owner. He made frequent trips to the United States, where he had several business interests (*DAB*, Supp. 5:538–40).

7. Sir Thomas Lipton issued his first challenge for the America's Cup, the premier trophy in yacht racing, in 1899. His unsuccessful annual attempts to claim the cup over the next thirty years cost him more than 1 million pounds but gained for him the reputation in the United States of being "the world's best loser" (*DNB*, Supp. 5:539–40).

8. Alfred Emanuel (Al) Smith (1873–1944), a popular reform Democrat, won election as governor of New York in 1918. He served from 1919 to 1921 but lost his reelection bid in 1920 in a relatively close outcome in a Republican landslide nationwide. He then served as board chairman of a trucking company in New York but remained active in politics. He ran successfully for governor in 1922 and served from 1923 to 1929 (*DAB*, Supp. 3:716–19).

9. *Blood and Sand* starred matinee idol Rudolph Valentino as a Spanish matador in mortal and moral conflict. The film, a Famous Players–Lasky release, opened in New York on 6 August 1922 and, despite criticism of its vampishness, scored exceedingly well at the box office (*FE*, 1400; *Variety*, 11 August 1922).

10. Pola Negri (Barbara Apolonia Chalupiec, 1894–1987), a Polish ballerina-turned-actress, appeared successfully on the stage in Europe in the 1910s and then in German films. A glamorous and exotic beauty, she arrived in New York on 12 September 1922 en route to Hollywood, where her on-screen talents and off-screen exploits would attract wide attention (*FE*, 999; *UDSSEP*, 403; *IDFF*, 3:465–66; *NYT*, 13 September 1922).

11. Adolph Zukor (1873–1976), Hungarian-born, pioneer motion picture exhibitor and producer, made his Famous Players Film Company one of the industry's most prolific studios by 1914. The dynamic Zukor, who preferred residing in New York over Hollywood, eventually consolidated his operations with those of Jesse Lasky and Paramount studios to become a dominant player by 1922 in film production, distribution, and exhibition (*DAB*, Supp. 10:870–73; *FE*, 1495–96).

12. Ogden Mills built and owned the Mills Hotel, as well as the Mills Building, which was located in New York at 15 Broad Street, the site of an edifice that his grandfather had constructed in the financial district. At the time of Rogers's writing, Mills was between marriages (*NYT*, 12 October 1937).

13. In the general election on 7 November, incumbent Ogden Mills defeated his opponent, Metz, 21,197 votes to 19,250 (*NYT*, 9 November 1922).

14. The dating of the document was determined by historical references in the text and a handwritten notation referring to the day of the week.

Remarks by Will Rogers in *Evening World* 4 November 1922 New York, N.Y.

Will Rogers' Sayings This Week

Item in all papers nowadays: "We know the guilty parties in the New Jersey murder and will make arrests within 24 hours."

Item in all papers Nov., 1934: "We have the guilty parties and will make arrests within 24 hours."[1]

Too bad the murderers didn't know the authorities didn't want them for a while. They could have gone into vaudeville until they were ready for them.

Man traded a Ford car for another man's wife. Well, a really good wife is worth a Ford car.

I am for Ford for President. He carries two-thirds of the country now.

Democrats are for light wines and beers in election. If they can get this beer you pay $2 a quart for any lighter than it is they'll have to put a prop under it to hold it up.

I'll bet Hughes will be glad when this election is over and he doesn't have to go around thinking up nice things to try to say about these Republican candidates.

I have had several offers to go into politics. Al Smith made me an offer to speak for Gov. Miller.[2]

This is the finish of Apple Week in New York. Next week is "Why Not Make Love to Your Own Wife Week."

PD. Printed in *Evening World*, New York, 4 November 1922. Scrapbook 15, OkClaW.

1. In the Hall-Mills homicide case in New Jersey, speculation as to the perpetrators continued to dominate the newspapers. One front-page story on 3 November focused on two warrants for murder pending in the case. No arrests took place (*NYT*, 3 November 1922).
2. Nathan Lewis Miller (1868–1953), an attorney and a former judge, served as governor of New York from 1921 to 1923. A Republican, Miller had defeated incumbent Al Smith in 1920 but faced him again two years later. With the Republican tide having weakened, Smith won the rematch in the general election three days after Rogers's article appeared in the *Evening World* (*DAB*, Supp. 5:493–94).

Remarks by Will Rogers in *New York American* 7 November 1922 New York, N.Y.

WILL ROGERS, cowboy comedian—"Lots of people ask me 'Who writes your stuff and where do you get it?['] The surprising answer is the newspapers write it! All I do is to get all the newspapers I can carry and then read all that is going on and try to figure out the main things that the other folks have just read, and then I talk and talk on that. I have found out two things: One is that the more up to date a subject is the more credit you are given for talking on it, even if you can't say anything very funny. But if it [is] an old subject all the gags have sure got to be funny to get over. And they've got to be founded on facts."

PD. Printed in *New York American*, 7 November 1922. Scrapbook 15, OkClaW.

Subtitles for Weekly Edition of *Selznick Newsreel* 10 November 1922 [New York, N.Y.]

Several months had passed since Rogers had last written a series of on-screen gags for motion picture theaters. David O. Selznick, a young man of twenty and a son of pioneer film mogul Lewis J. Selznick, approached the comedian in New York and asked him to produce some humorous topical comments for a new semi-weekly production, Selznick Newsreel.¹ *The following was Rogers's first batch.*

Sent Selznick, Nov   10th.

1. Miller made a mistake in the election²   he announced no crooked business.

2. Smith dident do anything like that   he said just go ahead and get all you can . Stick to the old Tammany Policy.³

3. I met some Women friends the night after the eleaction and they said they were all in from changing clothes and voting all day.⁴

4. Dr Copeland from New York was elected⁵   that means an Apple a day for all of us

5. Going to be a lot of trouble over that election   the Republicans are claiming now that the democrats dident notify them what day they were holding it on   Just like those Democrats   kinder dirty that way.

6. I dont know how that one fellow in N Y found it out that voted for Miller.

7. This election people getting all worked up over it will make a lot of change in our lives. the whole thing is Apple Suuce anyway.

8. Feel sorry for Pres H[arding]. Freylingh [Frelinghuysen]⁶ only fellow he could beat playing _G[olf].

TD. OkClaW, Early Articles by Will Rogers, Selznick News, 1922–23.

1. David O. Selznick (1902–65) was the youngest of the two sons of pioneer film producer Lewis J. Selznick (1870–1933). David and his brother, Myron Selznick (1898–1944), became involved in their father's motion picture business while still youngsters and over the years proved even more successful than their father. As editor

of the *Selznick Newsreel* in the late fall of 1922, young David, still in school, worked with minimal resources to produce the twice-weekly film, about one minute of which was devoted to Rogers's subtitles. Unaware that Rogers had a proven track record as a gag writer for the screen, Selznick thought he was doing the Ziegfeld performer such a favor by providing him publicity that he did not offer financial compensation until Rogers finally requested $100 a week. Rogers continued to produce titles for Selznick into January 1923 (*FE*, 1228–29; Behlmer, ed., *Memo*, 4–5; see Early Articles by Will Rogers, Selznick News, 1922–23, OkClaW).

2. In the general election on 7 November, Nathan Miller lost his bid for reelection as governor of New York by 390,000 votes, more than five times the vote margin he had scored two years earlier over the same opponent, Al Smith, then the incumbent (*DAB*, Supp. 5:493, 494).

3. Tammany Hall began in 1789 as a benevolent society but by the 1920s had become the most powerful and successful Democratic organization in New York, one strongly identified with corruption and machine politics. Deeply rooted in Tammany, Al Smith also won the support of many progressives through his promotion of certain labor, conservation, and welfare reforms (*HDPE*, 471; *DAB*, Supp. 3:717, 719).

4. Women won the right to vote with the ratification of the Nineteenth Amendment on 26 August 1920. They voted in a nationwide election for the first time in November of that year. The general election in 1922 was only their second such opportunity (*HD1920s*, 251; *HDPE*, 453).

5. Royal Samuel Copeland (1868–1938), a doctor of ophthalmology in New York, was elected as a Democrat to the U.S. Senate in 1922. He served from 1923 until his death (*DAB*, Supp. 2:120–22).

6. Joseph Sherman Frelinghuysen (1869–1948), an insurance executive, served in the U.S. Senate for just one term, 1917–23. A poker pal and golfing buddy of President Harding, Frelinghuysen was one of many Republican casualties in the general election on 7 November 1922 (*BDAC*, 1059; Murray, *Harding Era*, 15, 117–18, 318).

Manuscript for Newspaper Article
ca. November 1922
[New York, N.Y.]

Rogers departed abruptly from his usual writing style when he prepared the following manuscript in the late fall of 1922. Borrowing from the quaint Mr. Dooley, Rogers may have written the dialogue piece for the New York Herald, *which had shown interest in publishing his work, or for submission to the McNaught Newspaper Syndicate. He delivered a copy of the following article—or, more likely, a version of it—to McNaught as the first installment of a proposed weekly syndicated newspaper column.*[1]

Old Powder River and Soapy——They Settle The Affairs of the World

Old Powder River Powell was a ridin' into town on his old buzzard headed horse, a keepin' away over to one side of the road so these modern ranchmen's fenders wouldn't rake him over a cut bank down into a gulch. He was a middle aged waddie, kind of old-fashioned like, bein' still interested in live stock, politics and his first wife.

He was a goin' to town today because a Woman's Journal[2] had strayed away from the home range and drifted into hiswife's clutches. In it was an article by some old Maid where husbands should not be allowed to neglect thier personal apperance. So his wife was a going to try out this receipt by making Old Powder River go to town every Saturday to get a shave and another Journal.

This was not such bad medicine to take, ashe knew while he was in the Barber shop a getting' the buffalo grass amputated from his mug, that he would also get all the latest from his old friend, an Ex-Cowpuncher, who, when he quit punchin' Cows, took to the Butcher business, and naturally drifted from that into the Barber trade. His Barbering was the kind of a trust or monopoly, as it was not only the only one in town, but his nearest competition was a gallon of gasoline away.

But don't you go gettin' it into yourhead that old Soapy's shop was of the regualtion Police Gazette Variety, No sirree Old Soapy's Whisker dividends didn't all go for overhead or Hair Oil. It went for subscriptions for all the latest papers. While old Soapy might just be movin' and movin' around and around a barber chair and never getting' any where in particular, he sure wanted to know in which direction the rest of the World was headed.

Soapy was a sort of an Advance Agent for the World, as far as old Powder was concerned. While Soapy read the bare facts and laid them before old Powder, it was Old Powder that could tell him what he had missed between the lines.

So it was on this Saturday that old Powder rides up to this Death-on-Whiskers Emporium. Steps off his horse kinder slow, bein' long of stature, while old Soapy was of the [s]hort, bow-legged variety. He takes the toe of his boot and r[a]kes a couple of Fords under the porch out of the way, so he couldtie his old Crow Bait by the bridle reins to the barber pole, Soapy's sole advertising medium, which also doubled as a hitch rack.

"Hello, Soapy, how's business?"

"Why, Hello, Powder River; I sure am glad to see you, things sure is slow, been no rain to speak of, and I never saw hair and beard grow so slowin my life. If things keep on like this I am going to have to put in one of them see-sauges things."

"What is a mess-sauge?"

"Well, a Mess-suage is a sort of a Solution they have in the east, where if a man can't wash his own face and keep it clean why the barber laundries it for him."

"Soapy, don't you ever let my Wife hear of it or she would send and get one andmake me take a whole bottle of it. Already she says I have come in here every Saturday, and get shaved, whether I need it or not. So it looks like if my wife don't get over this rash she'sin now that I will be about your most constant customer. But say, Soapy, what's the World been a doin' since I was in last?"

"Well, Powder, there's a terrible lot of news. Then agin' there's a terrible lot in them daily Pamphlets that ain't news. You see, it takes me days sometimes to round up all them columns. The plum latest is Clemenceau is here.[3] You remember we used to talk about him during Wilson's and Col. House's invasion of Europe."

Powder--"What did he tell us, Soapy?"

Soapy--"Oh, he balled us all out and told us just what he thought.[4] He must be the Senator Borah of France. He said we left Europe too soon."

Powder--"Mayby he means we didn't leave Europe ENOUGH."

Soapy--"No, he says we didn't stay long enough after the War."

Powder--"Why we stayed till we was broke and that's as long as we are ever welcome anywhere. Don't he say nothing about and appreciate the seventy-five Thousand that did stay over there?"[5]

Soapy--"oh, yes, he seems mighty obliged to us as fur as we went. But he seems to have somethin' he wants and nobody can't fugure it out what it is."

Powder--"What's the matter, is heatalking French?"

Soapy--"No, but he im just as well might be as fur as anybody understandin' him is concerned. And say, he says there is going to be another War."

Powder--"Why, sure, anybody but a Fool knows that."

Soapy--"And say, Powder, what do you think he done while he was here? He got up every mornin' at 4 o'clock and had Onion Soup for breakfast."[6]

Powder--"Say, I'll bet that stopped a lot of them Society Women from imatating, didn't it? But say, Soapy, don't you ever let my Wife hear of that, either. She is gettin' awful high-fangled. She wants to move where she can get in one of those Women's Clubs. I canget up at 4 o'clock, but my own Mother couldn't make me gnaw into Onion Soup that early in the mornin'. Besides, Soapy, it's a sort of a Frogs dish anyway, ain't it? As a food I don't think it has any standing among Civilized Nations. Over here we have always considered it more as an Odor than as a Delicacy."

Soapy--"And say, that ain't halfem of it. He would eat Six and Eight soft boiled eggs for breakfast, too."

Powder--"You say you don't know what he come after? Why from what you say he must have come after eggs. You know France never has got their hens back to normalcy since the War. You know what it is, Soapy, to try to get things backto normalcy. Look at Warren, in Washington. You know that Normalcy has just about been the Ruination of him."[7]

Soapy--"Newberry, he resigned from the Senate.[8] I wonder what he will do now."

Powder--"Why, he will aboutgo back home and turn honest. You know that may be just the makin' of that man, to catch him before he gets too deep into Politics. You cansave 'em sometimes if you get 'em early enough. Course where I bal blame him is buyin' a seat in that body of men. That's like payin' admission to go in a jail. Who did they put in to take his place?"

Soapy--"Why Jim Couzens,[9] the Millionair Mayer of Fordville, Michigan."

Powder--"You mean the fellow who put 500 dollars in with Ford and took out 75 Million[10] and sued Ford and claimedhe didn't know how to run his business?[11] He is my idea of what they calls a real Pessimist. It's ▲a▲good thing he ain't a puttin' any money in that Senate. Wait till he sees how they do business. He will give Ford credit yet. But I tell you Soapy I am awful glad all these things is a happening in there. If they could have a shootin' inthere every once in a while, it would add a lot to people's confidence in that body. Do you know I meet a lot of people that things that Senate Prong of our Government has been plum annulled."

Soapy--"I sure am glad she is a percolating, cause I got a freind that got the empty Bottle privilege in there. Best privilege in Washington."

Powder--"How about Europe Soapy? You can generally depend on them foreign Nations for everything but Interest."[12]

Soapy--"Well, they ain't disappo inted you none. They been a goin' right ahead with their Wars. Our Newspapers have moved them over on the Sporting Pages now, and there is certain Coutries you can get odds on. Now Greece, since you was in here last, has dropped away down in the second division. They lost a whole series with Turkey."[13]

Powder--"You know, Soapy, that's just about the way I had 'em do ped. That Greece, she makes awful pretty Statues but she has booted away a lot of wars. She is what I would call the Philadelphia Athaletics[14] of Europe. Who is Turkey matched with this week?"

Soapy--"Nobody. They got an open week. They triedto get a date with England. But Ireland was fighting a Home Talent war[15] so England couldn't go to war without their Army. So it left Turkey with an open Schedule."

Powder--"no, it don't Soapy, that's one thing about Turkey. While I know it is a big Disappointment to Turkey to not have some big-time war on their handsthis week, the week wont be entirely lost as they go right back into Asia and start rehearsin' on those Armenians."

Soapy--"And what Turkey didn't kill off for Greece, why Greece took it upon themselves and shot six of their own Cabinet."[16]

Powder--"And Englands Cabinet, they resigned didn't they?[17] I tell you Soapy, those two things ought to be a lesson to Ours."

Soapy--"Do you want Bay Rum or Witch Hazel?"

Powder--"Gimme Bay Rum. It seems like my old courtin' days to smell that agin. And say, I like to forgot to ask you , did ~~you~~ they ever hang them People that killed that Hall and Mills in New Jersey?"

Soapy--"Hang 'em! Why the authorities in them two counties ain't never found 'em yet. The Grand Jury turned in a verdict sayin' 'We found the two Parties thoroughly killed. And Recommend additional funds to carry on this case.'"[18]

Powder--"Why don't the two Murderers go into Vaudeville till the Authorities find out who they are? That would give 'em a good long season. Now say Soapy, I am a goin' to take all these old Papers out home with me and kinder hash through 'em myself. You might a overlooked some news. Good night, Soapy. If you can get me the right kind of a bet and don't have to give too much odds, get me Turkey in next week's war.

- - - -

TM.[19] OkClaW, Early Articles, 1916–22. "1921 or 1922" is handwritten on the first page above the heading. Editorial markings appear throughout the document. They were disregarded for the transcription.

1. See Croy, *Our Will Rogers*, 173–77. In his book Croy included a transcription of the story of Powder River and Soapy, but because of possible editing by Croy the version in the book differs from the present one. (See also Manuscript for Syndicated Newspaper Article, ca. 31 December 1922, below.)

2. *Woman's Journal*, founded in Boston in 1870, was one of two publications of the American Woman Suffrage Association (Mott, *History*, 3:394, 4:355).

3. Georges Clemenceau (1841–1929) served in the French Senate from 1902 to 1920 and as premier of France from 1906 to 1909 and 1917 to 1920. Hard-nosed, Clemenceau was credited for his decisive and confident leadership in wartime France, but his popularity at home evaporated in the wake of concessions he was forced to make at the postwar peace conference at Versailles, over which he presided. After leaving office in 1920, he spent many months traveling abroad, including a tour of the United States in the late fall of 1922 (*BDWWI*, 117–18; Watson, *Georges Clemenceau*, 15, 388–89).

4. Clemenceau arrived in the United States on 17 November. Speaking in several major cities in the Northeast and Midwest, he defended the heavy reparations imposed upon defeated Germany and argued that the repayment of the huge French war debt to the United States should be tied to the reparations. He warned against American aloofness and pleaded for full participation in international associations like the League of Nations. Although Clemenceau was enthusiastically received as a war hero throughout the tour, his message made little impact. He sailed from New York on

12 December (*NYT*, 18 November, 3, 13 December 1922; Watson, *Georges Clemenceau*, 389; *HD1920s*, 336).

5. With the failure of the U.S. Senate to ratify the Treaty of Versailles, the United States and Germany remained technically at war until Senate ratification of bilateral peace terms, the so-called Treaty of Berlin, in October 1921. However, 15,000 U.S. troops continued to occupy the Rhineland of Germany, ostensibly to maintain stability in the region. President Harding did not withdraw the men until French and German hostilities boiled over in January 1923 and France sent troops across the Rhine (Trani and Wilson, *Presidency*, 144–45).

6. Every moment of Clemenceau's daily schedule became first-page news throughout his stay in the United States. Newspapers reported his bedtime and awakening hours, his breakfast menu, the volume of messages from well-wishers, his topics of conversation. After his first morning's breakfast of onion soup, Gruyere cheese, two soft-boiled eggs, bread, butter, and water, no coffee, newspapers began reporting such exaggerations as the eighty-one-year-old Clemenceau consuming a meal of eight hard-boiled eggs (*NYT*, 20 November, 1 December 1922).

7. President Harding had introduced the term *normalcy* during the presidential campaign of 1920 to describe, as he defined it, "a regular steady order of things . . . the natural way, without excess." After a long period of a disillusioning war, economic stress, growth of government, and social upheaval, Harding's utterance of normalcy gave promise of stability and tranquility. The phrase "return to normalcy" became a winning theme for the Republicans in 1920 and a historical label for the Harding administration and the government's probusiness policies during the decade (Murray, *Harding Era*, 70; Trani and Wilson, *Presidency*, 101; *HD1920s*, 253).

8. Truman Newberry, facing a renewed effort to unseat him for violations of campaign expenditure laws, submitted his resignation from the Senate on 19 November 1922. He returned to Michigan, retired from politics, and concentrated on his business affairs (*DAB*, Supp. 3:550; *NYT*, 20 November 1922).

9. James Couzens, a reform Republican who had been elected mayor of Detroit in 1918, had long desired to serve in the U.S. Senate. When Truman Newberry resigned, the governor of Michigan appointed Couzens to the position on 29 November. He took office about a week later (*DAB*, Supp. 2:126; *NYT*, 30 November 1922).

10. Couzens was one of the original investors in Ford Motor Company when it was incorporated in 1903. A man of moderate means at the time, Couzens could raise only $500 but with financial help managed to invest a total of $2,500. When he sold his shares to Henry Ford in 1919, he received $30 million, a return of better than 12,000 percent. The transaction was part of a larger effort by Ford at the time to purchase all outstanding stock. To help accomplish the buyout, he had secured a credit line of $75 million (Barnard, *Independent Man*, 41–42, 130; Nevins and Hill, *Ford*, 2:110–11).

11. Despite heated differences that had arisen between James Couzens and himself, Henry Ford issued a statement on 2 December commending his former business associate and endorsing Couzens's selection for the open Senate seat. Ford had sought the same position in 1918 (*DAB*, Supp. 2:125; *NYT*, 3 December 1922).

12. The United States had loaned more than $7 billion to European nations during the war and an additional $3.3 billion for reconstruction. Although the United States had prospered because most of the funds were spent in the country to purchase goods, American public opinion favored full repayment of the debt, plus interest. The debtor countries began to balk, however, when the prospects of receiving reparations from Germany faded with the collapse of that country's economy in 1921. Even payment of interest on the debt appeared doubtful by late 1922 (*HD1920s*, 336).

13. Greece and Turkey had fought a vicious war since 1921, but Turkey had gained the upper hand by September 1922, inflicting heavy casualties, including the massacre of several thousand Christian civilians at Smyrna. The age-old enemy states finally agreed to meet at Lausanne, Switzerland, to discuss peace. At the conference, which opened in November 1922, Greece surrendered all of its territorial gains in Asia Minor, and Turkey stabilized its foothold in Europe. The Treaty of Lausanne was signed in July 1923 (Dakin, *Unification*, 234–37, 242; Palmer, *Decline*, 262–63).

14. The Philadelphia Athletics finished next to last in the American League in 1922, the eighth consecutive season the baseball team had ended the year at or near the bottom of the league (*TB*, 47).

15. Civil war erupted in Ireland in June 1922 when republicans rebelled against the limited self-government permitted in the newly formed Irish Free State. The Irish Republican Army used guerrilla tactics against Irish government forces and assassinated some leaders. The government reacted strongly by executing 77 rebels and imprisoning 12,000. Although called off in May 1923, the civil war left a legacy of deep division in Irish society (*CHE*, 308, 309).

16. A military coup in Greece in September 1922 led to the overthrow of the king, the installation of a new monarch, and the establishment of a new government. The revolutionary committee then arrested, tried, and convicted the eight cabinet members in the former government, apparently to solidify the authority of the revolutionaries and to place blame for the military disaster that Greece had suffered in its war with Turkey. The executions on 27 November 1922 of six of the cabinet ministers caused an international outcry (Dakin, *Unification*, 238–39).

17. David Lloyd George and his cabinet of ministers resigned on 19 October when the coalition that he had built as prime minister collapsed amid rising European tension over the conflict between Greece, supported by Great Britain, and Turkey, backed by France and Italy (*DNB*, Supp. 6:525–26; *NYT*, 20 October 1922).

18. In the Hall-Mills homicide, a grand jury convened on 20 November in Somerset County, N.J., to determine if sufficient evidence was available to bring charges in the case. After listening to the testimony of sixty-seven witnesses, the jury deliberated less than an hour on 28 November and voted not to issue any indictments. With the refusal to indict, public interest in the case declined, although references to it continued to appear in print (Kunstler, *Hall-Mills*, 94, 102, 104).

19. Dating of the document was determined from historical references in the text.

Gags for *Life* Magazine
ca. November–December 1922
[New York, N.Y.]

Rogers reached a different kind of national audience when he began in the late fall of 1922 to supply gags to Life, *a venerable magazine of humor published in New York.* [1] Life *provided Rogers with an opportunity to connect with a weekly readership of almost one-quarter million people and to gain his first regular exposure in a national magazine.*

1. Turkey had hard luck this month   they had a war all booked and got it cancelled on them.

2. You cant get a War with Turkey on a days notice. You got to book your Wars way ahead with Turkey.

3. Winning or losing one War dont mean anything to Turkey. Its what you can average up at the end of the season that counts.

4. England is liable any time to go to War with Turkey. But Ruddy Kipling[2] seems to think America did so bad in the last War I dont suppose they would have nerve to ask us to go into another one.

5. Why drive the Turks back into Asia? There is no Humanity in a War like that. He would just start in rehearsing on those Armenians again.

6. Secretary Denby[3] says our Interests should be protected so he sent over 24 Battle Cruisers to protect our Interests in Turkey.[4] Thats 6 ships to each Interest.

7. Mr Hughes said the Dardenelles should be kept open.[5] Years ago it is said an American sailing Ship come pretty near going through there.

8. When Congressman Herrick[6] from my home state of Oklahoma heard them argueing over these Dardenelles. He said it was alright to keep them open during the week but that he was for closing them on Sunday

9. You would never get this Country to go to War over the Dardenelles unless they had to cross them going from their offices to their Golf Course.

10. The only War you will ever interest this Country in will be one on the Home Grounds. Why pay transportation to a War.

11. Look how much cheaper you could put on a War here. Instead of paying men a Dollar a year to help run it. Just pay them what they are worth   look what a saving.

12. Look   why it would almost be a pleasure to have a War with no Shipping Board connected with it.

13. Then fight alone without any help. So they wouldnt have to have three more Wars over who won that one.

14. Russia is a tough Country to fight as they are the only Country that carry their own Brush entanglements with them.

15. Well I see they let Lloyd George out in England. I never saw it fail when a Man starts selling his Memoirs he is about through.[7]

16. But we could use him in America. A bih [big] Man would be a novelty in this Country.

17. Their whole Cabinet resigned   funny we cant ever have any luck like that.

18. The more we cuss ours the longer they stay.

19. See the King is still in over there. England feels safe as long as her social affairs are taken care of.

20. Lot of people think a King aint much use. But I tell you in case of Parades they come in mighty handy.

21. They have outriders. Men on horseback ridding [riding] all around their carriage   And I tell you   sometimes their Horses are well worth looking at.

22. Of course as far as the King having anything to do with the Government I doubt if he knows Lloyd George is out.

23. Everybody cant get over Iowa beating Yale playing football.[8] Why they would have beat them sooner than this but it was only ten years ago that some Tourist left a football in Iowa.

24. Good thing they didnt beat Harvard[9] or they would have protested the game. Would have claimed it was against TRADITION.

25. Been having all kinds of weeks in New York   had one "Dont get hurt week"   Taxi Drivers couldnt hardly wait till the following Monday to run over you.

26. During the Campaign I read all of Gov. Miller of N.Y. and his opponent speeches till I found out they were both written by the same man.

27. I think the Democrats are the wisesr. They are trying to find somebody to run who aint known.

28. Certainly glad to see Womens skirts getting longer. A lot of men on the street seem to see where they are going now.

29. And you would be surprised at the beautiful faces Women have now which you never noticed before.

30. About 6 weeks after Congress closed Pres Harding sent a letter complimenting Floor Leader Mondell on what Congress had done.[10] He said "I would have written this letter sooner but I know you fellows had left here"

31. Allies Peace terms made Germany take all Engines out of Airships.[11] Now they are staying up three hours without anything. They [took?] all of her Gold and she is doing great on paper money.[12] They overlooked their biggest chance to ruin Germany   that was to have made them Prohibitioni[sts]

32. Nothing great about Germanys engineless flying machines   Henry Ford did the same thing on land.

33. See where Prohibition boats been going out beyond the three mile limit to seize Booze. Couldnt supply the demand with what they could catch inside the three miles.

34. They are underselling the Bootleggers now. They got no overhead.

35. Better look out going out 12 miles   They will get in trouble searching Englands Boats on Their Sea.

36. If we do get into War with England over Booze on Boats it will be stronger than the last war which was over tea.

37. The Literary Digest held a Poll on the Wets and Drys. The Wets won They would have won further than that but the stuff the wets are drinking nowadays after a fellow drinks it he aint able to vote.

38. Lasker[,] head of our ships[,] says taking Drinks off our boats will ruin them[13]   he says "You dont suppose People go to Europe just for the trip

39. An awful lot of traffic to Europe this year. Well there was a lot in [19]18 too. But this is a different bunch.

40. All bringing back souvenirs of the War. And we dont properly support the ones we have.

41. Everybody from Europe brings back a German Police Dog. I dont see why Germany dont pay their National Debt   they have sold enough dogs to pay for it.

42. I wanted to go over this summer but I figured after I paid my fare I wouldnt have enough left to get a dog. So I couldnt go.

43. See where Mr Ford has reduced his cars 50 Dollars.[14] Thats to discou[ra]ge petty thievery.

44. He is still trying to get Mussell Shoals.[15] But Congress cant decide whether the country needs High priced Senators. Or cheap fertilizer

TM.[16] OkClaW, Magazine Articles, Folder UCMA. I–UCMA. II. Typewritten, top margin, center, page 1: "Gags sent to life". Handwritten, not in Rogers's hand, upper right corner, page one: "Please return". Editorial marks, apparently not in Rogers's hand, appear throughout the document; they were ignored for this transcription. Handwritten, not in Rogers's hand, top margin, left side, page 2: "Fall of 1922". Hand-inserted, wavy vertical lines appear immediately left of the text of gag numbers 1–19, 20–25, 28–29, 31, and 32, all on page 2. Handwritten, not in Rogers's hand, immediately above gag 26, center: "Smith elected". Handwritten, not in Rogers's hand, immediately above gag 31, left side: "aviation".

1. Launched in 1893, the black-and-white weekly *Life* had become by the mid-1910s a leading and respected literary humor and cartoon magazine. Published in New York, the periodical reached its peak of popularity in 1916, but with the death of its founder two years later, it began to decline. By 1922 the circulation had dropped to 227,000, a respectable number but less than one-half of what it had been two years earlier. Rogers as presidential campaigner in jest in 1928 brought some renewed attention, but even "The Bunkless Candidate" could not halt the inevitable (see *HCTR* for the complete collection of Rogers's articles in *Life* in 1928). Sold in 1936, *Life* evolved into the famed photo-essay magazine of the *Time* organization (Sloane, ed., *American Humor*, 141–51; Mott, *History*, 4:556–68). For further evidence of Rogers's relationship with *Life* magazine, see Notes for Banquet Speech, ca. 3 January 1923, and Letter to Louis Evan Shipman, ca. January 1923, below. For Rogers's other writings in *Life* see *HTBF*, 6–12.

2. Joseph Rudyard Kipling (1865–1936), British author, wrote his first eight books by the age of twenty-two as a journalist in India. Among the most honored and recognizable of modern British writers, he was awarded the Nobel prize for literature in 1907. In an interview published in a New York newspaper on 11 September 1922,

Kipling criticized the United States for entering the war years late and profiting hugely from it. The remarks, which Kipling quickly disclaimed, provoked intense reactions on both sides of the Atlantic (*DNB*, Supp. 5:512–14; Birkenhead, *Rudyard Kipling*, 296–97).

3. Edwin Denby (1870–1929), an attorney and a former congressman from Michigan, served as U.S. secretary of the navy from 1921 to 1924 (*DAB*, 5:234–35).

4. Feelings quickly escalated in the United States in the fall of 1922 following reports of massacres of Christian Armenians in Turkish territory. As Americans pressed hard for the protection of Christians in the region, the Harding administration responded by dispatching a squadron of destroyers to Constantinople in October to evacuate women and children in a gesture of humanitarianism (Murray, *Harding Era*, 357; *NYT*, 15 October 1922).

5. Secretary of State Hughes directed American negotiators in the peace talks that began in November 1922 at Lausanne to obtain from Turkey freedom of transit through the Straits of the Dardanelles and the protection of Christians. At the same time the new nationalist government in Turkey demanded an end to foreign spheres of influence in its country. The American position proved moderate compared to that of the European allies, and the United States and Turkey eventually concurred on major points. They signed a bilateral agreement on 6 August 1923, but the Senate rejected the treaty in 1927 (Pusey, *Charles Evans Hughes*, 2:574–75; Trani and Wilson, *Presidency*, 168, 169).

6. Immanuel (Manuel) Herrick (1876–1952), an eccentric and a self-described attorney whose mother believed he was Christ returned, was swept into office as a U.S. representative from Oklahoma in the Republican landslide of 1920. Known as the "Okie Jesus Congressman," Herrick won election virtually by default because the popular Republican incumbent had died just before the primary and Herrick was the only other Republican candidate in a district and year where no Democrat stood a chance. Colorful but tactless, Herrick became stock material for newspapers. He lost his bid for reelection in 1922 (*BDAC*, 1206; Aldrich, *Okie Jesus*, 17, 93–98, 210–11).

7. David Lloyd George signed a contract with an American publisher in August 1922 to write his memoirs of the war, the book to be first serialized in the *New York Times* and the *Chicago Tribune*. When he became obligated to donate his profits to charity, his enthusiasm for the project waned. He then signed a new contract on 24 November 1922 with United Press Associations of America to write a periodic newspaper column. Holders of the first contracts protested, but their agreements were canceled by court action and Lloyd George was free to start a new career as a highly paid columnist. More than ten years passed before his *War Memoirs* appeared in print (Rowland, *David Lloyd George*, 572–73, 593, 703).

8. The University of Iowa football team defeated Yale, 6 to 0, at New Haven, Conn., on 14 October. The Iowa team finished the season unbeaten (*BDASFoot*, 298–99, 301; *NYT*, 15 October 1922).

9. Yale lost to its greatest rival, Harvard University, 10 to 3, on 25 November, leaving the Yale football squad winless for the season (*NYT*, 26 November 1922).

10. In a letter released to the press on 15 October, President Harding wrote House Majority Leader Franklin Mondell to commend the Republican-dominated Sixty-seventh Congress for the volume and quality of legislation it had enacted, especially a new tariff, tax revision, and budget reform. Coming only three weeks before the general election, Harding's letter reminded many Americans of a similar message by President Wilson just before the wartime election in 1918, a move that precipitated

cries of partisanship at the time. The Republican party fared little better in 1922 (Murray, *Harding Era*, 315; *NYT*, 16 October 1922).

11. Gliders, or engineless planes, enjoyed renewed popularity in Germany after the war because of the restrictions that the Treaty of Versailles had imposed on other types of aircraft. German and French glider contests in late 1922 had attracted the attention of U.S. aviation experts and had spurred interest in staging such competition in the United States (Josephy, ed., *American Heritage*, 207; *NYT*, 17 December 1922).

12. Germany had few gold reserves in the postwar period. That, coupled with a weakened economy, burdensome reparations, political upheavals, and ineffective fiscal administration, led to a spiraling, crippling inflation during which the exchange rate ballooned from 4.2 marks to the U.S. dollar just before the war to 17,972 marks in January 1923 (*HDGWR*, 221–22, 394–95).

13. Albert Davis Lasker (1880–1952), chairman of the U.S. Shipping Board during the Harding administration, faced the onerous task of liquidating the government fleet in the midst of a depressed postwar maritime economy. His troubles were exacerbated when the U.S. attorney general issued an opinion on 6 October 1922 that barred liquor from all U.S. vessels anywhere, public and private. American-owned passenger ships, including the government's, now had to find a way to compete with foreign liners that could offer well-stocked bars (*DAB*, Supp. 5:410–11; *NYT*, 7 October 1922; Trani and Wilson, *Presidency*, 75).

14. The Ford Motor Company reduced the price of the Model T six times between 1921 and 1925, bringing the cost of its basic runabout down to $260 in December 1924. Responding to a public predominantly focused on price and dependability, Ford produced 56 percent of all cars sold in the United States in 1921. The company increased its production by 26 percent in 1922 and close to 55 percent a year later (Nevins and Hill, *Ford*, 2:264).

15. Henry Ford offered in July 1921 either to lease or acquire from the government uncompleted hydroelectric facilities and an unused nitrate plant at Muscle Shoals, Tenn., and other related operations nearby, all dating from the war. Ford stated that he intended to finish and operate the dams and plants to produce affordable fertilizer for farmers. Although his initial offer was rejected, Ford continued throughout 1921 and 1922 to push for some sort of operational control of the Muscle Shoals facilities. He won the support of many farmers, laborers, and community boosters hopeful of better economic conditions locally, but congressional opponents of privatization blocked the deal because it offered Ford favored status and ran counter to the idea of public development of electric power. After years of stalemate, Ford finally withdrew his offer in October 1924 (Nevins and Hill, *Ford*, 2:305–11).

16. Dating of the document was determined through historical references in the text.

Statement of Earnings from Ziegfeld Corporations
13 December 1922
[New York, N.Y.]

December 13th,1922.
Re:- Will Rogers salaries &
royalties paid by the Ziegfeld Corporations during the
calendar year 1922.

Salary:-)
Ziegfeld Midnight Frolic-(Roof Show) Week Ending 1/7/22- $-1000.00
Salary:-)
Ziegfeld Midnight Frolic-(Rogers Show) Week Ending 1/14/22- $- 437.50
"   "   1/21/22-   500.00
"   "   1/28/22-   500.00-   2437.50

Royalty-10% of Gross)
Ziegfeld Midnight Frolic-(Rogers Show)   "   "   1/14/22- $-1450.00
"   "   1/21/22-   1876.80
"   "   1/28/22-   1758.51
"   "   2/4/22-   2037.00
"   "   2/11/22-   2519.30
"   "   2/18/22-   1807.70
"   "   2/25/22-   2106.95
"   "   3/4/22-   1561.95
"   "   3/11/22-   1985.70
"   "   3/18/22-   1520.60
"   "   3/25/22-   2462.60
"   "   4/1/22-   2401.00
"   "   4/8/22-   2124.50
"   "   4/15/22-   1788.50
"   "   4/22/22-   1886.90
"   "   4/29/22-   1671.00
"   "   5/6/22-   1658.40- 32617.41

Salary:-)
Ziegfeld Follies of 1922:-Twenty Seven Weeks from the week-
ending June 10th,1922 to the week ending December 9th,1922-
@ $-2000.-per week -- 54000.00
Salary to be paid by the Ziegfeld Follies ending the calendar
year of 1922-as follows:-
Week Ending December 16th,1922-$-2000.00
"   "   "   23rd,1922-   2000.00
"   "   "   30th,1922-   2000.00 6000.00- 60000.00
Total paid by the Ziegfeld Corporations during
the calendar year of 1922-- $-95054.91

GSS

Dear Mr. Rogers:-

Kindly fill in and sign the enclosed New York State Certificate of Residence. Return,in the addressed envelope enclosed,to this office.

Very Truly Yours,

George S. Savage

[*handwritten, in Rogers's hand, in bottom margin:*][1]

4,500 Detroit.

3,000 Chicago.

7,500[2]   Ichabod Crane about $18,000[3]   will send you that later.

But figure it out on basis of about $120,000.[00] Total.[4]

[*handwritten, not in Rogers's hand, on reverse side:*]

2 weeks rehearsing NY.

Life[5] 225[00]

Selznick[6]

1st Natl Bank Claremore

$1500.00– assessed $1000.[00]

Oklahoma, Agent

$5000

Garage $200-

TDS. OkClaW, Income Tax Returns, 1922 & 1923. Hand-inserted check marks appear to the right of the handwritten copy "Life 225[00]" and "Selznick" on reverse side.

1. Rogers likely wrote this note to his secretary/bookkeeper, Edward Hayden, and sent the document to Hayden in Los Angeles in anticipation of completing and filing Rogers's income tax return for 1922. See also Statement of Income and Deductions, ca. 15 March 1923, below.

2. Although not listed in the Ziegfeld organization's accounting of payments to Rogers, the $7,500 attributed as "Detroit" and "Chicago" does appear in Rogers's tax documents for 1922 as income received from the Ziegfeld Corporation. The income probably derived from road productions (see Income Tax Documents, 1922–25, OkClaW).

3. Rogers starred as Ichabod Crane in an independent film production, *The Headless Horseman,* based on Washington Irving's *The Legend of Sleepy Hollow.* Filmed in the summer of 1922 near New York, the movie provided Rogers an opportunity to earn extra money—he actually received $19,583.20—while also appearing in the *Follies.* The motion picture opened in New York on 5 November 1922 (Yagoda, *Will Rogers,* 191–92; *WRHolly,* 75; Charles W. Atwater to Will Rogers, 27 December 1922, OkClaW).

4. Rogers reported to the Internal Revenue Department a total salary income in 1922 of $122,138.11 from two sources, Ziegfeld Corporation and Sleepy Hollow Corporation, the latter the producer of *The Headless Horseman* (see Statement of Income and Deductions, ca. 15 March 1923, below).

5. Rogers provided a series of gags to the popular humor magazine *Life,* beginning in late 1922 (see Gags for *Life* Magazine, ca. November–December 1922, above).

6. See Subtitles for Weekly Edition of *Selznick Newsreel,* 10 November 1922, above.

Rogers at cookout fire on location of *The Headless Horseman* near Tarrytown, N.Y., in summer 1922. Standing immediately to Rogers's left are Ed Venturini, the director, and Ned Van Buren, cameraman. (*Gordon Kuntz Private Collection*)

Notes for Banquet Speech
16 December 1922
New York, N.Y.

An increasingly busy after-dinner speaker, Rogers found his usual audience at banquets to be members and guests of fraternal societies, trade associations, charities, service groups, or civic organizations. Only rarely did he address the officers and employees of a single company. In December 1922 he spoke to one such group, representatives of a favorite target of his populist-flavored humor—banking.

The American Bond and Mortgage Co.[1]

You Birds are so prosperous looking one would think you were the Buyers of the Bonds instead of the sellers. There aint a one of you thatdont lok better than than these men who own the Company. Not only that but your mind seems more at ease. Why if a Man told People in N Y that some of you come from Columbus and Grand Rapids wouldent believe you. But if you ever told them you ahd men in here that. come from the wilds of Rockfordand.Davenport. Why it would be unbelievable.

[I am the] Only man that had never heard of it.I had never had anything to mortgage and never had anything to buy a mortgage with.It ahs never been my idea of happiness to make money by having a mortgage on something somebody else was trying to make a living out of.

I only loan to the man who I think will pay it back.If I had to take a Mortgage I wouldent loan it to him. A man shouldent be allowed to borrow who wouldent pay back.

Did you ever figure that Banking. Loans Mortgages.Interests of any kind are the most nonessential industries in the world. Interest eats up half the earnings of the world. Suppose nobody borrowed anything and if they did they paid back just what they borrowed.If you live by a Neighbor and need asack of flour or some Potatoes you borrow from your neighbors and when you pay it back you pay one sack of flour not one and 8/100ths. now this neighbor only borrows when he needs it. and you only loan him when you have confidence in him.

every man owns his own business he is in   he dont owe anything on it. no interest to pay. so he dont have to charge as much for his goods.You work[,] buy what you need[,] save up[,] buy just what you can pay for and no more . see eliminate all business worries. Dont say it couldent be done for 2 thirds of the world live now without receiving a cent of Interest   well let this other third live or go to work without receiving any.

Now I am not a saving [saying?] anyhting against you salesmen.You are a working hard trying ~~to~~ [sell.] its these Capitalist[s] here who I am trying to convert.I want to try and get them to turn honest. Now take my graft   its about the same thing   its Non essential.I want to get out of it as soon as I can find something else.No man should spend Money for Amusements or to see anything funny on the Stage. My Lord aint there enough Funny looking things off the Stage and aint most of the things that Men say seriously funny enough to suit any one.

Now they kidded you fellows saying we are going to take you back east on a trip.We are going to give a lot of you fellows a chance to come to N Y   We are going to have a Convention. Convention that is the curse of all business is Conventions   thats what makes the overhead on all we poor buy is the rich holding Conventions. The minute a firm gets big enough to hire over two men why they call a convention. Where they herd you around like a lot of sheep and pin a Badge on you and make speeches to you and tell you what the organization is going to do during the coming year. That You have jipped so many people during the past year and that by putting your shoulders to the wheel you should go out this year and do more

They tell you what great guys you are but that next year you are expectedto do better.And maby all thetime they are telling you this they are figureing on some other fellow on an opposition firm to take your place. Now you know why they brought you back here because its so they could charge it off on yourincome tax.

I remember tgose [those] two Towns [Columbus and Grand Rapids?]. I lived in Oklahoma and we used to send missionaries to those places. But you take them in a bunch like this they are all right   the Company wisely brought you all through some of the smaller towns like Washington so would be about House Broke by the time you agot here.

Got an Inventio[n:] how to get rid of a Bo[n]d Salesman. Some people in small towns have Dogs that protect them but even tha[t] is no good as most Slesm an [salesmen] are so hard boiled yhey [they] got to bighting the dogs . For awhile people used to say they were broke   then they figured out a plan to sell them on credit   [My invention is] A highly tuned instrument you carry in your Pocket. and when a Bond Sal[esman] comes in the same Block it rings and gives you warning.

Senator Fess elected to be Senator[2]   that is about. the smallest job I ever heard of an Ohioan accepting. thay generally dont stop at anything less t than the ~~Senate~~ White House. There were Two Republicans elected he and Congressman Mills that I personally put over.[3]

Only business no Capital.

Bu ilding consern. so you can underbid any other firm. Guy name Beck he plans the Theatre.[4] Fellow spends so much on the Theat[r]e he has nothing left for the Show.So many Theatres if you get a Party of 10 you can get a whole Theatre to yourself.

Fox Studio. then puts on Pictures nothing but storms in em[5] what good is S[torm?]

Moore Family[6] you acn [can] always tell when a M n [man] has a good graft he lets all the family in on it. Only two brothers th[a]t ever kept speaking to each other.

Headquarters in Chicago.

TD. OkClaW, 1975.14.0010. Paragraph 13 ("Bu ilding consern, so . . .") was encircled by pencil.

1. The American Bond & Mortgage, which was organized in Chicago in 1905, provided first mortgage real estate bonds for large commercial properties. The company purchased a building in New York in late June 1922 to house its first permanent office in the city and to serve as its East Coast base of operations. After several months of remodeling, company employees first occupied the building on 18 December (*NYT*, 6 June, 18 December 1922).

2. Simeon Davidson Fess (1861–1936), a former university professor and administrator, served as U.S. representative from Ohio from 1913 to 1921. A Republican, he was elected to the U.S. Senate in 1922 in a general election that saw his party's majority in the Senate reduced by 4 seats and its majority in the House cut by 163. Fess left the Senate in 1935 (*DAB*, Supp. 2:180–81; Trani and Wilson, *Presidency*, 80).

3. See Article in *New York Times*, 27 October 1922, above.

4. For Martin Beck see *PWR*, 3:53–55n.20.

5. The epic drama *Orphans of the Storm* had opened in Boston a year earlier. Much more recently, *Tess of the Storm Country*, a melodrama with Mary Pickford as producer and star, premiered on 12 November 1922 and became one of the most popular movies of 1922–23. Neither film was a product of Fox Studios (*AFIC*, F2FE:792; Koszarski, *Evening's Entertainment*, 33).

6. C. E. Moore was senior vice president of American Bond & Mortgage Company in 1925 (*NYT*, 5 December 1925).

Remarks at Anti-Prohibition Meeting
17 December 1922
New York, N.Y.

. . . "I have a good act that I put on for the drys, . . . but this act to-night is for the wets.[1] Now, this prohibition law came about something like this: A man in the Legislature at Washington said: 'Let's take up this prohibition question. There is nothing else to do right now.' And so they sent around to the bars and got a quorum and passed the Volstead act.[2] Mr. Volstead lived up to the terms of his act and got only one-half of one per cent. of the votes in the last election.[3]

"I don't drink myself, but I do like to play to an audience that has had a few nips, because they seem to catch the point quicker and have enough intelligence to applaud. Miss Marbury[4] has spoken of the part the American armies played in the world war. Going back into history I find that all armies have used liquor. France ran her armies on wine; the Italians went over the top on Chianti, and Canadian Club put the Canucks over and the English went over on Scotch. The Americans were inspired by Green River and other good brands of rye. Germany, with beer, was affiliated with Turkey, and lost. The Russians were going fine until their vodka was taken from them and then they flopped.["] . . .

"Unlike Gus Thomas,[5] I am not referring to the Constitution of the United States. I am going further back than that. I get all my dope from way back—from the Bible itself. Take up your Bible, and in the ninth chapter of Genesis, twentieth verse, you'll find where Noah was soused. Now, this guy Noah was the Water Commissioner of his time. He was the first man to recognize that water has no value as a beverage.

"Because Noah got on a hard liquor spree the Lord picked him to collect two of every kind of animal to put on the Ark. He was the only man who ever saw two of each kind. If it hadn't been for Noah people wouldn't be going up to The Bronx Zoo now to see the baby elephants. The wine Noah drank, you'll notice, had such an ill effect that he lived only 950 years. Outside of Methuselah and Bill Bryan's speeches he is the only man who ever lived that long. Bryan's speeches were used 900 years before he started using them, and he has been hanging on to them fifty years.

"We read about where Nero fiddled as Rome burned. If he hadn't been soused he never would have fiddled during that fire and if the people hadn't been pretty well liquored up they wouldn't have applauded. Coming down to modern times, though, I can point to Gov. Edwards[6] here. The Harding Cabinet came into New Jersey to beat him. The Brunen murder case[7] has shoved the Hall-Mills case out of the papers and that State is the hardest place in the world for a man to tell the truth and not be believed. A guy comes forward in this Brunen case and admits he did the killing and the courts won't believe him.[8] The only bird they ever believed over there was Gov. Edwards. He walked up to the polls waving a bottle and shouted: 'Come on, boys.'["] . . .

"One bottle of liquor has more authority than a barrel of oratory. The only thing that is better than a bottle of liquor is two bottles. Senator Frelinghuysen had two bottles, but he gave them to Harding's Cabinet instead of to the voters.[9] This light wine and beer thought is a beautiful thing, but it's impossible. The prohibitionists after three years of hard liquor are not going to be content to go back to a beverage that is so light it has to have a prop to hold it up." . . .

PD. Printed in *New York Herald*, 18 December 1922. Scrapbook 8, OkClaW. Ellipses inserted by editors.

1. Rogers delivered his remarks to a packed crowd at the Thirty-ninth Street The-atre in New York on the evening of 17 December. The occasion was a rally of the Molly Pitcher Club, a women's group that was linked to the Association against the Prohibition Amendment, a national group formed in 1920 and the most active anti-Prohibition organization at the time. The name of the local group derived from the Revolutionary War heroics of Mary Ludwig McCauley (1754–1832), whose constant toting of water to relieve the thirst of her husband and other soldiers at the Battle of Monmouth earned her the sobriquet of "Molly Pitcher" (*HD1920s*, 19; *NYT*, 18 December 1922; *DAB*, 11:574).

2. Andrew John Volstead (Andrew John Wraalstad, 1860–1947), U.S. representa-tive from Minnesota from 1903 to 1923, virtually singlehandedly drafted the enabling legislation for the enforcement of the Prohibition amendment. Passed in 1919, the National Prohibition Enforcement Act, more commonly known as the Volstead Act, prohibited beverages containing more than one-half of one percent of alcohol. Much to his disappointment, Volstead became a hero of the drys and a symbol of scorn of the wets (*DAB*, Supp. 4:852–53; *HD1920s*, 329).

3. Volstead, like many incumbent Republican congressmen, lost his seat in 1922. Although targeted for defeat by anti-Prohibitionists, he was as much a victim of the depression in the farm economy and opposition from the labor front (*DAB*, Supp. 4:853).

4. Elisabeth Marbury (1856–1933) enjoyed a long, successful career as an agent for actors and playwrights in both the United States and Europe. Preceding Rogers to the podium at the event, Marbury, an ardent opponent of the Eighteenth Amendment, described Prohibition as "a widespread hypocrisy" (*DAB*, Supp. 1:538–39; *NAW*, 2:493–95; *NYT*, 18 December 1922).

5. Augustus Thomas (1857–1934), an American dramatist most active in the 1890s and 1910s, wrote or adapted about seventy plays. Widely noted and sought as a public speaker, Thomas also spoke at the anti-Prohibition rally. He termed the Prohi-bition amendment as "the most un-American, the most destructive thing that was ever written into the statutes" (*DAB*, 18:421–22; *NYT*, 18 December 1922).

6. Edward Irving Edwards (1863–1931), Democratic governor of New Jersey, ran on a strong anti-Prohibition platform in 1922 and defeated incumbent U.S. Senator Joseph S. Frelinghuysen, a close friend of President Harding. Also a speaker at the anti-Prohibition gathering, Edwards attributed his electoral victory and that of others to strong discontent with the new law. He served in the Senate from 1923 to 1929 (*BDUSCong*, 952; *NYT*, 18 December 1922, 27 January 1931).

7. "Honest John" Brunen, a circus proprietor, was shot and killed at his New Jersey home in March 1922. His wife, Doris Brunen, her brother, Harry C. Mohr, and a third man eventually were arrested for the murder. The trial of Brunen and Mohr opened on 11 December 1922 and ended nine days later in the conviction of

Mohr and the acquittal of Brunen. The presiding judge sentenced Mohr to life imprisonment, but the defendant was granted a writ of error in late January 1923 (*NYT*, 12 March, 12, 21 December 1922, 10, 27 January 1923).

8. Charles M. Powell, a former worker in Honest John Brunen's circus, who was deeply in debt to Harry Mohr, had confessed to firing the fatal shot, but he turned state's witness in the case. He testified that the crime had been conceived by Doris Brunen and Mohr and that both abetted the death of Honest John, allegedly slain because he had been "getting on the nerves" of his wife and daughter. After the trial Powell was committed to a state hospital for the criminally insane (*NYT*, 12 December 1922, 10 February 1923).

9. President Harding and his Washington friends, who included Senator Joseph Frelinghuysen of New Jersey, flaunted Prohibition by openly consuming liquor in the White House, especially during late-night poker sessions. The frequent episodes of drinking became public knowledge. In deference to the law, however, Harding eventually curtailed his consumption of alcohol during his presidency (Trani and Wilson, *Presidency*, 179).

4. RETURN TO HOLLYWOOD
December 1922–May 1924

"The house that jokes built," the Rogers family home in Beverly Hills, with riding ring in the foreground. (*OkClaW*)

WILL ROGERS'S FIRST VENTURE INTO FILMS HAD PRODUCED MIXED RESULTS. The critics had received him warmly, although not effusively, as in the case of the reviewer who noted that "the pleasing personality of Will Rogers, enhanced by quite a little acting, brightens 'Jubilo.'"[1] Theater-goers seemed less enthusiastic; box office receipts were moderate at best. Rogers's experience at Goldwyn Pictures was perhaps shorter than he might have hoped, but the nonrenewal of his contract was not unique. Other major players at the financially strapped studio also found themselves out of a job. His venture into self-production likewise was not uncommon; some stars in Hollywood, including his neighbors, Douglas Fairbanks and Mary Pickford, had successfully launched their own studios.[2] Granted, Fairbanks and Pickford had tallied a few more years in the business. Rogers's misfortunes as producer of his own films did not dim entirely his interest in motion pictures. He would continue to accept opportunities to appear before the camera; indeed, during the period covered here he would sign another movie contract and become the well-compensated star of a series of two-reel comedy films for Hal E. Roach Studios.[3] He would have to wait, however, until an advancement in technology occurred—motion pictures with sound—before he would enjoy the same level of success on film that he achieved on stage or in writing.

A new venue presented itself to Rogers in December 1922: a nationally syndicated newspaper column. For years he had succeeded in placing a few scattered articles in newspapers. Some of the pieces appeared in semisyndicated format, more often on an individual, freelance basis. Most consisted simply of recycled stage material, one- or two-liners that appeared in abbreviated paragraph form and that originated from the gags he used at the *Frolic*, the *Follies*, speaking engagements, and benefit performances. Occasionally, he contributed an article focused on one or two specific topics. He might tackle politics, Prohibition, foreign affairs, traffic, sports, but even in these a trademark joke or two would likely appear. Rogers's entry into the realm of newspaper syndication in December 1922 offered him a regularly scheduled voice and a potential audience of millions of readers nationwide. It gave him coveted space in the pages of the *New York Times*, the most respected newspaper in the country and the only one at the time that could possibly claim the title of a national read.[4]

The debut in syndication of what was to become commonly known as the "Weekly Article," Rogers's few to several hundred words in each Sunday edition, became a milestone in his development as a national political voice, although his first offerings proved less than auspicious. Over time he moved away from the retelling of his stage routine—what was familiar and easy to him—and into that of political commentary with theme, substance, and depth. He became a writer. McNaught Syndicate, a new company, initially signed a few handfuls of newspapers, but the numbers would continue to grow and the territory broaden until within a decade Rogers could claim a few hundred papers across the country as subscribers to his column, making him one of the most widely read political commentators in the United States.

Even before Rogers sat down and typed his first effort as a syndicated colum- nist, he had succeeded in becoming a regular contributor to a nationally distrib- uted magazine, *Life*.[5] His material in the weekly humor periodical, however, deviated little from the jokes he delivered on stage. Not all of his submissions made it into the pages of *Life*, a situation that so irked Rogers that he chided the editor for possibly having deposited more humor in his wastebasket than in his magazine.[6] Although Rogers's time as a featured contributor to *Life* was brief, his relationship with the New York publication did not end there. A few years later he made a return appearance in a mock political role that helped to revive momentarily the sagging fortunes of the magazine.[7]

Rogers's reach and skills as a writer expanded appreciably during the eighteen months that followed his initiation as a syndicated columnist. In addition to his newspaper and magazine writings, he continued to have a presence on the nation's bookstore shelves. His first two books remained in print, and he and wife Betty Blake Rogers took steps to add a third, *The Illiterate Digest*, contin- uing in the public consciousness a clever title that Rogers had exploited on the movie screen as well as the printed page.[8]

Rogers's lack of success at fully connecting with movie theater audiences may have had much to do with the fact that his comedy was conveyed better verbally than visually. While his body language and facial expressions accented well his remarks on stage, they fell short in silent film, where they were dis- connected from the spoken word. Throwing a subtitle on an otherwise blank film screen—the text necessarily abbreviated for the available space—did not suffice to convey the full Rogers. He would need the combination of sight and sound to fully succeed as a film actor. In the meantime, during this period of his career, the spoken Rogers found a way into the homes of many Americans through sound recordings. Rogers had previously appeared on radio, but those opportunities to enter the living rooms of his fans had occurred infrequently thus far and they certainly were not replayable. In February 1923, however, the first of a handful of recordings appeared on the market. These were phonograph records that Rogers had made for the Victor Talking Machine Company, a leader in the industry. Little of Rogers's material on the sound discs was original; rather, it came from his stage act or after-dinner speeches. Nevertheless, it allowed his spoken word to reach a sizable segment of the public and in a repeatable format.[9] Unfortunately, his entry into the world of sound recordings came at a time when that particular market had begun to decline as the popularity of radio sets and the number of radio stations climbed dramatically.[10]

Rogers's new ventures during this period contributed significantly to his improving finances. He had earned more than $100,000 in 1922 after returning to the Ziegfeld organization. The next year he increased his income by about one-third, earning more than $165,000 in all from several sources. His syndicated writings, Victor recordings, and after-dinner speeches produced a generous portion of the revenue flow. The largest amounts for 1923, however, came from three show business sources: the Ziegfeld organization, as he ended during this period his most recent association with the *Follies*; Pathé Exchange, which had finally taken on the distribution of his self-produced films; and Roach studios, where he began work once again as a film star at mid-year.[11]

During his first eighteen months as a syndicated newspaper columnist, Rogers developed his skills as a writer and commentator and built a national readership and reputation. The "Weekly Article" provided him with a steady, reliable income stream, and established for him a relationship with the national press that he would exploit on many occasions in the future. In the short term, however, his return to motion pictures may have brought greater satisfaction to Rogers, more so for personal reasons than for career enhancement. Roach studios not only offered him the chance to star again in films but also presented him with the welcome opportunity to return to Hollywood and to his family—and to come home in far better shape financially than when he had left many months earlier.

1. *NYT*, 8 December 1919.
2. *DAB*, Supp. 10:635.
3. Rogers signed with the Roach studios on 26 January 1923 to appear in two-reel comedies. He earned a weekly salary of $2,000, the highest among all Roach performers and more than even the studio owner took home (Charles H. Roach to Will Rogers,

10 March 1924, OkClaW [see below];Yagoda, *Will Rogers*, 205;Weekly Payroll Summary, Hal Roach Studio, ca. 16 June 1923, CLSU [see below]).

4. See Manuscript for Syndicated Newspaper Article, ca. 31 December 1922, below. Having his material published in the *New York Times* probably had sentimental value to Rogers: his father had subscribed to the newspaper when Will was a youngster (Yagoda, *Will Rogers*, 195).

5. See Gags for *Life* Magazine, ca. November–December 1922, above.

6. See Letter to Louis Evan Shipman, ca. January 1923, below.

7. See Telegram from Robert E. Sherwood, 6 June 1928, below; see also *HCTR*.

8. See Letter from V. V. McNitt to Edward H. Hayden, 17 October 1923, below.

9. For example, see Transcript of Recording for Victor Records: I, 6 February 1923, below.

10. Read and Welch, *From Tin Foil*, 255.

11. Income Tax Documents, 1923, OkClaW.

Manuscript for Syndicated Newspaper Article
ca. 31 December 1922
[New York, N.Y.]

The first of Rogers's so-called "Weekly Articles," the series of several hundred words of topical commentary and humor that he wrote without fail each week, appeared in the New York Times *on Sunday, 24 December 1922.[1] The first one to be syndicated, however, was published a week later. The following was taken from the manuscript that Rogers provided V.V. McNitt and the McNaught Syndicate for general release on 31 December.[2]*

Settling the affairs of the World as they should be.

By

WILL ROGERS.

Everybody is a writing something nowadays. It used to be just the Literary or Newspaper men who were supposed to know what they were writing about that did all the writing. But nowadays all a man goes into office for is so he can try to find out something and then write it when he comes out. Now being in Zeigfeld Follies for almost a Solid Year in New York has given me an inside track on some of our biggest men in this Country who I meet nightly at the Stage Door.

So I am breaking out in a rash right here in this Paper every Sunday. I will cite an example to prove to you what you are going to get. Last week there was a mess of Govenors here from various Provinces. And a Good friend of mine brought back on the Stage and Dressing Room Gov. Allen. (hurry up and print this story or he wont be Govenor) of Kansas[3]

Well I stood him in the wings and he was supposed to be looking at my Act but he wasent   he was a watching what really is the Backbone of our Show. he any way heard some of my Gags about our Government and all who are elected to help missrun it, So at the finish of my act I dragged him out on the Stage and introduced him to the audience. He made a mighty pretty little speechand said he enjoyed Wills Impertinences,and got a big laugh on that, Said I was the only man in America who was able to tell the truth about our Men and Affairs.When he finished I explained to the audience why I was able to tell the truth. It is because I have never mixed up in Politics. So you all are going from time to time get the real Low Down on some of these Birds who are are sending home the Raddish seed.

You know the more you read and observe about this Politic thing You got to admit that each Party is worse than the other, the one thats out always look the best. My only solution would be to keep em both out one term and hire My Good friend Henry Ford to run the whole thing   give him a commission on what he saves us.Put his factory in with the government and instead of Seeds every spring mail out those Things of his.

Mail Newberry one every morning Special Delivery.

I tell you Folks all Politics is Applle Sauce.

The President give a Luncheon for the visiting Govenors.where they discussed but dident TRY Prohibition.

It was the consensus of opinion of all their Speeches that there was a lot of drinking going on and that if it wasent stopped by January that they would hold another meeting and try and get rid of some of the stuff. Senator Curtis proposed a Bill this week to stop Bootlegging in the Senate[4] making it unlawful for any member to be caught selling to another Member while on Goverment property.While the Bill was being read a Goverment employee feel [fell] just outside the Senate door and broke a Bottle of Pre War stuff(Made just before last weeks TurkiskWar)   Now they are carpeting all the halls with a heavy material so in case of a fall there will be no serious loss.

Well New Years is here now   I suppose we will have to hear and read all these big mens New Year greetings . such as Swab[5] and Gerry[6] and Rockafeller[7] and all of them. Saying the same old Apple Sauce. That they are Optomistic of the coming year and everybody must put their shoulder to the wheel and produce more and they predict a great year . Say if we had those Birds Dough we could all be just as optomistic as they can. But its a good Joke and its got in the papers every year and I suppose always will.

Now the Klu Klux is is coming into New York and kinder got it in for the Jewish People,[8]Now they are wrong   I am against that, If the Jewish People here in New YorkCity hadent jumped in and made themselvs good fellows and helped us Celebrate our Xmas, The thing would have fell flat.

They sold us every Present.

The Klu Klux couldent get much of a footing here in New York.If there was some man they wanted to take out and Tar and Feather. They wouldent know where he lived. People move so oftenhere their own folks dont know where they live.

And even if they found out the Elevator man in the Apartment wouldent let em up.

See where there is Bills up in Congress now to change the Constitution all around elect the President in a different way and Have Congress meet at a different time.[9] It seems the men who drew up this thing years ago dident know much and we are just now getting a bunch of real fellows wh[o] can take that old Parchment and fix it up like it should have been all these years, It seems it just been luck thats got us by so far. Now when they get ~~that~~ the Constitution all fixed up they are going to start in on the 10 Commandments, Just as soon as they find somebody in Washington who has read them.

See where they are talking about another Conference over here. The Social Season in Washington must be ~~dr~~ lagging.

Well I think they ought to have it, those Conferences dont really do any harm and they give certain Deligates pleasure. Of course nothing they ever pass on is ever carried out (Except in Greece then they are all carried out)   But each Nation gets a certain amount of Publicity out of it, and us masses that read of it get a certain amount of amusement out of it.

Borah himself admits he dont know what its for or what they should do.[10] But it looks like a good Conference season and there is no reason why we shoulent get in on one.

BESIDES DID YOU EVER REALIZE THIS COUNTRY IS 4 CONFERENCES BEHIND NOW.

Next Sunday I will tell you about Ambassador Harvey,[11] I am going down to HEAR him land.and see if he has on his Knee Breeches.[12]

[handwritten, not in Rogers's hand, in bottom margin of last manuscript page:]
P.S. — Rube Goldberg[13] has promised to ~~make~~ ▲draw▲ a cartoon to illustrate this article[14] & we will send out the mats tomorrow, and hope that they will reach the papers in time for *use* – McNaught Syndicate

[handwritten, including bracketing, in same hand as above, on reverse side of final page:]

[Editor's Note.— The famous cowboy monologist, Will Rogers, has under-
taken to write for this paper a weekly article of humorous comment on contemporary affairs. The Literary Digest recently quoted ▲an editorial from▲
the New York Times thus: "Not unworthily is Will Rogers carrying on the
tradition of Aristophanes on our comic stage."][15]

———

By Will Rogers

TM. OkClaW, Weekly Articles. Editor's markings appear throughout the original document; they
were ignored for this transcription.[16] Handwritten in top margin of the first page: "Release Sat,
or Sunday, Dec. 30 or 31."

1. Rogers's first "Weekly Article" appeared in the *New York Times* on Sunday, 24
December 1922, in section 7, page 2, under the heading, "Batting for Lloyd George"
(see *WA*, 1:1–3). Although original writings by Rogers had long before been published
in such other local newspapers as the *Evening World* and the *American*, the piece on 24
December marked Rogers's writing debut in the venerable *Times*, a paper not known
for providing space for a column of humor. Rogers wrote a follow-up piece to his original Lloyd George article, but it did not appear in print at the time (see *WA*, 1:3–5).
2. Virgil Venice McNitt (1881–1964), a veteran of the newspaper service business,
and his partner, Charles V. McAdam (ca. 1892–1985), founded McNaught Syndicate,
Inc., in January 1922. Headquartered in the then *New York Times* building at Forty-second
and Broadway, across the street from the New Amsterdam Theatre, McNaught distributed columns, comic strips, and other features (*NYT*, 16 June 1964, 20 June 1985; *Time*,
26 June 1964; *WhJour*, 267; *ID*, xix; reminiscences, Charles V. McAdam, OkClaW). In
the late fall of 1922 McNitt and McAdam approached Rogers with an offer of $500 a
week to write a weekly newspaper feature. Rogers initially showed only mild interest,
but then McNitt's mention that the *New York Times* might run the column clinched the
deal. The first manuscript that Rogers submitted, the story of Powder River Powell and
his barber, Soapy (see Manuscript for Newspaper Article, ca. November 1922, above),
met with a tactful rejection. At some point thereafter, Rogers delivered to McNaught the
present manuscript, which was then marked and readied for release to the subscribing
newspapers, a handful initially. Four hundred newspapers subscribed to the series by the
time of Rogers's death (*Time*, 26 June 1964; Croy, *Our Will Rogers*, 173–74, 177;
telegram, Charles B. Driscoll to E. B. Garnett, 17 September 1935, OkClaW; Yagoda,
Will Rogers, 195).
3. Henry Allen did not seek reelection in 1922 as governor of Kansas. After leaving
office the next year he became a commissioner for Near East Relief. Several governors
visited New York in December 1922 while on the East Coast to attend an annual conference of state chief executives (*DAB*, Supp. 4:12; *NYT*, 17 December 1922).
4. Charles Curtis (1860–1936), a Republican and former congressional representative, served as U.S. senator from Kansas from 1907 to 1929. Curtis seldom submitted legislative measures. His strength lay in his ability to work behind the scenes to
craft and mold legislation (*DAB*, Supp. 2:136).
5. Financier Charles Schwab announced in early November 1922 that the outlook for business in the United States appeared better than at any time in the previous
forty-three years (*NYT*, 7 November 1922).

6. Elbert Henry Gary (1846–1927), a corporate attorney and steel magnate, helped organize the United States Steel Corporation, the largest business enterprise in the world at the time. He served as chairman of its board of directors from 1903 to 1927. In his annual business forecast on 10 December, Gary hedged on predicting prosperity in 1923; instead, he warned of labor unrest and laws adversely affecting business growth (*DAB*, 7:175–76; *NYT*, 11 December 1922).

7. John Davison Rockefeller (1839–1937) founded and developed what became Standard Oil Company, a mammoth business combination that dominated the industry and left Rockefeller one of the world's wealthiest individuals. By the 1920s Rockefeller had retired to private life, but his son, John Davison Rockefeller, Jr. (1874–1960), continued the family's postwar focus on public service and philanthropy (*DAB*, Supp. 2:568–76, Supp. 6:547–49).

8. The Ku Klux Klan originated in the post–Civil War South as an organized, violent response by ex-Confederates to Reconstruction and the enfranchisement of blacks. Although the original Klan died out with the end of Reconstruction in the late 1870s, the positive portrayal of the group in the film *The Birth of a Nation*, released in 1915, inspired a rebirth. In addition to blacks, hundreds of thousands of whom had migrated northward during World War I, the new Klan, which numbered 5 million by 1925, also targeted what it considered other "inferiors": immigrants from southern and eastern Europe, Roman Catholics, and Jews. Although more prominent in other northern cities, the revived, highly secretive Klan scored some success in New York, appearing there as early as March 1921 and operating as many as twenty-one cells, or klaverns, by December 1922 (*HD1920s*, 200–201; *ENYC*, 645).

9. On 5 December 1922, within three years of the ratifications of the Eighteenth and Nineteenth Amendments, proponents of further constitutional change introduced in Congress additional amendments. One called for advancing by thirteen months the date for convening a new Congress. A second proposed amendment would provide for the direct election of the president and vice president, thus eliminating the Electoral College. Both proposals failed to gain sufficient support to move forward (*NYT*, 6 December 1922).

10. Senator William Borah introduced in the Senate on 21 December a proposal for a new international disarmament conference to reduce the size of armies and navies as a way to solve the worldwide economic crisis. He withdrew the legislation eight days later, after receiving assurances that the Harding administration was working with European governments to settle the problems (*NYT*, 22, 30 December 1922).

11. George Brinton McClellan Harvey (1864–1928), a New York magazine owner and editor, helped orchestrate the presidential nomination of Warren G. Harding at the Republican national convention in 1920. Harvey was appointed ambassador to Great Britain in 1921. He resigned soon after Harding's death in August 1923 (*DAB*, 8:372–73; Murray, *Harding Era*, 451)

12. Harvey suddenly announced on 14 December 1922 that he was returning to the United States for a short visit, ostensibly because of his wife's health. Although pundits conjectured about the real nature of the trip, Harvey, not a favorite of Secretary of State Hughes, remained in the country for only a brief time. He returned to England on 18 January 1923 (*DAB*, 8:372–73; *NYT*, 15, 20 December 1922).

13. Reuben Lucius (Rube) Goldberg (1883–1970) created such successful comic-strip characters as "Mike and Ike," "Lala Palooza," and "Boob McNutt," the last of which ran as a syndicated feature in newspapers nationwide from 1915 to 1934. Thanks to his *Inventions*, a series of complex drawings of unusual contrivances, his

name became associated with any seemingly improbable machine, and became listed in dictionaries as an adjective for such (*DAB*, Supp. 8:217–18).

14. Goldberg, whose work was distributed by McNaught Syndicate, helped introduce Rogers to V. V. McNitt. Rogers's first "Weekly Articles" in the *New York Times*, however, featured the work of illustrator and architect Stuart Hay (ca. 1886–1969), not Goldberg (Croy, *Our Will Rogers*, 173; *NYT*, 24, 31 December 1922, 7 February 1969).

15. The *New York Times*, in an editorial published on 13 November 1922, likened Rogers to Finley Peter Dunne's "Mr. Dooley," a nineteenth-century character of heavy dialect and homely expressions. The *Times* piece praised the astuteness, decency, and humor of Rogers's political observations and ended with the line, "But Will Rogers in the Follies is carrying on the tradition of Aristophanes, and not unworthily." Aristophanes (ca. 448 B.C.–ca. 385 B.C.) ranked as the foremost ancient Greek writer of comedy and satirist of current events (*NYT*, 13 November 1922; Avery, ed., *New Century*, 162).

16. Without the editorial markings, the original manuscript bears the authentic typographical imprint of Rogers for this period of his life at a keyboard: all flush left, misspellings, transpositions, type-overs, missing apostrophes, hodgepodge and misplaced punctuation, liberal capitalization, uneven lines of type. The staff at McNaught made several editorial changes in this first syndication effort of Rogers—inserting apostrophes, lowercasing or uppercasing where appropriate, correcting spelling, indenting, moving words around. But soon McNitt, with Rogers's encouragement, came to understand the uniqueness of his style, whose genuineness was expressed as much through the use of the third-person-singular *dont* as through the overall thought. McNaught minimized its editing and encouraged its subscriber newspapers to do likewise (Yagoda, *Will Rogers*, 196–97).

Draft of Speech or Newspaper Article
ca. 1922
[New York, N.Y.]

As a well-established and popular speaker and entertainer at luncheons and banquets, Rogers had accumulated numerous opportunities by late 1922 to observe the usual routine at such events. The following manuscript, in which he satirizes the behavior of the presiding officer at a civic club function, suggests that he departed such dinners more than once with a feeling of frustration.

A man gets up and announces that he is not going to make a speech and it takes him longer to to tell that he isnt than it would if he made one.

Did you ever think of the time consumed at a dinner by all the different speakers announcing that they were no sppeechmakers.and that   they were not going to try to spek *but*   they just want to say. Those fel ws [fellows] that announce for a half an hour that they are no speechmakers. always try to leave the impression with you that while they are alittle short on speechmaking thwt in all worth while pursuits they are men who get things done. and and they can hardly conceal their contempt for the man who can do nothing but make speeches. they know that you have no wwy of making them prove that there is anyhting else that they can do.

Henry Ford the effenciency Man. should give some thought to this time saving business of afterdinner speaking.

For instance there is the President of the club who is generally the Toastmaster. He always starts off by teeling at each and every dinner why and how he awsc [was] made President and that there is so many more that would have been more worthy of the thing than he is. But as he is the chosen one he is not going to bore them with any long winded talk as we must get down to the business at hand as he has so many worthy speakers who he knows the Audience would much rather hear than him. But that he has always tried to give the Club the best that was in him in Time (And he is proving it for he has been 10 minutes now and hasent said on e word that he dident say at the last meeting[)] (He was elected because no one elese would havve the darn thing) Now as I said before I am not going to detain you with any of my Oratory   I know that I am voicing the sentiments of this club when I say that we are proud to have with us today such men as we have (he speaks as they were the best they could get) As all of you know wh[a]t our club stands for we are for the best in everything. I dont [t]hink there is an organization in this City that can show the same amount of Civic pride and accomplishments that our Organization has shown since I have been at your head. And I dont want to receive ~~that~~ all that credit .I wwnt to say that had I not been at the head of such a body of men as I am we cold not hav e accomplished the things we have done . So I wnt to take this means of thanking you for your wonderful work and   Cooperation and we are able to start the new week with a vim and Vigor that I know would not be present if it were not for the loyal backing of a bunch of the best fellows on earth. And dont think that I am unmindful of the hard work done by the lesser officers of our Organization and I want to take this means of thanking them not only for myself but for the entire Organization   For I can assure you that they are as worthy bunch of Lieutanants as ever it has been my good fortune to be associated. If we but steer our ship in the rightly direction which it has been headed for the last year I am sure we not only keep up our high standard but we will advance. Go forward as that is a Slogan that I should like to see adopted by this Club   " UP and onward never Backwards"   And I am sure with the type of manhhod we have here and with the right kind of Leadership we cant help but carry out that little Original Slogan of mine. Now as I said I am not going to take up any of your valuable time by having to listen to Little Me. For we have men with us today who carry a Message of instruction   thaey are of the same high type men who have whomwe are accustomed to having at our former meetings. It is only through having a Club of our High Caliber and effenciency that we are able to get such men to give up their time and business to be with us for a few minutes. and I am sure when you hear them you will agree with me that this has been one of our most entertaining and instructive meetings . And I am sure you will give them the strict attention and appreciation which it has for which th s organization has been noted in the past.

Now before I introduce the guests of the evening we have one little bit of Business that has been brought to the attention of the Club has been acted on in committe and must be passed or rejected in open meeting by the Club. The Resolution as I have it here is. Resolved that as it is reported in each of our Daily Papers there is alikelyhood of War being perprtated [perpetrated] someplace in the Near East by Turkey and Various other opponents. That it be the Voice and Sentiments of this (The BoHunk Civic and Commercial Club[)] That we hereby go on record as being opposed to any such undertaking. And do furthermore recomend and advise President Warren G Harding President of these United States to use his influence in conjunction with our support That if suchWar is entered into it will not have the sanction of the United States Of America.

Now Gentlemen you have heard the resolution. I dont need to stand here and insult your intelligence by telling you what this Organization stands for We are not only for the betterment of our own City and own State but we are broader our influence reaches out and out even beyond the confines of our bordering Oceans . The Entire World is our sphere.

Now is our chance to let the World know how and where this Organization of which I am proud and happy to be called President stands on And I wouldent be able to speak with such feeling if it were not for the class and loyalty and effeciency and suupport of such members as I know composes this Body of Men.

Other Clubs may haggle and quibble over a matter of this magnitude. But I think I spaek the voice of this entire Organization when I say that we are can take a question and with the effeciency and Caliber of Intelligence that we ahve re represented in this Organization go directly to the bottom of it. Now this question has been in Committee only 2 weeks but has been argued Pro and Con and I am sure when after due Deliberation by such a body as this commitee represented. Picked bydthe flower of our entire organization. which cant be beat as a whole by any like number of men in the World whole State. Yes I go further than that I say the whole United States. Now in drawing up this resolution some thought we were a little too strong that we should only advise that they postpone the war untill business Conditions adjust themselvs to normal. Amd that the Club should do nothing as a Whole that might antagonize Foreign Governments. But it was argued on the other hand that an Organization of our dimensions should not straddle any question that it was up to us to come out four Square one way or the other. So I think that they have drawn up the right kind of a document. It may not be ▲as▲ conservative as some weaker spined Club would suggest but remember we are not represented in our organization by any of the ordinary od [or] weak spined variety. We got a bunch of Red Blooded argueing fighting members who can come out into the open and and declare themselvs . Not only that but put themselvs on record[,] a thing a lot of Clubs I could name would be afraid to do. Thats what makes me proud   I am a club Man. and prouder still that I head one of the most progressive and effecient organizations in the Stae. yes or even in the United States. Now it aint any little thin skinned organization that can come out and take a chance on antagonizing a Foreign Government. No why because the havent got the class of Men that we have here and that I am am proud to be the spokesm n for,

I know that we have a sentiment represented here that are against any foreign entanglements. But its firmness that keeps us out of them we if we live up to the Slogan which I have coinned for you . we have got to look at Issue in the face. Now its not only for Humanity sake that we are against this uprising (And I know that I can speak for all of you that we are as human as any body on earth   in fact I can go farther and and say humaner than any other body of men.) As I say its not only the Humanity side but we must look at these Wars from a Commercial angle as after all Wars in our time are Won and Lost financially.Now a great many organizations would not be Broad minded or far sighted enough to see that a War in even the Near East would effect us indirectly. Our exports and imports would be int[er]fered with and even though we may haveno concern in the outcome of such Coflict you must concede that any war has a very demoralizing effect on business conditions and we havent a member here who sooner or later would not feel the effect of it even though none of your goods come from the East. I mean Near east.

N w I realize that this is a question that deserves every consideration and you must look at it from every angle. But if you will take advice and consul from me and I think that I can say without any tinge of egotism that my leadership has not led you astray so far. Why I wany [want] you to go on record as getting behind this resolution and putting it over in a whole hearted and unamamous fashion. I not only think it advisable in a Business or Humanitarian sense but I think it will be of untold assistance and moral suupport to our President and Government in Washington.

Now no matter what your Political affiliations are we want this club to be big enough and strong enough to stand behind either of our Political Parties no matter how bad we know them to be.

Now I am about ready to put thequestion to vote. and I dont think there is any need of me discussing it or going into detail so I will not take up any of your valuable time as you know we have men here with us today who have come a long way to speak to you.

Now the Secretary will just read the resolution over to you so you will understand exactly what you are voting on.

Resolution read.

Now just one moment before we take the vote   as I said I am no speaker and dont want to take your time. But I want each of you to give due delibera tion

TM, dc.[1] OkClaW, 1975.14.0097. Typewritten, top margin, page 1 and successive pages with respective change in pagination: "Page 1, Toastmaster and President."

1. Dating of the document was determined by historical references in the document and in relation to Rogers's activities as an after-dinner speaker.

Notes for Banquet Speech
ca. 3 January 1923
New York, N.Y.

Dont know what I am doing here at a Celebration of lifes 25 Birtday.[1] Suppose I am too late with the joke[s,] I read the Jokes in it and thought it was older   The Paper increases in Circ every week   While I have only been on it 6 weks those have been its most valuable and prosperous[2]

Dont owe you anything. This is too fast company for me . You have no doubt been listening to speeches all night here by Otto Kahn[3]   how did he horn in on one of our dinners   its almostt, impossble nowadays tfor two men to get togeather without one of them having a Mallet and calling on Otto Kahn for a speech. You dont mean he is backing us like he does theopera.[4] I should think he could get enough laughs over there   Optimistic.

I see our Manager and owner is here[5]   You know I always think its good policy to mention the Host in affairs like this because after all the Check is very little nourishment or consolation because after all even if he does only do this every 25 years we owe something to him. Now J D on his 83. on his every

83 . he gave a lot of little boys a dime .[6] and told them to share that among you. Now Mr Gibson since I met him he is a wonderful man, I had read so much of him that when I met him I felt kinder like you would feel if you were going to meet Will Hayes[7] or Mayor Highland[8] or Valentino, But here when I get in there is this big Double fisted fellow[9]   why he is really a rough neck in appearance   why I felt if that big guy can draw pictures he must do it with a Pick handle. Hisroughness however was offset by the rather effeminite manners of theres [the rest] of the staff.

Mr Gibson is the Dady of all of them   he is the first fellow to think of the Idea of calling a Cartonnist an Illustrator. and it was only his idea in namesthat distinguishee them today . The Cartonnist has to make his Picturres so people can tell what the figures are. While with an Illustrator you get three guesses and if you cant guess its a good Picture.

He has lately come into quite some prominence by feeding a prominent Frenchman whos diet attracted more attention than his pseeches.[10] After speaking here for three weeks no one seem to know just what he come after   well by the looks of his Breakfast Menu he come after eggs. He seemed to have solved the indijestin problem by eating a dozen eggs for breakfast and using Onion Soup as CHaser   We over here had always considered the onion more as a odor than as a Breakfast food and Mr gibson had the sympathy of the entire U S when we would think of you being awakened in your own home at 4 am by the ~~rovingof the~~ roving Aroma of the rotund bermuda. And you and Mrs Gibsom wilp always be considered Martyrs to the cause of Indijestion.

Now you have another face here that it seems I have seen distributed arounnd on our Ask Cans and out buildings during October and the early November.[11] I am not surprised to see him here at a Dinner of contributors of a humorous paper. He belongs here   I have read some of his Articles. I think he writes under the Non De Plume of Doctor Crane,[12] now that the dr has gotten in the senate that means an Aple a day. too late fora Dr   what we need is a Executione[r]   No selling to each other. Carpet. Newberry. Cousins.

TD. OkClaW, 1975.14.0090. "LiFES BiRTHDAY" is written, perhaps in Rogers's hand, in pencil at the bottom of page 1. The word "*Date?*" is also written at the bottom of the same page, but it is not in Rogers's hand.

1. Founded in 1883, the literary and humor magazine *Life* celebrated its fortieth anniversary at a dinner at Sherry's restaurant in New York on 3 January 1923. In describing the uniqueness of the event, the *New York Times* noted that *Life* "weakened

at the last and did not carry originality to the point where there were no speeches, they came late and were short and funny" (*NYT*, 4 January 1923).

2. See Gags for *Life* Magazine, ca. November–December 1922, above.

3. Otto Hermann Kahn (1867–1934), German-born American financier and patron of the arts, joined Kuhn, Loeb & Company in New York in 1897 and remained with the prominent banking firm until his death. Kahn spent considerable time speaking before groups in both the United States and Europe on subjects ranging from the arts to economics to foreign affairs (*DAB*, Supp. 1:457–58; Kobler, *Otto*, 11, 146).

4. Kahn used his great wealth in support of several charitable causes, mostly in the arts, but the Metropolitan Opera Company in New York ranked as his foremost philanthropy. He became president of the company in 1918, and at his death he owned 84 percent of the stock. He contributed millions to the Metropolitan and paid generously to buy out rival organizations (*DAB*, Supp. 1:457).

5. Charles Dana Gibson (1867–1944), creator of the famed Gibson Girl, sold his first illustration to *Life* magazine in 1886 and over the years contributed hundreds of cartoons and drawings to the publication. He led a syndicate that bought *Life* in 1918, and two years later he became owner and chief editor (*DAB*, Supp. 3:300–301).

6. In his later years, the elder Rockefeller earned a well-publicized reputation at his home in Florida for giving dimes, often shiny, newly minted ones, to golfing friends, guests, casual acquaintances, and, especially, children, the latter usually on Sunday mornings on the lawn outside the church he attended. Cynics belittled the dimes coming from someone so fabulously wealthy, but Rockefeller found it a chance to show humor and to convey his notion of thriftiness (Nevins, *Study*, 414).

7. William Harrison (Will) Hays (1879–1954), a Republican and former postmaster general of the United States, became the first "czar" of the motion picture industry in January 1922 when Hollywood film moguls named him to head the Motion Picture Producers and Distributors of America (MPPDA). The MPPDA, created to counter demands for censorship in the wake of scandals in Hollywood and perceived immorality in films, became known as the Hays Office and drew up a code that shaped motion picture content for decades (*DAB*, Supp. 5:280–82; *FE*, 606; Moley, *Hays*, 32).

8. That is, John F. Hylan, mayor of New York.

9. Gibson stood more than six feet tall and had a well-developed physique. An athletic man, he had been devoted since youth to such sports as rowing, swimming, and weight lifting (*DAB*, Supp. 3:300).

10. Gibson and his socially prominent wife, Irene Langhorne Gibson (ca. 1873–1956), a model for the Gibson Girl, hosted the former French premier, Georges Clemenceau, at their home on East Seventy-second Street during his stay in New York in the fall of 1922 (*NYT*, 20 November 1922, 21 April 1956).

11. Royal Copeland, physician and newly elected senator from New York, had contributed a syndicated medical column to Hearst newspapers beginning about 1918 (*NYT*, 18 June 1938; *DAB*, Supp. 2:121).

12. Rogers may have referred to Frank Crane (1861–1928), a Methodist minister from the Midwest who achieved fame through his syndicated writings in the early 1900s. Holder of a doctor of divinity degree, Crane produced hundreds of short, simply written newspaper and magazine columns of advice, inspiration, and patriotism that became known as the "Four Minute Essays" (*NYT*, 4 January 1920, 7 November 1928; *DAB*, 4:504–5).

Notes for Banquet Speech
9 January 1923
New York, N.Y.

Well Gentlemen I suppose most men addressing an Audience like this would consider it quite an honor and a Privalege,[1] But being a Motor Car owner and understanding something of your Indusrry and how you do business I really dont want it known that I am here, If an officer of the law saw me talking to you I could be pinched for you are the highest class bunch of Jips in the United States. Some of the junk you are selling over there under the Title of Motor Cars, You should be just 10 miles out of Atlanta,

Now if any of you think I have anything nice to say about you, You are missing, They brought a Lawyer here Mr Martin Littleton[2]   he will get up here in a minuute and tell you what a wonderful Industry you ahve a [have and] what a fine bunch of men is in it, Sure he will. a Lawyer will say anything   he figures if he makes a hit with some of your big men here he can help defend them sometimes (and they all need it), If there is a Manafacturer in this room that can honestly say with his hand on a Bible that he never infringed on a Patent) Not a one of you   we not only cant get anybody to swear it but we would have to send outside the Industry to get the Bible,

Now My Opponent here tonight started as a Barefoot boy in Tenessee, And if it had not been for saving the neck of Harry Thaw[3] he would be back in Tenessee with the same Bare feet only bigger, The next Crazy case he got was defending Newberry of Michigan, He was responsible for getting Newberry out of the Sen[a]te[4]   So you see he works in direct opposites, Thaw he got into a Lunatic Asylum and Newberry he got out of one, So you see he specializes in Lunacy Cases   thats why he reppresents this Organization, Newberry, Cousins,

Now with me its different, you acant buy me off. Thats what keeps me out of P Politics.

You hold these things which you call a show every year, When the Show is not on you can go in and look at any of the cars   take your time and see them under much more comfortable surroundings.you can also see more styles and Models, the only difference between a Show and a Display is the Dollar Admission. The only show I saw there last Night was the Dress suits that some of the Salesmen wore,Haynes said he made the first Car,[5] he di[d]ent make the first one of those dress suits cause he aint old enough,

Now most men start in their Automobile career by buying a Ford. Well I wasent so fortunate   I had to break in on an Overland,[6] It took me two weeks to learn to drive it and by then it was an Old Car, I decided that as I dident know any thing about a Car I wasent ever going to try   and make it worse by Monkeying with it   so no matter what happened I never stopped or looked into it till I got to the nearest Highway Station,the Garage, My Next jump   now most people go up but I reversed   I went down   I got a WiLLys Night,[7] A Silent Night they called [it.] I could drive up to deaf and dumb asylum and wake all the inmates up at 12 at night, It developed so many knocks and sounds I would bring it in to Silver (By the way what ever become of him) He was the Marion Davies[8] of male Adveti sers   well you know what a Service Station is   " We will take care of you right away,["] You can go away get married have a Son and send him back for the car and it will be reday [ready] tomorrow, And Charges they are BLACK JACK of the industry. Now you would think a Man would have gotten discouraged after that and had gone as low as he could go but no you couldent guess in a year what else had to happen to me   I got BUICK,[9] I made a trip up in the Mountains and half wayip up the mountain I had to hire a man to drive it while I sat on the Radiator and poured in water. It burned up just before I got to the top, Niagra falls wouldent save one of those things on a ~~Hil~~ long hill.,

Somebody said get a Franklin[10]   you dont have to bother about the water.

I said when I get so far gone that I have to get into a Coffin turned upside down the cooling system wont worry me,

Lots of cars you dont have to worry about   the water in the Franklin aint the only one   look at the old Studebakers[11] , When you ~~couldent g~~ cant get a car out of a Garage it dont need water either,

Well then I got a Moving Picture Contract and got prosperous and was going to California so I ~~was playing Buffalo so o~~ decided the only way to do was to to have two cars   so while one was in the Garage getting fixed you could be st▾tuck▾ on the road with the other one so you always had something to look forward too, So I got kinder flushy and ordered a Closed Cadillac[12] (By the way I am responsible for closed bodies   I lost so many of my Children bouncing out of these first cars I had I got a roof put on this one,[)] So got the Cadillac for my wife and then we played Buffalo and I bought a Pierce[13] one of those new ones that had just come out. 24 Valve   had it delivered in Cal the first one, I got this Pierce so I could Tow in the Cadillac   you know Towage on cars is the biggest item of expense. Well they told me get a Pierce   they are conservative   they wont change a Bolt unless it has been tried for years   a 1910 Pierce looks just like a 1920, we dont change them, well I was all all broke and swelled up over this . Fairbanks wanted to get it   it was the first one in L A. So one day about 6 months later my   Chouffer, Oh yes I h[a]d graduated to the in debt class , Well I got tired fixing these cars myself   The Chouffer said did you see the New Pierces. I said no for Iknew there could [not] be much change, well he showed me one   My God they had the thing looking like an Essex.[14] Here I had saved all my joke money for years and had thought I had a Car that would always be the same and here is this Burlesque on it, It looke like some guy had written a Porody on a Pierce,I said those Hewbrew Gentlemen must have got in this and want to spped up Production and cut the Price. Then I learned the truth   Mr (Clifton[15]   )   Here had resigned from the Presidency and wwnted to devote all his time to the good of Mankind witha wonderful Hospital, He is the first Automobile man to repent and he deserves a world of Credit   no wonder Buffalo loves him and all of you love him   When one of the 40 thieves turns honest it is worth your respect even if you havent got yours yet, Well they had to get him back as President and today they are trying not to improve on them but make them as good as they used tooo,

Today has been one of the off days in the Industry. Durant[16] only took over two new cars the Flint and the Princeton[17] and of course a few minor Truck companies, then he has the Fisher Bodies.[18]They asy the Fisher Bodies are the best but I tell you when it comes to Bodies Zeigfeld has em in his Follies

He[19] has promoted more things than any man alive. Niagra Falls was his Original Idea. He is the first man to have the Lords Supper a 12 Cylinder affair, If he lives 30 more years he willeither own the World or be in Jail, Then he would sell the stock and the people couldent sell it till they got out   He is the first fellow to discover that you can sell people some share in a pice of stock and still you keep the Stock, Fellow name Downs with him who gets his name from 3 dollars down and $ a week,

Started in to undersell the Ford[20] . Buy a Pierce. Parts.enough to make it pay   He is a wonderful man and they say he is honest and well loved in the Industry   has vision of every man woman and child owning a Motor, He has his production now on that Basis, now all he has to do is regulate the Birth rate,

TD. OkClaW, 1975.14.0175. First four paragraphs bear editor's marks not included in the transcription.[21] Handwritten, top margin, page 1: "Auto speech".

1. Rogers addressed members of the National Automobile Chamber of Commerce, an association of automobile manufacturers, at a dinner at the Hotel Commodore in

New York on the evening of 9 January 1923. The group had been formed in 1915 to replace a similar organization that had become a casualty of a patent dispute. Headquartered in New York, the chamber administered an industry-wide cross-licensing agreement and published an annual report on automotive and related statistics (Rae, *American Automobile Industry*, 41; Smith, *Wheels*, 48; National Automobile Chamber of Commerce, *Facts*).

2. Martin Wiley Littleton (1872–1934) left behind the extreme poverty of his youth in Tennessee to become a successful lawyer in New York who also dabbled in politics. He served one term in Congress as a Democrat but gained his greatest fame as a defense attorney and public speaker (*DAB*, Supp. 1:501–2).

3. Harry Kendall Thaw (1871–1947), a wealthy playboy, married chorus girl and occasional Gibson model Evalyn Nesbit in 1901. In June 1906, in a fit of rage, he shot and killed famed architect Stanford White because of his affair with Nesbit years earlier. Littleton served as Thaw's lead defense attorney in a trial that ended in 1908 with Thaw being declared innocent by reason of temporary insanity. After his release from a psychiatric institution in 1915, Thaw divorced Nesbit. An attempted suicide two years later, however, led to several more years in institutions for the insane (*DAB*, Supp. 4:826–27).

4. After Senator Truman Newberry was found guilty in March 1920 of criminal conspiracy involving campaign expenditures, Littleton succeeded in having the conviction reversed by the U.S. Supreme Court in a split decision in May 1921. Despite unrelenting pressure to resign, Newberry remained in the Senate for another eighteen months (*DAB*, Supp. 3:550, Supp. 1:502).

5. Elwood Haynes (1857–1925) claimed to have built the first American gasoline automobile in 1894 in Kokomo, Ind., but the Duryea brothers, Charles and Frank, had achieved the feat a year earlier in Springfield, Mass. An engineer by training, Haynes later formed a company to manufacture cars, but the pioneering venture never became a major producer. The company ceased operations in 1924, not long before Haynes's death (*NYT*, 14 April 1925; Rae, *American Automobile Industry*, 12–13; Smith, *Wheels*, 87).

6. Overland, like other car makers, originated as a wagon builder. The company began producing automobiles in 1906 in Indianapolis. Four years later, under different ownership, production of the Overland more than quadrupled, reaching 18,000 units. Popular and low-priced, the car continued to be manufactured even after World War II (Rae, *American Automobile Industry*, 25, 49, 64).

7. John North Willys (1873–1935) purchased the Overland Company in 1908, relocated the firm to Toledo, Ohio, and began producing the Willys-Overland with great success, generating large profits. In 1919 the company began to experience challenges with increased competition, labor difficulties, and overextension of commitments. It survived as an independent manufacturer until its acquisition in 1953. One of its models, known as the Willys-Knight, used an engine designed by Charles Y. Knight that was much quieter than other engines of the day (*DAB*, Supp. 1:709–10; Rae, *American Automobile Industry*, 49, 102).

8. Marion Davies (Marion Cecilia Douras, 1897–1961) captured the romantic eye of publishing magnate William Randolph Hearst as a chorus girl on Broadway in 1915. Although his wife would not permit a divorce, Hearst formed a film production company to launch Davies's movie career and used his newspapers to publicize her films. His relentless promotion of Davies antagonized theater owners and brought scorn from the public (*DAB*, Supp. 7:165–66; *FE*, 331–32).

9. David Dunbar Buick (1855–1929), a plumbing supply dealer in Detroit, started Buick Motor Car Company in 1903. Within a year he had exhausted his finan-

cial resources and sold the business. The Buick automobile, a relatively high-end car, became a division of General Motors Corporation in 1917 (Rae, *American Automobile*, 20; Rae, *American Automobile Industry*, 26, 34; Smith, *Wheels*, 23, 280).

10. Herbert H. Franklin (ca. 1867–1956) produced the first air-cooled Franklin in 1902 in Syracuse, N.Y. He continued to promote the superiority of air cooling long after water-cooled engines had established supremacy in the market. The firm failed to survive the Great Depression (*NYT*, 17 April 1956; Smith, *Wheels*, 20, 21).

11. The Studebaker Brothers Manufacturing Company of South Bend, Ind., was already established as the world's largest producer of horse-drawn vehicles when it began marketing cars in 1904. Well-financed, the company survived the postwar depression in good order and entered the 1920s as the country's third largest automobile manufacturer (Rae, *American Automobile Industry*, 25, 62, 64).

12. The Cadillac Motor Car Company was organized in 1905 and named for the founder of Detroit, Antoine de la Mothe Cadillac (ca. 1658–1730). A leader in automotive design and engineering, the company offered the first closed body as standard equipment in 1910 (Rae, *American Automobile Industry*, 26, 35–36; *OCAH*, 129; Smith, *Wheels*, 281; General Motors Corporation, "GM Corporate History").

13. George N. Pierce (1846–1911) turned from manufacturing bicycles to automobiles at his factory in Buffalo, N.Y., in 1901. His company was best known for the Pierce-Arrow, an early luxury car widely respected for its quality (Rae, *American Automobile Industry*, 18, 65; Smith, *Wheels*, 19, 133; "George N. Pierce").

14. The Essex was introduced by the Hudson Motor Car Company of Detroit in 1918. Although more expensive than the industry leader (Ford), the Essex, priced at $895 in 1924, found a market among buyers seeking more amenities and style. It continued in production until 1933 (Smith, *Wheels*, 89, 215; Rae, *American Automobile Industry*, 61).

15. Charles Clifton (1853–1928), president and chairman of the board of the Pierce Arrow Motor Car Company of Buffalo, N.Y., headed the National Automobile Chamber of Commerce from its organization in 1912 until his resignation in 1927 (*NYT*, 22 June 1928; *NatCAB*, 21:186).

16. William Crapo Durant (1861–1947), founder of General Motors, served as the president of the automobile manufacturing firm from 1916 to December 1920, being forced out, in part, because of financial pressures from his overbuying. By 1923 he had formed a new company, Durant Motors, and had acquired several small firms (*DAB*, Supp. 4:243–45).

17. The Flint Motor Company, a subsidiary of Durant Motors, showed a prototype of its new Flint sedan during the National Automobile Chamber of Commerce convention in New York in January 1923. The first cars left the factory in October, but the Flint line ceased production just four years later. The Princeton, another Durant Motors product and a lookalike of the Flint, came and went in 1923 (*AmCar*, [287, 340]).

18. Frederic John (Fred) Fisher (1878–1941) and his brother Charles organized the Fisher Body Company in Detroit in 1908. The firm dominated the market for closed automobile bodies by 1916. Three years later, Durant's General Motors purchased controlling interest, and in 1922 Fred Fisher joined the executive committee of General Motors. He served as its vice president from 1924 to 1934 (*DAB*, Supp. 3:273–74).

19. That is, William C. Durant.

20. Henry Ford, who had backed and encouraged the opposing litigants in the automotive patent fight, never joined the National Automobile Chamber of Commerce (Rae, *American Automobile Industry*, 41).

21. For an example of Rogers's use of speech material in a published article, see *WA*, 1:13–14.

To Louis Evan Shipman
ca. January 1923
[New York, N.Y.]

Mr. Shipmann.[1]

Dear Friend.

Enclosed find some Volstead or Near Jokes.[2]

Now I read the ones you used last week (both of them) And you have *some* man on your Paper whos Geninus I dont believe you fully appreciate. The way he can [read] 48 jokes and pick out the absolut poorest is postively uncanny. You see I try them on the Stage.so ~~you see~~ I am in a better position to appreciate his his flawless picking than you are.

Now this time I am *fooling him* I am not sending *any* bad ones So that means that none of these will see the advantages of LIFE. Kindly have them return to me the list I sent with the ones marked off which they used.Also the Bankers S peech[3] as I have no copy of either

What~~v~~ will Life take for their Waste Paper Basket.I want to buy it. There is a field for a Humorous Magazine.

~~YourHs in a Show without an Editor.~~

Yours in the Follies Uniedited.

If Benchley[4] and Sherwood[5] have had the same Experience I have We can take that Basket and Start a Humorous Magazine.

If A theatrical Manager had him as a Picker. And Worked on the direct opposite from you ~~he~~ It would make Producing an Absolute Cin[ch.]

TL, sc. OkClaW, 1975.05.0013.

1. Louis Evan Shipman (1869–1933), a successful playwright, became editor of *Life* magazine in May 1922. He remained in the position for two years (*NYT*, 4 August 1933).

2. See Gags for *Life* Magazine, ca. November–December 1922, above, for a sample of jokes Rogers submitted to *Life* for publication.

3. See Notes for Banquet Speech, 16 December 1922, above.

4. Robert Charles Benchley (1889–1945), widely regarded for his irreverent wit, served as managing editor of *Vanity Fair* magazine from 1919 to 1920. He then moved to *Life* as drama critic, remaining with that periodical until 1929 (*DAB*, Supp. 3:53–54).

5. Robert Emmet Sherwood (1896–1955) worked briefly for *Vanity Fair* before becoming a regular contributor to *Life* as a motion picture reviewer, the first in the

magazine industry. He wrote for *Life* for eight years, beginning in 1920, and also contributed film reviews to several other magazines and the *New York Herald*. He became editor of *Life* in 1924 (*DAB*, Supp. 5:623–24; Meserve, *Robert E. Sherwood*, 27).

Transcript of Recording for Victor Records: I
6 February 1923
[New York, N.Y.]

Rogers found a new way to reach the public in early 1923: phonograph recordings. Between February and June of that year, the Victor Talking Machine Company[1] made six studio recordings of Rogers's remarks, from which the company produced three records.[2] The first two of Rogers's recordings, including the one from which the following transcript was prepared, likely derived from his stage act, while the remaining four originated from among the sixty after-dinner speeches he made in the fall and winter of 1922–23.[3]

Hello, folks. I've looked out at you from the movie screen and the stage, but I never got a chance to talk to you at home before. And I'm not goin' to tell you any jokes, I, I just want to get acquainted with you and talk over the affairs of the day with you.

Now you take wars, they're a terrible thing, but as long as women are crazy over an officer's uniform there's going to be war.

If we ever have another war, it's going to be right here on the home grounds. No use paying transportation going to Europe huntin' a war. Just think how cheap we could put on a war without a shippin' board. Instead of payin' rich men a dollar a year to help run it, why just pay 'em what they're worth. That would be a big savings.

Foreign nations, they wondered how we could train our soldiers so quick. That's because we only train 'em to go one way.

Of course, what they need in the next war, and should have had it in the last one, is a referee. And the minute the war is over, let him announce who won and how much.

Now Turkey had a hard luck lately. They had an extra war all booked and got it canceled on 'em. You have to engage a war way ahead with Turkey. She likes to finish a war Saturday and open one some other country Monday, so there's no overhead a-tall. Turkey don't care about winnin' or losin' one war, it's just how they average up at the end of the season. Then when they have any time off, they put it in by rehearsin' on the Armenians.

Last fall England kinda wanted us to join in with 'em and help 'em fight Turkey. We couldn't go into another war. Haven't got any slogans. We couldn't go into war anyhow. We're two bonuses behind as it is. Besides we might win it. We couldn't afford to win another one.

I got a plan that will stop all wars. When you can't agree with your neighbor you move away. With your wife, she either shoots ya or moves away from you. Now that's my plan. Move nations away from each other. Take France or Germany. They can't agree. Well, take France and trade places with Japan. Let Japan live there by Germany. And if those two want to fight, why, let 'em fight. Who cares? We'd run excursions to war like that.

We don't always agree with Mexico. Well, trade Mexico off with Turkey, harems and all. Now, we got men in this country who'd get along great with Turkey.

Then that would solve the Irish problem. Take England and move 'em away from Ireland. Take 'em over to Canada and let 'em live on their son-in-law. When you move England away from Ireland, don't you let Ireland know where you're takin' 'em or they will follow 'em and get 'em.

SRT.[4] OkClaW, cassette 1975.20.0002.

1. The Victor Talking Machine Company began operations in Camden, N.J., in 1901 and used forceful, highly recognizable advertising to become the market leader by the postwar years. Falling prices and rising incomes helped to make phonographs a prominent item in millions of American households by the early 1920s (Millard, *America*, 49, 56–57, 61–62, 65, 74).

2. "New Slant on War" and "Timely Topics" (see Transcript of Recording for Victor Records: II, 6 February 1923, below) were listed as record number 45347, Sides A and B, respectively, in the Victor catalog for 1924. The same publication also included record 45369, which featured "Will Rogers Nominates Henry Ford for President" (see Transcript of Recording for Victor Records: III, 31 May 1923, below) on Side A and "Will Rogers Tells Traffic Chiefs How to Direct Traffic" (see Transcript of Recording for Victor Records: VI, 2 June 1923, below) on Side B. In the following year's catalog, Victor added a third Rogers record, number 45374, which included "Will Rogers Talks to the Bankers" (see Transcript of Recording for Victor Records: IV, 31 May 1923, below) and "Will Rogers's First Political Speech," Sides A and B, respectively (W. R. Moran to Anne Moffat, 23 October 1973, OkClaW; Ann Baker Horsey to Steven K. Gragert, 14 May 2003, OkClaW). The latter Victor recording derived from Rogers's remarks at a campaign rally for Representative Ogden Mills in October 1922 (see Article in *New York Times*, 27 October 1922, above) and, thus, has not been reproduced here. Victor reportedly paid Rogers a royalty of five cents per record, the same rate that opera star Enrico Caruso received (clipping, Scrapbook 15, OkClaW).

3. Like its major competitors, Victor used recordings by celebrities to validate the quality of its records and the prestige of its labels. Of great value in the acoustical days before electrical amplification were artists like Rogers, who were accustomed to projecting their voices in a large venue, such as a vaudeville hall. Although Victor led in the field of operatic and classical music, it also pushed the records of Rogers and other entertainers with more mass appeal. One full-page company advertisement

championed them as "popular music and comedy at their best." The recordings by Rogers were among the last of the acoustical period. In 1925 Victor switched almost entirely to electrical technology (Millard, *America*, 61–62; *NYT*, 4 December 1923; Read and Welch, *From Tin Foil*, 258).

4. Dating of the document corresponds to the release date of the original sound recording.

Transcript of Recording for Victor Records: II
6 February 1923
[New York, N.Y.]

You know, these talkin' machines are great things. When you come to a theater or movie to see some of us and you don't like our act, you just kinda out of courtesy you have to stick and see us through, but on one of these if you don't like us, you just stop the machine, take the record off, and accidentally drop it on the floor. Then the only annoyance we cause you is the sweepin' up.

Now, folks, all I know is just what little news I read every day in the papers. I see where another wife out on Long Island here in New York just shot her husband. The season opened a month earlier this year. Prohibition caused all this. There's just as many husbands shot at in the old days, but women were missin' 'em. Prohibition's improved their marksmanship ninety per cent.

Never a day passes in New York without some innocent bystander being shot. You just stand around this town long enough and be innocent and somebody is goin' to shoot ya.

One day there was four shot. That's the best shootin' ever done in this town. It's hard to find four innocent people in New York, even if you don't stop to shoot 'em. That's why a policeman never has to aim here. He just shoots up the street anywhere. No matter who he hits, it's the right one.

Robberies, did you, did you ever read about so many robberies? I see where some of our cities and towns are talking about being more strict with these robbers. When they catch 'em from now on they are goin' to publish their names.

They've been havin' every kind of a week here in New York: "Smile Week" and "Apple Week" and one called "Don't Get Hurt Week." Taxicab drivers couldn't hardly wait 'til the followin' Monday to run over you.

Everybody's talking about what's the matter with this country and what the country needs. What this country needs worse than anything else is a place to park your car. What our big cities needs is another orange in these orangeade stands.

See where a New York society woman is suing her ex-husband again. Claims she can't properly support that child on fifty thousand a year alimony. Somebody's been feedin' that young one meat.

Lots of people wondered why we left our soldiers in Germany so long. That's so they could get the mail that's sent to 'em during the war. We had to leave 'em over there. Two of 'em hadn't married yet.

I'm off Ireland for home rule from now on. I read an Irish paper the other day and it says liquor is eighteen cents a quart. Can you imagine a nation wantin' more freedom than that?

See where the Ku Klux is coming into New York. Yep, they're, they're here. I'm no fool. You ain't goin' to get me tellin' no jokes about them.

SRT.[1] OkClaW, cassette 1975.20.0002.

1. Dating of the document corresponds to the release date of the original sound recording.

Notes for Banquet Speech
ca. 13 February 1923
New York, N.Y.

Dont wish to graduate into the realms of Automobile manafacturing. where you can have scandal and Income Tax Dodging,and advertising agents saying you have the best cars in the world,Dont get into that filthy rich class . som of them their Golf is bad as their Cars,

Now go along making your Millions   thats enough for anybody, Keep the sa same wife and make just as good Bycicle as you used to make, Please the Children,Your Industry meant something   you dident pick up a paper every moring and have to raed how many peo[p]le your makeof cars had killed the day before,Yours is a h[e]alth giving [one;] theirs is ahealth destroying industry   its made most of our people so lasy, when he learns how to shift his gears he thinks his lifes education is over,

I dont generally boost an organization because it is so seldom that I can ever find one who will get down to earth and be on the level,Every thing now adays is to exagerate and four flush, Everybody is telling you where their Business ranks

There is only one branch of this wonderful organization that I can thin[k] I come h[e]re to compliment but I cant think of a singlething to say and thats these Darned Motorcycles,

[*handwritten:*]

No Man has ever been able to discover a good Word for a Motor Cycle– its the Prohibition *Motor* Travel engineer.

[*typewritten, third page:*]

I can take the wildest Broncho in this wild old Wooly west
I can ride him I can tame him let himdo his level best
I can handle any Cattle ever wore Coat of hair,
And Ive had alively tussle with atarned opd [old] Grizzly Bear,
I canropw [can rope] and tie a Longhorn of the Wildest Texas Brand ~~an~~
And in Indian Dissagreements I can hold a likely hand,
But at last I met my equal. And he sure did make me squeal,
when the Boys got me astraddle of that tarned old Wheel

It was at the Eagle Ranch on the Brazos.
When I first met that darned contrivance,
A Tenderfoot had it he was wheeling all the way from
Sunrise end of Freedom out to San Francisco bay
He had tied up at the Ranch to gey [get] outside a meal
Never figureing anybody would monkey with his darned old wheel.
Arizona Charley started it when he said to Jack McGill
there was feelows [fellows] forced to limit bragging on their riding skill
and he would venture the assertion that the same fellow that he maent
was a very handy cutter as far asriding Bronchos went
but he would find that he was up a different sort of deal
If he threw his leather leggings over that Gal Darned Wheel

Well such a slam against my talents made me hotter than a Mink
And I swore I would ride him for amusement or for Chink,[1]
That it was nothing but a plaything for the Kids and such about an
and they would have their Ideas shateered if they led the Creature out,
Well they held it while I mounted and agev [gave] the word to go
but the start that they give me warnt unreasonablly slow,
But I never spilled acuss word and I necer [never] spilled a Squeal,
I was going to make areputation on that Gol Darned Wheel.

Holy Moses and the Prophets,How we split the T[e]xas Air
And the wind it made whipcrackers of this same old Canthy Hair
I sort of comprehended as down the hill we went,
that there was bound to be a smask [smash] up that we couldent well prevent
Oh How them Punchers Bawled Stay with her Uncle Bill
Stick your Spurs in turn her muzzle up the hill
But I never made an answer I just [let] the cussses squeal.
I wae [was] a going to make areputation on that Gol Darned wheel.

The grade was mighty sloping from the Ranch down to the creek
And I wenta Gallifalutin like acarzy lightnin streak,

Went a whizzing and aDarting first this waya nad [way and] then that,
The Darned Contrivance sorter wobblin like the flying of a Bat
I pulled up on the Handle Bars but I couldent check it up
I yanked and sawed and hollered but the darn thing wouldent stop
Then asort of meaching in my Brain begin to whirl that the Devil had a
a Mortgage on that Gal Darned wheel.

Ive asort of dima nd [dim and] hazy remenberance of the stop.
with the World all a going round and the Stars all atngled [tangled] up.
Then there acme [came] an intermission that lasted till I found,
I was lying at the ranch house with the Boys all gathered round
And a Doctor was a sewing on the skin wher it was ripped
And old Arizona whispered " Well old Boy I guess you are whipped[."]
I told them I was busted from Sombrero down to Heel.
He grinned and said you ought to see that Gol darnned Wheel.

TD.[2] OkClaW, 1975.14.0022. Handwritten, in Rogers's hand, top margin, center right, first page: "BYCYCLE DiNNER." Handwritten, top margin, center, third page: "BICYCLE."

1. By "Chink" Rogers probably meant "money" but capitalized it in his usual loose style.
2. Rogers likely prepared these remarks for a dinner or other event held in conjunction with the National Motorcyle, Bicycle and Accessory Show, which opened at the Sixty-ninth Regiment Armory in New York on 13 February 1923 (*NYT*, 14 February 1923). Although rare among Rogers's writings, this work of verse was not his first use of that literary device (see Guest Newspaper Column by Will Rogers, 10 May 1917, above).

Statement of Income and Deductions
ca. 15 March 1923
[Beverly Hills, Calif.?]

Will Rogers.

INCOME:

Zeigfeld Corporation	$ 102,554.91
Sleepy Hollow Corporation[1]	19,583.20
	$ 122,138.11

DEDUCTIONS:

SALARIES PAID:

Betty Rogers.	$ 15,600.00
E. H. Hayden	2,600.00
John Marcian[2]	1,560.00

J. M. Bates	1,600.00
Captain Mori	1,600.00
Theatrical valets	1,300.00
Bon[u]ses	1,400.00

$ 25,660.00

TRAVELLING EXPENSES:

Los Angeles to New York: to Philadelphia: to Detroit: to Chicago:
to Rochester: Hotel expenses,
railroad fares, meals aboard trains

Pullman fares	6,358.69
Taxes paid to city and county	1,727.49
Interest paid on notes	2,292.47
Professional dues	266.00
Charitable contributions	800.00
Make up	349.52
Wardrobe (character)	755.04
Laundry (theatrical)	356.32
Automobile expense	4,627.08
Upkeep of horses used in profession	928.42
Ropes (estimated[)]	300.00
Bad debts	500.00
Telephone, telegrams etc	431.20
Publicity photographs, mailing etc	900.00

Theatre tickets, dinners, books, newspapers
entertaining expense to Governors, members
of the press etc.   4,800.00

$ 51,552.23

TD. OkClaW, Income Tax Returns, 1922 & 1923, Folder 16-C. Hand-inserted immediately beneath the final figure is a slanted line, below which is the figure "70585.88," the difference between net income and net expenses.

1. The Sleepy Hollow Corporation, an independent film producer, had previously borne the names of the Rare Entertainment Company and Legend of Sleepy Hollow Corporation. It was created to produce *The Headless Horseman*, a movie adapted from Washington Irving's well-known story, *The Legend of Sleepy Hollow*. Shot on the estate of John D. Rockefeller, site of the original Sleepy Hollow, the motion picture opened in November 1922 and gained praise for Rogers's performance as the lead character,

Ichabod Crane, along with complaints that "once more the title writer has done what he could to spoil the pictures" (script, *The Legend of Sleepy Hollow*, OkClaW; Yagoda, *Will Rogers*, 191–92; *WRHolly*, 75; *NYT*, 25 December 1922).

2. John Marcin was the Rogers family driver (Rogers, *Will Rogers*, 203).

From Charles M. Schwab
20 March 1923
New York, N.Y.

As with his stage act, Rogers found his newest forum, the syndicated weekly column, an opportunity to "lasso" the most prominent men and women, to recognize them at the same time that he poked gentle fun at their foibles and follies. Several made a point to acknowledge the printed mention, the following letter being one of the earliest such instances. Schwab's letter illustrates the usual tone and character of the notes of acknowledgment. It also provides very early evidence of the reach and prominence of Rogers's new "Weekly Article."

March 20, 1923

Mr. Will Rogers,
New Amsterdam Theatre,
New York City.
My dear Mr. Rogers:

I read with great interest your article in the Sunday Times and want to thank you for your kindly reference to me.[1] Your friendship and good will are deeply appreciated, I assure you—the more so perhaps because I have always regarded you as a very acute minded, witty, entertaining and philosophical gentleman.

With every good wish, I am

Sincerely yours,
C.M. Schwab

TLS, rc. OkClaW, 1975.21.0002. On letterhead of Charles M. Schwab, ▼25▼ ~~111~~ Broadway, New York.

1. In his "Weekly Article" of 18 March, which was titled "Banking and After-dinner Speaking; Two Non-Essential Industries," Rogers characterized financier and steel magnate Charles Schwab as possessing "the greatest personality of any man in America." He then added, "Of course Charlie don't hardly come under the heading of Banker. He only owns just the ones in Pennsylvania" (*WA*, 1:41).

Carroll Mansfield offered a caricaturist's view of the *Ziegfeld Follies of 1922*, which opened on Broadway in June 1922 and ran a full year. (*OkClaW*)

To William C. Durant
ca. 1 April 1923
[New York, N.Y.]

My Dear friend Mr. Durant:

I been wanting to write to you some time and just tell you personally that I think you are a H - - - of a fellow and so do a lot of other people who I have heard speak of you, and you sho made a real hit the good natured way you took all my little Gags, Andy Toombs[1] and I received your very thoughtful memento the Cards.[2] I can't use the darn things to do any good but they are pretty to look at.

Say I am going to California about April first to get back in Pictures.[3] I have a Pierce Touring Car and a closed Cadillac. This Cadillac I have had three years and if you will instruct those Jips of yours out there to do right by me I will trade it in on a Locomobile.[4] I think they are a real car.

Yours any time (FREE) you got somebody you want knocked,

WILL ROGERS

PD. Printed in *Durant Partner*, April 1923. Scrapbook 8, Part 1, OkClaW.

1. Andrew (Andy) Tombes (1889–1976), comic actor and veteran of Broadway productions, headlined with Rogers in the *Ziegfeld Follies of 1922* (*HFVVC*, 1081; Ziegfeld and Ziegfeld, *Ziegfeld Touch*, 252, 257).
2. Durant and a group of his car dealers from Long Island, N.Y., visited the *Follies* in January, likely during the occasion of the annual car show and convention of the National Automobile Chamber of Commerce (see Notes for Banquet Speech, 9 January 1923, above). During his performance, Rogers apparently singled out the automobile mogul in the audience and threw a good-natured barb or two in his direction. In return Durant sent to Rogers a set of souvenir whist cards (clipping, *Durant Partner*, April 1923, OkClaW).
3. Rogers signed with Hal E. Roach Studios on 26 January 1923 to appear in two-reel comedies, but the terms of the contract did not take effect until the close of the *Follies*. The *Follies of 1922*, however, enjoyed such success that Flo Ziegfeld extended its run well beyond the usual length. Rogers, however, did not stay until the show closed. He left the *Follies* on 1 June and headed for California two days later (Charles H. Roach to Will Rogers, 10 March 1924, OkClaW [see below]; Yagoda, *Will Rogers*, 191, 205; Insurance Inspector's Report, ca. 31 May 1923, OkClaW [see below]).
4. Locomobile, one of the earliest names in automotive history, originated as a steam car in 1899 in Bridgeport, Conn., but was converted to gasoline three years later. A luxury car, one of the most prominent ones on the market, the Locomobile went out of production in 1929 (Smith, *Wheels*, 98, 109, 233; Rae, *American Automotive Industry*, 18–19).

Statement of Moving Picture Receipts
14 April 1923
[New York, N.Y.]

Pathé Exchange began to distribute two of Rogers's self-produced films to exhibitors in late 1922, a year after their production. The Ropin' Fool *opened in New York on 29 October, and* Fruits of Faith *followed on Christmas Eve.[1] The following statement of receipts, the earliest available showing evidence of full nationwide distribution of both movies, suggests that Rogers, at long last, had a chance to reap a financial return at the box office.[2]*

Apr. 14, 1923

PATHE EXCHANGE, Inc.

In Account with WILL ROGERS
Period Ending 3/24/23

NO.	BRANCHES	THE ROPIN FOOL	FRUITS OF FAITH
1	Atlanta	55.00	43.75
2	Dallas	74.00	67.75
3	Chicago	62.50	590.25
4	Minneapolis	37.50	26.00
5	New York	217.00	1254.00
6	Boston	78.50	282.50
7	Los Angeles	65.00	425.00
8	St. Louis	41.00	8.00
9	San Francisco	122.00	268.75
10	Albany	54.00	77.75
11	Pittsburgh	50.00	203.13
12	Cincinnati	145.00	216.25
13	Cleveland	183.50	62.50
14	Oklahoma City	82.63	53.25
15	Philadelphia	344.00	542.50
16	New Orleans	16.50	6.00
17	Washington	57.50	459.50
18	Kansas City	57.50	103.50
19	Denver	125.00	86.75
20	Omaha	10.00	25.00

21	Seattle	55.90	37.50	
22	Salt Lake City	13.00	18.00	
23	Indianapolis	52.50	113.50	
24	Detroit	13.50	147.50	
25	Des Moines	67.50	23.75	
26	Newark	82.50	300.00	
27	Charlotte	58.50	41.50	
28	Buffalo	10.00	25.00	
29	Milwaukee	44.00	98.75	
30	Spokane	32.50	80.75	
31	Memphis	24.00	25.00	
32	Portland	6.00	35.00	
33	New Haven	81.50	44.00	
34	Illinois & Indiana	119.00	197.50	
35				
36				
TOTAL U.S. COLLECTIONS		2538.53	5989.88	8528.41
Less Expenses 35 %		888.48	2096.46	2984.94
Net U. S. Royalty		1650.05	3893.42	5543.47
Add Foreign Royalty		260.00		260.00
TO YOUR CREDIT				5803.47
Balance Previous Statement			473.61	473.61
Our invoices		409.74	633.31	1043.05
Credited		1910.05	3893.42	5803.47
Balance this Statement				
Check Enclosed for		1500.31	2786.50	Our check 4286.81

PD, with typewritten insertions. OkClaW, 1975.24.0201. San serif typeface indicates printed matter. Printed in upper left corner: "Form No. 30[*obliterated*] 12-27 1M". Underscoring indicates typewritten copy inserted on preprinted lines. Printed and stacked (/) to the right of "Add Foreign Royalty": "Statement / Attached".

1. *WRHolly*, 47, 49. See also Notes for Premiere of *The Ropin' Fool*, ca. 7 November 1921, above.

2. Pathé received negatives of *The Ropin' Fool* and *Fruits of Faith* in July 1922. In preparation for their general release, the company then secured approval from censorship boards in various locales, which meant incurring expenses for shipping and application fees, costs borne ultimately by Rogers. Although the statement of receipts shows that both films had reached full distribution by that date, the level of activity for the first release, *The Ropin' Fool*, five months into its run, had slowed considerably (J. K. McDonald to Betty Blake Rogers, 9 July 1922, OkClaW; Business Statements Re Movies, OkClaW).

Transcript of Recording for Victor Records: III
31 May 1923
[New York, N.Y.]

Toastmasters, gentlemen, you too politicians:[1] The Democrats are the middle-of-the-road party, the Republicans are the straddle-of-the-road party, so I hereby nominate Mr. Henry Ford for president and christen the party the All-Over-the-Road Party.[2]

In the first place it's too bad he is so competent. That is the only thing that'll beat him.

Mr. Ford's a good friend of mine and years ago he overlooked a suggestion that would have made him immortal. It was when he went over to stop the war. I wanted him to take the girls we had in the *Follies* and let them wear the same costumes they wore in the show and march them down between the trenches. Believe me, the boys would've been out before Christmas.

He has made more money than any man in the world by paying 'em the highest wages. Yet, he don't even manufacture a necessity. Neither would you call it a luxury. It just kinda comes under the heading of knick-knacks.

I was in his home last year and happened to ask him that in case of stiff opposition just how cheap he could sell his car. He says, "Why, Will, by controlling the selling of the parts, I, I could give the cars away." He says, "Why, those things would shake off enough bolts in a year to pay for themselves. The second year, that's just pure profit."

People think Dr. Couee was the originator of auto-suggestion,[3] but Mr. Ford is. He originated auto-suggestion when he made the synopsis of a car.

He has just recently lowered the price, fifty dollars.[4] That's done to discourage thievery.

He's the first man that ever took a joke and made it practical. So let's let him take this country; maybe he can repeat.

He should make a good political race. He carries two-thirds of this country now.

There's no reason why there shouldn't be a Ford in the White House. They're everywhere else.

He's the only man that could make Congress earn their salary. He would start a bill through and give each one something to tack on to it. When it come out, it would be ready to use.

He's the only man that when Congress started stalling could lift up the hood and see what was the matter with it.

Some are against him because he don't know history.[5] What we need in there is a man that can make history, not recite it.

Now if Mr. Ford will just take another one of my suggestions, he can be elected. If he will just make one speech and say, "Voters, if I am elected, I will change the front on 'em."

SRT.[6] OkClaW, cassette 1975.20.0002.

1. Rogers apparently prepared a script for the Victor production of his Ford remarks. The recording follows closely a one-page, typewritten document that is in the files of the Will Rogers Memorial and was likely produced by Rogers (see 1975.25.0117, OkClaW). He probably worked from similar scripts for other Victor recordings. Rogers commented about Ford as a presidential candidate during a frolic of the Authors' League on 7 January 1923 in New York. Some of the other topics he mentioned that night mirror those he made in the Victor recording (see *NYT*, 8 January 1923).

2. A grassroots movement booming Ford for president began in 1922 and progressed strongly until Ford himself deflated it by announcing in December 1923 in favor of Calvin Coolidge, who had succeeded to the presidency in August on the death of Harding (Nevins and Hill, *Ford*, 2:305).

3. Philip Emile Coué (ca. 1854–1926), a French pharmacist and drugstore owner, was a leading practitioner of healing by so-called auto-suggestion, the idea of improving oneself by way of imagination triumphing over will. Coué toured the United States in the early 1920s, touting his theories and gaining fame with his phrase "every day, in every way, I'm growing better and better" (*NYT*, 3 July 1926; Sutherland, *International Dictionary*, 42).

4. Faced with falling sales in the postwar economic slump, Ford Motor Company bucked a trend in the automotive industry when it began in 1920 to reduce annually the prices of its vehicles. Its latest reduction, a cut of $50 across the board, had come on 17 October 1922, and other companies reluctantly followed suit to stay competitive. Although Ford lost money on every car sold, the company made up for the loss by selling with each new vehicle several dollars' worth of parts at no price reduction (Nevins and Hill, *Ford*, 2:152–53, 154; *DAB*, Supp. 4:301; *NYT*, 18 October 1922).

5. Ford was quoted in a newspaper interview in 1916, "History is more or less bunk. It's tradition." The statement became embedded in the Ford legend (Nevins and Hill, *Ford*, 2:138).

6. Dating of the document corresponds to the release date of the original sound recording.

Transcript of Recording for Victor Records: IV
31 May 1923
[New York, N.Y.]

Loan sharks and interest hounds: I have addressed every form of organized graft in the United States, excepting Congress, so it's naturally a pleasure to me to appear before the biggest.

You are without a doubt the most disgustingly rich audience I ever talked to, with the possible exception of the bootleggers union, local number one, combined with the enforcement officers.

Now, I understand you hold this convention every year to announce what the annual gyp will be. I have often wondered where the depositors hold their convention.

I had an account in a bank once, and the banker, he asked me to withdraw it, said I used up more red ink than the account was worth.

I see where your wives come with ya. You notice, I say come, not were brought.

I see where your convention was opened by a prayer. You had to send outside your ranks to get somebody that knew how to pray. You should've had one creditor there. He'd shown you how to pray.

I noticed in the prayer the clergyman announced to the Almighty that the bankers were here. Well, it wasn't exactly an announcement. It was more in the nature of a warning.

He didn't tell the devil, as he figured he knew where you all were all the time anyhow.

I see by your speeches that you're very optimistic of the business conditions of the coming year. Boy, I don't blame ya. If I had your dough I'd be optimistic too.

Will you please tell me what you all do with the vice presidents the bank has? I guess that's to get anybody more discouraged before you can see the main guy.

Why, the United States is the biggest business institution in the world. They only got one vice president. Nobody's ever found anything for him to do.

I've met most of you as I come out of the stage door of the *Follies* every night. I want to tell ya that any of you that are capitalized at under a million dollars needn't hang around there. Our girls may not know their Latin and Greek, but they certainly know their Dun and Bradstreet.

You have a wonderful organization. I understand you have ten thousand here, and with what you have in the various federal prisons brings your membership up to around thirty thousand. So, goodbye, paupers. You're the finest bunch of shylocks that ever foreclosed a mortgage on a widow's home.

SRT.[1] OkClaW, Victor Records, transcripts.

1. The origin of Rogers's remarks was not determined. He made scores of speaking appearances from October 1922 through May 1923, but none, according to available

records, involved bankers. The annual convention of the American Bankers Association did meet in New York in early October 1922 and Rogers may have spoken at an event during the meeting, but no evidence of such a speech was found (see Chronology, 1920–22, 1923–25, OkClaW). Dating of the document corresponds to the release date of the original sound recording.

Insurance Inspector's Report
ca. 31 May 1923
New York, N.Y.

He is about the most prominent vaudeville actor in the profession, and for the past five years has been under the management of Florenz Ziegfeld, Jr. appearing in his annual Follies. His act consists of rope dancing, lariat throwing and a monologue in which he is always chewing gum. There is nothing hazardous about his act, he does no acrobatics or stunts. When he first appeared in this city he did an act with a horse, but later discarded this and has appeared in the same act which he is doing at the present time for the past ten years. From time to time during off seasons he has appeared in the moving pictures, taking star parts in all productions in which he appeared. While at times he has taken cowboy parts, riding horses and so forth, he has never done any trick riding or stunts, or other hazardous parts. Lately he has acquired quite a reputation as an after dinner speaker for which he is well paid. He made pictures for the Goldwyn Picture Corporation and several other well known film companies. His contract with Ziegfeld expires the 1st of June 1923 and he is to leave on Sunday, June 3rd, to go to California to appear in moving pictures for some time.

He was under contract with Ziegfeld for $2,000 a week and extra pay for special performances. In addition he has appeared in pictures for which he was well paid, and is said to be very close in money matters and saves his money very carefully. He works continuously and is in great demand. How much he is worth nobody knows, but he has had an income of at least $150,000 a year, most of which he is said to have saved.

Some of my informants are Paul Swinehart, Editor, Zits Weekly,[1] Sam Kingston,[2] manager Ziegfeld's Follies, Max Hart, booking agent, formerly manager of applicant. Eddie Keller,[3] booking agent, Palace Theatre Building, Mr. Dietch,[4] manager Goldwyn Pictures Corporation, and H. S. Hechheimer,[5] attorney, 1540 Broadway.

Respectfully submitted,
Jos. J. F.[6]

TLS, rc. OkClaW. On form of Bureau of Inspection and Revision, Inspector's Report. Printed, upper left corner: "R 110 10M-6-22". Typewritten below letterhead: "-2-". Rubber-stamped in ruled box at right angle, right side of letterhead: "SEEN BY COMMITTEE MAY 31 1923".

1. *Zits*, a weekly periodical for the theatrical trade, started publication in 1921 and reflected the colorful style of its founder, Carl F. Zittel (1876–1943), a veteran vaudeville critic for the *New York Journal*. Never successful, the publication folded in 1938 (*EV*, 574; *NYT*, 4 December 1924, 31 January 1943).

2. Samuel F. (Sam) Kingston (ca. 1869–1929) became a friend of Flo Ziegfeld when both were young men in Chicago. He worked for Ziegfeld off and on from the 1890s, including many years as general manager of the impresario's theatrical organization (*NYT*, 18 June 1929; Ziegfeld and Ziegfeld, *Ziegfeld Touch*, 30).

3. Edward H. (Eddie) Keller (ca. 1892–1942) worked as treasurer for several theatrical playhouses, including ones in New York, Philadelphia, and Washington, during a career spent mostly in theater (*NYT*, 15 December 1942).

4. The writer may have referred to Howard Dietz (1896–1983), a composer and motion picture producer who once worked as a publicist for Sam Goldwyn (*UDFT*, 69; Easton, *Search*, 197).

5. Harry Saks Hechheimer (b. ca. 1873) was a New York attorney who had ties to the theatrical business. He filed for bankruptcy about seven months before the insurance inspector's report (*NYT*, 8 October 1922).

6. For a similar document from the same unidentified source, see Insurance Inspector's Report, 2 October 1918, above.

Transcript of Recording for Victor Records: VI
2 June 1923
[New York, N.Y.]

Mr. Toastmaster, traffic chiefs from all over the world:[1] I'm here to represent what is left of a vanishing race, and that is the pedestrian.

Now, while you birds have been directing traffic in all of our big cities, I know more about it than the whole mess of you do. I've been dodging it. Why, you even have towers[2] built up in the air so you won't get run over yourselves, but [that] I'm able to be here tonight is not any thanks to you. I owe it to a keen eye and a nimble pair of legs. But I know they'll get me some day cause I am not as young as I used to be and they're missin' me closer every day. Just yesterday, I had to run in a store and shut the door in a driver's face to keep him from gettin' me. Another chased me into a buildin' and I hopped into an elevator. That's all that saved me. Now, in my younger days I could've stayed on the sidewalk and dodged these fellows fairly.

Taxicab drivers nowadays are the same fellows who run the submarines during the war. They duck down and they don't come up for three or four blocks.

Some towns have the streets all marked off with white lines. It's a sort of a game. If a fellow running the car hits you while you're inside those white lines, it don't count. He's got to come back and run over you again.

Before we had traffic officers, there was not near as many people killed outright as there is now, but there was more hurt, which proves that by having a traffic officer to properly direct you, the driver can finish his victim, where in the old days he could only hurt him. So, I think your association can well report progress.

Prohibition has helped the pedestrian a little as the drivers are afraid to run over just anybody because it might be a bootlegger and they would get the tires all cut up.

Here are a few rules which I want you to adopt.

Eliminate all right and left hand turns; make everybody go straight ahead.

Rule two: eliminate all street cars from the streets. They only get in people's way who are in a hurry walking home.

Third, to speed up traffic have a man hired by the city in each block to do nothin' but crank stalled Ford cars.

Four, nobody is to drive on Sunday but just the weekend drivers who don't drive any other day. Then all they can hit is each other.

Have everybody going east, go on Mondays. Everybody going west, go Tuesdays. And so on.

That's the only way you will ever make the streets of the United States safe for democracy.

At the present rate in two years there will be no pedestrians left, so where will you birds' jobs be?

I see the time is up to go, so, so long.

SRT.[3] OkClaW, Victor Records.

1. As the *New York Times* described the occasion, "Will Rogers poked fun at the police chiefs" at a luncheon during an international conference of law enforcement officers in New York on 3 May 1923 (*NYT*, 4 May 1923).

2. To combat a growing problem with traffic congestion, police officials in New York began to erect and staff towers at key intersections to regulate vehicular flow. The first tower on Fifth Avenue was dedicated on 19 December 1922. A single officer occupied the twenty-four-foot, bronze structure at the intersection of Forty-second Street and Fifth Avenue and manually changed mounted signals in the tower at regulated intervals. Other towers, each manned by a police officer, soon appeared elsewhere on Fifth Avenue and throughout the city. In May 1926 New York began experimenting with a centralized system whereby a single officer could simultaneously switch several electrically connected signal lights within a zone (*NYT*, 19 December 1922, 25 February 1923, 16 May 1926).

3. Dating of the document corresponds to the release date of the original sound recording.

From Florenz Ziegfeld, Jr.
2 June 1923
New York, N.Y.

June 2, 1923

Mr. Will Rogers-
New Amsterdam Theatre-
New York City.
My dear Will:

It is with sincere regret that the time has come where you are leaving The Ziegfeld Follies, after one solid year in New York City. I want you to know that I appreciate the fact that your word is good for anything on this earth, and to have you say you will do a thing is the same as if it was done. I knew when you gave me your word you would stay for the run of the play in New York City you were under the impression The Follies would run in New York until the last of September, as it usually does. But we are all surprised that we are still at the old stand where we started last June,[1] and my great regret is that you are not going to continue with us.

I have never had anyone appear in any of my attractions that was a greater joy to be associated with than you, and I trust when the time comes for you to return to the stage you will know I am always ready to let you do whatever you want to do behind the footlights.

If there is a possibility of my getting to California before you come back, I will certainly look you up. In the meantime, give my love to your family, and it is with regret that I must say au revoir to my friend. ►a REAL MAN.◄

Very sincerely yours,

FZiegfeldJr

TLS, rc. OkClaW, Ziegfeld Correspondence. On letterhead of New Amsterdam Theatre, New York. The interpolation was handwritten.

1. The current production of the *Follies* had opened on 5 June 1922 and did not close until 23 June 1923. It set a company record of sixty-seven weeks on Broadway and forty on the road (Ziegfeld and Ziegfeld, *Ziegfeld Touch*, 102–3, 252).

"The Rope Dance," which featured Rogers and the girls of the *Follies*, was the finale number of the first act in the summer edition of the *Ziegfeld Follies of 1925*. (*C. White Studio photo, OkClaW*)

Weekly Payroll Summary, Hal Roach Studio
ca. 16 June 1923
Hollywood, Calif.

Each production unit at Hal Roach Studios constituted a "company," sometimes named after the lead actor. The initial assignment for the "Wm Rogers Company" was Jus' Passin' Through,[1] *and the following payroll statement was the first issued for the unit and the studio's newest star.*

P A Y R O L L   S U M M A R Y

June 16th, 1923

Wm Rogers-Co[2]

Actor	Will Rogers[3]	2,000.00
"	Earl Mohan[4]	100.00
Actress	Marie Mosquini[5]	200.00
"	Marguerite Bourne[6]	75.00
Director	Chas Parrott[7]	500.00
Asst "	Chas Oelze[8]	50.00
Cameraman	Rob't Doran[9]	125.00
"	Otto Himm[10]	40.00
Prop Man	C A Rudd[11]	45.00
		$3,135.00

TD, excerpt. CLSU, Hal Roach Studio papers.

1. Rogers played a work-dodging hobo in his first Roach two-reel comedy, *Jus' Passin' Through.* The company started work on 11 June and finished in less than a month. The picture was released on 14 October 1923. No copies in English are known to exist (*WRHolly*, 58; Chronology, 1923–25, OkClaW; Hal Roach Studio files, CLSU).

2. The "Wm Rogers Company" later was renamed "Will Rogers Company" (Hal Roach Studio files, CLSU).

3. In addition to a weekly salary of $2,000, the most Hal Roach had ever paid and $250 more than his own, Rogers also received a 25 percent share of the film's profits (Yagoda, *Will Rogers*, 205).

4. Earl Mohan (also Earle Mohan, d. 1928), a boxer and actor, was credited with only one feature-length motion picture, *Love Makes 'Em Wild*, in 1927. He made at least four other two-reel comedies with Rogers for Hal Roach Studios (*VO*, 17 October 1928; *AFIC*, F2CS:1268, F2FE:458; *WRHolly*, 55, 59, 62, 69).

5. Marie Mosquini (ca. 1899–1983) was a veteran performer in silent film comedies, mostly two-reel productions, with occasional supporting roles in feature-length movies. She was a regular cast member in Rogers's comedies for Roach (*VO*, 30 March 1983; *AFIC*, F2FE:305, 699; *WRHolly*, 54, 55, 59, 61, 64, 65, 69).

6. Marguerite Bourne's part in *Jus' Passin' Through* apparently was minor. Her salary went from $75 in the first week down to $12.50 in the second, and thereafter her name disappeared from cast lists at the Roach studios. Also listed professionally as Margaret Bourne, she received credit for only one feature-length film, *Souls for Sale*, in 1923 (Hal Roach Studio files, CLSU; *AFIC*, F2CS:983, F2FE:749).

7. Charles Parrott (1893–1940) was more popularly known by his slapstick comedy star name of Charley (also Charlie) Chase but used his real name as director. He started in motion pictures in 1914 and primarily appeared in short comedies. Multitalented, Chase/Parrott directed, scripted, and acted in scores of films (*FE*, 244; *VO*, 26 June 1940).

8. Charles Oelze (1885–1949) assumed more than one job during his film career at Roach studios. He was listed as assistant director during Rogers's early months with the company but appeared in later company records as property man or assistant cameraman. Although his work responsibilities might have changed over time, his salary between June 1923 and May 1924 remained constant at $50 a week (*UDFT*, 199; Hal Roach Studio files, CLSU).

9. Robert (Bob) Doran (1890–1938), a veteran cinematographer, was chief cameraman throughout Rogers's first year at Roach studios (*VO*, 7 September 1938; *UDFT*, 71; Hal Roach Studio files, CLSU).

10. Otto Himm (1890–1940) began in films in Chicago in 1912, but left three years later to return to his native city of Los Angeles, where he worked in several studios as a cinematographer. He contributed camera work for Rogers's early films at Roach (*VO*, 10 April 1940; *UDFT*, 122; Hal Roach Studio files, CLSU).

11. C. A. Rudd was listed as prop man for Rogers's production unit at Roach until mid-October 1923; thereafter, the name no longer appeared on payroll charts (Hal Roach Studio files, CLSU).

Telegram from Florenz Ziegfeld, Jr.
29 August 1923
New York, N.Y.

B23S SH 233 BLUE 4 EX DUPLICATE OF TELEPHONED TELEGRAM

NEWYORK NY 257P AUG 29 1923

WILL ROGERS

WILL CALL HD OFS HOLLYWOOD CALIF

ITS TIME YOU WERE BACK YOU MAY NOT REALIZE IT NOW BUT EVERYBODY AGREES WITH ME THATS ITS A SHAME TO BURY YOURSELF AT A TIME YOUR NAME WAS GETTING A HOUSEHOLD WORD AS AMERICAS GREATEST HUMORIST AND EVERY NEWSPAPER WAS MAKING YOU AS SUCH IF I HAD HELD YOU TO OUR ORIGINAL AGREEMENT YOU WOULD STILL BE PLAYING IN THE PRESENT FOLLIES AS WE DONT LEAVE NEWYORK UNTIL SEPTEMBER FIFTEENTH I AM PUTTING ON AN ENTIRELY NEW FOLLIES TO OPEN AMSTERDAM THEATRE OCTOBER EIGHT[1] FEEL THAT YOU

CAN TAKE ALL THE MOVING PICTURES YOU WANT AROUND NEWYORK AT THE
SAME TIME KEEPING YOUR ENVIABLE POSITION IN THE HEARTS OF THE THEATRE
GOING PUBLIC PLEASE WIRE ME IMMEDIATELY AFTER TALKING TO YOUR BOSS
MRS ROGERS YOUR DECISION AS IT WOULD BE NECESSARY TO MATERIALLY
CHANGE THE NEW FOLLIES WITH YOU IN IT AS I WOULD ENDEAVOR TO GET TWO
GREAT SCENES FOR YOU IN ADDITION TO YOUR SPECIALTY AS WE WOULD ALL
CONCENTRATE ON YOUR MATERIAL PRACTICALLY MAKING YOU THE STAR OF THE
ORGANIZATION IN THE FOLLIES THAT I HAVE IN MIND WITH YOU IN IT I MUST
OPEN OCTOBER EIGHT SO THERE IS NO TIME TO LOSE AND I HOPE YOU REALIZE
THAT YOUR PICTURES SHOULD COME SECOND TO YOUR PUBLIC APPEARANCE I
HAVE JUST SEEN ERROL[2] I WANT YOU TO COME WITHOUT FAIL BILL ANSWER QUICK

ZIEGFELD

223P

TG, rc. OkClaW, 1975.21.0209. On Western Union Telegraph Co. letterhead. Metered below letterhead and near printed "Received At": "BRANCH OFFICE, 6360 HOLLYWOOD BLVD TELEPHONE HOLLYWOOD 45". Metered to the right of recipient's name: "195". "SHEET TWO B23 233 BLUE WILL ROGERS" appears at the top of page 2.

1. Because of the extended run of the *Follies of 1922*—opening 5 June 1922 and closing 23 June 1923—Florenz Ziegfeld staged a summer edition at the New Amsterdam Theatre from 25 June to 15 September 1923. A little more than a month later, 20 October, a new presentation, the *Follies of 1923*, began a lengthy run that would last until 10 May 1924 (Ziegfeld and Ziegfeld, *Ziegfeld Touch*, 252, 254, 257).

2. Leon Errol (1881–1951), an Australian-born comic, made his first appearance for Ziegfeld in the *Follies of 1911*. Over the next several years, he appeared successfully in more editions of the *Follies* and in other musical comedy productions on Broadway (*OCAT*, 235–36; Ziegfeld and Ziegfeld, *Ziegfeld Touch*, 294).

V. V. McNitt to Edward H. Hayden
17 October 1923
New York, N.Y.

Rogers's secretary, Edward H. Hayden, wrote the McNaught Syndicate in mid-September on behalf of Betty Blake Rogers. She had decided that a book featuring several of Rogers's weekly newspaper articles and a few speeches might prove highly marketable, especially if available by Christmas. As the following letter shows, McNaught head V.V. McNitt tried to sell the idea to book publishers in New York but encountered resistance. The book, eventually titled The Illiterate Digest, *finally found a publisher and a market by Christmas—of a year later.[1]*

October 17, 1923.

Mr. Edward H. Hayden,
412 Hollywood Security Building,
Hollywood, California.

Dear Mr. Hayden:

We wish to report to you on our efforts to secure publication for a book containing Mr. Will Rogers' newspaper articles and speeches. Immediately after receiving your letter we submitted the proposition to the George H. Doran Company,[2] and when we found that there was no chance in that quarter we tried Putnam's.[3] That house concluded that it cannot make the venture and we are now about to approach Doubleday Page & Company.[4] We are optimistic over the chances of finding some one to bring out the book. Please accept our assurance that we are not losing any time but are doing our best to hurry matters along.

The objection raised by the publishers we have seen is that articles that have been widely circulated in the newspapers are not apt to find a ready sale in book form. We are now striving to find a publisher who has not such doubts.[5]

Very truly yours,
V. V. McNitt

M-S

TLS, rc. OkClaW, Income Tax Returns, 1922 & 1923, Folder 16-C. On letterhead of The McNaught Syndicate, Inc., V. V. McNitt, Pres., Times Bldg., New York.

1. In his letter to V. V. McNitt, Edward Hayden mentioned that Betty Blake Rogers had considered the idea of such a publication "for sometime past." She sought "a very attractive book . . . one not too expensive and yet one that would not look cheap" (18 September 1923, OkClaW).

2. George Henry Doran (1869–1956) founded George H. Doran Company in 1908 in Toronto, Ont., but moved the publishing firm to New York a year later. The company prospered by taking chances on new, unconventional authors and helping to establish their reputations (*DAB*, Supp. 6:171–72).

3. George Haven Putnam (1844–1930) became head of the New York publishing firm G. P. Putnam & Sons on the death of his father in 1872 and continued at the helm until his own death. One of the most prominent publishing houses at the time, Putnam's was noted in the 1920s for its books on exploration and adventure (*DAB*, 15:278–79; *HBPUS*, 3:94).

4. Frank Nelson Doubleday (1862–1934), a veteran book publisher, and Walter Hines Page (1855–1918), a journalist and diplomat, organized Doubleday, Page & Company in 1900. By the 1920s the New York house ranked among the largest publishers in the country with a diverse list of distinguished and popular writers (*DAB*, 14:142, Supp. 1:259–60; *HBPUS*, 3:108).

5. Apparently a manuscript was produced that McNaught shared with publishers. The syndicate wired Edward Hayden in early November to report that a publishing house was considering the "Rogers material" and showing interest in accepting it. Overall, however, McNaught had "not found it easy to get action." Albert and Charles Boni, who founded the publishing house A. & C. Boni in 1923, published *The Illiterate Digest* a year later. One of the first best sellers for the new house, the book earned a long and favorable review in the *New York Times*, received praise from other critics, and underwent five printings in six weeks. A. L. Burt, a much larger New York publisher, printed a lower priced, facsimile edition, also in 1924 and apparently in cooperation with Boni (telegram, McNaught Syndicate to E. H. Hayden, 6 November 1923, OkClaW; *HBPUS*, 3:145, 447; Yagoda, *Will Rogers*, 215; *NYT*, 14 December 1924).

From Lee Keedick
5 December 1923
New York, N.Y.

December 5, 1923.

Mr. Will Rogers,

c/o Lambs Club,

New York City.[1]

Dear Mr. Rogers:-

If I remember correctly, during our last conversation, you suggested that I might write you about this time as to the possibility of your being able to do a lecture tour for me or at least fill some engagements enroute from California to New York.

I believe that we can make a tremendous success of such a tour and I hope that you are now in a position to consider the matter favorably.

I shall appreciate hearing from you.

With my kindest regards, I remain,

Very sincerely yours,

Lee Keedick[2]

TLS, rc. OkClaW, Income Tax Returns, 1922 & 1923, Folder 16-C. On letterhead of Lee Keedick, Manager of the World's Most Celebrated Lecturers, 437 Fifth Avenue, New York City.

1. At the time Rogers was busy in California with the production of *Big Moments from Little Pictures*, his seventh comedy for Hal Roach Studios. The two-reel film was released on 30 March 1924 (Chronology, 1923–25, OkClaW; *WRHolly*, 62).

2. Lee Keedick (1879–1959) opened a lecture bureau in New York in 1907. Through the years he booked and managed lecture tours in the United States for many prominent international and American personalities, especially writers and polar explorers (*WhAmer*, 4:514; *NYT*, 18 August 1959). Although Rogers did not sign with Keedick, the idea of working the lecture circuit apparently appealed to him. Within two

years he would contract with another manager and embark on a successful stint as a "lecturer" (Yagoda, *Will Rogers*, 221–28; see Letter of Agreement with Charles L. Wagner, 4 June 1925, below).

Newspaper Article
ca. 9 December 1923
[Los Angeles, Calif.?]

ACTOR DEBATES WITH PREACHER[1]

A debate on "Movies and Preachers" degenerated into a four-round battle of insults for the merriment of many hundred Optimists in the Biltmore banquet room yesterday noon.

Principals—Will Rogers, the Lariat Kid, versus Rev. James Whitcomb Brougher, the Temple Baptist Foghorn, at catchweights. Referee, Federal Judge Bledsoe.[2]

Round one: Rogers was on his feet at the gong. He charged his ministerial adversary with dealing him a foul blow. Contrary to Marquis of Que[e]nsberry rules, Dr. Brougher had "fixed" the referee to allot Rogers only ten minutes for his opening tirade on preachers.

ONLY TEN MINUTES

"Ten minutes," he complained. "We go to church and sit there for two hours, listening to him say nothing—yet they give us only ten minutes to tell what we think of preachers. It's another example of supreme court justice."

Referee Bledsoe ducked and the blow went wild—also the audience. Rogers attacked his adversary in his own corner.

"Brougher says I'm a better liar than he is. That's a compliment when he admits I can beat him at his own game. He makes a living by lying. With me it's only a diversion."

"Doc" Brougher grinned under this assault.

"By coming here I will be ostracised by all the movies," Rogers continued. "It's below the dignity of our profession to argue with any preacher. But it will go down in history as the most one-sided debate in the world. I see Brougher has his gang with him."

URGES INSURANCE

The Lariat Kid, the chief contender for the Wrigley[3] trophy, advocated insurance for preachers. He said it was being taken up everywhere.

"They're the poorest paid of all professions. Which shows what a generous race of people the Americans are. They always pay what a thing is worth—no more."

"Doc" Brougher escaped this one, but a follow-up blow caught him on the chin.

"The churches send missionaries to heathen countries. But the heathens know right from wrong. They shoot a preacher and laugh at a funny picture."

The gong saved the challenger.

Round Two: The round was Brougher's by a shade.

"Rogers says he is a unique actor. He gets it from the Latin. Unus means one. Equs means horse—one-horse actor. Will Rogers makes a million without the use of brains. He shoots a gun and twirls a rope and gets a million. A preacher has to think. He must think out his sermon. When I see Rogers's salary and then see my own, I often wonder what's the use of having brains."

Rogers staggered, grabbing a table knife to steady himself.

Round three: Rogers leaped to his adversary's corner. He did not give him a chance to get to his feet, so Brougher was on the defensive, sitting down through the entire round.

Rogers said preachers are not dignified as are those in the motion-picture profession.

INTELLIGENCE DEBATED

"What is a preacher? He's an intelligent man. Intelligent people do only what they have been told to do in schools. An uneducated man thinks for himself. A preacher preaches what some old theologian has told him to preach. They give their own interpretations to the Bible. Now—if they let me read the Bible in my own dumb way, I may put the interpretation to it that God expected to be put.

"How intelligent is a preacher? Brougher went to see a motion-picture of The Ten Commandments.[4] Though he was intelligent enough to see where God stopped and where the scenario writer started in, Brougher thought the title writer was a whiz. His name was Exodus.

"And they continue to send missionaries to heathen countries. I tell you— it will take three years for the picture to offset what the preachers have done with the heathens.

"Look in the jails. You'll find them full of preachers. They haven't got sense enough to keep out. Yet, you'll not find one word of scandal that ever passed over the threshold of the movies.

"You are indebted to the motion-pictures for what this town is. They opened up Los Angeles. "Doc" Brieglieb[5] and Bob Schuler[6] have closed it up. Look out. Don't lose a 3 o'clock industry in a 12 o'clock town!"

Rogers was still pummeling the preacher at the bell.

Round Four: Brougher tried something new in the ring battles. He stood in his corner and heaved a bushel of "chestnuts" at Rogers. Rogers squinted and chewed gum vociferously under the bombardment.

Brougher wound up the struggle with a clinch. It was more like a loving embrace.

"The motion pictures are one of the greatest institutions for doing good," he said. "Motion pictures of a high type, clean, wholesome and entertaining, are the mightiest influence to the upholding of a moral life."

Referee Bledsoe's version of the verbal tilt was that it was a draw. His decision in full was:

"If the movies would go to the church more often, and if the church would go more often to the movies, there would be greater harmony between these two great institutions. And, anent this subject, my personal opinion is that decent people should be permitted to dance as long as they please—and people who dance indecently should not be permitted to dance at all."

Though Referee Bledsoe termed the debate a draw, the reporters gave a newspaper decision to Rogers.

PD.[7] Unidentified clipping. Scrapbook 8, Part 2, OkClaW. The sub-headlines read: "Optimists Hear Four-Round Battle at Biltmore"; "Will Rogers Tells Views of Minister's Calling"; and "Dr. Brougher Speaks Mind on Motion Pictures."

1. See Notes for a Debate, 7 September 1920, above, for an earlier encounter between Rogers and the Rev. James Whitcomb Brougher.

2. Benjamin Franklin Bledsoe (1874–1938) served as U.S. district judge for the Southern District of California from 1914 to 1925 (*WhAmer*, 1:106).

3. William Wrigley, Jr. (1861–1932), a Chicago businessman, began aggressively marketing and selling chewing gum in the 1890s, when gum began to gain popularity. By the early 1910s he could claim credit as the world's largest producer of gum (*DAB*, Supp. 1:715). Chewing gum became a Rogers trademark, both on and off the stage.

4. Although *The Ten Commandments*, a major motion picture spectacle directed by Cecil B. DeMille, officially premiered on 21 December 1923 in New York, it is possible that Brougher attended a prescreening. A depiction of the biblical exodus amid interpretations of contemporary life, the movie ranked second in popularity for films released in 1923 (Koszarski, *Evening's Entertainment*, 33, 34, 186, 203).

5. Gustave A. Briegleb (ca. 1882–1943) was a politically active member of the Presbyterian clergy in southern California. He became minister of Westlake Presbyterian Church in Los Angeles in 1917 and later served as president of a local ministerial alliance (*NYT*, 22 May 1943).

6. Robert Pierce (Bob) Shuler (1880–1965), Methodist preacher and evangelist, became minister at Trinity Church in Los Angeles in 1920 and built the church into one of the largest Methodist congregations on the Pacific Coast. An outspoken voice for fundamentalism, he attacked modernism and immorality in Hollywood and campaigned vigorously for Prohibition and its enforcement (*WhAmer*, 6:375; *EWMeth*, 2:2151–52).

7. The dating of the document was determined by Rogers's mention in his "Weekly Article" of 16 December 1923 that the debate with the Rev. Brougher would occur the "next week" (see *WA*, 1:168). Usually there was a two-week lag between Rogers's writing of a "Weekly Article" and its appearance in print.

To Lester Markel
ca. 15 December 1923
[Beverly Hills, Calif.]

TO: L. MARCO,[1]   NEW YORK TIMES

I read in the New York Times which I receive away out here in California every day, Their appeal[2] for the 100 most neediest Families[3]   Now there is a Real Charity. I cant think of and I dont think any one else can of a more satisifying feeling when you sit down to a big Xmas Dinner, than to know that you have not only provided for yourself but you have contributed to 100 of the poorest and neediest Families out of Four Million, If[4] this dont help your conscience and make you enjoy your xmas better then I wantb some Judge to sentence me for 60 days for Slander. I know you all have other Charities and many obligati ions on Xmas but ~~you must remember that the ones you are helping is not these 100 neediest or they would be on the list So~~ no matter who you may be helping   it is someone who is not one of the poorest, for if they were ~~it~~ they would be on this list, So if you are not contributing to this Fund you are not helping the most needy, Along with this list of 100 of the poorest Families should be kept a list of 100 of the richest in New York, And ~~if~~ those 100 of the richest in that great City of ours ~~dont~~ ▲should▲ contribute to the 100 of the poorest, Because every rich Man in New York no matter what business he might be in has New York to thank for his Fortune in some way, Every one of these 100 neediest have ~~have~~ in some shape or form ~~contributed~~ in the past,contributed to his Fortune, New York is one ~~vast~~ big ~~Familye~~ family, and if the most fortunate 100 cant give to the most unfortunate 100 then I want you to give me their names and when I come back to New York I will tell ◄[*handwritten*:]JOKES► ~~jokes stuff~~ on each one of them as long as my Chewing Gum holds out.

They might escape the poor but they cant ~~ecape me~~ escape me. ~~The reason~~ ~~I~~ I would suggest that each ~~give~~ of these 100 Richest ▲contribute 1/1▲ contribute 1/100 th of their Revenue from Non Taxable Securities, That would make a very suitable Xmas Present for those 100 Families who have not been fortunate enough to get in on any Tax Ehempt Bonds, Perhaps if they had always been NonTaxable they wouldent be the 100 Poorest. This giving the rich preference in this by no means excuses the rest of us, I was only thinking how lovely if the 100 Richest did provide for the 100 Poorest. But every person in New York should contribute somethin g to the Poorest Kiddies of his Home Town, I have worked hundreds of Benefits in New York and know that New Yorkers are the most Charitable People on Earth, I have seen you give thousands to every known cause in the World. Now dont just by chance over-look your very own. I dont think there is a New Yorker living that wouldent give something to the poorest other New Yorker. So good fortune to these needy and Merry Xmas to all of you, I am mailing my Check,[5] New York has been mighty good to thousands of us, And to those who feel that it hasn not been sog good too, Why remember that it was not these 100 poorest Families fault   they never hindered you. So I cant see how anybody is going to con-scienciously gete out of this, No matter who or what you are, Whether you are Bronx or Brooklyn. Giant or Yankee.[6] Subway or Limousine. Christian or Jew, Big Time or Small. Erlanger or Shubert. Astor or[7] Automat.[8] Klu Klux or Knights of Columbus. Tiffany[9] or Teckla.[10] You every single one of you owe the Poorest Kid in New York something and unless Prohibition has changed you in the last Year I believe you will give it to them.

WILL ROGERS.

TLS. OkClaW, 1975.05.0020. The salutation was hand-printed. Hand-printed immediately above the body of the letter, right side, stacked (/): "PRESS. RUSH. / COLLECT." Interpolations were typewritten, unless otherwise indicated. Hand-inserted editorial marks appeared throughout the body of the document. They were ignored in this transcription. Dating of the document was determined by the date of its publication in the *New York Times*, 16 December 1923. The pub-lished version contained several editorial alterations, both cosmetic and substantive. The latter are given in the endnotes and cited as *NYT.*

1. Lester Markel (1894–1977) became editor of the Sunday edition of the *New York Times* in 1923 and supervised its editorial design, content, and direction for more than forty years (*NYT*, 24 October 1977).
   2. *NYT*: ". . . *Times* the appeal . . ."
   3. The *New York Times* had introduced its Christmas-time appeal, the "Hundred Neediest Cases," in 1912 as a way to tell its readers that poverty existed in New York and to stimulate thinking about the issue. In most of the succeeding years enough funds were raised to provide for twice the number of cases as planned. The newspaper estimated that the program since its inception had provided relief for more than seven thousand persons in New York (*NYT*, 16 December 1924; Johnson, *Honorable*, 257).
   4. *NYT*: ". . . out of nearly six million people. If . . ."
   5. The newspaper reported several days later that Rogers had sent "a substantial contribution" (*NYT*, 27 December 1923).

6. The New York Giants major league baseball team, which long had overshadowed the New York Yankees, swept their city neighbors in the World Series in 1922. The Yankees, however, overcame the Giants in seven games in the series the following year. Over the next four decades the Yankees would win twenty-nine league titles and twenty World Series and become the dominant team in major league baseball (*ENYC*, 84; *TB*, 2129).

7. *NYT*: "... or small, Astor or ...." The heirs of fur trader and real estate mogul John Jacob Astor (1763–1848) ranked among the wealthiest residents in New York in the early twentieth century (*ENYC*, 62–63).

8. Automat, a chain of self-service restaurants operated by the firm of Horn & Hardart of Philadelphia, first opened in New York in July 1912. A revolutionary concept for the times, they initially offered less than a handful of food and beverage choices, each individually displayed in glass compartments and costing five cents. The help-yourself operations started as a novelty and eventually became a way of life (*ENYC*, 67).

9. The famed New York jewelry firm of Tiffany & Company was founded in 1837 and was located at the corner of Thirty-seventh Street and Fifth Avenue in 1924. The founder's son, Louis Comfort Tiffany (1848–1933), a renowned stained-glass artist, became vice president and artistic director of the company on his father's death in 1902 (*ENYC*, 1183; *DAB*, 18:534–35).

10. M. Técla & Company, a jewelry company based in Paris, operated a prominent retail store on Fifth Avenue in New York in the 1920s. The name Técla became synonymous with imitation pearls (Mason, *Illustrated Dictionary*, 358; *NYT*, 20 November 1929).

Telegram to Henry Ford
19 February 1924
Los Angeles, Calif.

An offer by Henry Ford in early 1924 to present Rogers with a new luxury car prompted a flurry of telegrams between Los Angeles and Detroit, a few of which are included here. Rogers's ambiguous response to the offer caused confusion in the executive offices of Ford Motor Company but eventually was interpreted, correctly, as his unique way of rejecting the gift.

LOS ANGELES CALIFORNIA 19th 9:03A M

WU-105-3extra FBK

HENRY FORD

THANK YOU FOR YOUR KIND OFFER BUT WOULD PREFER INSTEAD OF ONE LINCOLN[1] TWELVE FORDS AND ONE TRACTOR AS I DID ALWAYS WANT A SELECTION OF CARS SHOULD I WEAKEN AND DECIDE TO MACCEPT THIS COLOSSAL BRIDE [BRIBE] WILL DO SO ONLY ON ONE CONDITION THAT I BE PERMITTED TO TELL THAT IT WAS GIVEN FOR TWELVE YEARS OF VALIANT WORK IN TELLING FORD JOKES AND NOT FOR ANY INFLUENCE THAT I MIGHT HAVE IN GEETING MUSCLE SHOALS PLEASE DONT SEND THE CAR OUT IN A BLACK BAG BY EDSEL[2]

AS THAT MIGHT BE MISUNDERSTOOD YOUR FRIEND AS LONG AS THE THING ~~RUNS~~
KEEPS RUNNING[3]

WILL RODGERS

1:00P M
2/19/24

TG, rc. BFRC-HFM. On letterhead of Ford Motor Company Automobile Manufacturers
Telegram.

1. Ford acquired Lincoln Motor Car Company, a struggling manufacturer of luxury
cars, in 1922, with the idea of entering a market entirely different from that of the mid- to
low-priced models, which Ford then dominated. The Lincoln would long rank at the top
end of Ford products (Rae, *American Automobile Industry*, 54, 56, 60, 110).
2. Edsel Bryant Ford (1893–1943), the only child of Henry and Clara Ford,
became secretary of Ford Motor Company in late 1915 at the age of twenty-two and
thereafter assumed more important roles in the company's operations. On his father's
resignation in 1918, he became president of Ford, although his father retained considerable power. Edsel Ford saw the Lincoln as a luxury alternative to the low-priced
Model T and took a leading role in its acquisition (*DAB*, Supp. 3:283–84; Rae, *American
Automobile Industry*, 56).
3. Rogers's reply to the offer caused a stir at the Ford Motor Company headquarters
in Dearborn, Mich. Within a few days, Henry Ford's private secretary telegraphed the
company's branch manager in Los Angeles: "I am unable to tell from this whether he
has passed the whole thing off on to a joke or whether he is sincere. Will you kindly let
me know what there is to this" (telegram, Ernest G. Liebold to B. L. Graves, 25 February
1924, BFRC-HFM). For the manager's response see Letter from B. L. Graves to Ernest
G. Liebold, 13 March 1924, below.

Telegram to Henry Ford
5 March 1924
Los Angeles, Calif.

LOS ANGELES CALIFORNIA   8:29A M   5th

WU-59-FBK   a

HENRY FORD

DEAR~N~ MR FORD I AM SORRY TO [THAT YOU?] MISINTERPITED MY FIRST WIRE
AS USUAL I WAS ONLY KIDDING AND THOUGHT IT MIGHT HAND YOU A QUITE
LAUGH NOTHING IN THERE WAS OF COURSE MENT SERIOUSLY STOP THERE IS
NOTHING I VALUE HIGHER IN THE WORLD THAN YOUR FRIENDSHIP WILL SEE YOU
PERSONALLY IF I EVER~Y~ GET BACK EAST BEST REGARDS

WILL RODGERS

SA 12:20PM
3/5/24

TG, rc. BFRC-HFM. On letterhead of Ford Motor Company Automobile Manufacturers Telegram.

From Charles H. Roach
10 March 1924
Los Angeles, Calif.

As the following document illustrates, Hal E. Roach Studios was prepared to extend Rogers's contract for another year. For Rogers, however, the medium of silent film, feature length or short, did not offer the best opportunity to convey his humor. He chose not to sign up again.[1]

Los Angeles, California
March   Tenth   , 1924.

Mr. Will Rogers
Dear Sir:

Referring to the agreement made and entered into the 26th day of January, 1923, by and between Hal E. Roach Studios as first party and yourself as second party, for your employment as actor in the production of a series of two-reel motion picture comedies featuring yourself, the Hal E. Roach Studios does hereby give you notice that said Hal E. Roach Studios has exercised and does hereby exercise its right and option under and pursuant to and in conformity with the terms of said contract, to extend and continue the term thereof, and of your employment, for an additional year, commencing with the expiration of said term, to the end that the aforesaid agreement shall be construed and understood as if the term of two (2) years were specified and referred to in said contract; subject, however, to the provisions in said contract contained with reference to the participation in the net profits from the comedy films produced under said agreement to be accounted for to you during the second year of the term of said contract as hereby extended; and subject also to all of the other terms, covenants and agreements contained in said contract.

HAL E. ROACH STUDIOS
By <u>C H Roach S[e]cretary</u>[2]

TLS, rc. OkClaW, 1975.26.0068. On letterhead of Goudge, Robinson & Hughes, Attorneys at Law, 622-627 Charles C. Chapman Building, Broadway and Eighth Street, Los Angeles, Cal. "Tenth" in dateline appears to have been typewritten at a different time than the rest of the letter and with a different machine. The signature of C. H. Roach is inscribed on a signature line. Seal of the Hal E. Roach Studios appears at the left of the signature line.

1. See Yagoda, *Will Rogers*, 207.
2. Charles H. Roach (1860–1936), a former insurance and real estate broker, was the father of Hal Roach and for sixteen years the secretary-treasurer of his son's film studio (*VO*, 3 June 1936; *UDFT*, 224; *NYT*, 3 November 1992).

B. L. Graves to Ernest G. Liebold
13 March 1924
Los Angeles, Calif.

Mar 13 1924

Mr E G Liebold[1]
General Secretary to HENRY FORD
Dearborn, Michigan
Dear Mr Liebold:

Referring to yours of the 25th ult., relative to Will Rogers.

Upon returning to California, I got in touch with Mr Rogers immediately to carry out Mr Ford's instructions, i.e., to present Mr Rogers with his choice of a Lincoln Car. I met Mr and Mrs Rogers in their home at Beverly Hills, and they were highly pleased over the fact that Mr Ford saw fit to present them with such a wonderful gift. However, both appeared considerably reluctant to accept the car at once; in fact, Mr Rogers stated he would much prefer to wait a while, and said he would send Mr Ford a telegram along the lines of the one which you received, and defer taking delivery for a time.

Mrs Rogers came down to the plant a few days later and looked over the various models, seeming to show a preference for a Fleetwood Sedan, but would not allow me to turn it over to her without Bill's consent. She stated that Bill was very busily engaged in making a picture that it would take him about three weeks to finish,[2] and that as he is putting his best energies into this picture, she would much prefer to wait until he had a little leisure time before pressing him for a decision as to accepting the car. I was very careful to explain to both Mr and Mrs Rogers that Mr Ford was actuated by no other motive than friendship, pure and simple, in presenting the car to them, and that he did not expect anything in return for the gift and did not care who knew about it.

After numerous attempts, I finally succeeded in meeting Rogers again yesterday, who stated that he had again wired you, explaining the joking wire. I did not see a copy of this latter wire, hence wish you would send me one at your earliest convenience. Rogers stated he expected to go to Detroit shortly, and at that time would take the matter up in person with Mr Ford.

Suggest that you have Mr Ford write Bill a personal letter, if this has not already been done, explaining his motive in presenting the car as being purely one of friendship, for there is no question that Mr Rogers holds Mr Ford in the highest esteem. For your information, Rogers is well thought of and respected by the citizens in this community, being far above the average of moving picture actors as far as morals and general conduct are concerned.

He has a lovely wife and two nice children, and spends his spare time with his family at his beautiful home in Beverly Hills.

Yours very truly

B L Graves

Manager

LOS ANGELES BRANCH

BLG M

. . .

TLS, rc. BFRC-HFM. On letterhead of Ford Motor Company, Manufacturers of Automobiles, Trucks and Tractors, Los Angeles, Cal. The ellipsis inserted by the editors concerned a hand-written note unrelated to Rogers.

1. Ernest G. Liebold (ca. 1884–1956), private secretary to Henry Ford since 1910, wielded much influence within the company (*NYT*, 5 March 1956).
2. Rogers may have been working at the time on *Don't Park There*, his tenth film for Roach studios. The two-reeler was released in June 1924 (Chronology, 1923–25, OkClaW; *WRHolly*, 65).

From Joseph P. Tumulty
14 March 1924
Washington, D.C.

14 March 1924.

Mr. Will Rogers,

Los Angeles, California.

Dear Will:

In an envelope postmarked "Los Angeles" came your story of your meetings with Woodrow Wilson.[1] I had already seen it in the New York Times. It was a fine, generous thing to do and, as one of Woodrow Wilson's friends and admirers,[2] I wish to thank you for all the kind things you said. There is no doubt but that Woodrow Wilson loved the theatre and everything about it. I am sure it will be pleasant for you to recall that in the critical days of the war you helped a tired, weary President over a rough road. He not only admired the comedian, Will Rogers, but he had a deep feeling of affection for Will Rogers, the man and pater familias.

If you ever should come my way, don't fail to drop in on me.

With warmest regards,

Cordially and sincerely yours,

J. P. Tumulty[3]

TLS, rc. OkClaW, 1975.21.0217. On letterhead of Law Offices, Joseph P. Tumulty, Federal-American National Bank Building, 1317 F Street, N.W., Washington, D.C.

1. Former president Woodrow Wilson died on 3 February 1924 at the age of sixty-seven (*DAB*, 19:352). Two weeks later, in his weekly newspaper article of 17 February, Rogers eulogized Wilson by recounting his performance before the president in Baltimore during the war. It had been Rogers's first occasion to entertain a sitting chief executive (see *WA*, 1:192–96). See also Notes for Appearance in *Friars' Frolic*, 30 May 1916, above.

2. Joseph Patrick Tumulty (1879–1954), an attorney and a Democratic politician, served as personal secretary to Woodrow Wilson during Wilson's years as governor of New Jersey and as president. His ties to Wilson weakened during the second presidential administration, and he began to wield less influence with the president. Tumulty, however, remained an admirer of Wilson, even after the two split publicly a year after Wilson left office (*DAB*, Supp. 5:696–97).

3. Tumulty and his wife, Mary Catherine Byrne Tumulty, were in the audience the night Rogers entertained President Wilson in Baltimore in May 1916 (*NYT*, 31 May 1916).

Draft of Telegram to Florenz Ziegfeld, Jr.
ca. 12 May 1924
[Beverly Hills, Calif.?]

Mr Zeigfeld.

New Amsterdam Theatre.

New York

Dont know yet if I can make arrangements , If so the Salary is Three Thousand One Hundred Per week.[1] I have been offered three Thousand several times back there for next Season and would not go, But for the small raise of one hundred will give you benefit of not competing with other Managers. This Hundred Dollars is in the Nature of a Fine for not engageing me ~~when I left for 3 thousand,~~ in advance when I left for 3 Thousand. Also Transporatat[ion] for Myself,▲One▲Wife Three Kids. 2 Cars, and not over 12 Horses, and a retinue of Dogs. and Cats.

TG, dc.[2] OkClaW, 1975.21.0207. A typewritten "4" appears in the top margin, near center.

1. The salary of $3,100 per week made Rogers the highest paid entertainer in the Ziegfeld organization. The *Follies of 1924* opened in New York on 24 June after several days of trial performances in Atlantic City, N.J. (Salaries Statement, 21 March 1925, OkClaW; Yagoda, *Will Rogers*, 209; Chronology, 1923–25, OkClaW).

2. Dating of the document coincides with the day the Rogers Company completed its work at the Hal E. Roach Studio and the production group was terminated. All but Rogers received another week's pay. His relationship with Roach apparently remained cordial. The studio used the Rogers house and property for a location shoot in 1925 (Hal Roach Studio files, CLSU; W. B. Frank to Will Rogers, 24 April 1925, OkClaW).

Proposal for "Will Rogers Weekly" Newsreel
26 May 1924
[New York, N.Y.]

OUTLINE OF PROPOSITION SUBMITTED

BY WILL ROGERS
AT A CONFERENCE, MONDAY, MAY 26TH, 2:30 P.M. [1]

———

PRESENT: Messrs. Noble
Rogers
Cohen[2]
Parke[3]
Pearson.[4]

———

Mr. Rogers:

My idea is to make a satire on anything, to be issued weekly, and I thought the length of the thing to make it fit in would run 400 or 500 feet.

The idea is, account it being a political year, to call this series "WILL ROGERS WEEKLY". Right under that I wanted to put, if possible, either "A MOVIE MADE AS A MOVIE", or "AS A STEAL", using as a trademark a skunk.

I have not got these things routined or even worked out. My idea was to take a lot of this, then put it together and see what we have got.

Start from a political angle. For instance, we pick out three prominent democrats like Harrison,[5] Caraway of Arkansas,[6] etc. (two or three comedians). Title reads: "Washington, D.C. June 1st, Senators Harrison, etc. call at the White House to discuss the tax problems of the day." Up they are, go in through the door. Title comes on "Even a Weekly with the prestige we have cannot tell you what happened at the meeting – we would portray [betray?] the confidence of the Government." Show any little White House. Follow with hokum.

Another idea you see an awful lot of in pictures is our presidential candidates at their favorite pastime. For instance, title reading "Candidate for Political Purposes Spends Day on Farm." You see him arriving at farm, silk hat, etc. Cameraman coming. He puts on old hat, overalls, etc., is seen milking cows, feeding chickens, giving horse a lump of sugar. The flash title: "Even a future President will not see an animal go hungry." (Do not mention names at any time.)

Another scene that would work in along similar lines is an Investigating Committee. Title: "Congress in Session, Washington, D.C." "United States Senate, the Most Dignified Body in the World." Doorway. "Investigating Room No. 1" -- then cut to a line of people waiting to go in to testify, all of whom have been subpoened. Fellow drives by – "What is that?" – "That is the Oil Investigation"[7] – "This Is the Chair" – "This is the Party that has been investigated" "What is all the crowd?"

There are, of course, all kinds of other things, that do not necessarily have to be along political lines.

I thought of a satire on the titles in pictures, which every critic kids about nowadays. "The Most Exceptional Extraordinary Unique Pictures Corporation Presents So and So (some name which would get the idea over). "The original title of this was THE HOLY BIBLE. They have changed it. It was not well enough known." Then it goes on down. "The Most Exceptional Extraordinary Unique Production directed under the personal supervision of So and So." "The locations on the exact spot in which the story was laid." "The shoes by So. and So." "The Wigs by So and So." ---- Finishes up by saying "We'd love to show you Some Pictures, but owing to the fact that our footage is limited, we haven't the time." (nothing in this entire thing except titles).

Another idea. Mention big name of a Company. It presents Will Rogers himself in person in a dramatic title "Walking", taken from the book, "The Pedestrian", Directed by "Western". You see Rogers coming down the street. Title: "Introducing our Principal Character, Will Rogers" (Get some title that has to do with walking –for instance "Johnny Walker". [)] Then camera. Steps off sidewalk, in all seriousness continues walking, looks about – beautiful drives, cliffs, sky, etc. – keeps on walking same pace. Comes to large building, continues walking. Keep this up for couple hundred feet. Then fade out to end. Title: "Next week RUNNING". Fade out.

Another thought: "How they photograph Game." "You have seen how they shoot game in Africa, but you have never seen how one of these is photographed." You see Rogers coming along with camera. Fellow runs out from behind. Sets up camera behind bushes. The camera which is taking scenes moves back and forth in all expectancy. Brook nearby. Along comes horse, takes a drink. Title: "(Some latin name for horse) Known to Become Domesticated." "The Most Ferocious Speciman of its Kind." Horse walks away in all calmness.

Remember, all this carried on in entire seriousness.

Fellow landing from Europe. (Charlie Chaplin gave me this gag). Take anyone who is receiving any amount of publicity in the daily pictures. For instance. "So and So from Russia. This man has made his name in Russia from manufacturing nail files (when as a matter of fact there is probably not a nail file in all of Russia). When he lands, Committee at dock, high hats and everything, to greet him. The Russian all dignity steps ashore. One asks him a question. Other three cheer. Then title goes on "Mr. Vickavitch has just announced that he is in this country and is not going to lecture."

Another idea. Satire. Daily News, Society Folks. "Mr. and Mrs. So and So on the golf links, Palm Beach, Florida." (names that don't mean anything). Or, "So and So at the Races (make them funny) Or, "Somebody laying a corner stone". (just a repetition of what they have looked at the week before, only retitled).

"Will Rogers Returns to New York City from California. After one year in the Movies, he decides to go back on Stage." Have cameraman shoot street early in the morning, from a prominent spot – say Times Square. Nobody in the street. Title following "Town turns out to greet him." (not a soul around.[)]

(Must always have the date and place at opening of this hokum, just like the Weekly.)

Another one: "Mayor of New York City arrives at office." Car drives up. Someone alights, dashes in door. No one knows who it is. Title: "Mayor Hylan just entered." Camera keeps turning on door. Audience keeps looking at door, but sees nothing. Keep this up for about 100 feet. Finally title flashes: "We couldn't wait all day for him to come out." Then quick flash of fellow rushing out. Title: "He just left."

Another: Title – "There is an old adage – Half the World doesn't know how the other half lives." "The other half are living off prizes, picture puzzles, etc." Another title: – "We are offering a prize here in this theatre which the management will give to the person in the audience who picks out the most objects in this picture whose name begins with a 'W'[.]" Show in rapid succession barnyard scenes, animals, mountains, lakes (everything under the sun). Camera keeps on moving so fast, no one could pick out anything. Fade out. Title follows: "For Those who did not win anything in the last picture, we are having a Consolation Contest." "The next prize is for the one who can give the exact number of people in this picture whose first name is Isadore. Use as a scene a Sunday afternoon at the polo grounds – the crowd watching a baseball game. Finish up with a gag something like "Winners kindly go to the Box Office and Try and get your Prizes."

You can burlesque a picture. Take an important scene from a picture like "America"[8] – a lot of people can't see American at all although they live in it. Take some scenes that were cut out of thepicture – for instance where the horse didn't jump. Title: "This scene was in 'America', but Mr. Griffith cut it out."[9]

Another idea. Take a typical Western picture. They all run so long. We must cut them down and make them shorter. Show villain and the chase. The hero rescues the girl.

Burlesque a colored film.[10] Open up with title: "People love beauty and color, and we spare no expense." Use the hardest and most grotesque (Bull Montana type) looking people for characters, dressed in gaudy colors. Show beauful [beautiful] flower gardens, water falls, pretty sky, etc.

We could run a burlesque on fashions and on scenes of eqtiquette.

Another thought. Take one scene out of "THREE WEEKS."[11] Rogers is *the* fellow. Woman made up like Elinor Glynn is supervising and directing.[12] Love scene of Rogers and girl playing lead. Elinor Glynn is disgusted with girl, but Rogers is just the kind of a fellow she had in mind when she wrote the book. The girl is too base. Elinor Glynn shows girl how it should be done and rehearses scene with Rogers. Rogers is married, his kiddies are at the Studio, see this love-making act, run home to the mother, who comes just in time to believe her own eyes.

Another gag. Take afellow who has tried for the leading part in a big picture like "Ben Hur."[13] Flash title "Why I wasn't picked for "Ben Hur" and show some little thing why he was not chosen.

Show a friend the sights of New York City. Keep pointing out things that no one has ever seen or heard of – things that don't mean anything. Show the Hudson and East Rivers as the same thing – a small stream. Point out a concrete railing mentioning this is where Brooklyn Bridge starts. Turn around and before you know it – this is the end of the bridge. Stop before some unheard of restaurant. "This is the O.K. restaurant", etc. etc.

I would like to do this. It is something along the line that nobody has touched and has unlimited possibilities. Exhibitors surely cannot kick on account of the length of it. We should get a lot of this stuff ready, then screen it and start off right. Work in the nut gags gradually. Start particularly with the topical things, then sneak in the others.

Mr. Cohen suggested starting the Pathe Review Drive with this as an issue. Get the Sales Force to help put the Drive over.

Mr. Pearson's idea was to put something in the Review that audience will laugh at without saying anything about it. Let the audience sell it to the exhibitor, in other words. That would beat any drive the salesman could make in advance. Finally make it a separate issue, because at first it will be hard to make the public realize sufficiently the value of this novel idea, to pay Mr. Rogers fairly and adequately.

Mr. Pearson suggested that inasmuch as these Reviews run practically exclusively in the high-class theatres only today, if this thing develops, as it probably will, we can go back to those Review numbers – the Branches can do it themselves – and make up 500 or 600 feet lengths of this, or even 1000 feet, for introduction into some of the other theatres. The salesman can carry this around with him when calling on the exhibitor. He can say to him "I think I have a little reel that your audience will laugh at." Put it on, then surprise the audience. Do not give too much on any one evening.

Mr. Cohen suggested that topical subjects of only three months endurance be used as a side light for the News.

Mr. Rogers feels he can land this series in the Follies, first-run, this city.

When we start advertising, have salesman tell exhibitor "I am not going to ask you to take this film if you or your audience haven't any sense of humor, because you won't like it.["]

TD. OkClaW, Miscellaneous Letters. Stamped on the upper left corner of page one is a clock face showing 4:00 with "RECEIVED PATHÉ EXCHANGE INC." above and "MAY 27 1924" below.

1. Rogers submitted the "Will Rogers Weekly" proposal to representatives of Pathé Exchange at a meeting in New York within a couple of weeks of returning from California. He apparently hoped to produce the film "weeklies" while starring in the *Follies*, thereby staying active in the film business despite his absence from Hollywood. Pathé Exchange had distributed Rogers's self-produced movies, as well as the Hal Roach shorts (*NHD*, 156; see also Statement of Moving Picture Receipts, 14 April 1923, above).

2. Emanuel Cohen (or Emmanuel Cohen, 1892–1977) was editor from 1914 to 1926 of *The Pathé Weekly*, a popular newsreel of international and national current events (Koszarski, *Evening's Entertainment*, 167; *UDFT*, 50; *NYT*, 11 September 1977).

3. William Parke, Sr. (1873–1941) was a long-time stage actor who also directed plays and films (*VO*, 30 July 1941; *UDFT*, 204).

4. Elmer R. Pearson (ca. 1884–1954), a veteran of film production and sales, was vice president and general manager of Pathé Exchange (*NYT*, 1 January 1955; *UDFT*, 207).

5. Byron Patton (Pat) Harrison (1881–1941), a former congressional representative, was elected to the U.S. Senate from Mississippi in 1918 and served from 1919 until his death. A Democrat, he gained national prominence for his strident opposition to the Republican presidential administrations in the 1920s (*DAB*, Supp. 3:334–35).

6. Thaddeus Horatius Caraway (1871–1931), a Democrat from Arkansas, served in the U.S. Senate from 1921 until his death ten years later. Caustically outspoken and intensely partisan, Caraway took a leadership position in exposing the scandals of the Harding administration (*DAB*, Supp. 1:151–52).

7. The secret leasing to private interests of naval oil reserves at Teapot Dome, Wyo., and Elk Hills, Calif., constituted the most infamous scandal of the Harding administration. Rumors of graft in the leasing arrangements led to the exposure in early 1924 by a senatorial investigating committee of what became commonly known as the Teapot Dome scandal. A federal grand jury indicted Secretary of the Interior Albert B. Fall in June 1924 for his involvement in the affair. He was eventually convicted (*HD1920s*, 314–15). For Rogers's thoughts on the oil scandal, see *WA*, 1:190–92, 196–203, 212–14.

8. *America*, an epic-length historical drama of the American Revolution, premiered in New York on 22 February 1924 and had its general release in August. Produced and directed by D. W. Griffith, it ranked among the five most popular movies of the year (*AFIC*, F2FE:17; Koszarski, *Evening's Entertainment*, 33).

9. Griffith often cut scenes and shot new ones even after a film had progressed through a few preview showings and the premiere. *America* was copyrighted at a length of fourteen reels. Eventually it was pared by three reels and a few thousand feet (Koszarski, *Evening's Entertainment*, 135; *AFIC*, F2FE:17).

10. The first American motion picture shot entirely in color, *Toll of the Sea*, opened in New York in late November 1922, but reluctance in the industry to add color because of unrealistic results and problems with projectors meant that by mid-1924 there were few other examples. A new process introduced within three years brought about greater acceptance of color cinematography (*FE*, 275; *AFIC*, F2FE:818; Koszarski, *Evening's Entertainment*, 130).

11. *Three Weeks*, released by Goldwyn Pictures in February 1924, was based on Elinor Glyn's novel of the same name. Published in 1907, the scandalous best seller about royal infidelity and murder was filmed at least twice, but the version in 1924 earned the most notoriety (*AFIC*, F2FE:806; Koszarski, *Evening's Entertainment*, 309).

12. Glyn's presence and influence in Hollywood had grown since her arrival there in 1920. She became known as the discoverer of motion picture sex appeal, which she called "It." Not surprisingly, a corporation was formed in March 1924 in England to acquire and market the copyrights of her literary works (Glyn, *Elinor Glyn*, 279; *NYT*, 20 March 1924).

13. Although it did not open in New York until December 1925, *Ben-Hur* was in production at Goldwyn Pictures, soon to be known as Metro-Goldwyn-Mayer, as early as 1923. Changes in stars, directors, scenarists, and location sites, all chronicled widely in the press, contributed to the film's production delays and monumental cost. Despite the nightmarish setbacks, the religious spectacular became the biggest movie attraction of 1926 (*AFIC*, F2FE:51; Koszarski, *Evening's Entertainment*, 33, 241; Marx, *Mayer*, 46–48, 71–72).

5. ON TO EUROPE
June 1924–September 1926

Rogers took a ride aboard the plane of Brig. Gen. William L. (Billy) Mitchell at Bolling Field in Washington, D.C., 24 April 1925. Five months later Mitchell, a leading advocate of military aviation, was dismissed from active duty for his public criticism of army policies. (*OkClaW*)

THE SUMMER OF 1924 LIKELY BECAME ETCHED IN WILL ROGERS'S MEMORY. FOR three long, grueling, hot weeks in June and July, he sat in a stuffy, overheated convention hall and watched and listened as the Democratic party tore itself apart trying to nominate a presidential candidate and to debate Prohibition and the Klan. Each day he tried to make sense of what he observed and then worked to peck out a column that could relate with humor the confusion, deadlock, frustration, and anger that had unfolded before him.[1] By the end of the experience his exasperation had probably overtaken his usual light-heartedness. From the chaos of Madison Square Garden he hurried to the bright lights of the New Amsterdam Theatre to perform every evening in the newest edition of the *Ziegfeld Follies*. Always one to stay topical, he made sure his nighttime stage act included a gag or two about what he had witnessed that day on the convention floor.[2] Often several of the folks who had been on that same floor made their way to the *Follies* in the evening for a chance to laugh at themselves.

Through his syndicated articles, other writings, after-dinner speeches, and stage acts, Rogers had gained by the summer of 1924 a growing and well-deserved reputation as a shrewd, sensible, down-to-earth commentator on politics and the political scene. Being shoulder to shoulder and face to face at the Democratic convention with some of the most recognizable politicos and pundits in the country guaranteed him a place in the mainstream of the political community. Not surprisingly, after the final, 103rd ballot had been cast, he took time to contact the major players and to offer a clever word of advice. He received replies in kind.[3]

Rogers's national prominence had risen with every passing year and every new means of communicating that he attempted. Now, he continued to expand his presence on the national scene, to pursue opportunities to reach new audiences, to tap additional resource streams. Some of the work he under-took during this period had already proven a success for him, as when he returned to the stage at the *Ziegfeld Follies* in July 1924, opening at the New Amsterdam Theatre the same day as the Democratic national convention. He continued to produce his weekly syndicated article, although in 1924 he lost the *New York Times* as a subscriber (but he did pick up Hearst's New York

World). During those same months he remained a favorite on the banquet circuit and accepted several after-dinner speaking invitations.

As he continued with the tried and true—and at $3,100 a week for the *Follies*, the high-paying—he could afford to have Betty and the children join him on the East Coast. They left behind their house in Beverly Hills and newly acquired property in the Santa Monica hills.[4] Instead, the Rogers family rented a place on Long Island for a year and settled into life back east. Once firmly replanted in New York, Rogers could pursue a few new options. One arrived in the summer of 1924, when the American Tobacco Company sought him out to write advertising copy for its popular pouch tobacco, Bull Durham.[5] After a little dickering, Rogers agreed; he began producing short pieces of nontestimonial material, pocketing a few hundred dollars per ad. The series, "The Bull's Eye," debuted in early 1925 and continued for more than a year.[6]

Another writing turn, equally unnoteworthy, came in the spring of 1925. Rogers approached his syndicator with an idea for a daily column of jokes that weren't, or, as the title of the series explained, "The Worst Story I've Heard Today."[7] For some reason McNaught bought the concept and signed some newspapers to carry the piece. Rogers's first effort at a daily syndicated column originated in print on 25 May 1925, but he later wearied of the project and allowed it to expire quietly after nineteen months.[8]

Despite such writing misadventures during this period, Rogers continued to maintain an enviable position in the national consciousness, as well as back in his home state. In the summer and fall of 1925 his name was proposed for governor of Oklahoma, although he quickly put a damper on the idea.[9] The brief flurry of political foolishness, as Rogers described it, happened as he was about to embark on one of his more successful ventures.[10] On 1 October he launched the first of several seasons of "lecturing." The gig came about through the work of Charles L. Wagner, a highly successful talent manager in New York.[11] Wagner arranged a national tour for Rogers and The de Reszke Singers, a quartet of young male vocalists.[12] Together, they spent two and one-half months in the fall of 1925 touring the country, with Rogers as the main attraction delivering his usual, unique monologue of topical humor.[13] He would perform on the lecture tour circuit for about three years, crossing and recrossing the country, telling his gags, commenting in his inimitable way on politics and myriad other subjects, making his humor even more relevant with asides of local interest. His performance at prestigious Carnegie Hall in New York in April 1926 capped a successful first year on the lecture circuit.[14] Many years later, long after he had broadened his act and his appeal, Rogers would tell interviewers that his "greatest personal satisfaction" came from the concert hall lectures. It "was the hardest work, but it was the most gratifying."[15]

During this period in his life, Rogers also began to build an international reputation, consciously or unconsciously, by striving to understand issues, people, and politics in other countries so that he could better communicate the same to his audiences in the United States. World affairs offered him further grist for his mill of humor, one that he constantly needed to feed and freshen. In September 1924 he made one of his most important overseas contacts, one that he would use to great advantage for several years. That September the Prince of Wales, as closely followed in the press as any major celebrity of the time, visited the United States and made the social rounds.[16] For several months before the royal visit, in his writings and monologues, Rogers had defended the heir apparent for the frequent, highly publicized falls he had suffered during steeplechase competitions. Rogers, known to take an occasional tumble himself in the heat of a polo match, commiserated with His Highness and cracked jokes about the likelihood of a rider staying up in the air until the horse recovered from its fall.[17] Aware of Rogers's empathy and defense, the prince requested that Rogers speak at a banquet given in his honor. The evening proved exceptional; Rogers and the Prince of Wales scored as a team that night and remained friends thereafter.[18]

His friendship with the Prince of Wales surely gave Rogers whatever confidence he might have lacked to take on other stars on the international stage. He had made previous trips to Europe, but the one in the summer of 1926 proved more productive and likely of greater lasting value to his work. In the nearly five months he spent there, he visited at least nine countries and conversed with heads of state and other national leaders throughout the continent. He delivered several banquet speeches, appeared on the London stage in a musical revue, and starred in a motion picture produced in England and in a group of twelve travelogues shot on location in several different countries. He initiated two series for the *Saturday Evening Post* that would eventually involve eleven articles and result in two books, and continued to write his syndicated weekly column (by this time an unattributed editor at McNaught was likely ghost-composing "The Worst Story"). Throughout this busy time, he maintained business correspondence with associates back home, escorted his family on sightseeing excursions, and sent to the *Times* the first of what would become his trademark piece of writing, the "Daily Telegram."

Rogers's European tour in 1926 allowed him to connect intimately with dozens of influential individuals and to add immeasurably to his fodder of topical material. He returned to the United States and to the lecture circuit that fall overflowing with observations and views, right or wrong. He had solidly established a national identity; he could now add to it a credible international perspective. Perhaps charged by his European experience—both the preparation for it and the results—his productivity had increased amazingly, but remarkably he had yet to reach his full stride.

1. See *CA*, 48–88; see also Telegram to William Jennings Bryan, 3 July 1924, below.

2. For example, see Notes for *Ziegfeld Follies* Skit, ca. 20 June 1924, below.

3. For example, see Telegram to John W. Davis, 10 July 1924, below.

4. See Letter from Gladys Dowling, 21 June 1924, below.

5. Bull Durham smoking tobacco was sold in small, tied, five-cent sacks. The brand, with a picture of a bull sandwiched between the words "Genuine" and "Durham," originated in Durham, N.C., after the Civil War and, through heavy advertising, became the best-selling tobacco for hand-rolled cigarettes. The American Tobacco Company, the leading maker of factory-produced cigarettes, acquired Bull Durham in 1899 (Heimann, *Tobacco*, 233, 235; *"Sold American!"* 17–18, 23; Winkler, *Tobacco Tycoon*, 103–6). See also Letter from Frank W. Harwood, 29 September 1924, below.

6. For an example, see Advertising Proof for Bull Durham Tobacco, ca. 1 January 1925, below.

7. Yagoda, *Will Rogers*, 215.

8. See Manuscript for Newspaper Column, ca. 25 May 1925, below.

9. See Telegram to J. S. Leach, 13 July 1925, below.

10. See Letter to James S. Davenport, 7 September 1925, below.

11. Charles Ludwig Wagner (ca. 1869–1956) had achieved considerable renown by 1925 as a lecture and concert manager. His clients included some of the most prominent figures from politics, literature, business, and music. In the 1920s he also began producing plays on Broadway (*NYT*, 26 February 1956; Wagner, *Seeing Stars*, 12). See Letter of Agreement with Charles L. Wagner, 4 June 1925, below.

12. The de Reszke Singers, an American male quartet who performed unaccompanied a wide-ranging repertoire, took their name from Jean de Reszke (Jan Mieczyslaw, 1850–1925), an acclaimed Polish operatic tenor who had retired from the stage in 1902. The quartet members had been the last pupils of de Reszke before his death. The group spent two seasons in England and France before their debut tour of the United States in January 1925. When Rogers's lecture tour began in Elmira, N.Y., on 1 October, the printed program listed Hardesty Johnson, Floyd Townsley, Erwyn Mutch, and Harold Kellogg as members of the group. By the time the tour reached Kansas City, Mo., six weeks later, bass Harold Kellogg, baritone Mutch, and tenors Townsley and Francis Luther made up the quartet. The same four were listed on the tour's program in November 1926. On other occasions Sigurd Nelson (or Nilssen) was listed as a member (*NYT*, 26 January 1925; *ODM*, 232; *EA*, 2 October 1925; program, Will Rogers Lecture Tour, OSU; *KCS*, 14 November 1926; program, Scrapbook 21, OkClaW; Wagner, *Seeing Stars*, 315).

13. A typical show during the lecture tour consisted of two segments with The de Reszke Singers opening each, followed by Rogers who did an hour or more of commentary while occupying a virtually empty stage (Yagoda, *Will Rogers*, 226).

14. Carnegie Hall was finished in 1891 and named in honor of industrialist Andrew Carnegie who underwrote its construction. Located at Seventeenth Street and Seventh Avenue, it became known as one of the premier concert houses in the country and was home for seventy years of the major philharmonic orchestra in New York (*ENYC*, 180–81). See also Notes for Lecture Tour Appearance at Carnegie Hall, 11 April 1926, below.

15. *NYT*, 14 October 1934.

16. Edward Albert (Edward Albert Christian George Andrew Patrick David, 1894–1972) became Prince of Wales in 1910 on the death of his grandfather and the succession to the British throne of his father. Extremely popular as crown prince, he ascended to the throne in 1936 as Edward VIII but was forced to abdicate a few months later because of his intention to marry a twice-divorced woman (*DNB*, 9:272–77). The trip in 1924 was the Prince of Wales's second to the United States. He arrived on 29 August in New York and traveled immediately to Washington, D.C., to meet President Coolidge (*DNB*, 9:273; *NYT*, 30 August 1924; Edward, *King's Story*, 199).

17. Edward, *King's Story*, 196.

18. The dinner on 3 September 1924 was held at the exclusive Piping Rock Country Club on Long Island, N.Y. (*NYT*, 4 September 1924). See Notes for After-Dinner Speech, ca. 3 September 1924, below. For an account by Rogers of his experiences with the Prince of Wales, see *WA*, 1:290–93.

Notes for *Ziegfeld Follies* Skit
ca. 20 June 1924
[Atlantic City, N.J.]

Pardon me Ladies and Gentlemen for stepping out of my Character,yo [to] make a direct appeal to you, (I will lay aside my Trade mark as a National Lawmaker) [(]Lay asidemy public character)   Now tha [then] I am out of my Character as a Politican. The plot needs just a shade of explanation here, right here   Six Months are supposed to haveleapsed [have elapsed] between the time you saw me in front of that Lemon Colored Capitol and this time here, Not are supposed to have elapsed but really have elapsded. This is Mr Zeigfleds first experiance with Plots   He knows Women as good as any manin the World but he dont know plats. Now I coming direct from the Movies are the direct opposite, I know plots   I have worked in hundreds of them with eight reels of plot and one reel of Story,

I have been in Washington 6 months and am already on an investigating Committe   all the Rooms are so gfull of investigating I have to use this one, Its the Chloride Gas room, Manafactured for the sole purposes of curing Mr Coolidges Colds after a hard days Vetoeing.[1]

Chloride gas is made by a combination of Senate and House of Representatives and Investigang Room, The more they Talk up there the Bigger it registers down here, we only use one half of one percent, Mr Ford offered to buy the whole thing, But he wabted [wanted] a 500 year lease on it,[2] at the expiration of the 500 years it wa do reveryt [was to revert] back to Uncle Joe Canon and Chauncy Depew,[3] Thank you   I will step back into my Governmental Character.

Oh One other little thing   might I add that I just wrote this little scene in her[e] to give Mr Tom Lewis[4] a ~~chan~~ legitimate excuse to do his League of Nations Monologue. I thank you.

I dont hardly know what to do   the jokes I had in last night are out, I introdeced all the prominent people in the audience last night but I am a bit handicapped.

About 5 sketcehs~~m~~ , and and I believ we did take out two car lo[a]ds of Scenery, . Oh yes and I like to forgot, a Plot   we had a plot, I tried to help Mr McGuire[5] write it, I was so nervous about the presentation of my first p[l]ay.I have heard of plays that just run one night, but this plot of oyrs [ours] only run half of one night   they cut it out between the first and the seconda Act. It wasent so bad on him as he has written lots of successes, ~~and~~ but being my first, it has discouraged me so I dont think I will ever write again, A Plot in this show would be as useless as a Corset. I wish it had stayed in, I had a great part, it would have been the making of me, They talked about me all during the first hour and a Half, the whole plot revolved around Me Alfaflfa Doolittle, eveybody kept asking where ~~A~~ is Alfaflfa, Then just befor intermission they had abig torch light procession and I ~~come~~ was carried on . Oh it was   acorking entrance,then I was carried right out, oh It was great Part.

Then I made a Speech to the people, They cut it out, It was just like all Politicians speeches, thats why they cut it out,

To Pick a man to run second to Coolidge,

In cleveland they tried to pick a man to run Second with him,[6] but this one is too pick a man to run wecond [second] against him.

Opening with a Prayer,

TD. OkClaW, 1975.33.0014. On letterhead of Hotel Traymore, Atlantic City, N.J. Typewritten below letterhead, first of two pages: "(Plot Talk at opening of Chlorine Gas Scene)".

1. Calvin Coolidge (1872–1933), former Republican governor of Massachusetts, was elected vice president of the United States in 1920 and succeeded to the presidency on the death of Warren G. Harding in 1923. He won election in his own right in 1924 and served until 1929. In May 1924 Congress passed over Coolidge's veto a controversial compensation package for war veterans (*DAB*, Supp. 1:191–98; *HD1920s*, 4).

2. Ford had aroused indignation in 1922 when he had asked for a one-hundred-year lease on the hydroelectric and nitrate facilities at Muscle Shoals, Tenn. (Nevins and Hill, *Ford*, 2:308).

3. Chauncey Mitchell Depew (1834–1928) was president of the New York Central Railroad for fifteen years and chairman of its board of directors from 1899 until his death. A former Republican senator from New York and a popular wit, Depew remained a much sought-after banquet speaker past age ninety (*DAB*, 5:244–46).

4. Tom Lewis (Thomas Lewis Maguire, ca. 1863–1927), a comedian, performed in vaudeville and Broadway productions for fifty years. He appeared with Rogers in both editions of the *Ziegfeld Follies* in 1924 and in the spring edition in 1925 (*NYT*, 20 October 1927; Ziegfeld and Ziegfeld, *Ziegfeld Touch*, 257, 258).

5. William Anthony McGuire (1885–1940) was a playwright and screenwriter who collaborated with Rogers in writing the dialogue for the *Follies* in 1924 (*NYT*, 17 September 1940; *UDFT*, 171; Ziegfeld and Ziegfeld, *Ziegfeld Touch*, 257, 258; *WhAmer*, 1:814).

6. The Republican party held its national convention in Cleveland on 10 June 1924. With incumbent Coolidge as the only presidential nominee, the main interest centered on the vice-presidential choice. The delegates took three ballots to settle on dark-horse candidate Charles Dawes. The Democratic national convention was scheduled to open on 24 June in New York. Rogers attended both conventions as a correspondent (*CA*, 31; *EAH*, 335).

From Gladys Dowling
21 June 1924
Los Angeles, Calif.

Having recovered financially from his experiences as a film producer and with the family feeling settled in California as their permanent home, Rogers decided to purchase property in a newly developing area in Santa Monica, a few miles from the family's home in Beverly Hills. The following letter was one of the earliest confirmations of Rogers's purchase of the real estate that eventually became the Will Rogers Ranch.

June 21st, 1924.

Mr. W. P. Rogers,

c/o Mr. Lou Rose,[1]

Beverly Hills, California.

Dear Sir:

We enclose herewith statement of interest due this Corporation on account of your purchase of Parcel #32, Santa Monica Mountain Park, as per agreement dated January 29th, 1924.[2]

The interest is figured to July 1st, 1924, for while the agreement called for a contract to be signed by March 15th, 1924, it was not signed due to reasons which we believe both parties understand.[3]

The attached blue print gives the necessary data for you to decide on the amount of acreage you wish, and we suggest that the contract to be entered into at this time be dated as of July 1st, 1924, with interest payable on the total acreage involved from that date forward. You will note that we have figured the interest in the statement we are now rendering, only on 150 acres.

If, therefore, you will advise us of your acceptance of this survey, we shall immediately prepare the contract.

Very truly yours,

ALPHONZO E. BELL CORPORATION[4]

by <u>Gladys Dowling</u>

Secretary.

Statement and blue print attached.

TLS, rc. OkClaW, 1975.24.0009. On letterhead of Alphonzo E. Bell Corporation, 530-531 Pacific Mutual Building, Los Angeles, Cal. The sender signed on a type-inserted line, as indicated by underscoring.

1. Lou Rose was associated with the real estate industry in Los Angeles (1975. 14.0196, OkClaW). He may have served as an agent for Rogers in the selection and purchase of the property in the heights of Santa Monica.

2. The contract provided for the purchase of 159.721 acres at $2,000 per acre or a total of $319,442. Rogers was to make a down payment of $30,000, and interest would be assessed at 6 percent. Parcel #32 rested between the mountains and the sea, six miles from Beverly Hills and less than two from the Pacific Ocean. Although mostly untamed and barren, it was a beautiful site, steep and rugged and bordered by canyons, a spot that Rogers called "'my Shangri-La.'" At the time, no paved roads ran near the property (1975.24.0007, OkClaW; Yagoda, *Will Rogers*, 207–8).

3. The failure to sign on 15 March may have been related to developments at Roach studios. The deadline date was very close to the final day, 13 March, for Rogers to agree to a contract extension offered by Roach. He declined the offer, possibly activating an automatic extension that would have bound him to the company for ninety days. He also may have decided not to sign the real estate deal until his financial livelihood beyond 15 March could prove more certain (Hal Roach Studio Ledger, 1924, CLSU).

4. Alphonzo Edward Bell (1875–1947), real estate promoter and oilman, developed in the Los Angeles area several exclusive residential enclaves, including Bel-Air. He co-owned the Los Angeles Mountain Park Company, which in 1924 began to develop and market several thousand acres in the mountains along the Pacific Coast, including property that became part of the Rogers family ranch (*NYT*, 28 December 1947; *NatCAB*, 36:450–51).

Telegram to William Jennings Bryan
3 July 1924
New York, N.Y.

The Democratic national convention of 1924 began in Madison Square Garden in New York on 24 June, the same day the new production of the Follies *opened at the New Amsterdam Theatre on Broadway. In a neat balancing act, Rogers was able to appear in the* Follies *and also cover the convention for the newspapers. The political show, however, became somewhat of a marathon, marked by endless speechmaking, balloting, and deal-making.[1] Rogers's frustration, echoing that of much of the country, was reflected in the following few words.*

NKB601

[*obliterated*] 3 144P

WILLIAM JENNINGS BRYAN

      CARE CONVENTION MADISON SQUARE GARDEN NEWYORK NY

WE WANT AL SMITH AND NO MORE HOT AIR

TG, rc. OkClaW, 1975.31.0311. On Western Union Telegram letterhead. Metered below the letterhead, upper right: "1924 JUL 3 PM 1 52."

1. The Democratic national convention of 1924, the longest political convention in American history, turned into a divisive, destructive struggle among the northern and southern, urban and rural, wet and dry, Catholic and Protestant sectors of the party. Delegates took 103 ballots to settle on a compromise presidential candidate and departed New York embittered and divided (*HD1920s*, 91; Finan, *Alfred E. Smith*, 182–83). For Rogers's coverage of the convention, see *CA*, 43–88.

Telegram to John W. Davis
10 July 1924
New York, N.Y.

MR JOHN W DAVIS[1]

      6 EAST 68 TH ST NEWYORK NY

WOULD HAVE CONGRATULATED YOU SOONER, BUT WAS AFRAID SOMEBODY WOULD CALL FOR A POLL OF THE DELEGATES, AND THEY NEVER POLLED, LIKE THEY HAD VOTED. SO I WAS IN MORTAL FEAR FOR YOU UNTIL THEY GOT OUT OF TOWN, STOP HEAR ONE OF THE BRYAN BROTHERS[2] ARE TO BE ASSOCIATED WITH YOU INDIRECTLY.

FOR GOD SAKE PICK THE RIGHT ONE. STOP WANT TO SEE YOU BEFORE IT
BECOMES NECESSARY FOR YOU TO DEGENERATE INTO A POLITICAL CAMPAIGNER.
CONGRATULATIONS AND REGARDS.

WILL ROGERS

TG, rc. OkClaW, 1975.13.0004. On Western Union Telegraph Co. letterhead. Handwritten on
right side of letterhead: "Copy". Metered below right side of letterhead, stacked (/): "ASTOR
HOTEL / JUL 10 1924." A double-depth "HT" appears on the left side of the metered copy and
"NY" on the right side. Typewritten below body and closing of the telegram: "[*obliterated*] THANKS
FOR YOUR KIND WIRE& WILL PICK THE RIGHT BRYAN AND& WATCH THE OTHER ONE. IF I AM
ELECTED I WILL APPOINT YOU AMBASSADOR TO ENGLAND& I HAVE THE KNEE BREECHES." Immedi-
ately below "I HAVE THE KNEE" is the same text handwritten with a short, hand-inserted arrow
pointing to "BREECHES."

1. John William Davis (1873–1955), a former congressional representative from
West Virginia, served as ambassador to Great Britain from 1918 to 1921. A dark horse
at the Democratic national convention of 1924, Davis won the nomination on the one
hundred third ballot, essentially as a compromise candidate (*DAB*, Supp. 5:155–56).
2. Charles Wayland Bryan (1867–1945) was a younger brother and chief advisor
of three-time presidential candidate William Jennings Bryan. Charles was elected
governor of Nebraska in 1922 but declined renomination two years later to seek the
Democratic presidential nod. Although he failed in his bid, he accepted the vice-
presidential slot, which had been offered to him to appease the Bryan wing of the
party (*DAB*, Supp. 3:114–15).

Telegram to Charles W. Bryan
10 July 1924
New York, N.Y.

MR CHARLEY BRYAN

WALDORF ASTORIA HOTEL NEW YORK NY

CONGRATULATIONS, THE DEMOCRATS ACCIDENTALLY PICKED ITS BEST TWO
MEN. IS THERE ANY WAY THAT WE CAN GO THROUGH THE BIRTH RECORDS, AND
SHOW THAT YOU AND MY GOOD FRIEND W J, ARE ONLY COUZINS, IF SO THIS WILL
HELP US IMMENSELY IN THE CAMPAIGN. YOURS FOR PARTY HARMONY

WILL ROGERS

TG, rc. OkClaW, 1975.13.0002. On Western Union Telegram Co. letterhead. Metered below
right-side of letterhead, stacked (/): "ASTOR HOTEL / JUL 10 1924". "HT" appears on the left side
of the metered copy and "NY" on the right side. A vertical line has been hand-inserted between
"AND" and "MY" in second sentence. The word "COUZINS" has been underscored by hand. Typewritten below body and closing of the telegram: "Thqnks for Wire   will do as you suggest
about records   thats a graet idea. In the meantime i have bought him a one way Ticket to
Floridaa.[1] Govenor Bryan".

1. William J. Bryan, a native of Nebraska, purchased 20 acres of land near Miami, Fla., in 1916. He eventually built a home there and became involved in Democratic party politics in the state. He served as a delegate-at-large to the Democratic national convention in 1924, but his declining health made the convention his last major political effort (Wilson, *Commoner*, 357–58, 363–64, 394–95, 407–8).

Telegram to William G. McAdoo
10 July 1924
New York, N.Y.

MR W G MCADOO

HOTEL VANDERBILT NEWYORK NY

CONDOLENCE TO A FELLOW DEFEATED CANDIDATE,[1] I TOO KNOW WHAT IT IS TO SUFFER. LACK OF WHISKEY, AND HARMONY, IS ALL THAT BEAT US. STOP BUT JUST THINK OF WHAT WE HAVE TO BE GRATEFUL FOR. WE CAN RETURN TO CALIFORNIA WHILE THESE OTHER POOR DEVILS HAVE TO STAY EITHER HERE OR IN WASHINGTON. YOU ARE TOO GOOD A FELLOW W G TO BE SPOILED BY BEING A MERE POLITICIAN. HELL IS FULL OF POLITICAL CANDIDATES, BUT IT WILL BE SEVERAL YEARS BEFORE THEY HAVE A W G MCADOO. BESIDES YOU WOULD HAVE GOTTEN TIRED JU▲S▲T HOLDING ONE LITTLE POSITION LIKE PRESIDENT. REGARDS TO MRS MCADOO, WANT TO SEE YOU BEFORE YOU GET SWELL AND GO TO EUROPE. P S WHEN YOU GET TO ENGLAND FIND OUT WHO JOHN W DAVIS IS FOR ~~ME~~ AND CABLE PARTICULARS. A BEATEN BUT NOT HUMILIATED CANDIDATE

WILL ROGERS

TG, rc.[2] OkClaW, 1975.13.0003. On Western Union Telegraph Co. letterhead. Handwritten on right side of letterhead: "Copy." Metered below right side of letterhead on both sheets, stacked (/): "ASTOR HOTEL / JUL 10 1924". "HT" appears on the left side of the metered copy and "NY" on the right side. Handwritten numbers, apparently inserted when counting words in the telegram, appear above the body text at ten-word intervals. The interlineation was handwritten. Double strike-through indicates hand-deleted text.

1. Rogers received a single vote on 4 July during the sixty-eighth ballot at the Democratic convention. The tally came from the ballots of two delegates from Arizona, who each represented one-half of a vote, and earned the *Follies* comedian and convention reporter an interview by the *New York Times* (*NYT*, 5 July 1924; Yagoda, *Will Rogers*, 212).
2. William McAdoo replied the next day: "DEAR WILL I APPRECIATE YOUR TELEGRAM DON'T FEEL BADLY ABOUT YOUR DEFEAT I CAME HERE WITH 530 DELEGATES AND COULDNT GET A SHOW HOW COULD YOU EXPECT TO HOLD YOUR ONE" (telegram, William G. McAdoo to Will Rogers, 11 July 1924, OkClaW).

Telegram to Alfred E. Smith
10 July 1924
New York, N.Y.

MR AL SMITH

MANHATTAN CLUB(IN REACH OF SPEAKERS PLATFORM MADISON SQUARE)[1]
NEW YORK NY

GIVE ME CREDIT, DIDNT I PREDICT FROM THE FIRST THAT YOU WOULD BE THE LUCKY ONE.[2] I KNEW THEY WERE GOING TO NOMINATE DAVIS. TRIED TO SEE YOU DOWN THERE, AND ALL THAT PREVENTED ME WAS NEW YORK AND ALBANY POLICE FORCES COMBINED. WELL LET US AT LEAST SHOW THE WOR[L]D THAT WE ARE A COUPLE OF GAME BUT DEFEATED CANDIDATES. WE CAN BOTH RETURN TO OUR RESPECTIVE FOLLIES. YOU AT ALBANY AND ME AT THE AMSTERDAM THEATRE. PERSONALLY I AM GLAD YOU WAS NOT NOMINATED, IT WOULD HAVE TAKEN TWO YEARS TO HAVE CLEANED THE PAPER OFF THE STREETS HERE. HAD MANY A PLEASANT CHAT WITH YOUR WIFE[3] AT HER BOX DURING THE THREE WEEKS READINGS OF STATES INSANITY STATISTICS. PERSONALLY I BELIEVE SHE IS GLAD YOU ARE BEATEN, WHAT SMART WOMAN WOULD WANT TO LEAVE NEW YORK TO GO TO WASHINGTON. REMEMBER 1928 IS A DIFFERENT YEAR WE WILL MAKE A JOINT CAMPAIGN. I AM GLAD YOU FOLLOWED MY EXAMPLE AND WITHDREW. YOURS IN MOURNING P S I HAVE TO SEND HYLAND ONE TOO.[4] I DONT HARDLY KNOW WHAT TO SAY TO HIM

WILL ROGERS

TG, rc. OkClaW, 1975.13.0014. On Western Union Telegraph Co. letterhead. Handwritten numbers, apparently inserted when counting words in the telegram, appear above the body text at ten-word intervals.

1. During the Democratic national convention, Al Smith stayed on the top floor of the Manhattan Club, where he could easily monitor convention proceedings across the street at Madison Square Garden (Finan, *Alfred E. Smith*, 182).
2. Al Smith entered the Democratic national convention of 1924 as a front runner with significant support in key states, but the religious division at the convention effectively crippled the chances of Smith, a Catholic, winning the party's candidacy. The loss of the nomination stung him, and the religious bigotry evident at the convention angered him as much (*DAB*, Supp. 3:719; Finan, *Alfred E. Smith*, 183–84).
3. Catherine A. (Katie) Dunn Smith (ca. 1879–1944) and Alfred E. Smith were married in 1900 (*NYT*, 5 May 1944).
4. Mayor John Hylan had once enjoyed Al Smith's support, but in 1924 when the governor rose to leadership in Tammany, Hylan lost favor with the powerful Democratic organization because of the mayor's close association with William Randolph Hearst, a political thorn of Smith's. Without Tammany's endorsement, Hylan lost the mayoral primary the next year (*DAB*, Supp. 2:331).

Notes for After-Dinner Speech
ca. 3 September 1924
Long Island, N.Y.

One of Rogers's most personally satisfying speaking engagements came in 1924 when he was invited to headline a dinner for the visiting Prince of Wales. Although Rogers made the crown prince a target of much of his humor that night, the Ziegfeld star proved a resounding hit with the guest of honor and the 150 others in attendance. The following notes, which Rogers re-created later for publication, show that he did not hesitate to rib royalty firsthand anymore than he did a president.[1]

Well here it is, I remember it from a few noted I made before I went, and also the impromptu ~~ones~~ remars that come to me while talking, The reason is I dont play before one of those things every day,

There had been so much talk over the speech that we asked Will if he would not write the whole thing out in full exactly as it occured, including the side lights on how different points of it were taken,

Gentlemen, and Polo Players, and Guest of Honor, You see I am stuck already   its terrible to get stuch this soon in a speech, But I am   I dont know what to call our distinguished Guest, In the mornings he is the Prince of Wales, in the afternoon, he is Lord Renfrew,[2] and as I have not read the last edition of the Papers, I dont know what he is here tonight, ▲TRAVELING UNDER AN ALIAS&▲   Well anyway he is a Prince in his own Country, He was Lord Renfrew on the trip over here, But with us here he is just a Regular Guy. ▲[*handwritten*:]Have that Translated and you will find its not lost T[ranslation?].▲ (IF I DIDENT THINK YOU WAS I wouldent b[e here.)]

Now I know a lot of you thought I would be all nervous up here appearing before Royalty, but I am not, because it is not the first time I have appeared before Royalty, One time Sir Harry Lauder[3] was in the audience where   I was playing, somebody had given him a Pass to get in. Well of course I was all swelled up over appearing before a Sir, and later on I got to reading some English book and found that a Sir was about the lowest form of Royalty there is, Its the Ford of Titles. (Note. That by the way was one of the biggest laughs ~~I got,~~ the Little Prince just doubled up, and waht made it universal there was several Sirs among the English Guests present)

But I am broadminded   if a Man can get out and make himself popular in spite of his birth, I am for him, I admire any man that can rise above his surroundings,

I dident know he was here untill just by accident I happened to see a little squib down in one corner of the paper, in akinder out of the way place, It said you were over here, otherwise I wouldent have known it,

▲Only danced with one others   try to get money BK [back?]▲

Now if you think I am coming here to tell you alot of Jokes about the Prince f falling off his horse [you're wrong].   Editorial Writers couldent swim it, I couldent climb it with a Ladder,   My falls dont attract as much attention but they hurt just as bad,

This Boy has the nerve, Look on the Boat danced with one Girl,

If you want to ~~ridesomebody about~~ see some funny riding go to Central Park

we dont have to wit for the Prince   Wlaes,

We cant kid Englishmen about their Horsemanship, If I cant find something funny in an Englishman besides his riding I [*obliterated*] wont consider myself much of a Comedian,

I am the Worlds worst Polo player, I dident take up the Game for its social purposes, or to be pointed out as a Man about Town, (He stopped me and said No I am the worst,) so anyway we played the next day and hewaon [he won] so I am the Worlds worst,. I told him we shpuld be compolimented, its not much distiction to be the best, as there is only about 10 around the table here tonight who are the absolute headliners, But look at the hundreds of them that are the Dubs,

So when you and I can point out that we are the worst, that means something   look at the oposition, we have got, Its like you Prince winning that Booby Prize on the boat, in a Masque Ball costume, any one could havw won the 1 st Prize but when you win a Booby prize you have done something, for look at the the nimber of Boobys,

Now any of you that think I am going to kid or tell any jokes about the Prince here toniht are wrong for I read where he had been practicing all the way over boxing in the Gymnasium, so you wont get m[e] telling any Jokes about him,

Another thing alot of you think I am kinder out of place talking to Royalty, Why say I know all about the workings of Raoyalty and high Society over in Eng[land.] I know all the Scandal, dident I hear Margot Asquith[4] on two of her Lectures in this Country, the first one a Fox Hunt, So you see I am the Margot of America   Slept during Loyd Georges, Lecture so i dont know much of the   Politics,

They dont play polo all the time, I will tell you alot on the Long Islandres, That will be the biggest Social gathering ever put [on], Husbands will meet

Wives who never met before, for 4 or 5 marriages, a person introduving two people are liable to have them say to each other after introductions Pardonme but was you not my first Husband, wasrnt I married to you one time, Old Wives will come to see how the new ones dress, Long Islnd you know Prince is A wondeful Island   it is maintained just by Alimony and potatoes,

Now this welcome that you got over here, Prince i dont want to have yoy missunde[rstand] it, part of the welcome was for your personal Popularity, part for the respect for the Country you represent, but most of this big Wholesome spontaious part was for the reaso you were not coming here to Lecture, Yoy are the first Englishman that ever come to our Shores that was not going to advise us how to run our Country, So as long as you dont Leacture you will always be welcome   But God help you if you start lecturing,

You dont know it Prince but you did me quite a favor, it was while you were in India, I wanted to see afew intimate views of the night life in that Country,

The polo game is supposed to start Saturday,[5] but I doubt if they can start as the English ittakes them as long to pick their team as it did the Democrats,

Polo you know is a Gentlemans game, Gentlemans Game, the man that named it had a sense of Humor, Take for Instance dev Milburn[6] , or this fel ow Lacey,[7] or Tommy Hitchvock,[8] They are just as gentle as kittens, all they would do in a Game would be to ride you right over the palisades of the Hudson river,

I happened to hear the American team in conversation theother day, I was sitting in the club and they dident think I could hear and the instructions to them from Captain Milburn was to miam but not quite kill, a Gentlemans game,

~~and say by~~ the way British Folf [golf] players are here too,[9]

I understand there is in the party here tonight some Golf Players, How did they get in here with the men, I thought this affair was a stag,

You know the other night at the Theatre I introduced the British team, Great bug [big] men, I just thought if a Co ntry could just get men like that to work what a help they would be if you could get them to work at something, Carry 19th Hole in your pocket, drink at every hole, Longer to play that [than] to explain,

I want to apoligise for my clothes, only Polo player with no dress suit or Polo coat, Dev Milburn,

Hospitality, made me tell theone on hospitality, no place for hired help,

Metcalf the Equerry[10] come back, he is the mEcghnician [mechanician], only one got sorem   I should have known better, because I have aformula that I always wotk on, that is always kid the big fellow, but never the littleone,[11]

Women want him to marry, WE are changing Govermemnets so often, just as soon [*text ends*]

TD. OkClaW, 1975.14.0078.

1. Soon after the dinner Rogers queried the publisher of the *Saturday Evening Post* about using his speech in the magazine. A senior staff member replied that editorial policy would not allow it because "all material published in the magazine must be entirely new." Even with the small attendance at the dinner, he explained, Rogers's remarks might reach a part of the readership of the *Post* ([Wesley W. Stout] to Will Rogers, 15 September 1924, DLC-MD, Wesley Stout Papers). Rogers may have typed these notes as an early draft of the article for the *Post*. The first two paragraphs probably were intended to provide a background to the piece and a third-person introduction.

2. Although he crossed the Atlantic under his official title, the Prince of Wales, in a vain attempt to travel incognito, assumed the name Lord Renfrew once he arrived in the United States (*NYT*, 10, 12 August 1924).

3. Harry Lauder (1870–1950), a hugely popular Scottish comedian and singer, made successful annual tours of the British Isles and the United States. He was knighted in 1919 for his countless troop concerts during the war and for his tireless efforts as a recruiter (*DNB*, Supp. 6:486–87).

4. Emma Alice Margaret (Margot) Tennant Asquith (1864–1945), the wife of a former prime minister and Liberal party leader, was a writer, lecturer, and commentator, noted for her unrestrained candor. She considered fox hunting her greatest pleasure (*DNB*, Supp. 6:23–24).

5. Teams from the United States and Great Britain vied for the annual International Polo Cup in a competition that began at the Meadow Brook Club in Westbury, Long Island, on Saturday, 6 September (*NYT*, 31 August 1924).

6. Devereux Milburn (1881–1942), American polo player, was considered one of the greatest competitors in the history of the sport. He played on the team in 1909 that first captured the International Cup for the United States (*NYT*, 31 August 1924, 16 August 1942).

7. Lewis Lacey (or Luis Lacey, b. ca. 1887) was a Canadian-born Argentine. A ten-goal polo player (the highest ranking), he helped lead a team from Argentina to international victories in 1922. He was a late addition to the British side in the International Cup matches at Meadow Brook in 1924 (*NYT*, 31 August 1924; Edward, *King's Story*, 199).

8. Thomas (Tommy) Hitchcock, Jr. (1900–1944), the son of an accomplished polo player, began competing in the sport at age thirteen. A ten-goal player, Hitchcock played on the American team in the International Cup competition in 1924 and captained the United States in the Olympics the same year (*DAB*, Supp. 3:360–61; *NYT*, 31 August 1924; *BDASOut*, 260).

9. The United States defeated Great Britain in Walker Cup golf competition in mid-September 1924. Named for George H. Walker, an American who had donated the trophy, the Walker Cup had begun two years earlier. The British had yet to win the series, which after 1924 became biennial (*NYT*, 13, 14 September 1924; *EG*, 284).

10. Edward Dudley Metcalfe, an Irish cavalry officer, met the Prince of Wales during his celebrated tour of India in 1921–22. Known by the nickname of Fruity, Metcalfe developed a close bond of friendship with the prince in India. He soon joined Edward's staff and served him as equerry, or personal attendant (Edward, *King's Story*, 170).

11. Rogers's opinion of Metcalfe soon changed: "He was at our Show the other night and after the Show come around to my dressing Room and said i am Major Metcalf Equary to the Prince, well ~~I dident know whether~~ he might just as well been talking Zulu to me, I dient know what an Equerry was, Of course I found out after he nexplained it to me that he was akind of Mechnician   Kept everythingbin running order, He seemed might nice   he compilimented me about what i had said about the Prince only falling when the Horse falls, Then he showee me how many falls he had gotten, where nothing was ever sad [said] about it, Scars all over, He started to take off his clothes to show me more but I stopped him and told him i would take his word for it. . . . But this Equerry cartainly was alive wire, I thought sure he was an Insurance Agent" (Original Follies Routine file, OkClaW).

From Frank W. Harwood
29 September 1924
New York, N.Y.

Rogers continued to find new ways to communicate. At some point in the summer of 1924 he began exploring an opportunity to write advertising copy for a maker of tobacco products. As a nonsmoker Rogers assumed a certain risk, not only in reputation but also in credibility. Given the remuneration described below, he may have found it a risk well worth taking.

September 29, 1924

Mr. Will Rogers
C.o New Amsterdam Theatre
New York   N.Y.
Dear Mr. Rogers:

In consideration of $500.00 handed you herewith, you engage yourself to write for us 26 pieces of BULL DURHAM copy, each to be signed by you and each to be approximately 150 words in length,[1] and to permit the publication of an illustration of yourself as a part of each advertisement.

We will pay you at the rate of $500.00 for each such piece of copy, or a total of not more than $13,000.[2]

We will require the copy at intervals of two weeks, beginning January 1, 1925, except for the first three pieces of copy which we may desire earlier so as to permit advance use being made of the advertisements.

It is understood that for a period of 26 weeks from January 1, 1925, you will write advertising copy exclusively for The American Tobacco Company, with the further understanding that The American Tobacco Company can, at the expiration of 26 weeks from January 1st, 1925, renew this exclusive arrangement for a period of 26 weeks at the same terms, if they so elect.[3]

We   are to have the right to cut out of the copy matter which we deem might not be good advertising.

Very truly yours,

THE AMERICAN TOBACCO COMPANY

Frank W. Harwood[4]

Manager- Advertising Dept

ACCEPTED _____

TLS, rc. OkClaW, 1975.26.0066. On letterhead of The American Tobacco Company, Incorporated, 111 Fifth Avenue, New York.

1. For a sample of Rogers's work see Advertising Proof for Bull Durham Tobacco, ca. 1 January 1925, below.
2. The American Tobacco Company had doubled its offer in a month. In August the company had proposed to pay Rogers $250 each for ten pieces of advertising copy (Frank W. Harwood to Rogers, 27 August 1924, OkClaW).
3. Rogers produced advertising copy for Bull Durham well into 1926. One such advertisement appeared in the *Claremore* (Okla.) *Weekly Progress* on 17 December 1926 (Bull Durham Original Ads, OkClaW).
4. Frank W. Harwood (ca. 1882–1935) served as the advertising manager of American Tobacco Company until his retirement in 1931 (*NYT*, 17 January 1935).

Article by Will Rogers
ca. 30 October 1924
[New York, N.Y.?]

TWISTS FROM THE COIL OF ROPE

By Will Rogers

All of old Eli's and the Army Alumni have been asked to contribute something (their presence on a 10 dollar ticket preferred) to the big yearly Dog fight.[1] Loving my old Alma Mater as I do but unable to come because it is Saturday (every big event is always held on Saturday a matinee day, I bet you when the world comes to an end it will be on Saturday, and I will be having a Matinee and will miss it). As I can't come I thought I would just write. I never attended Yale personally but I have met so many of its shining youths at the stage door of our Show for years, that I feel that I know most of you. Then, too, I feel close to old Eli[2] (do they still call it that) because in my early stage career I played the Poli Circuit of Vaudeville up there so much and so often. You see I used a Horse in my act in those days, well on account of Poli[3] having all his Theatres close together, I rode the Horse from one place to another. I had too. So I used to often ride by Yale coming from Waterbury or Bridgeport. I have often felt since that perhaps for social reasons, I wish I had stopped and got expelled. I dident realize at the time what it meant to one. As for West Point you have to be appointed by a Congressman to go there, and I would rather not have a Football education, than have it publicly known that I was acquainted with a Congressman. And a Senator, if one of those claimed acquaintanceship with me I would sue him for slander. They are both good Schools, of course of an entirely different character. Yale has beautiful old Trees and West Point has The River, and also a new modern Hotel adjoining built for John Smith and Pocahontas. Then West Point also has its Tack Officers, what a cheerful bunch of Porcupines they are. I went up to West Point years ago to speak to the Cadets one Sunday afternoon. Oh it was years ago. Well, I tell you how long ago it was. It was when this present Football Team they have now, was just graduating from other colleges and coming to West Point so they could retire in a couple of years on a Pension. They may use Oliphant[4] again. If you go away from there and forget everything you know that makes you eligible to enter again. Not that he forgot it, but its permissable if he did. I offered to write a letter for the Yale-Harvard Game, but I was told that it would be necessary to have my letter translated into English for the Crimson Alumni. If translated then Yale couldn't read it.

I love Football, I love it because I never heard it reffered to as Gentlemanly. You got to always watch out for these Games they call Gentlemanly. Because they never are. I see where Yale's authorities spoke of the Sportsmanlike conduct in the Dartmouth Game.[5] I dident see anybody speaking about the playing. You seem to have been better Sports than players. By the way, where did that school come from. It was as unknown as a Vice President. Then dident some Georgians come up there and like to beat you.[6] They dident even have any substitutes, they couldent have, they havent got enough Pupils, only for one eleven. Why for years they could only play Base ball at Georgia, then two more Scholars entered and they took up Football. They call it sportsmanship in Football when the Coach advises his men to maim, but not kill, unless absolutely necessary. I hope there will be no bribery exposed. Games have goten to be so untrustworthy nowdays. Craps is about the only dependable game we have. You can't fix the players, you can only fix the dice. The Army cares nothing in particular about beating Yale. Its that Dissarmament Conference Navy of ours that the Army wants to sink, still I kinder hope Yale wins as I don't like to see our Army go into the next war too confident.

I had a friend in Yale—he was cheer Leader, and he stayed an extra year to take a Post Graduate course in Public Speaking. But they wouldent let him lead the howling the 5th year, they claimed he was a professional.

I had another friend had to stay there 5 years too, he dident have his Mearcheum [Meerschaum] Pipe colored yet.

Football is wonderful, one forms so many friendships on the field. Nowhere can you come in such contact with men of other colleges as you can in a Football Game. There is a kind of a spirit you gain at College that stays with you untill you get out in the World and try to get a job.

A visiting Oxford Alumnus,

WILL ROGERS

Who is now contributing the only moral support to The Follies.

N.B.—This junk may be terrible, but it was the best I could do with the coaching I have had this year. I lost some of my best jokes last year through graduation and this year's jokes are slow on their feet.

PD. Printed in unidentified publication, ca. 30 October 1924. Scrapbook 8, Part 1, OkClaW.

1. The football squads of Yale University and the U.S. Military Academy played to a tie, 7 to 7, before a crowd of eighty thousand in the Yale Bowl at New Haven, Conn., on 30 October 1924 (*NYT*, 1 November 1924).

2. Yale University derived its name and nickname, Eli, from that of Elihu Yale (1649–1721), a wealthy English trader, whose donated goods helped to underwrite a new building in 1718 and led the appreciative trustees of the then struggling school to rename the institution in his honor (*DAB*, 20:590–91).

3. For Sylvester Z. Poli see *PWR*, 2:403–4n.1.

4. Elmer Quillen (Ollie) Oliphant (1892–1975) starred at halfback for Purdue University and the U.S. Military Academy in a collegiate football career that spanned seven seasons, 1911 to 1917. After graduation from Purdue in 1914, Oliphant won an appointment to West Point, where he continued his athletic success at a time when no limitations existed on years of eligibility (*BDASFoot*, 439–40).

5. Yale University and Dartmouth College, which had not competed in football in twenty-five years, tied, 14 to 14, at New Haven on 18 October. The game included the first touchdown ever scored by Dartmouth against Yale (*NYT*, 19 October 1924).

6. The Yale University football team defeated the University of Georgia by just one point, 7 to 6, at New Haven on 11 October (*NYT*, 12 October 1924).

From Will James
ca. October 1924
San Francisco, Calif.

Throughout his public life, Rogers received scores of new, personally inscribed books from authors, many hoping for an instant sales spike by Rogers's mention of their book on stage or in print, others seeking a return compliment that might merely boost an ego. The first effort of western writer Will James may have been sent for the usual self-serving reason or simply out of fondness and admiration for a former cowhand who had succeeded in life beyond the range.[1]

Franktown

Nevada—

Dear Mr. Rogers–

This is just me writing— I'm the author of this new book "Cowboys, North and South"[2] and drawed the pictures that's in the book too

Now I'm asking – have you seen, heard of, or got the book I'm speaking of here–?–

I'm thinking it'd tickle you– or any cowboy that's rode before the contest saddles come out. and for that reason I'd like to send you a complimentary copy of it– if it's O.K. with you.

The address where it'd reach you for sure is what I'd like to get— also a word as to wether you've got the book—

Sincerily

Will James—

ALS, rc.[3] OkClaW, 1975.21.0083. A line drawing of a male figure with western clothing, hat, and boots appears in the upper right one-quarter of the sheet, below which is hand-lettered "*JUST ME.*" The sender's address appeared in the original letter in the lower right corner. Handwritten in the opposite corner and stacked (/): "~~Present / 250 Taylor Street / San Francisco — Cal.~~" Handwritten just to the right of the first line of the deleted address is "Permanent address," from which a long, slightly curving line with arrow leads to "Franktown".

1. Will Roderick James (or Joseph Ernest Nephtali Dufault, 1892–1942) lived a checkered, partially self-created life that included a successful career as a western author and artist. James's first published article, which he also illustrated, appeared in 1923 (*DAB*, Supp. 3:382–83).

2. *Cowboys, North and South*, James's first book, was published by Charles Scribner's Sons in October 1924 and proved a success in terms of both financial returns and critical acceptance. A nonfiction, illustrated account of western range life, the book was characterized by one reviewer as having been written "in about the same dialect as that used by Will Rogers" (Amaral, *Will James*, 65–66; *NYT*, 12 October 1924).

3. The dating of the document was determined by the publication month of James's book.

To Edward T. Bishop
ca. October 1924
[New York, N.Y.?]

Mr Edward T Bishop.

Dear Mr Bishop,

Your Letter rec,d   Now I note what you say about the average price of the land being $380. but you did not state that the piece on each side of mine was valued at 400. my piece has nothing to do with other land further down the beach,[1] Now all I want is just what is fair   I want $400. the same as the others. I dont see why it should make any difference because I did not engage Counsel and fight the case, why that should lessen the value of my land, I am 45 years of age and have yet to ahve to have a Lawyer assist me in my business, I have always been fair and have gained quite a few friends by it who will testify to the fact I bought the land in good faith, expecting of course to keep it and hold it it for years, because I knew, a blind man would know that it was a good investment. You cant find Beach stuuf like that any more, and if you think 400 is a high price I will put up a Bond to the County to buy it back in 3 years at $750. a foot . I also had clippings sent to me from Papers "Where Will Rogers the Comedian trying to hold up the County, that I wanted ~~H~~ $I000. a foot, that ~~I must~~ he must think it sells by the p[o]und"   Now you know that is not so. and it had no business to be said, I dident try to do anything of the kind, I always said that I just wanted what the others got. I dident buy it to hold anybody up with   I bought it to keep. Now if you people dont like it because I did not engage Lawyers and fight the case, why I cant help it, If you think that I would be ashamed of the facts in the case ~~being~~ gaining publicity in the papers why you are misstaken, I write for over a hundred Newspapers and I can perhaps help you gaining wide publicity, because touching on a subject humorously will sometimes attract more attention than simply trying to be vindicitive:

Now as for the case coming to trial, and me having to ~~rr~~engage Counsel, and witnesses, and prepare the case, there will be nothing like that, If any Judge in the United States says that my I50 feet of Beach is not worth as much as was paid for the piece on either side of it why he can have it, I will only ask him to tell me one thing, What is the matter with it, and if there is something the matter with it, Why do they want it,

Now Mr Bishop I know that I have tried to do what was right about this and ~~whatever you dicide to~~ that you will explain to me whats the matter with my land, From what I can see all I needed on it was a Lawyer to make it worth 400. Personally I still think its worth as much without a Lawyer on it as it is with one on it. I may be wrong but I would like to hear from you about it.

Yours without advice of Consul
Will Rogers.

TLS, dc.[2] OkClaW, 1975.05.0014.

1. Los Angeles County apparently had condemned property that included beach frontage of Rogers and others. The purpose of the condemnation was not determined nor was the outcome of Rogers's protest.

2. Dating of the document was determined by the notation "1924" that appears on another draft of the same letter (see Folder 16-C, OkClaW) and the reference within the document to Rogers's age.

From Maud Rogers Lane
16 November 1924
[Chelsea, Okla.]

Maud Rogers Lane, a favorite and dear sister of Will Rogers, suffered a stroke soon after the death of her husband, Cap, in July 1924.[1] The stroke, which she describes in the following letter, left her an invalid and bedridden. Her condition naturally provoked the concern of Will and Betty Blake Rogers, who despite their distance from Chelsea, monitored closely her health and family situation. As this and subsequent correspondence show, members of the family stayed in close contact throughout the ordeal.

My Own Dear Betty Willie Miss Dick[2] and children.

I havent been very well since Oct 30   when I got up that morning I had such a strange feeling in my head so light and felt as if it were disconnected from my body and floating all around in the room far above my body. I went to Taylor.[3] There was no pain or nausea just a light feeling. Taylor thought it might be from my teeth two of which I had drawn Nov. 4[,] one Nov. 7. and two drawn Nov. 10   after the first two were drawn I had no further trouble with my head but during the day of Nov 4 I noticed I had no controle of my left hand or foot   there was absolutely no pain and neither was there any numbness or tingling sensation just I dident seem to be able to make them do as I wanted them to.

Taylor has seene me daily[,] took blood tests and all kinds of kidney tests but I cant get rid of that falling around habit my arm and leg has   I some time[s] walk out of my house slipper and never know it is off. and my hand seemes so heavy I cant lift it. While Taylor was out here last night I asked him if it would do any good for me to go to Mayoes[4] for an examination and he said yes that was the very thing to do   The children all want me to go so Ethel[5] and I are leaving tomorrow noon Monday Nov. 17 due in Rochester abo[ut] Wednesday AM. Nov. 19   we will stay at the Brown Hotel. Taylor dosent think we will have to be gone more than ten days and he dosent seeme the least bit alarmed about my condition so I dont want you to worry at all. and as to finances I have more than enough $3000 in the bank that I can check against and another thousand in savings I can get any time. Ethel is going with me   Stelle and her children have come up to keep house[6]

Lasca is so anxious to do any thing but her baby has been so desperately ill all summer she will have her hands more than full to take care of him.[7] Gunter wanted to go with me but there wasent one thing he could do and Belle and these babys need him all the time[8]

The national Supply Co. is moving Jim[9] to Independence Kansas the first of Dec. he will have a great deal more work[,] more responsibility and we hope more money. Now dont you worry one moment about me   I am so well and strong there cant be so very much the matter with me. But if this should prove my summons home I want you to know I am ready and feel all will be well.

My darling you havent the slightest idea what your every day life has ment to me each act an inspiration   you have come nearer my idea being a true follower of Jesus. Always doing for some one else. How proud I have always been of you and Oh! how I do love you and darling Betty. May Gods richest blessings be with you and yours always.

Devotedly

▶Maud.◀

ALS, rc. OkClaW, 1975.12.0002.

1. For Maud Ethel Rogers Lane see *PWR*, 1:499–501; for Captain (Cap) Lane see *PWR*, 1:498.

2. For Theda (Dick) Blake see *PWR*, 3:403, 405.

3. J. C. Taylor had operated a medical practice in Chelsea, Okla., as early as 1919 (Meyer interview; *CR*, 21 May 1925).

4. The Mayo Clinic grew from a small Catholic hospital, founded in Rochester, Minn., in 1889. Through the work of two brothers, Dr. William James Mayo (1861–1939) and Dr. Charles Horace Mayo (1865–1939), the institution acquired an international reputation for excellence of surgery, quality of care, and advancements in medical procedures. By 1912 it boasted about two hundred doctors, each a trained specialist in a particular field and all engaged in a cooperative practice (*DAB*, Supp. 2:438–41).

5. For Ethel Lane Hedges see *PWR*, 1:494.

6. For Estelle Lane Neal see *PWR*, 1:521–22. She had two children, James Lane Neal (1916–85) and Betty Maud Neal (b. 1920) (Lowe, *Will Rogers*, 53; Rogers family genealogy records, OkClaW).

7. For Lasca Gazelle Lane Luckett see *PWR*, 1:506. A son, Harvey Cap Luckett (d. 2003), was born 21 April 1924 (Lowe, *Will Rogers*, 46; Rogers family genealogy records, OkClaW).

8. For James Gunter Lane and Jennie Belle Mooney Lane see *PWR*, 1:499. At the time the couple had four children: Ethel Marie (b. 1918), Doris Lolita (b. 1919), Robert Rogers (1922–97), and Elsie Jane (1923–2004) (Lowe, *Will Rogers*, 43; unidentified clipping, RFP-DLM; Meyer interview; Rogers family genealogy records, OkClaW).

9. Lane referred to James Thomas Neal, the husband of her eldest daughter, Estelle (Meyer interview; see *PWR*, 1:521–22).

Telegram to Maud Rogers Lane
19 November 1924
New York, N.Y.

14 Ck 54   ——U——

St New York Ny 455Pm 19

Mrs C L Lane

Chelsea Okla.

My darling Sister you have been wonderful and brave all your life and I know you will bear it I cant possibly come we have decided you are to come to us turn entire placeover to gunter and come here to rest just as quick as you can all our conserlation [consolation] and love

Willie and Bettie[1]
505PM

TG, rc. LC-UT, IV:A:1. On Western Union Telegraph Co. letterhead.

1. Rogers sent a similar message at the same time to another sister, Sallie Rogers McSpadden, in Chelsea. He asked her to let him know how much money their sister Maud needed "for everything" (LC-UT, IV:A:1).

From Maud Rogers Lane
19 November 1924
Rochester, Minn.

Wednesday Noon.

My Dear Betty and Willie,

Well here we are in the city of health and it sure seemes to work like magic   we got in at 7 this AM. and at noon I [was] discharged   Th[r]ee

Dr. have looked me *all* over and told me word for word what Dr Taylor told me before leaving home.

My trouble is caused by the bursting of a very small blood vessel on the right side of my brain causing a dead numbness in my left foot and hand. there is absolutely no treatment   my system may absorb the blood and I may not get any worse but will probably not be any better.[1]

Now please donot let this worry you for I can get around quite well. The Dr told me I should not do any work now. that just delighted me   I am to eat plenty of vegtables and fruit   now what could be better   I insisted on Ethel going through the clinic and she is to have a blood test tomorrow[;] otherwise we could be on our homeward way tonight. Now I feel more than paid for our trip up here. there is so many things I can do and I have had 55 years of naught but pleasure   then with all due respect to all these high and mighty Dr. I know after a time I am going to get better use of myself. Dont you dear ones worry over my condition one moment for I was never happier in all my life

Devotedly
Maud.

ALS, rc. OkClaW, 1975.12.0003. On letterhead of The Damon Hotel, Rochester, Minn.

1. Doctors at the Mayo Clinic determined that Rogers's sister, Maud, showed "slight residue of hemiplegia," a paralytic condition that results from a stroke. The prescription was simple: "Believe rest at home most beneficial at present. Nature usually best physician in these cases" (telegram, Mayo Clinic to Will Rogers, 22 November 1924, LC-UT, IV:A:1).

Telegram to Maud Rogers Lane
21 November 1924
New York, N.Y.

30M D 95 NL

NEWYORK NY NOV 21 1924

MRS C L LANE

BROWN HOTEL ROCHESTER MINN

DONT YOU THINK YOU COULD COME HERE I KNOW THEY CAN DO SOME-THING IN NEWYORK AND IF THE TRIP IS NOT TOO HARD IF ITS REST YOU NEED YOU ARE NOT GOING TO STAY HOME YOU AND ETHEL AND A NURSE WILL HIKE RIGHT STRAIGHT TO BEVERLYHILLS ALL THE CHILDREN ARE CRAZY TO GO OUT

THERE WITH YOU ALREADY FROM HERE I AM WIRING YOU A THOUSAND DOLLARS
IF YOU COME HERE OR GO HOME HAVE A DRAWINGROOM ALL THE WAY YOU GET
WELL NEVER MIND THE FINANCIAL WORRY LOTS OF LOVE FROM BOTH

BILL AND BETTY

753A22

TG, rc. LC-UT, IV:A:1. On Western Union Telegraph Co. letterhead. Stamped to right of recipient's name: "221."

From Maud Rogers Lane
ca. 24 November 1924
[Chelsea, Okla.]

My Own Dear Betty and Willie

how I do wish you could look in and see me this AM. I am alll cleaned up and have had a wonderful breakfast. Willies dear letter came some days ago and I dont know how he can think of so many lovely things to do for me   It is so wonderful to want me to go to California and I am most assuredly going very soon but not till I can get around a little better which will be very soon   Taylor wants me to stay very quietly in bed for three weeks and have only liquid diett   now there isent any thing hard about that for I can so easily sleep ten and twelve hours at a time. Ethel hasent left my bedside ten moments since the morning I got up with that dreadful[l]y light feeling in my head Oct 30. I am just as sure I am going to be quite well again and since I donot suffer and you two darlings are seeing to it I donot want for any comeforts or luxuries   Oh! I just cant ▼tell you▼ how grateful we all are for all you are always doing for me and mine.

Now I am going to talk a litttle [b]usness and I want you to [t]ake close heed to every word I am saying for I mean it   Yes indeed I am going to take care of the getting well end of this game   When I came home Taylor told me he w[an]ted me to go to bed and *stay* there   well that is just what I did[,] jumped into the middle of my bed and havent wiggled so much as a toe. eat[:] I was told to have nothing but liquids   word went out I wanted butter-milk   twenty different women made a skedule to churn every thirty moments a part so I am getting ten gal[l]ons of buttermilk every ten hours   That dosent sound much like reducing do[e]s it   I am afraid when I do get up I will have to be crated with wheeles on the crate for me to move around, but any way I am obeying orders.

My room is so sunny and comefortable   [*illegible*] day my negro man keeps
the house at summer heat   he got all the cole [coal] off the place   gave all
the negros in the hollow half to help him fill our basement   he was so
delighted because it dident cost us any thing. we had ten young heffiers that
did not promise much as milk an ▲he sold them to the▲ butcher   got $25 a
piece payed for [*text ends; no continuation*]

ALS, rc. OkClaW, 1975.12.0001.

Transcript of After-Dinner Remarks
4 December 1924
New York, N.Y.

(Mr. Rogers was second on the program, following President Butler.[1] Dr.
Butler had mentioned Mr. Rogers by name in his salutation to the audience,
and the mention of the name in this connection had caused considerable
laughter.)

◖✺◗

Education, and Wealth: (Laughter) President Butler paid me a compliment
a while ago in mentioning my name in his introductory remarks, and he put
me ahead of the Columbia graduates. I am glad he did that, because I got the
worse of it last week. The Prince of Wales last week, in speaking of the sights
of America, mentioned the Woolworth Building,[2] the subway, Will Rogers, the
slaughter house, and the Ford factory. He could at least put me ahead of the
hogs, anyway.

◖✺◗

Everything must be in contrast at an affair like this. You know to show
anything off properly you must have the contrast. Now, I am here tonight representing poverty. We have enough wealth right here at this table, right here at
the speaker's table alone—their conscience should hurt them, which I doubt
if it does—so that we could liquidate our national debt. Every rich man
reaches a time in his career when he comes to a turning point and starts to
give it away. I have heard that of several of our guests here tonight, and that is
one of the reasons that I am here. I would like to be here at the psychological
moment.

◖✺◗

Now, another reason I am here is to represent another kind of contrast.
You see, by contrast at a college demonstration you must illustrate ignorance

too. So I am really here in a double capacity: my presence is an indication of ignorance and poverty. That is the reason for my being here.

We are here, as I see by the speaker, not only to keep cool with Coolidge, but to do honor to Alexander Hamilton. Alexander Hamilton, as Mr. Butler just said, has a statue erected to him finally in Washington.[3] They finally erected one there in the Treasury Building and forgot to say when he graduated. Now, as I read by this morning's papers to get some information on this affair, I read by the World that it was ~~it was~~ a hundred and fifty years ago when he entered Columbia College.[4] Then I read in the Sun that it was a hundred and fifty years ago when he finished from Columbia College, or left there. So if both papers are right,which they must be, he left the day he got there. So he is really not a Columbia man. We have yet to hear from the Hearst papers. I have no doubt they will add at least a hundred years to his age. We will find that he went to Columbia before he was born.

Now, he was the first Secretary of the Treasury. The reason he was appointed that was because he and Washington were the only men in America at that time who knew how to put their names on a check. Signing a check has remained the principal qualification of a U. S. Secretary of the Treasury.

(As Mr. Mellon[5] was one of the guests, this remark brought much laughter.)

We see next that he had a duel. I am glad Mr. Butler referred to it in this way. The principal reason, of course, was that the man he fought against wanted to be President.[6] He was a ~~Princeton~~ ▲Harvard▲ man—or I believe it was ~~Harvard~~ ▲Princeton▲.[7] I knew it was one of those primary schools. (Much laughter. Cheers) In fighting a duel, he forgot that in America our men over here could shoot. So unfortunately one of them was killed, which had never happened in the old country. So they did away with dueling. It was all right to protect your honor, but not to go as far as you like. They really fought over Mr. Burr's wanting to be Governor of New York, and Mr. Hamilton was against this. Their politics were not the same. He did not want Mr. Burr to be Governor of New York. The same situation is here now. I do not know whether it will go as far as a duel.

If you are speaking of finances here tonight, I do not believe that you could look further than Mr. Butler. Butler is the word—to dig up the dough.[8]

Columbia was nothing twenty years ago. Now, he has gone around and got over a hundred buildings, and has annexed Grant's Tomb. He was the first man to go around to the graduates and explain to them that by giving this money to Columb▶b◀ia it would help on the income tax and also perpetuate their names. We have an Alexander Hamilton Building. He landed these buildings and ran that place up to ninety millions or something like that. There are more students in that university than there are in any other in the world. It is the foremost university. It is remarkable to have thirty-two hundred courses there. You spend your first two years in deciding what courses to take, the next two years in finding the building that these courses are given in, and the rest of your life in wishing you had taken another course. And they have this wonderful society called the Alumni Society,[9] a bunch of men who have gone to school and after they have come out formed a society to tell the school how to run it.

ᗧᗣᗧ

TD. OkClaW, 1975.14.0216. The words "the slaughter house" in the second paragraph were circled by hand, and hand-drawn lines from the circled copy lead to a point immediately preceding "Will Rogers," in the same paragraph. Double strike-through indicates hand-deleted text. All interpolations were handwritten.

1. Nicholas Murray Butler (1862–1947), a former dean of philosophy at Columbia University, served as president of the university from 1901 to 1945, the longest presidency in the history of the school (*DAB*, Supp. 4:133–37).

2. The sixty-story Woolworth Building, erected by chain-store magnate Frank Winfield Woolworth (1852–1919) at Broadway and Park Place in New York, was until 1929 the tallest building in the world. Completed in 1913, it became a model for skyscrapers and transformed the skyline of New York (*DAB*, 20:523; *ENYC*, 1273).

3. The statue of Alexander Hamilton, standing at the southern entrance of the U.S. Treasury Building facing the White House, was dedicated in May 1923 (*NYT*, 18 May 1923).

4. Alexander Hamilton entered King's College, the colonial-era name of Columbia University, on an accelerated program of instruction in the fall of 1773. He left the school sometime in 1774 and became involved in the revolutionary movement (Hendrickson, *Hamilton*, 50–51).

5. Andrew William Mellon (1855–1937), Pittsburgh industrialist and banker, became U.S. secretary of the treasury in 1921. Mellon, one of the richest men in the world, effected a highly conservative, probusiness fiscal program. He served as secretary for eleven years and became a dominant force in the Republican administrations of the period (*DAB*, Supp. 2:446–52).

6. Alexander Hamilton's public attacks against his chief political rival, Aaron Burr, finally led Burr to issue a challenge to a duel. Armed with pistols, the two faced off at Weehawken, N.J., on 11 July 1804. Each man fired a single shot, but only Hamilton fell, mortally wounded. He died the following day. Burr fled, but eventually returned to resume his duties as vice president (*DAB*, 3:314–20).

7. Aaron Burr graduated with honors in 1772 at the age of sixteen from the College of New Jersey, much later known as Princeton University (*DAB*, 3:314).

8. Columbia experienced much growth during the presidency of Nicholas Butler. By 1911 the university boasted more students than any other higher education institution in the world, and within three years it had amassed the largest endowment among American universities. The school also greatly expanded its physical facilities during the Butler years. Fifteen new buildings opened between 1905 and 1934 (*DAB*, Supp. 4:134; Coon, *Columbia*, 107–8).

9. The Association of the Alumni of Columbia College sponsored the Alexander Hamilton Dinner. Rogers was not listed on the original schedule of speakers, but the alumni group's president, Chester W. Cuthell, wrote Rogers the day after the event to commend him: "It has been my good fortune to listen to many of the country's great orators deliver so-called impromptu speeches, which probably took months of preparation, but never before have I heard a speech, that I knew had been so hurriedly prepared, prove such a genuine success before such a highly intelligent and critical audience" (*NYT*, 23 November 1924; Chester W. Cuthell to Will Rogers, 5 December 1924, OkClaW).

From Charles A. Otis
18 December 1924
Cleveland, Ohio

December 18,1924.

Dear Will:

When I stop to think of the amount of money spent to convince people that a ninety-nine per cent. soap can really float, I wonder how much I am indebted to you for compelling the nation to ask that burning question "Who the hell is "Charlie Otis?"[1] I will say, regardless of my banker's caution regarding the bill, that I feel quite close to the top of the Christmas tree when I have for a press agent the man who put over the Prince of Wales and Mr. Bryan of Florida. In all modesty, and lest you should fail to appreciate your latest subject, let me say I am willing to go the limit in the interests of advertising—even to the extent of falling off a horse or drinking grape juice. If either of these two acts are too closely associated with the individuals named above, I might say that I have the same name as a darned good elevator.

In defense of Cleveland I can only attribute this to the discontented population of Cleveland and since females are voting and we have a great many old maids here, who are always discontented because so many of the best men are married, I presume they joined the others voting LaFollette.[2]

I enjoyed so much meeting you and look forward sometime to coming in back and talking [*obliterated*] you and taking a glance at the sables and minks that will be hanging around, with a careful eye at what they contain when in their stage costumes. I always enjoy your humor, and think it the best there is and the kind I most appreciate. I note there must be many others like me as my greetings on the street and my mail have been full of congratulations on the publicity obtained. If you are not careful, you will make me quite a national figure. However, "It Pays to Advertise" has always been my motto, so go as far as you like.

With the season's greetings and best wishes to you for years of happiness, I am

Very truly, your friend,
Chas. A. Otis.

[*handwritten:*] Also,
[*illegible*] Stock range
Mesa Co. Colorado[3]

TLS, rc. OkClaW, 1975.21.0085. On Charles A. Otis, Cleveland, letterhead. In the margin below the handwritten copy at the end of letter is the word "*Brand*," followed by what appears to be an uppercase, underscored "A" and a horizontal figure eight with smaller figure eights on the inside bottom of each loop, also underscored. The preceding ends with "E.M. —".

1. Charles Augustus Otis, Jr. (ca. 1868–1953), known as "Mr. Cleveland," was a millionaire investment banker, former newspaper publisher, and scion of a family of iron and steel producers (*NYT*, 10 December 1953; Rose, *Cleveland*, 6, 1032). In his newspaper column of 30 November, Rogers singled out Otis among other former "dollar-a-year" businessmen who had recently attended a performance of the *Ziegfeld Follies* while in New York for a reunion of the War Industries Board (see *WA*, 1:327).
2. In his "Weekly Article," Rogers kidded Otis, a Republican leader in Cleveland, for allowing Senator Robert M. La Follette, a third-party presidential candidate, to carry the city in the general election in 1924. La Follette finished second in the county that contained Cleveland, the city in which he had been nominated and had concluded his campaign (*WA*, 1:327; *NYT*, 2 November 1924; Thelen, *Robert M. La Follette*, 191).
3. Otis spent a brief time in the West as a cowboy after graduating from Yale University in 1890. Although he returned to his hometown of Cleveland to enter business, he maintained an interest in cattle raising and eventually owned and operated a working ranch in Colorado (*NYT*, 10 December 1953).

Advertising Proof for Bull Durham Tobacco
ca. 1 January 1925
New York, N.Y.

I know people are going to say "What do you think of Will Rogers writing and endorsing Bull Durham?"[1] That's where you're ~~wwrong~~ ▲wrong▲. I am not endorsing it, I never smoked any tobacco in my life, not even Bull Durham. If you want to know the real truth why I signed up to write a lot of pieces for these people, it's because I love animals. Have you ever studied that picture of the 'Bull' carefully?....have you ever seen such a kind-looking animal? I thought this:-certainly no ө one who cares as much about dumb creatures as they do would put out anything but the best smoking tobacco possible—so I said all right, I'll write your stuff. Honestly, the money part of it didn't have much to do with it. That is, not very much. Seriously, though, out where I come from, unless a male member of the population has got that Bull Durham tag hanging from the shirt pocket, he's liable to be arrested for indecent exposure. And, you believe me, you can't sell those western hard-boiled eggs much and keep on selling them unless it's got class. Guess maybe this not smoking thing has sort of got me winging. Wonder if that's why things has turned out this way. Come to think of it, it may be a moral lesson to the Youth of this country. The moral in my case being, if you want to grow up and know nothing but telling jokes and have people laughing at you all the time, don'd smoke. But who want to go through life acting the fool?

TD. OkClaW, Bull Durham Original Notes, Ads and Copy. Typewritten, top margin, center, stacked (/): "- 1 - / THE BULL'S EYE." The interlineation was handwritten. Ellipsis inserted by Rogers.

1. For the agreement to write advertising copy for Bull Durham tobacco, see Letter from Frank W. Harwood, 29 September 1924, above.

From Arthur Brisbane
30 January 1925
New York, N.Y.

January 30th, 1925.

Mr. Will Rogers,
Ziegfeld Follies,
New Amsterdam Theatre,
West 42nd Street,
N.Y.City.
My dear Mr. Rogers:

You will learn by the enclosed that your advertising is read — at least by one reader. I saw that advertisement of Bull Durham, where you probably never saw it, in the Hamlet News-Messenger, an excellent little paper published in the active town of Hamlet, North Carolina.

I am particularly glad to see that Mr. P.S.Hill,[1] who I suppose is your boss,puts his advertising in [*obliterated*] ▲many▲ of the smaller newspapers of the country. Those are the most important newspapers, and incidentally,in proportion to their circulation,their advertising results are the biggest,and their advertising rates are the smallest in the country. They are read through from end to end. Every copy of circulation means an entire family,not a family that lives in one room with a can opener,but a family that owns its own house,and land around it,at least ninety times out of a hundred, a family that buys everything,from the roof on the house,to the cement on the cellar floor,from the hat on the mother's head to the skates on the boy's feet. I hope you will persuade Mr. Hill and those that represent the advertising department of his big company to continue and to send advertising to what are called "the country newspapers." They not only pay well, but the service that their publishers render to the public,is in my opinion the most important service rendered by any class of citizens in the United States. The country editors are distributors of information,they reach the minds of the boys   that leave the farms,and they are the nation's mental police force.

Thissounds like a sermon,but I am writing on the train on my way through North Carolina,and your smiling face in the advertising column is responsible for this.

Yours sincerely,

Arthur Brisbane[2]

P.S. I enclose page of the Hamlet News-Messenger   I think you will be interested to see what excellent printing these smaller newspapers can do,and what a fine position the picture and your writing gets "next to pure reading matter" on a good page.

TLS, rc. OkClaW, 1975.21.0126. On letterhead of NewYork Evening Journal, Office of A. Brisbane. Handwritten at top of page 1, center to right margin: "I wrote this and it was not mailed until now, Feb 19." Handwritten below postscript, page 2, in same handwriting: "The page has been lost, but it was one of a series".

1. Percival Smith Hill (1862–1925), an executive in the Bull Durham organization, became a sales manager for the popular smoking tobacco brand after the American Tobacco Company acquired the label in 1899. He was named president of the parent company in 1912 and remained in that office until his death (*NYT*, 8 December 1925; Winkler, *Tobacco Tycoon*, 107–8).

2. Arthur Brisbane (1864–1936) started in journalism as a teenager in 1883 and worked for various newspapers before switching to the *New York Journal* in 1897. He became the chief editor at the *Journal* and wielded considerable editorial influence at other Hearst newspapers as well. Rogers and Brisbane worked as correspondents at the Democratic national convention in 1924 and became friends (*DAB*, Supp. 2:62–64; Carlson, *Brisbane*, 327).

From Arthur M. Ireland
7 March 1925
Long Beach, Calif.

With their relocation to New York, Rogers and his family left behind on the West Coast their house in Beverly Hills and their newly purchased acreage in the Santa Monica Mountains. Initially, Rogers had viewed the latter real estate as merely a retreat. By the fall of 1924, however, the prospects of a new road adjacent to the property had prompted Rogers to think of something more permanent. Over the next few months, he began to envision a house on the land, where to build it, and how to access it.[1] The following letter from his foreman provides a glimpse of plans for the property and some of the issues related to its development.

Long Beach Calif.,

393 Mira Mar Ave.,

Friday,3/7/25.

Dear Bill and Betty:-

I am enclosing herewith a statement of how you stand on the ranch deal. The money from the county was finally paid over to Bell[2] but the expense and interest to the Santa Monica Land Co was a good deal more than I expected, $600.00 being deducted. Havent received the statement from the escrow department yet and cant get over there during banking hours this month as I ►am► working days. I thought there would be available for Bell about $48,400 and had you send me $350 to make up the difference to $48.750 but interest was working on the $11,250 all during this delay and you had to pay ¼ of the title expense as your profit on the land was ¼ of what the County paid. These title birds are the ones that know how to add on the expense and the Santa Monica Land Co helped with the expense too I think. I am writing the bank for an i̶t̶ itemized statement on this escrow and will know just where all this $600 went. The Land Co expense on the same frontage was over $6,000, counting their court costs, lawyer fees,etc, so you cant complain much on the $600, considering everything. Will send you the escrow statement when I get it.

Now about the interest. Bell wants the interest paid up to the date of the new contract, Jan.29th. They charged you interest on the extra acreage from July 1st, 1924 and interest on the $270,000 from Jan 1st to jan 29 which all amounts to $1,933.99. I bucked like a steer on this back interest but your old contract never   specified the number of acres you were to buy and under that old contract the►y◄ could have collected interest from March 15th. Under the new contract your semi-annual interest payments are Apr. 15th and Oct.15th so you will have an interest payment in a short time from Jan.29 to ~~March~~ Apr. 15th which I figured will be $1,712.70.

Now the taxes.

Your taxes began with the date of your old contract, ▲[*typewritten:*]Jan. 29th,1924.▲ the last half of the 1923-24 tax period. Wayne[3] estimated the amount at about $2,700 which you sent me. I got this figured down to $2,570.26 which is at the rate of $17.55 per acre being figured on an assessed valuation of $500 per acre.

The $2,570.26 pays for the last half of the 1923-24 taxes from Jan.29th to July 1st and for the first half of 1924-25 to Jan.1st,1925. Now the second half is due amounting to $1,401.47 which will clean up the taxes to July 1st, this year. The whole thing amounts to~~t~~ this:- $250 which the County money lacked of paying Bell, $1,933.99 interest to Jan.29th,$2,570.26 taxes for last year and $1,401.47 taxes for the first half of this year, totaling $6,155.72, from which $2,700 is subtracted which you sent me, leaving $3,455.72 to be paid. Bell is holding the new contract until this is paid in. Send this to me by return mail and I will have everything cleaned up to date and mighty glad of it. While Bell charged back interest on the additional acreage, he did not charge any interest on the ~~on the~~ $48,000 coming from the county which was due on the 29th of Jan and whic▲h▲ he did not get for a month so it is nearly a stand off.

I saw Hayden the day before I got your message and if you havent got your tax statement from him by the time this reaches you, let me know and I will get after him.

There is another matter that is worrying me a lot. We will have to get rid of the Japs on the ranch or run a chance of getting into very serious trouble.[4]

If the authorities should start an investigation and find that we are renting on the old basis to the Japs, the state will comfiscate your land. That is the law. The cases that were appealed to the Supreme Court were all decided against the Japs so there is no way we can keep them on the place except to hire them straight~~e~~ out and give them no share in the crop whatever.

The chance of trouble is too great to take the risk because you have too much at steak. The first of next month, when I get off this shift, will look into the whole thing and try to figure out some way. Think I can have the land put in ~~a~~ alfalfa and get as much net income off it as the Japs are paying.

One thing is sure and that is, it wont do to go on this way now for if any trouble should come, you will suffer most by loosing your land and the Japs and and your humble servant would have to goto San Quentin for a spell.What?

This state law is very interesting reading. I will try to get you a copy of this Jap act and send it to you.

As I told you in my last letter, if your income tax and these land taxes and interest bills havent got you cleaned, you had better grab some more of this land out here for it sure looks good. One crew on the Beverly Blvd[5] work has a steam shovel at work widening the road up the long hill out of Santa Monica ~~Ca~~ Canyon to Riviera and expect to be in front of your land in less than 60 days.

Sandy and his family[6] will be here not later than the 20th of this month. He is to be checked out the 15th. The girls are looking for a flat near us for them. He wrote they would be here at least 3 months.

Rush the balance of the interest and tax money along and let me get the Bell matter wound up. Have been going to the bat with them since last October.

The folks send love to all of you.
Art.[7]

TLS, rc. OkClaW, 1975.24.0011. All interpolations were handwritten, unless otherwise noted.

1. See Yagoda, *Will Rogers*, 208–9.
2. That is, Alphonzo E. Bell.
3. The writer may have referred to Claude A. Wayne, who would later be identified with the Los Angeles Mountain Park Company, a firm that apparently succeeded the Santa Monica Mountain Company as developers of the properties of Alphonzo Bell in the Santa Monica Mountains (see for example, Claude A. Wayne to Betty Blake Rogers, 18 June 1926, OkClaW).
4. The Alien Land Law, anti-Japanese legislation enacted in California in 1913, prohibited ownership of land by aliens ineligible for citizenship. Loopholes in the law, however, allowed continuing growth in the Japanese population in the state and the leasing and subleasing of farm acreage. Nativist anxieties about Asian demographics finally led to the federal Immigration Act of 1924 aimed at ending Asian immigration to the United States. Rogers collected $961.50 in 1924 from leasing of his ranch property (Rolle, *California*, 165; Individual Income Tax Return, 1924, OkClaW).
5. Beverly Boulevard would later be renamed Sunset Boulevard (Yagoda, *Will Rogers*, 208).
6. For James K. (Sandy) Blake and family see *PWR*, 3:403, 405.
7. Arthur M. (Art) Ireland was caretaker of the Rogers property near Santa Monica and husband of Waite Blake Ireland, a sister of Betty Blake Rogers (*PWR*, 3:403–5).

From Edward F. Albee
4 May 1925
New York, N.Y.

May 4th, 1925.

Mr. Will Rogers,
New Amsterdam Theatre,
New York City, N.Y.
My dear Will:

I understand you had to have a guide last night to show you around New York. You know it takes a long time for these Western guys, particularly the ones who wear the big hats, spurred boots and lariats, to know New York as it really is.

You are one of the best fellows that ever lived. A man who proposes that he will go around to the five different theatres where the wonderful benefits were given last night and give his services if somebody will be sent with him, has humane attributes in his make-up. It is such attributes that have always made this country safe and sound.

You and I who knew vaudeville in its early stages can visualize and appreciate what last night's celebration means to the vaudeville business. Five houses packed to the doors. People turned away from every one of them, shows the advancement that can be made by injecting into our business the principles of the National Vaudeville Artists' Association[1] and the Vaudeville Managers' Protective Association,[2] which has been religiously carried out for the past eight years. You, by your gracious and liberal interest are one of the great exponents of this splendid organization which cares for the unfortunate. You are a source of pride to the entire theatrical business, exalting yourself as you have by your intelligence and your God-given gift of humor bringing laughter as you do to the highest and lowest classes.

Thanks a thousand times for your splendid interest. I am saying thanks for the whole vaudeville profession who admires you as a man and a wonderful artist. Thanks again, and all good wishes.

Cordially and faithfully yours,
E F Albee[3]

TLS, rc. OkClaW, 1975.21.0048. On letterhead of The Keith-Albee Circuit of Theatres, Palace Theatre Building, 1564 Broadway, New York.

1. The National Vaudeville Artists, organized in 1916 as an in-house union of performers on the Keith-Albee Circuit, staged an annual benefit each year that involved simultaneous performances at multiple theaters in New York on the same

night. In 1925 the event to aid the group's charitable funds was held on Sunday evening, 3 May, at the Metropolitan Opera House, Manhattan Opera House, Hippodrome, New Amsterdam Theatre, and Knickerbocker Theatre. The event featured an average of forty acts per program. Rogers and other principals from the *Follies* participated (*EV*, 368; *NYT*, 4 May 1925).

2. The Vaudeville Managers' Protective Association included management from much of the vaudeville industry in the United States. The group took an active role in the organization of the National Vaudeville Artists and worked to break and prevent independent associations of vaudeville performers (Laurie, *Vaudeville*, 313–14).

3. For Edward Franklin Albee see *PWR*, 2:465–66.

To Florenz Ziegfeld, Jr.
ca. 19 May 1925
New York, N.Y.

My Dear Mr Zeigfeld–

I knew you were away and I understood for I know you to well to think you dident think of me in my trouble.[1] I had such a lovely letter from your Wife and got your wire when you heard of my misfortune. I was sorry to be out of the show but I couldent help it. I am so glad I went. Thank you *Boss*, you are a good Boss;

yours as ever

Will

ALS, rc. OkClaW, 1975.31.0001. On letterhead of Will Rogers, New Amsterdam Theatre, New York.

1. Rogers's sister, Maud Rogers Lane, died early Friday morning, 15 May 1925. Rogers immediately left the *Follies* to attend the funeral in Chelsea, Okla. Other performers took his place on stage until his return early the next week (*CP*, 15 May 1925; *NYT*, 16 May 1925). For Rogers's thoughts about his sister's passing see *WA*, 2:33–34.

Manuscript for Newspaper Column
ca. 25 May 1925
[New York, N.Y.?]

In the spring of 1925, Rogers committed to write a second newspaper column, a daily piece that McNaught syndicated as "The Worst Story I've Heard Today." He prepared the following draft as the first entry in the series. It proved typical of the more than five hundred that would follow: a joke, usually attributed to a celebrity or pal, with a background blurb about the contributer and an apology or two about the story's lack of humor—in other words, why it qualified as "the worst story I have heard today."[1]

THE WORST STORY I HAVE HEARD TOADY
by
WILL ROGERS.

Somebody is always stopping me and telling me a Story and saying,"
You can switch that around and tell it in your Act", Now I have never in my
life on the Stage   ~~ever~~ told a ~~straight out~~ Story, Mine has always been   just
observations on the days news, But still I have to ~~go through life~~ listen~~ing~~ to
them, I hate a Story and I hate the Guys that are always telling them, There is
not [*obliterated*] a new one in 10 years.yet people go through life inflicting
them on everybody they meet,

———

When the Prince of Wales was over here he ~~even~~ pulled some [stories] on
me, and in return for his courtesy in laughing at some of mine ~~(which by the
way was not as funny as his)~~ I had to pretend to laugh at his, One that he
told me I will   repaet as being the worst I heard from him that day,

He had just been up to the Polo Grounds[2] to see a ball Game and like e very-
body that tells Storys he thought it would be a good time to tell his Base Ball
Story, In fact I think he went to the Game just to get an excuse to tell me the
Story,   he related [it] as folows,

"An Englishman over in America (as they generally are) was persuaded
to see a Game of Base Ball, (Its really nothing you know Will but our old
English Game of Rounders) and during the duration of the encounter he
chanced to turn [his] profile to the Game for just the merest instant, a Foul
Tip caught him on the ear and [*obliterated*] rendered him totally sensless ~~for~~
for several moments. On regaining his mental equilibium, he interogated
faintly. What was it ~~?~~ ►HiT ME?' ◄

A Foul, only a Foul, his American friend remarked,

Good Heavens he exclaimed. A FOWL?. I though[t] it was a Mule.

We   parted Friends the Prince and I but it was on account of his other
good qualities that I admire him. He certainly got even with me for those I
told on him.

Now how is a Mule going to be in a Ball Grounds, So you see the Story
has no sense to it, A Mule would be bust as much out of place at a Ball Game
as an Englishman would.

TM.[3] OkClaW, Worst Story file. Handwritten, not in Rogers's hand, above heading: "Release
Monday. May 18; 1925". Handwritten, not in Rogers's hand, and stacked (/) above first paragraph: ~~Italic~~/ To be run before each day's story". Double strike-throughs indicate hand-deleted
text. Handwritten, not in Roger's hand, in right margin of first paragraph with a hand-inserted
bracket offsetting the paragraph: "Indent it". The interpolation was handwritten. Other editorial

marks appear throughout the document but have been ignored in this transcription. Handwritten, not in Rogers's hand, in bottom margin: "Copyright &c".

1. Among newspapers that carried the "Worst Story" was the *Tulsa Daily World*, which published the first column on 25 May 1925 and the final one on 15 January 1927. The *World* ran all but 6 of the 516 that made up the full series. Although McNaught paid Rogers $300 a week for his efforts, material to fill the space became increasingly difficult to find, while the pressure of producing a daily column of 300–500 words in the midst of his other work took its toll. His wife, Betty Blake Rogers, who helped by scouring for joke books, would later recall that Rogers grew to dislike the "Worst Story" series. Near the end he finally quit producing manuscripts. McNaught then used an in-house editor to write the column under Rogers's name before eventually killing the series. Years later, the syndicate rereleased old "Worst Story" columns for use in small-town weekly newspapers. Betty questioned the arrangement and the financial return, and McNaught pulled the deal ("Worst Story" binder, OkClaW; Rogers, *Will Rogers*, 187–88; Yagoda, *Will Rogers*, 215–16; Frank J. Murphy to Betty Blake Rogers, 12 September 1930). See also Manuscript for Newspaper Column, 26 November 1925, and Manuscript for Newspaper Column, ca. 15 April 1926, below.

2. The Polo Grounds, a name given to four different sports facilities in New York through the years, was first used in 1876 for a polo venue in upper Manhattan. In 1925 the name applied to the home of the New York Giants baseball team (*ENYC*, 916; *DBD*, 307).

3. Dating of the document was determined by the date of its publication in *TDW*.

Letter of Agreement with Charles L. Wagner
4 June 1925
New York, N.Y.

Just when it seemed that Rogers had tapped almost every available medium to reach the public, another opportunity presented itself in mid-1925. Charles L. Wagner, concert manager, approached Rogers with the chance to take his monologue into lecture halls nationwide, to share his humor in front of an audience on a far broader scale than the Follies *had ever afforded and at much greater length, a minimum of fifty minutes contrasted to the fifteen on a typical night at the New Amsterdam. Compared to Rogers's $3,100 per week from Ziegfeld, the proffered pay of the lecture circuit must have overwhelmed any hesitation Rogers might have felt about the new venture.*

June 4-1925.

Mr. Will Rogers
New York, N.Y.
Dear Mr. Rogers:-

This letter will confirm our verbal agreement; that I am to manage a Concert tour for you beginning October 1st,1925 ending November 30th,1925, guaranteeing you sixty (60) performances, during this period, for which you are to

The de Reszke Singers performed with Rogers during his first several months on the concert lecture circuit in 1925–26. The members who helped launch the tour—Floyd Townsley, Hardesty Johnson, Harold Kellogg, and Erwyn Mutch—took time to sign a publicity photo and inscribe it: "To The Chief With our Eternal Good Wishes, From the quartet with eight legs *and* voices which will never sing 'Asleep in the Deep.'" (*OkClaW*)

receive Sixty Thousand ($60,000) Dollars, proportioned, and payable weekly in cash or New York check. Railroads and Pullman's when required, for two people. All extra performances above the sixty (60) during this period, to be paid for at the rate of One Thousand Dollars ($1.000) per performance. I further agree to extend this engagement for a further term of sixteen days from Dec.1st,1925 to December 16,1925, during which period I guarantee you not less than Fifteen (15) performances for which you are to receive Twenty-two Thousand Five Hundred Dollars ($22,500.) proportioned and payable weekly in cash or New York check, and for all extra performances above the fifteen guaranteed you are to receive Fifteen Hundred ($1500.) Dollars for each and every appearance.[1]

It is mutually agreed and understood that you are to appear on the programs, all told for at least fifty minutes, during the evening, and not less. Program to be arranged in two parts and to be assisted by The de Reszke Singers, who shall receive prominence, billing. It being understood and agreed that you are to [be] the sole star at all times and given such prominence in all advertising and billing matters and publicity connected with this tour, andthat I am to pay for all printing and advertising connected with this tour or any extention [*sic*] thereof.

It is further agreed and understood that this is to be exclusive management during the period of this contract, and that you will make no other appearances ofany kind, without my written consent.   Providing the foregoing terms and conditions have been fulfilled on my part, it is agreed and understood that I am to have an option on your services until October 15,1925, for the months beginning March 1st,1926 and ending April 30th,1926, on the following terms: Fifteen Hundred Dollars ($1500.) a performance guaranteeing six performances a week, and all extra performances during that time to be paid for at the same rate,$1500. each. Also Railroads and Pullman's and compensation payable as in the Fall tour.

Your acceptance below by signature, makes this contract legal and valid. It is understood that we enter into this contract to make a great success and to bind ourselves to give our very best to its fulfillment.

Yours very truly

Chas L. Wagner

Manager.

I accept the above: _____

Witness: _____

TLS, rc. OkClaW, 1975.26.0071. On letterhead of Charles L. Wagner, 511 Fifth Avenue, New York. The signature of Charles L. Wagner was inserted on a signature line.

1. Rogers opened the lecture tour at Elmira, N.Y., on 1 October, and closed in New York on 17 December. He made seventy appearances in two and one-half months and reported $75,000 in earnings from Wagner. At some point after the date of this agreement the terms were altered. Wagner offered local sponsors two options, either a $1,000 guarantee to Rogers or a cut of the gate, as much as 75 percent (Chronology, 1923–25, OkClaW; Yagoda, *Will Rogers*, 222; New York State Income Tax Statement for Will Rogers, ca. 15 April 1926 [see below]; *WDT*, 4 November 1951; Croy, *Our Will Rogers*, 194). See also Telegram from Betty Blake Rogers, 1 October 1925, and Article in *Elmira Advertiser*, 2 October 1925, below. For Rogers's account of his first season on the lecture circuit see *WA*, 2:94–118, 132–35.

From James W. Gerard
15 June 1925
New York, N.Y.

As Rogers's influence as a commentator on stage and in print began to widen in reach and scope, prominent public figures targeted in gibes by Rogers sought to assuage his feelings and to appeal his verdict. Two such cases arose in June 1925 after Rogers rebuked former ambassador James W. Gerard and financier Otto H. Kahn for alleged verbal indiscretions while traveling in France.[1]

June 15th 1925.

My dear Will Rogers:

I hear that, in your entertaining monologue, you are saying that I talked too much in France.[2]

This report is based on a dispatch in the "Evening Post", is absolutely without foundation and was promptly denied by me both in the newspapers and in a cable to the President.

I write to you because you are now a National Institution with large initial letters.

Anyway do you think that I would, in Paris, in the Spring, with all the museums to visit, be prattling about the French debt? I have worries enough with my own.

Besides, *you* ought not to be talking against free speech— how do you make your living?

As a fellow candidate before the last Democratic Convention, I rely on you to correct this false charge of undue loquacity. Shall be around to see you all soon– keep my usual seat.

Yours ever,
James W. Gerard.

ALS, rc. OkClaW, 1975.21.0038. On letterhead of Union Club, Fifth Avenue & 51ˢᵗ Street.

1. Two wealthy New Yorkers, James Watson Gerard (1867–1951), a Democrat and former U.S. ambassador to Germany, and Otto H. Kahn, banker and industrialist, had reportedly criticized the Republican administration's tough stance on the French war debt to the United States. Both men denied the story after their return from abroad (*DAB*, Supp. 5:241–42; *NYT*, 9 and 10 June 1925). See also Otto H. Kahn to Will Rogers, 19 June 1925, OkClaW.

2. Rogers, the newspaper columnist, wrote on 31 May: "There has been a terrible pack of Americans over in Europe the past few weeks telling them that we don't want or need the money they owe us, not to take us too seriously and that we are only kidding. Now I am sorry to hear this, because it happens to be two good friends of mine, Mr. Otto Kahn and Mr. Jimmie Gerard. . . . They are my friends, but the boys are wrong. They are letting Society and Social prestige run away with them. You know it's always popular when in a foreign Country to boost it to the detriment of your own Country. But you want to be sure that what you say is not going to reach back home, because, after all it's home that Counts" (*WA*, 2:36–37; ellipsis added).

Telegram to J. S. Leach
13 July 1925
New York, N.Y.

A former Oklahoma congressman suggested that Rogers should be the next governor of the state.[1] This led to a mini-boom in July 1925 that found its way into newspapers throughout the country.[2] Before the news could die in Oklahoma, a second boomlet emanated from neighboring Arkansas, where a civic club in Betty Blake Rogers's hometown lightheartedly asked Rogers to consider a run for governor of its state.[3] In both instances Rogers's comic but polite rejections by wire received as much press attention as the initial proposals.

135 KM X 112 NL 1-70

NEW YORK N Y JULY 13 1925

J S LEACH[4]

BARTLESVILLE ENTERPRISE BARTLESVILLE OKLA.

SURE I AM A QUALIFIED VOTER OF OKLAHOMA. I HAVENT VOTED THERE FOR YEARS BECAUSE YOU NEVER HAD THE RIGHT MEN UP FOR ME TO VOTE FOR. BUT YOU PUT ME UP FOR GOVERNOR AND YOU WILL SEE HOW QUICK I WILL COME BACK HOME AND VOTE FOR MYSELF.

THAT'S WHAT BRYAN USED TO DO AND LOOK WHERE HE IS TODAY.[5] GOVERNOR TRAPP HAS BEEN OUT OF THE STATE LONGER THAN I HAVE.[6] IF THERE IS ANY CAMPAIGN FUND ALREADY BEEN RAISED KINDLY SEND SOME ON NOW. I HAVE

TWO DEMOCRATS HERE IN NEW YORK I CAN BRING OUT WITH ME   REGARDS
TO JOHN STINK OF PAWHUSKA.[7] YOURS FOR A BETTER GOVERNOR'S MANSION.

WILL ROGERS

825P

PD. Printed in *Bartlesville Enterprise*, Bartlesville, Okla., 14 July 1925. On Western Union Telegraph Co. letterhead. Typeset below the letterhead, left side: "RECEIVED AT 106 W. THIRD ST., BARTLESVILLE, OKLA."

1. James Sanford Davenport (1864–1940), a Democrat, served in the U.S. House of Representatives from 1907 to 1909 and from 1911 to 1917. Davenport was an attorney in Vinita, an eastern Oklahoma town often visited by Rogers in his youth and young adult years. He probably was well acquainted with Rogers's family, especially his father, Clem, because of Davenport's service in the prestatehood Cherokee Nation legislature. In early July 1925 Davenport created a publicity bonanza for Will Rogers with his suggestion that he should be nominated as the Democratic candidate for governor of Oklahoma in 1926 (*BDUSCong*, 874; *NYT*, 4 January 1940; Scrapbook 25, OkClaW). See also Letter to James S. Davenport, 7 September 1925, below.

2. The Associated Press wire service picked up the Rogers-for-governor story on 9 July. Newspapers nationwide carried it the next day. Two home-state papers, the *Bartlesville Enterprise* and the *Oklahoma News* of Oklahoma City, quickly wired Rogers in New York for follow-up comment. Rogers's telegraphed response to the *Enterprise* was reproduced on the newspaper's front page under the heading "Will Rogers Seeks Information Regarding Campaign Funds for His Sooner Gubernatorial Race as Outlined by His Oklahoma Friends." He telegraphed the Oklahoma City newspaper, "I must have election guaranteed before I will give up my present job. Wire best offer at once" (*ON*, ca. 14 July 1925, and various other clippings, Scrapbook 25, OkClaW; see also telegram, J. S. Leach to Will Rogers, 10 July 1925, Scrapbook 25, OkClaW).

3. The Kiwanis Club of Rogers, Ark., wired Will Rogers on 24 July 1925: "FROM PRESS REPORTS YOU HAVE CONSENTED TO BE GOVERNOR OF OKLAHOMA AND KANSAS IF YOU INCLUDE ARKANSAS YOU WILL HAVE OUR UNANIMOUS SUPPORT" (Scrapbook 25, OkClaW). The Associated Press picked up Rogers's reply, and it appeared in newspapers throughout the country on 2 August: "Thanks for your offer to govern Arkansas. That's one state I could not govern. I got the best part of Arkansas here now, but I have never been able to govern her, but I do thank Arkansas, especially Rogers, for furnishing me a governor for eighteen years. Rogers is the Claremore of Arkansas and that's the last word in towns. . . . Good luck. WILL ROGERS" (various clippings, Scrapbook 25, OkClaW).

4. Jess S. Leach (d. 1935) purchased the *Bartlesville* (Okla.) *Enterprise*, an evening daily newspaper, in 1907 and continued to publish it until his death (Carter, *Story*, 32).

5. At the time William Jennings Bryan was serving on the prosecuting team in Dayton, Tenn., in the much publicized trial of John Scopes, a schoolteacher who had been indicted for violation of a state statute forbidding the teaching of evolution in opposition to the creation story in the Bible (*DAB*, 3:197). For Rogers on the Scopes trial see *WA*, 2:57–60.

6. Martin Edwin Trapp (1877–1951), a Democrat and lawyer, served as governor of Oklahoma from 1923 to 1927 (Blackburn, "Martin Edwin Trapp").

7. John Stink (Ho-tah-moie or Ho-tok-moie, ca. 1863–1938) was an Osage Indian who lived as a recluse near Pawhuska, Okla. Despite a substantial income from his full headright share of the millions the Osage tribe received from oil revenues from its lands, Stink made little contact with humans and preferred to roam the countryside with his pack of dogs (Wilson, *Underground Reservation*, 168–69; Franks, *Osage*, 142; *WWOkla*, 479).

To Sallie Rogers McSpadden
ca. Summer 1925
[New York, N.Y.]

Dear Sis,

Your nice newsy Letter just come, and was sure glad to hear from you, Excuse me writing on this thing but its got to be about the only way I can write,[1]

We are all getting along fine and having a dandy Summer, Along with my work I am playing a lot too, I was in the game the other day on his side when that Young Hitchcock Boy got hurt~~m~~[2]   I guess you have read it, We had had ~~Di~~ Lunch Betty and I at their home that day, He is still unconscious, It looks just like that Fall Steve McClellan[3] had over at the old McClellan place that time when he laid so long,

I am enclosing you a Check for a Thousand Dollars and you just go right ahed and use this any way you need it and I aill send you more as the Children need it in School this Fall, Dont you by any means let either one of them miss that education, Keep them at it as long as they will stay, Never mind about any land, Give that to them and some day it willbe worth something, Dont you ever get a Dollar from a Soul Bank or aything, You and Tome have done the most wonderful thing in the World bringing all that Family up on and   educating them and certainly is going to be fin[i]shed, Why thats no reflection on anyone not to have all they want at that age, Its a crefit [credit] when they can show what they have done with it like you all can, Thats what I want to do things like this so I can ~~point to~~ feel in my old age that out of all the money I made I did do some good with some of it anyway,

And I am going to fix Herb out in some way, and I bet you he wins out with those places, and comes out on top, ~~M~~ Why my Lord Sis this is the happiest thing I [e]ver did,

I wish I could write you a long letter and tell how wonderful you and Tom have always been to me , But I want to get this away, before I leave Town tonight, You see I dont come in town only at nights, and Matinee days,

I am wiring Herb to buy those Cattle, I want to let him in on it some way,

You and Tom have the greatest treasures on earth to have raised the Family you have and have them all turn out so wonderful like they have, I tell you thats a real lifes ambition realized,

Best Love to all of you, Now use this any way you need and remember I am taking care of that Schooling, There may be atime when those Nephews will have to take care of me,[4]   and I know they will do it too,

Well so long all of you, and lots and lots of Love,

From Betty and Billy,

TL, rc.[5] LC-UT, IV:A:1. Handwritten, not in Rogers's hand, top margin: "To Mrs. Thom McSpadden – Will's Sister Sallie – *1925*–."

1. The letter was typewritten on plain, white paper.

2. Frank Hitchcock (b. ca. 1909), a member of a famous Long Island, N.Y., family of polo players, was severely injured on 15 July when he was thrown from his horse during a match. The sixteen-year-old remained in a coma for at least two days (*NYT*, 15–16 July 1925).

3. For Stephen Frank (Steve) McClellan see *PWR*, 1:197n.6.

4. For Maurice Rogers McSpadden, nephew of Will Rogers, see *PWR*, 1:514–15.

5. Dating of the document was determined by historical and chronological references in the text.

To James S. Davenport
7 September 1925
New York, N.Y.

September 7, 1925

Hon. James S. Davenport,

Att'y. At Law and Reformed Congressman,

Vinita, Oklahoma.

My dear Jim:

Why did you want to slander me?[1] I was going along in my own way and not bothering anybody when you and some accomplices headed a black cat across my trail.

Now, you might have meant well by knowing I couldn't be elected, but if you thought that I could then it was malacious.

I am down there this fall for five days in various parts of the state, and if I last that long I will be doing well, much less four years.

Jim, I couldn't be a Politician in a million years. I like to go my own way, and I don't believe I could take dictation. It sure would be an honor, and worth all the monetary sacrifice, but I am going through life making up my own mind, even if it is foolish enough to be considered worth paying for.

But I sure thank you, and will see you soon. Best regards to you and Mrs. Davenport.[2]

Sincerely yours,
Will Rogers.

WR:Q[3]

TLS, rc. OkClaW, 1975.05.0012. On letterhead of Will Rogers, New Amsterdam Theatre, New York.

1. See Telegram to J. S. Leach, 13 July 1925, above.
2. Like Davenport's late first wife, his second wife, Byrd Ironside Davenport, was a member by blood of the Cherokee Nation. The couple had married in 1907 (*WhAmer*, 1:296).
3. Bruce W. Quisenberry (ca. 1906–89), the son of a sister of Betty Blake Rogers, worked as a secretary to Will Rogers, beginning approximately the late summer of 1925 as Rogers prepared to embark on his lecture tour. He continued to assist his uncle on the road throughout the course of Rogers's lecture tour (see *PWR*, 3:405–6; Yagoda, *Will Rogers*, 222).

Notes for Radio Broadcast
ca. 16 September 1925
[New York, N.Y.]

Although Rogers had made his first appearance on radio a few years before, the following notes represent one of the earliest records of his broadcasts. He delivered the remarks at a banquet in New York for several hundred representatives from the radio broadcasting industry.[1] True to his usual routine, Rogers prepared almost verbatim notes in advance of his appearance.

Ladies and Gentlemen I ahev been forbidden to make speech to you over the Rodeo tonigyt, by my manager who I am soon to start on a Concert Tour for, He figures if you ever heard me once you would never want tonhear me again,[2]

But I wanted to come   and explain it to you in person, and show you that I ~~am~~ that it is a bigger dissappointment to me than to you, Because when you make an Actor keep his mouth shut he is in pain,Its like an after Dinner Speaker going to a Banquet and not being called upon,

I am sorry my Radio friends cant see me, as you here at the Tables are privileged to do, Hearing me is nothing in comparisson to seeing me, Well I will try and describe myself to you, I am 6 foot five and half inches, horizontal, weight I95 all ►b◄rawn, color of eyes azure blue, Hair jet black and wavy, features strong, complexion perfect, Hands two, feet two, waist before meals 34, Home Hollyowood, Politics, highest bidder, religion, (wait till I look around here abefore I announce it, Jewish.

I dont know what this Dinner is for, Somebody stung some Sucker with a new Radio set and siad lets have a Dinner.

Nevr mind a Dinner get rid of Static, A Dinner is all right for those of you that are here, but how about the millions that tune in on your machines and all they can hear is ,Whistle___------------.

Besides there is a Senator here with you tonight,[3] and my Contract says I am not allowed to go o utside and appear ~~with an inf~~ in inferior company. There is a Moral clause where we are judged by our associates, There has never been a breath of scandal touched me untill lately I was named as Govenor of Oklahoma, I hushed that up as soon as I could,[4]

I thought I would find Jimmy Walker the newly nominated Mayor of New York here tonight,[5] But I guess he has got what he wanted now and he wont notice ua [us] any more,

I thought I would hear Jimmy announcing that he was rsponsible for ~~allowing~~ putting the Bill through Albany that ~~there was~~ allowed the air to carry Radio.

Radio is a great thing   the best thing about it is that you can tune anybody out when you want too,

I am leaving New York to try and get out of the Wve lengths of W H n and Grantlund,[6]

There is illions yes billionsmade in radio and all out of just selling the s tes [sets?], Theere must be some profit in those things,

I will be in every town   I dont care where you live   i will be there, Talk about seeing America first, I may not see it first but If I live i will see it this winter, all of it,

---

TD. OkClaW, 1975.25.0025. Typewritten with different machine, top margin, stacked (/): "Speech: / Radio Industries Banquet. September 16, 1925".

1. Rogers was a featured speaker on 16 September 1925 at the second annual radio industries banquet in New York held in conjunction with the yearly meeting of the National Association of Broadcasters and a large radio trade show. The dinner program was carried by twenty-six radio stations throughout the country, the largest broadcast to date (*NYT*, 16–17 September 1925, 21 August 1927).

2. Although concert impresario Charles Wagner had forbidden Rogers from speaking at the radio function, organizers of the banquet were unaware of the restriction and

panicked late in the afternoon of 16 September when it became known that Rogers had decided not to show. Believing he had balked because he had not been offered pay for his services, representatives rushed to the nearby New Amsterdam Theatre to catch Rogers off-stage, offer him all the money the group could afford, and try to persuade him to change his mind. For Rogers money was not the object; instead he felt an obligation to honor his contract with Wagner (see Letter of Agreement with Charles L. Wagner, 4 June 1925, above). He also understood, however, the predicament of the radio men. He thus agreed to tell the nation by radio that night why he could not speak publicly under the terms of his contract. His "nonspeech" proved one of his most unusual and humorous (*NYT*, 21 August 1927).

3. Rogers likely referred to Clarence Cleveland Dill (1884–1978), a Democrat who served as U.S. senator from Washington from 1923 to 1935. Dill was one of the scheduled speakers at the broadcasters's dinner (*BDUSCong*, 910–11; *NYT*, 21 August 1927).

4. See Telegram to J. S. Leach, 13 July 1925, and Letter to James S. Davenport, 7 September 1925, above.

5. New York state senator Jimmy Walker won the Democratic nomination for mayor of New York in the primary election on 15 September. He carried the general election in November by a wide margin and took office on 1 January 1926 as the city's one hundredth mayor (Fowler, *Beau James*, 147, 149, 153, 155).

6. WHN, a pioneer radio station in New York, was owned by a major entertainment company, Loews, Inc., which used it to promote its vaudeville acts and motion pictures. Nils Thor Granlund (ca. 1892–1957), a former yacht skipper and motion picture publicist, was an announcer at WHN who often broadcast from entertainment spots in the city and filled air time with comedy and poetry. Known as NTG or Granny, Granlund became recognized—and criticized—for his aggressive on-air style (*EAR*, 235, 541, 548; *NYT*, 22 April 1957).

Telegram from Betty Blake Rogers
1 October 1925
New York, N.Y.

As Rogers prepared to launch his initial lecture tour with a debut appearance in Elmira, N.Y., he received several messages of best wishes.[1] Probably none meant more to him than the following one.

412N H 13

HT NEWYORK 715P OCT 1 1925

WILL ROGERS

CARE THE PARK CHURCH[2] ELMIRA NY

GOOD LUCK DEAR I AM THINKING ABOUT YOU AND SEND ALL MY LOVE

BETTY

727P

TG, rc. OkClaW, 1975.12.0008. On Western Union Telegraph Co. letterhead. Imprinted immediately below letterhead: "RECEIVED AT 210 EAST WATER ST., ELMIRA N. Y." Metered immediately below recipient's name: "192."

1. Rogers opened his lecture tour on 1 October 1925 in Elmira, N.Y., which had been the home of Mark Twain's in-laws and a frequent summer residence of the humorist. Impresario Charles Wagner had selected Elmira in the belief that the residents of a town so closely identified with Twain would appreciate Rogers and his humor (Croy, *Our Will Rogers*, 189–90; *OCMT*, 192). See also Letter of Agreement with Charles L. Wagner, 4 June 1925, above, and Article in *Elmira Advertiser*, 2 October 1925, below.

2. Park Church served as the venue for the premiere of the lecture tour. Twain's parents-in-law, antislavery advocates, had helped establish the nondenominational Christian church in the mid-1800s after their previous congregation had split over the issue of slavery (*OCMT*, 193).

Article by Will Rogers in Lecture Tour Program
ca. 1 October 1925
[New York, N.Y.?]

A WARNING

I have been asked by Mr. Wagner to contribute something to this Programme. Now in the first place, it was a surprise to me to know that we would have a Programme. There are only two of us Acts, the Quartette and myself, and I didn't think the audience would be very apt to confuse one with the other. The Quartette is the one where there is four in it, that's in case they all show up, (which is rare) and I am the single individual, the man who will come out and enthrall you with his command of the English Language, with his unmatched dignity, with an oratorical delivery that is second only to Ben Turpin. So I couldn't personally see any need of a Programme. Then he told me why they used one. It was so they could advertise the next attraction in it. That people always looked at the coming attraction with hope, and it sometimes takes the sorrow from the present one. The Manager told me it was surprising what an audience would stand for if you only would promise them something better in the future. Then again it gives them evidence against the performers, or Managers, if the Patron is fortunate enough to get them into Court. I didn't know it until I come out on this Tour, but you would be surprised at the number of people who read Programmes. I just watched it when I was up there talking. There would be at least 50 per cent reading; (Well, maybe more than that) it depended on the per cent that could read. Sometimes it might run as high as 60 per cent. So I would advise smart business men to advertise in Theatre and Concert Programmes. Don't worry about it not being read—it's read—and I want to say it's a Godsend for the performers that their audiences have something to occupy their minds. If they didn't, I would hate to see what would happen some time, because there is an old Moth-eaten Law on the Statute Books, where if a Speaker, or Actor are attacked by the audience it still constitutes a crime. Politicians have always fought the repeal of this Law. So let's be grateful for the Programme, ESPECIALLY TONIGHT.

PD. Printed in *Will Rogers: The Prince of Entertainers and Entertainer of "The Prince"* lecture tour program. OSU. Rogers's byline appeared below heading, centered.

Article in *Elmira Advertiser*
2 October 1925
Elmira, N.Y.

SEYMOUR LOWMAN[1] AND I
GET MOST FREE EATING
SAYS JOLLY WILL ROGERS

NATION'S FAVORITE HUMORIST STARTS COUNTRY-WIDE TOUR AT
THE PARK CHURCH—WOULD REORGANIZE COOLIDGE CABINET.

It is somewhat of a leap from the stage of Flo Ziegfeld's "Follies," to the pulpit of the Park church, liberal though the latter is, but Will Rogers, America's best-liked funster, accomplished that feat deftly and graciously, Thursday night, to the great pleasure of an audience that nearly filled the place. Mr. and Mrs. George B. Carter, also courageous people, were responsible for the engagement, and present also, was Charles L. Wagner, Mr. Rogers's manager, who wished to see his latest star perform on a platform for the first time.

Mr. Rogers was accorded a hearty welcome. He had left his familiar lariat in Mr. Ziegfeld's barn back in New York, but he had his equally well-known quid of gum with him, which lent local atmosphere.

Mr. Rogers announced it was the first of a series of seventy-five appearances he was making outside of New York and that he hoped to return to Elmira next year, and annually.

"It seems odd for me to be talking in a church," said Mr. Rogers, "and yet I am pleased to know that I don't have to change much from the material I use in the 'Follies.'

"I don't know what to call this thing. I suppose it's got to have a name. If I were a smart man you would call me a lecturer and if I happened to be a politician, you would call me a debater. I want to say at the start that I am not trying to displace any lecturer. So we might as well call it 'With Charity to None and Malice to All" and let it go at that.

NEWSPAPER MAN.

"I am somewhat of a newspaper man. I was at the last Republican national convention in Cleveland, where they went to select a candidate for vice-president. The late William Jennings Bryan[2] was there writing for a paper also, and we got quite chummy. He said he understood I wrote humorous stuff, which showed to me he never had read any of it. He said that being the case he would slip me anything funny that he saw happen for my column, and I told him I would tell him of anything serious that happened, for his column. But it didn't.

"With the passing of Mr. Bryan the evolution scare has quieted down.[3] I am glad of it. After all, we are not so much concerned as to where we came from and to where we are going.

"I am glad to be in Elmira and to see so many here. Of course, you are not all here but those who think they are going to Florida will come back. Florida is the only place I know of where they have to use a ladder to get into the ocean.

"I like your traffic towers in Elmira. That is the only way to protect a police officer—to put him in a traffic tower. The traffic problem looms big and I'm for changing the traffic regulations. I would eliminate all right and left hand turns and insist that if you are going to a place to keep on going straight until you get there. We might have 'em use a certain street on Monday, another street on Tuesday and so on.

TELLS OF LOWMAN

"I am glad to be in the home of Lieutenant Governor Seymour Lowman. I meet him at dinners often and I suppose he and I get more eating for nothing than any two men I know of.

"I am not a party man. I think both parties are terrible. The one in power is usually the worst. I met President Coolidge at a dinner the other night[4] and he said he had met me before. I didn't remember it, so I told him that if I had met him before it must have been while he was vice president.

"Colonel William Mitchell was kicked out of the army[5] and right into the hearts of 11,000,000 people. Colonel Mitchell once asked me to take a spin around Washington with him and I accepted, supposing, of course it was in an automobile.[6] But it was in an airplane. We circled around Washington's monument and I tell you that if the monument had had handles, Colonel Mitchell would have lost a customer.

"I don't think Calvin Coolidge had a happy time on his vacation this summer.[7] Who could have had all dressed up in white trousers and yachting cap? Mrs. Coolidge[8] is a splendid woman, but I think she made Calvin wear those things and in that way spoiled his vacation.

"Charlie Hughes is the only man who ever resigned voluntarily from the United States government. He said he wanted to get back into private law practice to make some money. But the other day he bought a house in New York with 12 bathrooms and so I don't think he did so badly as Secretary of State.[9]

GLAD OF FORD CHANGE

"I am glad Henry Ford is going to change the shape of the things he makes.[10] They are to be seven inches longer, and I have figured out that means 183 less to the mile. But they are to be four inches wider and haven't you often missed them by just four inches. Henry wants Muscle Shoals for an assembling room for the things he makes. He proposes to throw in the parts above the dam and they will come out finished products below.

"Henry Ford is one of my best friends. I visit him often in Detroit. Once I was out at my home in California and he wanted to give me a Lincoln car. But it was during the oil scandal and I telegraphed him he could not bribe me that way. But I did tell him I would rather have 16 Fords and a tractor. I wanted 16 Fords because it has always been my ambition to be able to go out of my home of a morning and choose my car.

"I got one vote for the Democratic nomination for President at the Democratic national convention at Madison Square Garden in New York. But I am not proud of it because that convention got to the point where it was no credit to be voted for. My vote consisted of two half votes cast by two delegates and I will say that of all the 1,100 delegates in attendance, these two stood far above the others in intelligence.

"After the convention I telegraphed Al Smith congratulating him that he did not have to run. He replied that the only thing that beat him for the nomination was honest counting. He said they should have had Tammany tellers.

VISITS REFORMATORY

"I visited your Reformatory today and I want to say I never felt more at home anywhere. Dr. Christian[11] is doing a wonderful work there. I am going to speak to the boys Friday morning. They probably won't be interested much in what I say but I know they will be glad to see me because they won't have to work.

"I see they want to get Wilbur out of the cabinet.[12] Well, I'm for reorganizing the cabinet. I want Jack Dempsey made secretary of war and then there never will be any war. I would like to see Peggy Hopkins Joyce[13] secretary of the treasury. I know Peggy real well. I never have been married to her, but I know her. For secretary of the interior I would name one of the Mayo Brothers.

"The other night at the 'Follies' we had the President of Mexico.[14] He was a great sight, for think of seeing a living President of Mexico. I understand he was elected in the afternoon and left the country the same night. That's how we got him.

"Rudolph Valentino's wife, speaking about her divorce,[15] says a wife with an active mind should take a vacation occasionally. So you women of Elmira who have been living happily with your husbands are dumb and you don't know it. I am the only motion picture actor who has the same wife he started out with. My wife is not bragging about it but I am.

"Recently they filmed 'The Ten Commandments.' They ran shy of money before it was completed and one of the owners wanted to cut it off at the eighth commandment. I suppose they picked 'The Ten Commandments' so they wouldn't have to pay the author a royalty.

COOLIDGE WANTS JOB.

"Will Hays recently signed a new contract as motion picture boss for $200,000 a year. I hear he asked Cal Coolidge if he had better accept and that Cal told him to go to it and to look around and if he could find any other job he would come in too.

"I am going out to California to make pictures in January and February for Hal Roach, a former resident of Elmira.[16] Then I want to come back to Elmira next year and talk. I heard Margot Asquith give her first lecture and her talk was worse than mine is tonight. She talked an hour and a half on fox-hunting in England and half her audience had never seen a horse, let alone a fox.". . .

PD.[17] Printed in *Elmira Advertiser*, Elmira, N.Y., 2 October 1925. Scrapbook 8, Part 2, OkClaW. Ellipsis inserted by the editors.

1. Seymour Lowman (1868–1940), a Republican politician and attorney from Elmira, served as lieutenant governor of New York from 1925 to 1927 (*NYT*, 14 March 1940).

2. William Jennings Bryan died on 26 July 1925 (*DAB*, 3:191).

3. Bryan, a biblical literalist, took the stand on 21 July as a witness in the Scopes trial in Tennessee. In a relentless cross-examination, he showed his ignorance of science and the simplicity of his religious beliefs. He died in his sleep five days later (*DAB*, 3:197). For Rogers's tribute to Bryan see *WA*, 2:63–65.

4. Rogers and Coolidge shared the dais at the annual Gridiron Dinner of the Washington press corps on 23 April 1925. Before that night's event the two met in the president's office at the White House for several minutes (*NYT*, 24 April 1925). For an account of that meeting see *WA*, 2:22–25.

5. William Lendrum (Billy) Mitchell (1879–1936) joined the army at the outbreak of the Spanish-American War, rose through the ranks, and became a leading proponent of military aviation during World War I. He continued to promote and demonstrate its effectiveness in the postwar period, but his criticisms of the defense structure and military aviation policies of the United States led to the downgrading of his rank in March 1925. In early September he issued a more pronounced condemnation of incompetency in the U.S. military command. His public charges led to his dismissal from active duty on 21 September (*DAB*, Supp. 2:460–62; *HD1920s*, 235; *NYT*, 7 March, 22 September 1925).

6. Rogers made the flight with Mitchell at Bolling Field in Washington, D.C., on 24 April 1925. On landing, he declined Mitchell's offer to fly him to New York and instead took the train (*WES*, 25 April 1925). For an account of the flight see *WA*, 2:27–29.

7. Coolidge spent his summer vacation in 1925 at Swampscott, Mass. He returned to Washington on 10 September (McCoy, *Calvin Coolidge*, 299; *NYT*, 11 September 1925).

8. Grace Goodhue Coolidge (1879–1957), the wife of the president, met Coolidge in Northampton, Mass., where she taught at a school for the deaf and he practiced law. They were married in 1905 (*NYT*, 9 July 1957).

9. When Hughes submitted his resignation in January 1925 as U.S. secretary of state, he announced that he would resume his legal practice in New York to rebuild his wealth so he could provide for his family (Pusey, *Charles Evans Hughes*, 2:613).

10. The Ford Motor Company, beset with two years of declining sales, announced on 26 August the most radical changes in the Model T in six years. Although the alterations offered customers greater variety of style and even color, sales climbed only momentarily in the fall of 1925 before beginning to sink again in early 1926 (*NYT*, 27 August 1925; Nevins and Hill, *Ford*, 2:406–7). For the changes in Ford cars see also *WA*, 2:74–77.

11. Frank L. Christian (ca. 1876–1955), a surgeon, was superintendent of the state reformatory at Elmira from 1917 until his retirement in 1939. Christian received acclaim for his progressive administration of the reformatory (*NYT*, 20 October 1955).

12. Curtis Dwight Wilbur (1867–1954) became secretary of the U.S. Department of the Navy in 1924, at a time when the navy was trying to recover from the oil reserve scandals of the Harding administration. Although his outspokenness on a variety of topics brought him frequently under attack in Washington, he remained in office until 1929 (*DAB*, Supp. 5:746; *NYT*, 9 September 1954).

13. Peggy Hopkins Joyce (1893–1957) enjoyed some roles on screen and stage, including the *Ziegfeld Follies*, but gained greater attention for her many marriages and romantic escapades, several involving men of financial substance. In November 1925 she brought suit for divorce from her fourth husband, a Swedish nobleman (*NYT*, 16 November 1925, 13 June 1957).

14. Plutarco Elías Calles (1877–1945), a veteran army officer, won election as president of Mexico in 1924. Known popularly as the "Jefe," the Mexican revolutionary leader left office in 1928 but strongly influenced government affairs well into the 1930s. He visited New York in late October 1924, shortly after his election to the presidency (*NYT*, 28–30 October 1924, 20 October 1945; *EM*, 1:181–83).

15. Natacha Rambova (Winifred Shaunessy, 1897–1966), an occasional actress and set designer, married Valentino in 1922. Her temperamental personality and her marriage to the foremost screen idol of the time kept her in the spotlight. News of a possible divorce hit the newspapers in September 1925; the dissolution of the mar-

riage became official in early 1926 (*NYT*, 8 June 1966; *FE*, 1400–1401; Shulman, *Valentino*, 234, 247).

16. Rogers did not resume his film career with Hal Roach, a native of Elmira, N.Y. Instead, in January 1926 Rogers returned to the lecture circuit to begin a three-week tour of Florida. From there he proceeded through the Southeast and then on to the southwestern United States (*FE*, 1156; Chronology, 1926, OkClaW).

17. For an account by Rogers of his lecture tour appearance in Elmira, see *WA*, 2:95–96.

Telegram from Florenz Ziegfeld, Jr.
26 October 1925
New York, N.Y.

145N   243 BLUE

S1 NEWYORK 407P OCT 26 1925

WILL ROGERS

PARK THEATRE YOUNGSTOWN OHIO

MY DEAR BILL GLAD TO GET YOUR WIRE[1] AND DELIGHTED BEYOND WORDS OF YOUR GREAT SUCCESS AT SAME TIME AM DISAPPOINTED YOU ARE NOT READY TO COME BACK WE OPEN CHICAGO DECEMBER TWENTIETH YOU WILL HAVE SO MUCH MONEY BY THAT TIME YOU WILL WANT TO WORK FOR ME FOR NOTHING BECAUSE YOU KNOW I SHOULD HAVE BEEN ON ON THAT TOUR I AM OPENING A PLAY LIKE MIDNIGHT FROLIC IN A NEWLY CONSTRUCTED BUILDING BY URBAN ESPECIALLY DESIGNED FOR PURPOSE HAVE HICKMANS BAND[2] FROM LOSANGELES AND OPEN JANUARY 14TH FOR TEN WEEKS IF YOU DONT WANT TO PLAY THE TEN WEEKS PLAY PART OF IT YOU HAVE ALWAYS WANTED TO GO TO FLORIDA AND YOU CAN MAKE UP YOUR SALARY BY TEN MILLION DOLLARS IN REAL ESTATE DOWN THERE I HAVE PARIS SINGER INTERESTED WITH ME IN THEATRE DOWN THERE[3] AND HE HAS INSIDE TRACK ALL. REAL ESTATE THERE JUST PUT THAT THINKING CAP OF YOURS ON AND FIGURE OUT BEST WAY FOR YOURSELF OF COURSE I WOULD LOVE TO HAVE YOU WITH FOLLIES IN CHICAGO BILL FIELDS FOUND OUT CONTRACT BREAKING NOT SO EASY HE WALKED OUT IN BOSTON AFTER THIRD WEEK BUT IS PREPARED TO WALK BACK AGAIN IN PHILADELPHIA TONIGHT[4] IT IS FUNNY IN THIS WORLD EVERYBODY HAS IT COMING TO THEM GOOD OR BAD HOPING TO HEAR FINALLY YOU WILL COME TO FLORIDA AND MUST KNOW WELL IN ADVANCE AND HOPE YOU WILL WITH SINCERE REGARDS

FLO

515P

TG, rc. OkClaW, 1975.21.0205. On Western Union Telegraph Co. letterhead. Metered to the right of recipient's name: "470."

1. The telegram from Rogers to Ziegfeld was not found.

2. Art Hickman (ca. 1887–1930), a dance orchestra leader in San Francisco before the war, took his band to New York in 1919 at the invitation of Ziegfeld. Performing in the *Follies*, and in hotels and cafés, the group became a hit on the East Coast with its up-tempo, jazz-like style (*VO*, 22 January 1930; *EPM*, 2516).

3. Paris Eugene Singer (d. 1932) was the youngest of twenty-four children of the inventor of the sewing machine. Active in the Florida land boom of the 1920s, especially in Palm Beach, Paris Singer invested generously in various developments in the state, most of which failed in the real estate collapse that followed a devastating hurricane in September 1926. Ziegfeld announced on 26 October 1925 that he, Singer, and other investors would open a new theater, Ziegfeld's Palm Beach Nights, in early 1926 in the Florida resort city (*NYT*, 27 October 1925, 25 June 1932; *HD1920s*, 132).

4. Fields left the *Follies* in Boston in early October 1925 after accepting a film contract with Paramount studios. Ziegfeld promptly sued, causing Fields to return to the *Follies* stage after an absence of just two weeks. Within a few months he was back in front of the camera (*NYT*, 25 October 1925; Louvish, *Man*, 271).

Article in *Times-Picayune*
11 November 1925
New Orleans, La.

From the first stop in Elmira, N.Y., and throughout his lecture tour, local newspapers, from big cities to small towns, gave Rogers strong coverage and growing publicity. Interviews, pre-event stories, and postlecture accounts, some of them facilitated by Rogers's nephew and road manager, Bruce Quisenberry, brought Rogers to much larger audiences than the ones that filled the lecture venues. In a departure from the usual practice, donation of advertising space in a New Orleans newspaper afforded Rogers the following opportunity to thank the city and its mayor for their reception during his lecture tour stop on 8–9 November.[1]

THANK YOU MAYOR BEHRMAN[2]

--- Will Rogers

I thank you, Mayor Behrman, for your wonderful welcome to New Orleans. I want to thank you with all my heart—if a Comedian has a heart. I don't think ever was a mere Comedian welcomed to a city by full page ads in all your newspapers, and I appreciate it—I appreciate it just as much as if I didn't know that you were using me just as a means of getting some one to tell the benefits of your city to. It was a wonderful thought on the part of the newspapers who had the page and couldn't sell it, but, knowing you had an appropriation to spend on boosting, decided to relieve you of some of it.

You say Oklahoma was "a part of the Louisiana Purchase"—a part. It was the part they purchased, your end of it was thrown in.

You welcome me to the "Capital of Beautiful Women." An amendment to our Constitution drew women down to the level of men, and lipstick and powder have hid the beauty as well as the flaws, and made them equal.

You say "how interesting it would be if Mark Twain were here, and could see the city he loved and wrote about,[3] and how if he stood with me and you, looking out of the window of the New Roosevelt Hotel, and that I might tell him of the Follies, the Democratic Convention, and various things."

Mark Twain did know New Orleans, and then moved to Connecticut. In all fairness to you, however, I bet you he is the only man in the world that ever moved from Louisiana to Connecticut. Still Twain was a smart man. But if he were here today, as you suggest, we wouldn't be standing at our window looking out at the beautiful city. I am doing that right now, and I can't see anything but smoke, and you know Mark Twain made his own smoke. He wouldn't take anybody's smoke.

I could, as you say, "tell him of my Oklahoma." I could tell of its assortment of Governors, its outlaws who were caught, and those that were not. Yes, I could tell him of New York. But he was a pious man and I doubt if he would listen to me. I could relate how Tammany counts her votes, the price of hotel rooms, the "Couver" charges in a "Night Club." Yes, and as you also suggest, "I could tell him of the Follies." But you have business men right here in New Orleans that could tell him more of the Follies than I could. Yes, also I could tell him of the Democratic Convention, but I think too much of him to do so. I might tell him just about the first year of it. Then, if he didn't go to sleep, why tell him a little of the second year.

You say "Mark Twain's conversation might drift to Pirates, gathered in the Old 'Absinthe House'."[4] Yes, probably our conversation would drift to Pirates, especially if either of us had anything, we would perhaps have been robbed here that day. In the old days they did gather in the old "Absinthe House." Now that's the only place they don't gather.

You remind us, dear Mayor, "that we could talk of the days when Sazeracs and Gin Fizzes were a feature of local life." Why, Mr. Mayor, do you say "when they were a feature?" They are still a feature with "Outsiders," but, of course, they are just a plain common "Nuisance" with you all. While their names are the same, the amount consumed is the same; only the quality of the Gin and Absinthe have changed. Oh yes, and the price.

You say "Mark Twain's River Packets are gone." Mark's may have gone, but Andy Volstead's are here. Washington sent 300 revenue agents here to suppress the trade for a week.

You say, "We could tell him how we had spent ten million dollars in hotels." You could tell him, but I doubt if you could show him. If a million is spent in America nowadays, by the time the second edition announcing the expenditure reaches the streets the amount will have jumped to three million.

We could tell Mr. Twain how Income Taxes have made us pad our original investments. Income Tax has made more liars out of America than Golf. You could tell Mark Twain how you are having a convention here this week composed entirely of patriotic Americans who are trying to induce the Government to lower the taxes on their particular industries, and leave it on the others. Your hotels and restaurants might interest him, because in his day and time people lived at home and most of them knew where their own dining room was. You are right, "Your ten million dollars in office buildings" would interest him, with every office filled with men full of schemes to sell something to their fellow men. Yes, "we could tell him how twenty-five million dollars had been appropriated in water, sewerage and drainage system." But on account of it being Public Works we might not be able to show him over five million actually spent, but you could point with pride to that much, for that is a larger percentage by far than most cities get out of their appropriations. "You could tell him of the building of your canals east to Florida." And if he didn't believe you, you could take him to your soft road highways, and show him the avalanche of Fords going to Florida. "You note that I arrived by the L & N."[5] I did, one hour and fifteen minutes late. I note you say, "By the way, there is a twenty-seven million dollar real estate project under way at Lake Pontchartrain."[6] You speak as casually of millions as a Florida ad. But we must not forget, Mayor Behrman (and your Commission accomplices), while you are telling Mark Twain what you are going to do, that Mark could remind you of what you were going to do when he was here. He could tell you when these bridges you now propose, were first proposed. In fact, he knew the original proposer. So let's not have New Orleans tell what they PROPOSE to do. Florida is surviving on proposals. You go ahead and bridge the Mississippi River and the world will find it out without either Ad or Proposal.

You say, in welcoming me, "No man can ask either mercy or immunity from me." Now, Mayor, you are wrong. You have given me a wonderful welcome in this town (not town but city). Some thirty or forty of your most prominent men have dined me.[7] Gathered around our generous feast board (served by the master hand of America) was Jew, Gentile and Catholic—a commendable thing. You have patronized generously my little performance, you have laughed more than liberally at my foolishness; and I would be, indeed, an ingrate if I didn't publicly thank you. You are the only perpetual Mayor in the United States. Other cities have their problems of who to run for Mayor; New Orleans never has hers. You were out one term[8] and business dropped off to almost a level of Houston and Galveston. You are the only Mayor in America that seems to be able to hit a happy medium of being "liberal" enough for the "wide-opens" and "conservative" enough for the "shuts." I most heartily agree with you when you say "Louisiana envies neither California nor Florida." You, Mayor Behrman, are the head of the most unique and most beloved city in our entire Union. There is not an American pulse that doesn't quicken and a heart that doesn't beat livelier when they arrive in this city of such historical traditions. The new world will never have but one New Orleans. Don't try to make it just like other cities. If we keep on our cities will be just like Fords, where you can ship a block of one town and it will fit right down in the heart of another. Keep New Orleans so you can't get spare parts for your town anywhere. You are your only model. Don't have a standard-built town. Even some of our laws and customs which should apply to other towns should not apply to old New Orleans. Size and population should not be your goal. No American city can ever reach New York, so why want to be the second, or the fifth, or the tenth largest city? You won't be any happier; you are bountifully supplied for all your needs. So, instead of trying to make it a "typical commercial club town," keep it New Orleans. Maintain its traditions. The Old Timers that founded it knew what they wanted. There are thousands of ordinary cities striving for population and trade. Don't be just another bustling town. The Almighty located you—you weren't laid out by a Real Estate development. Let's keep one city for tradition and pleasure. You are it now. You can lose it, or keep it; it's up to you. I unfortunately can't describe your benefits and your beauty like dear Mark Twain did, but I like you as much. Everybody likes you. We feel an interest in you we don't feel in any other city in America. You stand first, and San Francisco next as cities we expect to find different. Surely America can have one Babbittless Town.[9]

Thank you for your hospitality. I am for you heart and soul as long as you stay "OLD" New Orleans.

PD. Printed in *Times-Picayune*, New Orleans, La., 11 November 1925. Scrapbook 21, OkClaW.

1. Various clippings, Scrapbooks 8 and 21, OkClaW; Yagoda, *Will Rogers*, 222; Chronology, 1923–25, OkClaW.
2. Martin Behrman (1864–1926), a powerful figure in Louisiana politics, served a record five terms as mayor of New Orleans. Known as "Papa," Behrman died in office two months after Rogers's lecture tour performance in the city (*WhAmer*, 1:78; *NYT*, 13 January 1926; Huber, *New Orleans*, 13).

3. Mark Twain first visited the port city of New Orleans in February 1857, like Rogers in 1902 hoping to find a ship headed to South America. Twain stayed and took an apprenticeship on a riverboat. Over the next four years, as he worked on boats plying the Mississippi, he visited New Orleans on many occasions, often staying for days at a time. Later, Twain mentioned the city many times in his writings (*MT*, 334).

4. The Absinthe House, built in 1806 on Bourbon Street in the French Quarter of New Orleans, was famous for the thousands of drinks of absinthe, a green liqueur, served from its bar (Huber, *New Orleans*, 125–26).

5. Rogers probably referred to the Louisville & Nashville Railroad (Huber, *New Orleans*, 300).

6. A $27 million project to dredge and develop the southern shore of Lake Pontchartrain, immediately north of New Orleans, was announced in late September 1925. Plans called for parks, parkways, homes, and hotels to be built on the 2,000 reclaimed acres over five to six years (*NYT*, 22 September 1925).

7. Rogers was the guest of honor on 8 November at a private banquet at Antoine's, a renowned restaurant in the French Quarter of New Orleans (Chronology, 1923–25, OkClaW; Huber, *New Orleans*, 185).

8. After sixteen consecutive years as mayor of New Orleans, Behrman failed to be reelected in 1920. He was returned to office five years later (*NYT*, 13 January 1926).

9. In the novel *Babbitt*, published in 1922, author Sinclair Lewis characterized business life in small-town America as provincial, materialistic, self-satisfied, and beset with crass local boosterism. "Babbittry" and its derivatives became synonyms for such phenomena (*HD1920s*, 23).

Telegram to Amon G. Carter
17 November 1925
Hennessey, Okla.

Rogers met newspaper publisher Amon G. Carter[1] during a lecture tour stop in Fort Worth, Tex., on 12 November. The two became fast friends, just in time for Carter to use his news connections on behalf of the circuit-riding Rogers.

GIVE THIS TO YOUR AP MAN MISSED TRAIN AT WAWIKA AND HAD TO CHARTER SPECIAL TRAIN FOR FIFTEEN HUNDRED DOLLARS TO MAKE NIGHTS PERFORMANCE AT WICHITA KANSAS.[2]

WILL ROGERS

TG, transcription. AGC-TCU.

1. Amon Giles Carter (1879–1955) helped merge two Fort Worth newspapers to form the *Star-Telegram* in 1909. He became controlling owner, president, and publisher in 1923. A brash showman, he used the newspaper and other business interests to become a leading booster of Fort Worth and west Texas (*NYT*, 24 June 1955; *WhAmer*, 3:141).

2. Rogers's performance in Wichita Falls, Tex., the night of 16 November went overtime, causing him to miss the train to Wichita, Kans., the next stop on the tour. Someone commandeered a car to take him to Waurika, Okla., to catch the midnight passenger train north. This, too, Rogers failed to make, so at considerable cost he chartered an engine and a spare car or two and finally arrived in Wichita in time for the show. Rogers's figure of $1,500 for the special train differs from that reported much later by Quisenberry and in at least one newspaper account. Whatever the cost, Rogers may have passed it along to Charles Wagner, who then tried unsuccessfully to be reimbursed by the local sponsors in Wichita Falls. Amon Carter obliged Rogers with a front-page story in the *Star-Telegram* on 17 November and a release to other newspapers throughout the country through the Associated Press. He wired Rogers with a caution, however: "dont let it happen again the item is only worth one story" (Croy, *Our Will Rogers*, 196–97; *WDT*, 4 November 1951; telegram, Amon G. Carter to Will Rogers, 17 November 1925, AGC-TCU).

Telegram to Betty Blake Rogers
25 November 1925
Ann Arbor, Mich.

AA875 96 NL SUB FREE 1/64

ANNARBOR MCH 25

MRS WILL ROGERS

925 BEVERLY DRIVE BEVERLY HILLS CALIF

YOU KNOW WHAT DAY I AM SENDING THIS LETTER AND YOU KNOW WHAT DAY[1] YOU WILL RECEIVE IT THIS IS ONE BARGAIN WE MADE WHERE WE DIDNT SELL OUT TOO QUICK THE LONGER WE HOLD IT THE MOREVALUABLE IT SEEMS TO BECOME HOPE YOU HAD A GOOD TRIP WE HAD IT GREAT LAST NIGHT IN UTICA AND IT LOOKS GOOD TONIGHT I DO.

A875 2/32 [*page 2*]

WISH I WAS THERE TOMORROW I WOULD BREAK REDUCING FOR ONE DAY LOTS OF LOVE TO YOU ESPECIALLY ON THIS WONDERFUL DAY AND A MIGHTY LOT OF THOSE WONDERFUL LITTLE NESTERS GOODNIGHT

DADDY.

TG, rc. OkClaW, 1975.12.0009. On Western Union Telegraph Co. letterhead. Metered immediately below the letterhead, page 1, and to right of "RECEIVED AT": "MAIN OFFICE 608-610 SOUTH SPRING ST., LOS ANGELES." Metered below the letterhead, both pages: "1925 NOV 25 PM 8 50." Metered above recipient's addresss: "1243." A slash mark was hand-inserted between the "E" and "V" in "MOREVALUABLE" on page 1 to indicate word break.

1. Will and Betty Rogers celebrated their seventeenth wedding anniversary on 25 November 1925. As in the year they were married, the next day, the twenty-sixth, was Thanksgiving (Chronology, 1923–25, OkClaW).

Manuscript for Newspaper Column
26 November 1925
Buffalo, N.Y.

Rogers was not without his detractors. Often he ignored their thrusts, but occasionally he would respond publicly, especially if he felt the criticism had been unjustified, as in the following instance.

~~NOTE) Be sure and send this just as written, Name address and all.~~
The Worst Story I heard today was not ~~told~~ ▲MEANT▲ to ~~me~~ ▲BE▲ ~~by the man I am writh writing about~~. The Man I am writing about just wrote me the following letter "Please give a long suffering Public a rest from the old mushy moth-eaten alleged funny Stories, which you are inflicting on a blasi [*obliterated*] and pessimistic Public. They are given out under ~~flase~~ ▲FALSE▲ missrepresentation, and not true, You dont meet the alleged Authors of these Stories, When you say you meet Mr So and So in Dallas, yesterday, and the King of England in Denver, it does not add to the humor of the story, by dragging in ▲PLACES YOU COULDENT [*vertically inserted in right margin:*]--BE AT YOU WERE NOT EVEN THERE▲~~an impossible person,~~ for the lovamike let up". signed C Gaylord 906 Williamson Bldg. Cleveland Ohio, and written on E Warner White Real Estate stationary ~~of Clev~~ Now we dont need any more joke than that in one day, Gaylord has furniseh todays humor, If my friends would work for me like my enemies I wouldent have to do anything myself. For the information of Mr. Galyord I am today as I write this in Buffalo, ~~N.Y,~~ and just passed through his city of Cleveland not over ~~three ho~~ five hours ago, coming from Ann Arbor Michigan, I have been ~~in~~ already in 55 Towns in 55 days covering over 22 States, I was in Dall▲[*typewritten:*]a▲s 10 days ago, and Denver a month ago, I will present to ~~any Charity~~ ▲you▲ Mr. Gaylord ~~might mention 5,000 five thousand~~ ▲[*typewritten:*]a thousand▲ dollars if ~~he~~ ▲[*typewritten:*]you▲ will name me one man that I have used a Joke about on this trip that I havent met and know personally. (If I said in the Story that I met them,)sometimes I say in the Story So and so sent me the following, but if I receive it in the mail I say so. As for the Stories generally they are told to me by the parties, if not they are taken from THE BEST STORIES OTHER PEOPLE Hear. You see Gaylord ~~when~~ if you ever got out of Cleveland you would find you would meet a lot of people, Even in Clev[eland] I have met a lot of them, just for example call up Charley Otis, Jim Wigmore,[1] of the Wigmore Bldg, Tris Speaker,[2] They might be able to throw some light on your troubled

brow as to my limited acquaintance, They are among the ones I have told jokes on, This is thanksgiving day, I am just going out to have Thanksgiving Dinner with Norman Mack[3] of Buffalo, One of the thrre big Leaders in the Democratic ▲PARTY▲if not the biggest of the threr, I am telling you this Gaylord so you ~~won~~ wont be suprised to hear of one he told me, I amalso going over after [dinner] to see an old broken down actor friend, that I havent seen in years, ▲~~You see Gaylord some of~~▲ you see Gaylord some of our best friends are not among the well known, Now ordinarily I wouldent pay much attention to this, but there might be ~~some fellow ju~~ another fellow just as bad off as you, Because no matter how skeptical and suspicious of everybody some people are ~~of everything~~ there is always somebody worse off than them. Now Gaylord if there is something ▲IN THE PAPER▲ you don't like. dont let it get your Goat, just dont read it, take that same time off that you use reading it and make you some friends and you will soon ~~see how many realize~~ be surprised at the amount of people you have met that you could write jokes about, ~~that you have really met,~~ For instance I dont like the Jokes in the Congresssional Record, But I dont sit down and ~~take my sore headiness out on the Congressmen that~~ write em, I just dont read it. Well Gaylord you unconsciously furnished us the worst Joke we heard today, By the way if you are a Real Estate man as the letter head shows, why aint you in California or Florida where you can be doing business and keep your mind occupied,

---

TM.[4] OkClaW, Worst Story file. Double strike-throughs indicate hand-deleted text; single strike-throughs indicate type-deleted copy. Editorial marks appear throughout the document but have been ignored in this transcript. All interlineations were handwritten, unless otherwise noted. Hand-printed, in Rogers's hand, at bottom of page 1: "NEXT PAGE". Typewritten and hand-encircled at top of second page : "Continued." A handwritten "2" immediately follows the preceding. Handwritten, not in Rogers's hand, at the bottom of the final page: "Copyright etc".

1. James A. Wigmore was a veteran polo player from Cleveland, Ohio, and a breeder of horses for the sport (*NYT*, 25 July 1929; Rose, *Cleveland*, 850–51).
2. Tristram E. (Tris) Speaker (1888–1958), professional baseball player, starred in center field for the Boston Red Sox from 1909 to 1915 and then the Cleveland Indians for eleven seasons, setting several fielding and batting records. He also managed the Indians from 1919 until his forced resignation in 1926 (*BDASBase*, 528–30).
3. Norman Edward Mack (1858–1932), a Canadian-born newspaperman, founded the *Sunday Times* in Buffalo, N.Y., in 1879 and the *Daily Times* in the same city four years later. He served as publisher and editor of both newspapers until his retirement in 1929. Politically influential, Mack was a member of the Democratic National Committee for thirty-two years (*NYT*, 26 December 1932; *WhAmer*, 1:762).
4. Dating of the document was determined by historical references in the text. The piece was printed in *TDW*, 7 December 1925.

Telegram to Betty Blake Rogers
26 November 1925
Buffalo, N.Y.

A46 85 NL 1/63

BUFFALO NY 26

MRS WILL ROGERS

925 BEVERLY DRIVE BEVERLYHILLS CALIF

RECEIVED YOUR WONDERFUL WIRE ALSO YOUR MORE WONDERFUL LETTER FROM STPAUL CERTAINLY DID MISS YOU TODAY HAD A FINE AUDIENCE HERE TONIGHT MR WAGNER HERE AND VERY WELL PLEASED WANTS TO BOOK ABOUT TEN DATES IN FLORIDA STARTING LATTER PART OF JANUARY THEN WORK WAY BACK WEST AND PLAY CALIFORNIA ABOUT LAST FEBRUARY THAT LOOKS LIKE BEST PLAN IF WE STARTED IN CALIFORNIA

AA46 2/22 [*page 2*]

WE WOULDNT GET BACK THERE AGAIN UNTIL WE FINISHED THIS WAY BRINGS ME BACK IN FEW WEEKS LOTS OF LOVE TO ALL

BILLY.

TG, rc. OkClaW, 1975.12.0012. On Western Union Telegraph Co. letterhead. Metered immediately below the letterhead on both pages and to right of "RECEIVED AT": "MAIN OFFICE 608-610 SOUTH SPRING ST., LOS ANGELES, CAL." Metered below the letterhead, both pages: "1925 NOV 27 AM 1 00." Metered above recipient's addresss: "1221."

Notes for Speech or Stage Appearance
ca. 17 December 1925
[Wichita, Kans.?]

Mitchell.

I see where they had him on trial today,[1] If he had cruticised the ~~Army~~ Navy instead of the Army he would have come clear on the first ballot.

If they convict him for talking too much . Lets try the Senate.

The reason Mitchell is shut up is because he said something worth while thats why the Senate never is bothered,

They say Mitchell talks too much   where can you get a Jury of Americans to try a man for talking too much.

They say Mitchell was wrong about the Shendoah,[2] they had an entire investigation to find out about the Shenandoah, and dident find out what it was, but still they say Mitchell is wrong,

Coolidge says I had nothing to do with the Mitchell investigation,[3] Oh No, No more than I had any idea of being here tonight, I just happened to be passing through town and saw this Place and come in, it was such a suprise when I saw you allhere, No more than the kaiser had to do with the War,

Say the heads of any deprtment in Washington cant change shirts till Cal gives em the high sign, He makes out their Menus.

If Mitchell had been a private and said the same thing he would have bee[n] considerd effiminate,

The Navy has a Slogan, "Watch your Testimony if you want to stay in the Navy".

OUR NEXT WAR WILL BE FOUGHT IN AN INVESTIGATING ROOM.

We cant have another branch, The Secretaries we have are changed so fast ~~w~~ they have all never met each other.

TD.[4] OkClaW, Will Rogers, Jr., Collection, Miscellaneous Original Writings, Folder 8.

1. Colonel Billy Mitchell stood trial for court-martial on charges stemming from his public criticism of the Departments of Navy and War. Relieved of duty, he attempted to use the trial, which lasted from 28 October to 17 December 1925, to air his views. The court returned a verdict of guilty and levied a sentence of five years' suspension. He resigned from the army on 1 February 1926 (*DAB*, Supp. 2:461; Levine, *Mitchell*, 342, 370).

2. The *Shenandoah*, a U.S. navy dirigible, crashed on 3 September 1925 in the midst of severe storms over the Ohio River valley. Forty-three airmen perished. The widow of the commander soon after leveled charges that the men had been forced to fly in inclement weather because of political pressures. Mitchell and others criticized the flight, while the secretary of the navy claimed that the disaster proved that the country was safe from an air attack (Levine, *Mitchell*, 324–25).

3. The judge advocate stated at the start of Mitchell's trial that President Coolidge had ordered the court-martial. A newspaper headline declared, "Coolidge Revealed as Actual Accuser of Mitchell" (Levine, *Mitchell*, 346, 349).

4. Dating and place of origin of the document were determined by historical references in the text and Rogers's known chronology at the time (see Chronology, 1923–25, OkClaW).

Telegram to George H. Lorimer
27 January 1926
Daytona Beach, Fla.

PA74 80 BLUE

CLARENDON HOTEL DAYTONABEACH FLO JAN 27/26

MR LORIMER

EDITOR SATURDAY EVENING POST[1] PHILADELPHIA PA

LIFE NOT FINISHED YET[2] MUST SEE FLORIDA HOWEVER THE LONGER I LIVE
THE MORE LIFE YOU GET ALL AT ORIGINAL PRICE I HAVE NO OTHER THINGS
WOULD LIKE TO SPOIL TWO ISSUE WITH ONE CALLED FLORIDA VERSUS CALI-
FORNIA WHERE THEY BOTH LOSE AND OKLAHOMA WINS IT IS ALLEGED TO BE
HUMOROUS AND THE OTHER ONE IS CALLED THE SOUTH IS EATING AT THE
FIRST TABLE AGAIN[3] WHAT DO YOU THINK OF THESE[4] ADDRESS NEXT FEW DAYS
KING COLE HOTEL MIAMI

WILL ROGERS

115P

TG, rc. DLC-MD, Wesley Stout Papers. On Postal Telegraph–Commercial Cables letterhead.

1. The venerable *Saturday Evening Post* flourished during the long tenure of editor George Lorimer. The mass-market, general-interest periodical rose in circulation from 2,000 in 1897 to an average of more than 2.4 million in the 1920s. The weekly magazine dominated its market and recorded unprecedented earnings (Cohn, *Creating America*, 4–8, 165; Mott, *History*, 4:696).
2. Lorimer earlier had asked Rogers to write his memoirs for publication in the *Post*, but the effort never progressed beyond a few words. Years later, when Lorimer visited Will and Betty Blake Rogers in California and again asked for his life story, Rogers replied, "How can I write my life? I haven't lived it yet. I've got too much life to live before I do my memoirs" (Yagoda, *Will Rogers*, 217; Rogers, *Will Rogers*, 22).
3. The *Saturday Evening Post* published two articles by Rogers in the spring of 1926. The first, "My Rope and Gum for a Democratic Issue," ran in the 1 May edition, and the second, "Florida versus California," four weeks later (for the articles see *HTBF*, 13–39). The magazine did not publish a piece by Rogers about the South, although Rogers again mentioned such an article as late as October 1926 (see Letter to George H. Lorimer, ca. 27 October 1926, below), and a manuscript titled "South," complete with editor's marks, was found in his papers (see Manuscript for Magazine or Newspaper Article, ca. 1926, below).
4. George Lorimer wired Rogers to proceed, but to "REMEMBER THAT I AM STARTING FOR CALIFORNIA NOW AND MAY HAVE TO VISIT FLORIDA NEXT YEAR PLAY UP OKLAHOMA STRONG" (telegram, Lorimer to Rogers, 28 January 1926, OkClaW).

To John W. Harreld
8 February 1926
Greenville, S.C.

GREENVILLE, S. C., February 8, 1926.

DEAR SENATOR:[1]

I certainly was glad to hear of the bill you introduced,[2] and hope you will be able to put it through.

Now, I certainly want to do anything I can to help the old home town. How is it getting along? Who is against it that I might be able to write to and try to convince? Anything you would like to have me do, just let me know.[3]

Permanent address in care of my manager, Charles L. Wagner, 511 Fifth Avenue, New York.

Best regards.

Sincerely,

WILL ROGERS.

PD.[4] Printed in U.S. Senate, *Construction*, 31.

1. John William Harreld (1872–1950), an attorney and oil producer, served as a U.S. senator from Oklahoma from 1921 to 1927 (*BDUSCong*, 1137).

2. Harreld, a Republican and the chairman of the Senate Committee on Indian Affairs, co-sponsored legislation in late 1925 to build a hospital in Claremore, Okla., to be operated by the Department of the Interior for Indians from throughout the United States. The facility would include baths using the medicinal-quality water available in Claremore. Harreld's bill was not passed in that session, but Congress eventually appropriated $85,000 to construct a forty-five-bed hospital. Opened in 1929, the facility was razed in the 1970s and replaced with a larger unit (U.S. Senate, *Construction*, 1–2; Steve Barse to editors, 18 July 2003; *TDW,* 2 March 1975).

3. For Rogers's promotion of the legislation see "Worst Story I Have Heard Today," 20 April 1926, OkClaW.

4. Rogers's letter was introduced with other supporting correspondence during a hearing of the Senate Committee on Indian Affairs on 18 March 1926. The other endorsements came from tribal and government officials and medical professionals (U.S. Senate, *Construction*, 5–31).

Telegram to Carl Stearns Clancy
1 March 1926
Ogden, Utah

KHA259 53 NL

UD OGDEN UTAH 1

CARL CLANCY[1]

118 WEST 48 ST NEWYORK NY

PLEASE DONT PROMOTE ANYTHING IN CONNECTION WITH ME I WILL NEVER GET DONE MEETING PEOPLE THAT HAD STOCK IN THE OTHER ONE GO TO WORK CLANCY AND QUIT DREAMING IF I DID MEET ANYBODY IN ENGLAND YOU DONT SUPPOSE THEY WOULD WANT MOVIES TAKEN OF IT[2] BEST REGARDS HOWEVER TO YOU AND HAM

WILL ROGERS.

TG, rc. CSC-GKC. On Western Union Telegraph Co. letterhead. Metered below the letterhead, right side: "1926 MAR 1 PM 10 41." Handwritten in the bottom right margin: "Nevertheless I persisted & in July my cameraman & I met Will in London & made 10 single reel travel reels[3] with him in Ireland England Holland Germany Switzerland France & on the Leviathan[4] —to our great mutual profit."

1. Carl Stearns Clancy, motion picture producer and scenarist, worked with Rogers on the movie *The Headless Horseman* in late 1922. He produced the film and also provided the adaptation. Clancy contributed to three other feature films in the 1920s and later became a motion picture director for the U.S. Forest Service (Yagoda, *Will Rogers*, 191–92; *AFIC*, F1FE:940, F2FE:7, 330, 536; *CB*, 397).

2. The idea that he would spend the summer of 1926 in Europe either had already occurred to Rogers or was planted by Clancy or another party. No matter the inspiration, Clancy approached Rogers with the idea of a series of film travelogues starring the Cowboy Philosopher as he toured abroad. Clancy continued to pursue the concept, and eventually Rogers relented (see Terms of Payment for Travelogues, 22 April 1926, and Advertisement in *Exhibitor's Herald*, 5 March 1927, below).

3. Clancy produced twelve one-reel travelogues in syndication with partners in New York and Chicago. The travel comedies featuring Rogers were originally copyrighted and distributed by Pathé Exchange, with which Clancy had business ties and to which he eventually assigned the contract. Rogers was credited as writer of each film's subtitles (extension of contract, C. S. Clancy Production Syndicate, 21 December 1926, CSC-GKC; *WRHolly*, 85–96). See also Cablegram from Sailing W. Baruch, 23 June 1926, below.

4. Rogers sailed to and from Europe aboard the *Leviathan*, a premier ocean liner of the day. The ship originally sailed under the German flag as the *Vaterland*, but it was seized by the United States during the war and then was returned to service by its American owners as the *Leviathan* (*OCSS*, 477). See also Notes for Stage Appearance aboard S.S. *Leviathan*, ca. 6 May 1926, below.

Notes for Lecture Tour Appearance at Carnegie Hall
11 April 1926
New York, N.Y.

I just want to come out and have chat with you, a lot of old friends that I havent seen for almost a year, Hows it been with you anyway, I never thought we would meet in Carnegie Hall,[1] I am just as much out of place here as you are,

This thing was dedicated to Art, and to an audience that undrrstood Art, so we are both equally desecrating the Joint,

There has been a great lot of us great men spoke inhere, most of the biggest ones spoke free,

I was going to speak free   then I thought I better nake [make] a small charge to keep out an undesirable element, They think you aint any good if you do it for nothing,

This [is] a great place   Zeigfeld dont know where it is, It and the meseum o[f] Art, and the Library   That Follies audienc ehink [think] they are   secret Fraternity buildings,

Zeigfled wouldent understand my Lecture in a place like this. He would be looking for me to spring a joke on An Penningtons knees,[2] or is Dillingham going to crab my Follies with his sunny[3] all summer,

Its a different enviroment altogeather, I dont know how I ever remained among all that smoke and ~~unclothed~~ uncovered flesh   it s fuuny how long it takes one to see the light so etime,

Even Delligham Intellectualy would be lost at one of my discourses now   I wo nder sometime how I could ever have been so crude, and blu Mange [?], But ltes [lets] hie ourselvs away and see what has transpire   since my uplift of the Provinces,

Jimmy has been made Mayor,[4] That was good news to me, We have met behind many a Speakers Table, He always sit next to me when possible, and get my Cocktail. He was the most versatile man I ever sqaw in my life, No mater what the Dinner whether it be Jew, Catholic, Klu Klux. Senagambia[n,] Polok, or just plain Ticket Speculatirs why Jimmy always brought them t[o] their feet with the announcement that he was one of their race and that up at Albany the whole Legislature had been against them and that is [if] it hadent ben for ghim they would have been sent out of the Country as undesiravble Aelians, Jimmy is truly a Cosmopolitan, I have seen him weep at the plight of the Hebrews in Russia, Meet him the next night at a Friendly Sons of Saint Patrick.) Apparently Friendly) and he resposd [responds] to the Taost "Down wuth the Jew   he is seeking his own Political machine in New York City. I predict Jimmy will be the best Mayor New York ever had, he can promise the drys enough that they are satisfied, and still liberal minded enough that he wont be thought out of palce ~~at~~ among New York other 90 percent.

New York needs liberality and Jimi is the right man at the right place   He believes in the Political Machine, that"is *always leave the victim enough to get home on*"   Tammany never took a mans last Dollar,

They always figured with that he would earn another stake and soon be ready for them again.

And by the way what become of Red Mike, I hated to see him lose   I always like Mr Hyland, He was a good man , an honest man, I knew he was out of place in New York. I hope he has got into a legitimate business[5]

What else has happened, What has Al decided to do, Yes I know in 28 but I mean now   what he do till then, Too bad to waste a good man like like that on Govenor   States have gotten so almost anuyhing can be Gov, I had a serious offer from Oklahoma while down there, But I hushed it up soon as possible, for those things are very detrimental to a promising career.

I have felt out the entire Country on Al['s] chances, I have talked to every prominent politician and Gov in ever Capitol I have Played and I want to tell you that Al has the best chance of any Democrat, now you can figure that out yourself, Some have suggested that he would be elected if he changed his religion, and turned Protestant, I think it would do more good if he would keep his religion but turn Repiblican   They willput up a little holler for awhile aboyut his being wet and a Catholic, but those old Southerners are not so religious that they will vote for a Republican, They will tutn Aethist before that,

MUNSEY dyinf [dying][6]   No more Consolidation,

Irving and Helen[7] got married since I left, It would be agood joke on Her Father[8] if he made her aliving wouldent it.

That will be a big Boost for Inter--allied marriages,

I used to go with alittle Rifkie.

The Bath Tub, I read that while I was playing Tia Jauna Mex, znd [and] it shocked them todaeth [to death].

Earl[9] always struck me as nit [not] being the kind of boy that would tolerate anything like that.

I was in Kansas City trying to keep them ~~fro~~ normal while Marion Talley[10] Had otto[11] and gatti[12] by the aers [ears?],

I have been blazing the trail for Abies Irish Rose,[13]

I found George Whites Scandals[14] playing Cleremore Omlahoma,

I am the obly [only] person ever outdrew Abies Irsih Rose at Tulzsa Oklayoma,

Nwew Yorl means nothing to us, Its just another stop,

We are the only ones that ever made a one Night stand out of New York

We finally got this burg right, Thats what its good for is one night, Tulsa two nights New York one   thats the right ratio,

You mean nothing in our young lives, ~~We dident even get a shine~~ Talk about brughtening up the show and regersing [rehearsing] for New York   we dident even get a shine for this

We dident know where we were going to play till we got here, We thought it would naturally be in the Civic Auditorum,

And as for what the Critics say, We travel so fast it dont make any difference what the critics say,

We leave atown immediately after the show and go just as far as we can away from there by the next night so if a Critic wants to take his spite out on us ; There is nobody left there toread it but himself and that takes all the joy away from cricitising.

In fact we have been in most of the ~~homes~~ ▲Towns▲ whre they raise these Critics, Some of them come from smaller places than I did,

I dont care where [y]ou live　　we haveplayed your twon [town], If it only has 50 people in it I have enlightened 5 of them,

This is about one of the smaleest places we ever played in, The smaller the Town the bigger the Auditorium, They some of them just fence in 80 acres with a Bob [barbed] Wire fence and call it an Auditorium,

I have been in places that I couldent have shot the fellow in the bach row with a 300 30 even if they had been a feloow therem [fellow there.]

I always bunched them up, If there was 5 here and 8 there and I0 there *[text ends at bottom of page; no continuation found]*

TD. OkClaW, 1975.23.0032. Typewritten, top margin, flush left, page 1: "*Can Use in the New York act at Carnegie Hall.*" Typewritten, top margin, center, page 2: "For Carnegie Hall Act. New York (page (2)". Hand-inserted vertical lines appear in the left margin immediately adjacent to paragraphs 2, 3, 4, 7, 9, 10.

1. For an account by Rogers of his experiences at Carnegie Hall see *WA*, 2:188–90.

2. Ann Pennington (Penny or Tiny, 1894–1971), vivacious American dancer with famous dimpled knees, starred in several *Ziegfeld Follies* beginning in 1913, and in numerous other Broadway musical productions (*NYT*, 5 November 1971; Ziegfeld and Ziegfeld, *Ziegfeld Touch*, 308; Goldman, *Banjo Eyes*, 70). For Rogers's reminiscences of Pennington and her knees, see *WA*, 4:136.

3. *Sunny*, a musical comedy produced by Charles Dillingham, opened at the New Amsterdam Theatre on 22 September 1925, three days after the close of the *Ziegfeld Follies*. It enjoyed a successful run of nearly sixteen months (*CAMT*, 417; Ziegfeld and Ziegfeld, *Ziegfeld Touch*, 260).

4. Jimmy Walker was elected mayor of New York in 1925 with the strong backing of Tammany Hall. The popular, wisecracking Democrat remained in office until his resignation in 1932 (*DAB*, Supp. 4:855–56).

5. Hylan, although praised for his honesty, had been regarded as ill equipped to be chief executive of the nation's largest city. After his loss of the mayoralty in 1925, he returned to his law practice and eventually became a judge in a local children's court (*DAB*, Supp. 2:331).

6. Frank Andrew Munsey (1854–1925) was a highly successful publisher of magazines, including an eponymous title that once boasted the largest circulation and earnings in the world. A frequent buyer and seller of newspapers and magazines, he became known as "a dealer in dailies." Munsey died in December 1925 (*DAB*, 13:334–35).

7. Irving Berlin (Israel Baline, 1888–1989), popular Russian-born American songwriter, provided songs and composed full scores for many Broadway musicals and revues, including several editions of the *Ziegfeld Follies*. The marriage in January 1926 of Berlin, an Orthodox Jew, and Ellin Mackay (1903–88), a Roman Catholic, short-story writer, and daughter of a multimillionaire businessman, caused a great sensation in social and religious circles at the time (*EMT*, 1:111–12; *NYT*, 30 July 1980; Cantor, *Take My Life*, 75).

8. Clarence Hungerford Mackay (1874–1938), heir to a vast fortune derived from the telegraph and mining industries, was a successful businessman in his own right

and a Catholic lay leader. His daughter's marriage to Berlin so angered him that he threatened to disinherit her. They later reconciled (*NYT*, 13 November 1938, 30 July 1988; *DAB*, Supp. 2:415–16).

9. Earl Carroll (1893–1948), colorful American theatrical producer and director, wrote several musical hits and staged Broadway "girlie" revues, including the *Earl Carroll Vanities*, an almost annual series from 1923 to 1932 (*EPM*, 2:954–55).

10. Marion Talley (1907–83), a soprano from Kansas City, Mo., created a sensation among opera lovers with her work in an amateur production at the age of fifteen and in an audition at the Metropolitan in New York the next year. She made her debut at the Met as Gilda in *Rigoletto* on 17 February 1926. Although disappointing to critics, her performance drew enormous publicity throughout the country (*NGDO*, 4:638; Gatti-Casazza, *Memories*, 217–18).

11. That is, Otto Kahn, chairman of the Metropolitan Opera Company.

12. Giulio Gatti-Casazza (1869–1940), a distinguished Italian impresario of opera, served as general manager of the Metropolitan from 1910 to 1935. He was recognized as a discoverer and promoter of American operatic talent (*DAB*, Supp. 2:222–23).

13. *Abie's Irish Rose*, a three-act comedy about a marriage between a Jew and a Catholic, opened at the Fulton Theatre in New York on 23 May 1922 and ran for 2,327 performances, lasting five and a half years. The longest-lived Broadway show of its day, the sentimental farce also enjoyed success on the road (*ENYS*, 1:3–4; *OCAT*, 5).

14. George White (George Wietz, 1890–1968), versatile show business figure, produced the first *George White's Scandals* in 1919. A Broadway revue featuring popular American music, fast-paced comedy sketches, and beautiful chorus girls, *Scandals* was staged annually through 1926. That year's edition set a record for performances and introduced such notable numbers as Ann Pennington performing "Black Bottom" (*EPM*, 5797).

New York State Income Tax Statement
ca. 15 April 1926
(New York, N.Y.)

		From sources within N.Y. State
Income:		
Ziegfeld Follies, N.Y.C.	$115,087.50	$115,087.50
McNaught Syndicate, Times Bldg., N.Y.C.[1]	19,500.00	
A.& C. Boni, 39 W. 8 St., N.Y.C.[2]	7,379.68	
H.W. Kastor & Sons, 22 W. 48 St. N.Y.C.[3]	18,500.00	
C.L. Wagner, 511 5th Ave., N.Y.C. Concert-lecture tour – 70 Appearances – 4 in N.Y. State (5.71%)	75,000.00	4,282.50
	$235,467.18	$119,370.00

Expenses connected with income from
sources within N.Y. State

Entertaining & Publicity expense		$21,060.31	
Wardrobe and equipment		3,006.29	
Living expense in N.Y. for 10 mos. while with Ziegfeld Follies – residence maintained in California		20,522.05	
Horses used mainly for publicity and entertaining purposes:			
Depreciation (Cost $18,000 at 20%)	$3,600.00		
Salary of groom	1,200.00		
Upkeep, transportation, etc.	17,207.19	22,007.19	
Auto maintenance & expense:			
Depreciation (Cost $5,600 at 25%)	$1,400.00		
Upkeep	1,634.98		
	$3,034.98		
Two-thirds for business use		2,023.32	
Commissions paid		1,750.00	
5.71% of traveling expense on tour – C.L. Wagner – (3890)		222.12	
Salaries for secretarial-clerical assistants, etc.		6,209.75	
Contributions (statement attached)		5,784.00	82,585.03
			$36,784.97

Schedule "A"

Rent $ 1.078.12   Taxpayer deducted 421.88 whereas he should have properly deducted $ 1,500.00 which represents a portion of the rent of his home in Beverly Hills California or $ 12,000.00. As the taxpaper [*sic*] used several of the rooms for business purposes, - one-eighth of the total rent of $ 12,000.00 or $ 1,500.00 as been allowed.

Cost of films $ 2,760.00   In making this return the taxpayer overlooked the fact that the cost of the actual film should be deducted. This cost is as follows:

8000 feet of film @ 4½¢ per foot			$ 360.00
8000 feet of film @ 3¢ per foot	developed		240.00
8000 feet of film @2	per foot	printed	160.00
Services of camerman			1,200.00
Negatives bought developed "N.G."			800.00
		Total	$2,760.00

This expense was incurred in the production of the "Illiterate Digest" a "weekly".[4] Taxpayer has given his affadvait with reference to the item cost of film ~~as~~ ~~his~~ $ 2,760.00 as his records are lost.[5]

Schedule "B".

Expenditures	As reported	Corrected	Difference
Makeup	$ 50.00	$ 50.00	
Costumes	700.00	3,933.13	3233.13
Laundry and cleaning	200.00	200.00	
Advertising-Railroad fares travel enetertaining etc	5,000.00	10,160.80	5160.80
Horses and upkeep	3,000.00	3,950.00	950.00
Grooms-riders etc	1,800.00		1800.00
Horses killed	800.00	1,350.00	450.00
Hospital – vetinary	250.00	250.00	
Telephone and telegraph	150.00	150.00	
Automobile expense ½ half charged to business	2,000.00	3,330.05	1330.05
Attorney fees	150.00	150.00	
Cowboys and riders		3,225.85	3225.85
	14,100.00	26.649.83	12,549.83
Net income as reported	$ 125.025.00		
as corrected	112.475.17		
	$ 12,549.83		

Expensitures [*sic*]   difference

Costumes $ 3,233.13   Taxpayer failed to include all expenses in correction with wardrobe   which as been incurred as above

Travel, magazines, entertained etc $ 5,160.80 as follows:

Trips to New York	$ 3,595.80
Photographs	1,000.00
Magazines etc	365.00
Entertaining	5,200.00
Previously deducted	$10,160.80
	5,000.00
Difference	$ 5,160.80

On the item of trips to New York $ 3,595.80 and entertaining of $ 5,200.00 which the taxpayer has no record of   it has been necessary to get his affadavit which fully explains these expenses. The taxpayer made three round trips from Los Angeles to New York for business purposes and did considerable entertaining as indicated

Horses and upkeep   - $ 950.00. The taxpayer also fully explains this item stating that $ 2,750.00 is for grooms and upkeep such as feed etc and $ 1,250.00 for depreciation or 25% of $ 5,000.00 the cost of the horses. These horses due to hard usage will not last more than four years as also indicated in affadavit attached.

Grooms – riders etc included in above item.

Horses killed in stunts ($450.00) . This represents cost of horses killed in stunts and roping acts. Taxpayer understated this amount as indicated. No insurance on these horses.

Auto expense $ 1,330.05. Depreciation on automobile used. A Acquired 1919 Cost $ 6,000.00 Rate 25%. Total depreciation $ 1,500.00 one half allowance for business.

The balance of this item of $ 3,330.05 or $ 2,580.05 represents half the upkeep of the car such as repairs, gas oil etc.

Cowboys and riders $ 3,225.85   This is salarys paid to cowboys and particularly clever riders

Explanation of items changed

unchanged

Schedule "A"   "Illiterate Digest" Rogers Cartoons.

	As reported	As corrected	Difference
Sales	$ 10,650.00	$ 10,650.00	None
Salaries	$ 9,050.00	$ 9,050.00	
Rent	421.88	1,500.00	plus 1,o78.12
Other expense	465.00	465.00	
Cost of films		2,760.00	plus 2760.00
Total	$ 9,936.88	$ 13,775.00	plus 3,838.12
Net Income	713.12	(3,125.00)	plus 3,838.12
Other expense			
Stenographers	$ 100.00	$ 100.00	
Telephone-telegraph	365.00	365.00	
	$ 465.00	$ 465.00	

Schedule "E"
Income from rents.

	As reported	As corrected	Difference
Receipts	$ 3,400.00	$ 3,460.00	
Repairs	500.00	500.00	
Depreciation	752.00	920.00	168.00
Taxes	1,200.00	1,200.00	
Commissions	750.00	750.00	
Total	3,202.00	$ 3,370.00	168.00
Net income	258.00	90.00	- 168.00

As reported

Depreciations	Date	Cost	Rate	Amt. ded.
Frame house	1903	2,400.00	3%	$72.00
Garage and th atre	1903	25,000.00	2%	500.00
Barn and farm house	1903	4,000.00	3%	120.00
" "	1920	2,000.00	3%	60.00
				752.00

As corrected

Depreciations			Rate	Amt. ded.
Frame House			5%	120.00
Garage and theatre			2%	500.00
Barn and farm house			5%	200.00
" "			5%	100.00
				920.00

Schedule "K" Deductions

Interest	700.00	700.00	
Bad debts	1,500.00	500.00	$ 1,000.00
Taxes	933.00	933.00	
Total	3,133.00	2,133.00	$ 1,000.00

Contributions

Episcopal Church Pasadena	$ 200.00
Hoover Fund	550.00
Bpy [*sic*] Scouts	100.00
Crippled Children	100.00
Los Angeles Orthapedic	100.00
McKinley Home	25.00
Red Cross	500.00
Mutual Aid Union	425.00
	$ 2,000.00

Schedule "K"

Bad Debts $ 1,000.00   This is not a bad debt but is for the services of an appraiser to look into the value of certain property which Mr. Rogers was interested in, and is therefor addition cost of such property and has been disallowed as a deduction.

TD. OkClaW, Income Tax Documents, 1922–25. Typewritten on first page, centered and stacked (/): "*Schedule attached to New York / State Income Tax Return - 1925 / Will Rogers.*" Handwritten to the immediate right of "19,500.00" figure under Income from McNaught Syndicate: "- 1 of 2".

1. McNaught syndicated Rogers's newspaper articles.

2. Rogers's income from Boni represented his first full year of royalties from sales of his third book, *The Illiterate Digest*. A. & C. Boni published two further books by Rogers, *Letters of a Self-Made Diplomat to His President* (1926) and *There's Not a Bathing Suit in Russia* (1927).

3. H. W. Kastor & Sons, an advertising firm, represented Bull Durham smoking tobacco for the American Tobacco Company (W. L. Chesman to Will Rogers, 19 November 1924, OkClaW).

4. For Rogers's production of *The Illiterate Digest,* see Letter of Agreement with Marion H. Kohn, 18 February 1920, and Screen Subtitles for *The Illiterate Digest,* ca. 31 March 1920, above.

5. Rogers filed a deposition with the Internal Revenue Bureau in early January 1925 affirming the production costs of *The Illiterate Digest* (OkClaW, 1975.24.0202).

Manuscript for Newspaper Column
ca. 15 April 1926
[Philadelphia, Pa.?]

This is not a worrst story, Its a good story about a little woman that all the older generation remember, She was the reigning sensation of America and Europe during all the hey day of Buffalo Bills   Wild West Show,[1] ᴵᵗ ▲[*type-written:*]She▲ was their Star, Her Picture was on more Billboards than a modern Gloria Swanson,[2] It was Annie Oakley,[3] The greatest Woman Rifle shot the world has ever produced, Nobody took her place, There was only one, I went out to see her the other day as I was playing in Dayton Ohio,[4] She lives there with her ~~sister, and~~ Husband, Frank Butler,[5] and her sister,[6] Her hair is snow white, she is bedridden   from an Auto accident a few years ago, What a wonderful christian character she is, ~~Did you know that one time there was a woman of the streets arrested in Chicago, and she gave the name of Annie Oakley, and lots of papers published the story, for her name was the best known in America at that time, well she is collecting judgeemnets yet from apapers papers that used the story, Why the whole world rose up in arms to testify in her behalf,~~ I have talked with Buffalo Bill Cowboys who were with the show for years and they worshiped her, ~~She holds one of~~ ▲ᵀᴴᴱ ᴼᴺᴸʸ▲ ~~two judgements against a very large and influential publisher in the whole history of court trials. shows you how she must have stood,~~ She for years taught the fashionable people at Pinehurst N C to shoot,[7] America is worshiping at the feet of Raquel Meller the Spanish Lady,[8] Europe talked the same of Annie Oakley in her day, and she reigned for many a year, I want you to write her all of you who remember her, and those that can go see her, ~~She will be a lesson to you, She is a greater character than she was a rifle shot,~~ her address is ~~Annie Oakley,~~ 706, Lexington Ave. Dayton, Ohio. She will be a lesson to you, She is a greater character than she was a Rifle shot. ~~The open air end of the amusement world has always been able to have not only a higher moral standing than its sister the stage, but higher than any other profession there is,~~ Circuses have produced the cleanest living class of people in ~~th~~ America today and Annie Oakleys name, her lovable traits, her thoughtful consideration of others, will live as a mark for any woman to shoot at.

TM.[9] OkClaW, Worst Story file. Editorial marks appear throughout the document but have been ignored in this transcription. Double strike-through indicates hand-deleted text; single strike-through indicates type-deleted copy. Interlineations were handwritten, unless otherwise noted. Handwritten at the bottom of the page: "Copyright etc".

1. For William F. (Buffalo Bill) Cody see *PWR*, 1:487–88.

2. Gloria Swanson (Gloria Josephine MacSwenson, 1897–1983) began her film acting career in 1913 as an extra but by the mid-1920s had risen to the heights of silent screen stardom. A reigning queen of motion pictures, she captured considerable press attention, perhaps most notably after her return from a trip abroad in 1925 as the new wife of a marquis (*FE*, 1320–21).

3. Annie Oakley (Phoebe Ann Oakley Moses or Mosey or Mozee, 1860–1926) enjoyed a successful stage and Wild West show career as a markswoman. A remarkable trick shooter, she could knock a cigarette from a person's lips or strike a coin tossed in the air. Rogers's tribute to Oakley brought her hundreds of letters of reminiscences and best wishes. She died slightly more than six months later (*NEAW*, 808; Riley, *Life*, 1, 21; *NYT*, 5 November 1926; Kasper, *Annie Oakley*, 240). For Rogers's remarks upon the life and death of Annie Oakley, see *WA*, 2:272, as well as his foreword in Cooper, *Annie Oakley*.

4. The exact date of Rogers's visit with Annie Oakley in Dayton in 1926 was not determined, but it may have occurred on 8 April. He arrived in Huntington, W.Va., on 9 April for a lecture tour appearance. A local newspaper reported the next day that he had traveled by train to Huntington, having left Dayton on the ninth at about eight o'clock in the morning. Rogers may have performed in the Ohio city in the evening of 8 April and may have found time before the lecture appearance to visit Oakley (clipping, *HA*, 10 April 1926, Scrapbook 8, Part 2, OkClaW).

5. Frank E. Butler (ca. 1850–1926) was a noted professional marksman appearing at an Ohio theater when the much younger Oakley beat him in a shooting contest. The encounter led to their marriage and helped launch her career. He became her promoter and manager. Butler survived his wife by less than three weeks (Riley, *Life*, 15–26; Kasper, *Annie Oakley*, 24, 241).

6. At the time of Rogers's visit, Oakley and Butler lived in a house on Lexington Avenue in Dayton, where Irene, the daughter of Oakley's half-sister, Emily Brumbaugh Patterson, provided nursing care for Annie (Kasper, *Annie Oakley*, 234, 238; Riley, *Life*, 198).

7. The Butlers spent several winter seasons at Pinehurst, a resort community in North Carolina that by the early 1900s had become a favorite haven for well-to-do northerners. They stayed at the Carolina, the most fashionable hotel in the village, and paid their expenses by teaching at a local gun club (Kasper, *Annie Oakley*, 203–6).

8. Raquel Meller (Francisca Marques Lopez, ca. 1888–1962) was a Spanish singer who had become a favorite music hall performer in Europe by 1923 and then embarked on a much publicized visit to the United States in 1926. She arrived in New York on 5 April and made her debut on Broadway nine days later in a ballyhooed performance that commanded one of the highest ticket prices ever before charged (*NYT*, 9, 14 April 1926, 27 July 1962).

9. The dating of the manuscript was based on the approximate date of Rogers's visit with Oakley and chronological references in the draft. The item was published in *TDW*, 30 April 1926.

Advertisement for Rogers's single-reel travelogue series. Produced by Carl Stearns Clancy, the first of twelve film guides to Europe appeared on screen in the spring of 1927. (*OkClaW*)

Terms of Payment for Travelogues
22 April 1926
New York, N.Y.

(Confidential Memo.)

ASTOR HOTEL APRIL 22, '26

Terms of Payment for Will Rogers work in the series of 26 single-reel travel comedies to be made in Europe this summer and to be called A B R O A D W I T H W I L L R O G E R S As requested by Mr.Rogers and agreed to by Mr.C.S.Clancy this date.[1]

$20,000 to be deposited to Mr.Rogers' account in the East River Nat'l Bank, 41st St. and Broadway before production work starts.

$1,500 a week to be deposited to Mr.Rogers's account in the same bank each week for ten weeks during production work.

(making a total of $35,000 for ten weeks or $3,500 per week.)

Additional weeks, if any, to be paid for at the rate of $2,500 a week.

IMPORTANT NOTE: On account of the lowness of the above terms, which are less than half his usual ones, Mr. Rogers wishes them to be kept *strictly confidential.*

He wants it distinctly understood that if it were not for his commission from the Saturday Evening Post,[2] which enables him to earn between $4,000 and $5,000 a week by writing his articles evenings, he could not be hired for this work for less than $7,000 a week.

C. S. Clancy

TDS, cy. CSC-GKC.

1. See Telegram to Carl Stearns Clancy, 1 March 1926, above. See also Cablegram from Sailing W. Baruch, 23 June 1926, and Advertisement in *Exhibitor's Herald,* 5 March 1927, below.
2. Rogers and George Lorimer of the *Saturday Evening Post* met for lunch in Philadelphia on 15 April. The two men probably discussed Rogers's forthcoming trip to Europe and agreed at the time that Rogers would provide the *Post* with a series of articles about his experiences and observations as he toured the continent (Yagoda, *Will Rogers,* 228). See also Telegram to George H. Lorimer, 26 April 1926, below.

Telegram to George H. Lorimer
26 April 1926
New York, N.Y.

As his sailing date of 1 May quickly approached, Rogers hastened to contact and visit several well-connected friends and acquaintances, requesting letters of recommendation and credentials that would open doors and borders.[1] The following wire, conveyed in his usual self-effacing style of humor, shows his sense of urgency and his thoroughness.

NF185 75 NL

NEWYORK NY 25

G H LARRIMER

SATURDAY EVENING POST PHILADELPHIA PENN

MAY BE THERE AROUND NOON TO SEE YOU AM ALL HEADED FOR ITALY SATURDAY FOR THE SATURDAY EVENING POST AND WANT YOU TO DIG ME UP EVERYTHING YOU HAVE IN THE WAY OF A CREDENTIAL EVEN DOWN TO YOUR MARRIAGE CERTIFICATE AM GOING DOWN TO WASHINGTON AND EVEN TRY TO GET SOMETHING FROM CALVIN AND CONGRESSMAN UPSHAW[2] I WILL TELL THEM IN ITALY I AM A FRIEND OF SAM BLYTE[3]

WILL ROGERS.

TG, rc. DLC-MD, Wesley Stout Papers. On Western Union Telegraph Co. letterhead. Imprinted immediately below the letterhead: "Received at Western Union Bldg., 230 So. 11th St., Philadelphia, Pa." Metered below the letterhead, right side: "1926 APR 26 AM 3   18." Metered immediately above the recipient's address: "3092."

1. Rogers solicited diplomatic assistance from an array of influential individuals, among whom were the vice president of the United States, the secretary of state, members of Congress from both sides of the aisle, a leading New York banker, a prominent Roman Catholic cleric, the publisher of the *New York Times*, and the speaker of the House of Representatives. In return Rogers received a flurry of useful papers, including letters of introduction from European ambassadors, statements of recommendation to heads of state, notes of instruction to expedite border crossings, and even invitations to visit rarely accessible official sites (see various documents, OkClaW).

2. William David Upshaw (1866–1952), a Democrat, served as a U.S. representative from Georgia from 1919 to 1927. A militant Christian evangelist and writer, Upshaw embraced the Ku Klux Klan, Prohibition, and Americanism (*BDUSCong*, 1969; *DAB*, Supp. 5:701–2). There was no evidence that Rogers asked Upshaw for credentials or a letter of introduction.

3. Samuel G. Blythe (1868–1947), a political writer, was Washington correspondent for the New York *World* for several years, and political columnist and writer for the *Saturday Evening Post* from 1907 until his retirement in 1921. Blythe continued to submit contributions to the *Post* well into the 1930s and remained one of editor

George Lorimer's closest associates (*NYT*, 19 July 1947; Cohn, *Creating America*, 177–79, 283–84).

Adolph S. Ochs to Whom It May Concern
28 April 1926
New York, N.Y.

April 28, 1926

TO WHOM IT MAY CONCERN:

Mr. Will Rogers, scholar and philosopher, and one of the most popular writers and entertainers in the United States, is making a tour of European capitals, and wishes contact with public men and those who are active in world affairs for his information and guidance in writing a series of articles for some leading publications, of which The New York Times is one. We commend him to your kind attention and courtesy.

There is no one in this country who has so large an audience as Mr. Rogers. He has the happy faculty of presenting complex public questions in such a way as to bring them within the comprehension and understanding of the general public, whose confidence and respect he enjoys to a marked degree.

Those who may have an opportunity of meeting Mr. Rogers will find pleasure and profit in his acquaintance.

Adolph S Ochs[1]

TLS, rc. OkClaW, 1975.17.0133. On The New York Times, Times Square, letterhead.

1. Adolph Simon Ochs (1858–1935) purchased the *New York Times* in 1896. As publisher he built the newspaper's circulation and finances while maintaining its editorial credibility. By 1925 the *Times* had become an institution and Ochs had begun to leave its operation to others (*ANB*, 16:597–98).

Notes for Stage Appearance aboard S.S. *Leviathan*
ca. 6 May 1926
En Route to Europe

We have a very distinguised gathering on here[1] going to Geneva, to hold a conference,[2] ~~this one is to~~ There is 21 nations to meet there to ~~draw up~~ hold a confereence to see if we they can hold a regular Conference, on dissarmamanet.

You see almost every Nation has about built up to the   last Conference   So they will have to have another meeting so they can lay out what th[ey] are allowed to build in the next few years in the way of disarming,

You see by dissarming,th   ~~longer a war lasts the~~ the less arms you have the longer the war lasts, what the wotld [world] realy seems to want is longer and better wars,

Well we can have one more conference but we cant have two, if we ever had two we would have to borro w boat to go to the seconf one,

We havethree men from the Army and three from the Navy, and ~~three~~   we would have sent three from the aviation but we couldent spare all our aviation at once, a war might comeup.

Then we have three from the Diplomatic service, It is headed by Mr Gibson, who is our Minister to Awitzerland,[3] a very charming man, If any of you are in Switzerland and get out of funds or lost I would suggest that you either Yodle or wear a feather in your cap and Mr Gibson will see to it that you are sent to America at once, Switzerland is the ~~only~~ Country you   have to go to when you want to say what you want to about the rest of Europe, Its the cussing box of Europ.

We have two very Charming Real Admirals, on here, Mr Hilary P Jones[4] and admiral Long,[5] They are making their first European trip, You have seen very littleof them on here as both have been seasick sincethey cone [come] on.

Captain Hartley[6] took them up on the Bridge today to show them the bridge of a ship.

They asked how he could see how to steer without the sun shinging, Admiral Long has never married, when he joined the navy as a young man they put him in command of a abota and sent him out   he had a sweetheart in that Poart, They told him you will have to run this Boat yourself, and in all these years he has never been able to get it back home again, So as a consequenevc he has to remain single,

We have

Capatin Andrews, of the Mayflower,[7] He is the man that is responsible for keeping Mr Coolidge in such wonderful physical condition. He just grabs the matflower like we would the Subway and coasts down the Potomac till the Democrats kinder get tired of cus ing him and here he comes back.

This is a ver unique Theatre, Its the only Theatre in either America or Europe that neither Marcus Loew or Lee Shubert or [are] not financially inter ted [interested] in,

And they are on here at that looking for a spot to open up one, Imagine Loew who is the main one in Metro Goldwyn Pictures ~~being~~ having to sit here every night and look at Universal Pictures.[8]

Shubert is going to Russia to get Al Jolson some new Mammy Songs. Loew is going ti Italy to get Mussiloni[9] to come to America and stand and let Annie Oakley shoot objects from his mouty [mouth] and head.

We have a Mr Tood ▲of Boston▲ the Shipbuilder[10] on here, He would have made the trip on one of his own boats but he has never bult one that could get any furthet away ftom New England than Providence,

Then we have Col Root,[11] of Boston, He is the one who led the so called singing at Lunch, Hecis the Mr Rodheaver[12] of the Leviathan,

When they heard him doing that today a great many people thought that singing aws [was] his business, But I want to state he dont live as poorly as that, He is from Boston and lives on tradition.

We have Mr Minot.[13] the all American Fo tball Star of I9 I0, Harvard teaches the best English and thd poorest football of any college in America,

Mr Cunningham from Autstrlia [Australia], a Sheep Herder, and you know what we think of Sheep Herders,

TD. OkClaW, 1975.14.0042. Handwritten, in Rogers's hand, top margin, center right, page 1: "CONCERT ON BOAT".

1. Rogers traveled to Europe aboard the 60,000-ton *Leviathan*, the largest passenger ship of its day. Originally christened the *Vaterland*, the liner had been seized by the United States from its German owners during the war and renamed. Rogers had sailed to Europe aboard the *Vaterland* in May 1914. On this trip he was accompanied by his eldest son, Bill. Other members of the family joined them in Europe in June (*OCSS*, 477; *NYT*, 10 May 1957; *LSMD*, 15; Rogers, *Will Rogers*, 188).

2. The Preparatory Commission for the Disarmament Conference met in Geneva, Switzerland, from June to November 1926 to lay the groundwork for what became the Geneva Conference of 1932. Sponsored by the League of Nations, the preliminary meeting in 1926 brought together army, naval, and air delegates from nineteen nations but resulted in scant progress toward arms limitation, especially of air power (*HD1920s*, 145; Ellis, *Republican*, 182–83; *NYT*, 8 June, 10 September 1926).

3. Hugh Simons Gibson (1883–1954), a career foreign service officer, served as U.S. ambassador to Switzerland from 1924 to 1927. While posted in Geneva, the headquarters of the League of Nations, Gibson participated in many efforts to reduce armaments, including the preliminary conference in 1926 (*NYT*, 13 December 1954).

4. Hilary Pollard Jones (1863–1938), a career naval officer, was named commander-in-chief of the U.S. Fleet in 1922. A year later, he joined the General Board of the navy and began to assume diplomatic functions, including as naval advisor to the international disarmament discussions in 1926 and 1927 (*DAB*, Supp. 2:351–52).

5. Andrew Theodore Long (1866–1946), a rear admiral since 1918, served on the General Board of the navy from 1924 until his retirement in 1930 (*NYT*, 23 May 1946; *WhAmer*, 2:328).

6. Herbert Hartley (ca. 1876–1957), a veteran skipper of American passenger liners, commanded the *Leviathan* from 1923 to 1928 (*NYT*, 10 May 1957).

7. Adolphus Andrews (1879–1948), a Texan and a career navy officer, commanded the presidential yacht *Mayflower* from 1922 to 1926. Although not always comfortable

on water, Coolidge often used the *Mayflower*, especially on weekends, to escape from the pressures and burdens of the presidency (*NatCAB*, 48:467–68; *NYT*, 20 June 1948; McCoy, *Calvin Coolidge*, 163).

8. Formed in 1912, Universal Pictures had become a major film studio by the mid-1920s and a principal rival of prestigious Metro-Goldwyn-Mayer Pictures Corporation (MGM), founded in 1924. Universal counted Rudolph Valentino among its stars (*FE*, 1396; *NHD*, 124–26).

9. Benito Mussolini (1883–1945), an aggressive nationalist and anticommunist, was named premier of Italy in October 1922. A leader of the fascist movement, he gradually transformed the government into a dictatorship and reorganized the state economy. Out of the troubled postwar period in Italy emerged order but at great cost to individual rights. He was overthrown and executed in 1945 (*HDFI*, 358–64).

10. William Henry Todd (1867–1932) was founder and first president of the Todd Shipyards Corporation, a major American shipbuilding firm with operations in several ports (*WhAmer*, 1:1244; *NYT*, 24 November 1940).

11. William Henry Root (ca. 1879–1937), who went by the title of colonel, was a principal in a prominent, family-owned contracting company in Boston (*NYT*, 25 December 1937).

12. Homer Rodeheaver (1880–1955), a self-described "musical missionary," spent twenty years as music director for evangelist Billy Sunday (*NYT*, 19 December 1955; *WhAmer*, 3:737).

13. Wayland Manning (Dono) Minot, a member of the Harvard University class of 1911, starred at fullback for the Crimson football team in 1909 and played left guard the next season. He was named an All-America player in 1909, a year Harvard lost only one game, to its traditional rival, Yale (Bealle, *History*, 186–92, 490, 538).

Notes for Speech at American Club
12 May 1926
London, England

Americans, Both Amateurs and Professionals, and you too Englishmen.

I suppose I should start out with the usual about how honored I am to have this Club[1] pay tribute to me, Well that would ~~a~~ be a lot of Apple Aauce. I am not honored I was just ~~conscripted.~~ drafted.

If I hadent seen a lot of dinners and see who they give them too why I would feel elated, But the class of honor guests at Dinners was never at such a low ebb as it is now. Its the hardest thing in the World nowadays to find out who to give a Dinner too,

They are generally given to give the the President a chance to get a speech off his chest,

I consider it more in the nature of a Scandal than a Honor.

All about Clubs.

About getting Passports.

French Debts.

Turkey will start a war for me if I can get I0 others to go in with me

Polgrims Society. Personally I have always felt it a missfortune that the Pilgrims dident ahev return tickets.

PROHIBITION.

I settled the Strike.[2] and wired Coolidge where will I go from here.

I wouldent have missed being here for a anything, the people on the Boat changing to Cherburg.[3]

ENGLAND HAS THE GREATEST STATESMEN AND THE POOREST COOFEE OF ANY NATIO[N] in the owrld, I just hate to see Morning come because I know i will have to drink some of that Coffee.

England hadent started to suffer yet   they still ~~had o~~ were able to wear their Spats.

If I wanted to stop England I would puncture their Bicycles,[4]

Stop their Tea and you will hit at the very vitals of the Englishman. The only dissorder I saw was in the house of Commons,[5] I understnad tha[t it] is populated by the lower middle classes, and they are the lowest classes there is, They are pretty near as low as the upper classes,

You have a great heritage, You might think that with all your taxes yo[u] are bad off, you are not   you have a great blessing   you have great people,

YOU ARE BULLHEADED BUT NEVER BONEHEADED?

JUST AS MANY WOULD HAVR GONE TOWAR ?

I Only hope that you will be a as big in victory as they have been in defeat,

---

TD. OkClaW, 1975.14.0044. Typewritten, top margin, center: "AT   AMERICAN CLUB DINNER IN LONDON."

1. The American Club, made up mostly of expatriate Americans working and living in England, was located on Piccadilly in London (*LSMD*, 42).

2. A congress of trade unions in Great Britain called a general strike on 4 May in sympathy with coal miners who had been locked out by mine owners. The work stoppage affected almost every industry and most public services. The government declared the strike unconstitutional and implemented emergency measures that served to blunt the workers' action. The trade unions surrendered on 12 May without achieving any worthwhile results; the coal miners remained on strike until November (*CCBH*, 332).

3. Upon reaching Europe, the *Leviathan* docked first at Cherbourg, France, where all but 395 of the 1,450 passengers disembarked. One hundred seventy-eight of those who left the liner at Cherbourg had originally been scheduled to travel on to Southampton, England, but had changed their plans when they heard news of the general strike. The landing at Southampton occurred without difficulty despite concerns about labor disturbances (*NYT*, 8 May 1926).

4. The stoppage of public transportation during the general strike forced many Londoners to resort to bicycles (*LSMD*, 30).

5. Rogers visited the British Parliament on 11 May and spent time in the galleries of both the House of Lords and the House of Commons. In the latter especially he witnessed heated, rancorous debate about the causes and consequences of the general strike (*LSMD*, 23–28).

To George H. Lorimer
13 May 1926
London, England

Daer Mr Lorimer.

Hope you like the idea of this and that we get off to a ~~go~~ good start,[1] wish you would leave space open for next weeks after this for the second one as it is on this English Strike   I was here during the whole thing, Have met all the Leaders, Been boarding out at Lady Astors,[2] Havent seen the Prince yet[3]   I think he is going to "High Hat"me, I will mail the other in two or three days,

I am going to try to make that "Preliminary Dissarmamnet Confrence" at Geneva next week,[4] 2I Nations are there to "See if they can hold ~~ane~~ another Conference",

Then on down to Mussolini.[5]

Englands strike wasent a succes because they forgot to puncture ~~eh~~ the Bicyc;es.

I will start a rebelion if they dont get better Coffee.

Good luck to you and the wildcat,[6] and old Friend Sam Blythe, Tell him the American Club gave me a Great Dinner last night and all asked about him.

Hold any Check till I let you know where to get me out of hock with.

Will

TL, rc.[7] DLC-MD, Wesley Stout Papers.

1. The first installment of Rogers's series of articles about his trip to Europe appeared in the *Saturday Evening Post* in its issue of 10 July 1926, and the final one was published in the edition of 4 December. Lorimer's reception of Rogers's writing was enthusiastic: "The start is a running one and we are going to have a big series, I am sure, judging by this first installment" (*LSMD*, xi; Lorimer to Rogers, 26 May 1926, DLC-MD). For the complete collection of Rogers's *Saturday Evening Post* articles, see *LSMD* and *TNBSR*.

2. Nancy Witcher Langhorne Astor (1879–1964), the American-born wife of Waldorf Astor, was elected in November 1919 as the first woman member of Parliament (*DNB*, Supp. 8:43–44; *NYT*, 29 November 1919). Her brother-in-law, *Life* magazine editor Charles Dana Gibson, gave Rogers a letter of introduction to Lady Astor, and Rogers passed it to her the day he visited Parliament. Taken with Rogers's intelligence and wit, she hosted him often during his stay in England and introduced him to several

of the country's leading social, political, and literary figures (*LSMD*, 27–28, 31, 38–40; Yagoda, *Will Rogers*, 230).

3. The Prince of Wales used an intermediary to contact Rogers the next day, 14 May, and invite him to his London home for a visit. The two spent more than an hour together that afternoon renewing the friendship they had formed during Edward's visit to the United States in 1924 and discussing such topics as horsemanship, polo, travel, Prohibition, and the general strike (*LSMD*, 46–51). See also Notes for After-Dinner Speech, ca. 3 September 1924, above.

4. Will and Bill Rogers traveled to Geneva via Paris, arriving in the Swiss city on 18 May. During their two-day stay, they spent time observing the preliminary conference on disarmament, a bore that fourteen-year-old Bill described as "just talking about nothing" (diary, Will Rogers, Jr., OkClaW).

5. Rogers and his son left Geneva on 20 May and arrived in Rome the next morning. After a wait of several days, Rogers finally met with Premier Benito Mussolini on Friday, 28 May. He had used several resources to secure the meeting, one that George Lorimer had especially urged. The *Post* editor had long been intrigued with Mussolini and what he had supposedly accomplished in Italy (Chronology, 1926, OkClaW; *LAE*, 26 May 1926; *LSMD*, 56; Yagoda, *Will Rogers*, 228; Cohn, *Creating America*, 180–85). See also Letter to George H. Lorimer, ca. 24 May 1926, below.

6. Hugh (Wildcat) Wiley (1885–1969), a frequent short-story contributor to the *Saturday Evening Post*, produced a popular series known as "Wildcat," about a black labor battalion he had commanded in the war. One of George Lorimer's closest pals, the personable Wiley became widely known by the same nickname (*NYT*, 1 January 1969; Tebbel, *George Horace Lorimer*, 100–101).

7. The dating of the document was determined from chronological references in the text.

To George H. Lorimer
ca. 16 May 1926
Paris, France

My Dear Mr Lorimer.

Here is a mess of Junk I am mailing you from Paris,[1] I had a great time in London and would have stayed longer but am in a hurry to get to Italy and then will come back by London, I think I have some good stuff on the Prince, I was asked over to his house and sit and talked with him for over an hour, He said its no interview, I just wanted to say hello to you, but he asked a lot about thibgs over home, am to see Lloyd George when I get back,[2] and Bernard Shaw,[3] and say I had a great visit with Sir James Barrie[4]   he took me from a dinner party by his Apartment and he talked for an hour or more, Wish I had had Ike[5] there to take it down.

I am going by Geneva to that confrernec then on to Italy, and say I made application in London for Russia and I had long talk with them and I think that I will make it,[6] I told them I dident care nothing about their Politics or

Government that I wanted it from the human side, This main Guy knew me from over home and I may make its so if I do save Checks to help pay investigators to find out what ever become of me,

well so long, regards to wildcat and Sam Blythe,

P.S. Say how did you like that head Title, It dident do bad for you and maby it can help out both of e us.[7] So lets keep it as a regular one, I will split the Royalty with you for use of it?.

TL, rc. DLC-MD, Wesley Stout Papers.

1. The manuscript material that Rogers forwarded to George Lorimer from Paris probably consisted of the article that was published in the *Saturday Evening Post* issue of 17 July.

2. Although Rogers observed David Lloyd George in debate in the House of Commons on 11 May, he apparently did not personally meet the former prime minister during his time in England (see *LSMD*).

3. George Bernard Shaw (1856–1950), a British critic and playwright, had achieved international renown by 1914 with such plays as *Man and Superman* and *Pygmalion*. Although his writings during the war seemed adverse to Great Britain and brought him scorn at home, he regained acclaim and popularity after 1918 and became the best known dramatist of his time (*DNB*, Supp. 6:773–82).

4. James Matthew Barrie (1860–1937), Scottish author, first achieved international repute in 1891 with the publication of his novel *The Little Minister*, which he later adapted for the stage. He gained lasting fame for his play *Peter Pan; or, The Boy Who Would Not Grow Up*, which he completed in 1904. He was made a baronet in 1913 and appointed to the Order of Merit in 1922 (*DNB*, Supp. 5:46–52). For accounts by Rogers of his visit with Barrie, see *LSMD*, 39–40; and *WA*, 2:218–21.

5. Isaac Frederick (Ike) Marcosson (1876–1961), a frequent contributor to the *Saturday Evening Post* and other magazines, was a leading exponent of the interview style of journalism. Marcosson traveled widely and interviewed many of the most prominent political and business figures of the 1910s and 1920s (*DAB*, Supp. 7:512–13; Tebbel, *George Horace Lorimer*, 127–31).

6. The Russian consul general in London notified Rogers on 6 June that his application for entry into the Union of Soviet Socialist Republics had been approved. He eventually received a visa and made the trip in early July (*TNBSR*, viii; Chronology, 1926, OkClaW).

7. Rogers gave his *Saturday Evening Post* series the title of "Letters of a Self-Made Diplomat to His President," a heading he borrowed from George Lorimer's own *Letters of a Self-Made Merchant to His Son*, which was serialized anonymously in the *Post* and became a best selling book in 1902. Rogers's open missives to President Coolidge proved immensely popular with the magazine's readers. Later, A. & C. Boni, Inc., collected and published the articles and related Rogers material in two books: *Letters of a Self-Made Diplomat to His President*, published in 1926 and featuring his writings about the non-Russian segment of his trip; and *There's Not a Bathing Suit in Russia & Other Bare Facts*, which came out the next year and focused on his experiences in the new Soviet Union (*LSMD*, xi; Tebbel, *George Horace Lorimer*, 145).

To George H. Lorimer
ca. 24 May 1926
Rome, Italy

Mr Lorimer.

Dear *Boss.*

Here is a pack of Junk[1]— just this Minute received word from our ~~Ambasad~~ Ambassador[2] that I am booked to see *Mussoline* Friday at Noon 28th. Hurrah—

Hope you like this *Prince interview*[3]

I am going after the *King of Spain.*[4]

Best and many thanks.

Will.

ALS, rc.[5] DLC-MD, Wesley Stout Papers. On Excelsior, Roma, letterhead. Handwritten on vertical edge of right margin, page 1 (of two pages): "(over)".

1. Rogers likely had enclosed the draft for the third article in his series, which the *Post* published on 24 July.
2. Henry Prather Fletcher (1873–1959), a career diplomat, served as U.S. ambassador to Italy from 1924 to 1929 (*DAB*, Supp. 6:206–7).
3. For Rogers's interview with the Prince of Wales, see *LSMD*, 46–51.
4. Alfonso XIII (1886–1941) reigned as king of Spain from his birth until his resignation in 1931 with the establishment of the republic (*NYT*, 1 March 1941). Rogers and son Bill spent a week in Spain, including an afternoon watching the king play polo and chatting with him before and after the match (Chronology, 1926, OkClaW; *LSMD*, 97–98). For Rogers's experiences in Spain, see *LSMD*, 90–100.
5. Dating was determined by the date of Ambassador Henry Fletcher's letter to Rogers, 24 May 1926 (OkClaW).

Cablegram to George H. Lorimer
16 June 1926
Paris, France

327CD PX

PARIS 47 NFT JUN 16 1926

LCD LORIMER

SATURDAY EVENING POST PHILADELPHIA (PENN)

WIRE NET PROCEEDS OF SIX ARTICLES TO MRS WILL ROGERS AND STARVING CHILDREN OF BEVERLEY HILLS CALIFORNIA MUSSOLINI ARTICLE SHOULD BE

THERE ABOUT NOW[1] AND ANOTHER FOLLOWING SAW KING OF SPAIN AND PRE-
MIER REVIRA[2] BRIAND RESIGNED[3] AS I WALKED IN

WILL

616P

CG, rc. DLC-MD, Wesley Stout Papers. On Western Union Cablegram letterhead. Metered
above body of text: "2913."

1. Rogers's account of his visit to Italy and his audience with Mussolini was published in the *Saturday Evening Post* on 31 July 1926. For a republication of the *Post*
material and other writings by Rogers about Italy, see *LSMD*, 54–82.
2. Miguel Primo de Rivera y Orbaneja (1870–1930), a Spanish general, staged a
coup d'état in 1923 with the support of the king. He established first a military dictatorship and then in 1925 a civil one with himself as the sole ruler. Economic failures
finally led to his resignation and exile in January 1930 (*NYT*, 18 March 1930). For
Rogers's account of his visit with Primo de Rivera, see *LSMD*, 90–96.
3. Aristide Briand (1862–1932), French statesman and Socialist party leader,
served as premier of France eleven times, including briefly in 1926, and as foreign
minister from 1925 to 1932. His most recent resignation as premier had come on 15
June 1926 after the franc had dropped in value and he had failed to effect a coalition
government (*NYT*, 16 June 1926, 8 March 1932).

Cablegram from Sailing W. Baruch
23 June 1926
[New York, N.Y.?]

JUNE 23RD, 1926[1]

WILL ROGERS,

GRAND HOTEL,

PARIS,

WALTER W IRWIN[2] AND I SERIOUSLY CONTEMPLATE FINANCING YOUR SERIES OF
TRAVELOGUE MOTION PICTURE COMEDIES ▲entitled Abroad with Will Rogers▲
AS PER BUDGET SUBMITTED BY C S CLANCY WHO INFORMS ME THAT HE HAS A
CONTRACT WITH YOU[3] UPON THE FOLLOWING TERMS FIRST YOU ARE TO PRODUCE
⚎ ▲pathe▲ TRAVELOGUE SERIES CONSISTING OF TWENTY SIX REELS SECOND
TWENTY THOUSAND DOLLARS IS TO BE DEPOSITED TO YOUR ACCOUNT IN THE
EAST RIVER NATIONAL BANK BEFORE PRODUCTION BEGINS THIRD EACH WEEK
THEREAFTER FOR TEN WEEKS FIFTEEN HUNDRED DOLLARS IS LIKEWISE TO BE
DEPOSITED MAKING A TOTAL COMPENSATION TO YOU FOR TEN WEEKS OF THIRTY
FIVE THOUSAND DOLLARS. IN THE EVENT THAT ADDITIONAL TIME IS REQUIRED
◀for you◀ TO COMPLETE SERIES AND CUT AND TITLE YOU ARE TO RECEIVE TWENTY

FIVE HUNDRED DOLLARS FOR EACH SUCH ADDITIONAL WEEK STOP WILL YOU
KINDLY CABLE ME IMMEDIATELY BY FAST CABLE AT MY EXPENSE CONFIRMING
THESE TERMS STOP I OF COURSE ASSUME YOU WILL HAVE NO OBJECTION TO THE
ASSIGNMENT OF THE CONTRACT TO A CORPORATION WHICH I AND MY ASSO-
CIATES WILL CONTROL WITH MISTER CLANCY AND THAT IT IS UNDERSTOOD
OWNERSHIP OF THE MOTION PICTURES WILL BE IN THE ▼pathe▼ COMPANY STOP
IF I CLOSE THE MATTER WITH MISTER CLANCY I WILL IMMEDIATELY COME
ABROAD TO SEE YOU STOP MY CABLE ADDRESS IS SAILRUCH

KINDEST REGARDS

SAILING W BARUCH[4]

CG, rc. CSC-GKC. On Western Union Cablegram letterhead. A man's photograph, unidentified, was clipped to the upper left corner of the cablegram. Handwritten to the immediate right
of "Grand Hotel": "or American Express Co." All interpolations were handwritten in the adjacent margins of the text body—top, right, or bottom—as indicated. Double strike-through indicates hand-deleted text.

1. Will and Bill Rogers left Paris for Geneva on 17 June (diary, Will Rogers, Jr.,
OkClaW).
2. Walter W. Irwin (ca. 1881–1948), an attorney, was a veteran of motion picture
distribution and merchandising. Through the years, he had held top positions at various studios, including Famous Players–Lasky, with which Rogers had been associated
(*NYT*, 15 July 1948; Koszarski, *Evening's Entertainment*, 34, 74).
3. See Terms of Payment for Travelogues, 22 April 1926, above.
4. Sailing W. Baruch (1874–1962) was a New York investment banker and stockbroker who had connections in the entertainment industry (*NYT*, 15 June 1962).

To George H. Lorimer
ca. 1 July 1926
[London, England?]

Dear Boss.

Say I kinder think this one is ▲if▲ you run it at all ~~thou~~ would be better in
paragraphs, for it is all Gags anyway,[1] andb by dividing them it might help it
out, and it sure needs all the help it cant get. I am leaving in the morning for
Russia, I have left all Ike's letters in London.[2] So if I am hungryin Russia
ayou will be the cause of it.[3]

Best to you and all and the Wildcat/
going to try and come out through the south by the way of Turkey.[4] Flying
all the way from London to Moscow,

Willie.

TL, rc.[5] DLC-MD, Wesley Stout Papers. The interlineation was handwritten. Hand-inserted, double vertical lines appear between "am" and "leaving" in the first paragraph.

1. This submission by Rogers was not identified.

2. Ike Marcosson was known to have provided notes of introduction for Rogers to use in London and Berlin. He apparently had written other letters to help open doors in Russia (see Isaac F. Marcosson to Will Rogers, 30 April and 28 May 1926, OkClaW).

3. Rogers's account of his trip to Russia was serialized in three issues of the *Saturday Evening Post*: 23 October, 6 November, and 4 December 1926. The publisher of his *Letters of a Self-Made Diplomat*, A. & C. Boni, of New York, followed with a book edition of the Russia material the next year. See *TNBSR*.

4. Rogers apparently failed to reach Turkey during his trip overseas in 1926 (see Chronology, 1926, OkClaW; *LSMD*; *TNBSR*).

5. Dating of the document was determined by chronological references in the text.

Notes for After-Dinner Speech
ca. 11 July 1926
[Berlin, Germany]

Dont tell me the Germans have no sense of humor, A short time ago I read of an election they had here, One side got a half million votes   the other side got I6 million, ~~then I read down~~ I thought well that is the most overwhelming election I ever heard of, thats 32 to one, and finally down at the bottom of the Article it says the side with a hald [half] million won,[1] That takes the cake for humorous election for now and all time,

I suppose in horse race over here the one that dont run at all and stays in the stable wins,

I have always heard that europeans did everything backwards, But that was the greatest exaple of it I ever saw,

I know that the rule was that you are supposed to get more than ahlf of the ~~rigist~~ eligible [votes], why say if you was having an election on voting for Eternal Salvation, You couldent get over half the voters out, Nobody knows how many has died since the census

A sense of humor on somebodys part was certainly good to the Princes, So this is the Country that lost the war, More humor.

I have visited various countries, the ones that won the war,

I saw Poland one of the winners, They are so tivkled to death over winning it that they are shooting each other yet just to celebrate the victory,[2] They are going to have Liberty just as long as the ammunitionlasts,

They hollered for an alley to the sea,[3] Now none of them want to go to sea,

It [is] just   used for Paderwiski to go back and forth to foreign Concerts,[4]

Somebody told Pilsudski,[5] " Do you know a fellow name Mussolini took Rome, and he wasent as big a fellow as you are, He says why dont you take something?2 Pilsaidski saysm I will   I will take warsaw,

He divided the army up, All those that had light hair fought on one saide and all those that had dark hair fought on the other, and instead of fighting out of tonw why they decided to fight in the street[s.] Then they would be sure of hittimg somebody,

Then he got warsaw, he has had it eight weeks and is looking for some enemy that he hates bad enough and he will give it to him

He is talking about fighting his way out now,

Somebody dug up a History where there is some land in Prussia that e used to belong to Poloand 950 years ago, and Pilsudski he says I am going out and get that back, and when I get it back I have another fellow looking through old History and if he finds anything else in the me ntime why wel will go right on from there and get it, in that way we will have no lost time between wars at all.

Everytime he goes to call   a Cabinet meeting why the some of his Ministers are out fighting "So called Duesl",[6] He has issued an edist [edict] now saying " Next wecnesdat [Wednesday] there is to be no Duels or other pleasures   we are going to meet and decide where to go from here". The seconds in these Polish duels are the only ones that are put to any particular inconvenience, They have to arrange them, They are harder to arrange than they are to fight,

History has proven that there has never been one where where one Pole

[*bottom of page; text ends*]

TD.[7] OkClaW, Original Movie Notes. Handwritten, possibly in Rogers's hand, top margin, left side: "In Germany".

1. A plebiscite was held in Germany on 20 June 1926 to vote on a measure to expropriate the houses of German princes. The result was 15.5 million "yes" votes, but the constitution required at least a simple majority of the eligible electorate, approximately 20 million, for enactment; therefore, the referendum failed (Heiber, *Weimar Republic*, 141; Arlinger, *Die Grundrechte*).

2. Poland, a member of the Entente powers, had gained territory after the war through the peace treaty negotiated at Versailles. The country, however, was wracked during the postwar years by civil disorder and government instability, including a general strike and a presidential assassination. A military coup in May 1926 claimed 379 lives and toppled the civilian government (Lukowski and Zawadzki, *Concise History*, 196–97, 208, 209, 212).

3. By the Treaty of Versailles in 1919, Poland gained a narrow outlet to the Baltic Sea, although Danzig, its historic port and home to a large German population, became a free city under the League of Nations (Lukowski and Zawadzki, *Concise History*, 197).

4. Ignacy Jan Paderewski (1860–1941), internationally celebrated concert pianist and composer, served briefly as prime minister of his native Poland in 1919. Because of other responsibilities Paderewski did not touch a piano for several years during and after the war. He resumed his career in 1921 and toured often over the next ten years, frequently giving benefit performances in Allied countries in remembrance of their war casualties (*BBDM*, 1352–53; Zamoyski, *Paderewski*, 216, 218).

5. Józef Pilsudski (1867–1935), marshal of Poland and former chief of state, launched a coup on 12 May 1926 that in three days overthrew the parliamentary government and captured the capital of Warsaw. Pilsudski, officially minister of war, ruled as a virtual dictator until his death (*NYT*, 13 May 1935; Lukowski and Zawadzki, *Concise History*, 212–13).

6. A former premier of Poland and a general in the Polish army met in a duel in Warsaw at dawn on 15 June 1923. The confrontation, which arose over blame for the revolution in May, ended with the statesman being grazed and then choosing to walk away after having leveled his pistol at his opponent (*NYT*, 9, 16 June 1926).

7. Dating of the document was determined by historical and chronological references in the text.

Notes for Appearance in *Cochran's 1926 Revue*
ca. 19 July 1926
[London, England]

Main Street has come to London.

Everwhere I look I see a prominent Bootlegger from America,

I dont want my English Couzins to think that that is a knock against the Americans that are here to call them Bootleggers at home, That is indeed a compliment. They are making terms with the English for next years delivery, and sampletling as they go along,

Well lets get down to business   what am I doing here, I am here on a Diplomatic mission, You remember Col House used to do a lot of outside jobs for Mr Wilson, in fact he fixed up everything including the war, well I knew that Mr Collidge needed some one in Europe to do some outside work for him, So I am President Collidge['s] Col House,

I am the House detective of Europe for Calvin.

I was here in London during t what they humorously called the general strike. I settled that, That was the poorest excuse for a srrike I ever saw, I would like to bring over IO Chicago Taxicab drivers and show England a strike, what we mean by a strike in America, the man dont quit work he, when he strikes he just commences, he starts in throwing Bombs, and bricks,

Will and Betty Blake Rogers returned to the United States from Europe in September 1926 with Mary and Jimmy Rogers and the newest family member, Jock, a Sealyham dog given to the family by Scottish distiller Lord Thomas Dewar. (*OkClaW*)

and shooting, It compares with the war, Over here a man wouod go to another and ask him if he would drive a tram, No sir I am on strike, But I should be pleased to get you a man to drive it, But England come through it great, It was worth the advertising you got out of it, for what it cost you,

This Coal str ke I could settle that in a minute, I would use electricity with a Dinamo hooked uo [up] from the House of Commons,

If the Tiners [Miners] can win a strike in the Summer time when nobody is using Coal what could they have done in the winter when everybody wanted it, The only way the general strike   c uld have been madena succes would have been by punctureing the Bicycles,

But I got to tell you what I am doing out here, Mr Cochran[1] said to me, Will they know you over in America, but they dont know you over here so you go out and kinder get acquainted with them,[2]

So as nobody would introduce me, I will have to do it myself, The Prince of Wales kinder helped me out when he come back from America, he told them something at dinner that I has siad [had said] to him and they dident know who I was and he told them they ought to know me, He said that the Subway, Fords Factory , and the Flatiron building[3] and myself were the things that amused him more in America, Ghe [He] could at least have put me ahead of the fords, Well I thought when I had him for a Press Agen t Ihhad about the best in the world,

But he is off ~~unveiling a Monument,~~ opening a Bridge or christening a Boat, he dident have time to come and introduce me personally,

well here is about the caliber of fellow I am and about the position I occupy in America,

I am a fellow about Five feet, eleven inchinces, weigh I8o stone IO. I mean Pounds , Light blue eyes, Features not handsome but good dependable, Dress neat but not gaudy, I wear my clothes well sometimes a year,

Now I have no official position in America, I am a good deal like a man in England that has been Prime Minister and is now tolerated,

---

TD. OkClaW, Speeches in Foreign Countries, SPC.5. Handwritten, top margin, left side: "1926". Editor's marks, including those for paragraphing and punctuation, appear throughout document; they were ignored for this transcription. Paragraph 4 ("Well lets get . . .") was offset by a hand-inserted, partial bracket in left margin.

1. Charles Blake (Cockie) Cochran (1872–1951), colorful British theatrical figure, achieved great success between 1917 and 1937 as a producer in London of revues and musicals. He also recorded several losses, including in 1925 when he underwent his second bankruptcy. Within the year, however, he regained financing and began to stage new productions (*DNB*, Supp. 7:232–34; *EMT*, 1:287).

2. Rogers opened in *Cochran's 1926 Revue* on 19 July and continued in the nightly show for a month. His monologue act followed closely in style the one he had performed regularly in the *Ziegfeld Follies*, but in London his humorous critiques of things British did not always please the public and press (*NYT*, 15 July 1926; Rogers, *Will Rogers*, 195–96; Heppner, *Cockie*, 144). See also *WA*, 2:237–38.

3. Erected in 1902, the twenty-story Flatiron office building acquired its distinctive name from the triangular plot of land it occupied at Broadway and Fifth Avenue in New York (*ENYC*, 417).

From Nancy Langhorne Astor
ca. 29 July 1926
Aboard R.M.S. *Aquitania*

Dear Boarder

I could not make it out. I waited & waited until like the Lady of Shalott[1] "He Cometh not she said, I am a'weary I am a'dreary, I would that I were dead." I so wanted to meet Mrs Rogers & hear what stuff she is made of. There's a sort of rugged stubborness & which — even material want & war — won't make her budge. I tried getting back to it all– Yet I see my way Clear– Your wife will tell you what a help C.S. is— I hope you will come back soon & always your *Coffee* will be ready-& a Welcome waiting you

I am positivey that unless America helps in some way (not financially) we Shall have another war– You & I won't fight but our sons may– My heart aches for England. We[']re alone on that Continent & make no mistake about it. This coal strike– [*illegible*] of your latest news & you saw mine. I should have called you up again but you said you were leaving town [*illegible*] –Well there it is.–

I do hope that you will go slow about Europe. I feel exactly like you do– but I hear that the cotton outlook is bad in the South[,] also wheat— I wish you would pull the Republicans ~~League~~ ▲leg not League▲ about the World Court![2] I dont believe they see Ireland to Come in.[3] Tho' Mr Kellogg[4] vows he's all for it— He has no idea of resigning– [*illegible*] that 2 years ago–

I am having a glorious Crossing. Never have [*illegible*] except to take a walk, so I read[,] read & read & *mercifully* no newspapers.

Please congratulate Mrs. Rogers for me– You are lucky to have a *wife & home*— A steadfast light–

I've not forgotten your generous gift— *Tho* a woman of few words– I feel deeply!

[*illegible*]
Nancy Astor[5]

Nick L. will never never be President[6]   Smiths got a better *chance*!

ALS, rc. OkClaW, 1975.22.0083. On Cunard R.M.S. "Aquitania" letterhead.

1. "Lady of Shalott," a poem by Alfred Tennyson, Britain's foremost poet of the Victorian age, was first published in 1832. A second version, much revised, appeared a decade later (*OCEL*, 551, 980–81; Tennyson, *Poetic*, 27).

2. The World Court, or the Permanent Court of International Justice, was created after the war. Although prospects of U.S. participation in the League of Nations had virtually died with failure to ratify the Treaty of Versailles, the Senate voted in February 1926 to join the judiciary body but added several onerous conditions. The court refused them, and the United States remained outside (*HD1920s*, 350–51; McCoy, *Calvin Coolidge*, 359–63).

3. The Irish Free State, a member of the League of Nations since 1923, failed in 1926 to be elected to the executive council, which included permanent and nonpermanent member nations. It won election four years later (*DIH*, 301; *HD1920s*, 210).

4. Frank Billings Kellogg (1856–1937), a Republican and former U.S. senator from Minnesota, served as ambassador to Great Britain from 1923 to 1925 and then secretary of state from 1925 to 1929 (*DAB*, Supp. 2:355–57; Bryn-Jones, *Frank B. Kellogg*, 133).

5. Lady Astor was the subject of the first of what became popularly known as the "Daily Telegrams," Rogers's most recognized newspaper writings. On the same day that she penned the above letter, Rogers somewhat casually sent to the *New York Times* a four-sentence cable about Astor heading to the United States and deserving an enthusiastic American welcome (see *DT*, 1:1). The *Times* ran his brief message on the front page of section 2 on 30 July and continued carrying follow-up cables from him during his remaining time in Europe. The column eventually was syndicated by McNaught and picked up by newspapers nationwide with the *Times* as the primary conduit (Rogers, *Will Rogers*, 193–95; Yagoda, *Will Rogers*, 229, 237).

6. Soon after Nicholas Longworth was elected speaker of the U.S. House of Representatives in 1925, he publicly declared his lack of interest in the presidency, although his name occasionally was mentioned among prospective Republican candidates (Chambrun, *Making*, 287–89, 308–9).

To Adolph S. Ochs
ca. July 1926
London, England

Savoy Hotel. London.[1]

My Dear Mr Ochs,

I am having the Syndicate send you over this Article and I want to ask you as a favor to run it in next Sundays issue, It wont cost a cent, I think it will geta few "giggles" in view of your present situation over there, Now I would be insulting your intelligence by trying to assume that there was no method in my present attitude toward your paper, Its not generosity on my part   its nothing but propaganda. I dont need to thinly veil the suggestion that I want my Sunday Articles "Back Home" again,[2] I went away from you and I have paid for it so now "Uncle Tome" is back on his knees begging to ~~be taks~~ assist the Editorial writers of the New York Times to carry "Little Eva" across the pages of your intellectual ice pond.[3]

Dont drive me to Hearst and let me degenerate into nothing but a Brisbane, I get back the last of September and start on my Lecture tour again, Thanks for your letter you gave me on my departure I have nearly wore it out showing it, all your troop over in Europe have been very fine to me, Paris especially, also had a very pleasant 10 days with little Durante in Moscow,[4] If it hadent been for him to talk to up there I would joined Trotsky,[5] You also have a new man that is very good Dennewitz in Warsaw[6]   keep him   he is a good Writer.

Now I wish you would let your Sunday Editor take this up with my Syndicate people there, I feel that I have kept the jokes out of New York long enough that they have forgotten tham and we can start using them over again now, besides I want to be set for the coming election.

But please for my sake use this Article anyway,

Regards to all.
Will.

TL, rc. NYT-A, Publishers Collection. Handwritten check mark appears above body of letter, center. Hardwritten in margin below closing, with parallel lines above and below and check mark to immediate right: "Will Rogers." Handwritten directly below preceding notation, with hand-inserted arrow pointing to notation: "A S Ochs signature to indicate file".

1. The Savoy, one of the most elegant and fashionable hotels in London and a long-time favorite among wealthy travelers and local residents, dated from 1889 and stood on the north bank of the Thames in the central part of the city (Denby, *Grand Hotels*, 143–45). Rogers and his family often stayed at the Savoy during their stops in London.

2. The *New York Times* discontinued publishing Rogers's "Weekly Article" in October 1924 after the New York *World* had started to carry it, effective with its issue of 5 October. The *Times* never resumed running the column. With this note to *Times* publisher Ochs, Rogers may have enclosed a draft of a forthcoming weekly column that he hoped would lure the publisher and the *Times* back into the fold.

3. In his analogy Rogers borrowed two of the main characters and a critical scene from *Uncle Tom's Cabin, or, Life among the Lowly*, a novel by Harriet Beecher Stowe (1811–1896), published in 1852. Highly influential among antislavery advocates, the book ranked as one of the most popular in nineteenth-century America (*OCAL*, 812–13, 871; Gossett, *Uncle Tom's Cabin*, 100).

4. Walter Duranty (1884–1957), English-born journalist, joined the Paris bureau of the *New York Times* in 1913 and became the newspaper's Moscow correspondent

nine years later. Duranty covered the Soviet Union until 1934 and gained fame as an expert on Soviet life and affairs (*DAB*, Supp. 6:183–85; *BDAJ*, 204).

5. Leon Trotsky (Lev Davidovich Trotskii or Bronstein, 1879–1940), Russian revolutionary leader, was a primary organizer of the October Revolution of 1917 that overthrew the tsarist government. Although powerfully ruthless as commissar of war, he was outmaneuvered as successor to Lenin. He was forced from leadership in 1925 before Rogers arrived in Russia and was banished from the Communist party two years later (*NYT*, 22 August 1940; *BDSU*, 446).

6. Carl O. Dennewitz (ca. 1888–1934), American newspaperman, served as a managing editor of the Paris edition of the *Herald* and then in 1926 joined the *New York Times* as its correspondent in Berlin. Shortly afterward he was posted to Warsaw, but left the *Times* the same year. He returned to the United States and worked as an editor and a publicist (*NYT*, 2 November 1934).

Cablegram to George H. Lorimer
4 August 1926
London, England

CBA428 34 CABLE

LONDON

LCO LORIMER

SATURDAY EVENING POST PHILADELPHIA

MAKING MOVIE HERE[1] AND BIGGEST HIT OF LIFE ON STAGE HAVE ONE ARTICLE ON IRELAND[2] AND ONE ON RUSSIA[3] TO WRITE SUGGEST SOMETHING ELSE SAVOY HOTEL LONDON

WILL.

CG, rc. DLC-MD, Wesley Stout Papers. On Postal Telegraph–Commercial Cables letterhead. Metered, right side of letterhead: "1926 AUG 4 PM 5 12." Handwritten above text body, center: "B-45."

1. Rogers signed a contract on 14 July to act in the British National Pictures production of *Tip Toes*, a comedy about three American vaudevillians stranded in England. Shot in London in the summer of 1926, the film feature was released in the United States a year later and in England in 1928 (*NYT*, 15 July 1926; *WRHolly*, 77–78; Low, *History*, 188). For Rogers's experience filming *Tip Toes* see *WA*, 2:232–33.

2. Rogers's article in the *Saturday Evening Post* issue of 2 October 1926 carried a place-line of Dublin, Ireland, but the contents did not concern Ireland.

3. The *Saturday Evening Post* ran three articles by Rogers about his visit to Russia. They were published in the issues of 23 October, 6 November, and 4 December 1926.

Betty Blake Rogers to Will Rogers, Jr.
29 August 1926
Lausanne, Switzerland

Sunday Aug 29*th*

My dear Bill:

In a cable just received from daddy he tells us that you and Aunt Dick are leaving soon for Culver.[1] We are all so glad that you have decided to go there   Im sure you will like it very much, and will be glad of your decision when you see what a wonderful school it is—   I only hope you can make the ~~cavrely~~ ▲cavlary▲ but I am afraid you are too small,[2] but any way you can tell best you and Aunt Dick which course you think would be most interesting   your daddy is about the happiest man I know because he thinks the school is so wonderful—   Jim is already thinking about going, I think it will make him a little more ambitious about his school—

We have just come in from a row on the lake. It is so beautiful & Jim and Mary row very nicely   Maddy[3] is home for a few days visit with her family, and her sister is coming tomorrow to stay with us & let Maddy visit with her friends—   We like Switzerland very much. We were in Geneva ~~yesterday~~ ▲Friday▲, and I thought about you— & wished you could be with us   Mary does very well ▼with▼her french, and does all the talking—   She is quite pleased with herself and I am very proud of her—   I think Jim is very sorry he did not study—   I think you should have latin this year and I would like you to specialize in a literary course of some kind   I suppose this this year is just the grades of first year high—   I will come by to see you on our way from New york. We are sailing Sept 21ˢᵗ I think

I will send this to the school as I am sure you will be there by the time this arrives—   It may [be] a short time now until we will be leaving   Mr Clancy is in London, and I suppose he feels very happy to start his work.[4] Daddy is giving him only two wks as he has to work all next week on the Picture he is making with Miss Dorthy Gish[5]—   Daddy starts his tour the fourth of October & comes near you on the tour—   He says he will see you before the hollidays—   and Xmas you will get to come home for a vacation—

Jim and Mary are already talking about what kind of car you will get and asking if I think you will let them drive it—   Tell Aunt Dick to stay there for a while and see that you get everything you need—   I wish I were there to go with you dear—

Jim is send[ing] a card to you and Mary is going to write to you tonight Love from mother to her dear boy—

Mother

We are going to London next week[6]—

ALS, rc. OkClaW, 1975.11.0005. On letterhead of Beau-Rivage-Palace, Ouchy-Lausanne.

1. Bill Rogers had left his father in Europe and had returned to California by August 1926, while the other members of the family—his mother Betty Blake Rogers, sister Mary, and younger brother Jim—had landed in England on 7 August and then traveled to the continent later in the month, reaching Switzerland by 24 August. Bill was accepted for admission to Culver Military Academy on 7 September 1926 and began studies at the Indiana school that fall. He remained enrolled through the spring semester of 1928 (postcard, Mary Rogers to Bill Rogers, Jr., 13 August 1926, OkClaW; diary, Mary Rogers, 1926, OkClaW; William Van [*sic*] Rogers file, CMA).

2. Culver required that cadets in its cavalry unit weigh a minimum of one hundred pounds and stand at least sixty-three inches. On young Rogers's application to the school, his height was given as sixty-one and three-quarter inches and his weight as ninety-three pounds, but cavalry was indicated as his choice of service, not infantry or artillery. School officials apparently made an exception in his case; he was assigned to the cavalry (application for enrollment, William Van [*sic*] Rogers file, CMA).

3. Maddy (or Maddie), a friend of Mary Rogers, accompanied her to Europe and joined her own family in Switzerland (diary, Mary Rogers, 1926, OkClaW).

4. Carl Clancy and Rogers began work on the travelogue series, *Strolling Through Europe with Will Rogers*, in early September. Betty Blake Rogers traveled with them around Europe, including by plane, as they shot film of landmarks, themselves, and local residents over about a two-week period (Rogers, *Will Rogers*, 203–4; *WRHolly*, 84–96). To follow Rogers's itinerary see *DT*, 1:10–14; see also *WA*, 2:243–45.

5. Dorothy Gish (1898–1968), American actress, made her film debut with her sister, Lillian, in 1912 at the age of fourteen. Especially noted for her comedy roles, she starred in scores of motion pictures through the late 1920s. She made her final few films, including *Tip Toes*, in Britain (*FE*, 529; *DAB*, Supp. 8:213–14).

6. Betty Blake Rogers left Geneva for London on 3 September. Mary and Jim remained in Switzerland until the family's departure from Europe on the *Leviathan* on 21 September (diary, Mary Rogers, 1926, OkClaW; *NYT*, 21 September 1926).

To George H. Lorimer
ca. 1 September 1926
[London, England]

Daer Mr Lorimer.

Say I got your Cablegram about the debt Article[1] and I want to say that you are the most thoughtful man I ever saw   that was sure fine of you to do that, I dident know but what it was a little too serious like and it sure tickled me to get your news,

Now this is the start of this Russian mess, I dont know if I can get it in one more or not   it may take two more as there is a lot of junk there If I tell it just as it happened, I think I have some pretty fair dope on Russia from a *reeal* angle, The[n] after Russia I got one on Irelnad,

I leave Europe about the 21st and will see you on my arrival as I am going down to get the dope from Cal and the boys to tell them on the tour this fall,

Best to you and al your Gangm   Hows the wildcat,

Will.

TL, rc. DLC-MD, Wesley Stout Papers.

1. The cable from Lorimer was not found.

Betty Blake Rogers to Will Rogers, Jr.
13 September 1926
Berlin, Germany

Monday Sept. 13th

Bill dear:

We had a wonderful trip—   how I wish you could have been with us—

We left London at eight o'clock, it was a beautiful bright day—   We came down in Ostend for about thirty minutes—   we were two hours flying over from London—   Then up again in the same plane, arriving Amsterdam eleven thirty—   I never felt the least nervous or afraid   that is after we left the ground—   I will admit I was a little nervous as we motored out to the field, but the bright clear day gave me courage. We spend that afternoon and night in Amsterdam   I am sorry you did not get to go to Holland. The island[s] of Marnen & Vollendam are very picturesque & I never saw any thing so beautiful as when we flew over Holland as we left the next day at noon for Berlin—   It is a trip I want you to take sometime—   We were in a big nine seater, monoplane—   all metal, big comfortable leather chairs & after a thirty minutes rest in Hanover we arrived Berlin about 4 o'clock—

There were no bumps and it was all a marvelous trip   I think I have some good pictures   hope so anyway—   I get very tired flying & think a few hours at a time would be all I could stand—   The noise & vibration wears me out, but oh how wonderful to be able to cover such a distance in such a short time—   To night we take train to hamburg & fly to Zurich Switzerland—   We are wiring Mary & Jim to meet us there & then we will all go to Paris together—   May fly as Mary & Jim are anx[i]ous to have the experience & if weather conditions are favorable & I think they will not get "air sick" I will take them—

Aunt Dick[']s cavle [cable] was here, & it was good to have news from you. I may stay in N.Y. & let Daddy bring Mary & Jim by to see you—   Then I will come by later—   I hope you are happy and that you will get along all right—   Im sure of that tho—   Any time my big boy can't take care of himself & gets the best there is—   Im mighty proud of you dear & I know you will be glad in the end that you have entered such a wonderful school—

your daddy is certainly glad you are there—   Be a good boy now & don't get into trouble. be a sport, but don't go in far—   Its raining now & dad just came in   They could not get any pictures—   We had a good day yesterday and got some wonderful scenes.

We got some wonderful material in Ireland, also Holland. It rained most of the time in England but I think some of the stuff will be good—   I took changing the guards, but most of it was taken in the rain—

Mary & Jim have been in Lausanne for two weeks while I have been with Dad. Jim & Mary ▲are▲ having a good time in Lake Geneva & Jim is getting some good pictures with his little camera, you would be surprised how well he does—   I may hope mine will turn out as well with the movie camera—

I wonder if you would like to have the camera there   It would be fine to get some pictures there & I will leave it with you when I come by ▼if you want▼ it—   Then you could bring it home [at] Xmas. you must write to us at least once a week—   You should write 2 times each week, but I know what an effort it is—   Im going to cavle [cable] you when we leave & ask you to have a letter in N.y. for me on my arrival—   We are all fine dear, but anx[i]ous to get home & ₳ will all be so happy to see you. Love from your Daddy and a big hug & kisses from your mother who thinks about her boy every day—   Love—   Love

Mother

ALS, rc. OkClaW, 1975.11.0004. On letterhead of Hotel Adlon Berlin W., Unter den Linden 1, am Pariser Platz.

6. ON TO POLITICS—WITH A SMILE
September 1926–July 1928

Rogers was honored as "mayor" of Beverly Hills during a noisy, cold-weather celebration at city hall in December 1926. Son Bill Rogers, dressed in his military academy uniform, stands near his father, while in front of Bill are his sister and brother, Mary and Jimmy. Betty Blake Rogers holds a bouquet of flowers to the right of Jimmy. (*OkClaW*)

ON TUESDAY, 21 SEPTEMBER 1926, WILL AND BETTY BLAKE ROGERS AND TWO OF their three children left Cherbourg, France, aboard the luxury liner *Leviathan* for their return voyage to the United States. Undoubtedly exhausted, Rogers must also have felt considerable satisfaction as the family finally headed home. Almost five months had passed since he had left New York and crossed the Atlantic, but in that time he had accomplished much. The two-million-plus readers of the *Saturday Evening Post*, the leading mass-circulation magazine in the United States at the time, already had consumed six installments in his popular series about his experiences in Europe, and new "Letters of a Self-Made Diplomat to His President" were in the works. Followers of the prestigious *New York Times* had been reading since late July his exclusive dispatches to the *Times*—the first of his soon-to-be syndicated column, the "Daily Telegram"— relating in a cogent, clever style news and observations from the other side of the Atlantic. He had finished location work on what would turn out to be a dozen travelogues shot at a hectic pace in the final days of his trip. He had established new contacts and friendships, and had renewed and solidified many others. He had starred on the theatrical stage, on the motion picture screen, and at the banquet hall podium. He now held a special place in the hearts of the Irish for his response to a tragedy in that country. He had witnessed and recorded the rancor and impasse of an international disarmament conference and had conversed with many national leaders, such as Benito Mussolini, the dictator of Spain, and the president of Ireland. He had socialized with the Prince of Wales and spoken with leaders in Parliament. He had discovered in Europe the speed and convenience of commercial aviation, and would make it his cause back home. He had heard and digested the concerns of Europeans about the debts of war, the need to disarm, the urge to build navies, the justi- fication for reparations, the rise of communism, the hypocrisy of Prohibition, the emergence of nationalism, the lowering of tariffs, the crassness of American tourists. He had seen England suddenly immersed in a general strike but operating nicely, thank you, with good cheer, a tip of the pint, and a sea of bicycles. He had spent an enchanted evening as the sole guest of the creative Sir James Barrie and had hunted grouse on the Scottish estate of an American financier. Even on board ship bound for New York and home, he found time to stage events to benefit the victims of a natural disaster in Florida.[1]

Soon after landing in New York, Rogers would receive something totally unexpected, a special invitation that would validate the prominence he had achieved. Two days after disembarking from the *Leviathan*, on 29 September he took delivery of a telegram from Everett Sanders, secretary to President Calvin Coolidge, inviting Rogers to be the overnight guest of the president and first lady at the White House.[2] Thrilled and excited, the Self-Made Diplomat took his self-made label to heart and promised in his reply to provide Coolidge with a report of his travels.[3] What took place that evening Rogers recounted in a piece in the *Saturday Evening Post* a few months later, a kind of postlude to his travel series, one he entitled "A Letter from a Self-Made Diplomat to His Constituents."[4]

His stay in the White House and the rare, intimate moments he spent with the Coolidges provided Rogers with prime material when he returned to the lecture circuit just a few days later. His experiences in Europe, the people he had met there, their issues and concerns, even his opinion of the English excuse for coffee also fed his lecture tour commentary.[5] As with his previous seasons on the road, he covered considerable territory at a ceaseless pace, with the de Reszke quartet still along for musical interludes. A highlight of the fall tour occurred in November when Rogers was a featured performer during the debut of the National Broadcasting Company. The historic broadcast linked more than a score of radio stations nationwide, with entertainers performing from scattered locations. Rogers, joining the program that evening from a station in southeastern Kansas, was able to reach millions of listeners throughout the country in a single performance from a remote locale.[6] Although he would bemoan performing without a live audience,[7] he seemed to grasp the mass impact of the radio medium and would return to it in the future.

Near the end of the fall tour, Rogers received a telegram from neighbor and film icon Douglas Fairbanks that bestowed on him a title he would milk to great comedic effect for months to come: Mayor of Beverly Hills.[8] Intended by local civic leaders and citizens as a publicity stunt—publicity for what or who would remain unclear, since neither the city nor the person really needed more—the honorary designation came with no powers of governance. It did occasion on Rogers's return home from the lecture circuit a parade, banners, a cheering crowd, a fake swearing in, and of course, speeches, all staged in a December shower.[9]

Throughout his tour that season, and as it flowed into the next, Rogers continued to produce his "Weekly Article" for McNaught, and he succeeded in having the daily blurbs he had been submitting since July accepted for national syndication.[10] To his delight and satisfaction, the *New York Times* agreed to run the new column, which became known as the "Daily Telegram." It marked Rogers's much hoped-for return to the pages of the venerable newspaper after an absence of two years. Although the column continued to attract subscribing newspapers over the years and became Rogers's trademark piece, it drew criticism, especially from among the readers of the *Times*.[11] Another occasional target of censure, the "Worst Story," had been mercifully allowed to expire by early 1927.

As his contributions to newspapers expanded in reach over the next two years, Rogers also enjoyed a strong presence in the *Saturday Evening Post*. His initial "Letters of a Self-Made Diplomat" series concluded in late 1926, but he continued to feed editor George Lorimer and the *Post* with other articles, many of them serialized and some later republished in book form.[12] Rogers produced three books during this period, two stemming from his trip to Europe, *Letters of a Self-Made Diplomat to His President* and *There's Not a Bathing Suit in Russia & Other Bare Facts*, and a third, *Ether and Me or "Just Relax,"* originating from a near tragedy in the summer of 1927.[13] Although one of his funniest productions and a best seller, the last-mentioned volume recounted a critical time in his life, a moment when his survival was threatened by a severe gallstone attack, a complicated surgery, and an unsteady recovery. He did survive the ordeal, and in typical Rogers fashion, he made use of the whole episode, spun into humor, in his writing and lecturing over the next couple of years.

Earlier in 1927, in the midst of his developing health problem, Rogers oversaw the release of the first of the travelogues that he and producer Carl Stearns Clancy had filmed in Europe and had completed the previous fall. The film shorts began appearing in the nation's movie theaters at the same time that Rogers was touring on the lecture circuit.[14] Along with his syndicated writings and his mass-market publications, they contributed to his ubiquitous presence. His image, his voice, his words seemed to be everywhere, but their down-to-earthness, their genuineness made the total package palatable and popular. That popularity translated into a generous public response in the spring of 1927, when Rogers appealed to Americans in the wake of one of the most spectacular natural disasters to strike the country in the early twentieth century: the flooding of the Mississippi River valley. Hundreds of thousands of people fell victim to the catastrophe, and the American Red Cross struggled to respond. Rogers's efforts raised very large sums for the Red Cross relief fund, and the organization thanked him with a life membership, an honor he treasured.[15]

In the midst of his relief efforts, Rogers, along with a good deal of the world, spent many anxious hours waiting for news that a lone American aviator by the name of Charles Lindbergh had successfully flown the Atlantic.[16] His remarkable flight, one of the most amazing feats of the century, fueled Rogers's commitment to aviation, confirmed his belief in its possibilities, fired his emotions, and led to a lasting friendship. Later in the year, following a banquet in San Diego in his honor, Charles Lindbergh flew Will and Betty Blake Rogers and other guests back to Los Angeles. At one point, much to his delight, Rogers even shared the cockpit with the world's newest hero.[17]

Rogers and Lindbergh soon enjoyed another encounter. In early December 1927, not long after finishing his fifth season on the lecture circuit, Rogers traveled to Mexico at the invitation of President Plutarco Calles.[18] His visit stemmed from Ambassador Dwight W. Morrow's efforts to build goodwill in a country where the United States sorely lacked it.[19] Rogers's stay went well, but the high point came when Lindbergh landed in Mexico City on the first leg of an extensive flying tour of Latin America.[20] The two men solidified their friendship, one that would bind them through common interests and common cause for years to come.

On 4 January 1928, a little more than two weeks after his return from Mexico, Rogers again found himself involved in a national radio hookup, this time as part of the Dodge Victory Hour, an entertainment program linking personalities at sites nationwide. Rogers, seated in his Beverly Hills home, surprised everyone, broadcasters and listeners alike, when he assumed the persona of President Coolidge and delivered on-air remarks as if from the White House.[21] The resulting criticism, including editorial-page rebuke in the New York Times, stunned Rogers, in part out of incredulity that anyone could have believed it truly was Coolidge on the air.[22] He sent an immediate and lengthy apology to the president, and Coolidge responded graciously.[23] The incident, however, continued to bother Rogers for several months, and he replayed it and his disbelief often during his next, and final, lecture season.

Despite the furor over his impersonation of the president, Rogers remained interested in foreign issues and affairs, and sought other opportunities to explore them. Another such chance soon came when he and his wife attended a conference of Western Hemisphere countries in mid-January 1928.[24] He shared his impressions of that experience with the public through his commentary in print and on stage. The presidential election year of 1928 also offered much to expound upon in the arena of politics. Rogers once again worked as a correspondent at the national political conventions, his frustration with the Democratic debacle in New York four years earlier still in evidence.[25]

His sense of the "bunk" of politics was played out that election year when Rogers accepted the invitation of *Life* magazine to run as a sham candidate for president. His Anti-Bunk party and political slogan, "He Chews to Run," offered a much needed and lighthearted diversion from a real campaign that even as early as July 1928 promised to devolve into an angry fight over religion and drink.[26] It also guaranteed for Rogers an appropriate place in the American public mind. As a mock candidate and as himself, he hovered above the madness of real politics, yet as one connected to the insiders, he was able to interpret those realities accurately and in simple, concise, understandable terms. Regardless of its levity, the Anti-Bunk campaign and Rogers's mock candidacy for president spoke well of his national prominence and his credible position in the public consciousness. The future indeed looked bright for the forty-eight-year-old cowboy from Oologah.

1. For the Rogers family's return on the *Leviathan* and the shipboard efforts to benefit the Florida hurricane victims, see *WA*, 2:249–53.

2. Everett Sanders (1882–1950), an attorney and Republican politician, had served as a congressional representative from Indiana; he was secretary to President Coolidge from 1924 to 1929 (*NYT*, 13 May 1950; *BDUSCong*, 1764). See Telegram from Everett Sanders, 29 September 1926, below.

3. See Draft of Telegram to Everett Sanders, 29 September 1926, below.

4. For a reprint of the article see *ML*, 3–17.

5. For example, see typewritten transcript, *Spartanburg Herald*, Spartanburg, S.C., 18 October 1926, in Lecture Tour News Coverage, OkClaW.

6. See Article from *Kansas City Star*, 15 November 1926, below.

7. *WA*, 3:127.

8. See Telegram from Douglas Fairbanks, 3 December 1926, below.

9. *NYT*, 23 December 1926. See Notes for Remarks at Mayoral Inauguration, ca. 21 December 1926, below.

10. See Draft of Newspaper Column, ca. 7 October 1926, below.

11. For example, see Letter from John S. to Editor, *New York Times*, 29 October 1926, below.

12. For example, see the republication of the series "More Letters from a Self-Made Diplomat to His President" in *ML*, 21–92.

13. For Rogers's account of his gallstone attack and recovery, see *EMJR*. See also Telegram from Florenz Ziegfeld, Jr., 15 June 1927, below.

14. See Advertisement in *Exhibitor's Herald*, 5 March 1927, below.

15. See Telegram to Newspaper Editor, 28 April 1927, and Telegram from John Barton Payne, 1 June 1927, below. See also *WA*, 3:24–27.

16. Charles Augustus Lindbergh (1902–74), an American airmail pilot, flew *The Spirit of St. Louis*, a single-engine plane, from New York to Paris in thirty-three and one-half hours on 21–22 May 1927, completing the first solo, nonstop transatlantic flight. His remarkable feat brought him worldwide fame and adulation (*DAB*, Supp. 9:495–99; *HD1920s*, 215). For a sample of comments by Rogers on Lindbergh and his flight see *DT*, 1:90–99; and *WA*, 3:35–37.

17. See Notes for Speech at Dinner for Charles A. Lindbergh, 21 September 1927, below.

18. See Telegram from Thomas Arnold Robinson, 4 November 1927, below.

19. Dwight Whitney Morrow (1873–1931), attorney and banker, was appointed by President Coolidge as U.S. ambassador to Mexico in the summer of 1927. Possessed of diplomacy but without experience in the diplomatic service, Morrow immediately went to work to improve the grossly deteriorated relations between the two countries. Among his first moves, he invited Rogers to Mexico on a goodwill mission and then, concurrently, arranged to have Charles Lindbergh fly to Mexico City. American public image improved appreciably (*DAB*, 13:234–35; Ellis, *Republican*, 246; Sobel, *Coolidge*, 349).

20. For accounts by Rogers of his experiences in Mexico, see *ML*, 21–92; and Transcript of Lecture Tour Performance, 16 April 1928, below.

21. *NYT*, 4–6 January 1928. See also Telegram from V. V. McNitt, 6 January 1928, below.

22. *NYT*, 7 January 1928.

23. See Letter to Calvin and Grace Coolidge, ca. 10 January 1928, and Letter from Calvin Coolidge, 11 January 1928, below.

24. For example, see Telegram to Charles Evans Hughes, 17 January 1928, below.

25. For Rogers's coverage of the conventions, see *CA*, 89–117.

26. See Telegram from Robert E. Sherwood, 6 June 1928, below. For more on Rogers's mock campaign for the presidency, see *HCTR*.

Telegram from Everett Sanders
29 September 1926
Washington, D.C.

Within a day of his return from Europe, Rogers received the following telegram from President Coolidge's personal secretary, Everett Sanders. The unexpected message offered Rogers his first invitation to stay overnight at the White House.

75N FWG 22 GOVT

– THE WHITE HOUSE WASHINGTON DC 352P SEP 29 1926

WILL ROGERS

HOTEL ASTOR NEWYORK NY

TELEGRAM RECEIVED[1] THE PRESIDENT HOPES YOU WILL STAY AT THE WHITE HOUSE DURING YOUR VISIT[2] WIRE ARRIVAL AND CAR WILL MEET YOU

EVERETT SANDERS

403P

TG, rc. OkClaW, 1975.31.0215. On Western Union Telegram Co. letterhead.

1. The telegram was not located. For a description of its contents see *ML*, 4.

2. President Coolidge customarily invited U.S. ambassadors to visit him at the White House on their return to the United States. When he heard of Rogers's imminent

return, he instructed his secretary to extend a similar invitation to the Self-Made Diplomat (Coolidge, "Real Calvin Coolidge," 214).

Draft of Telegram to Everett Sanders
29 September 1926
[New York, N.Y.]

Everett Sanders.
White House.
Washington. D. C.

If that gentleman is not kidding me that is the greatest honor   tthat ever fell my way[1] and I not only appreciate it but I am going to take you up on it, I have to stop off tomorrow,(Thursday) and see Mr Lorimer in Philadelphia, Then I am~~m~~ coming on down there ~~an~~ in ~~t~~the afternoon, Just think the only non officer seeker that that ever slept in the White House. I have an awful lot to report.[2]

I will be there one night if I have to put a cot in the Blue Room. If he will run again I will carry the solid south for him. I will wire from Philadelphia, If this is not on the level you better stop me in Philadelphia. Just think it will be the first meal I ever had on the Government, and its just my luck to be on a diet now.

Its Mrs Coolideg I want to meet. regards till somebody wakes me up.

W. R.

TG, dc. OkClaW, 1975.21.0216. Large hand-written "x" in top margin, center right.

1. See Telegram from Everett Sanders, 29 September 1926, above.
2. Rogers related his experiences at the White House in "A Letter from a Self-Made Diplomat to His Constituents" in the *Saturday Evening Post*, 8 January 1927. For a reprint see *ML*, 3–17.

Draft of Newspaper Column
ca. 7 October 1926
[Toronto, Ont., Canada]

Rogers's "Daily Telegram" column first appeared, rather inauspiciously, in the New York Times *on 30 July 1926. It continued to be published exclusively in that news-paper until his return from Europe.[1] The following is his draft of the first "Daily Telegram" to be syndicated to the* Times *and other newspapers throughout the*

United States.[2] It includes Rogers's instructions to the staff at McNaught Syndicate in New York.

Make this the first one, and please dont cut out a word, leave that Peaches[3] in there,
Alw[a]ys put the date line, and the town I send from .

~~Toronto Canada.~~

~~Oct, (date)~~

Toronto, Ont. Oct. 11.—

HAD JUST A▲[*handwritten:*]R▲RIVED HOME AFTER FIXING EVERYTHING/▲UP ▲IN EUROPE WHEN WHITE HOUSE SPOKESMAN DISSPATCHED ME TO ~~CANADA~~ LOOK OVER CANADA AND MAKE ~~THEM~~ ▲ENGLAND▲ FOLLOWING OFFER FOR IT. ONE DOUBTFUL WORLD COURT SEAT. PROHIBITION INCLUDING ENFORCEMENT OFFICERS. "PEACHES".[3] HAYTI.[4] ALL STATES SOUTH OF DIXON LINE. AND THROW IN AL SMITH. DEAL PENDING, WILL WIRE TOMORROW.

WILL [*handwritten:*]Rogers

TM, dc.[5] OkClaW, Will Rogers, Jr., Collection. Interlineations were typewritten, unless otherwise noted. Double strike-through indicates hand-deleted text. Place and date line was handwritten, but not in Rogers's hand.

1. The *New York Times* published its forty-seventh and final exclusive daily dispatch from Rogers on 27 September 1926, the day of his return from abroad. For the initial group of Rogers's "Daily Telegrams," see *DT*, 1:1–15; for further background information see Letter from Nancy Langhorne Astor, ca. 29 July 1926, above.
2. No daily dispatches appeared for three weeks while Rogers planned and started his fall lecture tour and the McNaught Syndicate marketed and sold syndication rights to the new daily series. Although the first of the syndicated "Daily Telegrams" carried a dateline of "Toronto, Ont., Oct. 10" (or "Oct. 11" in at least one instance), Rogers had left that Canadian city two to three days earlier and was either in Montreal or headed across the border to Buffalo, N.Y. The place of origin of the initial three syndicated columns differed from the progress of his lecture tour, but by 14 October the published datelines had begun to align with the tour chronology (*DT*, 1:16, 322; Chronology, 1926, OkClaW). See also Letter from F. J. Murphy to C. V. Van Anda, 15 October 1926, below.
3. Peaches Browning (Frances Heenan Browning, 1910–56), a fifteen-year-old schoolgirl, married Edward West Browning (1874–1934), a millionaire New York real estate operator who was thirty-five years her senior, on 10 April 1926. She left him on 2 October, less than six months later, and soon sued for divorce. The marriage of Peaches and Daddy Browning and its troubled aftermath provided ample fodder for the sensational tabloid journalism of the period (*NYT*, 13 October 1934, 24 August 1956; Leinwand, *1927*, 2).
4. Since U.S. intervention in Haiti during the Wilson administration in 1915, a succession of American navy and army officers had effectively controlled the Caribbean nation's domestic and foreign affairs. The strong U.S. presence had resulted in

improvements in the social and economic life of Haiti by the mid-1920s, but a perceived misapplication of authority by the occupying power had caused considerable friction with the traditional leadership, the native elite (Ellis, *Republican*, 230, 232–33, 270–73).

5. Dating of the document was determined from the recorded date of Rogers's presence in Toronto (see Chronology, 1926, OkClaW).

To Will Rogers, Jr.
ca. 9 October 1926
Ottawa, Ont., Canada

Ottawa.   Canada.

My Dear Bill.

I got your fine letter before I left New York but I was just so busy I couldent get time to answer, You see I had to have a whole new new act this season and I was worried about it, But it is coming along pretty well, a lot of the european stuff we saw and wrote about over there is getting good laughs, your Gag about "No cats in the Alley in Venice" is a big laugh, and your other one about " Getting up earlier so you could see more Churches", is good too, We got the biggest laugh last night   old Bruce come on to move the Piano for the roping and as he was pushing it it off to the back why the whole thing fell apart, all the legs fell off and there was Piano scattered all over the stage, You know how scared old Bruce can look   well you should have seen his eyes, He thought he had ruined the hwole show, Theatre, act,and everything, Well I wish it would happen every night I got a dozen laughs out of it, John McCormack was in the audience and I was up in his room here at the Hotel after the show, he sings here tonight and I will hear him as we dont play tonight,[1] He was tickled to death for what I had done for Ireland, He liked the act very much but he sent for Much[2] and told him that the quarteete was "Rotten" and that they should be shot for not singing some Popular songs, That if he could afford to go out and sing Popular songs with what he thought was a better voice than they had why he dident see why they should object, I hope it does make them some good, they can pick out the poorest songs there is it looks like, I hope your boil is all right   eat a nickles worth of raisens every day and you wont have any boils, if you do have any get em on the outside where you can get at em,

Now I would like to have you get after that Cavalry[3] if its possible, they tell me they make you ride bareback   there a lot, Now the way we will work that Black Horse troop, I will get you a nice big horse just the size of theirs, I will get one from some Trick rider, and you watch and see just what they have to learn and then we will tke him and break him in for it and you can practice on him every day all next summer, We will make us a small ring right above the Polo field out at the ranch and we can do all our tricks in there, We will break old Jim in so when he goes there he will have it all before he starts, How do you think he would make out, He wont get there till about your last year,

Well I guess Mama is there and you are happy, and I know she is too, I wish I was there with you both, I will get down there some time in a few weeks, Now you are going to be mighty homesick and lonesome when she leaves you, But you just grit your teeth and stay with it, This is the hard time and you can always figure the longer you stay the easier it will get, Basket ball ought to be a good game for you to take up so play it all you can, and work on the&~~Bars and rings all you can~~ Bars and rings all you can, I want you to do everything thatwill make your arms and shoulders strong, Take any extra lessons in the way of Athletics that you can, I dont care what it cost if it is helping you out in any way, I guess you got a real swimming pool there, I think we can arrange so we can go home togeather Xmas, I guess you wont have long but you will have time to make it some way, they have shortened the time on the trains a little now, Well I will have to stop and start digging out some Gags, I will fix you a couple of ropes and send to you, Hope this reaches you before Mama goes   I am in Cincannatii Wednesday, I thought maby she would come over there, I hope she likes the school and thinks that it is best for you and I hope you beat Kemper[4] this fall, Well By By Son lots of love to you and Mama, write me when you get time   I know they keep you pretty busy, If you write you always want to pick out a town several days ahead on my route to give it plenty of time, love,

daddy.

TL, rc. OkClaW, 1975.11.0036.

1. For Rogers's visit with John McCormack see *WA*, 2:256–58.
2. J. Erwyn Mutch, a tenor in the de Reszke quartet, served as the tour's business manager during the time that the group teamed with Rogers (*HC*, 1 November 1926; *NYT*, 4 January 1976)
3. By the time he left Culver Military Academy in the spring of 1928, Cadet Rogers had become a member of the school's famous Black Horse riding team and a top competitor on the varsity swimming squad (clippings, William Van [*sic*] Rogers file, CMA).
4. Will Rogers had attended Kemper School, a military academy in Boonville, Mo., from mid-January 1897 to mid-March 1898 (*PWR*, 1:9; see Kemper School Matriculation Book Entries, 5 January–11 February 1897, and Kemper School Report Card, 26 March 1897, *PWR*, 1:131–35).

F. J. Murphy to C. V. Van Anda
15 October 1926
New York, N.Y.

October 18▲5▲, 1926.

Mr. C. V. Van Anda,[1]
The Times,
New York, N.Y.

Dear Mr. Van Anda:

This will confirm our verbal arrangement covering the Will Rogers daily dispatches. For a period of six months, effective from today, we will deliver to the Times, seven days a week,[2] a short dispatch from Will Rogers sent from wherever he may happen to be. The dispatches will be filed to the Times at night press rate collect early each evening. We understand that you will turn over copies to the Western Union for filing to newspapers in other cities that are also buying the service. We understand that the price for this service is to be one hundred dollars per week.

In case the services proves satisfactory to the Times, we will give you an option of continuing the arrangement for a longer period of time after the six months term is completed.

If the terms as stated in this letter are correct and according to your understanding will you kindly confirm by signing below?

Very truly yours,

F J Murphy[3]

Treasurer.

Accepted:
The New York Times
By C. V. Van Anda

TLS, with autographed insertions, rc. NYT-A, Publishers Collection. On letterhead of The McNaught Syndicate, Inc., and Eastern Office of The Central Press Association, Newspaper Features, V.V. McNitt, Pres., Times Bldg., New York. The interlineation was handwritten.

1. Carr Vattel Van Anda (1864–1945) held the title of managing editor of the *New York Times* from 1904 to 1932, but he took a leave of absence in 1925 and thereafter was not active in the position (*NYT*, 29 January 1945).

2. Many subscriber newspapers never ran the Sunday version of the "Daily Telegram," probably because several of them (though not the *New York Times*) were already carrying Rogers's "Weekly Article" on that day. The lack of demand contributed to the discontinuance of the Sunday edition of the daily column in April 1927 (see *DT*, 1:324–49).

3. Frank J. Murphy was treasurer of the McNaught Syndicate from the late 1920s through at least the mid-1930s (various correspondence, McNaught Syndicate binder, OkClaW).

To George H. Lorimer
ca. 27 October 1926
[Tulsa, Okla.?]

Dear Mr. Lorimer.

I been a terrible time on this but I hope it is O K. I am going tright on on this same series,[1] I am not going to drop the idea of it, But the next one i send may be the one on the White House visit[2] and would be under another heading, I am working on it, Then Ireland tocome and one on the South.[3] Sure doing fine on my trip much better than last year even,

Best to you all.
Will

TL, rc.[4] DLC-MD, Wesley Stout Papers.

1. With this letter, Rogers probably enclosed one or more of the final installments of the "Letters of a Self-Made Diplomat" series. The last three episodes, which embraced Rogers's trip to Russia, appeared in the *Saturday Evening Post* in the issues of 23 October, 6 November, and 4 December 1926. They were reprinted in *There's Not a Bathing Suit in Russia & Other Bare Facts* (for the complete Russia series see *TNBSR*).

2. Rogers recounted his visit to the White House in his series on Europe: "A Letter from a Self-Made Diplomat to His Constituents." The piece ran in the *Post* issue of 8 January 1927. See also Telegram to George H. Lorimer, 2 December 1926, and Draft of Telegram from George H. Lorimer, 2 December 1926, below.

3. No articles by Rogers about Ireland or the South were found in the *Saturday Evening Post* or in other publications. See, however, Manuscript for Magazine or Newspaper Article, ca. 1926, below.

4. Dating of the document was determined by the date of George Lorimer's reply (see Letter from George H. Lorimer, 27 October 1926, below).

From George H. Lorimer
27 October 1926
[Philadelphia, Pa.]

October 27, 1926

Mr. Will Rogers

Dear Mr. Rogers:

That's a fine piece that came to hand this morning.[1] There is only one fault to find with these articles and that is that they don't come often enough. I think it would be a good thing to shoot the White House piece as soon as possible even though it would run ahead of the remainder of the European series.

Yours sincerely,

[George H. Lorimer]

L/D

TL, cc. DLC-MD, Wesley Stout Papers.

1. See Letter to George H. Lorimer, ca. 27 October 1926, above.

John S. to Editor, *New York Times*
29 October 1926
[New York, N.Y.?]

The publication of Rogers's daily column in the New York Times *drew some letters of objection from readers of the venerable newspaper, especially in the early months of its run in the* Times. *The following criticism typified the stridency of the complainants and issues common among them.*

To the Editor, New York Times
dear Sir—
    With this as the slogan of your paper– 'All the *News*' that's fit to print–" emblazoned on evry page- how can you so offend the refined & better feelings of the public in printing those vulgar letters daily, signed "Will Rogers"–[1]   his P.S. today– "Where is Marie[2]– Did Peaches can her papa? How's Aimee[3] & Al Smith" etc. Could there be any thing more obnoxious! Paragraphing her beautiful Gracious Majesty the Queen of Roumania with "Peaches [*word illegible*] it is an insult, only exceeded by the bad taste of the one who publishes his letters–   While abroad this summer nearly evry day ~~thos~~ the same Mʳ Rogers published criticisms & fictitious interviews with our *President of the United States*, familiarly speaking of him as "Cal"—   A paper such as The New York Times should *suppre▼s▼* ~~them▲~~ [*overwritten*] rather▲ than encourage familiarity [?] of such a man–   Of course he knows no better–   The New York Times should know better– Should know better faster,

Sincerely

Mr— John S__

ALS, rc.[4] NYT-A.

1. The archival files of the *New York Times* contain at least thirteen letters of protest, dating from late October 1926 to late March 1927. As in the immediate instance, some readers objected to a specific column by Rogers, while others lodged more general complaints about his writings (see NYT-A). For a reaction by the management at the *New York Times* see Letter from Arthur H. Sulzberger to Adolph S. Ochs, 17 January 1927, below.

2. Marie (Marie Alexandra Victoria, 1875–1938), queen of Romania, was the wife of King Ferdinand and also a member of the royal families of both Great Britain and Russia. More popular in Romania than even her husband, Marie was noted for her diplomacy, patriotism, and charisma. She started a much publicized American tour on 12 October, and her openness with the scores of reporters who accompanied her entourage ensured that stories about the queen filled newspapers throughout her six-week tour (*NYT*, 19 July 1938).

3. Aimee Semple McPherson (Aimee Elizabeth Kennedy, 1890–1944), flamboyant Canadian-born American revivalist, founded the Foursquare Gospel movement. From a base in Los Angeles, she built a significant worldwide following for her new denomination, but she became enmeshed in a scandal in 1926. Her supposed drowning, her reappearance, her claim of having been kidnapped, and stories of a love tryst captured headlines for several months (*DAB*, Supp. 3:497–99; *HD1920s*, 228).

4. Filed with the letter were two clippings, one of the boxed slogan, "All the News That's Fit to Print," that appeared daily in the *New York Times*, and a second of Rogers's "Daily Telegram" of 29 October 1926, the one that prompted the complaint (see *DT*, 1:21–22).

To Will Rogers, Jr.
ca. 10 November 1926
Abilene, Tex.

Abiline.   TExas.

Dear Son.

I been waiting to try and get a chnace to write you for several days but I am just so busy, Mr Clancy has come on with his Pictures he made in Europe and I have been trying toTitle them for him, He brought his projection machine and we set it up in the room and run it, they look pretty good, I think the Irsih ones are the best   they will hav e the most Comedy,

Mama went home from Lub ock the other day   gues you have heard from her.[1] She will be coming back east pretty soon and will stop off on her way east, I dont know what day I will get there till I get up that way and see what my route calls for, Now I think that I may be able to come down t there and do a show for you all at the school ~~some~~   The chances are it would have to be on Sunday night as that is the only one I am off, But I will make it some way, so they needent come up to South bend, You can come up but I dont want the Boys to pay out anything just to come up there   I willcome down to your place and do them a show.

Say I sw what Kemper did to you, Hooray, you better let those good schols alone and play Urban.

Say am getting the old Home ranch fixed up fine for you in Oklahoma, Got 300 sheep. 250 goats long haired ones, angoras. and over a hundred head of cattle, it looks fine and will make us a fine farm some day.

How did you make out halloween, did they do much to you, I guess it is getting a little easier now is it not,

Well you stay with em   after Xmas you will feel almost like an old timer. Mr and Mrs Post have been out home to our place and they are crazy about it and may come back,

They say the Polo field is in fine shape and all the Uplifters are crazy to get a crack at it[2]   they are playing on an old dirt field no grass, do they play indoor Polo there,

Well I have to go over and annoy the Texans,   Write me as often as you can, I know how it is   you are pretty busy, here is a couple of dollars but dont get to reckless with it??.

Well goodnight Son, I tell you we are awful proud of you sticking away off there, but you will be glad in the finish,

Lots of love.
Daddy.

TL, rc.[3] OkClaW, 1975.11.0039.

1. Betty Blake Rogers wrote at least two letters within a few days to son Bill. She penned a note from Dallas on 3 November and then a week later wrote a brief message after returning home to Beverly Hills (1975.11.0014, 1975.11.0016, OkClaW).

2. The polo field at the Rogers ranch was the first such layout in the Rustic Canyon area of the Santa Monica Mountains. The nearby Uplifters Club soon followed suit with its own polo grounds (Yagoda, *Will Rogers*, 268).

3. Dating of the document was determined by references to Rogers's lecture tour itinerary.

Article in Unidentified Newspaper
ca. 14 November 1926
[Little Rock, Ark.?]

If time allowed during his lecture tour stops, Rogers often would make himself available for an interview with a local reporter, not coincidentally, one from a newspaper that carried his syndicated columns. His visit to Little Rock, Ark., on 13 November 1926 was typical. The interviewer, apparently from the Arkansas Democrat, *spent time with Rogers in his hotel room before his appearance the same evening at a local high school auditorium.*[1] *The interview sheds light on the personal side of Rogers the entertainer.*

Will Rogers, of Claremore, Okla., and points east, sat in his room at the Hotel Marion last night and talked of two people he likes real well—Mrs. Will Rogers and Mr. Calvin Coolidge.

Mrs. Rogers has a sense of humor, and still likes his stuff, the rope fondling humorist said as he chewed gum. He didn't know whether Mr. Coolidge fell for it or not because, as he explained:

"I didn't spill any of my junk when I went to see him. I went to listen, not to talk."

Rogers stole a few minutes from a busy evening to talk. He is likeable off the stage.

"Well, it wouldn't be hard to recognize you," his visitor said. "No," answered Rogers, "I can't deny it very well."

DEFENDS PRESIDENT COOLIDGE.

"Coolidge isn't cold or silent," said Mr. Rogers. He talked with the president at the White House recently. "He talks freely and you can't tell him much he doesn't know. I tried to tell a little about Russia, where I was recently, but I found out I didn't know anything about it. And we have no representatives there, either. Coolidge is a great politician. He looks further down ahead than any of them.

"Those birds are cuckoo who think Coolidge hasn't a sense of humor. He couldn't say the things he does without one. He's got too much humor for the rest of those birds in Washington," he said. Mrs. Coolidge is "wonderful" and Washington is "crazy about her," Mr. Rogers declared.

"Nobody is big enough to keep on America's front page more than a week," said Mr. Rogers, switching the conversation to Queen Marie of Roumania, and her trip to the United States.

"You seem to be doing pretty well at it," his caller said.

"Only in spots. Lots of times now you'll find me over between the markets and the want ads."

Mr. Rogers made a movie in England while on his recent trip abroad as President Coolidge's self-appointed, self-made diplomat. It will be released soon after the first of the year. He likes the movies, likes his work with the Follies, and likes the "one-night stands."

"I've tried everything," he said. "I'll find something, afterwhile, I can do."

STILL HAS STAGE FRIGHT.

Although the gray is rather thick in his hair that won't stay combed, Mr. Rogers says he has never reached the point where he doesn't have stage fright. On Follies first night he is apt to be found walking the river bank, fighting off nervousness. Even on "barnstorming trips," when he speaks night after night, he is nervous when he first gets on his feet.

"Audiences are different, too," he says. "Two towns right near each other will have exactly opposite audiences. One will be quicker than the other, more alert. I can't explain it. The Western audience is the best, if you know what I mean—an audience of cow men or oil men. Lots of towns in Texas ain't western towns.

"I try harder for a small, hard audience than I do for a good audience. Then I get to forcin' myself and the humor's forced, and the audience gets harder until something happens to get us all together."

The telephone interrupted and central told him it was Slaremore [*sic*] calling.

"Here's the old home town yapping aroun' about something," Rogers said as he held the receiver to his ear. "I can hear 'em dropping money. Somebody's going broke." And then, into the mouthpiece, "Now, you get on in here. You roll on in here. Leave that Lizzie somewhere and come on up to that hall where I'm talkin'."

He's got a great family, Rogers says, and they've all got a good sense of humor. But, he complains:

"It's pretty hard to be funny with your family. They laugh at me when I'm not tryin' to be funny, and then I get sore."

PD. Printed in unidentified newspaper, ca. 14 November 1926. Clipping, OkClaW, Scrapbook 15:77.

1. Although the newspaper from which the clipping came was not identified, the reference in the text to the Hotel Marion, a hostelry in Little Rock, Ark., and a comparison of the typography and layout of the text with clippings in Rogers scrapbooks that are identified as being from the *Arkansas Democrat*, help substantiate that the item in question came also from the *Democrat*. The same newspaper carried Rogers's weekly syndicated piece (Chronology, 1926, OkClaW; clippings, Scrapbook 21:140–41, OkClaW).

Article in *Kansas City Star*
15 November 1926
Kansas City, Mo.

Although not his first occasion at a radio microphone, Rogers's participation in November 1926 in the premiere broadcast of the National Broadcasting Company brought him the largest audience he had ever entertained in a single, live performance.[1] As the following record of his moments on the air attest, his on-air routine differed little from that of his lecture tour.

. . . Will Rogers speaking "to the world," from Independence, Kas., last night delighted those listening in on WDAF, The Star's radio station, with his comments on the great and on world affairs.

His speech was a part of the initial program of the National Broadcasting Company, a chain of radio stations of which WDAF is a member.

Will's "wise cracks" came a few minutes after Mary Garden[2] sang from her suite at the Hotel Belmont, Chicago.

Perhaps this was known to Will for he included the opera star among those he "kidded."

UP IN MARY'S DRESSING ROOM.

"I was on the way to Russia a while back," he said, "and Morris Gest[3] gave me a drink of vodka. Then he took me up to Mary Garden's dressing room in a theater in Paris and introduced me. What do you think. She just reached out and grabbed my arm, held it around her neck and kissed me. Think of Mary Garden perfume and then think of being that close to the real article. Maybe it was the vodka, I don't know. Do you hear that, Mrs. Rogers, way off there in California?

"Anyway when I got back in this country I got a telegram from Mary and she said she was going to be in Chicago to greet me, when I get there, vodka or no vodka." . . .

Mr. Rogers said that he "just come" from Claremore, Ok., and that he just as well could have broadcast down there but the town didn't need the advertisement. He explained he just had returned to this country recently from Europe where he was attending to some affairs for "Cal."

ROGERS HAS A PRACTICAL FACE.

Just to give his radio audience an idea of who was talking Will described himself as a "neat dresser but not gaudy."

"I ain't pretty, and I ain't striking," he said, "but I've got a practical face."

Taking up his recent journey to England he remarked that there was no one with whom they could compare in England except George Bernard Shaw.

"I and George both know the world is wrong but we don't know just exactly what is wrong with it. We're trying to fix it, all at so much a word. We kinda hope nobody will find out just what is the matter with it." . . .

"I don't write good, but I write a lot. Anyway, it's getting so writing is based on endurance, not ideas," he remarked.

Swinging across the ocean, Mr. Rogers's next comment landed him in Kansas City.

"Mr. Coolidge made pretty much of a speech in Kansas City on Armistice day," he went on. "He opened up that new memorial down there.[4] Leastways they call it a memorial. Looked more like a silo to me when I was there.

LEFT OUT JIM AND JAMES BOYS.

"He talked about all the Kansas and Missouri soldier boys but he forgot to mention Jim Reed or the James boys.[5] Mr. Coolidge said in his speech that in the next war we probably would draft capital as well as labor. It's too bad someone didn't think of that before the last war. I believe there are enough people interested in that proposition right now to get a unanimous consent to another war just to see if they would do it."

And back to England again, Will said it was a fine country with only one drawback, the dole.

"If you don't work they pay you. I told them that wouldn't do. We've tried it with congress and the senate for years and it's a failure."

Rogers told of his interview with the Italian premier[6] and in this connection he was reminded of his recent visit to the White House. A visit that just preceded that of Queen Marie.

"I can just imagine when the President and Queen Marie sat down to the dinner table," he said. "I don't know but I bet they sat there a long time and then Cal said: 'What country are you from, Marie?' or 'Marie, what do you do when your farmers want relief?'[7]

"They tell me Marie wore a diadem dripping pearls. You can imagine Mr. Coolidge in a case like that. He probably got his hat and tried to catch some of the drippings, what with his economy program."[8]

"I understand that the acting king of Rumania, Ferdinand, has told Marie to get out of 'the banquet halls by Christmas.'[9] One thing the queen's visit done for America that ought to make us all pray for her every night—she pushed Aimee and Peaches way back to the want ads."

From Marie, Will skipped to Russia, a country, he said, that still has its shirt tail out.

"In Russia," he said, "they all bathe together. Maybe if it hadn't been for this promiscuous sort of bathing I would have got to see more of Russia. I didn't see all of Russia but I did see all of some Russians."

Rogers ended his radio talk by warning his audience that he couldn't be with them much longer because he had to make some more trips for Mr. Coolidge. The President, he said, wanted him to go to China and Japan next to attend to a few little matters there.

PD. Printed in *Kansas City Star,* Kansas City, Mo., 15 November 1926. Scrapbook 8, Part 1, OkClaW. Ellipses inserted by editors.

1. The debut of the National Broadcasting Company (NBC) involved a four-and-one-half-hour entertainment extravaganza over a nationwide linking of nineteen radio stations. The broadcast reached an estimated 8 million listeners. Rogers, whose first radio broadcast had occurred in February 1922 over pioneer radio station KDKA in Pittsburgh, shared air time on 15 November with other performers at sites around the country (Craig, *Fireside Politics,* 30; Yagoda, *Will Rogers,* 188, 240; telegram, M. H. Aylesworth to Will Rogers, 16 November 1926, OkClaW, 1975.31.0440).

2. Mary Garden (1874–1967), Scottish-born soprano, made her American operatic debut in New York in 1907. Successful in both Europe and the United States, she began a long career with the Chicago Opera Association in 1910. She served one year as its director—the first woman to head a leading opera company—and continued to perform with the group until 1931 (*DAB,* Supp. 8:200–1; *NGDO,* 2:350). For Rogers on Mary Garden see also *WA,* 2:202–3.

3. Morris Gest (Moses Gershonovitch, 1881–1942), born in Russia, scored success and acclaim in New York in the 1910s and 1920s for his large, lavish, but tasteful theatrical productions (*DAB,* Supp. 3:296–97).

4. President Coolidge spoke on Armistice Day, 11 November 1926, at the dedication in Kansas City, Mo., of the Liberty Memorial, a 200-foot-tall tower to honor the men and women who had served in the war (*NYT,* 12 November 1926; Brown and Dorsett, *K.C.,* 179). See also *WA,* 2:274–76.

5. Senator Jim Reed and the nineteenth-century outlaw brothers Jesse and Frank James hailed from western Missouri (*DAB,* Supp. 3:621; *NEAW,* 564).

6. That is, Benito Mussolini.

7. The agricultural sector of the economy, saddled with huge surpluses, significant debt, and low commodity prices, struggled throughout the 1920s. Attempts to provide relief for farmers through federal purchases of crop surpluses failed to survive opposition within the Republican administration (*HD1920s,* 227–28).

8. For Rogers on Queen Marie and her visit to the White House, see *WA,* 2:259–62.

9. Ferdinand (Ferdinand of Hohenzollern, 1865–1927) reigned as king of Romania from 1914 until his death in July 1927. Ferdinand opposed his wife's tour of the United States, but as the more dominant personality in the royal family, she prevailed (*NYT,* 21 July 1927).

Statement of Payments for Articles in *Saturday Evening Post*
ca. 30 November 1926
[Philadelphia, Pa.?]

ARTICLES BY WILL ROGERS IN THE SATURDAY EVENING POST DURING 1926[1]

Date of
Statement

March 25th	My Rope and Gun for a Democratic Issue	$2,000
April 20	Florida Versus California	2,000
June 17	Letters from a Self Made Diplomat	6,000
	(#1-2- & 3)	
June 17	Letters from a Self Made Diplomat (#4)	2,000
July 30	" " " " " " (#5 & 6)	4,000
Aug. 31	" " " " " " (#7)	2,000
Sept. 14	" " " " " " (#8)	2,000
Oct. 5	" " " " " "	2,000
Nov. 2	" " " " " "	2,000
Nov. 30	" " " " " "	2,000

Total $26,000

[*initialed:*] nsf [?]

ACCOUNTING DEPARTMENT.

TDS. OkClaW, 1975.24.0224. Small, hand-inserted check marks appear to the immediate right of each of the dates.

1. The respective publication dates of Rogers's thirteen articles were: 1 May, 29 May, 10 July, 17 July, 24 July, 31 July, 21 August, 28 August, 2 October, 23 October, 6 November, and 4 December 1926 and 8 January 1927.

Telegram to George H. Lorimer
2 December 1926
Toledo, Ohio

HA 23 119 NL 1/78

TOLEDO OHIO 1

GEORGE H. LORRIMER

SATURDAY EVENING POST PHILADELPHIA PENN

RECEIVED MANUSCRIPT BUT DONT KNOW ANY MORE NOW THAN I DID BEFORE THEY HAVE GOT A LOT OF THINGS MARKED HERE BUT HAVE DONE NOTHING WITH

ANY OF THEM DO YOU MEAN TO SAY THAT YOU ARE GOING TO TAKE EVERYTHING OUT OF THE ARTICLE THAT COOLIDGE SAID[1] IF THAT IS SO I DONT THINK THE ARTICLE WOULD BE WORTH PRINTING WHAT I HAD REFERENCE TO IN REGARD TO WANTING TO SEE THE MANUSCRIPT WAS TO SEE WHAT YOU HAD CHANGED IT TO AND THOUGHT PERHAPS I COULD TELL ABOUT STAYING WITH THE WHITE HOUSE SPOKESMAN THE ARTICLE AS I HAVE RECEIVED IT IS EXACTLY AS I SENT IT IN WILL BE AT HOTEL STATLER CLEVELAND TODAY THURSDAY REGARDS

WILL ROGERS.

TG, rc. DLC-MD, Wesley Stout Papers. On Western Union Telegraph Co. letterhead. Metered below letterhead: "1926 DEC 2 AM 2 48." Typeset above text, page two: "HA23 2/41."

1. For Lorimer's response see Draft of Telegram from George H. Lorimer, 2 December 1926, below.

Draft of Telegram from George H. Lorimer
2 December 1926
Philadelphia, Pa.

December 2, 1926

Will Rogers
Hotel Statler
Cleveland
Ohio

Think we will have to eliminate all direct quotation when President touches on political or international affairs. When speaks on other things would call him White House spokesman. In other words let President stand whenever don't quote ~~directly~~ and call him White House spokesman when do. Think can get over article pretty well as stands by little judicious editing along these lines.

George H. Lorimer

Charge Post Editorial
WU

TG, dc. DLC-MD, Wesley Stout Papers.

Telegram from Douglas Fairbanks
3 December 1926
Los Angeles, Calif.

Although merely symbolic, the "election" of Rogers as mayor of Beverly Hills in December 1926 reaped for his hometown—as well as for Rogers—a wealth of publicity. Public announcement would wait for a few days, but the news probably first came to Rogers in the following telegram from film actor and neighbor Douglas Fairbanks.[1]

CC716 57 NL

LOSANGELES CALIF 3

WILL ROGERS

APPEARING AT THE THEATRE GRANDRAPIDS MICH

AM WIRING YOU CONFIDENTIALLY THAT YOU HAVE JUST BEEN ELECTED MAYOR OF BEVERLYHILLS BY BOARD OF TRUSTEES AS RESULT OF ENTHUSIASTIC MOVEMENT WHICH HAS BEEN UNDER WAY SOMETIME STOP PLANS NOW BEING FORMULATED TO SWEAR YOU INTO OFFICE UPON YOUR RETURN AND ARRANGE-MENTS FOR RECEPTION GOING FORWARD STOP WOULD APPRECIATE YOUR WIRING ME YOUR ITINERARY BEST REGARDS

DOUGLAS FAIRBANKS.

>TG, rc. OkClaW, 1975.31.0354. On Western Union Telegraph Co. letterhead. Printed immediately below letterhead, flush left: "RECEIVED AT MAIN OFFICE, 35-37 PEARL ST., GRAND RAPIDS, MICH." Metered below letterhead, right side: "1926 DEC 3 PM 10 23."

1. Fairbanks led a cabal of prominent film, real estate, and business figures that conspired to name Rogers as mayor of Beverly Hills, a community that under California law did not qualify to have a mayor (Rogers, *Will Rogers*, 206; Yagoda, *Will Rogers*, 240). See also Telegram from Calvin Coolidge, 18 December 1926, and Notes for Remarks at Mayoral Inauguration, ca. 21 December 1926, below.

Draft of Telegram to Florenz Ziegfeld, Jr.
ca. 6 December 1926
[Youngstown, Ohio?]

FLO ZEIGFELD.

ZEIGFELDS OWN THEATRE.[1]

ON THE RAGGED EDGE OF PARK AVENUE.

NEW YORK.

I SURE AM GLAD YOU ARE GOING TO HAVE YOUR OWN THEATRE. I DONT THINK ANY MAN CAN DO GOOD WORK IN SOME ONE ELSES THEATRE. I KNOW

HOW IT WAS WITH [*obliterated*] YOU, YOU COULDENT PUT ON AS GOOD SHOWS AS YOU WOULD HAVE LIKED TO~~O~~, FOR IF YOU HAD ~~THEY~~ WOULD HAVE ONLY MEANT THAT ~~YOU WOULD HAVE~~ THEY WOULD HAVE MADE MORE MONEY. AND WHY MAKE MORE MONEY WHEN YOU KNEW THAT THROUGH YOUR ARTISTIC EXPOSURE, CHARLEY AND ABE WOULD GET THEIR CUT OUT OF IT.[2] THE MINUTE YOUR MIND IS OFF RENT YOU CAN SETTLE DOWN AND DO SOMETHING WORTH WHILE. JUST THINK WHAT YOU WILL ACCOMPLISH ~~WHEN~~ ▲WHEN▲ THERE IS NO ARGUMENT OVER PERCENTAGE WITH ERLANGER. WHY YOU WILL FEEL LOST. I FEEL THAT THIS IS JUST THE STARTING FOR YOU OF A CHAIN~~,~~ JUST THINK WHAT SHUBERT AND SHULTE, AND LOEW AND NEEDICK AND THE OWL AND CHILDS, ALL DID WITH ONE IDEA. WHY FLO I FEEL THAT YOU ARE JUST IN YOUR INFANCY IN THEATRE OW[N]ING, YOU ARE JUST LIKE P-OOR ANNE NICHOLS[3] WHEN SHE ONLY HAD ~~ONE&ABIE ONLY~~ ONE ABIE. RESERVING YOU BEST CORNER LOTS IN BOTH CLAREMORE AND BEVERLEY HILLS AT SMALL INCREASE, ~~FOR WESTERN BRANCHES~~ PROMOTE LOCAL CAPITAL, THATS WHAT THEY ALL DO, YOU DONT FURNISH ANYTHING BUT NAME AND GIRLS. I HOPE YOU NEVER HAVE TO PUT IN ▼A▼ MOVIE SCREEN.[4]

YOUR OLD HIRED HAND.

WILL.

TG, dc. OkClaW, 1975.21.0210. Editorial marks appear throughout the document, although no evidence was found to verify its publication. All editorial marks have been ignored for this record. Double strike-through indicates hand-deleted text; single strike-through indicates type-deleted copy.

1. The $2.5 million, state-of-the-art Ziegfeld Theatre, considered one of the finest stage facilities ever built in New York, was dedicated on 9 December 1926 during a well-publicized event that attracted eight hundred people. Two years in construction and long a dream of Florenz Ziegfeld, the new theater owed its financing to newspaper mogul William Randolph Hearst and his associate, Arthur Brisbane (*OCAT*, 733; Ziegfeld and Ziegfeld, *Ziegfeld Touch*, 121, 134–35).

2. Ziegfeld had teamed with theatrical producers Charles Dillingham and Abraham Erlanger in the ownership of such theaters as the New Amsterdam, but his relationship with Erlanger, who was more financially astute than Dillingham, had proved especially vexing (Ziegfeld and Ziegfeld, *Ziegfeld Touch*, 40, 51, 76–77, 82, 120).

3. Anne Nichols (1891–1966), American actress and playwright, was best remembered for writing and staging *Abie's Irish Rose*, the highly successful comedy about the marriage of a Catholic and a Jew (*OCAT*, 506).

4. After Ziegfeld's death in the 1930s, the opulent theater bearing his name operated as a movie house until restored as a theatrical stage in 1944 (*OCAT*, 733).

Telegram from Calvin Coolidge
18 December 1926
Washington, D.C.

70S N 12 GOVT

THE WHITE HOUSE WASHINGTON DC 521P DEC 18 1926

WILL ROGERS

BEVERLY HILLS CALIF

CONGRATULATIONS UPON YOUR ELEVATION TO THE OFFICE OF HONORARY MAYOR OF BEVERLYHILLS[1]

CALVIN COOLIDGE

252P

TG, rc. OkClaW, 1975.21.0152. On Western Union Telegraph Co. letterhead. Printed immediately below letterhead: "Received at 1509 Burton Way, Beverly Hills, Calif. Phone 584292."

1. See Telegram from Douglas Fairbanks, 3 December 1926, above. President Coolidge's wire was one of several messages of congratulations Rogers received on being named mayor of Beverly Hills (see correspondence files, OkClaW).

Notes for Remarks at Mayoral Inauguration
ca. 21 December 1926
Beverly Hills, Calif.

A delegation of Beverly Hills citizens met Rogers and his family at the railroad station on their arrival from the East Coast and escorted them by parade to the site of the inauguration ceremonies, a park near the Beverly Hills Hotel. Rogers delivered his inaugural speech as mayor from a makeshift stage in the midst of a rain shower.[1]

(leve that gag   do last)
Gods gift to the People who dident see the Queen.

I am by no means the first Comedian Mayor, That seems to be the one requirement of aMyor, I have never seen a Moyor that wasent funny. [*handwritten:*] FUNNY PURPOSELY.

And the minure [minute] he puts on a Silk Hat he becomes SCREMINGLY funny.

[*handwritten:*] GROPING

Thats the only thing that has held this Joint back, It has everything to make a good town, Burglars, Poor parking Regulations[,] shortgae of water in the summer, poor Telephone service, Luncheon Clubs. Chamber of commerce, and everything that go to goes to handicap a 99 percent of the towns.

But what you really have needed is a Good mayor,

Too many Mayors have been elected on Honesty, That dont get you anyhwere, John W davis ran on that last time for the Democrats, and Coolidge dident suggest it at all and Davis lost by 70 mil. Now I dont say that i will give the old Burg a honest adminsitarti but I will at least split 50 50 with you,

I am bringing over a few of the syst[e]ms of Mussolini, There is the wisest cracking Wop in the world, every time he issues a statement it is a ifty [nifty?].

Real Estate men have got to go to work. I dont care who you work [for] but its got [t]o be [for] somebody.

I   want to introduce a law to make Real Estate men and Moving Picture people as good as aany other Citizens, there shall be no disscrimination against them,

The old City has really done great, I can remember it when   there wasent over 25 mortgages inthe whole town,

[*handwritten:*] NOT EVEN A MANICURIST, BEAUTY PARLOR

I remember in those old days we tried to make a living kout of som ~~some us~~ our own busines instead of out of Real esate.

I vcan rememebr when it was thought an honor to say you lived in hollytwood and not a disgrace,

I have been thinking over that reform thing and like all smart men I have changed my mind, there is nothing in it   everybody is going in for that, Hollywood ewent in for it and everybody that amount to anything moved out, I dont know of a single   Feature length inhabitant of Hollywood, Name me anybodt that is packing em in today and I will show you where he only has two more payments to make in Beverley Hills,

No sir come to think of it, I am for scandal,

If Tony Mix[2] wa[n]ts to flle [flee?] early in the morning with black bess or Silver [K]ing[3] pulls a party for the Wild Horse gang why let it be known,If Rin Tin Tin[4] gats mixed up with some tow [two] reel Comedy dog that is doing nothing but rescueing Babies why let him have his fling, Life is short in Beverley.

[*handwritten:*] CRYER[5] IS COMEDY RELIEF

JIMMY WALKER THE MAYOR OF THE BIGGEST MAYOR IN THE WORLD GOT IN BECAUSE HE COULD WITHSTAND MORE BANQUETS THAN ANY MAN IN N TY [NEW YORK].

SAY I HAVE REFUSED MORE BANQURTHS THAN JIMMY WALKER EVER HEARD OF?

[*handwritten:*] EVER TIME RING BELL

~~I KNOW YOU WILL ASK? WELL WILL HOW ARE YOU GOING TO RUN THE TOWN ANE YOU AWAY SO MUCH SAY I CAN RUN THIS TOWN BY TELEGRAPH? AND HOLLY WOOD OR LOS ANGLES I COULD RUN IT BY RADIO EVEN WITH THE SATATIC ON.~~

THERE IS GOING TO BE NO KEYS GIVEN OUT TO THE CITY. EVEN MARCO HELLMAN[6] AND DOUG FAIRBANKS HAVE GOT TO KNOCK WHEN THEY CONE IN.

I DONT W NT ANYBODY [R]INGING ME UP WHILE HERE TELLING ME THEY GOT A GOOD BUY ON WILSHIRE. I AM MAYOR NOT SANTA CLAUS TO TO SOME REAL ESTATE FIRM.

WE HAVE MORE SWIMMING POOLS LESS BIBLES THAN ANY TOWN IN AMER-ICA% WE IMITATE DUKE KOHANIMOKU[7] MORE THA[N] WE DO MOSES

WE HAVE POOLS [BECAUSE] WE LOVE TO BATHE COLLECTIVELY? BUT INDI-VIDUALLY WE ARE PRETTY DIRTY.

WE ARE THE HANDIEST TOWN IN THE WORLD FOR ELDERLY ACTORS WE ARE JUST TOW [TWO] MILES FROM THE OLD MANS HOME%[8]

IT DONT SPEAK VERY WELL FOR YOU[R] TWON [TOWN] WHEN THIS MANY OF YOU HAVENT GOT ANYTHING TO DO BUT COME TO MEET ME. WHATS THE MATTER WITH BUSINESS?

THE REAL ESTATE MEN ARE BETWEEN SALES. THEY HAVE A GOOD SALE COMING UP.

THE STARS HAD TO MOVE AWAY FROM HOLLYWOOD TO STAY AWAY FROM THE EXTRAS.

I MAY MAKE A GOOD MAYOR% I HAVE TRIED EVERYTHING ELSE? I AM WHAT YO CALL JUST GROPING IN THE DARK AND I AM REACHING FOR ANYTHING

THE SUCCESS OF MOVIES HAVE BEEN THE ANIMAL TRAINERS? MORE THAN DIRECTORS, THE MINUTE DEIRECTORS CAN TRAIN ACTORS TO ACT AS NATURAL AS A DOG OR A HORSE THEN THEY WILL HAVE ACOMPLISHED SOMETHING, THE SUCCESS OF PICTURTES AS I SEE IT BETTER ANIMAL TRAINERS,

I AM SORRY SOMEBODY REFERRED TO MOVIES AS AN ART? FOR SINCE THEN EVERYBODY CONNECTED WITH THEM STOPPED DOING SOMETHING TO MAKE EM BETTER AND THEY COMMENCED GETTING SERIOUS ABOUT THEM?

About Girls coming to meet me.

TD. OkClaW, 1975.14.0045. Typewritten, top margin, left center, page 1: "For Beverley." First two lines of text are circled. Handwritten "3" appears in left margin of paragraph 3 ("I am by . . ."). Handwritten "17" in left margin of paragraph 6 ("That's the only . . ."). Handwritten "3" in left margin of paragraph 11 ("I want to . . ."). Handwritten, stacked (/), "16 / OLD TIMES" in left margin of paragraph 12 ("The old City . . ."), with hand-inserted bracket connecting paragraphs12–15, left margin. Handwritten "12" in left margin of paragraph 16 ("I have been . . ."). Handwritten "3" in left margin of paragraph 20 ("Jimmy WALKER . . ."). Handwritten "1" in left margin of paragraph 25 ("I DONT . . ."). Handwritten, stacked (/), "15 / Tough / advantage" in left margin of paragraph 26 ("WE HAVE MORE . . ."), with hand-inserted bracket connecting paragraphs 26–28. Handwritten

"1" in left margins of paragraphs 29 ("THE REAL ESTATE . . .") and 30. Handwritten "3" in left margin of paragraph 32 ("I MAY MAKE . . .").

1. For a printed version of Rogers's inaugural message see *NYT*, 23 December 1926. For newsreel of the event see URL-CLU. See also *DT*, 1:39.

2. Tony, billed as the Wonder Horse, was the well-known equine companion of actor Tom Mix (see *PWR*, 2:494–98) and appeared with Mix in most of his films (Lee, *Not So Dumb*, 80–85).

3. Silver King, a magnificent white stallion, became famous in the 1920s as the horse of Fred Thomson (1890–1928), one of the most popular western film stars of the decade (*FE*, 1345–46; Lee, *Not So Dumb*, 89–91).

4. Rin Tin Tin (1916–32), canine film star, was a German shepherd who was rescued from a German trench in the war, brought to Hollywood, and launched into a motion picture career. Hugely popular, he received top billing and became the leading revenue source for Warner Bros. studio in the 1920s (*FE*, 1152).

5. George Edward Cryer (1875–1961), a Republican and former U.S. district attorney, served as mayor of Los Angeles from 1921 to 1929 (*NYT*, 25 May 1961; *WhAmer*, 4:218).

6. Marco H. Hellman (b. 1878), a member of a prominent old Los Angeles family, had been president of the Hellman Commercial Trust and Savings Bank since 1918 and chairman of the board since 1925 (Starr, *Material Dreams*, 97, 110, 130, 161; *WhAmer*, 6:188).

7. Duke Paoa Kahanamoku (1890–1968), a native of Hawaii, was considered the greatest swimmer of his time, winning medals in the Olympics of 1912 and 1920 and holding several freestyle records. In 1926 he was in Hollywood pursuing a career in motion pictures (*NYT*, 23 January 1968).

8. A National Home for Disabled Volunteer Soldiers was established in 1888 at the corner of Wilshire and Sawtelle in what became Santa Monica. Known also as the Sawtelle Disabled Veterans Home, it was open to men who had served in U.S. military actions since and including the Civil War (NARA, "Sawtelle Disabled Veterans Home"; Basten, *Santa Monica Bay*, 6).

Telegram from Evalyn W. McLean
28 December 1926
Washington, D.C.

AA42 75 NL WASHINGTON DC 28

WILL ROGERS.

THE MAYOR OF HOLLYWOOD CALIF.

MANY THANKS FOR YOUR WIRE AND CHRISTMAS CARD THEY HAVE JUST SENT UP FROM THE POST YOUR ARTICLE FOR NEXT SUNDAY AND I AM GOING TO PRINT IT IF IT LOOSES [*sic*] ME EVERY FRIEND IN WASHINGTON[1] ITS KILLING AND YOU HAVE MADE US SEE OURSELVES AS OTHERS SEE US GIVE MY LOVE TO MRS ROGERS AND THE NEXT TIME YOU COME TO DINNER I WONT LET THEM TOUCH YOUR PLATE UNTIL YOU BLOW A WHISTLE.

E MCLEAN.

TG, rc. OkClaW, 1975.31.0479. On Western Union Telegraph Co. letterhead. Metered immediately below letterhead, right side: "1926 DEC 29 AM 4 07."

1. In his "Weekly Article" scheduled for publication on 2 January 1927, Rogers described his adventures with his wife at a formal dinner at Friendship, the Washington, D.C., mansion of the fabulously wealthy Ned and Evalyn McLean. The couple owned the *Post*, a Washington newspaper that subscribed to Rogers's weekly column. Rogers chronicled for his readers several details about his visit to the McLeans, including the waiters' knack of pulling the guests' plates before they could finish their food. Rogers wished he had taken along a rope. He would have used it either to hogtie his waiter or to lasso some meat. The dinner probably took place on Sunday, 12 December, while Rogers was in the capital for speaking engagements (see *WA*, 2:288–91; Chronology, 1926, OkClaW).

Manuscript for Magazine or Newspaper Article
ca. 1926
[Beverly Hills, Calif.?]

"South"[1]

All I know is just what I read in the papers, But I been going so fast lately I havent had time ▲TO▲ even open a paper, much less read one, When I shook the maps of I400 Real Estate men out of my face and   le﬏t the State ▲OF FLORIDA▲ I8 hours late, I hit out for North Carolina, But I want to tell you all I had a great time in Florida, I think everybody has a good time in Florida, that is what they intend for everybody to have, You go to Florida sorter like you go to Paris   you expect to do nothing but enjoy yourself, and as long as it stays like it is   Thousands will always go there, I am asked every minute, "When is the big bust going to come down there Will?",[2] Say take itfrom a Californian, and an Oklahomanian at heart, there *aint going to be no* bust, Good stuff will always be worth money there, as for people going away back and subdividing mi▲[*typewritten:*] I▲es back in swamps why they are already in the poor house, California has no quar▲REL▲l with Florida, they are 3000 miles apart, if either one of them can get 5 percent of the population within I500 miles ~~of themte~~ to come and visit them, they will have more than they can care for, And here is a tip, ~~for you~~ both of them better quit argueing with each other and watch Texas Gulf Country, There is a country that is raising more than either one of them to the acre, I hear more of it traveling around than I do of either of the others, They have the same Gulf as the west coast of Florida, great climate and richer land than either one of the others, A lot of you feel like you got in too late for the California and the Florida boom and that stuff is too high in both those places   why try Texas or the coast of Mississippi, that is just what Florida was three years ago, Every Railroad in the south is t trying to reach the Gulf Coast at some place or another, Why Galveston is not as big a wineter resort as it is a summer [resort] is just because people dont know about it and have never been there in the winter, I was there the other day and it was exactly the same climate as Florida or Los Angeles and a beach that compares with Daytona, they drive on it for miles, Oh yes and Golf Courses. You have to have Golf Courses now before you do a place to sleep, Well ~~they~~ ▲GOLFERS▲ are out there cussing their luck every day in the year, Wonderful Hotel, fishing, bathing, very few Revenue boats,[3] (Thats a [*obliterated*] thing you want [to] give consideration to before picking a winter location)   It should be a great resort town,and Houston is right there nearby and it will be one of the great cities of the Country in a few years, I just want   to tell you people that havent been traveling through any of that Country lately, The whole south is certainly stepping, it would be hard to pick out any one locality that is going ahe▲[*typewritten*:]a▲d [ahead] of the other, If you have never been to North Carolina you have the surprise of your life awaiting you, I think they have made more real advancement in the last I0 years than any state in the Union, And say they got a pay roll, I never saw as many factories in my life, They are next to California in good roads, Climate[,] resorts . If the Architect of this old world has produced a prettier place than Asheville, N C he certainly is concealing it. Pinehurst another great place, I showed there one night and I thought I was playing to Park ~~Ae~~ Ave, Winston Salem, Camel's ship out 50, (thats fifty, not five, its fifty) car loads of Cigarettes a Day,[4] (thats a day, not a year, its each DAY)   What a live place that is, and then over to ~~our~~ our old headquarters, the ~~Ddand~~ Daddy of them all, Durham, N C, I visited OUR factory, (The American Tobacco Co and ~~IS~~ mine) and after you see what Bull Durham has done for Durham, just imagine what it would do for you, They are building more new buildings out at Duke University[5] than Harvard has lost Football games in the last few years, And say if you want to read a masterpiece of a Will read that man Dukes, There was one rich man that dident forget his home State that had made him rich, In this day and time when rich men are running to some other State just to keep from leaving their ~~home~~ ▲OWN▲ State a ~~fai~~ small sum of what they have accumilated in it, ▲ITS AN EXAMPLE▲. He left big sum▲[*typewritten*:]s▲ to every worthy thing in ~~the~~ ▲HIS▲state[6]

Then ~~down~~ to Raleigh, You not only see a real town but you see, Josephus Daniels, He took the whole Navy through a war and had less trouble with it than they are having now in peace, Raleigh like all the reast is growing fast, And South Carolina is right on their heels, They are behind their step brother state in roads but that is about all, I bet you dident know that at Rock Hill they have a University for Girls that is third in size in the United States͵ ▲NAMED▲ Winthrop College,[7] ~~and~~ ▲AT▲ Greenville, South Carolina, They have more textile mills and Industries than some New England Cities, its a " Little Boston"   Even ▲OLD▲ Virginia has found that Commerce will ~~not~~ go allright along with tradition, So they are building Factories and new Homes where they used to build nothing but Monuments, ~~This C~~ Mississippi under the careful guidance of Pat Harrison has discovered that if everybody else is selling ~~Cli~~ climate, "We got some of the best in the w͟p̶ ▸o◂rld [world] that we can offer to the purchaser,["] and as far as raising crops why they had never considered that any particular novelty before they read of other States thinking it was new, Just for a Novelty and to show that they were no cheap Skates in the natural resource line why the week I was there Jackson, Miss struck a Diamond Mine, If Florida had that they would make another 20 million dollar appropiation for advertsing, Columbus Miss is the place that the Discoverer of America arrived at when he made that famous remark, " Quite an Island you have here". Georgia has turned from Ball Players and Peaches to ~~convincin▲g▲ Northerners that Sherman made a mistake by marching through instead of stopping. For~~ Factory's, Farming, and Coca Cola, Up to now Georgia has generally been just considered a highway, either for Sherman,[8] or Fords going to Florida. Time has proven that both of them were wrong, they should have stopped instead of marching through . Atlanta is the Chicago of the South, (without the financial and physical risk of Murder or e robbery). Even Arkansaw has broken out into a heavy prespiration of Prosperity. Louisina stuck her head out from under the rice foields, and asked, " Whats all the advertising for"   they told her that Florida was selling Climate," "Selling Climate," Why come here and we will give ~~em~~ it to em," And we have things ~~to~~ you can raise to fee[d]   yourself on while you are findingbout that you cant eat climate. We have history, tradition, Gin Fizzes, the biggest Ri river and the biggest Harbor, and the Old Absinthe house, We have Oil[,] Gas, Lumber, Cotton, Rice, and an almost French Language, We hadent thought anything about the Gulf of Mexico but if everybody else is claiming it as a sales arguement,why come to think about it we have it too. Just as blue just a slaty [as salty], You know this Gulf of Mexico is no respector of States, it takes inall of them, i6 [It] doent even draw the line at Mexico, in fact i thi[nk] the thing givesm, (columbia and --------- a sales argument,)

Greeley said " Go west Young nman",[9] But I say, " Go South Old man" and if yo[u] can get the old man to go south, the young Flapper,[10] will follow him,(as sure as England follows the Oil,) and if youcan get the Young ~~Charleston~~ Girls doing the Charleston[11] between inhalesr you will get the rest of America following them, so cater entirely to Old men,

TM. OkClaW, Unpublished Manuscripts. Editor's marks appear throughout the document but were disregarded for this transcription. All interpolations were handwritten, in Rogers's hand, unless noted otherwise. Double strike-through indicates hand-deleted copy; single strike-through indicates type-deleted copy.

1. Rogers informed *Saturday Evening Post* editor George Lorimer at least three times in 1926 that he was preparing an article for the *Post* about the South (see Telegram to George H. Lorimer, 27 January 1926, Letter to George H. Lorimer, ca. 16 March 1926, and Letter to George H. Lorimer, ca. 27 October 1926, above). Although no such story ran in the *Post* or was found to have been published elsewhere, this manuscript bears the marks of an editor, lending credence to the idea that Rogers did submit it for publication. References in it to the chronology of his travels and to historical events strongly suggest that he wrote this draft of the manuscript in 1926.

2. The Florida real estate market experienced a tremendous boom in the early 1920s. New residential developments appeared throughout the state, and early investors reaped huge returns. Over-development and speculation, however, caused the market to slow in the summer of 1926, and then a devastating hurricane in south Florida that fall hastened a full collapse that led to a flood of bankruptcies, loan defaults, and bank failures by 1927 (*HD1920s*, 132). The travails in Florida dated many of Rogers's observations in his article and likely contributed to the failure of his manuscript to be published.

3. Coast Guard sailors had the right to board and search vessels suspected of carrying liquor that might be smuggled into the United States, but the agency's efforts, even after the reduction of territorial waters from twelve to three miles in 1923 and the addition of more ships and men in 1924, proved greatly inadequate. According to one estimate, the federal government halted only 5 percent of the smuggled liquor trade in 1925 (Pegram, *Battling*, 158; Behr, *Prohibition*, 132).

4. Camel cigarettes, a product of the R. J. Reynolds Tobacco Company, made their debut in 1913 and through the distribution of free cigarettes to soldiers during the war became the dominant brand by the end of the conflict. Aggressive marketing and clever sloganeering earned Camels more than half of the market by 1924 (*HD1920s*, 55).

5. James Buchanan Duke (1856–1925), fabulously wealthy North Carolina industrialist and organizer of the American Tobacco Company, donated several million dollars in December 1924 to what was then known as Trinity College. Its name was quickly changed to Duke University, and the private four-year institution in Durham, N.C., soon added new schools and degree programs and launched a massive building effort (*DAB*, 5:497–98; *PrivCU*, 1:381–82; Winkler, *Tobacco Tycoon*, 294–301).

6. Duke's estate eventually totaled almost $133.4 million. His will, which was probated in 1927, ensured millions for Duke University and various hospitals in North

Carolina, as well as creating an enormous trust fund for his only child (Winkler, *Tobacco Tycoon*, 314–16).

7. Winthrop College started in Columbia, S.C., in 1886, as a training school for women. It moved to Rock Hill, S.C., nine years later, and in 1920 became Winthrop College, the South Carolina College for Women, a public, four-year institution. The school changed its name to just Winthrop College in 1974 when it began accepting male students (*PubCU*, 879).

8. William Tecumseh Sherman (1820–91), Union army general, led his forces on a decisive march through Georgia in late 1864 that led to much destruction of civilian property and countless acts of violence but also contributed ultimately to the defeat of the Confederacy (*DAB*, 7:96–97).

9. Horace Greeley (1811–72), prominent American newspaper editor and liberal Republican leader, helped to promote the westward movement in the United States with the universally popular pronouncement, "Go West, young man." Although often ascribed to Greeley, the phrase had been used two years earlier in 1851 by an editor in Indiana (*DAB*, 7:528–34; Van Deusen, *Horace Greeley*, 173).

10. Although the term *flapper* appeared in literature as early as 1915, it became almost exclusively associated with the 1920s to describe the brash, stylish, liberated woman of the decade (*HD1920s*, 131–32; *RHHDAS*, 1:767).

11. The Charleston, an exceedingly popular dance form of the 1920s, originated among blacks in Charleston, S.C., before the war and then migrated north with them as they sought wartime employment. Marked by fast-paced, syncopated foot action, the Charleston came to symbolize the culture of the flapper and the hedonism of the decade (*DE*, 503; *HD1920s*, 65).

From Chester (Chet) Byers
3 January 1927
Brooklyn, N.Y.

Brooklyn, N.Y.
January 3 – 1927

Dear Friend Will:

Hearty congratulations on your election to Mayor of that fine Town.

Since we met last in New York many things have happened to us both.... You have become a "Mayor", and me... (please don't laugh) a composer of a small book on "Trick and Fancy Roping."—

Am engaged just now in putting to-gether a little volume on how to spin a rope with full explanation of rules, sketches, etc to every trick. Am emphasizing how good Roping is for exercise, and why I think other people ought to take it up as such. G. P. Putnam's Sons of New York are very much interested in the idea, and are giving me their support.

Would it be asking you too much, Will, as a special favor to send me a little forward [*sic*] to use with my Book giving your ideas of rope spinning as an exercise and sport?– I feel embarrassed to ask you this, but please understand,

Will Rogers on the driveway of his home in Beverly Hills, ca. 1927. (*OkClaW*)

Will, I am not trying to trade on your own wonderful reputation. I just feel that your standing as one of the leading Ropers of the world which all of us Boys have always known, makes my story incomplete without a small contribution from you. If you can see your way clear to do this, kindly send it on to me as soon as you can.[1]

Please remember me to Mrs. Rogers and family– and to you I wish all the luck in the world.

> Your friend as ever
> Chet Byers

Please address:
567 – 69th Street
Brooklyn, N.Y.

ALS, rc. OkClaW, 1975.22.0090. Ellipses appear in original document.

1. Rogers was one of three show business friends of Chester Byers (see *PWR*, 3:411–12) to provide introductory remarks for his book *Roping: Trick and Fancy Rope Spinning*. G. P. Putnam's Sons published it in 1928 (Byers, *Roping*, iii–x).

Arthur H. Sulzberger to Adolph S. Ochs
17 January 1927
New York, N.Y.

January 17, 1927

MR. OCHS:

Don't you think Will Rogers is getting pretty bad – and if so that we have been paying him long enough to feel that we have wiped out any obligation that we may have incurred last summer?

My suggestion would be that we give him due notice of desiring to stop at the earliest possible time.

> A. H. S.[1]

TN, rc. NYT-A.

1. Arthur Hays Sulzberger (1891–1968), the son-in-law of *New York Times* publisher Adolph S. Ochs, started as an executive assistant at the *Times* and became a vice president by the late 1920s. He took over as publisher after the death of Ochs in 1935 (*DAB*, Supp. 8:636–37). The exact cause of Sulzberger's remarks is unknown, but the *Times* had received several letters of criticism since the newspaper started carrying Rogers's daily column (for example, see Letter from John S. to Editor, *New York Times*,

29 October 1926, above). Although no reason was given, the newspaper failed to run the "Daily Telegram" of 17 January, the date of Sulzberger's note. In it Rogers had made a gibe at Secretary of State Frank Kellogg and his recent linkage of the Soviet Union with deteriorating relations between the United States and Mexico (see *DT*, 1:47).

To Will Rogers, Jr.
ca. 20 January 1927
[Norfolk, Va.?]

Dear Son.

Well how are they going since you got back, are you liking it   I bet you hated to leave home, I know i did, You know the better we get everything fixed up the more we hate to leave, Who come back with you, I was in Indiana but it was before you come, I played their University at Bloomington, I dont know if I will be out that way till along in March some time after I come from California, I am going into Florida in a couple of weeks, I havent heard from Mama   I dont know if she decided to build or not, I kinder hate to sell the old place but I think it is the best thing for us, it would help boost our other property out there if we built and lived there,[1] Are you keeeping up pretty well, how about the riding   have you taken that up yet   I hope you have, Guess you all are busy skating now, You will have it on Jim and Mary on that, They say they sold some of the polo ponies, I kinder hated to see old Cheyenne go, if it hadent been for his ringing his tail I would have kept him, he was not any too fast either, But he was agood Pony, I saw Man of War[2] yesterday, He is out here from Lexington, Now dont get too homesick   just keep right after them and we will all have a big summer when you get home, I am planning to be there all summer, I may go to Mexico later on in the spring and maby go down to Nicaragua and Central Amererica,[3] just to see all that and give me something to write about for the Post this [s]ummer, I would go to Panama and then come up the west coast to California on a boat, I could make the trip in about a month, maby the month of May.

Hva   e you started to taking shooting yet.

Well I must stop and write to Mama, I guess she is pretty busy out there tending to all that,

Write to me so I will get the letter by next Sunday, as I will be in New Yorkpassing through next sunday, so write me to Astor Hotel there,

                                                         Love and best wishes from Dad.

TL, rc.[4] OkClaW, 1975.11.0043.

1. The Rogers family remained residents of Beverly Hills for a few more years but did take steps in the spring of 1927 to develop further the property in the Pacific Palisades area of the Santa Monica Mountains. The Rogerses built a house at the ranch that spring, overlooking a stable, corral, and polo field. It became a favorite retreat for the family until replaced by a much larger, permanent residence in 1930 (Yagoda, *Will Rogers*, 266–67, 269).

2. Man o' War (1917–47), legendary American racehorse popularly known as "Big Red," won twenty of twenty-one contests in just seventeen months and record prize money for the time. After his retirement from competition in October 1920, he stood at stud at his owner's farms in Lexington, Ky. (*OCWSG*, 642; Hale, "Man o' War").

3. Rogers's trip to Mexico would wait for several more months. He spent eighteen days there in December, but he did not continue on to Central America. Instead, he returned to California (Chronology, 1927, OkClaW).

4. Dating of the document was determined by references in the text to Rogers's chronology.

Notes for Introduction of Charles Chaplin
ca. 23 January 1927
[New York, N.Y.]

Mayor Walker was to have gone onhere, But as his act was getting prettyold aeound hereand he had to do some time running his town   why they sent out for the Ma[y]or of beverley Hills, A town that has never been touched by Taxes Mortgages or Scandal, Never has the least whimpering of immorality ever reached the lily white pages of even our dwarfed sized papers for Lillliputin minds.

Beverley Hills is the respectable end of Holywood,

I was going along fine with not a breath of impeachment till My own little friend Charley Chaplin   kicked over our lily white reputation,[1]   Before I ▼(took offic[e]▼ Wife walking out. give two days notice,

Now Charley is up against it[2]   he is back here trying to think of all the bank[s] he had half million Dollar deposits in.

Charley lives in my Munipality, I know him pretty well, Ever since i have been on the stage I have heard of Art and Artisits, They make out they can do this or that, I have never seen one yet that it wasent put on, Charley Chaplin is the only person I have ever met that I believe is an Artist at heart, Its in him and he could no more changeit than fly, Most of them are Artistic for the publicity or money, say he spands his own money on these Pictures and takes two years if it aint right to suit him, If he had wanted to be commercial he could havehda 15 milion, He is responsible for all his own work, Now as for his family affairs I bet you tomorrow if you took eveey Mother or in law out of Hollywood you wouldent &have divorce to import a divorce, We have

beenn led to rect [respect] all Mothers but what you see what those old con-
niving ones out there will go to to advance their daughter and give them an
easy position through life it would make you almost lose faith in humankind,
Now I got to live there by him only a block or so, and raise a family and if his
Mayor dont condemn him why dont you till you know,

More people are interested in his next picture tha[n] are in his wives.[3]
Charley Chaplin is the only man on earth that makes the whole world laugh, if
we are going to condemn a man that has women trouble we better . Charley
does use up a lot of wives, but he makes lots of people happy, and he generally
leaves the second Husband with enough that they can make some other man
happy, You know lots of us you change wives and stil,you are not funny with it,

I want to introduce to you the best known man in the World[,] The best
known man that was ever on this earth, His face is known in every land under
the sun. You try to make Broadway Laugh, This little frail bit of humanity has
to make the entire world laugh, I dont know what he has done, ~~am~~ but he has
amused me enough that I owe him a hearing, So Charley You make gfunny
pictures, y you ke p on making the world more cheerful to live in and as
mayor of your ho[m]e town ~~I wil furnish you with wives~~ I dont care how
many wivees you have, [a]nd the funnier your Pictutes are the more wives we
will give you, Because we have lots more single women than we have gret
Conedians.

TD.[4] OkClaW, 1975.14.0099. Second of two pages on Hotel Astor, Times Square, New York,
letterhead.

1. The protracted, bitter divorce proceedings between film actor Charlie Chaplin
and his second wife, Lita Grey Chaplin (Lillita Louise MacMurray, 1908–95), whom
he married in 1924 when she was just sixteen and he was thirty-five, dominated newspaper headlines in early 1927. On 10 January, the day before Chaplin headed to New
York to continue work on a film, Lita's attorneys filed a lengthy, recrimination-filled
divorce complaint that named as defendants Chaplin, his studio, and several banks
and corporations with which he did business (*FE*, 241; *NYT*, 31 December 1995;
Robinson, *Chaplin*, 336–37, 372–74). For other observations by Rogers about the
Chaplin divorce, see *DT*, 1:45–46, 121, 128.
2. In addition to the divorce, Chaplin had to deal at the same time with action by
the U.S. government to recover more than $1 million in delinquent income taxes
(Robinson, *Chaplin*, 371, 374–75).
3. Chaplin and his first wife, actress Mildred Harris Chaplin (1901–44), who was
seventeen years old at the time of their marriage, had divorced in 1920 (*FE*, 241).
4. The Lambs Club hosted the embattled Chaplin at an entertainment event on
Sunday evening, 23 January, in New York. Rogers, a member of the men-only organi-

zation of theatrical personalities, was in New York that night and likely delivered this introduction at the club (*NYT*, 26 January 1927).

From George H. Lorimer
1 February 1927
Philadelphia, Pa.

February 1, 1927

Mr. Will Rogers

My dear Rogers:

As I wired you, we would rather that you stuck to the S. E. P. and did not appear in another weekly.[1] Your article could very well be syndicated or sold to one of the monthly magazines like American.[2] Incidentally, though I suppose it is of no[3] particular interest to one who is knocking them cold all over the country, we had planned to lift the ante or, as they say in literary circles, the honorarium, with the beginning of the new series.[4]

Yours sincerely,

[George H. Lorimer]

TL, cc. DLC-MD, Wesley Stout Papers.

1. Rogers had submitted to the *Saturday Evening Post* an article apparently about the American Legion and its scheduled annual convention in Paris in September 1927. After the magazine declined to publish it, Rogers asked if Lorimer would mind if he submitted it to *Collier's Weekly*, a mass-circulation competitor to the *Post*. At the time, *Collier's* was on an upswing, improving both editorially and financially. In a return wire, the *Post* editor gently suggested that Rogers consider a monthly (telegram, Will Rogers to George H. Lorimer, 28 January 1927, OkClaW; telegram, [George H. Lorimer] to Will Rogers, 29 January 1927; Mott, *History*, 4:472–73).
    2. *American Magazine* was a member of the same corporate family as *Collier's*. Although it did not publish Rogers's American Legion piece, it eventually ran six of his other articles, beginning with "The Hoofing Kid from Claremore" in its issue of April 1929 (Mott, *History*, 4:468; for "Hoofing Kid" see *HTBF*, 98–102). Rogers may have used the American Legion story as his "Weekly Article" for 24 July 1927 (see *WA*, 3:49–53).
    3. Part of the typewritten text was obliterated, and the words "is of no" handwritten over the erasure.
    4. If Rogers and Lorimer planned an immediate new series, nothing came of it in print. Several months passed between Rogers's "A Letter from a Self-Made Diplomat to His Constituents" in the *Post* issue of 8 January 1927 and his subsequent contributions to the magazine in November (*ML*, 3–17; *EMJR*, 1–32).

To Will Rogers, Jr.
ca. 11 February 1927
[Tampa, Fla.?]

Dear Bill.

I been g oing so fast I dident get to write you for some time, How are you making out, did you pass all your examinations, Mary wanted to come by Florida but she wanted to come by and see you worse so she decided to let Florida go, I hope you havetaken up riding, Now you tell Captain Rossow[1] that I said if there was any extra's in the way of what you take [for] riding that you can have it, I mean like lessons, I hope you can get strarted in at that " Monkey Drill" or trick riding that they do, Then we will work on it all summer and next fall you will be all set for the Troop, You want to work on everything you can, all that helps you, Get in all the boxing you can& too, and when the baseball starts go out and practice every day with them, I have had a very good trip through Florida and am heading now for California, but will only be at home for a night or so, then on up into the Northwest, Old Bruce is the Manager now and is doing all the business and is making a good one. I dont have the Singers with me any more, and wont have now, [2]

I like it much better alone, Florida is in pretty bad shape   it dont touch California

What date is your school out, I want Jim to come back and be down at the ranch in Oklahoma with Herb by the time you get out   then you &c can go by there, and stay a bit and then you can both come home togeather,

I want you all to see how you like it down there, we got Goats, Hogs, Sheep, and Cattle, and Horses,

I am going to have two or three new Polo Ponies by the time you get back   I am on the lookout for them now, just the kind I want, I am playing Sunday in Aiken, South Carolina, Thats wh[e]re Mr Post had his horses, Mr Russell Grace,[3] and Van Stade's and all of them are there,

Say I am in Fayetteville, Ark, next Tuesday night, thtas right by Rogers, It sure is hot down here in Florida just like summer in Cal[ifornia].

Well Son I must close, I wont be so lomg writing to you the next time, Here is some candy money for you, Lots of love.

Dad.

TL, rc.[4] OkClaW, 1975.11.0044.

1. Robert Rossow (ca. 1881–1960) joined the staff of Culver Military Academy in 1905 and served twenty-three years as commander of its Black Horse Troop. He became commandant of cadets in 1928 (*NYT*, 27 November 1942, 13 April 1960).

2. With the departure of The de Reszke Singers, Rogers's nephew, Bruce Quisenberry, replaced Erwyn Mutch as on-site manager of the lecture tour and eventually took over the bookings (Croy, *Our Will Rogers*, 194; Bruce Quisenberry to Carol Baker, ca. March–April 1980, OkClaW).

3. William Russell (Russ) Grace (1878–1943) was an executive with Ingersoll-Rand Company in New York and the son of a wealthy industrialist and former mayor of the city. The younger Grace maintained a home in Aiken, S.C., where he raised horses and played polo (*NYT*, 1 April 1943; *WhAmer*, 2:217).

4. Dating of the document was determined by references to Rogers's lecture tour chronology in the text.

Commentary in *Dearborn Independent*
12 February 1927
Dearborn, Mich.

Will Rogers dropped into The Office the other day,[1] same old Will, wearing the same old brown suit in which he interviewed all the rulers of Europe. Will may be making money, but there is no theatrical flashiness about him, none of the lingo of the Hollywood crowd. The reason for this is, of course, that he is not a theatrical man. He is simply Will Rogers. Typing his 'Self-Appointed Ambassador' stuff on the train—he uses one finger of each hand to run his typewriter—sitting in private and talking offhand about anything at all, or doing his two-hour stunt on the stage, he is precisely the same in voice, thought, speech, gesture—simply and only Will Rogers. Somebody who knows how to do it should classify Will with our times as the ancient satirists were classified in theirs. I saw the other day a book review in which John Jay Chapman[2] says that Peter Finley Dunne (you know—the Dooley man)[3] was the modern prototype of Lucian.[4] Well, I think Will Rogers will stack as high if not higher. Neither Dunne-Dooley nor Rogers is a clown. Take Ring Lardner, for example, or some other of the Sunday weekly humorists;[5] they are forever clowning. But Will Rogers is serious. Did you ever see him tackle a subject for comment that was not serious? And did you ever feel that he had failed to get at the very heart and nub of the matter and split it open with a laugh? The answer is twice in the negative. The fact is, Will Rogers is a philosopher; so much of a philosopher that he has left the mechanics of philosophy far behind and has graduated into a higher region of humor. The so-called philosophers of our universities are not philosophers—they are merely students of systems of philosophy. If they were real philosophers in operation they would be tackling life instead of textbooks. Will Rogers tackles life, because he can. Humor is the highest gift; it is without alloy; Rogers has it. The editorial last week, or whenever it was, in this paper, that suggested making Will Rogers Secretary of State for Pan-American Affairs is no joke. We need a serious-minded man like him in public affairs.

PD. Printed in *Dearborn Independent,* Dearborn, Mich., 12 February 1927.[6] OkClaW, 1975.21.0006.

1. Rogers made a lecture tour stop in Detroit on 13 January and spent part of the day visiting with Henry Ford at his home (see *DT,* 1:46).

2. John Jay Chapman (1862–1933), deeply intellectual American essayist and poet, contributed numerous articles to magazines and wrote twenty-five books (*DAB,* Supp. 1:168–69).

3. Finley Peter Dunne (1867–1936), American newspaperman and magazine editor, achieved fame in the 1890s and early 1900s for a popular series of books and writings that featured an Irish saloonkeeper, Mr. Dooley, ruminating on current events, politics, and society in a humorous, folksy, broadly Irish style (*DAB,* Supp. 2:158–60; *OCAL,* 188).

4. Lucian (ca. 125–after 180), an influential Greek writer of satiric prose, was the subject of one of Chapman's many books (*GLA,* 260–61; *DAB,* Supp. 1:169).

5. Ring Lardner's syndicated newspaper column of disparate subject matter, "Ring Lardner's Weekly Letter," made its debut in 1920 and reached a readership of 8 million by the middle of the decade. Lardner, however, eventually grew tired of it. The last one appeared on 20 March 1927, essentially concluding his career as a journalist (Yardley, *Ring,* 224–26, 305, 313).

6. The *Dearborn Independent* was a country weekly that Henry Ford purchased in 1918 and which he intended as a champion of social justice. Subtitled "The Ford International Weekly," the newspaper carried a hodgepodge of articles and illustrations on foreign topics, Wilsonian progressivism, and pro–League of Nations issues. Always a money-loser, in 1921 the *Independent* became an organ for Ford's anti-Semitic views. Although Ford discontinued the articles about Jews in early 1922, the paper ran another, equally virulent anti-Semitic series in 1924–25 that led to a defamation suit. The newspaper ceased publication in 1930 (Nevins and Hill, *Ford,* 2:124–29, 311–23).

Advertisement in *Exhibitor's Herald*
5 March 1927
[Beverly Hills, Calif.?]

Rogers touted his newly released travelogue film series with the following letter printed in an advertisement under the heading "A Message to you from Will Rogers."[1] The full-page ad in Exhibitor's Herald *also featured a cropped photo of a seated Rogers working at a typewriter.[2]*

Dear Exhibitors:

Now I haven't bothered you in a long time.I layed off you and let you all get rich and properous.When I used to play you were all in little hay barns in the winter and out on vacant lots with a fence around it in the summer.You didn't have a thing to worry or bother about till every once in a while a Will Rogers picture would hit you like a rainy night.Now I got out and let you go ahead and accumulate big houses and Mortgages and worry and high taxes and everything.They told me it was things like me that was retarding the business.

Now this little mess I got here now that these fellows are trying to sell you wont hurt you much.They will just about give you time to go out and get a smoke while they are on.As Pictures are all so good nowadays I thought just as a contrast there ought to be some old has been come along and have something pretty ordinary and it would show off the modern things more.

The Character I am playing here is one I tried out before.I first tried it about forty some odd years ago and it turned out good and bad,but in the long run it kept me out of the casting line looking for an extra day.I dont know what they are,they aint exactly travelogues,They aint comedies cause comedies are Gags the people are used to laughing at.

The plots are a little too clean for dramas.

Well to be honest they are just about nine hundred feet of celluloid and take up about the same amount of time that a couple of close ups in a love picture would take up.They aint good and they aint bad,they just take up about fifteen minutes of a class of peoples time that time dont mean a thing in the world too.

The Saturday Evening Post jas [has] already payed for the trip, talking all over the country hase made me more than I ever could have made in Pictures even if I had been a real ~~good~~ star.the book of the trip has brought enough to pay for another trip,the Vitaphone staggered me to tell about it before their double barrell contraption,and this is just another By product.[3]I wanted ~~in~~ the reels to keep myself to show at home in my old days,and I just had them make another extra print.The radio is another by product I just thought of that has already paid me for them too. I was raised on a ranch but I never knew before there was so many ways of skinning a calf.I like to forgot Bull Durham paying me to tell also about the same trip.

And oh yes my old friend Sam Goldwyn wants the dramatic rights to the book.I sold Keystone the still pictures,[4]the syndicated strip cartoon rights are being negotiated for now.

Well so long the Mayor has got to get busy,there is a lot of new divorced people standing right here waiting to get married again.Thats a better side line than all of them.

Your old friend.MAYOR Rogers

PD. Printed in *Exhibitor's Herald,* 5 March 1927. OkClaW.

1. For background on the travelogue series see Telegram to Carl Stearns Clancy, 1 March 1926, and Terms of Payment for Travelogues, 22 April 1926, above. Producer Clancy claimed that the travel films, styled loosely after Mark Twain's *The Innocents Abroad,* were the first to feature the star facing the camera and speaking directly to the audience, allowing movie-goers to feel they were part of the sightseeing tour (Carl S. Clancy to Theodore McDowell, 18 August 1960, CSC-GKC).

2. First published in 1915, *Exhibitor's Herald* was one of several motion picture trade publications printed in the 1910s and 1920s that catered to theater owners and operators. In addition to reviews, interviews, industry news, and business improvement columns, the *Herald* and similar weeklies carried considerable advertising promoting forthcoming films and recent releases. The *Herald* merged with *Motion Picture News* in 1931 to form *Motion Picture Herald* (Koszarski, *Evening's Entertainment,* 195, 197).

3. Vitaphone, a part of Warner Bros. studios, was created in 1926 to take advantage of new technology for incorporating sound in motion pictures. The company made history in 1927 with *Jazz Singer,* the first feature-length movie with sound. The Vitaphone system, however, did not survive past 1931 because of the development of more reliable sound technology (*FE,* 1417–18).

4. Keystone, a Hollywood film production studio active in the 1910s, was noted for its slapstick comedies, among the most popular of which were the absurd adventures of the Keystone Kops (*FE,* 744).

Telegram from Henry H. Ogden
22 March 1927
Detroit, Mich.

KB887 98 NL 11 EXTRA 1/62.TH DETROIT MICH 22

WILL ROGERS.

MAYOR OF BEVERLYHILLS BEVERLYHILLS CALIF.

HOW WOULD YOU LIKE TO PROMOTE A TRANSATLANTIC FLIGHT[1] WOULD PREFER YOU OR ARTHUR BRISBANE OR BOTH TO SPONSOR THIS AS YOU ARE OUTSTANDING AVIATION ENTHUSIASTS IN THE MINDS OF THE PUBLIC SEVENTY FIVE THOUSAND DOLLARS WILL COVER EXPENSES CAN YOU PROMOTE THIS OR MAKE ANY SUGGESTIONS HAVE IN MIND WORLDS FOREMOST NAVIGATOR AS PARTNER DOUGLAS PLANE TO BE USED EVERYTHING FIGURED

KB887 2/36 [*page 2:*]
OUT COULD START IN THIRTY DAYS IF INTERESTED WIRE IMMEDIATELY AIR MAIL
LETTER EXPLAINING DETAILS WILL FOLLOW BEST TO JOE HASKELL WHEN YOU
SEE HIM.

H H OGDEN MEMBER OF WORLD FLIGHT TWENTY SIX FIFTY[2]

EAST JEFFERSON DETROIT MICH.

TG, rc. OkClaW, 1975.31.0401. On Western Union Telegraph Co. letterhead. Metered on lower
edge of letterhead, right side: "1927 MAR 22 PM 8 48." Printed immediately below letterhead,
flush left: "Received at Main Office, 608-610 South Spring St., Los Angeles, Calif."

1. With many aviation firsts still to be recorded, a nonstop flight by airplane
across the Atlantic Ocean ranked among the most sought after by 1927. A $25,000
prize had been offered as early as 1919 for the first transatlantic flight from New York
to Paris or vice versa, but eight years had passed without a successful attempt and
with two fatalities. Nevertheless, intense public attention continued to be focused on
every transatlantic hopeful (Roseberry, *Challenging Skies*, 26, 79–85).

2. Henry H. Ogden, a staff sergeant in the U.S. Army Air Service, was the
mechanic aboard one of three army-sponsored planes, each with a crew of two, that
became in 1924 the first to circumnavigate the world. Flying biplanes specially built for
the project by Douglas Aircraft Company in Santa Monica, Calif., the men flew a total
distance of 26,503 miles—hence World Flight Twenty-Six Fifty—in an elapsed flying
time of slightly more than 371 hours. The success of the expedition, lasting from April
to September, brought renown to the aircraft manufacturer, as well as to the fliers,
including Ogden. He was not, however, one of the only two Americans to register to
compete for the money prize for the first transatlantic flight (Roseberry, *Challenging
Skies*, 69, 73, 85; Baker, *Flight*, 151, 153). No reply from Rogers was found.

From H. C. Wu and Edgar C. Tang
8 April 1927
New York, N.Y.

April 8, 1927

Will Rogers, Esq.,
Beverly Hills,
California.
Dear Sir:-

On behalf of the several hundreds Chinese Students in New York, we take
the great pleasure to express to you our hearty appreciation for your impar-
tial, righteous and sympathetic attitude and interest toward the recent situation
in China.[1]

We have been greatly dis▲ap▲pointed that the American public have been betrayed by the recent colored news dispatches from the American correspondents in China. It is only the intellectual leaders in this country like you that we are looking for the better interpretation of China and things Chinese and for the promotion of the long-established friendship and good-will of these sister republics.

Best wishes from

Cordially yours,

H. C. Wu,chairman,

Edgar C. Tang,secretary.

TLS, rc. OkClaW, 1975.22.0095. On letterhead of National Affairs Committee of Chinese Students in New York, Box 172, John Jay Hall, Columbia University, New York City. Interlineation was hand-inserted. Underscoring indicates signatures were placed on type-inserted lines.

1. Popular resentment in China against the intrusive presence of foreigners led by 1925 to several violent, deadly antiforeign demonstrations. Missionaries often became the targets of Chinese outrage, an aspect given strong coverage in overseas press. The disorder throughout China led to a long civil war between Nationalist and Communist forces beginning in 1926. Antiforeign attacks, especially against Christian schools and churches, continued to occur into early 1927 and led to more foreign military intervention. The United States and Britain stationed gunboats near Nanking as stories of atrocities against foreigners mounted in March 1927 (Botjer, *Short History*, 44–52, 61–64). Rogers often used his daily column in March to question foreign intervention in China and the presence there of American missionaries. In his weekly column of 10 April, which ran two days after this letter was written, Rogers expounded at greater length on the same issues (see *DT*, 1:62, 67, 70, 71, 72, 74; *WA*, 3:14–17).

Telegram to Newspaper Editor
28 April 1927
Richmond, Va.

RICHMOND, Va., April 28.

CITY EDITOR, AMERICAN.

Hello, Editor: Say, is anybody coming to our show Sunday night, at Zeigfeld's new temple of form?[1] It ought to be quite a novelty—a show on Ziegfeld's stage and not a girl on it. Ziegy will want to get some on there some way, but John and I (you notice I call him John since we are working together), but John and I got our wives,[2] and we had to promise them that we was not going into any Follies or "Rio Ritas"[3] if we went there. We are just going there to see if a New York audience will listen to nothing but two men sing and tell jokes.

And, say, wasn't it nice and wasn't it big of a man like Mr. McCormack to come clear from out West to help out in a good cause like this (a benefit for the flood sufferers). I certainly do appreciate it and I hope a big bunch will turn out to hear him. If his voice goes bad I can do a little rough and tumble singing myself. I am flying in there from Staunton, Va.; it is the only way I can make it. Casey Jones[4] picks me up on the last lap from Washington to New York. Yours,

WILL.

PD. Printed in unidentified publication,[5] 29 April 1927. Scrapbook 8, Part 1, OkClaW.

1. Rogers and John McCormack staged a benefit concert in New York to raise money for a Red Cross fund to relieve victims of a devastating flood along the Mississippi River. The catastrophe, brought on by melting snows and weeks of rain, inundated 4 million acres, caused hundreds of thousands of people to lose their homes, and destroyed crops and livestock. Rogers and McCormack's joint performance at the new Ziegfeld Theatre on 1 May raised several thousand dollars for flood sufferers (*NYT*, 28 April, 2 May 1927; *HD1920s*, 234; Sobel, *Coolidge*, 315). Rogers's telegram to the unidentified newspaper editor was one of several contacts he made in promoting the event (for example, see telegram, Will Rogers to Adolph S. Ochs, 27 April 1927, OkClaW, and telegram, Charles Evans Hughes to Will Rogers, 28 April 1927, OkClaW). For Rogers on the Mississippi flood calamity see *WA*, 3:24–27.
2. Lily Foley McCormack (ca. 1886–1971), a former soprano from Dublin, Ireland, was the wife of John McCormack. The couple had married in 1906 (*NYT*, 28 April 1971).
3. *Rio Rita* was a musical comedy produced by Florenz Ziegfeld and the first show staged at his new Ziegfeld Theatre. A major hit, it opened on 2 February 1927 and ran for 494 performances (*EPM*, 6:4549–50).
4. Charles S. (Casey) Jones (ca. 1894–1976), an aviation pioneer, competed successfully in many air races in the 1920s, while also working as a test pilot and flight instructor for the Curtiss Corporation (*NYT*, 28 April 1952, 14 February 1976).
5. Although the clipping was unidentified, it likely came from the *New York American*.

Draft of Telegram from John McCormack
ca. 1 May 1927
[New York, N.Y.?]

My Dear Will

~~I supp~~ I am a temperamental tenor but I love you and I was and will always be delighted to be identified with you for any cause stop when I think of the sacrifices you made to give that benefit on Sunday I feel ashamed that I should even appear temperamental, stop.[1] I love you Will and I admire you and I am delighted to have been with you on the same stage. Bless you old Pal

John

TG, dc. OkClaW, 1975.21.0090. Printed at bottom of the first of two note-sized sheets and between two ruled lines: "Guaranty Letters of Credit are known throughout the world." Printed at the bottom of the second page, also between parallel rules: "BUSH HOUSE, the new American-built London 'skyscraper', is the home of our Kingsway Office."

1. McCormack, known for uncontrollable nervousness and wide-ranging moods, apparently had exhibited such untoward behavior at some point during the evening of the benefit performance that he felt compelled to send a note of contrition to Rogers. As McCormack's manager later recounted, Rogers's reply caused the tenor to act "like a schoolboy" and to exclaim to his friend, "I had the sweetest telegram I have ever received, from Will Rogers. It almost made me cry" (*DAB*, Supp. 3:485; D. F. McSweeney to Betty Blake Rogers, 6 May 1927, OkClaW). Unfortunately, Rogers's note to McCormack was not found.

To Will Rogers, Jr.
ca. 7 May 1927
[Montpelier, Vt.?]

Dear Son,

Well I guess you think your old Dad is a fine one   you know I havent written you since I left, You see Mmam [Mama] has been with me and I have been kinder figureing on her doing the corresponding, Now if she hasent dont [done] it its not because I havent told her too,

How are you getting on, I hope you are working right along on your riding so we can keep it up when you get out hoem and you will be sure and mek [make] the troop next year, And the B[a]se ball playing I ma going to fix a Diamond right in front of our ranch House down at [the] ranch, So you and your room mate keep playing catch and you learning to throw. And dont give up the swimming, I wa t [want] you to work on all you can these 1st few weeks, you will need all the wind you ~~can~~ have to follow us through the summer, for we will have aregular routine. Lots of Polo. lots of Trick riding. Lots of Roping, We are going to have the best summer you ever saw, I am going to get some Roping Goats and some calvee▲s▲ too, just too rope at.

I think I will get home about the time you do maby a day or so b before, The Oklahoma ranch has been under water so mucg [much] I dont know whether it will be dried out if we went by there,

You havent got anything on me for counting the days, I dont mind working in Theatres in the winter time when its cold but when its nice and warm at nights I hate to go in them then,

I am away off up here in Vermont, thefirst time I have ever played in this State in my life, Guess you are pretty busy with your Exams,

I hope you make tgrade in all of them. I wondrr if old Jim will pass, Mr John McCormack and I got 20 thpusand dollars for the flood at the Benefit I put on last Sunday.

I guess they told you we was going to build a kind of a ranch house down at the ranch up there on the side of the hill, right where the Camp was that the graders that fixed the Polo field was camped, It will be near the Barn, and not so high up that we will have to drive up a hill to get too it, It will be just like a Club House looking down over the Polo field, Then I am putting a cover over that whole center part of the Stable lot, So that will all be enclosed in the shade   [It will shade] the whole of the space in between both sides of the stable, clear out to the Gate where you go into the barn lot, That will make it nice and cool in there to rope and play, and shady and cool.

In that way we wont have to build a new barn,

Well I will stop   here is I0 Bucks that I dont think you will send back to me on account of not needing them, This is sorter strong but on account of Vacation coming on I know you will need more,

Lots of love   you write me when you get this and send the letter to, Chas L Wagner, 5II Fifth Ave, New York. and they will forward it on to me, Lots of love to you Son and am waiting till we meet on the polo field.

Dad

TL, rc.[1] OkClaW, 1975.11.0047.

1. Dating of the document was determined by references in the text to Rogers's chronology.

Telegram to Editor, *New York Times*
10 May 1927
Northampton, Mass.

72NP FE   67

NORTHAMPTON MASS 449P MAY 10 1927

EDITOR NY TIMES

NY

WHY DIDNT THEY RUN TODAY'S TELEGRAM ABOUT THE AVIATORS ITS THE ONLY GOOD ONE I HAVE SENT IN ALL THEY HAD TO DO WAS TO CHANGE ONE

WORD AFTER THEY KNEW THEY HADNT ARRIVED THE LAST PART ABOUT THE
AMERICAN WIRING COOLIDGE COLLECT WAS A YELL LAST NIGHT ON THE STAGE
DIG IT UP AND RUN IT I DON'T MIND THEM LEAVING OUT A BUM ONE[1] REGARDS

WILL ROGERS

640p

TG, cc. NYT-A, Publishers Collection. On Western Union Telegraph Co. letterhead. Imprinted and stamped below letterhead: "Received at THE NEW YORK TIMES." Handwritten vertically below letterhead, right side: "Will Rogers". Handwritten below letterhead, right margin: "277".

1. In his "Daily Telegram" of 10 May, Rogers wrote about French military aviators Charles Eugène Jules Marie Nungesser (b. 1892), a popular war ace, and François Coli (b. 1891), a navigator. The two men had left Paris on Sunday morning, 8 May, in an attempt to be the first to fly the Atlantic nonstop. Rogers wished the Frenchmen well and joked, "It would be better for American aviation that the French cross first. If we crossed first we would think we done all that could be done and just stop" (see *DT*, 1:86–87). Nungesser and Coli failed, however, to arrive in New York as scheduled on 9 May; whereupon the *Times* probably chose to hold Rogers's column. Their plane was not seen again (*NYT*, 8 May 1927; Roseberry, *Challenging Skies*, 86–87). See also *DT*, 1:87–88.

Telegram from B. Patton (Pat) Harrison
1 June 1927
Chicago, Ill.

CB13 44 BLUE.CHICAGO ILL 1 812A

WILL ROGERS.

ROOSEVELT HOTEL NEWORLEANS LA.

THE MISSI[SSI]PPI VALLEY APPRECIATES YOUR GREAT LABORS IN ITS BEHALF
YOU HAVE DONE MORE THAN ANY ONE ELSE IN THE UNITEDSTATES EXCEPT
HOOVER AND THOSE DIRECTING THE WORK TO BRING TO ATTENTION AMERICAN
PEOPLE THE NEED AND DISTRESS OCCASIONED BY THE FLOOD BEST WISHES.

PAT HARRISON.

TG, rc. OkClaW, 1975.31.0513. On Western Union Telegraph Co. letterhead. Handwritten on lower, center edge of letterhead: "GR." Metered immediately below letterhead, right side: "1927 JUN 1 AM 9 41."

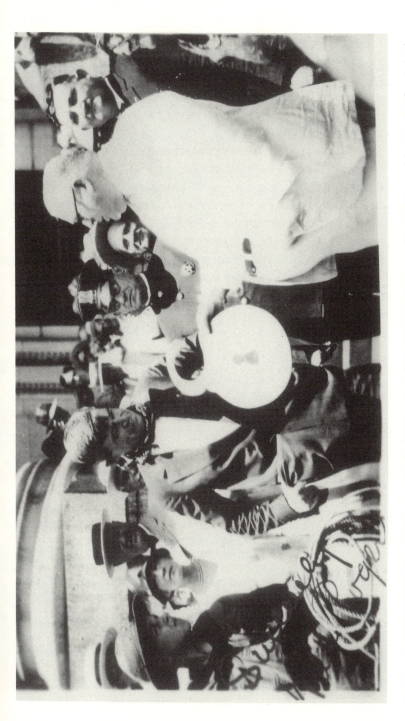

Rogers raised $48,000 in New Orleans on 1 June 1927 to benefit Red Cross efforts to relieve victims of devastating floods in the Mississippi River valley. In appreciation, Mayor Arthur J. O'Keefe, Sr., presented Rogers with a lock and key to the city. (*OkClaW*)

Telegram from John Barton Payne
1 June 1927
Washington, D.C.

JA119 84 5 EXTRA.F WASHINGTON DC 1 1137A

WILL ROGERS.CARE EARL F GATES.

RED CROSS RELIEF HEADQUARTERS 218 CAMP ST

NEWORLEANS LA.

.WE ARE MOST GRATEFUL FOR YOUR SPLENDID AND UNTIRING EFFORTS IN BEHALF MUCH NEEDED RED CROSS MISSISSIPPI VALLEY RELIEF FUND STOP MILLION AND HALF STILL TO BE RAISED BEFORE RED CROSS CAN SEE THE JOB THROUGH AND KEEP FAITH WITH THE PEOPLE STOP THIS REQUIRES RENEWED EFFORTS ON PART OF EVERYONE[1] STOP YOUR COMMENTS IN THE DAILY PAPERS[2] HAVE BEEN INSPIRATION TO ALL AND THE MONEY RAISED THROUGH YOUR SPLENDID BENEFIT PERFORMANCES IN NEWYORK AND NEWORLEANS MOST GRATEFULLY APPRECIATED.

JOHN BARTON PAYNE CHAIRMAN AMN NATIONAL RED CROSS.[3]

TG, rc. OkClaW, 1975.31.0515. On Western Union Telegraph Co. letterhead. Handwritten on lower, center edge of letterhead: "QC." Metered immediately below letterhead, right side: "1927 JUN 1 AM 11 15."

1. Rogers brought his spring lecture tour to a close on 1 June with a late-night show in New Orleans to benefit the victims of the Mississippi River flood. The performance set a record of $48,000 in proceeds for disaster relief (*NYT*, 2 June 1927; *DT*, 1:95).

2. See *DT*, 1:92–94. For Rogers's remarks about the New Orleans benefit see *WA*, 3:40, 42.

3. John Barton Payne (1855–1935), a former U.S. secretary of the interior, served as chairman of the American Red Cross from 1921 until his death (*DAB*, Supp. 1:594–95). Payne informed Rogers on 27 June that he had been elected a life member of the American Red Cross (John Barton Payne to Will Rogers, 27 June 1927, OkClaW). Rogers was so moved by the honor that he devoted a daily column to describing the award and extolling the work of the Red Cross (see *DT*, 1:108–9). On 1 August he wrote Payne a letter of appreciation that appeared in print. He told Payne, "[T]hat's just the biggest thing that I ever had happen to me, and it especially came at a time when it made me feel mighty good. The Red Cross is the only thing I can think of in America that we couldn't possibly get along without. If the people only knew one-half its worth we could raise any sum of money in 24 hours. My membership is already bearing fruit—I've booked 'twelve benefits.'" He added, "P.S. Hope I don't disgrace the organization" (clipping, Scrapbook 15, OkClaW).

Telegram from Florenz Ziegfeld, Jr.
15 June 1927
New York, N.Y.

23S C 214 BLUE

CP NEWYORK NY 1106A JUN 15 1927

WILL ROGERS

BEVERLYHILLS CALIF

I READ IN THE PAPERS YOU ARE SICK[1] I ALWAYS WAS WORRIED ABOUT THE TERRIBLE LIFE YOU WERE LIVING IN DUMPS AND ON RAILROAD TRAINS NO HUMAN BEING CAN STAND THIS LIFE I HOPE HOWEVER IT IS NOTHING SERIOUS ALL WE HAVE THAT IS WORTH WHILE IS OUR HEALTH AND I HOPE YOU WILL REALIZE IT IN TIME AND GIVE UP BARNSTORMING AND COME TO NEWYORK GO IN THE FOLLIES AUGUST FIRST AND GET YOURSELF A NICE

23S C SHEET 2

COUNTRY PLACE WITH A POLO FIELD AND REST FOR AT LEAST THREE OR FOUR MONTHS YOU CAN ALWAYS TAKE THAT PICTURE OF SAM RORKS[2] AND DO IT HERE NOW MAKE ME VERY HAPPY AND SEND ME A WIRE THAT YOU WILL OPEN WITH THE FOLLIES AUGUST FIRST I KNOW YOU REMEMBER THE DAY YOU TOLD ME THAT IF YOU EVER GOT FOUR HUNDRED DOLLARS A WEEK YOU WOULD BE SATISFIED BECAUSE YOU PROMISED YOURSELF WHEN YOU LEFT OKLAHOMA THAT SOME DAY YOU WOULD BE GETTING FOUR HUNDRED A WEEK NOW LOOK AT THE DARN SALARY I NEED SOME OF THE ROGERS LUCK IN

23S C SHEET 3

THE NEXT FOLLIES AND YOU HAVE TO GIVE IT TO ME IF ONLY FOR A MINUTE SORRY YOU ARE NOT HERE TONIGHT TO HELP ME WITH THE LINDBERGH RECEP-TION AT THE ZIEGFELD THEATRE LOVE

FLO

939A

TG, rc. OkClaW, 1975.31.0108. On Western Union Telegraph Co. letterhead.

1. In late May Rogers began to experience what he described as a stomachache, but the pain became more acute on his way home to California in early June. Doctors soon diagnosed the problem as gallstones and recommended surgery. Seriously ill, Rogers was taken to a hospital on 16 June and underwent surgery the next day. Although the operation went well, Rogers's recovery was not immediate. He remained in the hospital until 2 July and then was ordered to remain in bed at home for another

week (Rogers, *Will Rogers*, 212–13; *NYT*, 16–17 June, 2 July 1927). For Rogers on his illness see *DT*, 1:100–4; *WA*, 3:43–48; and *EMJR*.

2. Samuel E. Rork (1874–1933), Hollywood producer and director, engaged Rogers in 1927 to star in what would be Rogers's last silent film, *A Texas Steer*. A feature-length story of Rogers as a Texas congressman, the movie was released in December 1927, near the end of the silent era (*VO*, 1 August 1933; *UDFT*, 227; *WRHolly*, 79).

Telegram to Houghton Mifflin Co.
22 July 1927
Beverly Hills, Calif.

In the spring of 1927 Rogers became involved in a legal dispute between the famed Pinkerton's National Detective Agency and book publisher Houghton Mifflin and one of its authors, Charles Siringo.[1] With the following document Rogers sought to extricate himself and still remain on good terms with all parties.[2]

E15OC 6C 60 NL

BEVERLYHILLS CALIF JUL 22 1927

HOUGHTON AND MIFFLIN

THE RIVERSIDE PRESS BOOK PUBLISHERS[3] 16 EAST 40 ST NEWYORK NY

I SENT A LONG PERSONAL WIRE TO ALLAN PINKERTON WHOM I KNOW[4] HIS ANSWER WAS A LONG EXPLANATION BUT THAT THE INJUNCTION MUST STAND SO YOU BETTER ACT ACCORDINGLY I WOULD FIX UP SOMETHING TO REPLACE IT THERE AND NOT WORRY CHARLEY ABOUT IT AS I DONT THINK HE CAN STAND IT YOU FELLOWS GO AHEAD AND FILL IT IN[5]

WILL ROGERS

1150P

TG, rc. HL-MH, bMS Am 1925 (1530). On Western Union Telegraph Co. letterhead. Handwritten upper left: "*Mr Pickun*" [?]. Handwritten below letterhead, right side: "RN." Rubber-stamped in box lower right corner: "RECEIVED JUL 22 1927 HOUGHTON MIFFLIN CO."

1. Charles Angelo (Charlie) Siringo (1855–1928), a Texas cowboy and western historian, worked for Pinkerton's National Detective Agency from 1886 to 1907. He spent many of his later years chronicling his experiences and producing other books about the American West. His most recent work, *Riata and Spurs*, published in April 1927 by the venerable Boston firm Houghton Mifflin, had raised the ire of the Pinkertons because it used the company's name in print and mentioned clients of the firm and their cases, all issues that Pinkerton had addressed in an injunction against a previous Siringo book (Pingenot, *Siringo*, xvii, 13, 64, 129–30; *NEAW*, 1054).

2. Houghton Mifflin asked Rogers to provide a foreword for *Riata and Spurs*, but instead Rogers wrote Siringo in late March:

"Somebody in some town gave me the proof sheets of your book and wanted to know what I think of it. What I think of it? I think the same of it as I do the first Cowboy Book I ever read: 'Fifteen Years on the Hurricane Deck of a Spanish Pony.' Why, that was the Cowboy's Bible when I was growing up. . . .

"I camped with a herd one night at the old L. X. Ranch, just north of Amarillo in '98, and they showed us an old forked tree where some old Bronk had bucked you into. Why, that to us was like looking at the shrine of Shakespeare is to some of these 'deep foreheads.' Well, this one you have written now is just what that was then. Why, if you live to be a thousand years old, you couldn't write a bad book about the Cowboys. The stuff they did might be bad, but you could tell it so well it would almost sound respectable. My Lord! with Western stuff being written by Soda Jerkers and Manicure Girls, there must be millions who would like to read the straight facts if they could find the book that had them.

"This is to tell the world that your 'Riata and Spurs' is 'IT.' . . . Use this about the book any way you want to if it is any good to you, for I sure mean it" (transcribed letter, Will Rogers to Charles A. Siringo, 28 March 1927, HL-HU, bMS Am 1925 [1658], by permission of Houghton Library, Harvard University).

The publisher used quotes from Rogers's letter in their efforts to promote the book (Pingenot, *Siringo*, 122). For other thoughts by Rogers on Siringo and *Riata and Spurs*, see *WA*, 3:60.

3. Houghton Mifflin was founded by Henry Oscar Houghton (1823–95) as a printing and publishing firm, H. O. Houghton & Company, in Boston in 1852 with the headquarters on the Charles River known as Riverside Press. George Harrison Mifflin (1845–1921) became a partner in 1878. Two years later the firm's name changed to Houghton, Mifflin & Company and eventually Houghton Mifflin. The company was one of the largest and most respected in the industry by the 1920s (*DAB*, 9:255–56; *WhAmer*, 1:827; *HBPUS*, 3:121–22).

4. Allan Pinkerton (ca. 1876–1930), grandson and namesake of the founder of the famous Pinkerton's National Detective Agency, headed the New York office of the company and became president in 1928. A member of Meadowbrook Club, he was probably well acquainted with Rogers as a fellow polo enthusiast. When Siringo told Rogers in mid-July about the difficulties with the Pinkertons over his new book, Rogers became concerned and promised to wire Allan Pinkerton to drop the injunction against *Riata and Spurs*. Rogers's plea to Pinkerton failed to move the agency head (*NYT*, 8 October 1930; Pingenot, *Siringo*, 130–31).

5. Four days after Rogers's telegram, the editor-in-chief at Houghton Mifflin informed Siringo that the publishing house had deleted the offending portion of the book and had substituted new material. The revised edition was released in October 1927 (Pingenot, *Siringo*, 132–33).

George E. Akerson to Thomas T. C. Gregory
30 August 1927
Washington, D.C.

Washington,
August 30, 1927.

Mr. T. T. C. Gregory,[1]
Balfour Building,
San Francisco, California.

Dear Tom:

. . . I wish that you could have been with us in the Washington Auditorium last Saturday night when the National Press Club gave a reception in honor of Will Rogers.[2] There were about 8000 people present. The Chief and Mrs. Hoover,[3] the two boys, the daughter-in-law,[4] and I[5] occupied the President's box, this having been given to me by the President of the Club.[6] Mrs. Will Rogers was with us in the box. At the close of his kidding act Will Rogers said that he had had one of the greatest pleasures of his life that night, having met a man whom he considered one of America's greatest statesmen. He said he didn't want to humiliate this man but he would ask Herbert Hoover to stand up. The Chief had to stand up, and the position of the box was such that every one in the audience practically could see him. There was a tremendous ovation. After the Chief sat down Rogers went on to pull the stuff that he had already written, namely, that when a man is sick he calls for a doctor, but when the United States of America is sick they call for Herbert Hoover.[7] Then he said: "But, Mr. Secretary, I advise you to keep on your job. I know that you have the best chance in the country to become President, but if this man did mean it he could have said "I will not" instead of "choose".[8] Nothing finer in the world could have been staged. It was a magnificent personal tribute by Will Rogers to Herbert Hoover, and the audience of more than 8000 people enjoyed it.▲immensely.▲ . . .

Sincerely yours,
[George E. Akerson]

GA-M.

TL, cc. HHPL, George Akerson Papers, Campaign & Transition. Ellipses inserted by editors.

1. Thomas Tingey Craven Gregory (1878–1933), a friend and Stanford University classmate of Herbert Hoover, was a California attorney who had worked with Hoover in postwar Europe as a member of the American Relief Administration (*NYT*, 6 June 1933).

2. The National Press Club honored Rogers at a reception on 27 August in Washington, D.C., where Rogers was filming scenes for *A Texas Steer*. Just before he headed to the nation's capital, he had been informed that a new state law had voided his honorary office of mayor of Beverly Hills. In sympathetic jest, the National Press Club decided to bestow on Rogers the designation of "Congressman-at-Large for the United States of America" (*NYT*, 28 August 1927; Rogers, *Will Rogers*, 213). The new title immediately replaced "Mayor" in the closings of the "Daily Telegrams" (see, for example, *DT*, 1:122). For Rogers as new ex-mayor see *WA*, 3:68–70.

3. Lou Henry Hoover (1874–1944), like her husband a native of Iowa, met Herbert Hoover at Stanford University, Palo Alto, Calif., where both were students. They married in 1899 (*NYT*, 8 January 1944).

4. Herbert Clark Hoover, Jr. (1903–69), the older son of Herbert and Lou Hoover, received a master's degree in business administration from Harvard University in 1928. He later entered business and then government service. In June 1925 he married Margaret Eva Watson (*DAB*, Supp. 8:275–76).

Allan Henry Hoover (ca. 1907–93), the second son of the Hoovers, graduated in 1929 from Stanford University, the alma mater of his mother, father, and brother. Trained in engineering, he became a mining executive (*NYT*, 10 July 1969, 8 November 1993).

5. George Edward Akerson (1889–1937), a former newspaperman, began serving as secretary to Herbert Hoover in 1925 when the latter was U.S. secretary of commerce. He worked for Hoover until 1931 (*NYT*, 22 December 1937; *WhAmer*, 1:11).

6. Louis Leon Ludlow (1873–1950), president of the National Press Club in 1927, was a newspaper correspondent in Washington from 1901 to 1929, the year he became the first member of the congressional press gallery to move to the floor of the House as an elected congressman (*NYT*, 29 November 1950). For Ludlow's remarks in honoring Rogers see *WA*, 3:70–73.

7. Herbert Hoover supervised flood relief efforts in the Mississippi River valley in 1927. He secured public and private funding; worked to provide food, clothing, and housing for hundreds of thousands of people affected by the catastrophe; and made recommendations to improve flood prevention in the area. Given prominent attention in the national press, Hoover's forceful response to the tragedy reinforced his credibility as a presidential candidate in 1928 (*DAB*, Supp. 7:360; *HD1920s*, 234).

8. President Coolidge issued a typewritten statement to reporters on 2 August that read, "I do not choose to run for president in nineteen twenty-eight." Debate immediately began as to Coolidge's intentions: whether he was refusing outright to seek reelection, equivocating so as to allow for a popular draft, or opening the possibility of a run four years later. Regardless, Herbert Hoover became the front-running alternative (Sobel, *Coolidge*, 368–70; *HD1920s*, 173). For Rogers on Coolidge's choice of words see *DT*, 1:115.

Telegram to George H. Lorimer
6 September 1927
Beverly Hills, Calif.

79P FDW 34

BEVERLYHILLS CALIF 934A SEP 6 1927

EDITOR LORIMER

SAT EVE POST

SAVE ME AS EARLY SPOT AS POSSIBLE I AM SENDING YOU IN NEXT FEW DAYS
THREE ARTICLES THAT I AM FINISHING TWO ON OPERATION[1] AND ONE ON POLI-
TICS[2] PROVERTY [*sic*] DROVE ME TO WORKS REGARDS

WILL ROGERS

142P

TG, rc. DLC-MD, Wesley Stout Papers. On Western Union Telegraph Co. letterhead. Handwritten below recipient's name: "79."

1. "A Hole in One," Rogers's two-part story of his gallstone operation, appeared
in the *Saturday Evening Post* of 5 and 12 November 1927. G. P. Putnam's Sons published it in book form in 1929 under the title *Ether and Me or "Just Relax."* See also
Letter to George H. Lorimer, ca. 18 September 1927, below. For a reproduction of the
original manuscript see *EMJR*, 35–61.
2. The *Post* published Rogers's article on politics, "Duck, Al! Here's Another
Open Letter," in its issue of 29 October 1927. In it, Rogers poked fun at a common
form of political punditry of the time and the accelerated speculation about presidential candidacies, including Al Smith's, in the wake of President Coolidge's "choose not
to run" announcement in August. For a reprint see *HTBF*, 40–45. Lorimer's response
to Rogers was immediate and succinct: "SHOOT AND SHOOT QUICKLY NEED THESE
ARTICLES IN OUR BUSINESS" (telegram, George H. Lorimer to Will Rogers, 7 September
1927, OkClaW).

To George H. Lorimer
ca. 18 September 1927
[Beverly Hills, Calif.]

Mr Lorimer.

Dear Boss.

Here is the first dose of this two part operation.[1] Sending the other in a
day or so. Hope its good enough to use for I was kidding on the Level in
there. The next half is I think a little better than this. I will get busy now and

see what I can turn out. I want to go to Mexico and Central America before Xmas if I can. I am making a Movie now.

So long good Luck

Will.

P.S. Please dont change Main Title, and Leave Dr's names in there.[2]

TLS, rc.[3] DLC-MD, Wesley Stout Papers. On Excelsior Hotel, Rome, Italy, letterhead.

1. See Telegram to George H. Lorimer, 6 September 1927, above.
2. Rogers gave his manuscript the title of "Scarbelly," but the *Saturday Evening Post* published it under the serialized heading of "A Hole in One." The names of the physicians survived the editor's pen. For a reprint of the *Post* series see *EMJR*.
3. Dating of the document was determined by the dates of follow-up correspondence between Rogers and George Lorimer.

Notes for Speech at Dinner for Charles A. Lindbergh
21 September 1927
San Diego, Calif.

Rogers, accompanied by his wife, Betty Blake Rogers, met Charles Lindbergh for the first time at a huge celebration in San Diego to honor the aviation hero.[1] In typical fashion, Rogers used his remarks at a banquet that evening to kid the honoree. The speech delighted Lindbergh and sparked a lasting friendship.[2]

The biggest kick we will get during oyr [our] lifetimes, The armistace dident do it for it was looked for, but when we thought of this old lone long country boy away out there on the ocean alone where no human being had ever been before why, we will never have a greater thrill during our lifetime,

It was themost wished and prayed for event after it staretes [started] that ever was   He waas being prayed for in every known language,

If he had been lost it would have been the moost universally regretted [loss.] And what a sucker he made out a our Diplomats,

At his age and with his mechanical experience ~~we are~~ ▲he is▲ just start ing in to be of real value to this nation,

Glad he dident go in to the show buisiness,

get the biggest air force in the world and just sit here and take care of our own business and we will never during our lifetime shave [have] to use~~;~~ it.

We want people to get to traveling, never min d a letter, that gettin there quick dont mean anything, Its the people we want to get acustomed to flying,

Will and Betty Blake Rogers joined ten others on 15 November 1927 on one of the first flights of the Ford Tri-motor airliner. The group flew to Chicago from Detroit, where the Ford Motor Company had staged a special preview of its newest car, the Model A. Left to right: Howard Worth, Harry Clark, Jack L. Maddux, Helene K. Maddux, Charles Lindbergh, Betty Blake Rogers, Benjamin Bledsoe, George Eastman, Will Rogers, Harry Culver, C. C. Tanner, and B. F. Mahoney. (*OkClaW*)

We break our neck to hurry at everything else, we break our neck to reach a grade crossing and then stop at ahot dog stand and buy and a bottle of Coak,

We knock twelve men and women down to get one steeet [street] car ahead of some [b]ody then meet a friend on the corner and gab for w an hour, with somebody that dont want to li[s]ten,

Its the only clean thing that has been in the papres in years, We dide[nt] have to read about how many prominet men were endited [indicted] and who got away with all the ~~Poo~~ pools, dobody [nobody] murdered each other , nobody w lked [walked] on the sands and never made a track,

Come to Beverley and just buy a lot,

The Wop telegraphed Mussllini / ▲collect▲ and he had aplane there by next boat,[3] Congress would [have] held a Filibuster before they could have voted the money to even send him a ticket home,

So many kissee him   If coolidge had kissed him would have had to stand ona chair, or the mayor here,

We have ben waiting for ~~three~~ two things, in Cal[ifornia] for two months, Lindy and Henry Fords new car to arrive,[4]

Dont get the idea that because he have had three planes reach E-- [Europe] that [we] are ahed in Aviation, Its not how far three men can fly, but   , but what have you got for the other other hundred and nine million to fly in and where are they to light if they do,

Banquet chicken slowly getting [to] him,

Wait ~~and see if~~ till after the next war and see if Planes are prac▲t▲[ical.]

Thats pretty good ap lause to fly from nowhere but Chula Vista,

Ata Lindberg Dinner it must be terrible hard to find something new to talk about, ~~He has sit at these things for thre and a half months and listened to the local spell binders of every to in America,~~ So if you dont mind I would like to say a few words for Tia Juana, There['s] a twon [town] without Phtysical charms, you would never ina million years get an ey full of beauty, But yet its a mouthfull daily to thousands of poor unfortunates,

This Guy has sit at these dog fights for thre[e] and ab half months listeni[ng] to 5he spellbinndof [the spellbinding of] every ambitious Amateur Orator in America, He knows all that is a lot of Apple s[a]uce, You dont have to tell him he flew the Ocean, & ~~he knows~~ I imagine he can r mmeber it yet,

So I would like to say a few words about my Operation, after the dinne[r] I would like to have everyone that has made that ether flight remain especillay the ladies, we will get togeather and maby compare a little,

I been reading and listening to the speeches these Birds all make to you, thay read upmon [up on] their history and compare you with some old geeser that went somewhere years ago, they have you called the Napoleon of the air, Thats no compliment   Napoleon croosee [crossed] the alps with his army on its belly and then had a forced landing at Wtaerloo, He got in the air again, went into a tail spin and was completely washed out at St helena,

Some Guy in spoakne [Spokane] called you our nero, That Guy was nothing but a fiddler and the only non stop flight he ever made was to a afire, He was nothing buta fiddler at a fire house,

Columbus, why he was lost when the [he] found this country, what a fine aviator he would have been if he had missed this ~~w~~ the whole of Nortnh America fora landing filld [field],

You have be n called the Worlds greatest Ambassador, Why an Ambassor is [a] man that is sent to anothet country to fool them in favor ½of th[e] people of his own, There is nothing that will double cross you as quick as an Ambassador,

You have ben called an Inspiration to children, You will have every one of them getting up on top of the house tying something on their arms and and trying to make a non sytop jump to the next building, You will be the m eans of crippling more than any [?]

These Orators all mean well, But they dont know what they are talkint about, You have had more bum oratory wasted on you than the war,

Its must be a quiet laugh for you to sit here every night and listen to all this c hatter,

If I was you I would jump from these tables and satrt [start] a flight someh[ow.] I would fly the Pacific with ten gallon tank if I had to stand waht [what] you have~~n~~. No wonder you travel alone,

Youdont like it I can tell, you would loik [?]

TD. OkClaW, 1975.14.0050. On letterhead of Hotel del Coronado, Mel S. Wright, Manager, Coronado Beach, California. All text appears vertically on sheets. Hand-inserted "1" and "4" in top margins, center, of pages 1 and 4, respectively. Typewritten "2" and "3" in top margins, center, of pages 2 and 3, respectively. Handwritten, in Rogers's hand, in margin above text, left corner, page 3: "Lindberg Dinner Speech". Extra spacing between words occurs throughout text.

1. Lindbergh's visit to San Diego occurred in the midst of a triumphal tour of the country that covered 22,350 miles and attracted an estimated 30 million spectators. The now world-famous *Spirit of St. Louis* had been built in San Diego, and from the southern California city Lindbergh had launched a record-breaking, transcontinental flight that he completed just days before he set off across the Atlantic for Paris (Berg, *Lindbergh*, 98–104, 168–69; *DAB*, Supp. 9:496).

2. The day following the dinner, Lindbergh flew the Rogerses to Los Angeles but chose to avoid an awaiting throng at the main airport by using a new landing field. The flight went well, but the unexpectedly bumpy touchdown on an undeveloped runway embarrassed the seasoned pilot. His profuse apologies amused Rogers and further

endeared him to the aviation hero (Rogers, *Will Rogers*, 233). For Rogers's account of the flight and Lindbergh on the West Coast, see *DT*, 1:130; and *WA*, 3:85, 87–89.

3. Francesco de Pinedo (ca. 1890–1933), a nobleman and the head of the Italian air service, undertook an unprecedented expedition by flight in early 1927 that touched four continents. Flying on behalf of Premier Mussolini, he and his co-pilot by late April had landed in the western United States intending to fly across the country and then the Atlantic to Europe. In Arizona, however, a mysterious fire destroyed their plane. As Italians charged sabotage and Americans claimed otherwise, Mussolini sent a replacement plane and de Pinedo and companion continued their flight. It ended to cheers in Rome, but the Italians' success was dampened by Lindbergh's landing several days before in Paris (Roseberry, *Challenging Skies*, 168, 169–71; *NYT*, 3 September 1933).

4. To overcome sluggish sales, the Ford Motor Company decided to develop a new car to replace its venerable Model T. Rumors about the changes began to sweep the nation as early as May 1927, and anticipation snowballed when Ford started to shut down its factories to rebuild and retool. The company announced on 10 August that the car was ready for production and two months later reported that it would appear soon. The first public demonstration, however, did not come until 30 November. The slow, deliberate pace of Ford's production and unveiling of the new Model A created unprecedented public anticipation and consumer demand (Nevins and Hill, *Ford*, 2:429, 450–54, 459–60). See also *WA*, 3:104–7.

Telegram from Thomas Arnold Robinson
4 November 1927
Mexico City, Mexico

CDU423 86 NL.MEXICOCITY MEX 4

MR WILL ROGERS.

BEVERLYHILLS CALIF.

PRESIDENT CALLES IS IN RECEIPT OF A TELEGRAM FROM MR DOHERTY[1] ASKING HIM TO EXTEND TO YOU HIS CORDIAL GREETINGS TO MEXICO AND TO ENDEAVOR TO MAKE YOUR EXPECTED VISIT BOTH PLEASANT AND SUCCESSFUL[2] STOP THE PRESIDENT HAS REQUESTED ME TO SAY THAT HE WILL GLADLY COMPLY WITH THE FOREGOING AND THAT HE LOOKS FORWARD WITH GREAT PERSONAL PLEASURE TO SEEING YOU HERE STOP PLEASE KEEP ME ADVISED BY TELEGRAPH AT CASTILLO DE CHAPULTEPEC MEXICOCITY AS TO[ ]DAY AND HOUR OF YOUR ARRIVAL AT BORDER AND MEXICOCITY.

THOMAS ARNOLD ROBINSON.[3]

TG, rc. OkClaW, 1975.31.0306. On Western Union Telegraph Co. letterhead. Metered below letterhead, right side: "1927 NOV 4 PM 6 53." Stamped to right of recipient's name: "722."

1. The sender of the wire may have referred to Edward J. (Eddie) Doherty (1890–1975), a reporter for the *New York Daily News* in the 1920s who had previously

covered revolutionary activities in Mexico for newspapers in Chicago. He also had worked on assignments in Hollywood (*NYT*, 5 May 1975; *WhAmer*, 6:114).

2. Rogers arrived in Mexico on 1 December to begin a seventeen-day stay. He was met at the border by President Calles and Ambassador Morrow and spent a week aboard the presidential train en route to Mexico City. Several months later, the *Saturday Evening Post* ran Rogers's account of his experiences in Mexico in five successive issues of the magazine in May and June 1928. In the series Rogers again assumed the persona of the "Self-Made Diplomat" that had proved so successful with the reading public following his trip to Europe (see *LSMD*). For his complete series on Mexico see *ML*, 21–92. For other writings by Rogers on Mexico see *WA*, 3:114–16, 119–22; and *DT*, 1:154–60.

3. Thomas Arnold Robinson (ca. 1894–1934), an American businessman in Mexico, was married to the daughter of Mexican president Plutarco Calles. The couple divorced in 1931 (*NYT*, 11 May 1934).

Manuscript for Magazine or Newspaper Article
5 November 1927
[Gallup, N.M.?]

The birth daybhas just passed and even I was no t windy enough to blow ▼out all the candles,▼ ▲we run out of friends and had to na[me] some of the candles after our horses,▲ I was 48 years of old age yesterday, and in all that 48 I never can remember the time when I could do or go just wherever I wanted too,

What I me▲a▲n I was subject to the draft, I had nothing depending on me, There was no where I had to be a certain time, ~~I dident even~~ ▲I▲ knew ~~have a single free dinner engagement~~, I knew I wouldent have to ▲even▲ listen to the ~~original toastmaster~~ fol owing, " The next Genetleman I am about to introduce needs no introduction, He started out roping the Bulls and wound up by throwing them", There wasent an audience anywhere from then till Xmas that was going to have to listen to, " All I know is just what I read in the papers." Somebody has to act a fool for th e foolish but I was on a furlough, I can readlily understand the retired business man who sells out thinking"well I will take it easy now, I will just sit around and enjoy myself", He does for a few weeks, then the first thing he knows he ~~beallses he made~~ begins to wonder if he dident make a mistake by getting out too quick, That he is not so old he was a better man today than the man he sold out too, so he begins to get fig-ity, he acts like ~~he ha~~ he's got fleas, but he hasent, He just wants to be out and doing something, Well that['s] the way I was, I had purposely left these few weeks open with nothing on my mind but but politics(which has never con-stituted a burned [burden] to the bearer), So I says to wife ~~wou~~ right out of what would have been a clearsky, (if it had been anyhwre [anywhere] but in

California, but it was mighty hazy there)   "les you and I go somehwre [somewhere]," Well she being a kinder trooper [trouper] at heart, For all the Kids had been born in a dressing room and raised in a Taylor trunk,[1] A day coach was their idea of a preambulator, They all cut their teeth on Fred Harveys spoons,[2] Well the balance wheel comes back with " Where will we go"?. I am right there with   the comeback, and reply, " Any[w]here", I was tired argueing with the kids everynight as to whether they would study or go to the movies, and I was losing too many arguements, I figured by leaving and and leaving strict orders that there was to be no shows during ~~weeks night~~ school nights, it would save me the trouble of losing so many arguments, Well I says, Did you ever see the Navajahoes?", She says yes " I saw the two in Albequrque that they keep to meet the train for atmosphere", She says are they the ones that ~~make the~~ sell Blankets?2, I says ~~yes~~ they are the ones that ~~make~~ ▼(sell)▼ the blankets but the white folks are the ones that sell them

No they are the ones that make the blankets   the white folks sell them, She says well what has the Navajoe s got to do with the trip, Well says I les go see the navajoes, She says oh do you think we can get some blankets cheap,", right away she was reverting to type.

She syas [says] I saw the two the[y] have in Albequrque that meets the train for atmosphere, Now America is pretty big, and there is lots of places to go and why i happened to singleout the Navajoes is just another one of the mysterious workings of a Comedians mind,

When can we go says family spirit level, " Why   [let's] go tonight", " Oh I cant go tonight   I just sent my dress out to the cleaners and it wont be back till tomorrow", Isays cant you wear the other one", She syas, I hate too   I have wore it through Arizona ~~to the s~~ so much that I know every Conductor and dining car Steward knows it by heart, Besides we wanted to go see "Uncle", his picture opens tomorrow night". Now so that I am not keeping anything away from my myriad of readers, " Unlce" that she so affectionately spoke of was a strawberry roan Arizona and Old Mexico Steer. with Tarrasas brand on his side and a double diamond on his left hip, and various road brands, He had gone through three revolutions in Mexico, then come to Arizona in time to hear all the arguments on the Boulder Dam, and what else exciting was there forsa [for a] steer to do but go in to the Movies which he did, Dough Fairbanks was making the "Goucho"[3] and hee instead of going to a ranch and using their cattle he just went out and   bought 700 old long horned Mexican steers and took them right to the Studio to board during the making of the picture, He figures instead of usiung [using] a mob scene with hundreds of extras I will use steers instead, Instead of ha[v]ing a background of people that all cheersat the same time and all do the same thing at the same time I will get steers, and just let em do what they want too, Well"Uncle" was one of these Steers, He was a gentle and agreeable kind of a creature and hadent been on the Fairbaks studio lot more than a week till he was making his presence felt, He had been in Mexico ,omg [long] enough to know that the leader is the one that grabs off alnthe [all the] gravy, that is as long as he lives to lead, so old Uncle just announced that he was the " P[a]ncho Villa, Obregon,[4] and Calles combined". He was leading every steer revolution on the lot, and doing it a kind of a Coolidge way without making any fuss about it, Well he got hims[e]lf in so strong that Doug when the picture was a l finished hated to see him go to the guillotine with the rest of them so he puthim in a truck and sent him down to my littleranch at Santa Monica, Now there is one thing about California that if you have never been there will be a laugh to you, and that is that everything that is not on spring street Los Angeles ~~aa~~ or Market street San Francisco is called a Ranch,

Any other State or country in the world a Ranch, is a ranch, or it aint one, ~~but in~~ There is only three kind of raches anywhere else in the world, that is ~~S~~ a Cattle, Sheep or, Horse ranch, But in Califirnia, you may be invited to someones"ranch" and it will be a forty   foot lot with thre[e] ~~Prune~~ ▲(lemon▲ trees growing on it, and it will [be] "our Prune Ranch", If you get a pair of ~~Belgian har~~ cotton tail rabbits, Its " Our Belgian hare rancH",

Avacado ranches are all the go, you can go out and watch the Cowbosy round up the Avacado's, Then a ~~Walnut~~ ▼(prune)▼ Rodeo, on one of the big ~~walnut~~ ▼(Prune)▼ Ranches, is postively thrilling,

~~If its~~ The Prune Stampede in Fresno   every year, is oneof the biggest events in California, They drive in the prunee for miles and miles from other ranches,   and the old time "Pruners meet and talk over what the country was when it was wide open, and you could judt go out and raise Prunes anywhere, that now they theranches are getting small, and they are getting kindef high falutin, and are bre ding the prunes up, and they havent got the wild ones like they used to have   in the old days when   we first opened up this country and made it safe for prunes.

Then if you live near the ocean or beach it is a Fish ranch, You go out on the spring roundup with a good hook and line and it aint nothing to come back into the ranch house at night with your bait all gone and your lunch all eat up. You see therecis [there is] a monotony about ranches the world over, for maby you dont like seeing nothing but hundreds and thousands of cattle, or sheep or horses, or Cowboys, or sheephererds, So much sameness gets on your nerves, but with California rances it is different, For instance if you dont

like a chaicken ranch where you are visiting, why you can go across the the
street and [visit a?] goose and duck ranch, or if you like novelty8s there is
Skunk ranches, and Lion ranches, or if you dont like animal, or fowl or insect
ranches there   is the fellow next door who took his quarter of an acre   and
sowed it all to Alfalfa, and he has "His Alfalfa rancH2, Anything tha[t]   is
not a two family apartment house, or a fil[l]ing station, or a Piggly Wiggly, or
a Branch bank, or a Real Estate office, ~~why you will take no~~ is a ranch, and
you will not only make no mistake by calling it that but you will please the
ownder greatly by calling it that, Well we have a Ranch, There is nothing on it
but a Polo field, So its a ranch, I suppose it should be called a Polo ranch,
where we hope to raise other Polo fields,

we have been unsuccessful up to now, as we didesnt hardly know what the
cross was, and as Mr Burbank[5] had passed on we dont know ~~he~~ what to croos
graft onto a polo fild that might produce maby a golf course, In fact we dont
know what to croos it with to eve[n] produce a practice field, Well dough
[Doug] had heard of " Our Ranch" so he put old "Uncle " in a truck and he
was taken away from these other seven hundred Movie extras and he sent him
down to "Our Ranch", mind you there wasent a Cow on it or ever had been
on it but it was our " Ranch"   well "Uncle" looked around and started to
grin, and said, " So they ~~make fun of Mexico~~ call this a ranch, and ~~yet~~ these
are the people that make fun of Mexico, Well at least Mexico knows what a
ranch is anyway, "If this [is] a ranch I am asacred Ox", So Dough called me
up and told me he had given me Uncle, Well I went down and I never felt as
sorry for an actor in my life as I did for uncle   here he had just left the
night life of Holllwood, to spend the balance of his days on a Polo ramnch, I
could tell he either craved for company, or craved for Hollywood, so I just
went down to the stock yards in Los Angles and and bought some companions for " Uncle"   I sorted them out that ~~S~~ and picked the ones that I
thought would be good company, I got I5 head, I knew that wouldent be
many to Uncle but it would a be a lot to a California ranch, I selected Cows
and calves, ~~so the children could ride the calves at tmes whn the wasent at the
movies, and in case Father could~~ not so much with "Uncle" in view but so
that the Children could have a little Calf riding, and Father could have a little
Roping on the side, I got small ones so I would be sure in case of an acciden-
tal catch I could be able to take the rope off, Well now I I must get ~~back to the
original~~ fade back to the [point] where I left you awhile ago talking to may
[my] wife and sh ewas saying we couldnt go today on acc[o]unt of having to
go see Uncles opening at Graumans Theatre,[6] The children and all of us were
all hoppeed up and excited over seeing Uncle's opening, And I tell you we

sure was proud of him, dont miss him   go see "Uncle" in the Goucho, He runs by a camera jusr [just] like   it wasent there, he is the 2I2 one from the end, when they run through the twon [town], remember a big braod horned, strawberry roan steer, t.R.S. connected on the left side and a double diamond on left hip, left ear split and underslope the   right, you cant miss him,

Well with due honors done to Uncle and the dress cleaned, all we had to do was sign some blank checks ~~and leave~~, to leave, ask the children to please mind, and start out hunting Indiands, in November I927, My wife says, " dont you think we ought to have a few trinkets, and beads to trade, or give them", I says no   if they are anything like ~~our~~ my tribe the Cherokkes you will insult em if you offer em anything less than a Packerd car. We garb of   reseveations [grab off reservations] on the Chief   thats the Santa fees crack tr[a]in, Then they tell us, " You cant go to Gallup on this train, the nearest you can go is Albequrque," Well you go through Gallup dont you, "Y"Yes," Well you stop there dont you?,   Yes, well why cant we get off there then, "Well because we dont carry passengesrs just to Gallup, You have to ride ont to Albequrque", It seemed like if they get anybody on their trains they dont like to have em getting on or off all the time, they like for you to stay on there, So I fixed it by buying tickets to Albequrque, and ɡ when the conductors wasent watching fool him and get off at Gallup, Be a good   joke on that Conductor when he finds we paid to go clear to Albequrque and dident go clear there, a Comedian does think of the most original things,

---

TM, dc.[7] OkClaW, Unpublished Manuscripts. Typewritten, top margin, center, page 1: "Page one, I,   Navajo". Handwritten, not in Rogers's hand, upper left corner, stacked (/), page 1: "*Nov 5 / 1927 / Extract*". Handwritten, in Rogers's hand, upper left margin, page 1: "Use". Typewritten, top margin, right center, page 3: "A bee ranch". A typewritten "3" appears in the top margin of each of the last two pages. A few editor's marks for paragraphing and capitalization were hand-inserted in the first three pages but were disregarded for this transcription.

1. A Taylor trunk was a typical piece of luggage used by theatrical professionals. It took its name from that of the manufacturer (*IDTL*, 859).

2. For Frederick Henry Harvey see *PWR*, 3:71n. 2.

3. *The Gaucho*, a romantic adventure film set in Argentina and produced by Douglas Fairbanks, starred the swashbuckling actor in the title role. It opened in New York on 21 November 1927 and ranked among the five most popular movies of the year (*AFIC*, F2FE:283; *NYT*, 22 November 1927; Koszarski, *Evening's Entertainment*, 33).

4. Álvaro Obregón (1880–1928), a leading military commander in the Mexican Revolution in the 1910s, was elected president of Mexico in 1920 after the previous head of state had been overthrown by Obregón supporters. He left office four years later, but by 1927 he had become a candidate for reelection to the presidency in a vote scheduled for the next year (*EM*, 2:1031–33).

5. Luther Burbank (1849–1926), renowned California breeder of plants, developed over a career of almost sixty years numerous new species and varieties of fruits, flowers, vegetables, trees, and other plant life (*DAB*, 3:265–70).

6. For Sidney Patrick (Sid) Grauman see *PWR*, 2:453–54n.5.

7. The manuscript may have been intended for the *Saturday Evening Post*, but no record of its publication in that magazine or anywhere else was found. For a brief account of Rogers's experiences and observations during the trip to the Southwest, see *DT*, 1:146–47.

From George H. Lorimer
6 December 1927
Philadelphia, Pa.

December 6, 1927

Mr. Will Rogers

My dear Rogers:

You may remember from your boyhood that stuff in the Bible about the two women grinding at the mill -- how one was taken and the other was left. That's the way it is with these two articles. The flying stuff is fine and we are glad to have it,[1] but,with the greatest possible admiration for Henry and his new car,I cannot escape the conviction that it should appear next to pure reading matter instead of as pure reading matter.[2] Otherwise it would seem that we ought to go on with a snappy series on the Chevrolet, the Buick, the Packard,[3] the Pierce-Arrow, etc. ad infinitum.

Yours sincerely,

[George H. Lorimer]

L/D

TL, cc. MoU-WHMC, George Horace Lorimer Papers.

1. Lorimer likely referred to a manuscript that the *Saturday Evening Post* serialized and published on 21 and 28 January 1928 as "Flying and Eating My Way East" and "Bucking a Head Wind." In the two articles Rogers related his experiences crossing the country, both ways, as a passenger aboard airmail flights in October. He was charged his weight in postage. For a reprint of the articles see *HTBF*, 46–73; for other Rogers writings about the flights see *DT*, 1:140–41.

2. Although the *Post* chose not to run Rogers's piece on the much anticipated new Ford model, Rogers probably did not let his work go to waste. His "Weekly Article" of 22 January 1928 fits the description (see *WA*, 3:122–25).

3. Packards, first manufactured in 1899 by James Ward Packard (1863–1928), had become noted worldwide by the late 1920s as large, luxurious cars of quality construction and engineering (*DAB*, 14:128–29; *EABAuto*, 295).

To Internal Revenue Department
ca. 1927
[Beverly Hills, Calif.?]

To Internal Revenue Department,

Mr Andrews our income tax man[1] tells me that there is some doubt about allowing the living expenses in New York when we left our home in Cal, and went back there to work,[2] I couldent very well be asked to pay my expenses there wh[e]n my home was here, but I had to move there with my family in order to earn that money, And as for thePolo, Now in order to earn the money that I have been lucky enough to earn, it is like any other well advertised concern, they have to have some way of doing the advertising, Now of all the things that I have done in my career that has received national publicity without my having to pay for the actual space over the counter, Polo has been the best one, I am no polo player, I am not even fond of the game, I could ride a bit and I took it up solely for what there was in it from a publicity angle, It has been the means of my meeting and association with prominent people more than any thing I ever did, I just finished a letter now to one of our International Polo players whom I have been a guest of, It was absolutely and solely the means of meeting and association with the Prince of Wales, over here and in England, It w as through me dubbing around Polo that they asked me to speak at the big Polo Dinner before him at Piping Rock Long Island, and played with him in a game the next day, There was 200 other Comedians in N Y at the time that could have entertained him as well as I, But on account of my Polo connection I was the one thought of, The publicity that accrued from a the Prince alone was the means of my using it for weeks in the Follies in my act, On the road in my lectures, I used it in my syndicated articles lord knows how many times,

Went to England met the Prince again at a Polo game   wrote for the Saturday Evening Post about it, and used that in my lectures here, Met the King of Spain through Polo in Madrid, He had heard that I pla[y]ed and that was the entire conversation, All of my friends on Long Island and in various Cities throughout the Country to used to come to the Follies and now to see me on my own tours are over 90 percent Polo and horse friends, I certainly am not doing it for the exercise, the roping I do nightly on the stage keeps me in enough physical shape, It requires good horses to play and it requires lots of expense and men to keep a string of ponies, I am not able to do it if it wasent that I know that it has been a great asset for me in dozens of ways,

Out here in California I maintain a Polo field, I havent been able to play on it much last year and this year on account of my operation, not at all, But it is used three times a week, on Sundays there is thousands of people at the field, Its in all the papers, "At "Will Rogers Polo Field yesterday&"and so on. My stable and horses are visited by hundreds, All the high priced seats at my lectures are all these same polo people, I dont give big dinners and entertainments and charge them off as entertaining my clients, I dont go in for that, But they do use my Polo field absolutely gratis, with me bearing all the expense for I know it is good for me in my business, Now I am not trying to put anything over on you in this, I sincerely feel and know that it has been a tremendous help to me in my business, Us Birds that try to keep before and interest the public have various ways of doing it, The more you do anything that dont look like advertising the better advertising it is, I never take out adds in Theatrical papers, and in no oje [one] of my income tax blanks will you find one cent charged off to a Press Agents salary, and I think if you will notice that you will find that I am the only actor in America on your list with no charge for Press Agent, I cant charge it off on my tax because I have never had one, The shows I have been with have had Press men that were paid by the management, ~~But~~ and most actors, at least all that can afford it have private press Agents, which is their way of keeping their name well known,

I have never paid one cent to any man in my life for publicity, and I get paid for being fairly well known, Well I had to do it someway, and the reason I figure I have made myself maby better known that the majority is because I have done ~~it~~ the publicity end of it differently, With as much publicity as I have had I certainly feel out of all my earnings entirely out of my publicity that I have a just claim in charging this polo off,

If I dident have to make my living out of my name before the public you would see me hitch those polo ponies to a plow and turn that polo field into a corn patch, that['s] how much the game means to me outside what it brings me in, If Polo was not a means of getting me publicity what would you suggest would be a legitimate thing to charge off, I must have some thing, Any business concern that gets one tenth the publicity that I do would have three times the charge off, so what gets me all this. I dont calim [claim] that Polo got it all, But it got a lot, and it is the only thing that I am claiming for, Now I am writing this because I know you all are fair enough to want to get my angle, and not feel that something was being put over on you, I honestly feel that if anyone was ever legitimately entitled to a thing I am to this,

Yours very truly,
Will Rogers.

TLS, dc.[3] OkClaW, 1975.05.0002. On Will Rogers, Beverly Hills, California, letterhead.

1. J. L. Andrews maintained an office on Madison Avenue in New York (J. F. Callan to Will Rogers, 3 August 1927, OkClaW).

2. Rogers was asked in early August 1927 to meet with an Internal Revenue Service agent in New York to discuss his tax return for 1925. The letter requesting his presence was not specific about what issues had prompted the audit, but subsequent contact that Rogers's accountant must have made with the bureau apparently centered on the concerns Rogers addressed in this correspondence (see J. F. Callan to Will Rogers, 3 August 1927, OkClaW).

3. Although the announcement of an audit of Rogers's income tax return of 1925 came in August 1927, no record has been found to verify that Rogers personally attended an audit meeting or submitted a response to the concerns raised by the Internal Revenue Service. He likely prepared and sent this letter in 1927, sometime after 11 August, the date of the original correspondence from the bureau.

Telegram from V. V. McNitt
6 January 1928
New York, N.Y.

The public reaction to his good-natured imitation of President Calvin Coolidge during a national radio broadcast took Rogers by surprise. As the following wire reflects, Rogers as Coolidge fooled a large portion of the listening audience and left many unamused.[1]

39SM 67 BLUE

TZ NEWYORK NY 1116A JAN 6 1928

WILL ROGERS

BEVERLYHILLS CALIF

MR OCHS OF TIMES ASKS US TO CONVEY TO YOU FOLLOWING IDEA HE SAYS YOUR IMITATION OF COOLIDGE ON RADIO WAS SO GOOD THAT MILLIONS OF PEOPLE THINK IT WAS REALLY COOLIDGE TALKING AND HE THINKS YOU MIGHT WANT TO EXPLAIN IN DAILY DISPATCH THAT IT WAS NOT REALLY CAL BUT YOU[2] WE JUST TRANSMIT THE SUGGESTION TO YOU AT THE REQUEST OF MR OCHS[3] BEST REGARDS

V V MCNITT

1002A

TG, rc. OkClaW, 1975.31.0501. On Western Union Telegraph Co. letterhead. Printed flush left immediately below letterhead: "Received at 1509 Santa Monica Blvd., Beverly Hills, Calif. Telephone Oxford 4709."

1. Rogers served as the master of ceremonies on the evening of 4 January 1928 during the most widespread hookup to date of performers in a radio broadcast. The program, sponsored over the NBC network by Dodge, an automobile manufacturing company, linked Rogers, seated at his home in Beverly Hills, and program participants in New York, Chicago, and New Orleans. The comedian surprised everyone when he suddenly announced that Calvin Coolidge had joined the broadcast from the White House and then began imitating the president's New England twang. Rogers as Coolidge discussing foreign and domestic issues prompted letters and telephone calls of protest. Some people mistook the imitation for real and thought that Coolidge was appearing on the show in endorsement of the sponsor's product. Even among those listeners who knew it was a joke, there were critics who felt that Rogers's prank exceeded the bounds of good taste (*NYT*, 5, 6 January 1928).

2. Rogers did not immediately address the issue in a "Daily Telegram," but several days later he devoted a column to recounting the incident, the public reaction, an apologetic note he wrote the president and first lady, and Calvin Coolidge's response graciously dismissing the whole episode (see *DT*, 1:170; see also *WA*, 3:125–27). For Roger's apology see Letter to Calvin and Grace Coolidge, ca. 10 January 1928, below; for Coolidge's reply see Letter from Calvin Coolidge, 11 January 1928, below.

3. Not all reaction was critical. Sol Bloom, a Democratic representative from New York, sent a message the night of the broadcast that "all senators and congressmen" had listened and thought it was "the best thing they ever heard." Two days later, Edsel Ford, president of the Ford Motor Company, wired Rogers to express his enjoyment of the broadcast. As a competitor to the program sponsor, he may also have found amusement in the reaction to Rogers's mimicry of Coolidge (telegram, Sol Bloom to Will Rogers, 4 January 1928, OkClaW; telegram, Edsel Ford to Will Rogers, 6 January 1928, OkClaW).

To Calvin and Grace Coolidge
ca. 10 January 1928
Washington, D.C.

My Dear Mr and Mrs President,

I find that due to my lack of good taste, or utter stupidity, that I have wounded the feelings of two people who I most admire, and should have been the last ▲to▲ embar[a]ss, had I purposely started out to annoy the entire World,[1] If it will lessen the annoyance any to know that there was absolutely and postively no inkling of a thing of that kind intended, why I want you to believe me when I tell you that was the case,

Why Mr Coolidge you and your wife have benn nicer to me than any one in high public life in America , I was never invited to the White House by any other President, and in dozens of ways you have been kind to me,

Why I have just finished visiting in the home of your best friend, Mr Morrow, A man that I tremendously admire, anda family that I would cut off my right arm rather than have them think I had been in any way rude to you his friend, I am not as ungrateful as that, in all my little jokes and remarks of you, I had never felt that I passed the borders of good tas[t]e, I have had people say to me time and again, " Will I notice you joke a lot about Coolidge, but you generally wind up by having something mighty complimentaryto say of him before you finish, I believe you are a real admirer of him". And that is exactly the way I have felt about it,

If I dident have sincere admiration for you both and know the good you have been to our Country, regardless of the personal kindness's you had shown me, this thing wouldent hurt so bad, But it does hurt me, to think that I have to resort to bad taste to make my living from men who have befriended me, I did the little talk in a moment of jest, never for one moment thinking the most stupid of people could ever mistake it for anyone but me, On another page I want to write you the very remarks, and leave it to your judgement as to how anyone in any pa[r] t of their sane moments could possible picture the President of the United States uttering such words.

I just missjudged the intelligence of the people listening, and I cant lay all the blame to them, For I can see now after due thought that it was not the proper thing to do under any circumstances, Buts its the intent that I do ask forgivness for, I realize now that radio is not the stage, where they can see you, and I ~~aloo~~ also realize that the class of people who would come into a Theatre to see you are above the average o[f] some of the ones who would be listening overa radio, all this I have learn[ed] to my sorrow, And if you can see it in your heart, you and that dear wife of yours to forgive me, I will certainly see that it,or nothing approachin it will ever happen again, I have always so boasted of the friendship of all menthat I joke about, and said that I hope that I would never do anything that would cause them embarrassment, I lived in Mr Morrows home for over twow weeks and I think he will tell you that I am not quite as bad as I appeared. My wife and I knew nothing about it till we got here, I had heard nothing of it on the coast, everyone took it as I had meant it, We went to Mrs Longworths for dinner and we were told, and it certainly has been a gloomy night and day for us,   I hate to face the Jackson day dinner now for I know how the feelings of some of them will be that I will do something that will upset the affair,[2]

If there ever was a sad Comedian, I am one, and I do ask all the forgivness that its in your and Mrs Coolidges power to give,

Yours most respectfully,
Will Rogers.

[*Will Rogers's enclosed recollection of his radio remarks as "President Coolidge"*:]
Radio Fans,

I have a friend in Washington who on account of what the Automobiles have done for his Economy wants to speak to you, Mr Coolidge,

all right Mr Coolidge go ahead,

"Ladies and Gentleman, I am supposed to deliver a message every year on the condition of the country, I find the Country as a WHOLE prospero[us.] I dont mean by that, that the WHOLE country is prosperous, But as a ~~Whole~~ WHOLE, its prsosperous, That is its prosperous as a WHOLE. a WHOLE is not supposed to be prosperous, There is not a WHOLE lot of doubt about that,"

(Now can you picture anyone being so devoid of humor that they would picture ~~anyone~~ you uttering such nonsense)

" Mr Mellon has saved up some money for the country, and laid by some for himself".[3]

"Mellon is the only [Secretary of the] Treasury that the United States ever had that has saved faster than Congress can divide it up"[4]

"They are here now to split up the swag, The cheapest way would have been to have taken each Senators and Congressmans address and just mailed him his Pro Rata share, that would have eliminated any cause for holding this session at all, and been cheaper in the long run on the people",

" Pretty near all the men I come in contact with are *doing* we*ll*, Hoover, Dawes,[5] Lowden,[6] Mcadoo, Smith, Course none of them are doing as well as they hope to be doing this time next ~~year~~ year, But they are doing well".

"I sent Dwight Morrow to Mexico, He is doing good work, Smart Boy [that?] Dwight, One of the two smartest boys in our class at Amherst, where we were preparing for College".[7]

" Lindberg is down in Central America,[8] We seem to get in wrong faster than that Boy can get us out, Wish he was twins".

" I am leaving next week for Cuba,[9] Going to show South America that we are not as bad as we've been".

"Nicaragua, We are haiving a little trouble in Nicaragua, But I think we will soon get that buried",[10]

" Last summer I made a statement in which I said I dident "choose to run,["] Well/its seems to have been missunderstood, So at the opening of Congress I clarified it by stating, " I still dont "Choose" to run. I dont see how any one could missunderstand that statement".

"Prohibition,   Prohibition is going down about as well as usual".

Now there Mr President is an exact copy word for word of the nonsense i uttere[d] that night, HOW could it ever be misstaken for you?.

TLS, rc. FL-CCPLM. On The Willard, Washington, letterhead.

1. See Telegram from V. V. McNitt, 6 January 1928, above.

2. See Notes for Speech at Jackson Day Dinner, ca. 12 January 1928, below.

3. Andrew Mellon's unusually long service as treasury secretary, which came during a time of prosperity and peace, was marked by policies of debt and tax reduction and special considerations for accumulators of significant wealth (*DAB*, Supp. 2:448–49).

4. Federal expenditures in 1928 totaled $3.1 billion, but receipts reached $3.9 billion. In the same year the national debt fell to $17.6 billion, a $4.7 billion reduction in five years (Sobel, *Coolidge*, 392).

5. Charles Gates Dawes (1865–1951), a former banker from Illinois, served as vice president in the Coolidge administration from 1925 to 1929. He had shared the Nobel peace prize in 1925 for his successful postwar efforts to institute a reparations program for Germany (*DAB*, Supp. 5:159–60).

6. Frank Orren Lowden (1861–1943), Republican governor of Illinois from 1917 to 1921, declined several federal appointments in the 1920s to focus instead on rural programs and issues. He ran half-heartedly for the presidential nomination in 1928 but never emerged as a leading candidate (*DAB*, Supp. 3:467–68).

7. Calvin Coolidge and Dwight Morrow had been friends since their days as members of the class of 1895 at Amherst College, Amherst, Mass. (*DAB*, 13:234; Ferrell, *Presidency*, 129).

8. From Mexico City on 28 December Charles Lindbergh flew to Guatemala City, Guatemala, to begin a tour of Latin America. By the time he returned to the United States in mid-February 1928, he had logged 9,390 miles and touched down in fifteen countries and territories in Central America, South America, and the Caribbean (Berg, *Lindbergh*, 274).

9. President Coolidge addressed the opening session in Havana, Cuba, of the sixth International Conference of American States, commonly known as the Pan-American Conference. Held from 16 to 20 January 1928, the meeting came at a time of heightened American intervention in Latin America and extreme pressure on the United States to revise its policies (Ellis, *Republican*, 268).

10. The United States had withdrawn its marines from Nicaragua, a small Central American nation important as an alternative site for a canal, in August 1925 after an unprecedented intervention of thirteen years. Increased revolutionary activity, however, had brought two thousand American troops back to Nicaraguan soil by March 1927. The unsettled situation in the country between liberal and conservative elements led to continued U.S. intervention and promised American supervision of a scheduled election in 1928 (Ellis, *Republican*, 252–58).

From Calvin Coolidge
11 January 1928
Washington, D.C.

January 11 1928

Mr. Will Rogers.
Washington, D.C.,
My dear Mr. Rogers-

Your letter has just come to me.[1] I hope it will cheer you up to know that I thought the matter of rather small consequence myself though the office was informed from several sources that I had been on the air. I wish to assure you that your note makes it all plain that you had no [bad] intention[, only] some harmless amusement.

I hope you will not give the affair another troubled thought. I am well aware how nicely you have referred to me so many times.

Cordially Yours
Calvin Coolidge

ALS. OkClaW, 1975.21.0147. On The White House, Washington, letterhead. Includes envelope addressed to Mr. Will Rogers, New Willard, Washington, D.C.

1. See Letter to Calvin and Grace Coolidge, ca. 10 January 1928, above.

Notes for Speech at Jackson Day Dinner
ca. 12 January 1928
Washington, D.C.

Most people at a great affair [l]ike this[1] would consider it an honor, But I want to tell you I dontw nt [dont want] it known that I amhere, its just bordering o on disgrace,

Is there a oh [one] of you that could swear ona Bible that he never boughta vote or sold his own, you couldent swear it, and if you could you would have to send outside Politics to borrow the Bible,

My Opponents here tonight who were alsobarking for theer meals,[2] They said nice things , why because they had too, They are looking for something , even if its not President, they well [will say?] I can at least land " Secretary of State", most anybody can get that, they are never very particular,

I am not here to say anything nice abo ut you, I am not looking for a thin[g.] You have nothing I want, and from the looks of thi[n]gs you wont ~~get~~ be in ~~anything~~ a position to do anything for me anyway,

You know I like to talk to Democrats, They have a better sense of humor than the Republicans, Republivcans have been in office more than Demo[crats]- so that has always given us more to laugh at,

Us Democrats are jeust [just] as funny when in office m but we are never in office long enough for any one to muster up any continous laughter,

▲CANNIBAL.▲ No you are funny, Republicans are serious, for they never know at what moment they will get caught, beinvestigated and thrown out,

The Republicans take the Government serious, But the Dem— figure its just here today gone tomorrow witthem, so they dont worry mucg [much],

FOR OPENING OF SPEECH,

~~WELL GENTS I AM GOING TO BE A TERRIBLE DISSAPOINTMENT TO YOU, I'LL~~
~~SWEAR I dont know how I ever made sucha mistake, and it was just by listening~~
~~to some of the other speaker here that I found out my mistake, if I had spoke~~
~~first I wouldhave mde myself the laughing stock of the country, I have a speech~~
~~here based naturally on Jackson, and all of it hinged on how he " Stood like~~
~~Stom½ne wall" and wahat he meant to our civil war, and now I come , I think I~~
~~can go ahead and deliver it and nobody will ever know t the difference, O He~~
~~stood like Stone wall may mean Al Smith to them, we well I come here and~~
~~and find it wasent Stonewall Jackson at all, so my speech is practically a loss~~
~~inless I can find some gathering that want wants to celebrate the civilwzr,~~
~~Why lord its olsd Andrew Jackson,~~

~~That old rounder, why no wonder the party dont get anywhere celebrat~~
~~ing him, He is the Guy that run the Cherokee's out o my race out of Georgia,~~
~~and North Carolina, I will eat at his dinner but I have no compliments for~~
~~him, He is the first politicain that believed that every man that voted for you~~
~~should be ptovided with an Government officem, he originated the spoil system.~~
~~and just about spoiled the Democratic Party,~~

~~He thought a man should hold a Government on Politics and not on abil~~
~~ity, But I will give him credit forone thing, he is the inly man that ever~~
~~resigned from the S nate, the U S senate, He did it in1797 and again 23 years~~
~~later, he just would eg go in there, Now they are spening all can to get in,~~

~~We are here to open bids and pick the highest bidder,~~

I am a Candidate, I am not like these other[s], telling what the party needs and thinlu [thinly] veiling the fact that they are the ones to supp[l]y that need, I am not kidding you   I am aCandidate, I am the only one that comesright out in the open, I am not like my good friend, all [I'll] send my gang down to see if its safe, and then if it is I will come,[3] I am right here, Who wants a Comedian fo r President that admits he isa Comedian, and is a Comedian purposely, and not accidentally, or by nature, Good, You other Guys just ~~Lets at least eat in harmony even if we cant vote in harmony~~. ▶DRINK IN H–[harmony][4]◀

I hate to see a dinner or anyother thing where everybody does the same thing, We all like novelty, Now here to night most of the speeches are of a Democratic order, Well I want to say a few words for the Republicans,

If it wasent for them there would be no use havinga a harmony dinner,

If it wasent for them we wouldent have to have any party,

If it wasent for them creating all these various offices, there ▶would◀ ▼be no need of Politics.▼

[*typewritten:*]~~Everybody has some one to work on their speeches with them, Jim Reed had the advice of the Anti Saloon Legue on his,~~

~~McAdoo I dont know where he dug that one he had,~~

~~Georges I could see a touch of heflin, there, whn he~~

~~Davis thts one of the old 24 spe ches, Whata memory,~~

~~Well Collidge helped me on mine,~~

IAM the only person that will admit that I will take the vice Presidency and then figure on divine providence helping me from then on.

I got in wrong with Smith, by advising him not to run till 28, I meant well But you must bever [never] advise a politician to do anything that he dont want you to advixse [advise] him on, So from now on I am for everybody running regardless of his chances, when they ask me, "Have I got a Chance, Git a Chance why they cant beat you. Let em all run

~~I said to Calvin, "I want a speech, that will satisfy the Democrats, Well you tell em I am not going to run, Thats the best speech you can have for the Democrats", Its Economy.~~

I am tired having Conventions wait to see if the man will run for Vice P. and having them,

[Jim Reed (?), you might] as well wawh up and go home, Go back to the Smelly banks of the Kaw, Go back and listen to the Republivans cheering,

Go backa nd grind your teeth during the Republican convention in your City, Ritchie get back to Maryland to those Stills,[5]

We musent make the mistake of nominating a ~~ge~~ high class Gentleman [like?] last time, so lte [let's] dont make the same mistake again, dont be too particular, In fact I think any of these other ~~Gent~~ fellows here would answer.

But I want it known, I am to run the REPUBLIC[A]N

~~Outside of our Lady Speakers and Myself, I never saw sucha motley array of talent in my life, They have tried to swamp you with quantity, when they knew they were lacking in quality, They run their Dinners like they do their Conevntions, as they cant settle ona Candiadte they vote all summer ona ll of them and at their Dinners they cant settle on one or two to tell what the paryy stands for, they listen all night to all of them,~~

~~The Democratic Party dont needa Candidate, it a Warden.~~

first gag.

~~10~~

▲[*typewritten*:]Shows what restricted immigration[6] has done for this Banquet tables,▲

~~Outside the Lady Speakers ▲and myself▲ I never saw such a motley array of talent. They have tried to swamp uuo in quantity when they knew they were lacking in qualtity, They run their dinners like they do their Conventions, When they cant settle ona Candidate they vote all summer on all of them, when they cant settle on one or two men to present their case at a dinner they settle listen all night to all of them.~~

~~The Democratic Party dont need a Candidate, They need a stop watch, Warden~~

~~Look at these Politicains here, Local Bandits sent by their local voters to raid the Public treasuery, and if they come home with enough public loot they are known as Statesmen.~~

I read a hec½dline [headline] the other day that said, "What would foreign Countries do if we were in dire distress and needed help, " Thatwas the question, I should say they would give a celebration.

IF THE REP[UBLICANS] DONT RUN COOLIDGE THEY ARE MORE CONCEITED THAN I THINK THEY ARE.

I think the Fllod [flood] should have an asses ment [assessment] district, From both banks of th[e] river to the Oceans,[7]

Prohibition. If you think this Country aint dry watch em vote, and if you thisnk [think] this country aint wet watch em drink,

They will vote dry as long as they will stagger to the Poles,

If they could at the poles at election take peoples breath instead of their vote yoh [you] would get the true sentiment of this Country.

Nicaragua.

We are fighting Nicarague in the Preliminaries, and Cost[a] Rica in the finals. If you Democrats will nominatea good man, I will see that Nicaragua sends their Marines up here and see that he is is elected.

We will protect Americans in Nicar[a]gua even if we have to send somein there to be protected.

We will have enough Mariens in Nicar[a]gua so when the war is over they can dig the Canal them selvs,

Why dont we diga Can al from the head of the Columbia to the head of the Miss ouri, there is no Mexican Propaganda against that.

Whats become of of the time when we used to lay all our Ills on Russian propaganda.

66_____ If the Democrats are smart they will run Borah, ▼[*typewritten*:]Boths sides claim him and boths sides are afaisd [afraid] he will join em,▼

TD, dc. OkClaW, 1975.14.0051. Typewritten, top margin, center, page 1: "For Jackson Day Dinner." Handwritten, top margin, far right corner, page 1: "Notes". Handwritten, top margin, right corner, page 1: "*1928*". Hand-inserted horizontal line extends across much of page between second and third paragraphs, beginning in far left margin. Hand-inserted vertical mark appears in left margin adjacent to third paragraph. Double strike-through indicates hand-deleted text; single strike-through indicates type-deleted copy. Hand-inserted horizontal marks appear in left margin adjacent to paragraphs 5, 7–10, and 11. All interpolations were handwritten, unless otherwise noted. "Jackson" in paragraph 9 is hand-encircled.

1. The Jackson Day Dinner, held in observance of the anniversary of General Andrew Jackson's defeat of the British at the Battle of New Orleans on 8 January 1815, started in 1827 and became over time a chance to honor both Thomas Jefferson and Andrew Jackson, heroes of the Democratic party. The Democratic National Committee sponsored the dinner in 1928, which was held at the Mayflower Hotel in Washington on 12 January and attracted two thousand people (Stinnett, *Democrats*, 9–10, 33, 114).

2. Seventeen men and women, some touted as presidential candidates in 1928, were scheduled to speak, but at 2:30 the next morning when five had yet to approach the lectern, organizers wisely adjourned the program. Rogers addressed the throng at one o'clock (Stinnett, *Democrats*, 116).

3. Governor Al Smith, anticipating an unfriendly reception from dry forces, chose not to attend the dinner; instead, he sent a message. It received sustained applause (Stinnett, *Democrats*, 115–16).

4. The Democratic National Committee promoted the event as a "harmony dinner" in hopes that widespread differences within the party could be put aside for the evening and for the coming campaign. Speakers were told to avoid lightning-rod issues (*NYT*, 12 January 1928; Stinnett, *Democrats*, 115).

5. Albert Cabell Ritchie (1876–1936), Democratic governor of Maryland from 1920 to 1935 and a speaker at the Jackson Day event in 1928, gained national fame in the 1920s as an ardent opponent of Prohibition (*DAB*, Supp. 2:559–60).

6. A rising demand since the late nineteenth century to restrict immigration was finally manifested in the National Origins Act of 1924. The new law, enacted by a Republican-controlled Congress, reduced the total number of immigrants admitted to the United States each year and imposed a small percentage limit on immigration from any one country. More stringent limits were to go into effect in 1927, but the new restrictions were delayed for two years (*HD1920s*, 246–47).

7. Earlier in the day Rogers appeared in Washington at a hearing of the House Flood Control Committee that was considering the extent of the federal government's

responsibility to implement flood control measures. While entertaining House members with stories of his flood relief tour in the spring of 1927, Rogers also spoke seriously in support of the government assuming responsibility for effecting control measures and paying Mississippi flood victims in full for their losses (*NYT*, 13 January 1928).

Telegram to Charles Evans Hughes
17 January 1928
Havana, Cuba

PLAZA HABANA ENERO 17 DE 1927 [1928] LAS5.P.M.

SECRETARY CHAS EVAN HUGHES.

ALMENDARES HOTEL. ALMENDARES.

TOMORROW NIGHT THURSDAY MRS. ROGERS AND I ARE HAVING A LITTLE DINGER [DINNER] FOR DWIHT [DWIGHT] MORROW AND WIFE[1] MR FLETCHER[2] AND JUDGE OBRIEN AND WIFE[3] NOW IF YOU [W]ILL DO A LITTLE SLUMMING IN DIPLOMACY AND WILL REMEMBER MEAS YOUR VAUDEVILLE PARTIR [PARTNER][4] WE WOULD JUST BE TICKLED TO DEATH IF FOR A LITTLE RELAXATION YOU WOULD COME AND BE WITH US IT WOULD BE A GREAT CHANCE TO MEET YOUR DELIGATION YOU DENT [DON'T] EVEN HAVE TO DRESS UP SURE WOULD LIKE TO HAVE YOU[5]

WILL ROGERS.

BILMOORE HOTEL

TG, rc. NNC, Charles Evans Hughes Papers, Rare Book and Manuscript Library. On letterhead of Republica de Cuba Secretaria de Comunicaciones, Direccion de Telegrafos, Telegrama. Handwritten below letterhead, right side: "Pan American".

1. Elizabeth Reeve Cutter Morrow (1873–1955), a native of Cleveland and a trustee of her alma mater, Smith College, married Dwight Morrow in 1903 (*DAB*, 13:235; *NYT*, 24 January 1955).
2. Diplomat Henry P. Fletcher led the U.S. delegation to the fifth Pan-American Conference in 1923 and helped represent the United States at the sixth conference five years later (*DAB*, Supp. 6:207).
3. Morgan Joseph O'Brien (1852–1937), long active in Tammany politics, served as a justice of the New York Supreme Court for several years beginning in 1887. He left the bench in 1906 to resume a private legal practice and continued in that work for three decades. He married Rose Mary Crimmins (ca. 1855–1940) in 1880 (*DAB*, Supp. 2:496–97; *NYT*, 17 December 1955).
4. Both Rogers and Hughes, accompanied by their spouses, returned from Europe in September 1926 aboard the *Leviathan*. Although the two men had never met, they teamed up for a benefit performance aboard ship that raised $42,000 for the victims of a disastrous hurricane that struck Florida just before the *Leviathan* sailed. Rogers and

Hughes became good friends (Rogers, *Will Rogers*, 204–5). See also *DT*, 1:15; and *WA*, 2:249–53.

5. Hughes accepted Rogers's dinner offer, closing his reply with "Yours for more and better wise cracks" (ca. 17 January 1928, OkClaW).

Adolph S. Ochs to Arthur H. Sulzberger
15 February 1928
Los Angeles, Calif.

February 15, 1928.

Dear Arthur:

. . . With reference to Will Rogers -- I don't think that it is a very nice thing for MacNitt to sell special Sunday articles to the Tribune and Herald,[1] and I am quite sure that if he had conferred with Will Rogers he would not have permitted him to do anything that didn't meet our approval.

So far as our own interests in the matter are concerned, I would offer no objection had we been consulted, for if the weekly articles are of any value, it would stimulate an interest in his daily messages, for someone would quote what he read in the Sunday article, – he might be met by quotations from the daily articles that are more timely, and I believe more piquant.

I think Rogers is making a mistake in writing too much, but that's his business. You may recall that the weekly articles he used to supply us became almost valueless, and we were not at all disturbed by the World taking them up.[2] Perhaps you will also recall that after they had appeared in the World, Rogers came to me and begged to be taken back and said he had been a "bonehead" to have left the Times. I haven't seen him since I am here, but probably will before I leave. . . .

Sincerely,
Adolph S Ochs

TLS, rc. NYT-A, Publishers Collection. On The Ambassador, Los Angeles, letterhead. Ellipses inserted by editors.

1. The articles were not located.
2. When the *New York Times* discontinued Rogers's "Weekly Article" in September 1924, the New York *World* began carrying it. The *Times* never resumed publication of the column (see *WA*, 1:409).

Book Foreword by Will Rogers
ca. March 1928
New York, N.Y.

FOREWORD

By

Will Rogers

IT SURE DOES STRIKE ME KINDER ODD TO SEE an author writing a book about Europe that got his knowledge of the subject through constant visits and not through one visit, "just to learn conditions as they really are." I saw you[1] in Europe every time I was there[2] and I can get witnesses to prove it, and I can swear you wasn't there to study economic conditions or get "impressions." If I thought you was gathering impressions I wouldn't have spoke to you. The only thing that makes me doubt you will not sell a million copies of "Pleasure—If Possible" is that you know what you are talking about.

I am glad your book has a happy ending–America demands that. We are an intellectual people and we like things the same all the time.

Come to think of it from what I saw of you in Europe the title of your book should be "Pleasure Is Possible."

PD. Printed in Karl K. Kitchen, *Pleasure—If Possible, a Passport to the Gay Life Abroad* (New York, 1928) xiii–xiv.

1. Karl Kingsley Kitchen (1885–1935), a New York writer, was noted for his newspaper columns, magazine articles, and books about gastronomic pleasures in the city and in Europe, a favorite destination of his during annual travels abroad (*NYT*, 22 June 1935; McIntyre, "A Few Once Overs").

2. Kitchen, who had frequently caught performances by Rogers on stage and in banquet halls in New York, was present when Rogers addressed the American Club in Berlin in July 1926. Kitchen reported on the experience in his column, "Broadwayite Abroad," several days later (clipping, New York *Evening World*, 29 July 1926, OkClaW).

Draft of Telegram to Editor, *Cincinnati Post*
ca. 8 April 1928
[Louisville, Ky.?]

Perhaps not surprisingly, a press release from Rogers did not follow the usual format. He invented his own, often to great effect. The following draft of Rogers's unique form of self-promotion pushes some of the most important buttons in attracting a newspaper editor's attention: local news, politics, sports.

Editor Cincannatti Post.[1]

Cincannatti. Ohio.

I will hold the first Political rally of the Presidentail year in your midst Tuesday night, Everybody welcome, even Democrats. Come and vote, I take a straw vote of the audience, even if there is only tow [two] of them.[2] Come and see who your town wants for President,(if anybody)

I am putting in Nomination Tuesday morning all over the civilized nation including Chicago, the candidacy of Nick Longworth, late of Cincinnatti.[3] Remember come and vote at my election   its the only one wh[e]re you pay to vote   in most modern elections you are paid to vote. But you will pay me to vote or you dont vote, Hows the Reds, I saw Hendricks[4] training em in Daytona,[5] maby they are like a Politician, you cant learn em anything, But he was trying, They looked pretty good, I saw em at dinner there one night.

Who is Bugormaster of the old town now, They threw me out in Beverley Hills   I wanted to close up the town at four in the morning, and they accused me or [of] puritanism, Is Jonny Horgan, the silver voiced InnKeeper of the Sinton there yet. With every Bill paid for with a good check, he will sing you a song, and give you a box of Candy, so everybody goes away satisfied. Remember we launch Nick Tuesday night, On monday night In Columbus I nominate Donahey, who raises his won [own?] voters.[6] Come early and vote as often as you pay. Yours

Will Rogers,

TG, dc.[7] OkClaW, 1975.13.0015. On Western Union Telegraph Co. letterhead.

1. Elmer Plumas Fries (1884–1949), veteran of editorial staffs at several newspapers, served as editor of the *Cincinnati Post* from 1921 to 1929 (*WhAmer*, 3:304).

2. For an example of such a straw poll by Rogers, see Transcript of Lecture Tour Appearance, 16 April 1928, below.

3. Speaker of the House Nick Longworth was born in Cincinnati and held his first elected office in the Ohio city (*DAB*, 11:394).

4. John Charles (Jack) Hendricks (1875–1943) played only three seasons of major league baseball as a little-used outfielder before becoming manager of the Cincinnati Reds in 1924. His best year as manager came in 1926 when the team finished second. He left three seasons later (*TB*, 851, 2424).

5. Rogers made a lecture tour appearance in Daytona Beach, Fla., on 15 March (*DT*, 1:190).

6. Governor Donahey and his wife had ten children (*NYT*, 9 April 1946).

7. Dating of the document was determined by references in the text to Rogers's chronology.

Transcript of Lecture Tour Performance
16 April 1928
Montclair, N.J.

The following is an apparently verbatim record of a lecture tour appearance by Rogers. Although some elements of his act, especially local references, differed during the course of a tour, much of the body of his topical material stayed constant over a lecture season, from one city to another and one concert hall to another. By mid-April 1928 Rogers had his routine well set.

After introduction Mr. Rogers spoke as follows:

You'd think he was selling real estate or something. He's good. He's one of the best advance agents I've had.

Well now, folks, it's my duty to-night to - well, I want to tell you something about the man that brought me up here to-night. He says, "You know we are very near New York here." It didn't seem like it on this train that we were on. He said, "We are very near New York here, and," he says, "of course, most of our people have seen you in New York and that's why we had a little trouble selling tickets." I said, "Well, it's awful nice of you to come down to the train to meet me. I certainly appreciate that. I don't have that anywhere. I just sneak into a town, you know what I mean, just like anybody going to a job. I just go on the job, do it and go away, but it's awful nice of you to meet us." Of course, the taxi cab was occupied at the time. I think this fellow that got in it had it engaged by the year, and we were standing there looking around for something, and I says, I told him, I says, "I'm awfully glad you came down, Mr. Mondel,[1] it's awful nice of you. We don't get this everywhere. It's rather unusual." "That's all right," he says, "we'll meet anybody that will come here."

So I'm mighty glad to get here and I'm mighty glad to come right out, and everything, and even if my act is a failure it gives the members a chance to wear their suits to-night. You know the more practice you get in them the easier you will feel. I know I'm rather nervous to-night and keep doing that (indicating), you know, but I'm glad to get here with you anyhow.

I want to tell you something about this place, Montclair, New Jersey. Years ago I remember a book that fell into my hands way out in Oklahoma where I lived - we adjoined Texas at that time - written by a man, and in there - I happened to say to Mr. Mondell to-night, "Do you know how I remember this town?" He says, "No." "Well, I remember this town by the cow boy poems that was written by a fellow that was supposed to be kind of a cow boy, or a man who had gone out West and settled there, and he wrote these poems and became very famous. Some of them were about the West and one of them was about a cowboy coming back East, and it mentioned Montclair, New Jersey, and I come to find out that this man who had written these poems - I remember his name but I never met him - Larry Chittenden - they tell me originally his folks resided here, and he wrote some very famous poems.[2] One was called "The Cowboy's Christmas Ball."

Boy, I expect that's the most famous cowboy thing we have in Oklahoma - a kind of folk lore, you know, among the cowboys. I understand he lived here before. Here's where he came from. He went out on the Plains and located there. So that's how I remember Montclair, and he spoke of this Society here, and I never thought I'd have the pleasure of appearing before you.

To-night you're going to hear a lecture. A lecturer is any man who can memorize enough material to come out on a stage and insult an audience's intelligence for an hour and still have lack of conscience enough to take their money. I'm a lecturer. The difference between a lecturer and a comedian - a comedian entertains and a lecturer annoys.

I guess I'm about the only American lecturer in the world. Most of our lecturers come from Europe and most of them have written a book - generally on sex. I never wrote a book on sex but as soon as I find out something about it I'm going to write one - not that it is necessary to know what you're writing about, I don't mean that, but I'd just like to know about sex even if I wasn't going to write about it.

Well now, I also want to apologize for my appearance. I should - coming here and speaking to a nice-high-class audience, you know, in one of New York's best suburbs, I should have worn a dress suit, you know, because every lecturer has a dress suit. In fact, they get the suit before they get the ~~hat~~ ►act►. That's what gives them the idea of the ~~hat~~ ▲act▲ - is to get the suit, but I haven't got a dress suit. I'm going to be honest; I haven't got a dress suit, but I have got two street suits and plenty of underwear; and I have seen people in dress suits that I was doubtful about - not only doubtful about them have plenty but doubtful about them having any.

Years ago when I was playing in vaudeville an English lecturer came over here and he couldn't get a job lecturing. Well, he could get a job lecturing but he couldn't get anybody to listen to him. He thought it was a terrible thing, that he was really slumming when they put him in vaudeville. I happened to be playing on the same bill with him at the time and as we had an awfully full vaudeville bill we had to double up in the dressing rooms, so he had to dress with a very tough acrobat. He was rather an illiterate chap, this acrobat - I hate these illiterate people - and he was rather uncouth and illiterate, this acrobat, and he was named Scream Welch [Welsh].[3] So during the week we asked Scream - we were anxious to know, the rest of us on the bill, so we says, "Scream, how are you and this high-brow Englishman making out?" "Well, he says, "that guy speaks the finest English and has got the dirtiest underwear I ever seen."

Since then I've always been leery of anyone when they spoke perfectly.

Now to-night you're going to hear an awfully illiterate act, but it's sanitary. In other words, my performance is very ungrammatical but clean. That will be a blow to some of you. That's why I can't go into the drama, on account of the cleanliness of my performance. I'm a good actor but I can't get a job in the drama.

Well now, here, let's see what we are going to talk about. I've got an awful lot of politics I want to talk to-night. It's a political year. Every four years we have a Presidential Election and the country's upset and everybody's all turned around, and business conditions are unsettled just because we are going to elect a President, and it don't make a dime's worth of difference to anybody in America, outside of the fellow that's going to draw the salary, whose elected. It don't mean a thing in the world.

Our own forefathers one hundred and fifty years ago, you know, they laid out the Constitution, so that I don't care how incompetent you are you can't do much harm to the country. You can't. It just looked like those old fellows were so far sighted they could just look ahead about this far, about 150 years, and sense the type of baboon that would be living here now, and they made the Constitution almost fool-proof.

I have honestly and conscientiously believed, and always will believe that Ben Turpin would make a splendid President. In fact, he's the only one I know of that could look both ways, and he certainly would not be out of place because the country's cock-eyed anyway.

Anyhow some nut in a spirit of jest, or what he thought was jest or ridicule, suggested me for President, and I took it serious enough to consider: Now just what qualifications have I got for the President of the United States? Everyone of you, or anyone you can think of, know what it means, because way out in the Indian Territory in the early days before some nut come along and called it Oklahoma, I was born in Indian Territory of Indian parentage. My mother and father were both ~~Turkish~~ ▲Indian▲. My mother was a wonderful woman, like all our mothers were, you know, and we had kind of a modern frame house where we lived, and they tell me that when I was about to be born she had to move her bed into a log cabin - looking way ahead, thinking her son - poor old soul, she had me mixed up with Lincoln - and I was born in a log cabin.

Well, I got to thinking over my qualifications outside of the log cabin. I said, "What other things have I got to make me President?" And, you know, save my soul, I only have one. Out of the million things that a man's got to be to be President I only had one, and that is this: If elected President of the United States I'd be the only President the country ever had, you know, that would be funny purposely. Any time that I acted a fool I would, at least, know I was acting it anyhow, and we have had cases to the contrary. So I thought there'd be no novelty in a man running for President in a year like this - no, there'd be more novelty not to run, and so I says - now I never and I don't believe you ever did either ever hear of a man voluntarily wanting to be Vice-President. Did you ever hear of a guy wanting to be Vice-President? I never did. So I said, "Well, I'll take that," and it's not much of a job. I mean, you know, who wants to be Vice-President? Why don't you want to be Vice-President? Because it's a position that looks like no future to it, see. You're just Vice-President and you get nowhere else; you're just Vice-President and that's all. I said, "I'll take that and let Providence take its course." I says, "I'll just announce to the Lord, 'Lord, I'm Vice-President, do your duty,'" and I certainly have enough confidence in the Divine to feel that He would get me somewhere.

I must tell you all a little story about that, because the gentleman comes from your State; he lives over here, not so far from you now, and I want to tell you that if Calvin Coolidge never did anything in his administration - and he hasn't done much - if he never did anything in his administration but appoint Dwight Morrow to Mexico he's earned his salary. That's all there is to it.

I don't say that just because Dwight Morrow was nice to me in Mexico - I never met the man before in my life - but I say it out of real sincere admiration. I think Morrow is going to do a tremendous lot of things in Mexico, more than any Ambassador we have ever had down there. All the other ambassadors used to do was to sit there and wait till they got a note from Kellogg. Kellogg would send a note every morning to tell Mexico what to have for breakfast. Every time we get a note from England or France, why, we send one to Mexico. We can't argue back with England and France because they have a Navy but Mexico hasn't, but we take it out by sending a note to Mexico.

Now I want to tell you that since Morrow has been in Mexico there hasn't been a note sent down there, and he told me that he had confidential instructions from Coolidge - Coolidge told him, he said, "Dwight, go on down there. We don't want any war."

It seems good to meet an audience that's heard Coolidge, And so he said to him, "Dwight, go on down there. We don't want any war with Mexico," he says, "we're not going to jump on Mexico, but you just go on down there and keep them from jumping onto us." That was Morrow's only instructions in going to Mexico.

Well, Morrow and Coolidge went to school together in Amherst when they was preparing for college.

Oh, my Lord, you don't know how happy I am that you got that. I told that in Rochester the night before last, and it just laid right there (indicating). Amherst might have been the Montclair High School, as far as Rochester was concerned, and it speaks well for Rochester that none of their Alumni was there.

Well, they went to school together, and they graduated together, Coolidge and Morrow did. Coolidge and Morrow graduated in the same class. Morrow caught up with him.

A little slower on that - but they graduated, and, you know, the graduating classes take a vote on who in the class will, perhaps, some day amount to something. Now, that's what I heard they do. Mind you, when I speak of graduation, I am speaking from hearsay. This is not first-hand information at all. I never graduated. Yes, I did. I graduated from the Follies. It took me 12 years to finish a 4 year course, but I finally got out of there. They had me in the Follies 12 years. I was to come on while the girls changed their powder - costume, by amendment. But as I say I don't need to tell you I never graduated from anything in my life.

When I went to school it was so far back that we didn't call them grades. In the old days we called it readers. You said, "I'm in the third reader, McGuffy's third and fourth readers." A lot of you old guys out there didn't get any further than I did either. Many of you old birds out there running around in fine cars don't know anymore than I do.

Well, I never got any further than McGuffy's Fourth Reader. I don't need to tell you that after talking to you this long. In fact, I have had people who doubted that I got that far. I got there all right, even if I have forgot it. I got there, however, and, mind you, I'm not the usual Smart Alec that comes out, you know, on the stage in public or anywhere else, the usual Smart Alec who don't know anything and knocks people that has an education. I'm not like that. I have a sincere regard for people who have had the advantage of a splendid education. There's not a day in my life I don't regret I don't know more, because I have even gone so far as to have solved the educational problem in this country.

Take, for instance, your High School. This is a beautiful building. I have appeared in a good many of them but this is one of the nicest ones I've been into. Now, when a High School turns out - here's the way to solve the educational problem of this country - when a High School turns out a graduating class every June, let them say, "Half will go to college and half to work." Divide it up, say, split it in half - "You go to college; you go to work," and at the end of four years when the ones that went to college get out of college they can go to work for the ones that went to work first.

I am not knocking you fellows that come from college. I think a college degree is a wonderful thing. I don't think anything beats it. Suppose you have got a good college degree and have graduated from somewhere, and you go to a man and ask him for work, and the man you are asking for work maybe never had a grammar school education, and, you know, he don't give you the job. Then when you walk away you know that you know more than he does - that's an awful big advantage. You know it's a tremendous satisfaction to know that you're smart even if you aint working. You can go around and talk to some other fraternity brothers.

You know there are a lot of people who are against fraternities. They don't know anything about fraternities, sororieties, [*sic*] and all that, but I played a big college town a week ago, Ann Arbor, Michigan[4] - I'm pledged to a sororiety now. I didn't know what it all was, but these girls come running up to me and wanted me to be their Mother Superior, or something like that.

Mind you, I don't know nothing about fraternities. There are a lot of people agin them and there are some for them. I don't know nothing about them, but, personally, I think they must be a splendid thing. I think fraternities and sororieties are fine things - they keep you away from the common herd while you're in school. Of course, when you get out you seek your level.

I think college is a great thing. I think it is better for the parents, in fact, than I do for the students. I think colleges are wonderful for the parents. They take a child away from home just when they are at that arguing stage of life. Did you ever have a boy or girl, about 18 years old, look at you and say, "Look at old dad there. How did he ever live this long and not know any more than he does? Look at him! He can't even black-bottle. Look at him!"

Send them away for 4 years and then when they come back they know you don't know anything.

I am going to get a degree some day that will knock your eye out. You are going to pick up the Sunday Supplement sometime and see a picture of me getting a degree from one of the biggest colleges in the country, Columbia.

Nicholas Murray Butler - you all know Nicholas Murray Butler, the President of Columbia, the wet old thing - Nicholas and I are good friends. We have spoken at a good many dinners together, Nicholas Murray Butler and I have. I know that sounds egotistical to you - "Why, an ignorant thing like that ever talking with Nicolas Murray Butler at a banquet!" I have at a lot of them in

NewYork before I reformed, and I'll tell you what I was doing at the banquet. He was the usual Nicholas Murray Butler, the usual college professor, but the usual college professor when he gets up has to expound logic, and they had to have somebody to offset him with facts.

I met him over in Paris the Summer before last - I just happened to run into him - we happened to be standing right by each other at the time. I says, "Hello, Mr. Butler, how are you? I'm glad to see you." And he says, "Hello, Will, how are you? What are you doing here, Will; what are you doing in Paris?" "Just the same as you, President Butler; come on let's have another, what do you say?" Well, we had.

Then he says, "Do you know what I am going to do with you, Will, do you know what I am going to do with you when I get you over in NewYork some time? I'm going to have the College confer a degree on you." And I says, "I think that's a good joke on you, Mr. Butler. They can't confer any degree on me because I don't know nothing." He said, "Don't let that worry you. That's the only kind we confer them on." He says, "We have a degree for every branch of ignorance in the world."

They're not going to confer any degree on me. I've seen people getting those degrees; I've seen pictures of them. They don't get me wearing no gown in the day time.

All kidding aside, college is a great thing. I've got two boys, and people ask me, they say, "Will, are you going to send your boys to college?" And I says, "Yes, I'm going to send them one year and if the coach don't offer to pay their tuition I'll bring them home.

A man came up to me one day in a college town and he says - he was one of these boys that writes on a college paper - and he says, "Will do you advise a college man to turn professional, like Red Granger[5] and all those players?" I said, "No, not until he's earned all he can as an amateur.["]

But those were great times, the old days, when a college boy come out of college he couldn't get a job - that was an unsettled time in his career. There was nothing hardly suitable for him. But boys that come from college now are all settled. They go to work in a filling station. Now half of the unemployed in America are working in filling stations. It's a very confining job. You have to be there because you never know what moment it will be robbed. You've got to be there to hand over the money - perhaps, to another fraternity brother.

But Dwight Morrow - I've got to get back to my story - I'm like a movie; I start out with an idea and I wind up with something else. I started off telling you about Dwight and Coolidge. They graduated, and they took a vote, like all colleges do, as to who in the class will, perhaps, amount to something. You know college[s] do that, you know, they always vote on one in the class that will amount to something. I mean they never figure that there'll be more than one that will ever amount to anything. There may be 500 graduating but there is always just a vote on the one - that's a pretty big average - and so they voted on it, and this is what they voted on, "Who in this class, perhaps, will do something that will make people think he didn't come from Amherst," and Morrow got all the votes - Morrow got all the votes but two, and Coolidge got those two - Morrow voted for Coolidge!

I'm not accusing old Cal; I'm not accusing him but they went around and asked everybody in the class if nobody else had voted for him. I am just laying the evidence on the table, that's all.

It looks like - Coolidge has had a wonderful political career; he's never been defeated - looks like he started in with his own support. Here's what I'm going to tell you in politics. You're going to hear people say during this campaign, "Coolidge is for So-and-So;" "Coolidge is for Hoover;" "Coolidge is for Dawes" - and all these various things. Morrow told me this, he said - we talked politics down there - he says, "Will, you go back home and bet anything you've got that Coolidge won't come out until after the nominations are made."

During the Cleveland Convention four years ago - get this situation - Coolidge had been in for two years; he was re-nominated at the Convention, you know, and so they tried to pick out a Vice-President, and Morrow was with Coolidge in Washington at the time.

As you know, in picking a Vice-President they always pick someone who will be acceptable to the President who they have just nominated, so they called up Washington. They had a line through, you know - the Government was paying for it, and so they had a line through and they called up Washington and said, "Would Louden [Lowden] be all right? Would Louden be acceptable to you, Mr. President, as Vice-President?" "Yes, Louden's all right with me."

Well, they couldn't get Louden. He was too smart for a gag like that, and so they called up the next day about Hoover. They said, "Would Hoover be all right?" "Yes, Hoover's all right with me." That's all they could get out of Coolidge.

I was at Cleveland at the time writing for the newspapers, and it looked like a riot out there. Do you remember reading about it - the terrible time they had picking a Vice-President? It looked like they would have to draft the janitor to be Vice-President, and I think if they rang Coolidge up and asked about it he would say, "Yes, the janitor's all right with me." He knew he wasn't going to get anywhere anyhow, and nobody would take the Vice-Presidency under Coolidge because they knew what splendid care Calvin takes of himself, so finally Morrow turned to Coolidge and he said, "Calvin" - he calls him Calvin - I guess he and I are the only ones who calls him Calvin - he turned to him and he said, "Calvin, why don't you tell them who you would like to have? They want to abide [by] your wishes; why don't you tell them who you would like to have?" He said, "No, I'm not going to do any such thing. I'm not going to advise them at all." He said, "They done pretty well four years ago."

He's a hot sketch, this Morrow. The first time he met Coolidge he said a man took him in and introduced him, and, he said, "I tried to compliment Mr. Coolidge on how well he was looking. I said, 'Mr. Coolidge, you are certainly looking fine.' I said, 'This job of being President has been too much for a lot of our men but you seemed to have gotten by with less worry than anybody else.' He said, 'Yes, I never get mixed up with any of the big problems of the day.'"

I am asked every minute in the day by somebody I met, they say, "Will, has Coolidge got any humor?" He's got a lot of humor but Coolidge is too smart to use it, but he's got a lot of it. He knows that a comedian never got anywhere in politics, so he is too smart to use it. You know, I don't know, but everything Coolidge says is funny to me.

Well now, getting back to my little plot of being Vice-President, I'll show you my qualifications. A Vice-President goes to the dinners. When the President can't go the Vice-President goes, and he gets there and gets up and says, "I'm very sorry His Excellency, the President, is not able to attend - he got a better offer."

Well, I could do that. I could do that. You know, I could go to all the dinners. I could eat just as much as Dawes can; the only thing the Government would have to get me [is] a dress suit. I haven't got a dress suit, as I told you awhile ago and I couldn't go in a hired suit or they would mistake me for a Congressman.

Did you ever see those Congressmen in an affair, all in the evening? There's a masque ball for you!

Well, another thing, a Vice-President presides; a Vice-President presides over the Senate. He sits there with a hammer and hits it on a rock, a big mallet, and he hits it on a rock and calls it to order. If I were Vice-President I would use that hammer where it would do the most good, you know. The trouble with the Senate is, and you know it yourself, they have been there since the first Monday in last December; our Senate met and what have they done? Have they passed - can anybody in this house tell me one constructive bill our Senate has passed since last December, and they have been there all this time. They haven't done a thing - flood relief, farm relief, tax reduction - not a thing has been done about anything you can mention. They are arguing and arguing, always debating and messing around.

If I was Vice-President I would pass one rule - and you see if this rule wouldn't shorten debate. I'd say, "Every time a Senator tells all he knows he's got to sit down." I want to tell you right now I'd have some of them just getting up and nodding - there'd be about half of them that couldn't answer roll call.

Well now, that's enough about politics for awhile. Let's see what we are going to get off onto next. I'll tell you what I'd like to talk to you about. I see a lot of young folks here - and I want to distribute this talk around so it'll get everybody - you boys and girls, and, of course, you old ones, too, are just as much interested - now, I don't pose as a bosom friend or any pal, or anything like that, but I am a humble admirer, like you, but I did happen to be associated with him for a few days and I think you'd like to hear a few intimate details of our hero, Mr. Lindbergh.

I know I've heard people say, you know, I know they sometimes say, "Oh, give us a rest. Every time you pick up a paper you read about what Lindbergh did." Don't ever say that. You don't know the value of that boy to this country. You don't know what a tremendous asset that boy is until you've seen him in a foreign country. That's where you realize his real value to us.

I happened to be in Mexico with Mr. Morrow when that kid come in and I want to tell you that I never seen anything like it, and I never hope to see anything to equal what took place then. Early in the morning - I was stopping at the Embassy - Morrow dug us all out early in the morning. Lindy couldn't have got there before about noon, if he had been on time he couldn't have gotten there, but Morrow come around and dug us all out, "He may catch a tail wind and come in early." Well, I knew what chance a man has of catching a tail wind. I knew that Lindy could fly till his whiskers got caught in the propeller, and he wouldn't catch a tail wind, because the wind don't start - if you have ever done any airplaneing - the wind don't start until you take off and it sees which way you are going.

That's what happened to these fellows you have all read a lot about. I flew from Los Angeles back here and from Hadley Field over here back to Los Angeles in less than four days and there was a head wind bucking us all the way - I think it waited here till I got here. You thought I was joking about it. Well, you see what your head wind did to those great aviators coming over. That's all that stopped them, your head wind. I'm not kidding about it. It's there. Any time you fly it's there; it's right there, and it met them, and that's why Lindbergh went the other way. The reason our fliers all make it going to Europe is because they've got Congress behind them. There never will be a flier ever come this way until we send our Congress over and have them meet in Ireland.

And wasn't it nice, you know - talking about those wonderful brave fellows - wasn't it nice of that Irishman, you know, when he had this head wind bucking them, you know, and this tremendous load, wasn't it nice for him to let those two Germans stay on there, you know.[6] You know that's a great tribute to the Irish race, that he didn't throw those two fellows overboard - it was awful nice of him.

Well - so Mr. Morrow dug us out early and we got to the field about 7:15 in the morning, with no breakfast, you know, and we got there, and when we got to that field there was a little stand, about as big as this stage, built up over a beautiful hangar. You know they've got terrible planes there but an awful nice hangar, and they had this thing built up over that, and when we got there at 7:15 in the morning there was the President of Mexico already there; he had all his Cabinet and all of his staff officers, and everybody was there-there must have been 200,000 people on that field, and they stood there on that field from 7:15 in the morning until 3:45 in the afternoon, when Lindberg landed there. He was lost up in the clouds for 3 or 4 hours and he didn't know where he was but finally he found his way back in there and landed there, and these people stood there all that time with never a thought of anything to eat. There wasn't as much as a sandwich served on this stand even to the President or any of the folks up there. There wasn't even a pitcher of water, there wasn't a thing in the world. The idea of eating never entered those people's minds in their anxiety about this boy coming in there.

I stood out on the field waiting for these Germans that were coming, and what did the Americans do? - "I don't think they're coming; better go get some sandwiches."

Not the Mexican people. They said, "No, sir" - why, I heard the President turn to Mr. Morrow - this was through an interpreter - and he said, "It would be the most terrible calamity that ever befell this country if something happened to this boy while he was coming in here. He's coming to make friends with people he never saw, people that don't mean nothing to him, he's coming down here and let us all be here to see him. Just think of a man taking his life in his hands to do that!"

That's what Lindbergh looked like to all these countries. He was not a human being; he was a superman, a supreme being; and I never saw such a demonstration in my life as when he landed. Those Latins are kind of temperamental anyway - boy, they went cuckoo - and do you know what they did?

Now what does he do when he lands here? We have to put a police guard around his plane and we have to leave a police guard around Lindbergh's plane or we'd go up and cut the tail off, or put the carburetter in our pocket, but what did they do in Mexico? Not a thing. Do you know what the Mexicans did? Why, when there were no guards around there, the peons - that's the low class people - carried that plane over a quarter of a mile and put it in the hangar - they didn't let the wheels touch the ground. They didn't cut it up or anything - they're just ignorant that way, you know; they didn't have enough progress to cut it apart, you know, not at all; they didn't know about that. You could leave that plane out in the heart of Mexico for ten years and nobody would ever think of cutting anything off of it. That never entered their heads; that's the way they're there; first-class people.

Well, you know, I thought I would give up my bed - I had been living in the Embassy - and I told Mr. Morrow, I says, "I got a room down in the hotel; I got a room engaged in the hotel," and he said, "Will, you'll do no such thing; you'll not get out of here." I said "I certainly will. I've been here quite awhile and I understand Colonel Lindbergh is going to have these rooms. I'm leaving this morning." And he said, "You'll stay right here with us - and just to show you this guy was an ambassador, he never held a post before but he was an ambassador at heart, he said, "You will not; this room is not good enough for Lindbergh," and he took me in and showed me his room - he was giving up his room to Lindbergh - and after he showed me his room the thing I was in was kind of punk at that. I come pretty near leaving of my own accord then.

Well now, you hear a lot about the bull fights down there. Here's a people - some of you old women out there that belong to some old busy-body's society go yapping around, telling somebody what to do - pass resolutions even. Well, they wired me, knowing I was down there, I got wires, "Don't let Lindbergh go to a bull fight." What could I do about Lindbergh going to a bull fight. I was lucky to shake hands with Lindbergh, much less than telling him where to go. They sent more wires - I got a stack of wires that high - "It's a national crime if Lindbergh attends a bullfight. It will undo all we have worked for for years." I wanted to wire back, "What are you worrying about Lindbergh for? Why don't you stop the bull from going?" There's the head man in that show.

Well, Lindbergh came in one morning and he picked up the paper - there is one page in English; all Mexican papers have a page in English - he picked it up and it says, "America protests Lindbergh attending a bull fight." He looks at it and he said, "Well, that settles it. What time does the fight start?"

He never had an idea of going to the fight; he wasn't going to do [go]- that's one considerate thing about the Mexicans; it wasn't on his official program at all; he wasn't supposed to go but they made such a racket about it - why they made almost a diplomatic problem out of it, and he wasn't supposed to go at all, and after he saw that he couldn't go he went out there all right.

I think it is better to go to a bull fight when you're in Mexico, and when you come back and somebody says, "Did you see some bull fights? They must be terrible down there. Did you see one?" "No, but I heard they were terrible." When you come back you can tell them that the Mexicans are not all nutty over bull fights. There are lots of other things there. They've got as much tennis and golf and baseball - why, on every corner they've got kids playing baseball; and they've even got a Humane Society, and the Humane Society gave a benefit - they wanted to raise some money - and they gave a bull fight. Yes, sir, they did that, and they do a lot of that, you know.

And another thing I want to tell you: Lindbergh was not sent to Mexico by the Government. Somebody says all the time, "Well, I don't know but I think the Government ought to quit sending him around taking chances." Well, the Government did not send him. If you know this boy Lindbergh you know that nobody sends him anywhere. This guy aint sent anywhere; this bird goes; that's all.

He went down there through his friendship with Morrow, and the whole idea was framed up with Dwight Morrow after he came back from Europe. Mr. Morrow met him and they got acquainted, and in the meantime Morrow was appointed Ambassador, and one time he said to Lindbergh, "Colonel, I would like to have you go down to Mexico. I've been appointed Ambassador and it would be a great thing if you could come down, and Lindy said, "Marvelous, nobody has ever hopped from here to Mexico City" - and Morrow told me this illustrating this boy's will - Morrow said to him, "Don't hope to do it all in a day, but go to St. Louis, then to SanAntonio and then Monterey and on in," and Lindbergh turned to him and said, "Mr. Morrow, you take care of that end; I'll take care of the flying. Don't start telling me how to get down there." That's what he did, you know. Well, he come down.

You know I was out on the Presidential trip with Mr. Morrow, on this trip around the country, for about ten days, and I remember one member saying - at one place they stopped there were some engineers putting through a big irrigation project, Lindy had promised to come there, and he said, "This'd be a great time to have him come down," and they wired him - the President wired him, the President sent a direct wire - not through the State Department but a direct wire - and they got a wire back, "Will be there the first clear day." The funny part of it was he didn't even wait for the clear day; he come down.

Now another thing. One day - I'm going into the Embassy and he's coming out. He had his helmet and goggles on and he said, "I'm going to the field; come on and I'll take you up with me." He was going to take a Mexican plane up - and he turned to me in the car - this illustrates the diplomacy of this boy

- Herrick[7] didn't tell him this, you know what I mean. I've got great respect and admiration for our dear old Ambassador over in France, Mr. Herrick; he did a lot for that boy but he didn't tell him everything. This boy's got a few ideas of his own. Now get this: We were going out to the field - this was the first time he had been out to the field since he landed - and he turned to me and he says, "Will, I won't take you up first; it wouldn't look good to come to Mexico and take an American up first. I'll take some of them up first."

Think how far ahead that was! There wasn't one person in a hundred in Mexico or in any other country that would even think he had taken up an American first, but that one in a hundred he was figuring on.

You people go to Europe - in an audience like this to-night - in the Summertime and you go around on trips. Now, if you show one-twentieth part of the consideration for the feelings of the people in the country where you visit that Lindbergh does, we would be the most popular nation in the world.

We can learn a lot from that boy. I'm not saying these things about Lindbergh because he's an aviator - we can learn a lot from that kid besides flying. He has taught us more things than flying - flying is one of the poorest things he does.

What do we do when we go to Europe? The minute we get there we think because we are paying something - "Well, what a joint this is. Imagine putting a guy in a room like this! Where is the bathroom?" And we start yapping, "Why don't they tear these old dumps down and build new ones?"

No wonder Europeans sneak up and hit us in the head - after we pay our bill. We are the rudest people in the world. Absolutely. We just go yapping around all the time.

But Lindbergh don't think of a thing in the world only to please the people. When he lands in a country they see him through curiosity, when he leaves they see him through admiration. That's the difference - when he comes and when he leaves.

Well, after I saw him lead this Mexican plane out I was in favor of him taking all the Mexicans up first. I didn't care if he never got to me. They led this thing out and I looked at it.

Well, he took a Mexican aviator up first and then he brought him down and took another one up, one at a time, and then he hollered to me, "Come on, Will" - he hollered to me or I wouldn't have been there. I went over and I got in this thing. I looked at it and I got into the thing. Well, I'm going to tell you I was scared - you know it's almost sacreligious [*sic*] for anyone to say they are scared when flying with Lindbergh, and I shouldn't have been afraid because the only chance of my ever becoming immortal was to fall with Lindbergh, but even at that I was scared to fall with him.

I got in there, you know, and, well, this old thing certainly was rickety. They had bob [barbed]-wire on it and everything in the world nailed up, slats and everything - and, honest, when we were flying around up in the air it looked to me like these wings was going to say, "Brother, we are with you."

When we come down and we were going back, you know - he took about 20 people up after that, he flew around with them; he's wonderful that way; he flew until it got so dark he couldn't see; he must have taken 20 or 30 people up one at a time - and when we were going back that night, I said to him, "I don't know much about airplanes but it seemed to me that was kind of a weak sister, wasn't it?" And here's the only undiplomatic remark the boy ever made - and I don't think he would have made that if he had realized who he was with - he says, "I just wanted to fly that plane to see if a plane that old would fly."

He's a great aviator. I'll bet he could take the oldest Ford in the world and get it here and monkey with it - mess here with it for half an hour, tie a propeller here and one there and take off from here and land over there. He's a great kid. We've got some great men in our aviation. That's one thing. We've got great boys in our aviation. They're all wonderful. Take any of them that have graduated from the Kelley School or out of the Army School in San Antonio - the biggest coward in the world - and say to any one of these boys, "Will you go to Siberia?" "Come on, brother, I don't know where it is but I'll go."

It's a great thing; aviation is a coming thing. All you want to do, you prominent men out there, is to do everything you can for aviation. It is a coming thing. The next war is going to be in the air. Nobody will shoot anything at you in the next war; they are going to drop it on you. You've got to learn to fly or dig in. They aint nobody going to hand you puttees or a little gun in the next war. They're just going to slip an airplane in your hand and tell you to go aloft and see if you can come down purposely. That's all. We've got more air here than anybody in the world.

Here, I must tell you this. I know a lot - I've had young girls ask me, "What does Lindbergh look like? What does he talk about? What is he like?"

I'll tell you, girls, what he's got his mind on - I don't want to discourage you but his mind is on aviation. Morrow told me this - two months after I had been in Mexico I went to Cuba primarily just to visit Mr. Morrow again. He was going to be there at the Pan-American Congress and I went down there to see him. Now, get this situation: Lindy spent about three weeks with the Morrow's in Mexico. He had his mother[8] down there and they had a wonderful trip there together. He leaves, and Morrow showed me this letter in Cuba which he had gotten from Lindbergh after he had left Mexico City. I read it and memorized it:

"My dear Mr. and Mrs. Morrow:

"This is the first chance I have had to write you since I left. I left Mexico City this morning at six o'clock, arrived at Guatemala 7:13. I was in the air thirteen hours and thirteen minutes. It will take this letter 12 days to reach you by train and boat. If we had air mail it would reach you to-morrow night.

"Yours respectfully,
"Charles Lindbergh."

Not a word of thanks for the bed or buggy ride, much obliged for the fire-crackers, or anything; just "Get an air line to Guatemala." Why, I guess he's the only one that's ever been to Guatemala. If you put a bill in Congress to-morrow to do something in Guatemala I don't think you've got two men in Washington who could find it on the map.

The first time I met Lindy was when I was making a tour of the country and spoke at a banquet for him at ~~St. Louis~~ ◄San Diego◄, and I did want to say something different. ~~St.~~ Louis was making a big splurge because that is the town he started from. Well, I went down and I wanted to say something different than the Mayor or Governor for forty straight nights, "Our boy, our hero, who flew from here across the ocean." Well, I had an idea that the kid knew where he went. I couldn't see any need of bringing that up again, so I turned to him, I said, "Colonel, you've done all the wonderful things they say you've done, but, of course, your record can be beaten by far. Engines will improve and things ▲[*typewritten:*]will▲ get better. As engines improve you will be able to go over in a few hours and beat your time, but you have one record that I think will remain unsurpassed right on down through the ages - you are the only man who ever took a ham sandwich to Paris."

Then every time anybody introduces Lindbergh they say, "[']He's an inspiration to our boys.['] They all tell you what a great thing you offer our boys. Well, that's a lot of applesauce because if all our boys followed you they would be in the Atlantic Ocean." I said, "I've got two boys. I want them to admire you but I don't want them trying any of the stunts you are trying to do."

Did you ever hear - there aint a person in this room that ever heard Lindbergh introduced by somebody who didn't call him the Columbus of the air, our modern flying Columbus. These old speakers just get up and flare there away; they don't know what they're talking about - pick out some guy in history and bring him down and line his name up with some modern fellow. It's insulting Lindbergh to call him Columbus. Why, Columbus was lost when he found this country. He just touched the Queen for a lot of jewels and then lit out.

Well, the next day Lindy took us back to Los Angeles, some of us. He took a three-motored Ford plane;[9] he took 11 of us back there, and I happened to be sitting out on the pilot seat by him. It was a little enclosed place and we could hear each other talking, and he said he was going to land at a field where there was no hangar - and there was nothing to show which way the wind was blowing. He said, "In coming down the thing to do is to keep away from the crowds," and I said to him, "How can you tell how to land when there aint anything to show you which way the wind is blowing?" And he says, "Why, didn't you see the way those clothes were blowing on that line awhile ago?"

Didn't I see some washing that was blowing on the line about ten towns back? I didn't even notice what clothes was on there; so I said, "Well, suppose it wasn't Monday, what would you do then?" I said, "I guess we'd have to fly around till they washed, is that it?"

Say, listen, I wasn't kidding this boy; he's got a good sense of humor. He come right back at me. He said, "I wouldn't fly over such a dirty country."

An old lady out in Los Angeles about two months ago, just before I left there, a little, very dignified, old lady come into the book store, and she was walking around there, you know, and the clerk come up and said, "Madam, can I do something for you?" "I don't know but what you can. I am looking for Colonel Lindbergh's book 'It'".[10]

I didn't see Lindbergh land in Cuba. I didn't stay there until Lindbergh came in, but I saw Coolidge come in and they held a rehearsal for Lindbergh. No, I will take that back.

I must tell you a little joke about that. They gave Calvin a wonderful welcome in Cuba. They steamed in through the harbor coming into Havana - it was the first big battleship that had been in there since the Maine[11] - and the people were all up on the hillside at Machado's Castle.[12] It was a beautiful Sunday afternoon and they were parading the streets and cheering from the houses, and they took him up and put him in Machado's Palace, and when he got located in his apartment - he and Mrs. Coolidge - a Secret Service man who was near them, Mr. Espey, said, "Mr. President, this is the greatest reception I have ever seen anyone get. It is really marvelous the way the people received you here, and I just wanted to tell you that." Then he stepped back, thinking Coolidge would thank him, or something. "In fact," he said, "I've been with every President since McKinley; I've been on all their trips with them and I never saw a President get a more spontaneous reception than that, and I just want to tell you because I feel it is the real truth, and I want to tell you;" - and Coolidge, "Where's the luggage?"

Nobody wasn't going to hand him any bull, that's all. That was the first time he'd ever been out of the country in his life and he wasn't going to have somebody stealing his grip; he wasn't going to trust these foreigners. That's Cal, you know.

I talked over the radio about two months ago - you might remember, some of you, the trouble you had with the radio; and then I read your mail! Oh, Lord, I didn't know I was so rotten until I read my mail. Why, everything you do is wrong; you'll get letters saying that something is wrong.

I introduced Fred Stone,[13] you may remember, as a marvelous performer, a high-class gentleman and an excellent performer, and I got a letter saying, "What do we care about one actor boosting another one. Give us entertainment; that's what we are paying for" - "that's what we are paying for" - over the radio!

And I joked about Graham McNamee,[14] our great announcer who announces all the football games and all the prize fights. I have known him for years. He had dinner at my home that night - he kept pulling the microphone away from my face when I spoke too loud, and bringing it nearer when I read a little joke. He just announced a New Year's football game two days before, and I remember how he told about the beautiful hills, how the lowly mountains met the sea - you know there's nothing to prevent them - and, you know, he never did tell when the football - you remember, he never told anything about that. He told about the flowers blooming on the hillside and the little jonquils and johnny-jump-up's, but he never told who made any touchdowns, and I joked about that. Well, you ought to have seen what 500 of them had to say about that: "Where do you come in, kidding Graham McNamee? Why, he knows more about talking over the radio than you'd ever know."

I told jokes about Coolidge, and they hopped on me because I imitated Coolidge. Well, I've imitated Mr. Coolidge ever since Mr. Coolidge has been in public life - even before he was in public - when he was Vice-President - and I imitated Mr. Coolidge, and I have done it in Washington three times on little tours like this, and I didn't think there was anything wrong in that. They hopped on me and said I had shown bad taste, and everything. It hurt me very much for I am a great admirer of Mr. Coolidge - I really am - and it hurt me to think he had taken any offence at anything I did. He was awfully nice to me when I was entertained at the White House - well, I won't go that far but I have been there - so I wrote him a nice letter and I asked him, I said, "Mr. Coolidge," I says, "it would give me great pain if I annoyed you in the least;" and I got a nice letter right back from him. He said, "Never paid any attention to it."

No, I got a lovely two page letter from him, written in his own hand. He says, "Will, I knew that anything you did you did for good-natured amusement. Don't give a moment's thought to it." Then down at the bottom he thanked me for some of the nice things he had heard I had said at various times.

I like Coolidge. I could tell you a million jokes about him, but I'm really fond of the little runt, and Mrs. Coolidge I'm crazy about. If we've got a lady in this audience that's never met Mrs. Coolidge and she's anywhere within ten miles, you go to meet her. She's got more personality and more magnetism than any woman I've ever met in my life. She's marvelous. I'm crazy about Mrs. Coolidge. She could run it - Calvin couldn't - she could run it all right, a vindication ticket.

So I've got my little speech here and I am going to read it to you, if I can find it. A lot of you might not have heard this this night over the radio - maybe you didn't hear it, so if I've got it - that's the notes (indicating) and I won't read that, it aint so good. Now I'll read this to you because the chances are a lot of you didn't hear it. You may have had enough to go somewhere else, and the chances are the ones that were listening in had static.

Now, this is Mr. Coolidge delivering his yearly message - I'll put glasses on. This is an imitation of Mr. Coolidge. Mr. Coolidge always wears glasses - because it's the first time he's read the message.

"I am proud" - you know Mr. Coolidge don't move his lips very much in talking. He don't smoke cigarettes but if he did smoke cigarettes he could keep on smoking and talking at the same time, as somebody aptly said up in Vermont: One time a man went up there and said, "What about this fellow Coolidge? What kind of a guy is he?" "Well," they said, "he's an awful close chewer and a tight spitter."

Of course, you've all heard the wonderful joke Alice pulled about him - Alice Longworth. Alice - every time I come to Washington I go out to see Alice, and nobody - a little later she is going to talk out in Kansas - nobody knows who's going to run for President at this time; they even stopped them talking until they could hear from Alice, and Alice don't know. Well, when Alice don't know - She don't like Cal. She loves Mrs. Coolidge; she's a Republican, and everything, but she don't like Coolidge. She says so and she says she tells him so, and she's the one that made the famous remark that Coolidge was weaned on a pickle.

I had come back off of a little tour - back from one of my little tours around the country - I had been in every state in the country the first year I went in for this thing and when I got back I met Alice. Alice is very excitable and nervous, and she says, "Will how is it; I hear Coolidge is very strong?" I said, "Mrs. Longworth, the people have got a lot of confidence in him and he's pretty strong." "Is that so? All over the country?" I said, "No, up in Iowa, up in the farm-belt, especially in the corn section up in Iowa and Nebraska, they got it in for Coolidge. They don't think much of him." "Is that so, up in the corn-belt where they raise corn they don't like Coolidge?" I said, "No." I said, "Everybody raised corn."

Well now, here's Mr. Coolidge delivering his message: "I am proud to report that the country as a whole is prosperous. I don't mean by that that the whole country is prosperous, but, as a whole it is prosperous. That is, it is prosperous for a whole.

["]A hole is not supposed to be prosperous, and we are certainly in a hole. There is not a whole lot of doubt about that.

"Everybody I come in contact with is doing well. They have to be doing well or they don't come in contact with me.

"Mellon has saved some money for himself, and he gives the country that usual ten per cent. Congress is here to divide up what Mellon saved. Sometimes I wished he hadn't saved it.

"We are having a little trouble down in Nicaragua over Sardino.[15] I certainly wish that guy was canned.

"Foreign debts - I am sorry to report that foreign debts are just about as foreign as ever.

"Farm relief - I will give relief to any two farmers who can agree on what relief they want.

"Prohibition - the Dry's wanted Prohibition in the Constitution and they got it in here. The Wet's wanted a drink and they got that; so what's all the shooting about? I don't know what it's all about."

Now, can you imagine in your wildest moments - that's the very speech I read over the radio that night - now can you imagine our dignified little Mr. Coolidge delivering a lot of junk like that? Yet the New York Times comes out the next morning and denounced me - they said, "It would have been all right, Will, if you had announced that it wasn't Coolidge." Now, I want to tell you it's mighty hard for a comedian to make a living when he's got editorial competition like that.

How anybody could have thought that that was Coolidge - in the first place, I don't want to be egotistical but Coolidge can't write that good a message, and, in the second place, the message was delivered at 11 o'clock that night. I am glad you got that one. I generally have to go on and tell the answer. I generally have to say that he's been sleeping two hours. Lord, the way you are working we are going to get out of here early to-night. You know it don't take half as long to tell jokes if you don't have to explain them. You know you can get through with jokes in just a little while if you just tell them, but where you have to go through and explain them all it takes time.

Anyhow Mr. Coolidge - I am going to tell you about the people over the radio. You can't talk over the radio and use the same type of stuff that you do on the stage, because you haven't got that kind of an audience. Everybody listening in over the radio wouldn't laugh like this. A radio audience - and I'm not saying this to flatter you, but everybody, you all wouldn't have come in if you hadn't a sense of humor. There has to be something the matter with you or you wouldn't have come in. They don't have that over the radio. I am sure you all had to have a sense of humor; it is certain that sex appeal drew nobody in here, and I'm positive that nobody come in to whet their intellect. No, you come in here to get just a laugh, but over the radio you have people listening in there with no sense of humor at all. Anybody can tune in on that.

There ought to be a law, or somebody, a kind of judge - for instance, they thought I was wrong - now the next time I talk over the radio I've got a splendid imitation which I am going to do of Abraham Lincoln but I am certainly going to announce that it's not Lincoln.

Now wait - what did I do with my paper? Here it is - oh, I got another one I must read to you that I am going to deliver. I know I criticize too much over the radio, boss everything, take everything literally, tell jokes about England, also I talk too rough, I know that I haven't got the proper voice; I talk too rough, and everything; I ought to do it more like an announcer.

Well, here's my next radio speech I submit for your approval:

"Good evening, radio fans; good evening, radio fans and you, too human beings. Isn't it a beautiful night. I know that it's beautiful here in California and I feel that it must be equally beautiful in the various places where you are assembled.

"Isn't it a wonderful world we live in? Well, isn't it a wonderful world that everybody lives in, for there might be people listening in from other worlds and we certainly don't want to hurt anyone's feelings, no matter what world they are from.

"Isn't the radio grand, and isn't everybody that listens in on it marvelous? There is no branch of the entertaining world where you have such broad-mindedness which you have over the radio.

"Aren't all our candidates running for office just too wonderful. Al Smith is too dear, and the cutest thing, and Hoover - the women just love him. If it hadn't been for him we would have eaten ourselves to death during the war;

and Dawes - don't you love his plans; and Louden will do so much for the farmer the farmer won't even have to farm; all he need do is to harvest.

"And women's rights - haven't women got the grandest rights? They can't go wrong; they've got too many rights; and what an influence women have been on honesty and integrity in politics" - it's kind of blurred there, I think.

"Oh, I just love women; I love men, I love everybody; that's the kind of a guy I am. I even love the youth of this country who everybody wants to choke. There's an old saying that youth must have its fling. Well, just because a lot of us are getting too old to fling we shouldn't criticize those who are still flinging. Your mothers - before they landed what they finally did pick up - your mothers did some mean flinging themselves.

"Short skirts - we think short skirts is terrible. Well, long skirts hid more in your mother's day but provocation was there.

"Automobiles stopping by the roadside - we think that's terrible, but a horse would stop - not only would stop but did. You couldn't expect a livery horse to keep going all Sunday afternoon.

"Now my time is up. It's been such a pleasure to bring you this wonderful message. This hour is being sponsored by the Anti-Human Scratch Flea Powder Company. We are announcing our new non-skid anti-scratch powder in your favorite drug store on your favorite corner to-morrow morning. If you have no favorite drug store on your favorite corner to-morrow morning, wait till to-morrow afternoon and we will build one there. Remember it doesn't prevent the itching but it does stop the scratching. So good - oh, just a moment. here's some telegrams. Here's a telegram that just come in from the Kiwanis Club, "Program coming in fine." Good-night friends, good-night."

Well, sir, I'll tell you what we've got to do here to-night. I was like to forget it - and that's take a straw vote. All around through the country I take a straw vote. Now a straw vote is about the lowest form of voting. It really is not a vote, it is a threat, that's all it is. It is like beating yourself at solitaire. We are going to have a straw vote, and I am going to ask you all if you won't join with me and hold up your right hands and vote for the candidates you want. I'll tell you who is ahead in all the other towns because I have taken a straw vote in thirty states in different towns, and, in the first place, I want to start with the Republicans. I mean I imagine that they predominate, and I hope there's not been, you know, too many of the undesirable element sneaked in. I know in a wonderful audience like this there can't be many of the paupers here, and so we will start in with the Republicans.

I hate to start with an apology but I am going to have to apologize to the audience to-night, to you Republicans especially. I am going to apologize to you Republicans before I start on my straw vote - I won't be able to pay you anything for your vote. I know that's rather unusual for a Republican vote.

I'm a great friend of Will Hayes but it was all gone when I reached him, so I have nothing for you whatever. You will have to put yourself on a level with the Democrats. Now, the Democrats have been voting for nothing for years - not only have they not received anything for their votes but they have been voting for nothing. You'll have to do that to-night.

We are going to start in - I think I will not betray any confidences when I tell you that Mr. Hoover received more votes than anyone all around over the country on either Party, so we will start in on Mr. Hoover.

Before we start in on Mr. Hoover, though, I'm going to tell you something. I got another fellow here that I want you to vote on with Hoover.

Calvin Coolidge says, "I don't choose to run.["] I'll let you all go home to-night and borrow a dictionary, and you can read that dictionary until I meet you again, if it's ten years from now, and if you can find a word in that dictionary which means less than choose does, I'm wrong. It's absolutely the only word in any language that means, "Yes, No, I don't know whether I will or not, I don't care, I haven't made up my mind yet, I don't know whether to come in or stay out, Shut the door." It just absolutely don't mean nothing, and if you wanted to - well, it means something. Don't tell me that little guy picked that word accidentally. I want to tell you he did a lot of research work before he found that word.

I don't say that Coolidge wants to run; I don't say he wants to run, but why hasn't he clarified his statement? That's what makes me think he has - why, every time they dig him up he says, "I'll stick to my original statement." Nobody knows what his original statement is.

If any business man in this house to-night was quoted to-morrow by the newspapers, and to-morrow afternoon everybody says, "What did you say? We couldn't make any sense out of it" - you would say, "Here is what I said: I said this." Did anybody ever hear Coolidge explain? No. I don't say that he wants to run but I say he left this loop-hole where - take this, it's only a nut comedian's idea, take this: Hoover will go to the Convention with, perhaps 400 or 450 votes more than anybody else. It takes five hundred and some odd to nominate, and he will go there with, perhaps, 450. Lowden will go with 250 or 300 maybe. Of course, the minute they get started his strength will switch over to Dawes and the different ones. Curtice [Curtis] will have Kansas, and the various ones - Watson of Indiana[16] will have his district, and all the various ones - Edge[17] will have his precinct, and all the various ones.

Now then, they've got to nominate; they can't decide; it gets to where Dawes is against Coolidge, 450 each, and they can't nominate. Then a gentleman gets up at the Convention, apparently impromptu, but with only 8 months rehearsal - he will get up and say, "My fellow Republicans, are we going to stand here and make monkeys out of ourselves, like those Democrats? Are we going to stay here and argue and haggle all Summer over two splendid men when we have one man that we all know can carry a victory? What's the matter with nominating unanimously Calvin Coolidge?"

See, that's what they'll do, nominate unanimously. Wait till Hoover takes the baby and lays it at Calvin's doorstep. "Why, there's the nomination laying there, bundled up. I didn't know you was here. I had no idea they were going to leave you here." Then he takes it in and says, "Well, I don't want to be cruel so I will nourish you all I can."

That's the way it will be, see. I even went so far - that's not only my saying - you can write one way and read another - but I bet on it months ago. I bet $5,000. I can bet that much because I wasn't putting it up. I tried to land Brisbane. He kept writing that Coolidge aint going to run. I said, "Now wait, Arthur, bet me," but I couldn't land him. He kept saying, "Don't sell America short" - he was too busy. That's all he was preaching. He said, "Don't gamble, American people, just get some General Motors and hold it until it goes up but don't gamble;" but Hearst took it up. Hearst hopped on me. He said, "Will, you're crazy; I'll bet you two to one" - William Randolph Hearst and I - he bet $10,000 to $5,000. If I lose I'll say, "Lord, you don't think I was on the level, do you?" Boy, if I win that $10,000 you are going to hear a celebration. I sure will. Sure, I could win that $10,000 if I would split it with Coolidge.

All right, we will start voting. We will start on Hoover, see, start on Hoover. Mr. Hoover. All right - right hands up. We are going to take the balloting all around. We are going to vote for Hoover, then against Hoover. You Republicans can't vote both ways. We've got to watch you. I am going to play Hoover against Coolidge and see which one will win. Mr. Hoover - hold up your right hand; hold up your right hand. Thank you. All right. Now up in the balcony, Secretary Hoover. (Minority response). Thank you. Coolidge - (almost unanimous response.) All right.

Now I don't need to tell you that Al Smith is as far on the Democratic side - he's as far ahead as Hoover is on the Republican side. Now Al Smith - come on, you can vote. They have taken the sheets off Al Smith. (4 or 5 responses).

Now let's see who'll elect Dawes. Anybody for Dawes? Dawes. Any bankers here? Lowden; Lowden. Any farmers here? There's a farmer up there. If you'd plough instead of holding your hand you wouldn't need relief.

I don't want to discourage any of you people who are interested in agriculture but the Government is going to do nothing about farming. Out in Iowa and Nebraska, they are discouraged out there - they are going to fertilize instead.

The Government is not going to help you farmers at all, so you might as well go back to work. The trouble with the farmer in America is he belongs to so many relief organizations he's not raising enough to pay his dues. What the farmer needs is to pass less resolutions and more filling stations. He wants to trade his speedometer for an alarm clock.

Now, let's see who else we've got. I'll tell you a guy I'm for, if I were a Republican, Secretary Hughes. There's an old fellow I'm for. If you could all just look at the people that applauded then - that's the Intelligenzia of this audience. You riff-raff don't appreciate Hughes.

Hughes is a great man. The trouble with Hughes is people don't understand him. They think he's all intellect and whiskers. You know I come over on the boat with him the year before last, on the Leviathan, and while we were coming over Florida had a tornado the second day we had been out, so I gave a benefit - I gave a little show on the boat. I tried to raise some money and I didn't know whether Mr. Hughes would help me out or not, so I went to him, I said, "Mr. Hughes, come on, I want you to do something in a little show that I'm giving," and he come on and did it, and he made a hit. The next night when we played the Second-Class he come down and worked there, and then in the Third-Class and the sailors and everybody was crazy about him on the boat, and we raised $47,000 - that's coming this way. That means a million going the other way. When Europe heard there was $47,000 - - - - -

Well, I met him down in Cuba the other day when I went down there. You know I'm a great admirer of the old gentleman, and he was down there at the Pan-American Conference. You know we had another Conference. America has a very unique record - we never lost a war and never won a conference. We can lick any nation in the world and yet we can't confer with Costa Rica and come home with our socks on, but we did very well at the Conference. We did very well down there. The Conference was not a success but we didn't lose anything.[18] Any time we don't give up anything we win, and we got along all right, and I asked Mr. Hughes - I gave a little dinner party - I wanted to give a little dinner party for the Morrow's. My wife wasn't with me in Mexico but she went with me to Cuba and she wanted to meet the Morrow's. They are awful plain people for rich folks, awful ordinary, pretty near common; so I had a little party there. I had Mr. and Mrs. Morrow, and I had Fletcher, of Rome - when I was in Italy he took me in and showed me Mussolini - that's the time I found out about castor oil from Mussolini[19] - I had him down there, and Judge O'Brien, bless his dear old heart, over there in New York. So I said, "I'm going to ask Mr. Hughes. I know he's awfully busy and I doubt if he'll come to a thing like this," but I sent him a note, and I got a nice letter that evening:

"Mrs. Hughes[20] and I will be there. Yours for more and better wise cracks."

So he said he would come to our little dinner party, and we were worried to death - my wife and I. We never entertained prominent people. I had been to a few dinners myself - I mean the kind with hired help - but we never entertained anybody and we was very excited. My wife and I are old country folks, and we wanted a lovely dinner, and we told the man at the hotel to go the limit - you know what I mean - but look out.

We was a little doubtful what to serve and my wife said, "I wouldn't"; I said, "Yes, we always do." I says, "It isn't Cuba, it's perfectly permissible," and finally we decided. I said, "Well, we will have it there, bring it in and set it there and let them do as they like."

Well, I am not betraying any great confidence when I tell you that not a soul in this audience could have got soused on what was left. We really - of course, the one we doubted was Mr. Hughes. We were all looking at Mr. Hughe's [*sic*] cocktail sitting there, you know, and Mr. Hughes was telling a story. We were watching him very closely - we don't start till he does. Well, the old gentleman just parted his whiskers and went at it, and he didn't show - you know he didn't show anything like a detour either. Well, it was mighty nice.

I wanted to find out something about Nicaragua during the evening. I said, "Secretary Hughes, tell me something about Nicaragua. I'm one of the million up home out of the bunch that don't know what the marines are doing there; they're getting shot down there in Nicaragua and I want to find out what we are doing down there." Here we are going to Nicaragua to settle an election and we didn't have a marine in Chicago the other day.

I'll tell you it takes a sense of humor for us to go somewhere else to settle an election. Imagine us - here we are settling an election at Nicaragua - our going down there to settle an election, and I told him, "Look at Chicago. The other day they had an election and what did we do?" I am a life member of the Red Cross and a great friend of Mr. Paines, the head of it, and we sent our nurses out to Chicago. What to do? The doctors and nurses that went out there they formed relief stations; they established relief stations just about where they figured the booth would be blown to.

I met a man the other day going to Chicago. I met him on the train. He spoke with kind of a foreign accent and I got acquainted with him on the train, and I asked him what he was doing. He said he was representing the Krupp people in Germany, that he was going to get an ammunition contract in Chicago.

We've got our marines riding mules in Nicaragua. Can you imagine a marine on a mule. Those South American mules will kill more marines than the Nicarguans will. We've got them down there hunting this guy Sardino. When he comes in to vote they are going to nab him.

I asked Mr. Hughes, "What are we doing down there?" That old fellow is smart. He just sat there and explained Nicaragua at that dinner; he explained our position so well that, honestly, if I was ten years younger I would have enlisted and gone and fought those Nicaraguans, honest. I never heard people persecuted as much as we have been persecuted by the Nicaraguans. How we ever got anywhere, how we ever reached our present position in society with Nicaragua on our necks, I don't know. What he said - I don't remember it now - but it certainly sounded plausible then. A great old fellow!

I turned to him and I said, "Mr. Hughes, I wish you'd run for President." I said, "I'm for you." He's a very modest man - he said, "Oh, Will, I don't want to run. I had my chance." I said, "Well, if you'll run I'll go around the country and campaign with you, that's what I'll do. I think you are a very much misunderstood man. If I bring you out on the platform and shown the American people what an American guy you are, and shave you, I could elect you."

Well now, I must tell you about the candidate Hoover. How about Hoover? I'd love to see Hoover nominated just to see how far a competent man would get in politics. It's never been tried; it would be rather an experiment; and you women are all for Hoover. During the war when Hoover was pictured on the screen you used to applaud - you'd drop your knitting to applaud - remember you were knitting on a sweater which a soldier afterward wore for a sock - and you applauded Hoover. Hoover was our food dictator. Hoover really won the war for us. He ruined our stomachs but he gave us liberty with indigestion. He had us living on slogans. Every time you'd get up for breakfast there'd be, "Butter it thin and you are bound to win;" "Drink your coffee black and give the enemy a whack;" "A lump a days keeps the enemy away."

He's a politician. He don't know it but he's quite a politician. He won the Catholic vote when he made the Baptists eat fish on Friday.

He took the wheat out of bread and fed it to the hogs, and he had the Jewish soldiers eating pork. He did a lot during the flood. I was down in the flooded area and saw some of the splendid things Hoover did. He even personally saved people's lives, and when he got them out, shook them out, wrung them out, they were Democrats.

Well, that was discouraging, really discouraging. I know if I personally risked my life and saved anybody and found he was a Republican I would shove them back in again, and that he didn't shove these Democrats back in showed he was a humaritarian. Hoover is the only Republican that ever saved a Democrat's life.

I don't know how he could ever be President. He would have to resign every April and May and go down and take care of the flood.

If you've got any friends in the Mississippi Valley I'd advise you to assist them to get a boat. I'd rather have one canoe in a flood than a Senate behind me. There is going to be nothing - Congress is going to do nothing about the flood. They passed resolutions the other day denouncing floods.

Hoover is the only man that's been mentioned for the Presidency on either side that could make a living at something else if defeated.

Now we'll get over to Al. Now I'm going to tell you a little information. I don't think Hoover will be nominated because the politicians are against him. People all over the world are for Hoover; Hoover would get more votes than anybody but the politicians don't like him. They know he knows more than they know and that he knows that he knows more than they do, and they aint going to appoint him. They're afraid if Hoover was President it would be just like appointing some able man and upsetting the whole political machine.

As I say, ▲[*typewritten:*]the▲ people are for Hoover, but when did you ever have anything to do with nominating anybody? I'm certainly not going to insult your intelligence by trying to make you think you have anything to do with it.

Even the man from your own State - President Wilson - why, Champ Clark went there with over 700 votes[21] and Wilson goes from New Jersey and wins it. What good does it do for the people to be for some man?

Remember in New York, the Democrats? Between McAdoo and Smith they had 900 votes, yet neither one got it. A guy named Davis got it. That's a lot of applesauce.

When Harding was nominated he only had Ohio - and I don't think he had all of Ohio - still he was nominated. What do the people say - "We want So-and-So," and you send delegates, but that don't get you anywhere. Even if you were a delegate you couldn't get into the rooms where the President is going to be nominated. You couldn't get into those rooms that night, and even if you did get in you couldn't stand the smell.

Now, we'll get over to Al. What about Al? I can't tell you nothing about Al. You know better than I do. Al's been a great friend of mine for years - Smith is quite a fellow. He's got a lot of personality. He goes into Tom Heflin's territory[22] and stays there three days, makes a speech, shakes hands with everybody, and the night he left he was made Honorary Keagle of the Klan. He's got a lot of personality. Smith's a great fellow.

Now, I'm asked every once in a while, "Will, how about a Catholic running the country, us Protestants?" I don't know nothing about it, but I know he is Governor of New York State, and anytime those Jewish people trust you with a thing the second time you've got to show something. Any time they let you run their State, the State where they own 90% of the stock - if the Jews can trust you with New York where they own everything, I see no reason why us Protestants couldn't trust him with what little we've got left in the United States. If he took everything we've got and took it back to Rome we wouldn't be much of a loser, or anything.

He's a bright fellow. It's a funny thing but I like Smith. I like all of them, that's the thing. There aint a candidate you could mention that aint a good friend of mine. I go around and tell jokes about all of them, but I hate to see the election come on, I really do, because I hate to see anyone get defeated. I wish there was some way of giving them all a week apiece. That's enough, yes, sir, but there's one thing - if you ever read anything I write you say, "Oh, Will's always hopping onto somebody" - I like to joke about them, everyone of them - but I've even got a tombstone epicack, or whatever you call it, when I die - and I'm anxious to die just to see how you look when you pass by my grave. The chances are I'll be setting up there - I'll be out looking. No joke about it.

Well, here's what it is - I'm really sincere about it - and although I'm a Protestant Father Duffy[23] is going to put it on there for me.

I went around to see Father Duffy - he's an Irish priest over on 69th Street - a great friend of mine - I went around there yesterday. He has a Protestant confession box, too, and I went in there. He's got three there - Otto Kahn was over in another one. Anyhow, so I said, "Here's what I want on my tombstone: 'I've joked about every prominent man in my time but I never met a man that I didn't like'" - that's what goes on there and I am really sincere.

You know Tom Heflin is always blathering around - I like the old sucker, I really do, he aint a bad old fellow; he just gets off on the wrong track; he don't know what he's talking about. He means well; he's all right.

That's one thing, don't ever form a dislike for a fellow because you don't agree with him. "I'll tell you so-and-so" - now, don't disagree with him looking at him; walk around behind him and see the way he's looking.

Now Coolidge says there is prosperity in the country. See, Coolidge says the country is prosperous. Well, Coolidge isn't purposely lying to you; Coolidge is not lying. He's a sincere man; he's not lying to you about the country. It does look good from where he sits at home.

Give you $75,000 a year, free rent and a yacht, and things will look fairly rosy.

So that's what I say about old Tom Heflin. He and I got into an argument the other day. I told him, I says, "Tom, there aint no use of you getting sore at me. We're both in the same business. My jokes have never been poor enough to get me in the Senate but you never can tell when they are liable to deteriorate.

Now, let me tell you something: Tom is off on this Pope business. Tom don't know nothing about the Pope.[24] He's never been over to Rome. I was in Rome the Summer before last and I went through the Vatican. It's a tremendous building, as big as this town. The whole thing is magnificent - there are works of art and great treasurers there that they have been gathering for years from the four corners of the earth - they're all in there. Tom Heflin don't know it, but in case Al Smith is elected the Pope couldn't move over here in four years.

He really couldn't. If Al Smith was re-elected the second term the Pope couldn't make it, but Tom thinks he'd be here for the inauguration, but, Lord, he couldn't get over here. I never saw as much plunder in one house in my life.

Now people ask me, they say, "Will, do you think Smith's religion will be against him?" I don't think it will. That's not a very safe thing for a comedian to come out on the stage and discuss, but I don't think Smith's religion will be against him. I think Smith's politics will hurt him worse than anything else. I think his being a Democrat will be more against him.

Yes, sir, I know if I was a Democrat - you know if I was a Democrat and a Catholic and had Presidential aspirations, and somebody says, "You'll have to change one of those before you'll have a chance," it would only take me a tenth part of a second to tell what I'd change - I'd change my Catholicism and move over to the paying party.

I don't want to discourage you Democrats, after scratching up all you had to pay to get in here tonight; I don't want to be rude, or anything, to anyone belonging to your Party, but I'm going to be honest with you: After touring the country for two or three years and appearing in every State in the Union, I'm going to be honest, at least, it don't just look like our year.

Now when one guy reaches down and gives the Republicans $260,000, we can't compete with junk like that; we can't do it. If the Democrats had $260,000 in their whole campaign's boot we wouldn't even have a nomination, or an election either; we'd just knock off and divide up and celebrate.

Now then, people ask me, they say - now, mind you, I am not criticising Will Hayes. He had dinner with me before I left California. Will is all right;

he's just a good hustler; Will will go out and do that Patrick Henry stuff, "Give us liberty or give us death" - "Give us Liberty bonds or checks."

Will is all right; Will has not a crooked bone in his body; don't think Will Hayes isn't honest. Of course, there's been times - I will say this - being a politician there's been times when Will is walking on the edge, you know - a typical Presbyterian elder.

Now people ask me, they say, "Do you think the South will vote for him on account of him being a Wet?" I think they will. I don't believe they will be sober enough to notice it.

I'm not saying that - I'm casting no reflections on the South, because I come from down there - I'm from the lower side of this Montgomery-Ward[25] line myself - but the reason I am not casting any reflections on the drinking of the South, the South don't drink anymore than anybody else; you know what I mean?

Drinking in America is regulated by capacity, that's all. The North don't drink anymore than the South, and the East don't drink anymore than the West, and vice versa. No part of the country drinks anymore than any other part. Everybody drinks all they can hold. That's all, all they can hold.

Prohibition is not an issue, it's a commodity. The fact is it is taken care of by supply and demand, the same as shoes, or anything else, and the reason I bring up the South is on account of the stuff they drink, called corn liquor. Now, corn liquor is really not a drink; it is a character builder.

Corn liquor - those people that make that are the only people who have been able to bottle courage. Take corn liquor - now ordinarily you have to breed courage into a race through years of breeding; you are brave because your father was brave and your forefather was brave - but just pour some of that stuff out of a bottle and take a couple of swipes of it and you'll walk right out and meet a street car head on purposely.

Now just one bottle of corn liquor fell into the hands of the Riffs over in Morocco[26] - they declared war on Spain the next morning. Then they ordered another half quart and said, "Bring on France, we'll have an international war."

Well, I've joked about Prohibition but allow me to be serious for just a few minutes - this is the only time during the evening - and I can tell you of a little observation which I have gleaned from messing around the country all these years and talking to everybody.

I don't know whether this will agree with you but I'm going to tell you the sentiment of this country is dry. No joke about that. I am just telling you that the sentiment of the country is dry. I'll tell Edwards[27] that or any of the rest of them, you know; and that don't go on the moral issue at all; don't think that the country is getting better, you know, that we realize our moral responsibility - no, nothing like that. It is that way because it is economic. That's why we've got dozens of men in this house tonight who own factories or business concerns where they engage men - and you are for Prohibition. Why? Because your men will produce more dollars. You who are paying them know that they'll be there on Monday morning and give you more for your money than otherwise - and you are certainly not injured in any of your personal habits.

In other words, you are getting more per dollar and as much per drink, and you're going to have it dry. You know you are. You know what I mean? You're going to vote for the country being dry, that's what you're going to do. I've been all over the country - I don't say the country is dry - I say the voting sentiment of the country is dry, and it will always be dry.

There's not a child in the place, there's not a little boy here who will live to see the time when Prohibition will be taken out. It will always be argued about but nothing will be done about it because the voting sentiment of this country is dry.

There are millions of people in this country who will vote dry just as long as they are sober enough to stagger to the polls. The only way you will ever get the true sentiment of this country is for some man like Edison, or some wonderful statesmen, to invent - to fix up a place and have like a megaphone - instead of talking into it, breathe into it, it gets your breath.

You go ▲[*typewritten:*]to▲ the polls, and here's the box. You come up and vote - drop your vote in here and breathe in here, and your vote and your breath have got to correspond. You can't vote one way and breathe another. That's what I mean. Then you'll get the true breath of America. Somebody will invent it some day.

Now you can tell bad liquor. How can you tell? Why, you take a steel bar, hold it down in a bottle just two seconds, take it out and if the bar is rusty - you say, "Oh, my goodness, the bar is rusty; it must be terrible stuff" - well, if the bar is rusty it's all right, but if the bar isn't rusty you'd better dilute it.

You know I used to do two or three little tricks from a rope. I haven't done them for a long time. I want to apologize to you for not doing them, though I don't want you to think I'm trying to shortchange you in any way. I couldn't do but 2 or 3 and I got ashamed of doing those. Any kid in the audience could get up here and do the same thing - but I'm not allowed to jump around and do anything of an atheletic nature on account of my operation.

After the show is over in a little while I want all you ladies to gather around here - we'll all come around here and hold a little testimonial meeting after you men have gone out. Each one will tell how it struck you when you were operated on. We will have a little gathering all around here, and I know we will have much in common. I know we'll have a good time.

Mine really wasn't a disease, or anything at all. I had it since childhood - stomach-ache, that's all. I always had it, for years, and I had it even before we had a hot water bottle. We used to have to get these stove lids, you know, that you lift off with a hook and put the skillet on. We used to have to heat those flat stove lids, heat them up to so many degrees Fahrenheit and place that on your centre, you know, and I don't care which extremity that was in pain that was the cure. You get that thing hot enough and I have known it to cure a broken arm. I have seen it cure corns and headaches - the same treatment.

I come home one time after a little tour, last June, and I had a little stomachache. Meantime we had acquired a doctor. Tell you how we got him.

We got this doctor - our children are growing up, they're getting to be pretty good sized little old kids, and they wanted to go around to parties and they couldn't go around to any decent parties because they had adenoids and tonsils yet. So my wife got a doctor and she had their tonsils taken out. That's not a medical precaution, it is a social one; and she had that done, so they commenced running around with the white children then.

So I come home and we had this doctor. I don't know why she hadn't paid him - and he was hanging around there, and when I get my little stomach ache he bobs in - he evidently knows his way about the house - and he commenced feeling around, and I could tell by the way he was feeling he was looking for an appendicitis operation - scouting out in Southwest 40. I didn't know what I had but I had heard enough about appendicitis to know where it was, and I knew I didn't have it. It gave me great glee even in all my pain to see this guy, he was just looking to operate, and I said, "It's a good joke on you, it aint down there at all."

Well, he felt rather discouraged at the time but he shook his head and come in again, and he said, "Where is the pain?" I said, "Right up there; right in the middle." Well, he moved up there and found gall stones - a much more expensive operation than down there. I would have saved $1500 if I had left him where he was in the beginning.

Well, he got messing around down there and he says, "Now, Will, you've got to have an operation." That scared me. I said, "Wait a minute. I've heard that lots of times you fellows are too quick with these operations. I've read in the papers a lot of times where they would send a man down and operate on him and the first thing you know he dies, and he don't even die from the thing you are operating on."

"Oh," he said, "that'll not be the case with me. If I operate on you for gall stones you will die of gall stones."

So I says, "Well, Doc, is it a very dangerous operation?" "Many people have it," he said, "women have it all the time; women have it a lot, a lot of women have it, especially among Jewish women, lots of them have it."

I said, "Lord, I don't look like one, do I?" I thought maybe I'd been eating too much gafilter fish and running around with Eddy Cantor.[28] He said, "It's a woman's disease. Eight women have it to every two men."

Well, that didn't make me feel any too good. Here I was, a great big roughneck lumocks, laying there with an effeminate disease.

I says, "Well, Doc, if that's the case maybe you won't have to operate. Maybe a couple of bottles of Lydia's[29] will be all right," but, you know, he didn't believe in patent medicine, and I tried to compromise on Peruna.[30]

He 'phoned to somebody - I didn't know who he was 'phoning to, and the minute that somebody comes - we live on a little hill, on Beverly Hill. You come inside a gateway and drive up, and you have to drive up a steep little driveway, and I can tell the calibre of our guests by how many times they shift on this hill. If they make it up there on high, you know, no shift, why, you know, I am at home. If they grind and shift, why, the maid goes to the door - the maid, not a maid, just the maid, if she aint cooking, she goes to the door; and if they don't make it at all, if they have to back down the hill and walk up, there aint anybody home, they've all gone.

Well, this fellow evidently got up on high, because he come on into the room before we knew it was him. It was another doctor that this guy 'phoned for, another doctor. All doctors nowadays have accomplices. Very few robberies are pulled off single-handed. They don't need each other medically, but when they are sending their bill it loans moral support.

He come in - I was laying over here - this doctor - and the other fellow said, "I'm glad you come; it looks like business." So the new one comes over and he says, "Well, how are you, Will? Ha - ha - ha - ha- kind of sick? - ha - ha - ha - ha - that's good - ha - ha - ha - ha. You've had a pretty tough season? Haven't you worked pretty hard?" I said, "Yes, sir." "You done[ ]well?" And me like a fool said, "Yes."

Leave it to an actor to be so conceited that they hurt their own business. He said, "We'll send you down to-night and operate in the morning," and he went out. Well, my wife heard that - my poor wife - we have been married all these years, the same husband, you know, for twenty years, me and her have battled together all these years - she was a Southern girl. I met her down in Arkansas - and just getting used to wearing shoes.

Well, she went out of the room. I knew she was all broke up, so when they got through messing with me I went in to cheer my poor wife. I said, "Maybe I won't die at that, maybe I'll come out all right." And what do you think she was doing when I come in - looking at the insurance papers. Well, they take me down - you see I am paid up - I go to the hospital; they moved me down that evening, and the first thing they do when they put you in a hospital - a little girl comes in, not a nurse, with little short skirts, looks like a manicurist, and she says, "Give me your hand." That's a blood test, a little blood test.

Well, they kept coming like that after blood. Finally one old gal come and I said, "There ain't any more fingers." "All right, here;" and she took it from there. You know, I don't know what they were all going to do with it but I thought some of them was keeping a friend who was anemic.

So that night they didn't give me any dinner. They don't give you any supper when you enter a hospital; they starve you; then they wrap you all up with a bandage. Remember this? I can tell by looking at you that you've all been bundled.

They put a flannel bandage, wrap it all around you. Don't you know what that's for? That's to keep some other doctor getting into you before they get to it.

Well, they get me all wrapped up and my wife goes home that night and gets thinking, "Poor old Will, maybe I give him up too quick," so she calls up Mary Pickford. Mary is a good little friend of ours. Mary is a Christian Scientist but she has a doctor in case - and Mary says, "I'll send my doctor," so Mary sent her doctor.

And old Bill Hart - you remember old buck shooting Bill - well, he heard about me being sick. Now Bill is a Holy Roller by religion. His doctor is a veterinarian, so Bill come in the next morning with horse hair all over him. You couldn't tell from the odor of the place whether it was a hospital or a livery stable.

So they were getting me all ready and in comes the two new doctors. They ask questions about my condition and before I can say anything my two answer them, and they answer in such a way that it shows if I am not operated on within half an hour I will perhaps die, although I had the disease for 44 years.

Finally they file out, and when they get out - I don't need to say nothing, I am just laying there, Exhibit A, that's all; all I have to do is to furnish a stomach for them to practice on.

I asked the nurse, "Do you think there's any chance of a hung jury?" I knew I couldn't get acquitted. So they come back in. They was for hanging. They come in and they told me, "You'll feel much better, Will, after you get the operation over," and out they went.

I heard my two doctors thanking them outside, "Good boys, we'll do as much for you some time. Good-bye," and out they went.

Then they come back in and get ready for the operation. All I've got on is alcohol. I could just lick my arm and get soused.

Then they put boots on me - remember that - they put boots on me, kind of canvas or cloth boots that come way up there. You never know what they're for. I guess it's in case you jump up and run out of the operating room you won't get blood on the floor. Either that or to keep you from biting your toe-nails.

Well, they rolled me into the operating room, and just as they were rolling me in they were rolling another guy out. That will make you shudder, that will stop you, I don't care how tough a guy is. I wondered if he would live or die, I wondered what he was operated on for, then I heard him cussing. Well, of all the cussing I ever heard that man was doing the best job I ever heard. I never heard such beautiful cussing; he really had a rhythm to it. He was under the effects of ether but he timed it perfectly. I thought, "Well, even if you don't know what happens to you, you had the pleasure of telling what you thought of them anyhow.["]

Well, they rolled me on in there - and I said, "Well, if I last as long as you do I'll be happy."

You know they have a little balcony like in there where you can go and see operations. That must be where people with a wonderfully well developed sense of humor - imagine meeting somebody on the street, "Hello, Marjorie, what are you doing this morning?" "Oh, nothing." "Come on, I have got two seats for the operation."

Well, I looked up and there was nobody up there. That kind of hurt my pride. I thought as I was passing out, "This is the poorest business I ever did in my life."

Well, they get me all ready - and here's something, don't let people tell you they used so many hundred stitches to sew them up. That was when they opened them up and left something inside and kept on opening them up and closing them up, putting hooks and eyes on, and all that. There aint anymore of that nowadays.

One girl, one nurse, stands there at the table and she has a piece of paper and pencil, and when you are opened up everything goes down - she's really not a nurse, she's a bookkeeper. She marks it down - 12 packages of gauze, 11 clips, one pair of scissors, 3 cigarette butts - and before you're sewed up everyone of those has got to come out and she's got to mark it off, like that. She's got to account for every one. I don't care how big a surgeon you are, you're not sewed up till she says O. K.

People say they have had a severe operation - an hour and thirty minutes. They were operated on for 10 minutes and they were searching for 1 hour and 20 minutes. You didn't have an operation, you had an exploration, that's all. That's all they've been doing to you.

Before I went in there I didn't know what might happen to me, so I said, "Well, I've got a lot of laughs in my lifetime and I want to pass out with one.["] So I thought all night of a good joke; I was going to have a good joke and just before they operate I thought I'll pull this joke and they will all laugh hilariously and then they can say, "Well, old Will wasn't so bad at that."

So I got ready to pull the joke, and there was one fellow standing behind me - he's the fellow you can't see; he's the fellow that's going to knock you out; he's the fellow that's got a jar of ether in his hand just ready - well, I was all ready to set the world laughly [*sic*] uproariously and I thought when this old guy reaches over I'll just reach up and pull it off and tell my joke and then let him go ahead.

That was the little idea I had - it was entirely my own. Well, I reached up - I started to reach up - you know they have men in these hospitals that they call internes but they're really wrestlers, that's what they are - well, that's as far as I got.

Out I went, and from that day to this I have never been able to think of that joke. I would give thousands of dollars if I could think of that joke. It was the best joke I ever had.

I don't know what they operated on me for but they certainly took out that joke.

When I come to that night the girl said to me, "Good night, don't turn; be careful, Mr. Rogers." She said, "Look out for the tubes." I said, "What tubes?" "Why," she said, "you've got some tubes in there?" "Where? How many tubes?" She said, "Two."

Well, that discouraged me, you know, for you can't get far on a two tube set. Out in California if we could get Amie preaching that's all we could get with two tubes, but they sewed me up with so much catgut - I had an awful big scar - they sewed me up with so much catgut that when I went home I didn't even sleep in a room. I just went out on the back fence every night. I was a howling Mayor.

They operated on a woman the same day I was operated on - she was a very beautiful woman - and she got all excited when they were going to operate on her and she said, "Oh, Dr. Moore,[31] I want to ask you, will this scar show?" He said, "That's entirely up to you, Madam."

There's one thing I am glad of and that is the doctor didn't take my teeth out. You know you go to a doctor and tell him, you say, "Doctor, I've got lumbago." "Here, take this card; have your teeth X-rayed."

You go and have your teeth X-rayed and bring him back the card. "See that spot on that molar there?" Sure enough, there's a spot on the molar - maybe it's a piece of toast, you can't tell. "Just what I thought. We will take out that upper row." He says, "That may not be what's the matter but in case it aint we can always take out the lower one."

Everything nowadays when you go to a doctor is your teeth. "Doctor, I think I have water on the knee." "That's all right, we will take these two out and drain it off."

See that row of teeth there, that's for dandruff. All these front ones - those are for fallen arches. Pull those out and raise your arches.

Every doctor now is a specialist. You don't see a doctor that knows all about you anymore. For instance, a man doctors on the upper end of your throat - he don't know where the lower end goes to. Anytime the disease passes the Adam's Apple you are out of his range - you go into the hands of another physician. When you cross here then you've got a disease that goes clear down to the stomach, and you have to have six doctors then.

Then they have another doctor - he don't do nothing but just tell you which one to go to. He couldn't even open a boil. He's not a doctor; he's just really a traffic cop for doctors.

When you go to a doctor nowadays and you say, "Doctor, I believe I broke my leg." "Which leg is it?" "It's my left leg." "I am sorry, but you'll have to go to a left leg doctor; I'm a right leg doctor."

They're a great people. Listen, they're a great people, though you have to be pretty near dead to appreciate them, and when you have had them where they could bump you off, you've had a lot of confidence in them. I love doctors.

You all feel good here to-night, but let any of you go home and have a little pain. You ring up the doctor, "Come on over, I don't know what it is but it's terrible." And he's got to dig out and come over at all hours of the night. They are very self-sacrificing - anybody is who will relieve human suffering; it's a marvelous thing to do.

And they do a lot of charity work. We haven't a doctor in the room who doesn't at some time do something for nothing, and he knows he will get nothing for it. They're great that way.

That ought to square that other.

I really meant that. Listen, I'm not joking. I think it's great.

Now I just want to tell you ladies a few things. I met a lady at a dinner party not long ago and she said to me, "I love to go to your show, Will, but you don't tell any jokes about women; all your jokes are about men." You know that got me thinking that maybe I aint treating the men right.

Well, the next morning I pick up the Literary Digest and what do I read: "There was literally $400,000,000 spent in beauty parlors alone last year." Well, you certainly don't look it. Somebody's getting money under false pretenses; that's no lie.

You go in a barber shop and women have supplanted the old-fashioned Police Gazette for men to look at while they were waiting to get a shave. In the old days you would go in a barber shop and pick up the Police Gazette and you'd see an actress in tights - Della Fox[32] - and you'd look at it. Now just go in and sit down; you'll see the same thing but no tights.

The men are getting worse than women; they're all vain, and they have to go in and have their faces massaged. That's nothing but washing their face, that's all, it's the same thing that your mother used to do with a corn cob and some ashes, that's all; and here a big lumocks will sit and get a manicure.

You know that's a thing that always got my goat, to see a great big ape with the little manicure girls on each side of him. It would be all right if he were just getting a manicure but all he's thinking of is making a hit with the little girls that have to make a living. I love to see them make all they can and clean up, but what physical disability prevents a man cleaning one hand with the other one? Why have your nails cleaned anymore than you would have somebody come in and wash your teeth? There'd be some excuse for a one armed man getting a manicure.

I want to tell you that what this country needs is dirtier finger nails and cleaner minds. That's what we need.

Out in Los Angeles not long ago I went to a big banquet. I don't go to banquets very often but this was the Corset Manufacturers Association and I did go there. I said, "Here's an industry that's on its last legs."

Well, I said I'd go to this Corset Manufacturers' banquet and after I promised to go I was sorry I promised. I thought, I aint got any act that will do for corset manufacturers and their wives and families - and they come from all over the world - and I got thinking, and I just happened to think, What about your early married life?

You know I was married a long time ago and I can remember way back to the old corset. Many of you fellows my age, many of you fellows and older, what did we do the first ten years of our married life (illustrating). "You do it if you think you can get it any tighter. Don't argue with me. I've pulled all I can.["]

I really believe that if my wife had worn a corset till now I'd been a wonderful harp player.

Now you young girls don't know nothing about this. You might as well go on home. All you young girls and boys don't know what I'm talking about but your mothers do. This is old time stuff but it's good to see some of you remember.

That was the back lace - that was where the husband or friend - and then the single woman had to use the front lace. She couldn't get much of a purchase pulling this way. She used to walk up, tie a string onto the door knob and back off. She was really 3 inches taller.

Oh, Lord, they were awfully barbarous things. Remember women in the old times used to come along like that - this old whalebone, no elastic. It was really worth seeing one go through the torture of wearing it just to see the relief at night. Oh, they were so satisfied. They even quit arguing with you then.

I never saw a moment in the day that some man didn't remind me of a monkey, but that's the only time when I can really remember when a woman really reminded me of one. (Illustrating).

Those were great old times. I'll tell you something else. Remember in the early days before you knew enough to clip off the bottom, when you used to sit down, especially if you were the least bit fleshy, and they would come up?

I've seen women at dinner parties when they couldn't see out over them.

Oh, I'm glad I went to that dinner. I might have done some good. I'm not so modern that I think the corset should have been done away with. I'm kind of old-fashioned. I don't believe, you know, in just letting nature go where it wants to. That (indicating) might not look so good but it looks about as good as this (illustrating). You bet your life.

Any industry that can kind of assemble you somewhere, kind of round you up into some kind of a shape, deserves a lot of credit.

I went one night to a dinner party, and this woman was kind of fleshy - she was sitting right behind me. The first thing I knew - I thought she was moving over my way on the bench - it was one of these long benches - one of these strings had broken. She was just settling slowly. That woman come to that party in a coupe and they took her home in a truck.

Now then, I'm going to talk to you one more minute. I am getting tired of messing with you now. I don't care if you are so tired, people, I am tired of looking at you; you've got to get out. I don't know when I monkeyed with an audience as long as this. If anybody ever kept this town awake as late as this they would think you were crazy, but I'm glad to have been here with you. We've had a wonderful audience; it's mighty fine to have been here and I'm proud I played out here for you and I hope some time to come back. Any time that I come back I'll have some new jokes. I don't have the same old jokes. You won't have these old jokes anymore. I've talked a lot of politics, but a lot of these jokes that I've spoken here to-night will pass out between now and November - they'll all be gone but one.

You know people often ask me, "Will, where do you get your jokes from?" Why, I just watch the Government and report the facts. I never have found it necessary to exaggerate.

Now, you women are wearing your clothes too short; I'm telling you. I come out of the Follies, and I'm not an old prue, not an old granny, but what you're doing is to try to imitate the Ziegfield [*sic*] girls in the show. Let me tell you something: Any time Ziegfield put short skirts on a girl he picked the girl personally; you understand; I have been with him 12 years. He didn't just let anybody go buy a short skirt and wear it. He'd have a fine show if anybody could just walk on there. He picked the girls personally. I'm just telling you something: Don't follow fashion any further than you are physically able.

And that goes for a lot of you old women, too. A lot of you are waddling around in short dresses when you ought to have a barrel on.

I'm telling you that a lot of you girls and a lot of you women here - I know from the looks of you - haven't stood and turned your back to a mirror, like that, and looked back over your shoulder in a full length mirror. If you do you are going to learn something to your advantage.

Now there aint one in this house, the funniest legged one among you in here that don't look so bad, you know, from the front. You're always lined up at your mirror dabbing away at your nose. Three more generations and we aint going to have any more noses; we are just going to pound it right on in. Well, you just line up and you don't look so bad. Your legs are not so funny from the front, you know what I mean; you don't look so bad coming but you can't meet everybody; you have got to pass somebody once in a while.

TD. OkClaW, Will Rogers, Jr., Collection, Folder 12. Bound by three binding rivets, and the front and back covers consist of yellow card stock. Typewritten on the cover, centered near the top, stacked (/): "TALK / by / MR. WILL ROGERS, / MONTCLAIR HIGH SCHOOL, / MONTCLAIR, NEW JERSEY, / APRIL 16TH, 1928." Typewritten in the lower right hand corner of the cover, stacked (/): "Verbatim Report by / Convention Reporting Co., / 42 Broadway, / New York City, / Hanover 6104-5." All interpolations were handwritten, unless otherwise noted. Double strike-through indicates hand-deleted text. Some paragraphs in the document were bracketed in pencil, and handwritten exes occasionally appear in the margins. In addition, main topics have been written in pencil as the topics appear in the text. All of these markings have been ignored in this transcription.

1. Rogers might have meant John J. Blondel, a member of the Montclair Rotary Club, sponsor of the local lecture tour appearance. Blondel hosted Rogers at a reception at his home (clipping, *Montclair Times*, 18 April 1928, OkClaW).

2. William Lawrence (Larry) Chittenden (ca. 1862–1934) was born in Montclair, N.J., but left the area at age twenty-one and headed for Texas, where he eventually gained prominence as a rancher and as a contributor of poetry and other writings to magazines and newspapers. Among his many poems was "The Cowboys' Christmas Ball," a paean to life in nearby Anson City, Tex. (*NYT*, 25 September 1934; Gregg and Gregg, ed., *Best Loved Poems*, 79–81).

3. Scream Welsh performed a comedy acrobat act in vaudeville. To keep his diamond stud secure, he was known to attach it to his underwear before going out on stage (Laurie, *Vaudeville*, 29).

4. Rogers performed in Ann Arbor, Mich., on Monday evening, 2 April (Chronology, 1928, OkClaW).

5. Harold Edward (Red) Grange (1903–91) was one of the greatest collegiate and professional players in American football history. He starred for the University of Illinois from 1923 to 1925 and then left school to join the Chicago Bears of the National Football League. His gridiron exploits brought the professional game a significant boost in public attention. He retired as a player in 1934 (*BDASFoot*, 216–18; *NYT*, 29 January 1991).

6. James C. Fitzmaurice (1898–1965), commandant of the Air Corps of the Irish Free State, was a last-minute replacement as co-pilot aboard the *Bremen*, a German plane that landed in Ireland on 26 March 1928 as a prelude to a transatlantic flight. Fitzmaurice and fellow aviators, Captain Hermann Köhl (1888–1938) and Baron Ehrenfried Gunther von Huenefeld (1892–1929) of Germany, left Ireland on 12 April and became the first men to fly the Atlantic east to west (*DIH*, 173–74; *NYT*, 6 February 1929, 9 October 1938; Roseberry, *Challenging Skies*, 177–78; Davies, *Lufthansa*, 22).

7. Myron Timothy Herrick (1854–1929), a former Republican governor of Ohio, served as ambassador to France on two occasions, first from 1912 to 1914 and then from 1921 until his death. Lindbergh stayed at Herrick's official residence after his flight to Paris (*DAB*, 8:587–89; Berg, *Lindbergh*, 130–31).

8. Evangeline Lodge Land Lindbergh (ca. 1876–1954), a high-school science teacher in Detroit, was the mother of Charles Lindbergh. His father, Charles Augustus Lindbergh, a former congressman, had died in 1924 (*DAB*, Supp. 9:495; *NYT*, 8 September 1954; Berg, *Lindbergh*, 18, 24, 76, 173).

9. The Ford tri-motor, one of the few multi-engine aircraft in production, made its debut in June 1926 and became the focus of Ford's fairly recent entry into airplane manufacturing. The all-metal Ford tri-motor carried eight passengers and proved popular among the growing number of passenger air services (Nevins and Hill, *Ford*, 2:243–45).

10. Charles Lindbergh wrote a brief account of his life and the transatlantic flight that was published in the summer of 1927 as *We*. Almost two hundred thousand copies were sold within a month (Berg, *Lindbergh*, 166–67).

11. President Coolidge arrived in Havana, Cuba, aboard the battleship *Texas*. Thirty years earlier, the explosion and sinking in the same harbor of another U.S. war ship, the *Maine*, had precipitated the Spanish-American War. Coolidge addressed the delegates to the Pan-American Conference on 16 January and sailed home the next day (Ferrell, *Presidency*, 139).

12. Gerardo Machado y Morales (1871–1939) was president of Cuba from 1925 until his overthrow in 1933, by which time he had assumed dictatorial powers. Machado hosted the Coolidges at the presidential palace in Havana during the conference (*NYT*, 16 January 1928, 30 January 1939).

13. Fred and Dorothy Stone were among several entertainers who performed during the national radio broadcast on 4 January. The father-daughter duo sang in a dressing

room between acts of a musical in Chicago (*NYT*, 5 January 1928). See also Telegram from V. V. McNitt, 6 January 1928, and Letter to Calvin and Grace Coolidge, ca. 10 January 1928, above.

14. Graham McNamee (1888–1942) started working in radio in 1923 in New York. His colorful, highly descriptive style brought him considerable attention as a sportscaster, and he was one of the first announcers to broadcast sessions of a national political convention. He covered the first Rose Bowl game over a national hookup and was in Paris to announce Charles Lindbergh's arrival (*DAB*, Supp. 3:495).

15. Augusto César Sandino (1895–1934), Nicaraguan rebel leader, returned from exile in Mexico in 1926, joined antigovernment forces, and soon became leader of the liberal army. He ignored a truce negotiated by the United States in 1927 and created a separate republic within Nicaragua. When his forces were eventually overcome, he fled again to Mexico in 1929. He returned to Nicaragua the next year under terms of peace, but national guardsmen seized and executed him in 1934 (Hodges, *Intellectual*, 3, 12; *NYT*, 23 February 1934).

16. James Eli (Jim) Watson (1864–1948), a colorful, conservative Republican from Indiana, served in the U.S. Senate from 1917 to 1933 (*BDUSCong*, 2016; *NYT*, 30 July 1948).

17. Walter Evans Edge (1873–1956), a successful businessman and Republican leader in New Jersey, served as governor from 1917 to 1920 and as U.S. senator from 1920 to 1929 (*DAB*, Supp. 6:186–88).

18. U.S. intervention in Latin America, particularly in Nicaragua and Haiti, was an overriding issue at the Pan-American Conference in Havana in January. A nonintervention resolution reached the floor during the final session, but Charles E. Hughes, as head of the U.S. delegation, deftly succeeded in postponing the issue and effectively continuing American occupation (Ellis, *Republican*, 268–69).

19. To consolidate his power in Italy in the early months of his dictatorship, Benito Mussolini encouraged a reign of terror by his fascist supporters. Assassination by beating was commonplace, as was castor oil administered in sufficient amounts at times to cause death (Mack Smith, *Mussolini*, 63).

20. Antoinette Carter Hughes (ca. 1864–1945), daughter of a prominent New York attorney, married Charles E. Hughes in 1888 (*NYT*, 7 August 1945).

21. James Beauchamp (Champ) Clark (1850–1921), Democrat from Missouri, served in the U.S. House of Representatives from 1893 to 1895 and from 1897 until his death. The front-runner for the Democratic presidential nomination in 1912, Clark, speaker of the House, led his main challenger, Woodrow Wilson, 440 1/2 votes to 324, on the first ballot at the national convention. He continued to lead through fourteen ballots, but he lost crucial support and eventually lost the nomination (*DAB*, 4:121).

22. James Thomas (Tom) Heflin (1869–1951) served for many years as a Democratic congressional representative from Alabama. He served as U.S. senator from 1920 to 1931. An aggressive prohibitionist, anti-Catholic, and white supremacist, Heflin enjoyed the support of the Ku Klux Klan. He vigorously opposed the presidential candidacy in 1928 of Al Smith, a Catholic (*DAB*, Supp. 5:290–91).

23. Francis Patrick Duffy (1871–1932), the much decorated chaplain of the Fighting Sixty-Ninth Regiment of the New York National Guard, after the war served as priest at Holy Cross Catholic Church on West Forty-Second Street in New York. A well-regarded servant to the poor, Father Duffy also became a beloved pastor of the rich, famous, and influential (*DAB*, 22:267–69).

24. Pius XI (Achille Ambrogio Damiano Ratti, 1857–1939), a native of Italy, served as head of the Roman Catholic Church beginning in 1922 (*Papacy*, 2:1199; *LSMD*, 136–37n.196).

25. Aaron Montgomery Ward (1843–1913), a Chicago entrepreneur, started a mail-order dry goods business in 1872 that was generating annually $40 million in sales worldwide by the time of his death (*DAB*, 19:414).

26. The tribes of the Rif, under the leadership of the nationalist Abd el-Krim (Abd al-Kârim, ca. 1881–1963), defeated colonial forces in Spanish Morocco in 1921 and proclaimed a separate state the next year. Seeking full independence for the Rif peoples, they successfully struck outposts in the French part of Morocco in 1925, but a combined Spanish and French force of more than 800,000 troops led to the surrender of Abd el-Krim and the Riffian army in late May 1926 (*NYT*, 7 February 1963; *HDM*, 10–11).

27. That is, Senator Edward I. Edwards.

28. For Eddie Cantor see *PWR*, 3:412–16.

29. Lydia Estes Pinkham (1819–1883) developed a home remedy that she began bottling and selling in 1873 as Lydia E. Pinkham's Vegetable Compound. Aggressively marketed as a curative for "female complaints," it brought great wealth to the Pinkham family and made Lydia a household name (Holbrook, *Golden Age*, 58–66).

30. Peruna, a patent medicine touted as the cure for what its promoters seemed to consider the ultimate human affliction, catarrh, originated in Ohio in the late 1800s and became immensely popular. Detractors labeled it as nothing more than "cheap whisky," but as late as 1927 it was still being advertised on the radio (Holbrook, *Golden Age*, 94–102).

31. Edward Clarence Moore (1882–1944) was a noted surgeon in Los Angeles (*EMJR*, 63).

32. Della Fox (1872–1913) was a vaudeville and theatrical comedienne and comic opera star. Rogers appeared on the same bill with her on at least one occasion (*NYT*, 17 June 1913; *PWR*, 3:252n.2).

From Lena F. Winders
26 April 1928
Tulsa, Okla.

Tulsa, Oklahoma.
April 26th, 1928.

Hon. Will Rogers,
Beverly Hills,
California.
Dear Sir:-

Doubtlessly news items, as the one attached come to you in great numbers, but surely it will do no harm, for a former resident of Claremore to extend to you great thanks and appreciation for the very kind and benevolent spirit bringing about this act in which Andy Payne received this gift.[1]

Knowing the financial condition of the family, I know how much it would mean to them, for it has been hard for them to secure means to keep him in the race.

Very Sincerely,
<u>Lena F. Winders</u>
Former resident of
CLAREMORE, OKLAHOMA.

1103 So. Quimby,
Tulsa, Okla.

TLS, rc. OkClaW, Scrapbook 8, Part 2. Author's signature appears on a typewritten line.

1. Andrew Hartley (Andy) Payne (1907–77) was a young runner from Foyil, Okla., who competed in an endurance feat popularly known as the Bunion Derby, a transcontinental footrace that started in Los Angeles on 4 March 1928. Eighty-four days and 3,400 miles later, Payne ended up first, several hours in elapsed time ahead of his nearest competitor, when the fifty-five survivors finally reached the finish line in New York. When the runners neared Claremore, Okla., in mid-April, Rogers offered to split $500 among the lead runners entering his hometown. When the event organizer disallowed the purse because it had not been sufficiently advertised to all competitors, Rogers forwarded the full $500 to Payne for leading the others into Claremore (Thomas, *Bunion Derby*, 2–4, 6, 133; *DT*, 1:398; *NYT*, 5 March, 27 May 1928; unidentified clipping, 19 April 1928, Scrapbook 8, Part 2, OkClaW). Rogers published a tribute to Andy Payne and his amazing feat in *American Magazine*, April 1929 (see *HTBF*, 98–102). See also *DT*, 1:202, 212, 215, 216, 217.

Telegram from Robert E. Sherwood
6 June 1928
New York, N.Y.

In a good-natured parody on politics, Life, the humor magazine, spawned a new political party for Rogers and made him its presidential candidate in 1928, running on the slogan "He Chews to Run." The Bunkless party made its debut in the issue of 17 May, and Rogers's initial contribution appeared two weeks later.[1] Shortly thereafter editor Sherwood wired Rogers with news of a major endorsement.

77S BR 73

BN NEWYORK NY 259P JUN 6 1928

WILL ROGERS

BEVERLYHILLS

CLAIR MAXWELL[2] WILL BE IN KANSASCITY WEDNESDAY MORNING STAYING WITH DICK SCANDRETH[3] WHO IS DWIGHT MORROWS NEPHEW STOP HE IS VERY

The Rogers family and pets on their ranch in the Santa Monica Mountains. Jock, a Sealyham, was acquired during a trip to Europe in the summer of 1926. The Brahma calf was a gift of Sarah Kleberg Johnson in June 1928 and named Sarah in honor of the Texan. (*OkClaW*)

ANXIOUS TO SEE YOU THERE STOP PLEASE WIRE ME IMMEDIATELY WHERE YOU
CAN BE REACHED IN KANSASCITY[4] AND WHEN YOU WILL GET THERE STOP JUST
GOT MARVELOUS LETTER FROM HENRY FORD DEMANDING THAT YOU RUN
SERIOUSLY FOR PRESIDENT[5] WILL SEND YOU COPY STOP YOUR COPY ARRIVED
YESTERDAY IT IS THE BEST YET

BOB SHERWOOD

1244P

TG, rc. OkClaW, 1975.31.0494. On Western Union Telegraph Co. letterhead. Printed flush left
immediately below letterhead: "Received at 1509 Santa Monica Blvd., Beverly Hills, Calif. Telephone Oxford 4709." A curving line has been hand-inserted between the "s" and "c" in the first
instance of "KANSASCITY." "HENRY FORD" has been underlined lightly in pencil.

    1. The Rogers campaign series in *Life* was intentionally launched in advance of
the national conventions of the major parties, which Rogers attended as a correspondent. The series continued through the issue of 9 November. For the complete run of
articles see *HCTR*.
    2. Clair Maxwell (ca. 1892–1959), a member of the *Life* magazine staff in 1928,
became president of the publishing company in 1929 and eventually publisher (*NYT*,
12 May 1959; Mott, *History*, 4:567).
    3. Richard Brown (Dick) Scandrett, Jr. (1891–1969), attorney and corporate
executive, was the eldest child of Dwight Morrow's sister, Agnes, and a favorite
nephew of Morrow (Nicolson, *Dwight Morrow*, 5n, 43; *WhAmer*, 5:636).
    4. Rogers arrived in Kansas City, Mo., on Sunday, 10 June, to begin work as a
special correspondent to the Republican national convention. By the eighteenth the
convention had ended and he was in Oklahoma (Chronology, 1928, OkClaW). For his
account of the convention see *CA*, 95–103.
    5. Ford's letter was reproduced in the *Life* edition of 21 June (see *HCTR*, 26).

Book Foreword by Will Rogers
ca. Spring 1928
Beverly Hills, Calif.

FOREWORD

    I was asked to write a Foreword for this Beverly Hills High School Con-
gressional Record.[1] This is not really a Foreword it's a Warning. Every book
or magazine should have a warning, the same as we have at railroad crossings
where there are signs warning the trains to look out for cars. The electric lines
out there killed more people than the war. They don't run fast until they get
near a crossing—and they never will hit one person in a car, they can't monkey
their time away with only one they wait for a load. But that's got nothing to
do with this warning, this one is telling you to look out for this magazine. You

are liable to sneak up on it and read it before you know you have done it if it wasn't for the warning. Course people don't pay much attention to warnings, they think they are just put there by people with nothing else to do; but I want to tell you that is not the case with me. I am busy and when I take time to warn you to lay off this Almanac I mean it. Time is valuable nowadays, and people haven't got any time to be monkeying with this thing.

I want to warn parents especially, for if they read this they will wonder "Why do we send them to school." But if they don't read it why they will still think you are learning something. They get these illustrated hand-bills out every year in all the schools, just to keep their minds off any work that the teachers might have given them to do. Some high school started it as a substitute for study and the rest of course have followed. Now, Beverly is a new school, and I am glad of that for it [if] you don't take my warning and go read this you won't have to read about "Tradition". The school has absolutely no "Tradition". It was started to keep our children from going to Hollywood. In fact it cost us over a million dollars just to keep you out of Hollywood and its evil influences. You would have learned more if you had gone to Hollywood school, but it was not what we wanted you to learn. I want you to know we had to move two oil wells to make room for the thing. We could enlarge the school but it would interfere with the golf course. There are thousands of people learning to play golf to every one learning to read. You don't have to know about History to get along but you certainly do have to know how to "Putt". There are people playing golf in America today that think the word "Coolidge" is an add for some new fangled Refrigerator.

You all must be sure and go to College when you get out of High School. In the old days college boys had nowhere to go when they come out of college, but now they go to work in filling stations. All they have to do is to be there to hand over the money, whenever a robber appears (generally another college man). I think everybody ought to have a fine education, even if you can't make a living at it. It's good to know that you know more than the people that you have to ask for jobs from.

Not that this has anything to do with the subject, but how is the old town anyhow? How's the water, has it cleared up any? You never had any trouble with it when I was Mayor. That was the first thing I would do every morning was to see that the water was clear. I think they made a big mistake by ever letting me out. How is the Parents' Teachers' Association, still telling the teachers how to teach their children things that they couldn't teach 'em at home themselves. These high schools down south here where I am now[2] are coming along fine, they are getting some splendid Coaches. Who's got the most votes out there now, the North or the South side of the tracks? You might think the north side had more money, but they haven't, they only owe more. The south side pays rent and the north side pays interest on Mortgages. Now all this ought to be warning enough for anybody. After reading this they certainly would go on at their own peril.

Yours,

WILL ROGERS

PD, cy. Printed in *The Watchtower*, 1928 (Beverly Hills, Calif.: Beverly Hills High School, 1928). OkClaW, *Watchtower* file.

1. Rogers's contribution appeared in the first issue of *The Watchtower*, the yearbook of the new Beverly Hills High School. The name of the annual may have come from a distinctive architectural feature of the French Normandy design of the school, which was dedicated in November 1927 and had opened earlier that fall. Although none of Rogers's children at the time attended the school, Bill, Jr., graduated from it in 1931 (*Watchtower* file, OkClaW; Basten, *Beverly Hills*, 116; *PWR*, 3:439).

2. Rogers's lecture tour took him through much of the South in March 1928 (Chronology, 1928, OkClaW).

Frank J. Murphy to Betty Blake Rogers
24 July 1928
New York, N.Y.

July 24, 1928.

Mrs. Will Rogers,

Beverly Hills, Calif.

Dear Mrs. Rogers:

Thought I had better drop you a few lines to explain the enclosed check.

As you know, the weekly rate was increased to $2000.00 on June 3. We divided this evenly between the weekly articles and daily wires, making it $1000.00 each.

Up to this time►,◄on the 20th of each month wwe paid for the weekly articles released up to the last Sunday of the previous month, but payment for the daily wires ran for a couple of weeks into the current month. In other words, on June 20, we paid for the weekly article►s◄released up to and including Sunday, May 27, and for the daily wires up to the week ending June ►9◄. Therefore, we owe Will the difference between the old and the new rate for that one week from June 4 to 9. The total figure is therefore arrived at as follows:

Weekly articles for June 3, 10, 17, 24 and July 19, 2004
    5 weeks @ $1000.00 -   -   - $5000.00
Daily wires – balance due week June 4 to 9, difference between
    $1000.00 new rate and $700.00 old rate   -   300.00
Daily wires – 3 weeks ending June 16, 23 and 30
    3 weeks @ $1000.00 -   -   -   <u>3000.00</u>
    $8300.00
Daily Worst Stories   -   -   -   <u>293.25</u>
    $8593.25

For bookkeeping purposes it will be simpler if we pay in the future on the 20th of each month for the wires and weekly articles released up to and including the last Sunday in the preceding month. This will avoid confusion, and we are sure Will will have no objection to that arrangement. In other words, on August 20, our check will include payment for four weeks ending July 29, at the rate of $2000.00 per week.

We are collecting the money on the conventions and as soon as we have Will's share in, will forward check. We have been very successful in selling the convention material and hope to send along a check about three times the size of the one four years ago.

We had a great time in Kansas City and Houston,[1] although I suspect Will felt more at home among the Democrats. I will confess I did, although I have usually voted the Republican ticket.

With best regards,

Sincerely,
F J Murphy

FJM/EB

TLS, rc. OkClaW, Letters The McNaught Syndicate binder. On letterhead of The McNaught Syndicate, Inc., Features for Newspapers, Times Building, New York. All interlineations were hand-inserted.

1. For a complete record of Rogers's articles on the Republican national convention in Kansas City, Mo., and the Democratic national convention in Houston, Tex., in June 1928, see *CA*, 89–117.

Bibliography

The sources used in this volume are listed in three categories: books; articles and chapters in anthologies; and unpublished and miscellaneous sources. Titles given in quotation marks in the document endnotes may be found either in the "articles and chapters" section or among the "unpublished and miscellaneous sources." See also the list of symbols and abbreviations in the front matter of the volume.

BOOKS

Aldrich, Gene. *The Okie Jesus Congressman: The Life of Manuel Herrick*. Oklahoma City: Times-Journal Publishing, 1974.

Allen, Michael. *Rodeo Cowboys in the North American Imagination*. Reno: University of Nevada Press, 1998.

Amaral, Anthony. *Will James, the Last Cowboy Legend*. Reno: University of Nevada Press, 1980.

Arlinger, Kai. *Die Grundrechte im Spiegel des Plakats 1919 bis 1999*. Berlin: Deutsches Historisches Museum, 2000.

Arnold, Alan. *Valentino*. London: Hutchinson, 1952.

Arnold, Byron, comp. *Folksongs of Alabama*. University: University of Alabama, 1950.

Auer, Michel. *The Illustrated History of the Camera: From 1839 to the Present*. Translated by D. B. Tubbs. Boston: New York Graphic Society, 1976.

Avery, Catherine B., ed. *The New Century Classical Handbook*. New York: Appleton-Century-Crofts, 1962.

Baker, David. *Flight and Flying: A Chronology*. New York: Facts on File, 1994.

Barber, Lucy G. *Marching on Washington: The Forging of an American Political Tradition*. Berkeley: University of California Press, 2002.

Barnard, Harry. *Independent Man: The Life of Senator James Couzens*. New York: Charles Scribner's Sons, 1958.

Barns, Florence Elberta. *Texas Writers of Today*. 1936. Reprint. Ann Arbor, Mich.: Gryphon Books, 1971.

Barrus, Clara. *The Life and Letters of John Burroughs*. Vol. 1. Boston: Houghton Mifflin, 1925.

Basten, Fred E. *Beverly Hills: Portrait of a Fabled City*. Los Angeles: Douglas-West, 1975.

———. *Santa Monica Bay: The First 100 Years*. Los Angeles: Douglas-West, 1974.

Batty, Peter. *The House of Krupp*. London: Secker & Warburg, 1966.

Beach, Rex. *Spoilers*. New York: Harper & Bros., 1906.

Bealle, Morris A. *The History of Football at Harvard University, 1874–1948*. Washington, D.C.: Columbia Publishing Co., 1948.

Beardsley, Charles. *Hollywood's Master Showman: The Legendary Sid Grauman*. New York: Cornwall Books, 1983.

Beasley, Norman, and George W. Stark. *Made in Detroit*. New York: G. P. Putnam's Sons, 1952.

Behlmer, Rudy, ed. *Memo from David O. Selznick*. 1972. Reprint. New York: Modern Library, 2000.

Behr, Edward. *Prohibition: Thirteen Years That Changed America.* New York: Arcade, 1996.

Berg, A. Scott. *Goldwyn, A Biography.* New York: Alfred A. Knopf, 1989.

——. *Lindbergh.* New York: G. P. Putnam's Sons, 1998.

Berger, Robert, and Anne Conser. *The Last Remaining Seats: Movie Palaces of Tinseltown.* Los Angeles: Balcony Press, 1997.

Bernard, Jacqueline. *The Children You Gave Us: A History of 150 Years of Service to Children.* New York: Jewish Child Care Association of New York, 1973.

Billington, Monroe L. *Thomas P. Gore: The Blind Senator from Oklahoma.* Lawrence: University of Kansas Press, 1967.

Birkenhead, Lord. *Rudyard Kipling.* New York: Random House, 1978.

Bloom, Ken. *American Song: The Complete Musical Theatre Companion.* Vol. 1. 2d ed. New York: Schirmer Books, 1996.

Blum, John Morton. *Woodrow Wilson and the Politics of Morality.* Edited by Oscar Handlin. Library of American Biography. Boston: Little, Brown, 1956.

Bobinski, George S. *Carnegie Libraries: Their History and Impact on American Public Library Development.* Chicago: American Library Association, 1969.

Botjer, George F. *A Short History of Nationalist China, 1919–1949.* New York: G. P. Putnam's Sons, 1979.

Brands, H. W. *Bound to Empire: The United States and the Philippines.* New York: Oxford University Press, 1992.

Brown, A. Theodore, and Lyle W. Dorsett. *K.C.: A History of Kansas City, Missouri.* Boulder, Colo.: Pruett, 1978.

Browning, Frank, and John Gerassi. *The American Way of Crime.* New York: G. P. Putnam's Sons, 1980.

Bryant, Keith L., Jr. *History of the Atchison, Topeka & Santa Fe Railway.* Lincoln: University of Nebraska Press, 1974.

Bryn-Jones, David. *Frank B. Kellogg: A Biography.* New York: G. P. Putnam's Sons, 1937.

Buckley, Thomas H. *The United States and the Washington Conference, 1921–1922.* Knoxville: University of Tennessee Press, 1970.

Burrows, Edwin G., and Mike Wallace. *Gotham: A History of New York City to 1898.* New York: Oxford University Press, 1999.

Byers, Chester. *Roping: Trick and Fancy Rope Spinning.* New York: G. P. Putnam's Sons, 1928.

Cammaerts, Emile. *Albert of Belgium, Defender of Right.* New York: Macmillan, 1935.

Canfield, Leon H. *The Presidency of Woodrow Wilson: Prelude to a World in Crisis.* Rutherford, N.J.: Fairleigh Dickinson University Press, 1966.

Cantor, Eddie. *Take My Life.* Garden City, N.Y.: Doubleday, 1957.

Carlson, Oliver. *Brisbane: A Candid Biography.* 1937. Reprint. Westport, Conn.: Greenwood Press, 1970.

Carson, Gerald. *The Golden Egg: The Personal Income Tax: Where It Came From, How It Grew.* Boston: Houghton Mifflin, 1977.

Carter, Joseph H. *Never Met a Man I Didn't Like: The Life and Writings of Will Rogers.* New York: Avon, 1991.

Carter, L. Edward. *The Story of Oklahoma Newspapers, 1844 to 1984.* Oklahoma City: Oklahoma Heritage Association, 1984.

Carter, Randolph, and Robert Reed Cole. *Joseph Urban: Architecture, Theatre, Opera, Film.* New York: Abbeville Press, 1992.

Caruso, Dorothy, and Torrance Goddard. *Wings of Song: The Story of Caruso.* New York: Minton, Balch, 1928.

Caruso, Enrico, Jr., and Andrew Farkas. *Enrico Caruso: My Father and My Family.* Portland, Ore.: Amadeus Press, 1990.

Cashman, Sean Dennis. *America in the Age of the Titans: The Progressive Era and World War I.* New York: New York University Press, 1988.

Chambrun, Clara Longworth de. *The Making of Nicholas Longworth: Annals of an American Family.* New York: Ray Long & Richard R. Smith, 1933.

Clancy, Foghorn. *My Fifty Years in Rodeo: Living with Cowboys, Horses and Danger.* San Antonio, Tex.: Naylor, 1952.

Cohn, Jan. *Creating America: George Horace Lorimer and the* Saturday Evening Post. Pittsburgh: University of Pittsburgh Press, 1989.

Coletta, Paolo E. *William Jennings Bryan.* Vol. 3, *Political Puritan, 1915–1925.* Lincoln: University of Nebraska Press, 1969.

Collings, Ellsworth. *The Old Home Ranch: Birthplace of Will Rogers.* 2d ed. Claremore, Okla.: Will Rogers Heritage Press, 1986.

Colvin, D. Leigh. *Prohibition in the United States: A History of the Prohibition Party and of the Prohibition Movement.* New York: George H. Doran, 1926.

Coon, Horace. *Columbia: Colossus on the Hudson.* New York: E. P. Dutton, 1947.

Cooper, Courtney Ryley. *Annie Oakley: Woman at Arms.* New York: Duffield, 1927.

Corneau, Ernest N. *The Hall of Fame of Western Film Stars.* North Quincy, Mass.: Christopher Publishing, 1969.

Cowles, Virginia. *The Kaiser.* New York: Harper & Row, 1963.

Craig, Douglas B. *Fireside Politics: Radio and Political Culture in the United States, 1920–1940.* Baltimore: Johns Hopkins University Press, 2000.

Cramer, C. H. *Newton D. Baker: A Biography.* Cleveland: World Publishing, 1961.

Crane, Jonathan. *Submarine.* 1984. Reprint. London: British Broadcasting Corp., 1985.

Creel, George. *Rebel at Large: Recollections of Fifty Crowded Years.* New York: G. P. Putnam's Sons, 1947.

Croy, Homer. *Our Will Rogers.* New York: Duell, Sloan & Pearce, 1953.

Cuff, Robert D. *The War Industries Board: Business-Government Relations during World War I.* Baltimore: Johns Hopkins University Press, 1973.

Curran, Joseph M. *The Birth of the Irish Free State, 1921–1923.* University: University of Alabama Press, 1980.

Dakin, Douglas. *The Unification of Greece, 1770–1923.* New York: St. Martin's Press, 1972.

Daniels, Josephus. *Our Navy at War.* New York: George H. Doran, 1922.

Davies, R. E. G. *Lufthansa: An Airline and Its Aircraft.* New York: Orion, 1991.

Denby, Elaine. *Grand Hotels, Reality & Illusion: An Architectural and Social History.* London: Reaktion Books, 1998.

Diccionario Porrua de Historia, Biografia y Geografia de Mexico. 2d ed. Mexico City: Editorial Porrua, 1964.

Di Scala, Spencer M. *Italy: From Revolution to Republic, 1700 to the Present.* 1995. Reprint. Boulder, Colo.: Westview Press, 1998.

Dougherty, Barry. *New York Friars Club Book of Roasts, the Wittiest, Most Hilarious, and, Until Now, Most Unprintable Moments from the Friars Club.* New York: M. Evans, 2000.

Dulles, Foster Rhea. *The American Red Cross: A History.* New York: Harper & Brothers, 1950.

Dunbar, Willis F. *Michigan: A History of the Wolverine State.* Rev. ed. Edited by George S. May. Grand Rapids, Mich.: William B. Eerdmans, 1980.

Easton, Carol. *The Search for Sam Goldwyn: A Biography.* New York: Quill, 1975.

Edward, H.R.H., Duke of Windsor. *A King's Story: The Memoirs of the Duke of Windsor*. 1947. Reprint. New York: G. P. Putnam's Sons, 1951.

Ellis, L. Ethan. *Republican Foreign Policy, 1921–1933*. New Brunswick, N.J.: Rutgers University Press, 1968.

Farrar, Geraldine. *Such Sweet Compulsion: The Autobiography of Geraldine Farrar*. New York: Greystone Press, 1938.

Farwell, Byron. *Over There: The United States in the Great War, 1917–1918*. New York: W. W. Norton, 1999.

Ferrell, Robert H. *The Presidency of Calvin Coolidge*. Lawrence: University Press of Kansas, 1998.

Fields, Armond. *Fred Stone: Circus Performer and Musical Comedy Star*. Jefferson, N.C.: McFarland, 2002.

Finan, Christopher M. *Alfred E. Smith, the Happy Warrior*. New York: Hill & Wang, 2002.

Fiske, Turbesé Lummis, and Keith Lummis. *Charles F. Lummis: The Man and His West*. Norman: University of Oklahoma Press, 1975.

Fitzgibbon, Russell H. *Uruguay: Portrait of a Democracy*. New Brunswick, N.J.: Rutgers University Press, 1954.

Fowler, Gene. *Beau James: The Life and Times of Jimmy Walker*. New York: Viking Press, 1949.

Franks, Kenny Arthur. *The Osage Oil Boom*. Oklahoma City: Oklahoma Heritage Assn., 1989.

Fuhrmann, Joseph T. *Rasputin: A Life*. New York: Praeger, 1990.

Gallagher, Tom. *Portugal: A Twentieth-Century Interpretation*. Manchester, U.K.: Manchester University Press, 1983.

Garafola, Lynn. *Diaghilev's Ballets Russes*. New York: Oxford University Press, 1989.

Gatti-Casazza, Giulio. *Memories of the Opera*. New York: Charles Scribner's Sons, 1941.

Gehring, Wes D. *W. C. Fields, A Bio-Bibliography*. Westport, Conn.: Greenwood Press, 1984.

Genini, Ronald. *Theda Bara: A Biography of the Silent Screen Vamp, with a Filmography*. Jefferson, N.C.: McFarland, 1996.

Gilbert, Martin. *The First World War: A Complete History*. New York: Henry Holt, 1994.

Glines, Carroll V. *The Saga of the Air Mail*. Princeton, N.J.: D. Van Nostrand, 1968.

Glyn, Anthony. *Elinor Glyn*. 2d rev. ed. London: Hutchinson, 1968.

Goldman, Herbert G. *Banjo Eyes: Eddie Cantor and the Birth of Modern Stardom*. New York: Oxford University Press, 1997.

Gordon, Dudley. *Charles F. Lummis: Crusador in Corduroy*. N.p.: Cultural Assets Press, 1972.

Gossett, Thomas F. *Uncle Tom's Cabin and American Culture*. Dallas: Southern Methodist University Press, 1985.

Gregg, John J., and Barbara T. Gregg, eds. *Best Loved Poems of the American West*. Garden City, N.Y.: Doubleday, 1980.

Hanes, Col. Bailey C. *Bill Pickett, Bulldogger: The Biography of a Black Cowboy*. Norman: University of Oklahoma Press, 1977.

Hanesworth, Robert D. *Daddy of 'Em All: The Story of Cheyenne Frontier Days*. Cheyenne, Wyo.: Flintlock Publishing, 1967.

Harries, Meiron, and Susie Harries. *The Last Days of Innocence: America at War, 1917–1918*. New York: Random House, 1997.

Hatch, Alden. *Edith Bolling Wilson, First Lady Extraordinary*. New York: Dodd, Mead, 1961.

Hayne, Donald, ed. *The Autobiography of Cecil B. DeMille*. Englewood Cliffs, N.J.: Prentice-Hall, 1959.

Heiber, Helmut. *The Weimar Republic*. Translated by W. E. Yuill. 1966. Reprint. Oxford: Blackwell, 1993.

Heimann, Robert K. *Tobacco and Americans*. New York: McGraw-Hill, 1960.

Hendrickson, Robert. *Hamilton*. Vol. 1, *1757–1789*. New York: Mason/Charter, 1976.

Heppner, Sam. *"Cockie."* London: Leslie Frewin, 1969.

Hodges, Donald C. *Intellectual Foundations of the Nicaraguan Revolution*. Austin: University of Texas Press, 1986.

Holbrook, Stewart H. *The Golden Age of Quackery*. New York: Macmillan, 1959.

Huber, Leonard V. *New Orleans: A Pictorial History*. New York: Crown, 1971.

Hunt, Stoker. *Ouija: The Most Dangerous Game*. New York: Barnes & Noble, 1985.

Jackson, Stanley. *Caruso*. New York: Stein & Day, 1972.

Jessup, Philip C. *Elihu Root*. Vol. 2, *1905–1937*. New York: Dodd, Mead, 1938.

[Joffre, Joseph J. C.] *The Personal Memoirs of Joffre, Field Marshal of the French Army*. Vol. 2. Translated by T. Bentley Mott. New York: Harper & Brothers, 1932.

Johnson, Gerald W. *An Honorable Titan: A Biographical Study of Adolph S. Ochs*. New York: Harper & Brothers, 1946.

Jordan, David M. *The Athletics of Philadelphia: Connie Mack's White Elephants, 1901–1954*. Jefferson, N.C.: McFarland, 1999.

Josephy, Alvin M., Jr., et al., eds. *The American Heritage History of Flight*. New York: American Heritage, 1962.

Kasper, Shirl. *Annie Oakley*. Norman: University of Oklahoma Press, 1992.

Kawamura, Noriko. *Turbulence in the Pacific: Japanese–U.S. Relations during World War I*. Westport, Conn.: Praeger, 2000.

Keso, Edward E. *The Senatorial Career of Robert Latham Owen*. Gardenvale, Quebec: Garden City Press, n.d. [ca. 1938].

King, Bill. *Rodeo Trails*. Laramie, Wyo.: Jelm Mountain Press, 1982.

King, Willford I. *The Wealth and Income of the People of the United States*. New York: Macmillan, 1922.

Knock, Thomas J. *To End All Wars: Woodrow Wilson and the Quest for a New World Order*. New York: Oxford University Press, 1992.

Kobler, John. *Otto the Magnificent: The Life of Otto Kahn*. New York: Charles Scribner's Sons, 1988.

Koistinen, Paul A. C. *Mobilizing for Modern War: The Political Economy of American Warfare, 1865–1919*. Lawrence: University Press of Kansas, 1997.

Koszarski, Richard. *An Evening's Entertainment: The Age of the Silent Feature Picture, 1915–1928*. Vol. 3 of *History of the American Cinema*. Charles Harpole, gen. ed. New York: Charles Scribner's Sons, 1990.

Krasovskaya, Vera. *Nijinsky*. 1974. Translated by John E. Bowlt. New York: Schirmer Books, 1979.

Kunstler, William M. *The Hall-Mills Murder Case: The Minister and the Choir Singer*. 1964. Reprint. New Brunswick, N.J.: Rutgers University Press, 1980.

Landis, Marilyn J. *Antarctica: Exploring the Extreme: 400 Years of Adventures*. Chicago: Chicago Review Press, 2001.

Larsen, Karen. *A History of Norway*. Princeton, N.J.: Princeton University Press, 1948.

Laurie, Joe, Jr. *Vaudeville: From the Honky-tonks to the Palace*. New York: Henry Holt, 1953.

LeCompte, Mary Lou. *Cowgirls of the Rodeo: Pioneer Professional Athletes*. Urbana: University of Illinois Press, 1993.

Lee, Raymond. *Not So Dumb: The Life and Times of the Animal Actors.* South Brunswick: A. S. Barnes, 1970.

Leinwand, Gerald. *1927: High Tide of the Twenties.* New York: Four Walls Eight Windows, 2001.

Leopold, Richard W. *Elihu Root and the Conservative Tradition.* Boston: Little, Brown, 1954.

Levine, Isaac Don. *Mitchell, Pioneer of Air Power.* New York: Duell, Sloan & Pearce, 1943.

Lewis, David L. *District of Columbia: A Bicentennial History.* New York: W. W. Norton, 1976.

Lieb, Frederick G. *Connie Mack, Grand Old Man of Baseball.* New York: G. P. Putnam's Sons, 1945.

———. *The Detroit Tigers.* New York: G. P. Putnam's Sons, 1946.

Lieb, Frederick G., and Stan Baumgartner. *The Philadelphia Phillies.* New York: G. P. Putnam's Sons, 1953.

Lingenfelter, Richard E. *Death Valley and the Amargosa: A Land of Illusion.* Berkeley: University of California Press, 1986.

Link, Arthur S. *Wilson: Campaigns for Progressivism and Peace, 1916–1917.* Princeton, N.J.: Princeton University Press, 1965.

———. *Wilson: Confusions and Crises, 1915–1916.* Princeton, N.J.: Princeton University Press, 1964.

Link, Arthur S., et al., eds. *The Papers of Woodrow Wilson.* 69 vols. Princeton, N.J.: Princeton University Press, 1966–94.

Linton, George E. *The Modern Textile and Apparel Dictionary.* 4th ed. Plainfield, N.J.: Textile Book Service, 1973.

Louvish, Simon. *Man on the Flying Trapeze: The Life and Times of W. C. Fields.* New York: W. W. Norton, 1997.

Low, Rachael. *The History of the British Film, 1918–1929.* London: George Allen & Unwin, 1971.

Lowe, Pat. *Will Rogers Official Genealogy and Bibliography: Family Tree and Historic References.* Claremore, Okla.: Will Rogers Memorial, 1997.

Lukowski, Jerzy, and Hubert Zawadzki. *A Concise History of Poland.* Cambridge, U.K.: Cambridge University Press, 2001.

Lyons, Eugene. *Herbert Hoover: A Biography.* Garden City, N.Y.: Doubleday, 1948.

Mack Smith, Denis. *Mussolini.* New York: Alfred A. Knopf, 1982.

Maland, Charles J. *Chaplin and American Culture: The Evolution of a Star Legend.* Princeton, N.J.: Princeton University Press, 1989.

Marquis, Albert Nelson, ed. *The Book of Detroiters: A Biographical Dictionary of Leading Living Men of the City of Detroit.* 2d ed., rev. Chicago: A. N. Marquis, 1914.

Marx, Samuel. *Mayer and Thalberg: The Make-Believe Saints.* New York: Random House, 1975.

Mason, Anita. *An Illustrated Dictionary of Jewellery.* 1973. Reprint. New York: Harper & Row, 1974.

McCoy, Donald R. *Calvin Coolidge: The Quiet President.* 1967. Reprint. Lawrence: University Press of Kansas, 1988.

McGraw, Mrs. John J. *The Real McGraw.* Edited by Arthur Mann. New York: David McKay, 1953.

McNamara, Brooks. *The Shuberts of Broadway: A History Drawn from the Collections of the Shubert Archive.* New York: Oxford University Press, 1990.

Meserve, Walter J. *Robert E. Sherwood, Reluctant Moralist.* New York: Pegasus, 1970.

Metz, Clinton. *Freeport, As It Was*. Freeport, N.Y.: n.p., 1976.

Meyer, Karl E., comp. *Pundits, Poets, and Wits: An Omnibus of American Newspaper Columns*. New York: Oxford University Press, 1990.

Millard, Andre. *America on Record: A History of Recorded Sound*. New York: Cambridge University Press, 1995.

Miller, Nathan. *Theodore Roosevelt: A Life*. New York: William Morrow, 1992.

Moley, Raymond. *The Hays Office*. Indianapolis: Bobbs-Merrill, 1945.

Morehouse, Ward. *George M. Cohan, Prince of the American Theater*. Philadelphia: J. B. Lippincott, 1943.

Morell, Parker. *Diamond Jim: The Life and Times of James Buchanan Brady*. New York: Simon & Schuster, 1934.

Mott, Frank Luther. *American Journalism, a History: 1690–1960*. New York: Macmillan, 1962.

———. *A History of American Magazines*. 5 vols. Cambridge, Mass.: Belknap Press of Harvard University Press, 1938–57.

Murray, Robert K. *The Harding Era: Warren G. Harding and His Administration*. Minneapolis: University of Minnesota Press, 1969.

Myers, Margaret G. *A Financial History of the United States*. New York: Columbia University Press, 1970.

Nasaw, David. *The Chief: The Life of William Randolph Hearst*. Boston: Houghton Mifflin, 2000.

Nash, George H. *The Life of Herbert Hoover: Master of Emergencies, 1917–1918*. New York: W. W. Norton, 1996.

National Automobile Chamber of Commerce. *Facts and Figures of the Automobile Industry, 1924 Edition*. New York: National Automobile Chamber of Commerce, 1924.

Nevins, Allan. *Study in Power: John D. Rockefeller, Industrialist and Philanthropist*. New York: Charles Scribner's Sons, 1953.

Nevins, Allan, and Frank Ernest Hill. *Ford*. Vol. 2, *Expansion and Challenge, 1915–1933*. New York: Charles Scribner's Sons, 1957.

Nicolson, Harold. *Dwight Morrow*. New York: Harcourt, Brace, 1935.

Oderman, Stuart. *Roscoe "Fatty" Arbuckle: A Biography of the Silent Film Comedian, 1887–1933*. Jefferson, N.C.: McFarland, 1994.

O'Geran, Graeme. *A History of the Detroit Street Railways*. Detroit: Conover Press, 1931.

Palmer, Alan. *The Decline and Fall of the Ottoman Empire*. 1992. Reprint. New York: M. Evans, 1993.

Pegram, Thomas R. *Battling Demon Rum: The Struggle for a Dry America, 1800–1933*. Chicago: Ivan R. Dee, 1998.

Perry, John Curtis, and Constantine Pleshakov. *The Flight of the Romanovs: A Family Saga*. New York: Basic Books, 1999.

Pingenot, Ben E. *Siringo*. College Station: Texas A&M University Press, 1989.

Pound, Arthur. *Detroit, Dynamic City*. New York: D. Appleton-Century, 1940.

Pusey, Merlo J. *Charles Evans Hughes*. 2 vols. 1951. Reprint. New York: Columbia University Press, 1963.

Rae, John B. *The American Automobile: A Brief History*. Chicago: University of Chicago Press, 1965.

———. *The American Automobile Industry*. Boston: Twayne, 1984.

Read, Oliver, and Walter L. Welch. *From Tin Foil to Stereo: Evolution of the Phonograph*. Indianapolis: Howard W. Sams, 1959.

Renehan, Edward J., Jr. *The Lion's Pride: Theodore Roosevelt and His Family in Peace and War*. New York: Oxford University Press, 1998.

Riess, Steven A., ed. *Sports in North America: A Documentary History*. Vol. 6, *Sports in the Progressive Era, 1900–1920*. Gulf Breeze, Fla.: Academic International, 1998.

Riley, Glenda. *The Life and Legacy of Annie Oakley*. Norman: University of Oklahoma Press, 1994.

Riske, Milt. *Cheyenne Frontier Days: "A Marker from Which to Reckon All Events."* Cheyenne, Wyo.: Cheyenne Corral of Westerners International, 1984.

Roberts, Chalmers M. *The* Washington Post: *The First 100 Years*. Boston: Houghton Mifflin, 1977.

Roberts, Randy. *Papa Jack: Jack Johnson and the Era of White Hopes*. New York: Free Press, 1983.

Robinson, David. *Chaplin: His Life and Art*. London: Collins, 1985.

Rogers, Betty. *Will Rogers: His Wife's Story*. 1941. New ed. Norman: University of Oklahoma Press, 1979.

Rogers, Naomi. *Dirt and Disease: Polio before FDR*. New Brunswick, N.J.: Rutgers University Press, 1992.

Rolle, Andrew. *California: A History*. 5th ed., revised and expanded. Wheeling, W.Va.: Harlan Davidson, 1998.

Rose, William Ganson. *Cleveland: The Making of a City*. Cleveland: World Publishing, 1950.

Roseberry, C. R. *The Challenging Skies: The Colorful Story of Aviation's Most Exciting Years, 1919–1939*. Garden City, N.Y.: Doubleday, 1966.

Rowland, Peter. *David Lloyd George: A Biography*. 1975. Reprint. New York: Macmillan, 1976.

Russell, Francis. *The Shadow of Blooming Grove: Warren G. Harding in His Times*. New York: McGraw-Hill, 1968.

Schickel, Richard. *D. W. Griffith: An American Life*. New York: Simon & Schuster, 1984.

Schoenbaum, S[amuel]. *William Shakespeare: A Compact Documentary Life*. New York: Oxford University Press, 1977.

Schwarz, Jordan A. *The Speculator: Bernard M. Baruch in Washington, 1917–1965*. Chapel Hill: University of North Carolina Press, 1981.

Service, Robert. *Lenin: A Biography*. Cambridge, Mass.: Harvard University Press, 2000.

Shulman, Irving. *Valentino*. 1967. Reprint. New York: Pocket Books, 1977.

Slide, Anthony, comp. *The Films of Will Rogers*. Beverly Hills, Calif.: Academy of Motion Picture Arts and Sciences, 1998.

———. *Silent Players: A Biographical and Autobiographical Study of 100 Silent Film Actors and Actresses*. Lexington: University of Kentucky Press, 2002.

Sloane, David E. E., ed. *American Humor Magazines and Comic Periodicals*. New York: Greenwood Press, 1987.

Smith, Darrell H., and Paul V. Betters. *The United States Shipping Board: Its History, Activities and Organization*. Washington, D.C.: Brookings Institution, 1931.

Smith, Philip Hillyer. *Wheels within Wheels: A Short History of American Motor Car Manufacturing*. New York: Funk & Wagnalls, 1968.

Sobel, Robert. *Coolidge: An American Enigma*. Washington, D.C.: Regnery, 1998.

"Sold American!": The First Fifty Years. N.p.: American Tobacco Co., 1954.

Stansbury, Kathryn B. *Lucille Mulhall: Her Family, Her Life, Her Times*. N.p.: n.p., 1985.

Starr, Kevin. *Material Dreams: Southern California through the 1920s*. New York: Oxford University Press, 1990.

Stinnett, Ronald F. *Democrats, Dinners, and Dollars: A History of the Democratic Party, Its Dinners, Its Rituals.* Ames: Iowa State University Press, 1967.

Stout, Joseph A. *Border Conflict: Villistas, Carranistas and the Punitive Expedition, 1915–1920.* Fort Worth: Texas Christian University Press, 1999.

Stump, Al. *Cobb: A Biography.* Chapel Hill, N.C.: Algonquin Books of Chapel Hill, 1994.

Sutherland, Stuart. *The International Dictionary of Psychology.* New York: Continuum, 1989.

Tebbel, John William. *George Horace Lorimer and the* Saturday Evening Post. Garden City, N.Y.: Doubleday, 1948.

Tennyson, Alfred. *The Poetic and Dramatic Works of Alfred, Lord Tennyson.* Student's Cambridge Edition. Boston: Houghton Mifflin, 1898.

Thelen, David P. *Robert M. La Follette and the Insurgent Spirit.* Boston: Little, Brown, 1976.

Thomas, James H. *The Bunion Derby: Andy Payne and the Transcontinental Footrace.* Oklahoma City: Southwestern Heritage Books, 1980.

Thompson, Donald E., comp. *Indiana Authors and Their Books.* Vol. 3, *1867–1980.* Crawfordsville, Ind.: Wabash College, 1981.

Trani, Eugene P., and David L. Wilson. *The Presidency of Warren G. Harding.* Lawrence: Regents Press of Kansas, 1977.

U.S. Congress, House of Representatives, Committee on International Relations. *Hearing on the History of Armenian Genocide.* 104th Cong., 2d sess., 15 May 1996.

U. S. Congress, Senate, Committee on Indian Affairs. *Construction of a Sanatorium and Hospital at Claremore, Okla.: Hearing on S. 1833.* 69th Cong., 1st sess., 18 March 1926.

Van Deusen, Glyndon G. *Horace Greeley: Nineteenth-Century Crusader.* Philadelphia: University of Pennsylvania Press, 1953.

Wagner, Charles L. *Seeing Stars.* New York: G. P. Putnam's Sons, 1940.

Walworth, Arthur. *Wilson and His Peacemakers: American Diplomacy at the Paris Peace Conference, 1919.* New York: W. W. Norton, 1986.

Watson, David Robin. *Georges Clemenceau: A Political Biography.* 1974. Reprint. New York: David McKay, 1976.

Wertheim, Arthur Frank, ed. *Will Rogers at the Ziegfeld Follies.* Norman: University of Oklahoma Press, 1992.

White, John Albert. *The Siberian Intervention.* Princeton, N.J.: Princeton University Press, 1950.

Whitfield, Eileen. *Pickford, the Woman Who Made Hollywood.* Lexington: University of Kentucky Press, 1997.

Wilson, Charles Morrow. *The Commoner: William Jennings Bryan.* Garden City, N.Y.: Doubleday, 1970.

Wilson, Edith Bolling. *My Memoir.* Indianapolis: Bobbs-Merrill, 1938.

Wilson, Terry P. *The Underground Reservation: Osage Oil.* Lincoln: University of Nebraska Press, 1985.

Winkler, John K. *Tobacco Tycoon: The Story of James Buchanan Duke.* New York: Random House, 1942.

Woerner, Gail Hughbanks. *A Belly Full of Bedsprings: The History of Bronc Riding.* Austin, Tex.: Eakin Press, 1998.

Wood, James Playsted. *Magazines in the United States.* 2d ed. New York: Ronald Press, 1956.

Yagoda, Ben. *Will Rogers, a Biography.* 1993. Re print. Norman: University of Oklahoma Press, 1993.

Yardley, Jonathan. *Ring: A Biography of Ring Lardner.* New York: Random House, 1977.

Ybarra, T. R. *Caruso: The Man of Naples and the Voice of Gold.* New York: Harcourt, Brace, 1953.

Zamoyski, Adam. *Paderewski.* New York: Atheneum, 1982.

Zieger, Robert H. *America's Great War: World War I and the American Experience.* Lanham, Md.: Rowman & Littlefield, 2000.

Ziegfeld, Richard, and Paulette Ziegfeld. *The Ziegfeld Touch: The Life and Times of Florenz Ziegfeld, Jr.* New York: Harry N. Abrams, 1993.

ARTICLES AND CHAPTERS IN ANTHOLOGIES

Black, Roe C. "Introduction." In *100 Years of Farm Journal*, 1–3. Philadelphia: Countryside Press, n.d. [ca. 1977].

Blackburn, Bob L. "Martin Edwin Trapp, Governor of Oklahoma, 1923–1927." In *Oklahoma's Governors, 1907–1929: Turbulent Politics*, edited by Leroy H. Fischer, 147–71. Oklahoma Series, Vol. 16. Oklahoma City: Oklahoma Historical Society, 1981.

Castle, Irene. "My Memories of Vernon Castle." *Everybody's Magazine*, November 1918, 22–27; December 1918, 36–41; January 1919, 38–42; February 1919, 50–55; March 1919, 39–42.

Coolidge, Grace. "The Real Calvin Coolidge: A First-hand Story of His Life." *Good Housekeeping*, March 1935, 22–25, 214, 217–27.

Cruikshank, Jan. "Haviland: An American Tradition." *West Coast Peddler*, April 1999. Available at: http://www.colemanantiques.com/west.htm

Falls, Cyril. "Turkish Campaigns." In *A Concise History of World War I*, edited by Vincent J. Esposito, 187–219. New York: Frederick A. Praeger, 1964.

Garnett, E. B. "Will Rogers Began to Write His Gags after a Visit Here." *Kansas City Star*, 6 November 1949.

Habicht, Werner. "Shakespeare Celebrations in Times of War." *Shakespeare Quarterly* 52 (Winter 2001): 441–55.

Hamlin, Tom. "Jubilo." *Motion Picture News*, 20 December 1919, 4529.

Hay, James, Jr. "Graham Bright Nichol." *National Press Club Yearbook, 1932*, 18–22.

Jackson, Rebecca B. "The Politics of Gender in the Writings of Anna Louise Strong." Paper presented in History 498, University of Washington, June 1999. Available through Seattle General Strike Project at: www.faculty.washington.edu/gregoryj/strike/jackson.html

Kahn, Coppélia. "Remembering Shakespeare Imperially: The 1916 Tercentenary." *Shakespeare Quarterly* 52 (Winter 2001): 456–78.

McIntyre, O. O. "A Few Once Overs." *Tulsa Daily World*, 13 May 1928.

Nimmo, H. M. "Detroit: The Newest and Latest 'Whirlwind Success' among Cities." *American Magazine* 84 (December 1917): 36, 65.

Smith, Tom, as told to Jean Dean. "The Actors' Colony at Freeport." *Long Island Forum*, October 1947, 183–84, 198.

Walsh, Edward R. "Will Rogers on Long Island." *Long Island Forum*, Spring 1993, 32–34, 36.

Wells, Stanley. "William Shakespeare." In *British Writers*, Ian Scott-Kilvert, gen. ed., 295–99. New York: Charles Scribner's Sons, 1979.

Williams, Ben Ames. "Jubilo." *Saturday Evening Post*, 28 June 1919, 3–4, 101, 105, 108, 111; 5 July 1919, 24–25, 145–46, 149–50, 153–54; 12 July 1919, 24–25, 113, 117–18, 121–22.

UNPUBLISHED AND MISCELLANEOUS SOURCES

Barse, Steve, Indian Hospital, Claremore, Okla. E-mail to editors, 18 July 2003.
City of Detroit. "Belle Isle Timeline." Available at:
    www.ci.detroit.mi.us/recreation/centers/M/belle_isle/history.html
Crocetto, Heather, Archivist and Librarian, National Press Club Archives. E-mail to editors, 15 July 2003.
Freeport-Lights Club file. Freeport Memorial Library, Freeport, N.Y.
General Motors Corporation. "GM Corporate History." Available at:
    www.gm.com/company/corp_info/history/gmhis1910.html
"George N. Pierce." Buffalo Architecture and History. Available at:
    http://ah.bfn.org/h/pierce/pierce/
Hale, Ron. "Man o' War, 'He Rewrote the Record Books.'" Available at:
    www.equinenet.org/heroes/mow.html
Meyer, Doris L. Telephone interviews with editors, 4–5 August 2003.
Mitchell, Lisa. "Ties That Bind: Searching for the Motion Pictures Association." *DGA Magazine*. Available at: www.dga.org/news/v26_4/v26_4.php3
NARA. "Sawtelle Disabled Veterans Home, Los Angeles Case Files, 1888–1933." Available at:
    www.archives.gov/facilities/ca/laguna_niguel/disabled_veterans_files.html
National Press Club. "About the Club: History & Ethics." Available at:
    http://npc.press.org/abouttheclub/history-ethics.cfm
Rulinski, Mary, *Farm Journal* magazine. E-mail to editors, September–October 2002.
"Who's Who: Paul Bolo." Available at: www.firstworldwar.com/bio/bolo.html
Wid's Year Book, 1918–21. Microfilm. University of Houston Library.

General Index

References to illustrations are printed in **boldface** type.

References to notes that provide primary biographical information about an individual are preceded by an asterisk (*).

For page numbers of correspondence between given individuals and Will Rogers, see Documents list in the preliminary matter of the volume (*ix–xv*).

For Will Rogers's lecture tour and other travel itineraries for the time period covered by this volume, including the lecture venues and cities where he appeared, consult the Chronology in the preliminary matter of the volume (7–42). The Chronology and Documents list may also be used as guides to help locate particular documents of interest within the volume by date or time period.

A. & C. Boni (publishing house), 316n.5, 411, 415n.2, 428n.7

Abd el-Krim (Abd al-Kârim), *575n.26

Abie's Irish Rose (play), 409, 411n.13, 470n.3

Absinthe House, New Orleans, 396, 399n.4, 477

Acord, Art, 79, *80n.18

Actor and acting, 135, 137, 209, 240, 317, 318, 385, 389

Adamson Eight-Hour Act, 85, 87n.16

Ade, George, 148, 209, 210n.11

Adler, Felix, 174, *175n.2

Advertising, 205, 208, 369–70

Advertising Club of Los Angeles, 208 & n.1

Aero Club, 235

After-dinner speakers, 279–80

Aiken, S. C., 486

Airmail, 547

Akerson, George E., 502, *503n.5

Albany Hotel, New York City, 89n.2

Albee, Edward Franklin, 374

Albert I, King (of Belgium), 74, *75–76n.16

Albrecht, Duke (of Württemberg), *120n.1

Albuquerque, N.M., 511, 514

A. L. Burt (publishing house), 316n.5

Aldridge (or Aldrich), Charlie (or Charley), 82, *84n.13

Alfonso XIII, King (of Spain), 429, *429n.4, 430

Alien Land Act (1913), 227n.4

Allen, Henry Justin, 177, *178n.7, 274–75, 277n.3

Allied Nations (in World War I), 119, 147n.7

Alphonzo E. Bell Corp., 344

Amarillo, Tex., 136

Ambassadors, 508

America (film), 331, 333nn.8–9

"America First," 85, 87n.14

American Bankers Association, 307

American Bond & Mortage Co., 263–65, 265n.1

American Club, in Berlin, Germany, 530n.2; in London, England, 424–25, 425n.1, 426

American Legion, 485nn.1–2

American Magazine, 485nn.1–2

American Red Cross, 126, 127n.2, 176n.6; honors Rogers, 449, 498 & nn.1,3, 557; and Mississippi River flood, 493n.1. *See also* Red Cross

American Red Cross War Fund Committee of New York, 127

American Society for the Prevention of Cruelty to Animals, 82, 84n.9

American Tobacco Co., 338, 340n.5, 353–54, 354n.2, 370n.1, 415n.2, 476

American Woman Suffrage Association, 252n.2

America's Cup of Yachting, 245n.7

Andrews, Adolphus, 422, *423–24n.7

Andrews, J. L., 516, *518n.1

Animal trainers (in film industry), 473

Ann Arbor, Mich., 537

Anteater (bucking horse), 81, 82

Anthony, Daniel Read, Jr., 177, *179n.14

Anthony, Susan Brownell, 177, *179n.15

Anti-Bunk party. *See* Rogers, William Penn Adair (Will), and mock presidential campaign

Anti-Saloon League, 213n.1

Antoine's restaurant, New Orleans, 399n.7

Arbuckle, Roscoe Conkling (Fatty), 222–23, 224 & *n.2, 224nn.3–5,11

Argonne, Battle of the, 177, 178n.8

Aristophanes, 277, *279n.15